Smart Technologies:

Breakthroughs in Research and Practice

Information Resources Management Association
USA

Published in the United States of America by
    IGI Global
    Information Science Reference (an imprint of IGI Global)
    701 E. Chocolate Avenue
    Hershey PA, USA 17033
    Tel: 717-533-8845
    Fax: 717-533-8661
    E-mail: cust@igi-global.com
    Web site: http://www.igi-global.com

Library of Congress Cataloging-in-Publication Data

Names: Information Resources Management Association, editor.
Title: Smart technologies : breakthroughs in research and practice /
  Information Resources Management Association, editor.
Description: Hershey, PA : Information Science Reference, [2018] | Includes
  bibliographical references.
Identifiers: LCCN 2017008818| ISBN 9781522525899 (hardcover) | ISBN
  9781522525905 (ebook)
Subjects: LCSH: Technological innovations.
Classification: LCC T173.8 .S6139 2017 | DDC 600--dc23 LC record available at https://lccn.loc.gov/2017008818

British Cataloguing in Publication Data
A Cataloguing in Publication record for this book is available from the British Library.

All work contributed to this book is new, previously-unpublished material. The views expressed in this book are those of the authors, but not necessarily of the publisher.

For electronic access to this publication, please contact: eresources@igi-global.com.

List of Contributors

Table of Contents

Section 2
Corporate Innovation

Section 3
Culture, Society, and the Arts

Section 4
Educational Technology

Section 5
Urban Spaces and Energy Optimization

Preface

The constantly changing landscape surrounding smart technology makes it challenging for experts and practitioners to stay informed of the field's most up-to-date research. That is why IGI Global is pleased to offer this one-volume comprehensive reference collection that will empower students, researchers, and academicians with a strong understanding of these critical issues by providing both broad and detailed perspectives on cutting-edge theories and developments. This compilation is designed to act as a single reference source on conceptual, methodological, and technical aspects, as well as to provide insight into emerging trends and future opportunities within the discipline.

Smart Technologies: Breakthroughs in Research and Practice is organized into five sections that provide comprehensive coverage of important topics. The sections are:

1. Assistive and Wearable Technology.
2. Corporate Innovation.
3. Culture, Society, and the Arts.
4. Educational Technology.
5. Urban Spaces and Energy Optimization.

The following paragraphs provide a summary of what to expect from this invaluable reference source:

Section 1, "Assistive and Wearable Technology," opens this extensive reference source by highlighting the latest trends in assistive technology innovations. Through perspectives on indoor navigation, visual impairment, and patient monitoring, this section demonstrates the benefits and opportunities of assistive devices. The presented research facilitates a better understanding of how new technologies are optimizing the medical field.

Section 2, "Corporate Innovation," includes chapters on the optimization of business processes and environments through smart technology applications. Including discussions on public relations, business intelligence, and marketing, this section presents research on the impact of emerging innovations in the corporate realm. This inclusive information assists in advancing current practices in business settings.

Section 3, "Culture, Society, and the Arts," presents coverage on the application of smart technologies for social innovation and improvement. Through discussions on smart government, machine learning, and gesture recognition, this section highlights the growing role of technology in modern society. These inclusive perspectives contribute to the available knowledge on societal improvements through technological applications.

Section 4, "Educational Technology," discusses coverage and research perspectives on computational tools in classroom settings. Through analyses on language learning, wireless technologies, and speech recognition software, this section contains pivotal information on learning optimization through smart technologies. The presented research facilitates a comprehensive understanding of how to utilize emerging innovations in contemporary educational environments.

Section 5, "Urban Spaces and Energy Optimization," highlights the latest smart technology trends for urban and sustainable development initiatives. Through innovative perspectives on data visualization, energy consumption, and smart grid, this sections presents emerging research on development of smart cities. This pivotal information serves as a valuable resource in understanding the role of smart technology in urban spaces.

Although the primary organization of the contents in this work is based on its five sections, offering a progression of coverage of the important concepts, methodologies, technologies, applications, social issues, and emerging trends, the reader can also identify specific contents by utilizing the extensive indexing system listed at the end.

As a comprehensive collection of research on the latest findings related to *Smart Technologies: Breakthroughs in Research and Practice,* this publication provides researchers, practitioners, and all audiences with a complete understanding of the development of applications and concepts surrounding these critical issues.

Section 1
Assistive and Wearable Technology

Chapter 1
RFID and Dead–Reckoning–Based Indoor Navigation for Visually Impaired Pedestrians

Kai Li Lim
The University of Western Australia, Australia

Lee Seng Yeong
Sunway University, Malaysia

Kah Phooi Seng
Charles Sturt University, Australia

Li-Minn Ang
Charles Sturt University, Australia

ABSTRACT

This chapter presents an indoor navigation solution for visually impaired pedestrians, which employs a combination of a radio frequency identification (RFID) tag array and dead-reckoning to achieve positioning and localisation. This form of positioning aims to reduce the deployment cost and complexity of pure RFID array implementations. This is a smartphone-based navigation system that leverages the new advancements of smartphone hardware to achieve large data handling and fast pathfinding. Users interact with the system through speech recognition and synthesis. This approach allows the system to be accessible to the masses due to the ubiquity of smartphones today. Uninformed pathfinding algorithms are implemented onto this system based on our previous study on the implementation suitability of uninformed searches. Testing results showed that this navigation system is suitable for use for the visually impaired pedestrians; and the pathfinding algorithms performed consistently according to our algorithm proposals.

INTRODUCTION

Pedestrians who are visually impaired face numerous challenges whenever they are required to step out of their dwellings to move to another location. Assistive technologies exist to alleviate the mobility challenges faced by visually impaired pedestrians by utilising modern electronic innovations to guide the visually impaired user. With the advent of ubiquitous mobile and wireless technologies, there is a growing demand for assistive technologies from the visually impaired community. This is especially true whereby automotive navigation systems, along with many mainstream and modern pedestrian naviga-

DOI: 10.4018/978-1-5225-2589-9.ch001

tion systems implemented (e.g. on wearable technologies and smartphones) are evidently designed and developed for the sighted pedestrian, with little or no regard for the visually impaired. This, along with and other challenges faced in the mobility of the visually impaired is highlighted in (Williams, Hurst, & Kane, 2013), with extensive reviews and case studies. These reviews include those of assistive mobility aids for the visually impaired, where case studies are conducted by interviewing a selected group of visually impaired pedestrians across the United States. The authors queried the participants regarding their usage of smartphone-based assistive technologies and gathered that only 13% of the users do not use assistive navigation technologies. There is, therefore, a clear demand for assistive technologies.

According to (Dakopoulos & Bourbakis, 2010), navigation assistive technologies provides a form of visual substitution for the visually impaired. It can be categorised into three types of devices/aids:

1. Electronic travel aids (ETAs) for mobility and displacement,
2. Electronic orientation aids (EOAs) for orientation and bearings, and
3. Position locator devices (PLDs) for positioning and localisation.

The ETA is usually the main component in a navigation system for these pedestrians, and it is typically connected to an EOA and a PLD (aka ETA system). The ETA handles more vital processes for the system, which includes pathfinding computation and user guidance, among others. This chapter emphasises on pathfinding algorithms and their roles in ETA systems for blind pedestrians. An ETA system, like other pedestrian navigation systems, follows the process in Figure 1 to function.

ETAs remain an area of popular research interest, the growing smartphone adaptation rate, along with the ubiquity of navigation systems, catalysed the need of ETA systems for the visually impaired. These days, the processing capabilities of smartphones are improving immensely, with octa-core processors finding a commonplace within new smartphone launches. Hence, many current works on ETA systems proposed are smartphone-based (Au et al., 2013; Guy & Truong, 2012; Kamiński & Bruniecki, 2012; Uddin & Suny, 2015), where they are versatilely used to provide route calculation, speech input via speech-to-text, and speech output via text-to-speech, which is used in guidance (Ceipidor, Medaglia, & Sciarretta, 2010; Uddin & Suny, 2015). Alternative methods to guidance may involve external devices, such as a haptic device (Ando, Tsukahara, Seki, & Fujie, 2012; Todd, Mallya, Majeed, Rojas, & Naylor, 2014). ETA Route calculation (pathfinding) requires that the smartphone communicates with PLDs and EOAs such as a GPS receiver and a compass to localise and position the user before it can commence, as

Figure 1. Process of navigation in an ETA, texts on arrows depict the procedure for navigation

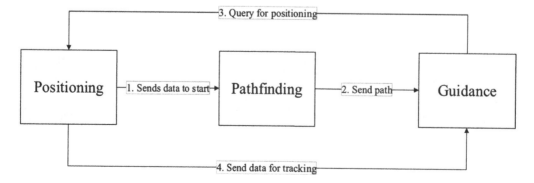

illustrated in Figure 1. Besides GPS receivers, PLDs can exist as different systems; in the case of indoor positioning, where GPS signals are unable to penetrate buildings, alternative positioning approaches are in active research. Examples include received signal strength indicator (RSSI) trilateration, where positioning is achieved by the measurement of signal strength from at least three wireless access points (AP) (Au et al., 2013; Ran, Helal, & Moore, 2004); radio frequency identification (RFID) arrays, where the pedestrian equipped with a RFID transponder traverses an environment fitted with RFID tags fixed on the floor (Di Giampaolo, 2010; Fernandes, Filipe, Costa, & Barroso, 2014; Liao et al., 2013); image positioning; where cameras are mounted on the pedestrian, which captures points of interests or barcodes that are matched within the database to achieve positioning (Beeharee & Steed, 2006; Filipe et al., 2012); dead-reckoning, which uses sensors to track the strides of the pedestrian (Hua, Marshall, & Wai, 2007; Kang & Han, 2015; Kourogi & Kurata, 2014); and visible light communication, where location data can also be relayed to the system (Hyun-Seung, Deok-Rae, Se-Hoon, Yong-Hwan, & Sang-Kook, 2013; Nakajima & Haruyama, 2012). A detailed review of the positioning methods for indoor navigation systems and their methods of pedestrian guidance is covered in (Fallah, Apostolopoulos, Bekris, & Folmer, 2013). Whichever the PLD system used, the positioning data obtained can then be sent to the ETA to start pathfinding.

Pathfinding is the computing process of finding the best route between two locational points on a map. The best route can be determined by a combination of the fastest route, the shortest route, and the simplest route (with the fewest number of turns). Pathfinding can either be informed or uninformed. Informed pathfinding is performed using informed search algorithms, where environmental information known as heuristics is fed into the algorithm to improve its search process. Examples of informed search algorithms include the A* search (Hart, Nilsson, & Raphael, 1968) and the iterative-deepening A* (IDA*) search (Korf, 1985).Conversely, uninformed pathfinding is performed using uninformed search algorithms, where pathfinding is performed sans the heuristics of informed algorithms, leading to an exhaustive search across the map. Examples of uninformed search algorithms include the Dijkstra's algorithm (Dijkstra, 1959) and the iterative-deepening depth-first search (IDDFS) (Korf, 1985). Out of the motivation to introduce a fast and memory efficient uninformed search algorithm, the boundary iterative-deepening depth-first search was proposed in (Lim, Seng, Yeong, Ang, & Ch'ng, 2015). Further improving on the speed of the BIDDFS, the findings in (Lim, Seng, Yeong, Ang, & Ch'ng, 2015) revealed that uninformed pathfinding is well-suited for use in indoor environments, especially when spaces are confined to corridors and walkways, and that indoor environments like these actually makes the heuristic calculation in informed algorithms redundant. Noting that most ETAs that implement pathfinding implements an informed search algorithm, this proposal of an ETA that uses uninformed search algorithm is a better alternative for indoor, path constricted environments.

On the prototyping front, an ETA that is built using modern wireless mobile technologies should incorporate recent devices such as a smartphone that is capable of performing route calculations and provides guidance for the user. The use of a smartphone should facilitate a wireless interface between the different modules and devices used within the ETA. For example, positioning devices can connect to the smartphone through ad-hoc Wi-Fi, whereby the smartphone will act as a hub for the positioning devices to connect to, which will then receive positioning data from these devices. A RFID positioning system is suitable for implementation for a wireless ETA, whereby ZigBee can be used to facilitate a many-to-many connection between the RFID tags. However, the accuracy of a RFID tag is limited to its effective tagging radius; increasing the signal output of the transponders using more powerful transponders, or by using signal amplifier is a method for improving the likelihood of successful tags.

In this chapter, the authors introduce an intelligent wireless ETA for visually impaired pedestrians with an emphasis on indoor environments, where positioning and localisation are achieved using a RFID/dead-reckoning hybrid model. This is a portable and mobile navigation system and user communication is incorporated using speech recognition and synthesis. The main function of this system is to guide a visually impaired from one point to another in an indoor environment, and its performance benchmark is measured in this chapter as its pathfinding efficiency. A visually impaired pedestrian will initiate the navigation process by saying his/her intended destination after a voice prompt, then the system will perform pathfinding, and subsequently guides the user to his/her destination. The motivation for proposing this ETA is to address the current issues pertaining existing RFID-based ETAs whilst acknowledging the demand of accessible ETAs from the visually impaired community; as well as to offer a test bed for the authors' pathfinding algorithms to run on real-world hardware and scenarios. This ETA aims to be easily deployed by premise owners and adopted by the visually impaired community while providing simple and accurate navigational guidance.

The remainder of this chapter is organised as follows:

- Section 2 presents an in-depth look at the ETA and its components.
- Section 3 discusses the software requirement of this ETA, including the smartphone application and pathfinding programming.
- Section 4 documents the testing methodology and results conducted on the ETA.
- Finally, future directions the concluding remark is given in Section 5.

SYSTEM ARCHITECTURE AND COMPONENTS

This ETA system is conceptualised based on the reviews on currently available ETAs for the visually impaired, and it is able to harness the high processing performance of new smartphones. A smartphone is hence the core of this ETA device, where it will be paired with two PLDs and an EOA. This is an Android-based smartphone, meaning that the pathfinding algorithm will be programmed as part of an Android app, which interfaces with the PLDs and EOA. This system concept for the visually impaired is as illustrated in Figure 2, where the user attached module is worn by the pedestrian and communicates with the floor deployed RFID system in a one-to-many configuration. The smartphone communicates with the RFID system wirelessly through ZigBee (using the XBee Pro (Digi International, 2008)), which facilitates one-to-many connection. Within the main module, communications with the user can be performed via the Bluetooth headset using speech recognition and synthesis from an Android smartphone (the Samsung Galaxy Note II (Samsung Electronics Co. Ltd., 2014)). Positioning and tracking hardware can be connected to the computing device via RS232 through a microprocessor board (e.g. an Arduino), communicating with the Android application. The RFID module provides positioning relative to the map through strategically placed RFID transponders such as the Texas Instruments TRF7960A (Texas Instruments, 2014) module. The DRM provides positioning and tracking relative to the user's location, and the user's orientation is supplied by a digital compass, the Honeywell HMC6352 (Honeywell, 2006). These components constitute the ETA and they are as photographed in Figure 3, with Figure 3(a) illustrating the physical connections between the hardware modules.

Figure 2. System hardware block diagram

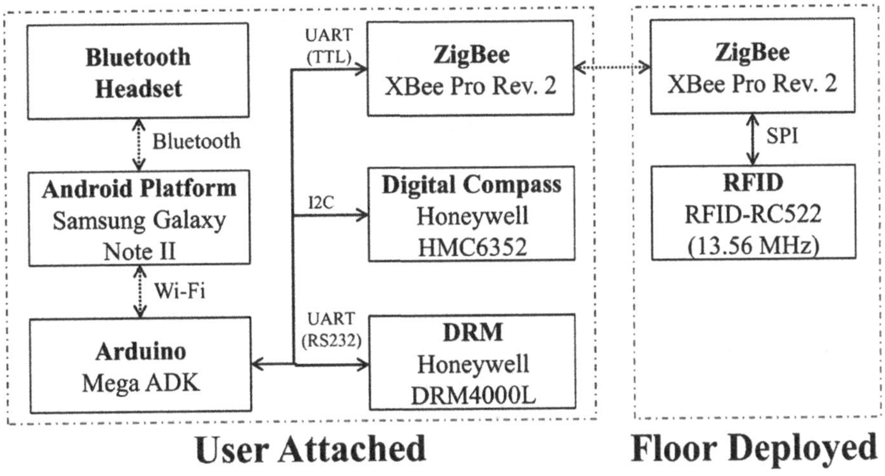

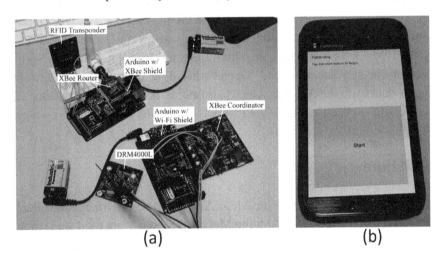

Figure 3. (a) The hardware components of the ETA (left), and (b) the Samsung Galaxy Note II smartphone

(a)   (b)

RFID Positioning With Dead-Reckoning Localization

This system employs two PLDs for positioning as an effort to reduce implementation cost and complexity when compared against conventional environment-wide fixtures such as using a dense RFID fixture layout. The PLDs consist of a dead-reckoning module (DRM) and a RFID positioning system. The Mifare RFID-RC522 (NXP Semiconductors, 2014) and the Honeywell DRM4000L (Honeywell, 2011) were used as the RFID transponder and the DRM in this system respectively. To alleviate the need of installing many RFID transponders for better positioning accuracy, the DRM is introduced in this system to complement the RFID transponders in tracking the pedestrian's movements. The DRM is able to ensure that the pedestrian is moving within his/her intended route (e.g. in a straight line) without having to resort to redundant RFID transmitters placed throughout the path of the pedestrian. The RFID positioning system then consists of a RFID tag (placed in the pedestrian's shoe sole), and RFID transponders; each successful tag positions the user on the map. Instead of installing the transponders with fixed distances from each other throughout the environment, they are installed on the floor at several critical locations within the navigation environment, such as at junctions, stairs, or dead-ends. This reduces the installation and maintenance cost on the navigation environment. The orientation of the user is provided by a digital compass, which is the dedicated EOA in this system. This is supplemented by the DRM, which is also able to provide orientation data.

The Android Platform

The Android platform is selected for implementation because of the wide availability of Android devices capable of fast mobile computing, and the ease of developing Android application using the Java programming language, royalty free. The recent advent of many multi-cored Android smartphone is an advantage for parallel processes such as pathfinding algorithms. The Samsung Galaxy Note II (Model: GT-7100) is used as the Android device for the development and implementation of this system. It functions as the main processing device in this navigation system. It is responsible for retrieving positioning data from the PLDs and EOA, and then processing it for pathfinding, and subsequently guiding the user over the Android application. Tethering is turned on and the smartphone functions as a Wi-Fi access point (AP), allowing the Arduino to connect to it, where the positioning data will be received. This allows the Arduino to find the Android AP and subsequently allowing User Datagram Protocol (UDP) communications over Wi-Fi. The user may then hold the home button to start the S-Voice to open the navigation application via the voice command "Open Pathfinding". Pathfinding will commence once the smartphone receives data from the Arduino. Once pathfinding is completed, guidance can be delivered by the device via Google's speech synthesis API, which is forwarded to the user via a paired Bluetooth headset (a wired headset works just as fine).

The Arduino Platform

This system prototype implements the Arduino Mega ADK for Android microcontroller board, with the ATmega2560 as the microcontroller. Two Arduino Mega ADK boards are used – one in the main module (attached with Wi-Fi shield, worn by the user), and another on the RFID module (attached with XBee shield, as a serial peripheral interface (SPI) to transistor-transistor logic (TTL) converter). This board is chosen for implementation due to its ability to support up to four serial communications simultaneously, along with SPI support. The Mega ADK features a Type-A USB port capable of connecting to an Android device via accessory mode. However, Wi-Fi was chosen over accessory mode to allow a wireless implementation, and that the Samsung Galaxy Note II does not support accessory mode.

Component Interfacing

Communications between the RFID flood-installed RFID transponders and the RFID module's Arduino handled via the ZigBee (IEEE 802.15.4) standard. For the purpose of this prototype, the XBee Pro Series 2 modules are used. ZigBee is chosen for this purpose due to its ability to support wireless data transfers in a mesh network with an advertised indoor range of 40m (Digi International, 2008). This is because multiple RFID readers will be interfacing with the navigation system simultaneously. The XBees are programmed in two ways, and each connects to an Arduino board – the XBee connected to the smartphone-connected Arduino is programmed as the coordinator, where it receives incoming signals from the routers; the second set of XBees connects to the RFID transponders (via an Arduino Mega ADK), and are programmed as the routers. The coordinator XBees connects to the DRM and the DRM outputs in RS232. These XBees are not able to support the RS232 and hence an MAX3232CSE RS232 to TTL converter is used in tandem with the devices, which are connected as shown in Figure 4. To interface the DRM4000L to the Arduino, an initialisation parameter is required to be sent. The parameter "INIP" is sent to the DRM4000L from the Arduino to receive latitude and longitudinal data, and beginning position error for a connection without GPS. The DRM4000L ensures that the user follows the path from pathfinding; any deviation from the path would be detected by the system. On the router XBees' side, each device is connected directly to an Arduino that is programmed to convert the SPI signals from the RC522 into a UART signal that can be processed on the smartphone. As soon as a RFID tag is read by the RC522, the unique identification number (UID) of the tag is obtained, thus identifying the user treading on the transponder. A complete navigation system will use multiple RFID transponders placed at POIs around the navigation environment, each connected to an XBee through an SPI to UART converter. To provide absolute localisation to the system, each transponder is assigned a unique identification number, which is passed to the Arduino in a string datatype via the ZigBee mesh network to the ZigBee coordinator, which is connected to the Arduino in the main module. The effective range of the RFID transponder was measured with a ruler with the RFID tag moving increasingly closer to the transponder until the tag is read. Ten measurements were taken for the card tag and coin tag and the result was averaged to be 2.4cm. To increase the accuracy of absolute positioning, the density of implementation of the RFID transponders is to be increased, requiring more Transponder-ZigBee combinations to be implemented in an environment.

The UDP (User Datagram Protocol) is used for communications between the Android and Arduino platforms. The Arduino streams data from the positioning devices to the Android to be processed for user guidance on the route from pathfinding. Hence, the Arduino is made the transmitter and the Android device is made the receiver. UDP communications on the Arduino starts by defining the SSID name of the AP to connect and the DHCP server upon connection provides the IP address. The Arduino defines a listening port during initialisation. The listening port is used to wait for incoming connections before the data is streamed to the Android, henceforth known as the data request. Each set of data received from the positioning devices by the Arduino is cast and parsed as a single string, delimited by underscores ('_') (e.g. "3.0_128.5_31.5_A"). The Android device then splits the received string into their individual data set (using the String.split function) to be stored as variables to be processed by the Android device.

Figure 4. The block diagram showing connections between the DRM4000L, MAX3232CSE, and the Arduino Mega ADK

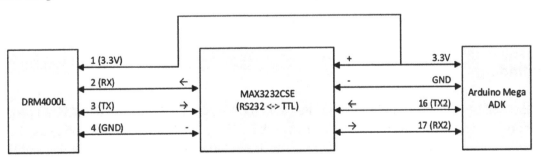

Each string passed by the Arduino represents a set of data for an instance. The listening of data is set as a dedicated thread pool on the Android device and it is constantly listening to the UDP broadcast from the Arduino, it is able to receive UDP messages up to an interval of 10ms.

Based on the hardware block diagram in Figure 2, on the user attached side, the Arduino Mega ADK connects serially to the XBee and the DRM module through the TTL UART standard. It connects to the DRM through an RS232 to TTL converter, as the DRM outputs in the RS232 standard. The digital compass interfaces via the I2C standard and is connected to the analogue inputs on the Arduino. The Wi-Fi Shield attached to the Arduino in the main module allows the Arduino to connect to the Android AP. Once a Wi-Fi connection has been established, the Android is assigned an IP address via DHCP by the Android AP. On the floor-deployed side, these RFID transponders use the Arduino Mega ADK alongside the RFID reader to convert its SPI output of to UART usable by the XBee. In other words, the RFID reader connects to the SPI ports on the Arduino, which are then converted and serially outputted in UART to the XBee.

SOFTWARE REQUIREMENTS

Programming the Arduino

The Arduino devices are programmed using Arduino 1.5.4 for Mac. Every Arduino source code is separated into two functions – the initialisation (start()) and an infinite loop (loop()). This section describes the programming of the Arduino worn by the user. (The Arduino connected to the RFID transponder simply reads the RFID tags in SPI and outputs the signal in TTL) Before the loop begins, the Arduino is programmed to initialise the three serial connections with their baud rate, using the Serial0, Serial1, and Serial2 headers for the USB (connected to the Mac), XBee, and DRM respectively. During this initialisation, the Arduino is required to send the initialisation parameters "INIP" to the DRM and "A" to the digital compass (if attached), which are sent in strings. Finally, the Arduino connects to the Wi-Fi access point on the Android device through the defined service set identification (SSID) name. When a Wi-Fi connection is established, a confirmation is printed to Serial0, which can be viewed using Arduino's serial monitor. The loop then begins.

In the Arduino loop function, the Arduino is programmed to first wait for a packet from the Android device to enable the Arduino to identify the source IP address of the device before a reply can be sent. Once the data is received, the packet string is read, saved, and displayed in the serial monitor, together with the Android's IP address. The Android device now listens for replies on positioning data from the Arduino. To receive positioning data, the data streams from each of the positioning device is read at every 10ms interval and saved in variables. At every other 10ms, the positioning data from the positioning devices is parsed as a single string and sent to the Android device. A sample pseudocode used for reading the packet data is shown in Figure 5.

Pathfinding

Here, the pathfinding algorithm is implemented onto the Android platform. The uninformed pathfinding algorithms are programmed in Java and then packaged as an application, incorporating the features required to communicate with the other hardware devices. During this stage, the pathfinding algorithms

Figure 5. A loop function for the retrieval of UDP data.

```
void loop() {

  receivePacket();

  if(packetReceived())

  {

     print("Received packet of size " + packetSize + "from " +
Udp.remoteIPAddress() + "from " + Udp.remotePortNumber());


     Udp.readPacketContent();

     print("Contents:" + contentBuffer);



     while (connection.isOpen()) {

       sendData();

     }

  }

  delay(10);

}
```

are programmed as independent classes with their own methods, which can be called from the main class of the application. This enables the programming of multiple pathfinding algorithms onto the application, working independently from other processes such as hardware communications. Classes that interface with other hardware modules in this system are then programmed independently, alongside the pathfinding classes. A single goal algorithm and a multi-goal algorithm are selected for implementation. The single goal algorithm selected is the parallel bidirectional BIDDFS and the multi-goal algorithm is the multi-goal BIDDFS that the authors proposed in (Lim, Seng, Yeong, Ang, & Ch'ng, 2015), and are ported to Java in the same way that they did for (Lim, Seng, Yeong, Ang, & Ch'ng, 2015). The algorithms are programmed individually, and they will be used according to the pedestrian's need. For example, if a pedestrian requests to navigate directly to a destination, the single goal algorithm will be used; likewise, if the pedestrian decides to survey the distance from each destination, then the multi-goal algorithm will be used instead (the user will be prompted) These pathfinding algorithms are programmed onto the Android application using Android Studio 0.2 (Google), and the application is then installed on the Android device.

Smartphone Application

An Android application is designed in this system to interface with other hardware components, along with performing pathfinding and pedestrian navigation. The user interface (UI) is designed with the visually impaired in mind, offering a single, simplistic button on the main screen, and a text area to show navigational data for debugging purpose for the prototype (see Figure 6). All other interaction with the user is controlled through speech recognition and synthesis. The Android application performs speech recognition (speech-to-text) and synthesis (text-to-speech) by utilising Google's speech recognition and speech synthesis application programming interfaces (APIs). The Android application is programmed with the headers android.speech.RecognizerIntent and android.speech.tts respectively to enable speech recognition and speech synthesis. To use the Google speech recognition API, the Android device is connected to the internet as the speech database stored on Google's servers; the speech synthesis API is able to function without an Internet connection, as the text-to-speech algorithm is already built into the device.

Speech recognition and synthesis are used after pathfinding, during guidance. During navigation, the application will listen for speech input from the user. If a speech is recognised, it will be returned as text, which is then stored as a string in the Android application. The recognised string can then be manipulated by the Android application into input commands – if a test is matched with valid commands (e.g. "start"), the input is recognised. Speech synthesis is used as an alternative to visual feedback in a navigation device. The programming of the speech synthesis module in the Android application reads strings from the program and outputs the speech as an audio feedback. Examples of synthesised speech in this prototype include directional commands ("turn left", "go straight", etc.). If the Android device is paired with a Bluetooth headset, the user will then receive the audio output via the Bluetooth headset. Otherwise, it will be outputted through the speaker. Speech synthesis is used to output responses from the Android application, such as directional guidance and application statuses.

Once pathfinding is completed, the Android device is required to interface with the Arduino to receive the user's current positioning data for guidance. A socket-programming module is programmed into the Android application as a standalone thread pool that is started after pathfinding. This enables UDP communications over the IEEE 802.11g Wi-Fi standard. The Android device acts as an AP using Android's tethering feature and the Arduino with an attached Wi-Fi shield connects to the Android device.

Figure 6. Android application user interface showing the time elapsed for multiple runs on the (a) parallel bidirectional BIDDFS runs (left), and (b) multi-goal BIDDFS runs using three goals (right).

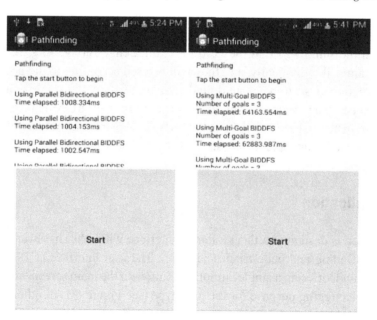

The media access control address (MAC address) of the connected Arduino is used to look up its IP address from the address resolution protocol (ARP) table. Once the IP address of the Arduino has been identified, the application uses that IP address to send the first packet to the Arduino. An initialisation string (e.g. "start") is sent to the Arduino to commence the inflow of positioning data. Subsequently, the Arduino recognises the IP of the Android device from the packet sent and returns the positioning data in replies back to the Android device. The reply packets from the Arduino are received by the Android and are stored as variables to be processed for guidance.

TESTING AND RESULTS

The ETA is assembled according to Figure 2 and 3(a) as a prototype, where it is then subjected to testing. Testing is focused on the pathfinding algorithms with reference to the functionalities of the prototype. The implemented pathfinding algorithms are tested in two parts – the parallel bidirectional BIDDFS and the multi-goal BIDDFS. Prior to testing, a user is equipped with the ETA according to Figure 7. His objective is to navigate from his current location to a room as shown in Figure 8. This room is set to be the goal for single goal testing on the floor plan map. For multi-goal testing, this goal is used along with other predetermined goals scattered around the map as described in section pathfinding test results, where pathfinding on the smartphone will be benchmarked for its time efficiency to compare with the same instance as performed on a PC. Before pathfinding starts, the navigation system determines the user's starting position, either by manual input or by a RFID transponder; for the purpose of this testing, the manual input method is used. Once the starting position is determined, pathfinding tests begin first with

Figure 7. (a) User carrying the ETA components, wearing the Bluetooth headset and holding the smartphone (left photo); and (b) user navigating in an environment with the navigation system prototype (right photo)

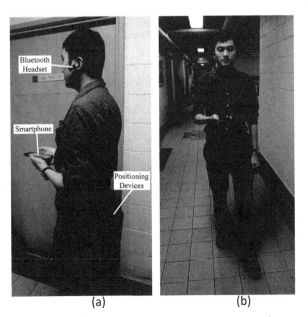

(a)   (b)

the parallel bidirectional BIDDFS, followed by the multi-goal BIDDFS algorithm. Multi-goal and single goal pathfinding provide difference experiences to the user. When the parallel bidirectional BIDDFS is implemented, the system expects a destination input from the user before pathfinding begins, and then calculate the route from that starting point to the destination (goal). Conversely, when the multi-goal BIDDFS is used, pathfinding begins as soon as a starting point is determined; a single search is used to locate all goals on the map, and the user is presented with the distance from each goal relative to the user before a destination selection is made. Simply put, the destination input happens before pathfinding when the parallel bidirectional BIDDFS is used, and after pathfinding when the multi-goal BIDDFS is used. Pathfinding times are printed on the screen of the application (see Figure 6), and these results are tabulated and discussed.

To test the functionality of the ETA prototype, the user carries two sets of devices – the smartphone and the Arduino with the DRM. The smartphone can be placed in the user's pocket during navigation as communication can be performed through a connected Bluetooth headset. The other device set consists of the Arduino, the DRM, and the ZigBee coordinator, which are for now placed in a pouch bag worn by the user, the enclosure is awaiting fabrication. Figure 7(a) illustrates a user wearing the ETA prototype. To open the Android application, the user double taps the home button, launching SVoice, and say "Open Pathfinding". Once the application is opened and the starting position is determined, tapping on the start button initiates the pathfinding process. The result is a path(s) connecting the goal(s) to the starting point (this path is stored in the phone's memory), and then guidance for the user begins. The user can alternatively start pathfinding using the implemented Google speech-to-text module, which is also used to specify the destination. During navigation, the Android device provides only voice guidance. While the user is in motion, the device supplies directional information to the user. This begins by ensuring the orientation of the user after the starting point is determined by an audio feedback (e.g. "turn around", "turn right", "turn left", "go straight"). Once the user hears "go straight", he/she will proceed to walk in a straight line until the next feedback is delivered at the next turning point. The user travels according

Figure 8. A simple illustration showing the devices worn by the user, and the path (in dashed line) obtained from pathfinding

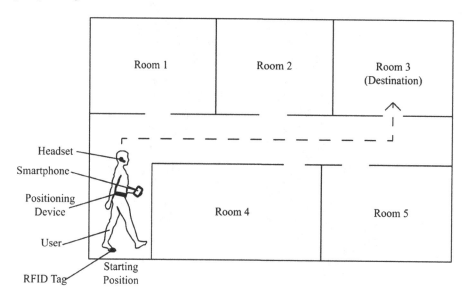

to the synthesised voice directions. This process continues until the goal is reached, where the RFID transponder is tagged. Turning points on the map are identified to set the locations to give directional cues to the user. The location of these turning points can be accurately identified by placing a RFID transponder at the location, allowing the absolute position to be delivered to the navigation system for directional cues. For testing purposes, the RFID transponder is placed on the goal and the DRM tracks the user's location, which is relative to the users starting location. The RFID tag placed in the user's shoe is detected by the transponder when it is within range. A successful tagging of the transponder will prompt an audio feedback to the user.

Pathfinding Test Results

The testing results of pathfinding algorithms running on the navigation system hardware are documented in this section. The algorithms are tested for the purpose to ensure their pathfinding times on hardware is consistent with the results obtained from (Lim, Seng, Yeong, Ang, & Ch'ng, 2015), where the single goal and multi-goal algorithms are run with maps of single and multiple goals, at varying sizes. The parallel bidirectional BIDDFS and the multi-goal BIDDFS are programmed onto the Samsung Galaxy Note II (N7100) Android device of the navigation system for testing. It is powered by a Quad-core 1.6 GHz Cortex-A9 processor with 2GB RAM, running on Android 4.3 Jellybean. Background applications are closed before running the pathfinding application, as they may interfere with the pathfinding speed.

The performance of pathfinding algorithms when the "Start" button is tapped on maps of different resolution is tabulated in Table 1 with different goal numbers using the two BIDDFS algorithms. Floor plans can be sub-divided into nodes for pathfinding, a division to more nodes constitutes to a higher resolution map. A map of higher resolution supports larger maps with a higher path and obstacle detail, but with longer pathfinding time, meaning that the user would have to wait longer before guidance begins. The maps used for testing introduces a virtual environment, where floor plans are superimposed on real environments for testing. A 50 by 50 node resolution map can be represented with 1 metre per node in a real environment; likewise, a 250 by 250 node map can be represented by 10 centimetres per node in a real environment. The pathfinding times are measured as an average of ten repeated runs on the Android device. The parallel bidirectional BIDDFS is faster than the multi-goal BIDDFS. On a 50×50 map, it is 10 times faster than the multi-goal BIDDFS and 4.4 times faster on the 250×250 map. This proves that the results obtained in this hardware testing between the algorithms and the map resolution are consistent

Table 1. Pathfinding times for different map sizes used in testing with the parallel bidirectional and multi-goal BIDDFS

Map Resolution	BIDDFS	Goals	Time (s)
50×50	Parallel Bidirectional	1	0.02696
50×50	Multi-goal	1	0.26807
50×50	Multi-goal	3	0.27872
250×250	Parallel Bidirectional	1	14.736
250×250	Multi-goal	1	64.855
250×250	Multi-goal	3	65.925

with the results obtained in the simulations in (Lim, Seng, Yeong, Ang, & Ch'ng, 2015). It should be taken into consideration that when the map size increases, pathfinding is slower on the Android smartphone since the computer has faster hardware. Therefore, it is deduced that a lowered map resolution on the Android smartphone allows it to perform pathfinding at speeds comparable with the computer.

CONCLUSION

This chapter presented a review of current ETAs and subsequently proposed an ETA system concept for visually impaired pedestrians. This ETA was developed and tested for indoor navigation with visually impaired pedestrians in mind. A detailed overview of the ETA is presented. The RFID-DRM indoor positioning solution reduces the need of installing many redundant RFID transponders while still being able to track the user's movements. With a focus on pathfinding algorithms, uninformed pathfinding algorithms were implemented onto this ETA. Testing results showed that the ETA is able to guide a visually impaired pedestrian for navigation, and pathfinding results are consistent with the tests performed during the authors' algorithm proposals. Further works relating to this ETA include more experiments to measure its hardware functionalities in the areas of positioning and guidance. For example, the PLDs will benefit from more experiments to measure their accuracy in positioning and tracking; whilst the guidance system can be subjected to a user experience survey.

ACKNOWLEDGMENT

This project has been supported by the Malaysian Ministry of Science, Technology and Innovation (MOSTI) eScienceFund number 01-02-16-SF0024.

REFERENCES

Ando, T., Tsukahara, R., Seki, M., & Fujie, M. G. (2012). A Haptic Interface "Force Blinker 2" for Navigation of the Visually Impaired. *Industrial Electronics. IEEE Transactions on, 59*(11), 4112–4119. doi:10.1109/TIE.2011.2173894

Au, A. W. S., Chen, F., Valaee, S., Reyes, S., Sorour, S., Markowitz, S. N., & Eizenman, M. et al. (2013). Indoor Tracking and Navigation Using Received Signal Strength and Compressive Sensing on a Mobile Device. *Mobile Computing. IEEE Transactions on, 12*(10), 2050–2062. doi:10.1109/TMC.2012.175

Beeharee, A. K., & Steed, A. (2006). *A natural wayfinding exploiting photos in pedestrian navigation systems*. Paper presented at the 8th conference on Human-computer interaction with mobile devices and services, Helsinki, Finland. doi:10.1145/1152215.1152233

Ceipidor, U., Medaglia, C., & Sciarretta, E. (2010). SeSaMoNet 2.0: Improving a Navigation System for Visually Impaired People. In B. Ruyter, R. Wichert, D. Keyson, P. Markopoulos, N. Streitz, M. Divitini, & A. Mana Gomez et al. (Eds.), *Ambient Intelligence* (Vol. 6439, pp. 248–253). Springer Berlin Heidelberg. doi:10.1007/978-3-642-16917-5_25

Dakopoulos, D., & Bourbakis, N. G. (2010). Wearable Obstacle Avoidance Electronic Travel Aids for Blind: A Survey. *Systems, Man, and Cybernetics, Part C: Applications and Reviews. IEEE Transactions on*, *40*(1), 25–35. doi:10.1109/TSMCC.2009.2021255

Di Giampaolo, E. (2010). *A passive-RFID based indoor navigation system for visually impaired people.* Paper presented at the Applied Sciences in Biomedical and Communication Technologies (ISABEL), 2010 3rd International Symposium on.

Digi International. (2008). *XBee™ ZNet 2.5/XBee-PRO™ ZNet 2.5 OEM RF Modules Datasheet.* Author.

Dijkstra, E. W. (1959). A Note on Two Problems in Connexion with Graphs. *NUMERISCHE MATHEMATIK*, *1*(1), 269–271. doi:10.1007/BF01386390

Fallah, N., Apostolopoulos, I., Bekris, K., & Folmer, E. (2013). Indoor Human Navigation Systems: A Survey. *Interacting with Computers*. doi:10.1093/iwc/iws010

Fernandes, H., Filipe, V., Costa, P., & Barroso, J. (2014). Location based Services for the Blind Supported by RFID Technology. *Procedia Computer Science*, *27*(0), 2–8. doi:10.1016/j.procs.2014.02.002

Filipe, V., Fernandes, F., Fernandes, H., Sousa, A., Paredes, H., & Barroso, J. (2012). Blind Navigation Support System based on Microsoft Kinect. *Procedia Computer Science*, *14*, 94–101. doi:10.1016/j.procs.2012.10.011

Google. (n.d.). *Getting Started with Android Studio.* Retrieved from http://developer.android.com/sdk/installing/studio.html

Guy, R., & Truong, K. (2012). *CrossingGuard: exploring information content in navigation aids for visually impaired pedestrians.* Paper presented at the SIGCHI Conference on Human Factors in Computing Systems, Austin, TX. doi:10.1145/2207676.2207733

Hart, P. E., Nilsson, N. J., & Raphael, B. (1968). A Formal Basis for the Heuristic Determination of Minimum Cost Paths. *Systems Science and Cybernetics. IEEE Transactions on*, *4*(2), 100–107. doi:10.1109/TSSC.1968.300136

Honeywell. (2006). *Digital Compass Solution - HMC6352 datasheet.* Author.

Honeywell. (2011). *DRM™4000L Dead Reckoning Module Datasheet.* Author.

Hua, W., Marshall, A., & Wai, Y. (2007). *Path Planning and Following Algorithms in an Indoor Navigation Model for Visually Impaired.* Paper presented at the Internet Monitoring and Protection, 2007. ICIMP 2007. Second International Conference on.

Hyun-Seung, K., Deok-Rae, K., Se-Hoon, Y., Yong-Hwan, S., & Sang-Kook, H. (2013). An Indoor Visible Light Communication Positioning System Using a RF Carrier Allocation Technique. *Lightwave Technology. Journalism*, *31*(1), 134–144. doi:10.1109/JLT.2012.2225826

Kamiński, Ł., & Bruniecki, K. (2012). Mobile navigation system for visually impaired users in the urban environment. *Metrology and Measurement Systems*, *19*(2), 245–256. doi:10.2478/v10178-012-0021-z

Kang, W., & Han, Y. (2015). SmartPDR: Smartphone-Based Pedestrian Dead Reckoning for Indoor Localization. *Sensors Journal, IEEE*, *15*(5), 2906–2916. doi:10.1109/JSEN.2014.2382568

Korf, R. E. (1985). Depth-first iterative-deepening: An optimal admissible tree search. *Artificial Intelligence, 27*(1), 97–109. doi:10.1016/0004-3702(85)90084-0

Kourogi, M., & Kurata, T. (2014). *A method of pedestrian dead reckoning for smartphones using frequency domain analysis on patterns of acceleration and angular velocity.* Paper presented at the Position, Location and Navigation Symposium - PLANS 2014, 2014 IEEE/ION.

Liao, C., Choe, P., Wu, T., Tong, Y., Dai, C., & Liu, Y. (2013). RFID-Based Road Guiding Cane System for the Visually Impaired. In P. L. P. Rau (Ed.), *Cross-Cultural Design. Methods, Practice, and Case Studies* (Vol. 8023, pp. 86–93). Springer Berlin Heidelberg. doi:10.1007/978-3-642-39143-9_10

Lim, K. L., Seng, K. P., Yeong, L. S., Ang, L.-M., & Ch'ng, S. I. (2015). *Pathfinding for the Navigation of Visually Impaired People. International Journal of Computational Complexity and Intelligent Algorithms.*

Lim, K. L., Seng, K. P., Yeong, L. S., Ang, L.-M., & Chng, S. I. (2015). Uninformed pathfinding: A new approach. *Expert Systems with Applications, 42*(5), 2722–2730. doi:10.1016/j.eswa.2014.10.046

Nakajima, M., & Haruyama, S. (2012). *Indoor navigation system for visually impaired people using visible light communication and compensated geomagnetic sensing.* Paper presented at the Communications in China (ICCC), 2012 1st IEEE International Conference on.

Ran, L., Helal, S., & Moore, S. (2004). *Drishti: an integrated indoor/outdoor blind navigation system and service.* Paper presented at the Pervasive Computing and Communications, 2004. PerCom 2004.

Samsung Electronics Co. Ltd. (2014). *Samsung GALAXY Note2 - Samsung Mobile.* Retrieved from http://www.samsung.com/global/microsite/galaxynote/note2/spec.html

NXP Semiconductors. (2014). *MFRC522 - Standard 3V MIFARE reader solution Product data sheet.* Author.

Texas Instruments. (2014). *TRF7960A.* Retrieved from http://www.ti.com/product/trf7960a

Todd, C., Mallya, S., Majeed, S., Rojas, J., & Naylor, K. (2014). *VirtuNav: A Virtual Reality indoor navigation simulator with haptic and audio feedback for the visually impaired.* Paper presented at the Computational Intelligence in Robotic Rehabilitation and Assistive Technologies (CIR2AT), 2014 IEEE Symposium on.

Uddin, M. A., & Suny, A. H. (2015). *Shortest path finding and obstacle detection for visually impaired people using smart phone.* Paper presented at the Electrical Engineering and Information Communication Technology (ICEEICT), 2015 International Conference on.

Williams, M. A., Hurst, A., & Kane, S. K. (2013). *Pray before you step out: describing personal and situational blind navigation behaviors.* Paper presented at the 15th International ACM SIGACCESS Conference on Computers and Accessibility, Bellevue, WA. doi:10.1145/2513383.2513449

This research was previously published in the Handbook of Research on Recent Developments in Intelligent Communication Application edited by Siddhartha Bhattacharyya, Nibaran Das, Debotosh Bhattacharjee, and Anirban Mukherjee, pages 380-396, copyright year 2017 by Information Science Reference (an imprint of IGI Global).

Chapter 2
Information Communication Assistive Technologies for Visually Impaired People

Li-Minn Ang
Charles Sturt University, Perth, Australia

Kah Phooi Seng
Charles Sturt University, Perth, Australia

Tee Zhi Heng
BP Castrol Lubricant, Malaysia

ABSTRACT

The information explosion era provides the foundation for a technological solution to enable the visually impaired to more independent living in the community. This paper first provides a review of assistive technologies for visually impaired people. Current technology allows applications to be efficiently distributed and operated on mobile and handheld devices. Thus, this paper also summarizes recent developments of assistive technologies in mobile interaction. It then presents the Wireless Intelligent Assistive Navigation Management System Using SmartGuide Devices for visually impaired people. The "SmartGuide" of the system is built as a standalone portable handheld device. The system is to assist blind and low vision people to walk around independently especially in dynamic changing environments. It also includes a camera sensor network to enhance monitoring capabilities for an extra level of security and reliability. Finally, the paper presents an improved system with some new designs involving mobile interaction.

INTRODUCTION

Visual impairment can result from damage at any time in the life cycle of human beings. Severe visual impairment leads to a person being totally blind. Less severe cases cause a person to have partial vision loss that cannot be corrected called "low vision". Genetic and developmental anomalies can cause blindness from birth. Visual impairment may also occur during adulthood when many diseases and genetic

DOI: 10.4018/978-1-5225-2589-9.ch002

patterns manifest themselves. These groups of people should not be excluded from the community. They should be encouraged to become valuable members of the community. It is often these groups that are left behind in the Information Age. The largest population of visually impaired people are the elderly because vision loss is the normal result of aging. Elderly people, although blind, have years of experience and can be valuable contributors to the community. In current public transportation centers, a tactile strip or paving is placed on the ground for the visually impaired person to follow. There are many limitations with this method. Firstly, it requires the person to already be familiar with the environment which may not always be the case. Secondly, even if the person is familiar with the environment, the person would not know when he or she has arrived at the desired location. The person has to constantly ask people along the way as to whether they have reached the correct place. If there is no one around, the person would be lost. The entire process creates anxiety and stress. Thirdly, in emergency situations such as fire, the paths may not be passable and there are no alternative paths to safely guide them. Therefore, it is important to use Information Communication Technology (ICT) for e-Inclusion in public transportation systems to tap new digital opportunities for the inclusion of visually impaired people. Public transportation systems like airports, bus terminals, LRT stations would be made more accessible to this segment of society. They would be able to travel in unfamiliar locations successfully and have a workable strategy for self-familiarization within complex environments.

Initially, most research and designs on smart walking sticks or smart canes focus on detecting obstacles in the path of visually impaired people (The Nation, 2007; Omar, 2006; Smart Cane, Ankush, 2007). In (The Nation, 2007), a smart cane is proposed to detect objects in front and warn the person through a vibration in the handle. The smart cane used ultrasonic sensors to detect objects at levels from waist to head. The work in (Omar, 2006) used a combination of ultrasonic and infrared sensors to increase the accuracy of the obstacle detection. The smart cane in (Smart Cane, 2005) developed in 2005 by Prof. M. Moghavvemi in University Malaya used 'bat technology' by sending out ultrasound signals so that when the signal hits an object, part of it reflects back and the system can calculate how far the object is from the cane. When the visually impaired person approaches an object less than three and a half meters away, a pre-recorded voice says 'watch out', closer than that and it says 'beware' and when they are about to hit something it says 'danger'. These smart canes are useful for obstacle detection. However, they have no function to inform the visually impaired person of his or her current location. Several researchers have proposed technological solutions using RFID or GPS technology to assist visually impaired people (D'Atri et al., 2007; Chang, et al., 2005; Ran, Helal & Moore, 2004; BrailleNote, n. d.; Cardin, Thalmann & Vexo, 2007). Amongst the assistive systems which have been reported are SESAMONET (D'Atri et al., 2007), iCane (Chang, et al., 2005), Drishti (Ran, Helal & Moore, 2004), BrailleNote (n. d.) GPS and Werable Systems (Cardin, Thalmann & Vexo, 2007). The works in (Kulyukin, 2005) and (Ulrich, 2001) uses robotics technology for visually impaired people. In (Kulyukin, 2005), a RoboCart is used to help visually impaired people navigate a grocery store and carry purchased items.

Around the year 2007, relevant trends in ICT included pervasive sensing networks, wireless sensor networks and ubiquitous computing. The reduction in costs for hardware and software allowed the creation of both novel uses for existing technologies and applications of completely new technologies including assistive technologies. Researchers from the Visual Information Research (VIER) in Nottingham University tried to address problems by research and developing a system called Wireless Intelligent Assistive Navigation Management System Using SmartGuide Devices for Visually Impaired People. Their research works could be considered as the first to utilize wireless sensor network, pervasive computing intelligent processing to develop assistive technologies for visually impaired. Their works could be found in (Tee Z.H, Ang L.M 2009a; 2009b; 2009c; 2009d; 2010, 2011) and the development of a lab-scale prototype tested in a university environment. One of the works also won an award at the IBM Assistive & Rehabilitative Technology Student Design Challenge 2009.

The use of commercially available mobile devices with powerful processors shows great promise to assistive technologies for visually impaired people. Around the year 2012, the research and development works from the group of researchers mentioned in the previous paragraph were further extended. The works were conducted by K. L Lim and K.P Seng from the Assistive and Affective Technologies (AAT) Research Centre at Sunway University (affiliated with Lancaster University) and L.M. Ang from Edith Cowan University. The work aimed to enhance works including the lab-scale prototype from previous phases. It also targets to enhance the work by utilizing new trends and technologies in ICT (e.g. smart phones). They hope to continue the system development to enhance the lab-scale prototype to have coverage of multiple buildings.

This paper consists of three main parts. The first part reviews various assistive technologies. The second and third parts focus on the research and development works conducted by researchers mentioned in the previous paragraphs. The Wireless Intelligent Assistive Navigation Management System Using SmartGuide Devices for Visually Impaired People is first presented. The first system consists of (i) SmartGuide devices to monitor the current locations of people in the environment. The SmartGuide is a small unit that is placed near the end of the walking stick of blind people or can be carried in the hand for low vision people; (ii) Wireless Technology consists of a mesh communications network to receive data from the SmartGuides and forward it using a low power protocol. Smart Nodes will be placed throughout the transportation environment to form the mesh network; (iii) Intelligent Assistive Navigation Management System which receives data from the mesh network and processes those signals. The Intelligent Assistive Navigation system allows the visually impaired person to input a desired location to go to and guides the person via speech technology to the desired destination.

The third part of this paper focuses more recent works on the above Wireless Intelligent Assistive Navigation Management System Using SmartGuide Devices for Visually Impaired People. Basically, enhancements to SmartGuide devices in (i) have been done. To overcome some weaknesses of the SmartGuide devices in the previous system, Shoe-Pack, Belt-Pack and Head-Pack have been proposed. A new Navigation Module is included in the (ii) of the previous system. The path routing is dynamic and in emergency situations (example, fire), this intelligent system can safely guide the person out through the safest path when other paths become not available. In the latest system, the work extends the coverage of the system to multiple buildings. Each building will have its own submesh network for the wireless topology. This also gives fault tolerance to the system because even if one submesh goes down the others will still function. The submesh topologies will have some overlap among buildings to further increase the reliability of the system.

REVIEW OF ASSISTIVE TECHNOLOGIES FOR VISUALLY IMPAIRED PEOPLE

This section presents a comprehensive literature review on assistive technologies for visually impaired people. The review focuses on technologies which involve guidance or navigation system. It first reviews the research and development or products within 2001-2009. During this period, the research and development work utilized RFID and GPS. The second part of the review covers the research and development or products from year 2010 onwards. More mobile applications for the visually impaired on the mobile platforms started to appear from 2010. A brief review on non-guidance technologies to assist visually impaired people on text, speech and typing is also provided.

Research and Development Works Within 2001-2009

In this subsection, the research and developments of assistive technologies both in academia and the commercial market from year 2001 to 2009 are summarized. Further details can be found in our publication in 2011 (Tee Z.H, Ang L.M, 2011). A comparison of the interactive assistive technologies for earlier years can also be found there. The Wearable Audio Navigation (SWAN) (Walker, 2006; Wilson, 2007) is also included in this review. It is important to note that most of technological solutions in earlier years involved only RFID or GPS. There is no mobile application for the visually impaired on the Android and iOS platforms in earlier years. An update of our review on the assistive technologies from 2010-2015 including those on mobile devices or platforms will be provided in the next subsection (2).

Wearable Audio Navigation (SWAN)

A recent system with a comparable level of sophistication is the System for Wearable Audio Navigation (SWAN), which was developed to serve as a safe pedestrian navigation and orientation aid for persons with temporary or permanent visual impairments (Walker, 2006; Wilson, 2007). SWAN consists of an audio-only output and a tactile input via a dedicated handheld interface device. Once the user's location and head direction are determined, SWAN guides the user along the required path using a set of beacon sounds, while at the same time indicating the location of features in the environment that may be of interest to the user. The sounds used by SWAN include navigation beacons (earcon-like sounds), object sounds (through spatially localized auditory icons), surface transitions, and location information and announcements (brief prerecorded speech samples).

Secure and Safety Mobility Network (SESAMONET)

The SESAMONET (Secure and Safety Mobility Network) system (D'Atri et al., 2007) was developed by the European Joint Research Centre and University of Rome's RFID lab of Sapienza. The system uses RFID technology for user localization and tracking. SESAMONET use a grid of RFID tags which are burrowed in the ground around a depth of 4cm. The tags are wrapped in ceramic cells and embedded at 65cm intervals. An RFID reader is attached to a cane to obtain the tag ID as the cane moves over the tag. This information is sent to a PDA where software looks up the navigation data for the tag ID in the data server. The data server holds the database containing all the information used for navigation. The server also has an interface for client data synchronization which automatically updates data on the client side whenever the user approaches a new tag. The navigation data is converted to speech using text-to-speech synthesis and it is sent back to the user via Bluetooth through a Bluetooth headset. The main barrier in the successful performance of 'SESAMONET' is logistical issues. The system is only available provided the user is on the RFID embedded pavement. Furthermore, the layout and the maintenance of the RFID embedded path can be labour and material intensive. There is also a problem where the user wandered away from the track (RFID Microchip Network) and cannot find an RFID transponder to get back on to the track.

iCane

The iCane (Chang, et al., 2005) system is developed by Tsung-Hsiang Chng of National Taiwan University. The 'iCane' is based on a walking stick which is capable of giving navigational help to user in terms of locating nearby services. It features an individual personal map in order to assist revisiting places of interest easily. The system functions similarly to SESAMONET. The system utilizes RFID technology for person localization, a PDA to store navigation data and Bluetooth headset as human voice interface. RFID tags are placed on tactile pathways to be read by the RFID reader on the cane. Unlike SESAMONET, iCane utilizes a local database map installed in the PDA in order words; it has a static data source. The accuracy of the system is proportional to the density of the RFID network. The RFID tags are categorized by storing significant lower nibbles as an indicator of different tactile paving. The tile type is differentiated by the least significant bits (LSB) of the tag ID. The iCane lags behind SESAMONET as it utilizes a static navigation data source which is unable to handle dynamically changing environments. Since the control is static, there are risks of user navigation in a newly changed area with the old data set; a situation where the physical situation mismatches with the logical situation depicted in the data base. This can be of an enormous danger if the user is guided in a wrong direction in a wrong environment.

Drishti

Drishti (Ran, et al., 2004) which is an integrated navigation system for visually impaired people uses the Global Positioning System (GPS) and Geographical Information System (GIS) technologies. It is designed to be used within the university premises and contains a GIS dataset of the university. This contains geographically referenced information for both static and dynamic environments and is referred to as a spatial database. A differential GPS receiver in the wearable device determines the localization of the user by obtaining the *(x,y,z)* coordinates. After localization is performed, the spatial database is accessible through a wireless network to a wearable device that is carried by the visually impaired person. Drishti uses the IEEE 802.11b protocol to connect with its GIS server. Drishti is an assistive device which is operable in dynamically changing environments and can optimize routes for navigation when there is an unforeseen obstacle in the path. Like SESAMONET, Drishti gives assistance to the user by means of speech. Drishti may be considered as the first reliable assistive technology system which is capable to provide navigation assistance for the visually impaired people in dynamically changing environments. However, there are two limitations with this system. First, the prototype weighs eight pounds. Second, the degradation of the RF signals inside buildings degrades the accuracy of the GPS localization.

BrailleNote GPS

The BrailleNote (n.d.) is an assistive device which is on the market since 2005. The BrailleNote is a commercial product with various functions to offer that comes in a small and compact package. The BrailleNote GPS uses the GPS satellites to relay information about user's position and nearby points of interest. The user can easily program personalized travel routes and locations as well as use the thousands of points supplied by the system. BrailleNote GPS provides direction to head or whose driveway the user is crossing, and even which location the user is currently at. The BrailleNote uses the new generation GPS maps which maps larger territories and are divided into regional maps for more convenience.

Multiple-maps can be activated and stored in BrailleNote's memory. The Trekker 3.0 also expands the sources of geographical information with the capability to integrate complementary points of interest coming from other users, or databases downloadable from the Web. The 'VoiceNote GPS' is a more advanced version which uses the TTS method to convey speech information to the user. The 'BrailleNote' suffers the same shortfall as Dristhi. The GPS's accuracy is the limitation within indoor environments.

Wearable Systems

Wearable Systems (Cardin, et al., 2007) is a system designed to aid visually impaired people focusing on obstacle detection especially obstacles at shoulder height. The system utilizes sonar sensors to sense dynamic obstacles surrounding the environment and feeding the information through a sensing interface. In other words, the system will serve as an extension of the user's body functions. The major drawback of the system is that it does not provide guidance to the user for travelling.

Research and Development Works From 2010-2015

This subsection provides an updated review of recent developments in assistive technologies targeting the blind community. Besides academia, the products in commercial market are also briefly reviewed. This subsection also considers assistive technologies on mobile platforms. A cross-section of trending mobile applications for the visually impaired on the Android and iOS platforms is also provided here.

Real-Time Assistance Prototype (RTAP)

Real-Time Assistance Prototype (RTAP) (Dunai, 2010) is a camera-based system. The system consists of stereo cameras applied on a helmet, a portable laptop with Windows OS and small stereo headphones. The RTAP uses 19 discrete levels for distance. It also provides the advantage of explicitly representing the lack of any obstacle within a certain distance, which can be very useful in reassuring the user that the system is still in operation. In addition, the RTAP has object classification capabilities. It can filter objects based on importance or proximity. Tests have demonstrated several important factors. One of the factors is the ability of users to remember auditory events. Another important factor is the amount of training and the level of detail with which the associated training protocols are designed and validated. Some disadvantages of RTAP are the limited panning area of ± 32o, the lack of wireless connection, the laptop-sized central unit, the use of headphones blocking the outside world, low resolution in distance, and the inability to detect objects at the ground level.

HiFiVE

HiFiVE is a complex vision support system that combines sound with touch and manipulation (Dewhurst, 2010, 2009, 2007). Visual features are mapped onto speech-like (but non-verbal) auditory phonetics (only not emotional in character). All such sounds include three syllables which correspond to different areas in the image: one for color and two for layout. For example, "way-lair oar" might correspond to "white-grey" and "left-to-right". Changes in texture are mapped onto fluctuations of volume, while motion is represented through binaural panning. Users are also enabled to explore various areas on the image via finger or hand motions due to the haptics and tactile feedback. The HiFiVE system has seen several extensions since it was originally proposed in 2007. Due to the rise to prominence of automated vision processing approaches, recent extension has enabled the creation of so-called audio tactile objects, which represent higher-level combinations of low-level visual attributes. Such objects have auditory representations, and can also be explored through 'tracers'— i.e., communicational entities which either systematically present the properties of corresponding parts of the image ('area-tracers'), or convey the shapes of particular items ('shape-tracers').

See ColOr System

Another assistive technology which involves tactile interaction is the See ColOr system. This system combines auditory feedback with tactile interaction (Gomez, 2014). In brief, it combines modules for local perception, global perception, alerting and recognition. The local perception module uses (i) various auditory timbres to represent colors, and (ii) rhythmic patterns to represent distance as measured on the azimuth plane. The global module allows users to pinpoint one or more positions within the image using their fingers, so as to receive comparative feedback relevant to those areas alone. On the other hand, the alerting and recognition modules can provide higher-level feedback on obstacles which pose an imminent threat to the user, as well as on "auditory objects" which are associated with real-world objects.

Talking Location

Talking Location is an android app which enables users to learn their approximate position through WiFi or mobile data signals by shaking the phone (Talking Location, 2015). It is designed mainly for blind or eyes free use. It is often highly inaccurate. The app only allows users to send SMS messages to friends with their location to seek help when needed. There is no indoor or outdoor navigation.

Guard My Angel

Guard My Angel is also mobile app adapted to visually impaired people. It is similar to the idea behind Guard My Angel, which sends SMS messages (Guard My Angel, 2012). In fact, Guard My Angel is a free mobile application which enhances people's security and safety. In case of any personal emergency, the app automatically sends alerts to pre-selected contacts, and directs them to the user's exact location utilizing "live" maps.

WalkyTalky

Several "walking straight" applications have been developed to facilitate straight-line walking (Panëels, 2013; WalkyTalky 2015). Such applications use built-in sensors (i.e. mostly the magnetic sensor) to help blind pedestrians. Through the augmentation of mobile capabilities with data services comes the possibility to make combined use of GPS receivers, compasses and map data. WalkyTalky is an accessible navigation aid. It can periodically updates the status bar with your current location to the nearest street address. It is one of the many apps created by the Eyes-Free Project that helps blind people in navigation by providing real-time vibration feedback if they are not moving in the correct direction (Paul, 2012). The accuracy based on the in-built GPS can be low, making it difficult to issue warnings within 3–4 m of accuracy. This can be eliminated by having a better GPS receiver connected via Bluetooth.

Intersection Explorer

Intersection Explorer speaks the layout of the streets and intersections in neighborhoods as you touch and drag your finger around the map. This helps blind and low vision users get an understanding of a neighborhood both before venturing out and while on the go (Intersection Explorer, 2015). Google WalkyTalky and Intersection Explorer (developed within 2010-2012) aid vision-impaired Android users. Two Android apps intended for assisting blind or partially-sighted users are getting some attention of late, with Google's WalkyTalky and Intersection Explorer both being praised for their useful functionality. WalkyTalky basically hooks into Google Maps navigation engine Google Maps (2015) which is voice-guided GPS navigation. It gives directions in spoken rather than just on-screen instructions. It also reads out the street names you should be passing, so as to help users keep track of where they're walking.

vOICe

A more comprehensive application is The vOICe for Android (vOICe, 2015). The application maps live camera views to soundscapes, providing the visually impaired with an augmented reality based navigation support. It includes a talking color identifier, talking compass, talking face detector and a talking GPS locator. It is also closely linked with the Zxing barcode scanner and the Google Goggles apps by allowing for them to be launched from within its own context. The vOICe uses pitch for height and loudness for brightness in one-second left to right scans of any view: a rising bright line sounds as a rising tone, a bright spot as a beep, a bright filled rectangle as a noise burst, a vertical grid as a rhythm.

VoiceOver

Apple's iOS incorporates several features that help the visually impaired access an iPhone. VoiceOver is a gesture-based screen reader that allows blind and low-vision users to touch the screen to hear a description of the item under their fingers (VoiceOver, 2015). They can then use a double-tap, drag or flick motion to direct the phone or app to perform an action. VoiceOver renders text on the screen and also employs auditory feedback in response to user interactions Importantly VoiceOver can easily be switched on and off by pressing the home button three times. This is key if the device is being used alternately by a visually impaired and a sighted user, as the way in which interactions work is totally different when VoiceOver is running. Visually impaired users can control their device using VoiceOver by using their fingers on the screen or by having an additional keyboard attached. The iOS platform also provides applications for navigation assistance.

Ariadne GPS

Ariadne GPS also works with VoiceOver (VoiceOver 2015). Talking maps allow for the world to be explored by moving a finger around the map. During exploration, the crossing of a street is signaled by vibration. The app has a favorites feature that can be used to announce stops on the bus or train, or to read street names and numbers. It also enables users to navigate large buildings by pre-programming e.g. classroom locations. Rotating maps keep the user centered, with territory behind the user on the bottom of the screen and what is ahead on the top portion. Available in multiple languages, Ariadne GPS works anywhere Google Maps are available. Similarly to WalkyTalk, low resolution GPS receivers can be a problem, however this can be solved through external receivers connected to the device (Talking Location, 2015).

GPS Lookaround

GPS Lookaround also uses VoiceOver to speak the name of the street, city, cross-street and points of interest (Brian, 2013). Users can shake the iPhone to create a vibration and swishing sound indicating the iPhone will deliver spoken information about a location.

BlindSquare

BlindSquare is the accessible GPS app developed for the blind and visually impaired. It provides information to visually impaired users about their surroundings (BlindSquare, 2015). It describes the environment, announces points of interest and street intersections as a user travels. The tool uses GPS and a compass to identify location. Users can find out details of local points of interest by category, define routes to be walked, and have feedback provided while walking. From a social networking perspective, it is self-voicing, announcing points of interest, intersections and user defined points through a dedicated speech synthesizer.

WIRELESS INTELLIGENT ASSISTIVE NAVIGATION MANAGEMENT SYSTEM USING SMARTGUIDE DEVICES FOR VISUALLY IMPAIRED

Wireless sensor networks and pervasive computing can be considered as rapid emerging research areas around year 2007. The VIER research group in Nottingham University also worked on the research and development of wireless sensor network and its applications. One of their projects was called wireless intelligent assistive navigation management system using smartguide devices for visually impaired people. Figure 1 gives an overview of this system. In this project, wireless sensor network, pervasive computing and intelligent processing were utilized to develop assistive technologies for the visually impaired. This section gives a review of the research works in (Tee Z.H, Ang L.M 2009a; 2009b; 2009c; 2009d; 2010, 2011) and present the final and complete system. The complete system consists of three main components: (i) SmartGuide Devices, (ii) Wireless Technology and (ii) Intelligent Assistive Navigation Management System to assist and monitor the visually impaired people to roam freely in an indoor environment. This section also provides the mapping of four core layers which are the hardware layer, wireless sensor network layer, speech layer and software layer in (Tee Z.H, Ang L.M, 2011) to three major components in the final system presented in this section.

SmartGuide Devices

The system uses SmartGuide devices to monitor the current locations of people in the environment. The SmartGuide is a small unit that is placed near the end of the walking stick of blind people or can be carried in the hand for low vision people. Each SmartGuide has a wireless transceiver and continuously queries the network to get its current position. The localization capabilities of the SmartGuides are improved by using RFID tracking in combination with Dead Reckoning Modules (DRM). The DRM modules are miniature, self-contained, electronic navigation units that provide the user's position relative to an initialization point. The SmartGuide sends the data via wireless technology to the Intelligent Assistive Navigation Management system which processes the data and sends back the current location. The SmartGuide has speech modules to give and receive speech. SmartGuide devices can be found in two core layers, the *hardware layer* and *speech layer*, in (Tee Z.H, Ang L.M, 2011).

Wireless Technology

This technology consists of a mesh communications network to receive data from the SmartGuides and forward it using a low power protocol. Smart Nodes will be placed throughout the transportation environment to form the mesh network. The Smart Nodes work wirelessly making it very easy to attach them throughout the environment. The networking protocols utilize the deep sleep modes of the transceiver and microcontroller making the communication extremely energy efficient. This sophisticated technology delivers low power wireless embedded networking that is reliable and self-configuring. (Tee Z.H, Ang L.M, 2011) presented the detail of wireless technology in *wireless sensor network layer* (Crossbow WSN).

Figure 1. Overview of the wireless intelligent assistive navigation management system using SmartGuide devices for visually impaired

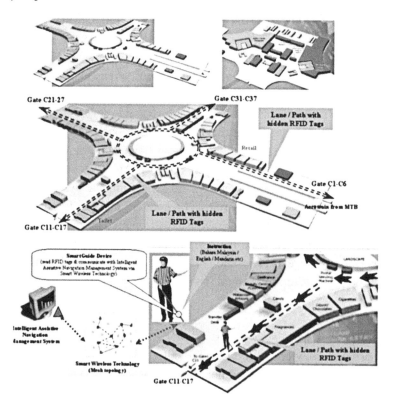

Intelligent Assistive Navigation Management System

This system receives data from the mesh network and processes those signals. The Intelligent Assistive Navigation system allows the visually impaired person to input a desired location to go to and the system guides the person via speech technology to the desired destination. The path routing is dynamic and in emergency situations (example, fire), this intelligent system can safely guide the person out through the safest path when other paths become not available. This system allows caregivers to view the movements of visually impaired people in the environment and automatically detect situations when they need assistance. The *software layer* (centralize server and intelligent management software) built in (Tee Z.H, Ang L.M, 2011) is part of the Intelligent Assistive Navigation Management System.

SmartGuide Devices

The system utilizes RFID tags as its indoor geographical information provider in order to achieve indoor localization. In other words, programmed RFID tags are placed strategically to mark points of interests in an indoor environment. By virtually connecting all the RFID tags, a 3D map is formed. RFID tags make up waypoints (the tags that the user must travel through) which is used during real time navigation to reach the requested destination. The speech layer acts as the main human interface of the system. Commands are given in speech to increase the user friendliness of the system. The hardware layer utilizes various technology and sensors to achieve the localization, navigation and extraction of positional data. The wireless sensor network (WSN) layer acts as the data transportation backbone of the system. Data transfer between the hardware and software layer can be achieved to increase system stability. Throughout the navigation process the user's position will be monitored there will be real-time and fault-tolerant data communication between all the four layers. The navigation starts with the hardware and speech layer where the user first requests a destination by talking into the microphone. The speech layer will handle the request by performing speech recognition, digitizing the speech into machine understandable command. At the same time, the hardware layer which consists of the SmartGuide devices obtained the user's current location. The current location of the user is obtained at the same time the requested destination is digitized into machine understandable command. These data are then relayed to the central server where to software layer is located via the wireless sensor network layer. The software layer on the central server then performs further processing, utilizing an algorithm to obtain the shortest travel path to the requested destination. The shortest path is a string of way points calculated by the system's algorithm which the user has to travel.

Smart-Guide Reader and Tracker

The SmartGuide device consists of two parts. One part is attached to the cane (Smart-Guide Reader) and the other part is attached to the person (SmartGuide Tracker). By splitting the hardware into two parts, the SmartGuide Reader is designed to be as compact as possible to increase portability and mobility. Core processing modules and interfacing modules are being installed on the SmartGuide Tracker which will be housed on a belt or a backpack of the user. The use of a belt/backpack system ensures ease of travelling. The two parts communicate wirelessly using Bluetooth technology. The SmartGuide Reader uses various technology and sensors to achieve the localization, navigation and extraction of positioning data. A combination of RFID technology, Global Positioning System (GPS) and Dead Reckoning

Module (DRM) tracking are used. The core processor for the system is a PIC Microcontroller. Bluetooth modules are used to replace the physical wires between the RFID Reader attached to the cane and the PIC microcontroller attached to the person. After the data extraction and measurement from the digital compass, GPS and DRM, the data are wirelessly transmitted to the host server via a wireless sensor mote. The host server will locate the current position and sends back the necessary speech information for user guidance and navigation. The SmartGuide device uses the RFID tags as localization points which are located on the floor in different areas. The RFID reader reads the tag ID from the RFID tags and the DRM which consists of gyroscopes and accelerometers is utilized to complement the positioning method by providing the position between those discrete points. After the data has been sent to the central server, acknowledgement of position and localization will be done by the server from the corresponding data entry in the database. The server data is then passed to the speech module. The speech module accepts voice activated commands from the user and generates synthesized speech to inform the user of position and navigation information.

Upon power up, the system attempts to request and establish the wireless connectivity between the Tracker and the Reader. Once the wireless connectivity is established, the LED indicator is shown by lighting on. The next step is to turn on the wireless mote to establish the connection for the database server. Once the GUI on the software layer indicates that the system is active and working, the positions of the user will be displayed on the server's map for monitoring. At the same time, the SmartGuide Tracker will have a message shown on the LCD to indicate that the RFID Tag is detected upon each designated location where the tags are fixed. RFID data reading, compass data reading, and DRM data collection is performed within the Mote interrupt service routine and these data will be sent over to the mote when requested by the mote through the interrupt. The mote will request this information periodically in the interval of few seconds. Once the reader detects an RFID Tag, the tag id is sent to the server via wireless mote. The correct position will be determined according to the RFID tag and necessary speech information is delivered to the user in voice form. Assistive data will be sent back to the SmartGuide Tracker in the form of bytes. The PIC saves the assistive data and sends them to the speech processor to be spoken out as words.

User Interface by Speech

The speech layer is responsible to perform speech recognition and speech synthesis. A microphone acts as the main human interface of the SmartGuide system but inputting speech commands for them user (recognition) while a speaker/headphone is used to output instructions to provide navigation assistance (synthesis). The speech processor is the VR Stamp RSC-4X RPM microcontroller and software development supported by Phython Project-SE IDE (Integrated Development Environment) which supports C language. Sensory Loader 4 is then used to burn the software into the VR Stamp via a development board. The VR Stamp RSC-464 speech processor is a 8 bit programmable microcontroller with built-in ADC, DAC, RAM and a basic interpreter (PBASIC) built into the ROM. Utilizing the new Fluent-Chip technology and optimized audio processing blocks, the VR Stamp is capable of providing high performance I/O speech features to cost sensitive embedded and consumer products with improved noise control. The VR Stamp supports the capability of creating speaker independent recognition sets by simple typing in the desired recognition vocabulary. For development, the speech processor provides an unprecedented level of cost effective system-on-chip (SOC) integration, enabling many applications that require DSP or audio processing which be used as a general-purpose mixed signal processor platform for custom applications. Speech recognition is done via a hybrid Hidden Markov Model and Neural Net methods.

The VR Stamp supports and recommends fast rapid deployment by using Quick T2SI speech recognition software to construct words and phrase that make up the speech and command library. The command library is built on predefined user response various user responses maps to various actions that will be carried out by the speech recognition application. The speech library is responsible for speech synthesizing, outputting predefined navigation instructions by voice. There are two types of speech interfacing methodologies, prompted recognition and continuous listening recognition. Command phrases are examples of prompted recognition where the application prompts for the user for further input to perform the required actions (initiative on application side). On the other hand, triggering phrases is an example of continuous listening recognition, and where the application reacts immediately once a speech input is received (initiative on user side). For either method, end-point detection is required to mark an end to the user's response. End point detection can be done via timeout (time elapsed with no input) and word spotting (predefined vocabulary).

Wireless Technology Layer

The wireless sensor network (WSN) provides the remote database and server connectivity. Data such as navigation requests and instructions are relayed on the fly between the hardware and software layer. The Crossbow Wireless Sensor Network is selected as the core hardware for data transportation for the SmartGuide system. In general, the architecture of Crossbow Wireless Sensor Network via nodes in connection with outside applications (server, PC, cell phone etc.), has three devices:

- **Node/ Mote:** Acquires data from associate data acquisition board and forwards the data upstream to the base station;
- **Gateway:** Aggregates data from the network; Provides connection to outside applications (PC, PDA, server etc.);
- **Router:** Extends network coverage; Re-routes in case of node failure or network congestion.

Wireless sensor networks have attracted a wide interest from industry due to their diversity of applications. Sensor networks are pervasive by nature; the number of nodes in a network is nearly boundless. Therefore, a key to realizing this potential is multi-hop mesh networking, which enables scalability and reliability. A mesh network is really a generic name for a class of networked embedded systems that share several characteristics including:

- **Multi-Hop:** Capability of sending messages peer-to-peer to a base station, thereby enabling scalable range extension;
- **Self-Configuring:** Capable of network formation without human intervention;
- **Healing:** Capable of adding and removing network nodes automatically without having to reset the network;
- **Dynamic Routing:** Capable of adaptively determining the route based on dynamic network conditions (e.g., link quality, hop-count, gradient, or other metric).

When combined with battery power management, these characteristics allow sensor networks to be long-lived, easily deployed, and resilient to the unpredictable wireless channel. With mesh networking, the vision of pervasive and fine-grained sensing becomes reality (Crossbow Technology Inc., 2007a). Crossbow defines a full featured multi-hop, ad-hoc, networking protocol called XMesh. Nodes or motes in XMesh terminology which are wirelessly connected with each other make up the XMesh Network. The XMesh is a true mesh topology (peerto-peer) which supports self-organizing and self-healing. The multi-hop technique supported by the WSN enables data relaying between nodes, maximizing signal coverage area at the same time provides fault tolerance. Typically, XMesh can route data from nodes "upstream" to the base station or "downstream" to individual nodes. If there is a node failure, XMesh will re-route the message through alternative path in order to reach the destination (Crossbow Technology Inc., 2007b).

Data routing on the XMesh is done using the Any-to-Base Routing Algorithm. XMesh expands all the available routes linked to the destination. The first goal is to measure the success rate/link quality of each of the links. Each mote will monitor its neighbouring and report the link quality. The route with better link quality ensures higher ratio probability to transmit the expected packets to the receiver node. The second goal is to minimize total path cost to determine the optimal route. The term "cost" is a measure of distance based on hop count, transmission and retries and reconfiguration over time. Crossbow WSN is an ideal solution for SmartGuide system as it provides intelligent, reliable networking with significant fault tolerance. The system is used to assist visually impaired people; thus any fault or delay in message transmission is not wanted and might cause safety issues. On the other hand, the ease of integration and low power consumption makes the Crossbow solution a good choice for the system.

Additional Monitoring: Camera Sensor Network

To enhanced real time monitoring by the caregivers and system administrators, a camera sensor network is implemented on top of the SmartGuide system. The caregiver monitoring system automatically switches to the camera nearest to the user for live user tracking. The camera system network operated wirelessly consists of two basic elements, the visual camera node and the visual base node. The visual camera node is made up of by the OmniVision OV9650 CMOS cameras connected to a Xilinx Spartan-3 FPGA. The Xilinx Spartan-3 FPGA used is part of a Celoxica RC10 development unit to process the captured images and control the ZigBee radio module. The information is sent wirelessly from the RC10 unit using the Telegesis ETRX2-PA ZigBee module to the data receiving end which is the visual base node on the PC/server side. For the vision nodes, the Telegesis ETRX2-PA module is configured as a ZigBee router while the base node is configured as a coordinator.

Intelligent Assistive Navigation Management System

This system receives data from the mesh network and processes those signals. It allows the visually impaired person to input a desired location to go to such as 'Platform 2' and the system guides the person via speech technology (e.g. 'go straight', 'turn left') to the desired destination. The path routing is dynamic and in emergency situations (example, fire), this intelligent system can safely guide the person out through the safest path when other paths become not available. For this proposal, only the Assistive component of the system will be implemented. This assistive system will inform the visually impaired person of his or her current location (e.g. 'at Platform 2', 'at ticket counter'). The Management system allows caregivers to view the movements of visually impaired people in the environment and automatically detect situations when they need assistance. Thus, pathfinding is an essential element in this assistive navigation and software which manages and monitors the navigation is also built.

Pathfinding: Search Algorithm

The search algorithm is performed after the RFID tags are properly mapped. The backbone of the search algorithm is the A* search algorithm. In the current scenario, A* is optimal (cost to the destination tag is never overestimated) and complete (all the tags and its positions are known) making it the best choice which minimizes the total estimated solution cost. The algorithm is enhanced further so that it will be able to perform search in a 3D environment as typical buildings consists of multiple floors. The A* is a form of informed search utilizing the known position and distance between tags to obtain the cheapest path from the current stage to the goal. The A* search algorithm is a type of best-first search in which a node is selected for expansion based on an evaluation function f(n). The node with the lowest evaluation function is selected for expansion as the value of the evaluation function is the measured distance to the goal. The A* search algorithm evaluates nodes by combining g(n), which is the cost to reach the node, and h(n), the cost to get from that node to the goal: f(n) = g(n) + h(n). Since g(n) gives the path cost from the start node to node n and h(n) is the estimated cost of the cheapest path from n to the goal, f(n) is defined as the estimated cost of the cheapest solution through n (Russell & Novig, 2002). A* is optimal in this case as the f(n) is an admissible heuristic. The heuristic function h(n) never overestimates the cost as it is basically the straight line distance (h_{SLD}) from tag n to the goal (shortest distance from one point to another). On the other hand, g(n) is the exact cost to reach n (total distance travelled). Thus it is an immediate consequence that f(n) never overestimates the true cost of a solution through n. The search is always complete in this case as the solution is the user requested destination that is always available.

Referring to Figure 2, if a user request to travel from the main door (point A) to the telephone (point F), the shortest travel path using the A* algorithm would be A -> D -> F. The search algorithm will check on the current tag (point A) and all its adjacent tags (in this case the adjacent tags will be B, C and D). Utilizing the tag coordinates stored in the database, the algorithm will then apply the evaluation function calculation and expand the nearest path as the one with the smallest heuristic distance (in this case it will be D with the smallest f(n)). Similarly, the algorithm will repeat itself by exploring all the adjacent tags of the subsequent state, in this case point D, and perform the heuristic calculation to decide which tag to expand until it reaches the goal state F. All the expanded tags will form the shortest path to the destination tag requested. The 3D A* search comes into action when the destination requested is not on the same floor as the current position of the user. The algorithm will perform a search to locate the nearest gateway that provides access to different floors, in this case, stairs, escalators or elevator. The system will then provide the user navigation either up or down to the appropriate floor. The search will then continue to guide the user from the particular exit point of the gateway till the final destination which is now on the same floor.

WEB-Based Intelligent Application Software

The web-based software, "IntelNav Web 3.0" is built using ASP. NET. The web application utilizes ASP. NET AJAX framework extensively for bandwidth and speed enhancing. The web application performs partial page updates that refresh only the parts of the web page that have changed. Thus, improving the

Figure 2. The 3D coordinates of a floor plan

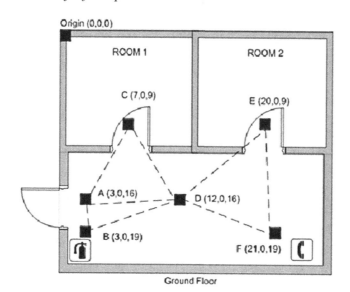

efficiency of the web application as part of the processing is performed by the browser. More detail of this software and its screen shots can be found in (Tee Z.H, Ang L.M, 2011).

Experiments and Prototype

Two experiments on were conducted in (Tee Z.H, Ang L.M, 2011). In the first experiment, the accuracy of the dead reckoning device was tested. Dead reckoning is a way of predicting the user's location while navigation assistance is temporarily lost when the user is travelling between tags. In the second experiment, the camera sensor nodes were tested. Important parameters such as data delay time and signal coverage ranges were obtained in order to determine the camera node network setup. Results and full discussion on these experiments can be found in (Tee Z.H, Ang L.M, 2011). This paper discusses the enhanced prototype of the system which has not been presented in any publication so far. Figure 3 shows the prototype of the Wireless Intelligent Assistive Navigation Management System and SmartGuide Devices. Figure 4 demonstrates the testing of the prototype in a university environment.

ENHANCEMENT OF WIRELESS INTELLIGENT ASSISTIVE NAVIGATION MANAGEMENT SYSTEM USING SMARTGUIDE DEVICES

In the previous system, SmartGuide Devices, Wireless Technology and Assistive Management System were developed. The enhancements to the previous system include:

1.   Re-design and development of new SmartGuide devices to replace those in the previous system. These include Shoe-Pack, Belt-Pack with Smart Track, Smart Link, Smart Phone and Head-Pack;
2.   Development of Navigation module for Intelligent Assistive Navigation Management System;
3.   Enhancement of the Wireless Technology developed in the previous system.

Figure 3. Prototype of the wireless intelligent assistive navigation management system and SmartGuide devices

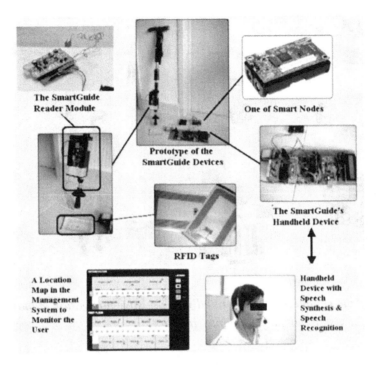

Figure 4. Testing of SmartGuide devices and wireless technology in university environment

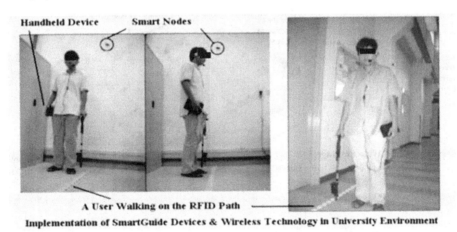

Figures 5 and 6 provide the overview of the Enhanced Wireless Intelligent Assistive Navigation Management System Using SmartGuide Devices for Visually Impaired People in Outdoor and Indoor environments. The technology allows applications to be efficiently distributed and operated on mobile and handheld devices, even in cases where computational requirements are significant. As a result, mobile technology can be combined with the technologies in the previous system to support assistive solutions for the visually impaired.

Figure 5. Overview of the enhanced wireless intelligent assistive navigation management system using SmartGuide devices for visually impaired people (outdoor)

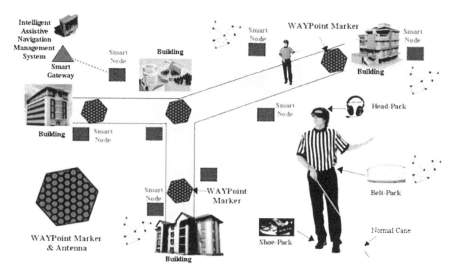

Figure 6. Overview of the enhanced wireless intelligent assistive navigation management system using SmartGuide devices for visually impaired people (indoor)

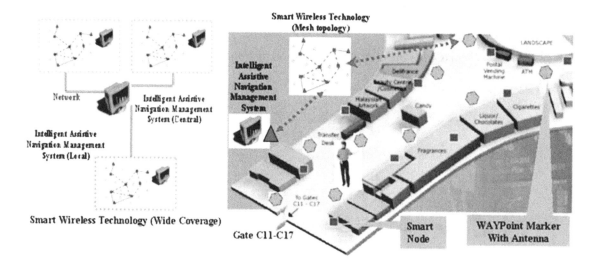

Enhancements of SmartGuide Devices

In the previous system, the SmartGuide was a small unit placed near the end of the walking stick of blind people. The unit contained a wireless transceiver and RFID reader and continuously queried the network to get its current position. The localization capabilities were achieved by placing RFID tags along the path and also used Dead Reckoning Modules to estimate position between tags. The unit also had speech modules to give and receive speech. There are three weaknesses with the previous system:

1. It requires many RFID tags to be placed along the path. This increases the cost of deployment and maintenance;
2. The swinging of the walking stick may miss the RFID tag and affect the localization accuracy;
3. Although small, the SmartGuide unit affects the natural walking way of the blind person.

To overcome the above weaknesses, the system is re-designed to have the following enhancements: Shoe-Pack, Belt-Pack and Head-Pack. Figure 7 illustrates (a) Shoe-Pack, (b) Head-Pack, (c) Interfacing with Smart Phone and (d) Belt-Pack.

Shoe-Pack

The RFID tag is attached to the shoe of the person. RFID tags to be embedded along the path as in the previous system are no longer needed. This reduces cost and maintenance. It is activated and read when the person is standing on a RFID Waypoint Marker. For the RFID Waypoint Marker, the RFID module from RFIdent or any equivalent module is used. Measuring only 38mm x 45mm, the reader module is ideal for battery operated handheld readers, mobile devices and printers. With a standard RS232 cable plus a USB connector, it is a ready "plug and play" product for desktop solution. The module also comes in RS422 and RS485 interfaces. The Waypoint Marker will also contain a custom antenna for the RFID module.

Belt-Pack

The localization and tracking is performed by the DRM and digital compass modules contained in the SmartGuide. The DRM module is a miniature, self-contained, electronic navigation unit that provides the user's position relative to an initialization point. GPS systems are not used because they do not work well inside buildings. It was observed in the previous system that DRM tracking was accurate for short distances and only became inaccurate for longer distances. The DRM is initialized at each RFID waypoint. As long as there are sufficient RFID waypoints, DRM tracking is accurate. The RFID waypoint contains a RFID reader and an antenna to detect the RFID tag. Compared to the previous system, the locations of the tag and reader are reversed. The person no longer carries the bulky reader but only needs to carry the small tag. This novelty is also one factor that distinguishes this project from others. The DRM localization data is transmitted to the Smart Phone via Bluetooth. The Smart Phone is a normal phone. The system uses the processing and speech capabilities in the phone itself. Thus, a dedicated microcontroller is not required. The data is then passed to the Assistive Navigation Management system via the mesh network which processes the data and sends back the current location.

For the DRM Module, the DRM5000 module from Honeywell or any equivalent module is used. The DRM5000 Dead Reckoning Module provides accurate position information for first responders and other people on foot in places that the global positioning system (GPS) is unable to reach. The small, easy-to-integrate unit contains ten sensors including three gyros, accelerometers and magnetometers as well a barometric altimeter to accurately deliver position location. The DRM5000 uses patented motion classification algorithms to analyze walking motion and compensate for unique user kinematics. The DRM5000 contains an internal Kalman filter for integrating onboard sensors and external GPS data. It nominally provides position data that is accurate to within 2% of the actual distance traveled by a user in environments without GPS. For the Digital Module, the HMC6352 module from Honeywell or any equivalent module is used. The HMC6352 is a two-axis, chip-scale digital compass for GPS applications, personal navigation, vehicle telematics, consumer electronics, and general two-axis compassing. Honeywell's digital compass combines the sensor elements and all the processing electronics in a 6.5mm square package to satisfy smaller, next generation applications.

Head-Pack

This is a wireless Bluetooth headset to receive speech information from the Smart Phone. The Smart Phone contains the text to speech synthesis software. In the previous project, dedicated speech chips were used. However, the project team has found that the speech synthesis capabilities of the chips were severely limited in its vocabulary. For the Smart Phone, the use of different smart phones from several manufacturers such as the Windows Mobile development tools and API from Microsoft can be investigated. Other alternatives could be Android from Google or iPhone OS from Apple. Unlike the previous system, the speech module is accomplished by text to speech synthesis and recognition software in the Smart Phone. The previous system used a dedicated speech chip which had severe limitations in its capability for recognition and synthesis.

Navigation Module for Intelligent Assistive Navigation Management System

In the previous system, only the Assistive Module of the system was implemented. The Navigation Module is software that allows a person to requests and the system gives information to guide him/her to the desired location. The effectiveness of various path-finding algorithms (A* search, Djikstra shortest path, etc) is investigated. An important safety feature of the system is its dynamic routing. In emergencies,

Figure 7. (a) Shoe-pack; (b) Head-pack; (c) Interfacing with smart phone; (d) Belt-pack

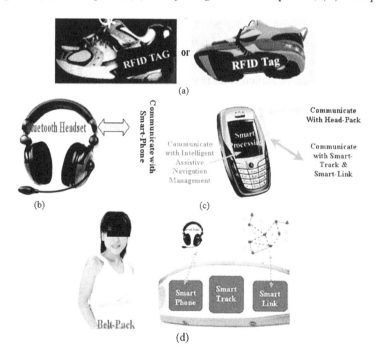

the system will guide the person out via the safest path when other paths become blocked. This safety feature is novel to our proposed system and gives more confidence to the visually impaired person to use the public transportation system. The system also allows caregivers to view the movements of people within the transportation environment so that they can give immediate assistance when required. The system can also detect the need for assistance automatically. This feature involves intelligent signal or information processing techniques. Caregivers can also select the option with instant notification technology. Soft alarm will be triggered to inform the person to view the screen. The system can also send SMS to inform the person via mobile phone.

Enhancement of the Wireless Technology (Coverage of Multiple Buildings)

In the previous system, the Smart Wireless Technology (Smart Nodes, Smart Mesh Network, Smart Gateway) which has been designed and developed. In the current system, the focus is to extend the technology to have coverage of multiple buildings using sub-mesh implementations. Each building will have its own submesh network for the wireless topology. This also gives fault tolerance to the system because even if one submesh goes down the others will still function. The submesh topologies will have some overlap among buildings to further increase the reliability of the system. Similarly, the wireless technology consists of a mesh network to receive data from SmartGuide devices and forward the data. It is important to note that information or data will be smartly routed using alternate path, if a single node fails for any reason. The Smart Gateway interfaces the wireless mesh network to the host PC or workstation, LAN or internet.

Experiments and Prototype

This subsection presents some research and development works in the Affective and Assistive Technologies (AAT) Research Centre in Sunway University.

Pathfinding: New Algorithms

New algorithms have been developed for pathfinding. The boundary iterative-deepening depth-first search (BIDDFS) is first proposed to compensate the memory requirements of the Dijkstra's algorithm and the search redundancy of the IDDFS. This algorithm utilizes the iterative-deepening feature of the IDDFS to reduce the memory requirements for pathfinding and the cost calculation feature of the Dijkstra's algorithm to guarantee the shortest path. A portion of memory is allocated for the algorithm to store the location of the boundary to minimize search redundancy. This means that while the IDDFS perpetually repeats its search from the starting point, the BIDDFS repeats its search from the saved boundary locations. The BIDDFS exhibits faster single-node expansion speed compared to the A* search, IDA* search and fringe search (Björnsson, Enzenberger, Holte, & Schaeffer, 2005), and it is faster than the IDDFS due to its minimized redundancy. To allow faster searching, the BIDDFS was enhanced for bidirectional searching. Bidirectional searching searches back and forth between the starting and goal locations, and these two searches meet at a distance in between and subsequently the route is then plotted from the meeting location. This approach of searching is able to reduce pathfinding times due to lesser number of nodes searched. Furthermore, the bidirectional BIDDFS is tested with a parallel approach to search from both the starting and goal locations simultaneously. The BIDDFS is also enhanced to search for multiple goals on a map.

A multi-goal BIDDFS is able to search for all goals on a map in a single search, whereas single-goal algorithms will need to repeat searching for different goal locations, introducing search redundancy. This eventually allows the multi-goal BIDDFS to save time and redundancy searching multiple goals. Many experiments on pathfinding were conducted. Results and discussion on some experiments can be found in (Kai Li, K. PSeng, 2015a). In (Kai Li, K.P. Seng, 2015b), the developed pathfinding algorithms were implemented on Android device. The pathfinding algorithms were programmed using NetBeans, an integrated development environment (IDE) by Oracle Corporation primarily for Java development. This simplified the implementation of the pathfinding algorithms onto a navigation system running on the Android platform. Furthermore, programming the pathfinding algorithm in Java allowed the identification of critical points that could be optimized for faster pathfinding. Java's thread functions allowed easy implementation of parallel programming for the pathfinding algorithms, increasing the utilization of multi-core processors found in smartphones and computers today. Therefore, the optimized BIDDFS was proposed. The optimized BIDDFS, called BIDDFS* was able to record drastic improvements in pathfinding speeds compared to the standard BIDDFS. The approach was further extended to the fast bidirectional BIDDFS*.

Lab Prototype

In this paper, the lab prototype of the enhanced system which has not been presented in any publication so far is included. Figure 8 shows some hardware components used to develop the lab prototype. Figure 9 illustrates the laboratory prototype and testing.

Figure 8. Hardware components of the lab prototype

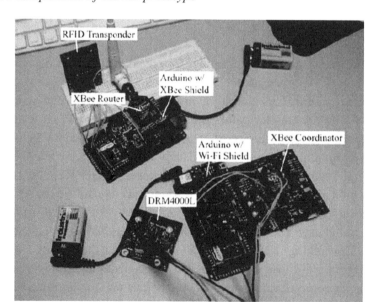

Figure 9. (a) Lab prototype for the enhanced SmartGuide devices; (b) Testing; (c) The RFID tag before embedding to the shoe; (d)Smart phone (Android)

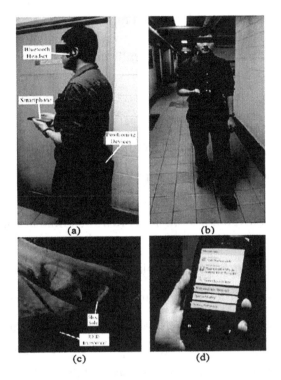

CONCLUSION

This paper has presented a comprehensive and up to date review of assistive technologies for visually impaired people. Recent developments of assistive technologies in mobile interaction have also been discussed. The Wireless Intelligent Assistive Navigation Management System Using SmartGuide Devices for visually impaired, developed by VIER group in Nottingham University has been presented. The system is able to assist blind and low vision people to walk around independently, especially in dynamic changing environments. The "SmartGuide" of the system is built as a standalone portable handheld device. The "Intelligent Assistive Navigation" of the system allows the visually impaired person to input a desired location to go to and guides the person via speech technology to the desired destination. The system also includes a camera sensor network to enhance monitoring capabilities for an extra level of security and reliability. The paper has also discussed more recent works to enhance the system, and improvements to SmartGuide devices to overcome some weaknesses of the SmartGuide devices in the earlier system have been presented. Prototypes of both systems have also been discussed in this paper.

ACKNOWLEDGMENT

Authors in this paper would like to thank Mr Lim Kai Li who was the postgraduate student of Affective and Assistive Technology (AAT) Research Centre Sunway University to provide some photographs of lab prototype from his thesis. Mr Lim Kai Li is currently the PhD student in UWA Australia.

REFERENCES

What is BlindSquare? (2015). BlindSquare. Retrieved from http://blindsquare.com/about/

BrailleBack. (2015). https://play.google.com/store/apps/details?id=com.googlecode.eyesfree.brailleback. Accessed Nov 2015

Braillenotes product information. (2009). *BrailleNote*. Retrieved from http://www.humanware.com/en-asia/products/blindness/braillenotes

BrailleType. (2011). Retrieved from http://www.ankitdaf.com/projects/BrailleType/

Voice Brief. (2015). *Dong Baik*. Retrieved from https://itunes.apple.com/HU/app/id423322440?mt=8

Cane, S. (2005). Retrieved from http://www.axistive.com/smart-bat-cane-for-the-blind-and-deaf.html

Cardin, S., Thalmann, D., & Vexo, F. (2007). Wearable system for mobility improvement of visually impaired people. *The Visual Computer: International Journal of Computer Graphics*, *23*(2), 109–118. doi:10.1007/s00371-006-0032-4

Chang, T. S., Ho, C. J., Hsu, D. C., Lee, Y. H., Tsai, M. S., Wang, M. C., & Hsu, J. (2005). iCane-a partner for the visually impaired. In T. Enokido et al (Eds.), Embedded and Ubiquitous computing, LNCS (Vol. 3823, pp. 393-402). Springer.

Color ID Free. (2015). *GreenGar Studios*. Retrieved from https://itunes.apple.com/HU/app/id402233600?mt=8

Colorblind Helper. (2015). *Angres Felipe Vergara Gonzalez*. Retrieved from https://play.google.com/store/apps/details?id=com.beanslab.colorblindhelper.helper

XServe user manual. (2007a). *Crossbow Technology Inc*. Retrieved from http://www.xbow.com/Support/Support_pdf_files/XMesh_Users_Manual.pdf

XMesh user manual. (2007b). *Crossbow Technology Inc*. Retrieved from http://www.xbow.com/Support/Support_pdf_files/XMesh_Users_Manual.pdf

D'Atri, E., Medaglia, C. M., Serbanati, A., Ceipidor, U. B., Panizzi, E., & D'Atri, A. (2007). A system to aid blind people in the mobility: A usability test and its results. *Paper presented at the Second International Conference on Systems*, Sainte-Luce, Martinique. doi:10.1109/ICONS.2007.7

Light Detector. (2015). *EveryWare Technologies*. Retrieved from https://itunes.apple.com/HU/app/id420929143?mt=8

Dewhurst, D. (2007) An audiotactile vision-substitution system. *Proceedings of second international workshop on interactive sonification*, York.

Dewhurst, D. (2009) Accessing audiotactile images with HFVE silooet. *Proceedings of fourth international workshop on haptic and audio interaction design* (pp 61–70). Springer, Berlin doi:10.1007/978-3-642-04076-4_7

Dewhurst, D. (2010) Creating and accessing audio-tactile images with "HFVE" vision substitution software. In: Proceedings of the third interactive sonificationworkshop. KTH, Stockholm, pp 101–104

Dragon Dictation. (2015). *Nuance Communications.* Retrieved from https://itunes.apple.com/HU/app/id341446764?mt=8

Dunai, L., Fajarnes, G. P., Praderas, V. S., Garcia, B. D., & Lengua, I. L. (2010) Real-time assistance prototype—a new navigation aid for blind people. In: Proceedings of IECON 2010—36th annual conference on IEEE Industrial Electronics Society, pp 1173–1178

Intersection Explorer. (2015). Retrieved from http://www.androlib.com/android.application.com-google-android-marvin-intersectionexplorer-qqxtC.aspx

Eyes-Free Shell. (2015). http://accessibleandroid.blogspot.hu/2010/09/how-do-i-use-eyes-free-shell.html Accessed Nov 2015.

Garg, A. (2007) *Smart cane project: knee above obstacle detection and warning system for the visually impaired* [Bachelor of Engineering Dissertation]. Indian Institute of Technology.

GomezValencia JD. (2014) Acomputer-vision based sensory substitution device for the visually impaired (See ColOr), PhD thesis. University of Geneva Google Maps (2015) https://play.google.com/store/apps/details?id=com.google.android.apps.maps&hl=en Accessed Nov 2015.

Guard My Angle. (2012). http://www.prlog.org/11967532-guard-my-angel-mobile-app-adapted-to-visually-impaired-people.html. Article in 2012, Accessed Nov 2015

Hameed, J. I., Naseem, B., Anwar, O., & Afzal, S. (2006). Assistive technology based navigation aid for the visually impaired. *Proceedings International Symposium on Practical Cognitive Agents and Robotics*, Australia. (pp. 192-199). doi:10.1145/1232425.1232450

Awareness! The Headphone App. (2015). *Essency.* Retrieved from https://itunes.apple.com/HU/app/id389245456?mt=8

Horowitz, B.T. (2013). 10 iPhone Apps Designed to Assist the Visually Impaired. *Eweek.com.* Retrieved from http://www.eweek.com/mobile/slideshows/10-iphone-apps-designed-to-assist-the-visually-impaired/#sthash.0GDG5TYh.dpuf

JustSpeak. (2015). Retrieved from http://eyes-free.blogspot.hu/

Kai Li Lim, K. P. (2015, April). Seng, L. S. Yeong, L.-M. Ang, and S. I. Ch'ng (2015b). Uninformed Pathfinding: A New Approach. *Expert Systems with Applications, 42*(5), 2722–2730. doi:10.1016/j.eswa.2014.10.046

Kai Li Lim, K. P. (in press). Seng, L. S. Yeong, L.-M. Ang, and S. I. Ch'ng (2015b). Pathfinding for the Navigation of Visually Impaired People. *International Journal of Computational Complexity and Intelligent Algorithms.*

Kulyukin, V., Gharpure, C., & Nicholson, J. (2005). RoboCart: toward robot-assisted navigation of grocery stores by the visually impaired. *Proceedings International Conference on Intelligent Robots and Systems* (pp. 2845-2850). doi:10.1109/IROS.2005.1545107

Talking Location. (n. d.). Retrieved from http://www.androlib.com/android.application.com-shake-locator-qzmAi.aspx

LookTel Money Reader. (2015). *IPPLEX*. Retrieved from https://itunes.apple.com/HU/app/id417476558?mt=8

Threads and threading. (2009). *Microsoft*. Retrieved from http://msdn.microsoft.com/en-us/library/6kac2kdh(VS.71).aspx

Nunal, P. (2012). Best Android apps for the blind and visually impaired. *Android Authority*. Retrieved from http://www.androidauthority.com/best-android-apps-visually-impaired-blind-97471

oMoby (2015). *Mashable.com*. Retrieved from http://mashable.com/2010/03/04/omoby-visual-search-iphone/.Accessed Nov

Panëels, S. A., Varenne, D., Blum, J. R., & Cooperstock, J. R. (2013). The walking straight mobile application: helping the visually impaired avid veering. *Proceedings of ICAD13*, Lódz (pp. 25–32).

Pun, T., Roth, P., Bologna, G., Moustakas, K., & Tzovaras, D. (2007). Image and video processing for visually handicapped people. *EURASIP Journal on Image and Video Processing, 2007*, 1–12. doi:10.1155/2007/25214

Ran, L., Helal, S., & Moore, S. (2004). *Drishti: An integrated indoor/outdoor blind navigation system and service.* Paper presented at the Second IEEE Annual Conference on Pervasive Computing and Communications. doi:10.1109/PERCOM.2004.1276842

Read for the Blind. (2015). Retrieved from https://andreashead.wikispaces.com/Android+Apps+for+VI+and+Blind

Russell, S., & Novig, P. (2002). *Artificial intelligence: A modern approach* (2nd ed.). Prentice Hall.

Seenesthesis. (2015). Retrieved from https://play.google.com/store/apps/details?id=touch.seenesthesiiis

Seenesthesis-blind exploration (2015). Retrieved from https://play.google.com/store/apps/details?id=touch.see&hl=en

Students set out to assist blind people. (2007, Sep. 27). *The Nation*.

TalkBack. (2015). Retrieved from http://www.androlib.com/android.application.com-google-android-marvin-kickback-FExn.aspx

TapTapSee. (2015). Retrieved from https://itunes.apple.com/us/app/taptapsee-blind-visually-impaired/id567635020?mt=8. Accessed Nov 2015

Tee, Z. H., Ang, L. M., & Seng, K. P. (2009a) SmartGuide System to Assist Visually Impaired People in a University. *Proc. Inter. Convention on Assistive Technology* (pp. 5-8). doi:10.1145/1592700.1592703

Tee, Z. H., Ang, L. M., & Seng, K. P. (2009b) Web-based Caregiver Monitoring System for Visually Impaired People. *Proc. MultiConference Engineers* (pp. 974-979).

Tee, Z. H., Ang, L. M., & Seng, K. P. (2009c) Wireless RFID and camera sensor network system to assist visually impaired people. *Proc. IADIS Conf. Applied Computing* (pp. 124-131).

Tee, Z.H, Ang, L.M, & Seng, K.P. (2010) SmartGuide Assistive Technology System to Assist Visually Impaired People in an Indoor Environment. *IETE Tech. Review*, 27(6), 455-464.

Tee, Z. H., Ang, L. M., & Seng, K. P. (2011). *A Novel Application of Information Communication Technology to Assist Visually Impaired People. Assistive and Augmentive Communication for the Disabled: Intelligent Technologies for Communication, Learning and Teaching* (pp. 103–126). IGI Global.

Tee, Z. H., Ang, L. M., Seng, K. P., Kong, J. H., & Ricky Lo, M. Y. Khor. (2009d) Web-based Caregiver Monitoring System for Assisting Visually Impaired People. *Proceedings of the International MultiConference of Engineers and Computer Scientists (IMECS 2009)* (Vol. 1, pp. 974-979).

Ulrich, I., & Borenstein, J. (2001). The guidecane - applying mobile robot technologies to assist the visually impaired. *IEEE Transaction on Systems, Man, and Cybernetics-Part A: Systems and Humans*, 31(2), 131-136.

Video Motion Alert. (2015). Retrieved from https://itunes.apple.com/HU/app/id387523411?mt=8

VizWiz. (2015). Retrieved from https://itunes.apple.com/HU/app/id439686043?mt=8 2015

VOICe. (2015). Retrieved from http://www.androlib.com/android.application.voice-voice-wiz.aspx

VoiceOver. (2015). Retrieved from http://appadvice.com/applists/show/apps-for-the-visually-impaired

Walker, B. N., & Lindsay, J. (2006). Navigation performance with a virtual auditory display: Effects of beacon sound, capture radius, and practice. *Human Factors*, 48(2), 265–278. doi:10.1518/001872006777724507 PMID:16884048

WalkyTalky. (2015). Retrieved from https://play.google.com/store/apps/details?id=com.googlecode.eyesfree.walkytalky&hl=en

Wilson, J., Walker, B. N., Lindsay, J., Cambias, C., & Dellaert, F. (2007) SWAN: system for wearable audio navigation. *Proceedings of the 11th international symposium on wearable computers (ISWC2007)*, USA

This research was previously published in the International Journal of Ambient Computing and Intelligence (IJACI), 7(1); edited by Nilanjan Dey, pages 45-68, copyright year 2016 by IGI Publishing (an imprint of IGI Global).

Chapter 3
Gaze–Based Assistive Technologies

Thies Pfeiffer
Bielefeld University, Germany

ABSTRACT

The eyes play an important role both in perception and communication. Technical interfaces that make use of their versatility can bring significant improvements to those who are unable to speak or to handle selection tasks elsewise such as with their hands, feet, noses or tools handled with the mouth. Using the eyes to enter texts into a computer system, which is called gaze-typing, is the most prominent gaze-based assistive technology. The article reviews the principles of eye movements, presents an overview of current eye-tracking systems, and discusses several approaches to gaze-typing. With the recent advent of mobile eye-tracking systems, gaze-based assistive technology is no longer restricted to interactions with desktop-computers. Gaze-based assistive technology is ready to expand its application into other areas of everyday life. The second part of the article thus discusses the use of gaze-based assistive technology in the household, or "the wild," outside one's own four walls.

INTRODUCTION

How exciting is the first eye contact with a new born baby and his parents. How overwhelming the moment when the eyes start exploring the world and the head movement follows the eyes. And how ground-shaking the effect once the baby's eyes can follow the attentive gaze of her parents (Corkum & Moore, 1998; Hood, Willen & Driver, 1998) or find the target beyond the pointing finger (Butterworth & Itakura, 2000).

Eyes are a powerful device for communication–they tell a lot about us, our intentions, what we are talking about, whom we are talking to, and they even reveal parts of our emotions. They are part of a multimodal communicative ensemble that is our human body.

For some, however, the eyes are also the one and only gate to the outside world. We humans are often very good in a situated reading of the intentions of others just by observing their eyes. If someone we care for is gazing at a glass of water, which to him is out of reach, we infer that he might be thirsty, offer

DOI: 10.4018/978-1-5225-2589-9.ch003

our help and give him to drink. If we talk to someone unable to speak or move, we can establish a pact and tailor our questions in such a way, that our interlocutor can answer them using eye blinks (e.g. one for no, two for yes) or eye movements (up/down or left/right).

This chapter addresses the question on how gaze-based assistive technologies enable us to make use of our eyes for purposes that are beyond their natural sensory use. It will show that today it is already possible to talk with our eyes and even to write letters. Someday we will also be able to interact with our (technically enhanced) physical environment based on eye gaze and first visionary steps into that direction will be presented.

Gaze-Based Interaction and the Midas-Touch Problem

A crucial task in interaction is the selection of the object to interact with. For a successful selection, one has to aim at a target and then trigger the selection (see e.g. Huckauf & Urbina, 2008). While aiming at a specific target is the example par excellence for an appropriate gaze-based interaction, it proves to be more difficult to actually trigger the selection.

The problem of providing a robust but also swift technique to trigger a selection is common for many gaze-based applications. The eye is predominantly a sensory organ which is now, in gaze-based interaction, used in an articulatory way. For articulation we want to have a high and exclusive control over our modality, so that we are not to be misunderstood. Gaze, however, wanders over the scene while we process it and it is highly attracted to changes in the environment. Users might thus look at a certain key on the screen because they want to type, but they might also just accidently look there, e.g. while listening to a response, or just because the keys' depictions of a virtual keyboard switched from lower to upper case after triggering the "shift"-key. Other visual changes might, e.g., be the result of the intelligent algorithm that rearranges the display to present the keys most likely selected next at a prominent position.

The problem of unwillingly triggering reactions is known as the Midas-Touch problem, since a prominent paper by R.J.K. Jacob (1993).

Parameters of Eye Gaze

Our eyes are active sensory organs. They are sensors that capture light that is cast from the objects in our environment and project them internally on a light-sensitive surface, the retina (see Figure 1). The resolution of the retina, however, is not equally distributed. We have a certain circular area of very high acuity, the fovea, and acuity diminishes the further away from the fovea the incoming rays hit the surface. The field of view covered by the fovea is rather small, only 1-2, which is approximately the area covered by 1-2 thumbs when extended at arm's length.

Interestingly, we are seldom aware of objects we can only see with a very low acuity. This is where the active part comes in: we constantly orient our eyes towards the area in our field of view we want to inspect. And we do it in such a way, that the interesting parts fall onto the fovea. These visual inspection movements are very quick – the eye is in general a very high speed device with a peek angular velocity of 900°/sec. That would be nearly three full rotations per second. Thus when we see something of interest in the periphery, which has a low visual acuity, we orient our eyes swiftly towards the target and will thus bring the target within our field of high visual acuity.

Figure 1. The eye is optimized to perceive the environment with a high acuity only in the area of the fovea

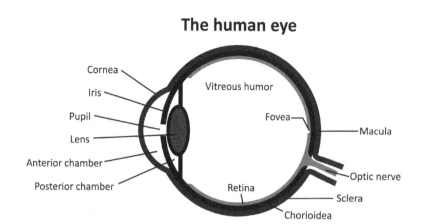

The fast eye movements are called *saccades* (from the French *saccadè*, meaning jerky). The moments of rest, when the eyes are aligned with our target of visual attention, are called *fixations*. The fixated area is called the *point of regard*, although it probably should better be called area or even volume of regard, to underline that it is not only a single point we have in our center of high accurate vision. When we visually inspect a scene, we produce a sequence of fixations and saccades, until we finally have satisfied our curiosity (and even then we will normally continue to produce them, just staying alert). If we connect the areas that have been the target of the fixations by lines representing the saccades, we can create a *scanpath* (see Figure 2) depicting the temporal sequence of our visual exploration.

Scanpaths are often used to depict the time course of visual attention over a certain stimulus (Norton & Stark, 1971; Yarbus, 1967). One area that is specifically interested in this incremental processing of the environment is usability research. When analyzing complex user interfaces, the scanpaths can tell the expert how the users perceive the interface and how the interface guides the visual attention of the users. For example, if the scanpath shows that the user has switched his gaze back and forth between two different buttons, this can be taken as a hint that the user was having difficulties to decide which action to take next and what the alternative actions were.

There are also qualitative visualizations that allow for the depiction of visual attention of a whole group of users. These visualizations come by different names and flavors, such as attention maps (Pomplun, Ritter & Velichkovsky, 1996), attentional landscapes, saliency maps or heatmaps (Wooding, 2002). Heatmaps (see Figure 3) are the most commonly known visualization type, as they are often used to depict the distribution of visual attention over webpages.

It has been found that the duration of a fixation correlates to the processing that is going on in the brain. The duration of a fixation thus helps us to differentiate between accidental gazes, gazes during visual search and, e.g., intentional gazes during communication (Velichkovsky, Sprenger & Pomplun, 1998, see Figure 4). The duration a fixation rests on a certain object is also called dwell time. As can be seen in Figure 4, during the localization and figurative processing of the visual scene, fixations durations are basically shorter than 250 ms. To avoid the Midas-Touch effect in gaze-based interactions, it is thus reasonable to use dwell-times well above 250 ms to trigger a selection.

Figure 2. Scanpath of a user reading a webpage. The circle in the center represents the initial fixation. From there, the eye moved up to the picture and only then back to the title of the section.

Figure 3. A heatmap summarizes the distribution of attention over time and/or several participants. Areas which received high amounts of attention are depicted in red (in print bright white) and areas with little or no attention are shaded.

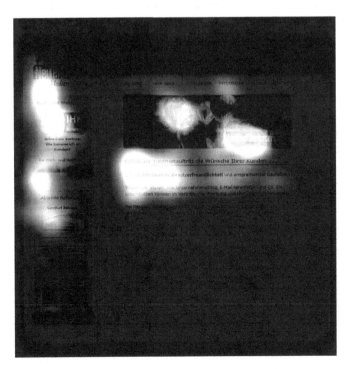

Figure 4. Fixation durations can be used to differentiate coarsely between typical tasks (Redrawn from Velichkovsky et al., 1998). Figurative: shape; Semantic: interpretation of meaning; Selfreferential: related to the subject; Communication: gaze with communicative function (e.g. joint attention).

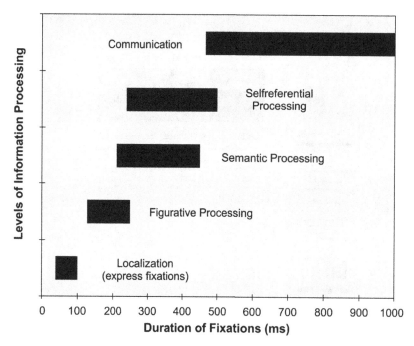

Another idea instead of dwelling is to use eye blinks as triggers. We have tested this idea in a 3D game of Asteroids we have implemented in our virtual reality environment (Hülsmann, Dankert, & Pfeiffer, 2011). It turns out, that this technique has some disadvantages. First, similar to fixations, our participants had to increase the time they closed their eyes when triggering the selection to let our algorithms differentiate between involuntary blinks and intentional blinks. Second, as the eye also moves during the initiation of the blinking, the accuracy of the aiming was affected and it was difficult to decide at what time before the detection of the blink to take the aim. In an alternative approach, we asked the participants to use a one-eyed blink to trigger a selection. By this we expected to cut down the timing, as one-eyed blinks do not occur naturally, and we also imagined that the eye remaining open could still provide a steady direction for aiming. Most participants, however, were not able to blink with one eye only, so this approach was also not very successful.

Devices for Gaze Tracking

Historically, there have been several technical approaches to eye tracking. A short overview of these systems can be found in Duchowski (2007). A very appealing approach, the electro-oculography (EOG), measures the electrical changes on the skin around the eye induced by the eye movements (e.g. see Young & Sheena, 1975). The advantage of this method is that it does not interfere with the line of sight. EagleEyes is an eye tracking system based on EOG developed at Boston College (EagleEyes, 1996; Gips & Olivieri, 1996).

However, the system is very sensitive to other movements of the face and thus of limited use in everyday activities, especially if the person being tracked has only limited control of his facial muscles. Electro-oculography, however, could be used to distinguish simple eye-based gestures (Drewes, De Luca, & Schmidt, 2007) where a high spatial precision is not required.

A more precise approach uses a contact lens instrumented with sensor technology, e.g. with a wire coil whose movement is then measured by electromagnetic tracking (Robinson, 1963) or an optical lever that amplifies the movements of the eyes which are then measured on a photo-sensitive receptor (Ditchburn & Ginsborg, 1953). The high precision, however, comes at the cost of a high intrusion. The system is also very delicate to handle, tends to drift over time and does not seem fit for the requirements of robust every-day interfaces.

The systems most commonly available today when measuring the point of regard are video-based corneal reflection eye trackers (Duchowski, 2007). The principles of this technology have been developed over 100 years ago (Robinson, 1968). This computer vision-based approach detects distinguishable features of the human eye, such as the pupil and corneal reflections of a stimulating infra-red light (also called first Purkinje image). This infra-red light is part of the eye tracking system and serves as external reference. By combining both features, the position of the pupil and the position of the corneal reflection, the eye tracking system can differentiate between movements of the head and the eye. There are many vendors of commercial eye-tracking systems. A good overview is provided in the wiki of the Communication by Gaze Interaction Association (COGAIN, 2012).

An advantage of this video-based approach is its use of inexpensive hardware – in principle such a system can be created from off-the-shelf electronic parts. In fact, there are several open source projects today that offer detailed descriptions and part-lists for the eye tracking enthusiast (EyeWriter, 2012; ITU Gaze Tracker, 2012; Li, Babcock & Parkhurst, 2006; openEyes, 2006; openGazer, 2012).

Tabletop Systems

Tabletop systems are bulky devices that are typically placed right in front of its user. They remind us of the devices used by eye doctors or opticians. They have an opening for the head with a chin-rest where the user is supposed to place his head. The chin-rest stabilizes the head and enables the system to make very precise measurements. This renders tabletop systems an interesting device for basic research. The user, however, has to acquire and maintain a certain position during the usage of the device. This might be suitable during the participation in a short scientific experiment, but not for every-day interactions. These devices are thus not very suited for gaze-based assistive technologies.

Head-Mounted Systems

Head-mounted stationary systems (see Figure 5) are a compromise, where the eye tracking gear is mounted on a small helmet which is strapped on the users head. This helmet is typically equipped with one or two eye tracking cameras attached to flexible mountings that allow for a precise adjustment of the gear to the position of the eyes. The cameras either require a direct view on the eyes or make use of a deflection mirror, which is typically transparent for the visible spectrum of light – which enables the user to see through the mirror – and only reflects the spectrum required by the tracking system. Professional head-mounted systems may support very high frame rates for tracking both fixations and saccades. However, they typically come with a powerful computer for the image processing and are thus more or less stationary.

Figure 5. SR research eyelink II head-mounted eyetracker with chinrest

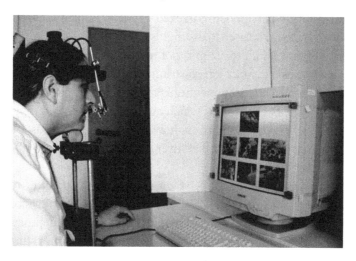

Figure 6. LC technologies eyefollower remote eye tracker with moving cameras

The mobile head-mounted systems available today are much smaller and more light-weight. They are either mounted on a helmet, a cap or are integrated in a pair of glasses. Not all of these systems allow for a real-time access to the eye tracking data. They are primarily designed for the recording of interactions and an offline analysis, e.g. for usability studies. They thus defer the expensive computer vision tasks to the offline processing unit. An example of a mobile head-mounted eye-tracking system with real-time tracking capabilities and a real-time software SDK are the SMI Eyetracking Glasses (see Figure 7). They come with a powerful laptop that handles all the computer vision tasks on the fly.

Remote Systems

Remote eye-tracking systems (see Figure 6) try to capture the image of the user's eyes from some distance. In computer-based set-ups, the camera system is typically placed directly under the screen of the

Figure 7. Mobile eye-tracking systems, as the SMI Eyetracking Glasses shown here, have become less obtrusive and more robust to use in the recent years. They feature a scene-camera (right between the eyes in the center of the frame) that provides a live-stream of the visual field of view in front of the user. And they feature one or two eye-tracking cameras (the SMI Eyetracking Glasses shown here feature two) which are used to provide real-time access to the fixations and the point of regards of the eyes.

computer. Remote eye-tracking systems can also be applied to monitor general desktop workspaces or areas with restricted human movements, such as the cockpit of a car or an airplane. For these more complex scenarios, systems that support camera arrays might be required to capture eye movements when the user turns his head sideways. Some systems use rotating turrets to adjust the cameras on-the-fly to the best viewing direction (see Figure 6). Remote eye-tracking systems allow for a restricted movement of the user and do not require any attachments to the user's body. They are thus very comfortable and unobtrusive to use. They, however, require an unobstructed view on the eyes and are disturbed (e.g. when the user is gesturing or placing objects, such as a coffee mug, in front of the screen).

GAZE-BASED ASSISTANCE FOR COMMUNICATION

The most prominent and most established example for gaze-based assistance systems are gaze-typing systems. Physically challenged people may be unable to hold or use tools, such as pens, in their hands, feet or mouth for written communication. Some might not even be able to press buttons on a keyboard.

Gaze-typing systems offer assistance for those still being able to perceive a display, such as a computer screen or a projection on a surface, and move their eyes voluntarily. The typical gaze-typing system presents an interactive keyboard to the user and tracks the point of regard of the user on this virtual interface. By changing the point of regard to a specific button and by some technique to trigger a selection, the user can, step-by-step, enter texts. The key ideas behind this are discussed in more details later.

Similar techniques can also be used to select elements in the typical user interface of the computer, such as menu entries or icons. Freely available examples, among many others, are Point-N-Click or ClickAid by Polital Enterprises LLC (2012), as well as Dwell Clicker 2 by Sensory Software Ltd. (2012) which realize a virtual mouse device and provide an interface to trigger mouse-related actions (click, double-click, etc.).

There are also special purpose environments available, e.g. SueCenter (2012), that offer a full integration of accessible input methods to tasks such as writing, research or e-mail communication. There are also specific dashboard solutions that present easy to select grids of common tasks, either for communicating with others (e.g. triggering speech output) or for launching programs (e.g. GazeTalk by ITU GazeGroup, 2012). These grid-based solutions offer also great opportunities for non-literate users, such as children, who would not be able to use a gaze-typing system. With a set of well-chosen icons, they could still use a gaze-based interface to communicate with others.

There are several approaches to gaze typing or virtual mouse movements which differ in the ways the gaze is being measured (e.g. via video or via electro-oculography), a pointer is moved around the screen, the keys are arranged and sized on the display, the intelligence behind the interface (e.g. T9 or other algorithms to support faster typing) and the interaction technique used to trigger the selection.

Examples of Gaze-Typing Systems

The typical gaze-typing system offers a virtual keyboard on which the user can type texts by selecting buttons. The individual systems differ in their visual layout and the level of advanced algorithms they offer to support the user in faster typing. A very basic virtual keyboard is offered by MidasTouch of Boston College (MidasTouch, 2009, see Figure 8). The keyboard shows all of the letters of the English alphabet (it is not configurable for international layouts), basic editing command such as delete or space and some resting points (green squares in the middle, shown grey in print) where the eyes can rest while thinking or talking to someone without accidently typing something. The program can be configured to pronounce each letter as it is typed using the Microsoft Speech SDK. Once the text has been entered, it can also be spoken by triggering either of the two Speak buttons. The text is also automatically copied to the clipboard, so that it can be swiftly pasted in the target application. MidasTouch can thus be used to talk to someone, to write messages or to enter text in applications. It is, however, not prepared for complex tasks, e.g., it cannot be used easily to enter WWW addresses or numbers.

Depending on the system for recognizing gaze-direction or the capabilities of the user, the virtual keys of MidasTouch (see Figure 8) might be difficult to hit. StaggeredSpeech (see Figure 9), also from Boston College, addresses this problem by dedicating more screen space to the buttons. However, now the user has to trigger two selections to type a letter: the buttons on the first screen only stand for a subset of letters and thus the letter has to be selected on a second screen which opens by the press of the first button.

The two examples discussed so far are static. They do not adjust to typical inputs of the user or word frequencies of a given language. Dynamic Keyboard by CanAssist at the University of Victoria (CanAssist 2008) is a Microsoft Windows program that comes with its own keyboard layout. Besides a semi-transparent overlay mode that allows the user to run the keyboard in full-screen while still seeing the application underneath, it has the special feature to adapt its layout to the typical inputs of the user. This adaptation can speed up the typing process. It also features several other helping aids, such as automatic capitalization after punctuation or adding matching suffixes to completions (copy is turned into copies by just adding s). Similar technologies can be found in many of today's virtual keyboard solutions for multi-touch systems, such as smartphones or tablets.

A more experimental system that also adapts both its keyboard layouts as well as the number of buttons available at each screen is UKO II by (Harbusch & Kühn, 2003). It is based on the platform independent XEmacs editor and has a rather conservative layout. It is, however, open source and could thus be interesting for a developer – or if the user chooses not to use Microsoft Windows. The more

Figure 8. The midastouch virtual keyboard for text input with head- or gaze-controlled access technology

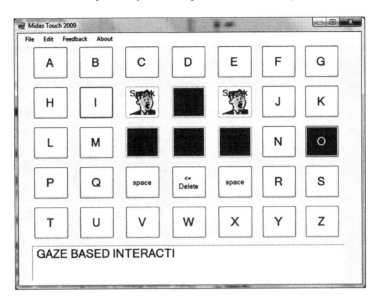

Figure 9. StaggeredSpeech (2009) is also from boston college and provides an interface with larger buttons for easier selection. It requires, however, two clicks to enter each letter.

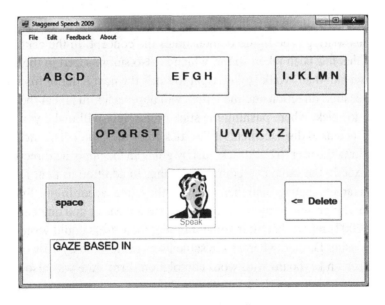

graphically advanced pEYEwrite system (Huckauf & Urbina, 2007, 2008) uses two level pie menues (similar to the two-level concept used by StaggeredSpeech) to allow text input.

There are also virtual keyboards that follow more closely the standard keyboard layout, at least for the arrangement of the keys. One example of such a free virtual keyboard that is also advocated to be used by people with disabilities is Click-N-Type (Lake Software, 2001). Click-N-Type has also some advanced features, such as word completion, however, the screen design is rather small, and thus a high accuracy is required when aiming for the keys.

Figure 10. Dasher offers a very unconventional interface, but it is easy to learn. In the center of the window is the resting position, to the left are the letters already written, which are also shown in the text box above. To the right are the different paths the user can take by extending the red line in the middle into the appropriate direction. This sequence of five images shows the starting position, the movement towards the initial 'G', progress to the letter 'a', further progress to 'a' and a later stage where the 'd' of the input 'Gaze based' has just been typed (or dashed) and the space is going to be next.

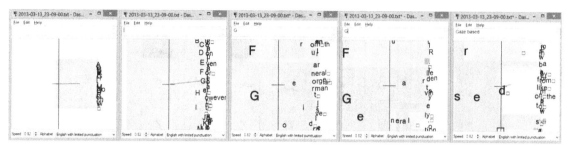

Continuous Zooming

A way to circumvent the Midas-Touch problem is to use continuous input instead of discrete selection events and provide means to backtrack. The text-input system Dasher realizes this concept (Ward & MacKay, 2002) and is compatible with several input modalities. The key idea is that the user navigates through a text universe where all the texts have already been written (see Figure 10). The path taken by the user will then be his writing. The figure demonstrates the concept. In the center the user is at rest. To the left is the path that has been taken so far, which is also summarized in the textbox below (here "Gaze based"). The user can then "walk" to the right towards the next letter of his sentence. For this he just has to look in the desired direction and the letters will approach him and at the same time zoom in. It is similar to using a joystick, where pushing the stick to the right will make you drive forward, with speed increasing with increased displacement of the stick from the center. The nice thing about this interface is that it also allows the user to backtrack, just by going in the opposite direction. Thus correcting your writing follows exactly the same procedure as writing. In addition to that, Dasher can also learn the probabilities of the target language and then arranges the letters accordingly. Succeeding letters that are more likely will thus be presented more prominently and are easier and quicker to find and walk to.

Ward & MacKay (2002) report that after some training, their users could write about 25 words per minute with their eyes using Dasher, whereas the same users achieved only 15 words per minute using gaze-typing on an on-screen keyboard with word completion. Error rate was also five times higher on the on-screen keyboard. Urbina and Huckauf (2007), however, report that novice users felt stressed confronted with the always changing Dasher interface.

A more recent project combined gaze-based Dasher with a speech recognition system (Vertanen & MacKay, 2010). In their system speech recognition comes first. If that fails, the user can use Dasher to correct the result. The model used by Dasher then integrates the hypotheses of the speech recognition system and thus supports a quick editing. The words per minute entered using speech Dasher depend on the word error rate of the speech recognition system. In their paper Vertanen and MacKay (2010) report that users achieved up to 54 words per minute and about 30 words per minute when the sentence contained at least one error.

The experimental approach StarGazer presents the input in 3D and uses pan and zoom to enable gaze typing (Hansen, Skovsgaard, Hansen & Møllenbach, 2008; ITU GazeGroup, 2007). Its basic idea is similar to Dasher, as the path a user flies, here through a tunnel in space, defines his writing. StarGazer, however, does not feature advanced text analysis algorithms as Dasher does. It also remains unclear, how backtracking is realized.

How Fast Can These Tools Be?

One of the fastest ways to communicate text would be speech. Users are reported to enter about 102 words per minute (Larson & Mowatt, 2003) into a dictation system – however without correcting the result of the speech recognition. As the error rate of speech recognition is still very high, the time required for the correction significantly reduces the input speed. Known input rates considering corrections are at about 14 to 17 words per minute (Karat, Halverson, Horn, & Karat, 1999; Larson & Mowatt, 2003). In their paper on Dasher, Ward, and MacKay (2002) report a 25 words per minute input rate for their gaze-based Dasher and 15 words per minute for gaze-typing. These results are, however, to be treated with care as they are not independently tested and the sample size is very small. For their pEYEwrite system, Huckauf and Urbina (2007) report about 8 words per minute for novice users and a maximum of 12.5 words per minute for experts.

Testing the Tools

Most of the described systems are available as public domain software and can thus easily be tried out. However, the hardware, that is the eye-tracking systems, might not be as easily available and the described systems only support a very restricted set of eye-tracking systems out of the box (if any).

An interesting alternative that can be used for evaluation purposes could be the Camera Mouse (2002) system developed at Boston College (Betke, Gips, & Fleming, 2002). This system uses a simple webcam to track the users face and map head movements to the mouse cursor. While this is not eye tracking but a very simple version of gaze tracking, the Camera Mouse could be a first inexpensive step towards gaze-based text communication. It is also a good way to get the feeling for the problems associated with this kind of input. Compared to an eye tracking system, the user has the advantage that the eyes are free to move and can be used to explore the visual interface without the Midas-Touch problem. On the downside, the head movements have to be highly controlled. In the long run, the Camera Mouse approach is expected to be more tiresome than an eye tracking approach. An alternative to Camera Mouse is the free Microsoft Windows program Head Mouse developed by Indra (2012). The same company also offers a free virtual keyboard.

Gaze Gestures

An alternative to gaze typing are eye gestures. Instead of establishing a reference with an external entity, the key, a less complex communication system can use the eye movements alone. The prototypical example is the communication with severely impaired interlocutors via eye blinks. A gaze-based interaction system can also recognize several other movements of the eyes, e.g. up/down, left/right, or patterns, e.g. diamond, circle, and trigger corresponding actions.

A couple of examples of such eye gestures have been considered by Isokoski (2000). He introduced the concept of off-screen targets for gaze typing. These are targets that are not shown on the computer display, but at the sides of the display. Although a good calibration only warrants precise point of regard measurements within the area of the calibrated display, eye gaze towards these targets can still be measured by the calibrated eye tracking system. The advantage of the approach is that the eyes can be used freely to explore the visual interface. The otherwise visually less important frame of the computer screen is used for static symbols. This is also the major disadvantage: as the targets are beyond the screen area, they cannot simply be changed to implement adaptive text input methods. The approach, however, could be extended by using LED displays or other methods for dynamic image presentation.

Isokoski (2000) describes, how three off-screen targets Dot, Dash, and End can be used in principle to realize gaze-based text input via Morse code. As it is basically only relevant to measure whether the user fixates to the left of the computer screen for a Dot, to the right for a Dash or above the screen for End, the precision of the measurement is less important than by typing on visual keyboards. In a similar way, Isokoski provided examples for the Minimal Device Independent Text Input Method (MDITIM) with five off-screen targets (instead of three for the Morse code) and QuikWriting for gaze input using eight targets. He also argued that a Cirrin-like (Mankoff & Abowd, 1998) arrangement of the full set of keys of a keyboard can be created, which would however increase the number of targets significantly and at the same time reduce their sizes, which would make them more difficult to find and hit. In a theoretical reflection considering character frequencies in English texts, he showed that QuikWriting and the Cirrin-like approach would require only a few numbers of gaze-based activations of interface elements (1-2.5), whereas MDITIM and Morse code would require more than three activations.

Wobbrock, Rubinstein, Sawyer, and Duchowski (2008) extended the work on EdgeWrite (Wobbrock, Myers & Kembel, 2003) for gestural letter input on mobile devices to create EyeWrite, a text input system inspired by Isokoski's MDITIM. Their work is similar to pEYEwrite (Huckauf & Urbina, 2007), however, it does not require a complex visual interface, such as a pie menu. The visual interface of EyeWrite shows only a small dialog window where text can be input via eye gestures connecting four dots shown near the edges of the dialog. The advantage of the system is, that it requires little screen space and is easy to learn and use. In a longitudinal study, they found that typing speed using EyeWrite (4.87 wpm) did not exceed that achieved on virtual keyboards (7.03 wpm). EyeWrite, however, was considered to be easier to use and less fatiguing. This could be due to the fact that no unnatural dwelling is required, which might be tiresome for the user.

Beyond Verbal Communication

Drewes, Hußmann, and Schmidt (2007) picked up the works of Isokoski (2000) and Wobbrock et al. (2008) to create an eye-gesture interface that does not require external references–and thus does not depend on an external calibration. Their eye gestures are in principle similar to those of Isokoski (2000), but the targets are now (invisible) within the eye space, i.e. pupil to upper left, pupil to upper right, etc., instead of being tied to visible targets surrounding a computer screen. It is thus no longer necessary to track the exact position of the head of the user. A robust detection of these eye gestures, however, does require gesture sequences that are recognizably slower than normal eye movements. The performance of the system, with nearly 2 seconds for simple gestures, is therefore quite low. Nevertheless, there are interesting applications for those gestures: currently, the management functions of the eye-tracking system, such as starting the calibration process, have to be triggered manually, as obviously the uncalibrated system is not able to detect a dwell-time gaze-based selection of any button. A predefined set of calibration-free eye gestures could give handicapped users the freedom to initiate their gaze-based communication sessions on their own.

The logical next step has been taken by Vaitukaitis and Bulling (2012), who adopted the work of Drewes, De Luca, & Schmidt (2007) and presented a first prototype on a portable device, an Android smartphone. In the near future, I envision handicapped users to have a personal mobile gaze-based interface, e.g. based on a smartphone, which supports a robust detection of a small but versatile selection of eye gestures. Depending on their context and location, e.g. when approaching the desktop computer, the mobile interface could then be used to turn-on the computer with gaze assistance. After the computer is running, the mobile interface again can be used to trigger the required calibration procedures. Only after that, the interaction is handed over to the stationary remote eye-tracking system, which provides the higher spatial accuracy required for gaze-typing.

A completely different problem with gaze-typing systems was addressed by Hornof and Cavender (2005). They realized that little to none gaze-based software solutions existed for illiterate and especially for children. They presented EyeDraw, a gaze-based drawing program for Microsoft Windows. In contrast to previous free-drawing approaches (Gips & Olivieri, 1996; Tchalenko, 2001), where the eye movements were directly mapped to strokes on the virtual drawing canvas, EyeDraw follows the approach of classic vector drawing programs in which line segments or other shapes are drawn by specifying a sequence of points. To solve the Midas-Touch problem, they use a dwell time of 500ms, which they found to be optimal for their application in a user study. They report, however, that especially the targeted audience of younger users did have problems with the high control of the eye movements that was required to operate the system. For early phases they suggest using a free-drawing mode to provide direct positive feedback. This could improve acceptability and increase motivation. Older participants of their study showed more stamina and were quite successful in using EyeDraw.

GAZE INTERACTION IN 3D WORLDS

Gaze-typing systems opened up the modern world of digital communication to people with certain handicaps. Communication, however, is not all one needs. Given the success of the gaze-typing approach, why are there not more mobile approaches that empower handicapped to be more autonomous in operating and handling common tasks, such as using light switches, doors or even media and kitchen equipment?

This is not an easy task. The power of gaze-typing systems lies in the fixed set-up of the dedicated eye-tracking system and the exact knowledge of the temporal-spatial environment: the tracked eyes and head of the user and the digital content presented on the screen. Only when all this information is known, the system can relate the orientation of the user's eye in the video cameras of the eye-tracking system with the position (in pixels) of the point of regard on the screen and finally with the key of the virtual keyboard that currently covers exactly that position.

In a household scenario, the user must be allowed to be mobile, to move around. To ensure that a gaze-based interaction system can always sense his eye movements, he would, presumably, be required to wear a head-mounted eye-tracking system. Movements (e.g. jerky movements) when accelerating an electric wheelchair, could then make the gear shift slightly around over time. This introduces a drift into the eye-tracking signal, which is a common problem of head-mounted (mobile) systems. After such drifts, the point of regard estimated by the eye-tracking system would deviate from the original one fixated by the user and thus mislead any gaze-based interaction. An even greater problem, however, is that the real world is dynamically changing, uncontrollable by the gaze-based interaction system. It is even difficult to exactly locate the position of the user in this dynamic world. There could, for instance suddenly be people standing in front of a light-switch or furniture might be moved. Rooms can also look totally different, just depending on the current lighting.

Gaze Interaction in Virtual Reality

There is a place where computers know all about the environment and they also can have an exact knowledge about all the changes that happened. And that is virtual reality. There we can already design and test gaze-based interactions as if computer vision could provide us a reliable 3D model of our environment.

In virtual reality, we have already tested algorithms that allow for a better detection of the point of regard in a 3D world by using binocular eye tracking. The idea is to exploit information about the vergence movements the eyes make when focusing at objects in different distances to estimate the 3D coordinates (Pfeiffer, 2008, 2011; Pfeiffer, Latoschik & Wachsmuth, 2009). Based on these more precise 3D point of regard measurements, the concept of attention maps (see above) can be transferred to spatial objects (3D attention volumes, Pfeiffer, 2012).

These technologies will be helpful for real world gaze-based interactions as well. Their key advantage is that the depth estimation is based solely on the orientation and vergence of the eyes. It does not require knowledge about the context. The system could e.g. decide whether the driver of a wheelchair focusses something on his body or the wheelchair (small vergence angle, pupils close together) as opposed to something in the environment (pupils further apart). In doing so the system would be able to get the right context for the interpretation of the eye gaze, like when the driver focusses on a screen attached to the wheelchair, a gaze-typing system could be started. As the system is able to tell gazes at close, medium and far distances apart, this could also be used to activate eye gesture recognition only when gazing at a certain distance, like when staring nearly straight as if looking at a horizon far away. This way the Midas-Touch problem would be further minimized.

Monitoring the current calibration quality of the eye-tracking system to detect drifts is also easier when exact information about the environment is available. We implemented a procedure in which we sample typical point of regards for a set of monitor objects (normal objects of the environment picked by us to play this special role) directly after the eye tracking system is calibrated (Renner, Lüdike, Wittrowski, & Pfeiffer, 2011). Later, during interaction, the user every now and then fixates at one of the monitor objects. We then compare these new point of regards measured under the current condition of the tracking system with the typically point of regards measured with a very accurately calibrated system. Based on the differences, we estimate the current drift of the system and trigger a calibration when the error is above an application specific threshold. For a more intuitive calibration in virtual reality, we let a dragonfly appear in front of the user (Renner et al., 2011). By following the dragonfly the eye-tracking system gets calibrated without the unnatural sequence of fixation point required by most desktop-based eye-tracking systems.

When we talk about our environment, it is natural that we fixate objects we are going to talk about just right before we refer to them verbally. In communication, our addressees will often follow our gaze and they might be able to infer which object we are talking about, just right before we do it. This can every now and then be nicely observed at a large dinner or breakfast table, when the right marmalade is already handed over while one was still struggling for the words. In virtual reality, we have realized a system that enables the virtual agent Max to achieve joint attention with the user on the objects of a small virtual world (Pfeiffer-Lessmann, Pfeiffer, & Wachsmuth, 2012). By this we mean that Max follows the user's gaze and shows an appropriate gaze behavior that supports the user in the belief that he and max share their attention on a particular object and that they are both aware of that. The user can thus be sure that he communicated a reference to an object to Max (as the representative of a computer system). This technology could be transferred to real world scenarios and, e.g., enable people to enter references to objects into a computer system just by gazing at them. For example, one could write "Give me" and then gaze at a cup on the desk to put a reference to the cup into the text. The system could then speech-synthesize "Give me a cup". This could improve gaze-typing based direct communication systems, because the gazing to the objects we talk about would be similar to that under natural conditions.

Gaze Interaction in the Real World

The analysis of visual attention in the real world is of interest to many areas of research. In marketing, for example, scientists want to know, how the placement of products in a shelf affects the decision of the customers. In other disciplines, such as ergonomics or architecture, they are interested whether people see and follow functional signage. Mobile eye-tracking systems with scene-cameras can be used to record the field of view in front and map the eye movements onto the recorded video. These gaze-videos can then be analyzed offline, which is a costly process when done manually: for every fixation recorded in the video, which might be several per second, a human annotator has to classify the visual content under the point of regard (e.g. whether a signage has been fixated and if so, which type and where), before a statistical analysis can be made.

Computer vision algorithms can help finding and tracking the objects of interest in the gaze-videos and count the fixations automatically (Essig, Seifert, Sand, Künsemöller, Pfeiffer, Ritter & Schack, 2011). Work in this area has just started. Major challenges at the moment are rapid or extreme changes in the lighting conditions, fast movements of the head (and camera), partial occlusions and the speed of the detection algorithms when large sets of common objects are to be identified. Brône, Oben, van Beeck, and Goedemé (2011) discussed these main issues and defined the starting-point of their "InSight Out" project, in which they also primarily aim at scientific studies, i.e. offline processing. They presented first results of their prototype system a year later (De Beugher, Ichiche, Brône, & Goedemé, 2012). While the described approaches do not focus on providing real-time performance on a mobile device, they are facing all of the computer vision (lighting, occlusions, and fast movements) and localization problems.

Mobile gaze-based assistive technologies can also provide help in common tasks. The system could remember where the wearer has left his keys by reviewing the last hours of videos upon request, until the keys appear. They could also offer help in challenging areas, such as games. Figure 11 shows an example of one of our current projects, where we investigate how gaze-based interaction can be combined with a multimodal dialog to provide coaching and support in complex cognitive interactions, such as chess playing. The idea is that the system recognizes the board and the current positioning of the pieces from the scene-camera of the eye-tracking system (see Figure 12). From the current point of regard (the circle in Figure 12) and the past scanpath, the system tries to infer the best context and the appropriate time to provide assistance. The hints given by the system should be just enough to support a proximal learning of the user.

Figure 11. The intelligent attentive chess assistant recognizes the board and the positioning of the pieces

Figure 12. The point of regard (here visualized by a circle to the upper right of the white pawn) of the user is then used to identify the appropriate context to give advice for

While this example might look rather artificial, the general principle of the system could later be applied to many different contexts: recognizing context and actions, inferring current cognitive processing by following the visual attention, planning and finally information presentation in a verbal dialog. For example to teach patients common daily practices in rehabilitation. The system could monitor the people's actions from their own perspective while they are washing, brushing their teeth or laying the table. Once the system detects moments of hesitation or that a required action is not taken, it reminds the patient according to a therapy protocol. Just like a hearing aid.

CONCLUSION

Gaze-typing is, as of today, still the most prominent gaze-based assistive technology. There are several competing approaches available, which enables the user to select the tool best matching one's own preferences or capabilities. While professional eye-tracking systems still come at some cost, the prices will come down drastically in the near future. In 2013, commercial eye-tracking systems will be available for less than 1000,- €. In parallel, there are already several open source eye-tracking systems available, accompanied by systems such as Camera Mouse that operate on head-movements.

There are many mobile areas of application, where gaze-assisted technologies could provide new ways of support for people with motor disabilities. Gaze interaction with technical appliances could extend the reach of our actions, e.g. by remotely triggering electrical switches. People in a wheelchair would then need less navigation to reach a button. In the same scenario, an attentive wheelchair could infer the intended target position by monitoring the point of regard the driver is looking at. A speech support system could create situated verbal expressions using text-to-speech for the objects looked at by the user. This way, the user could be enabled to refer to the objects in her surroundings more swiftly then by typing. Together with a tableau of verbs (eat, drink, give, take, like, I, you, etc.), simple expressions such as "I like a coffee" or "you take the bag" can be "spoken" with only a couple of fixations. The user would also appear more communicative to others, because her gaze would be more engaging, wandering around in the scene, than with the alternative of a mobile gaze-typing system, were she would have to dedicate most gaze to the user interface.

Research on promising applications for mobile gaze-based interaction has just picked up pace. In 2011, the first workshop on pervasive eye tracking and mobile eye-based interaction (PETMEI, 2011) was held at the ACM International Joint Conference on Pervasive and Ubiquitous Computing (UbiComp, 2011). In 2012, the MobiGaze challenge was announced, setting out prizes for innovative mobile systems and new implemented applications for gaze-based interactions. Looking – in the future – will be more productive and provide more freedom to many.

REFERENCES

Betke, M., Gips, J., & Fleming, P. (2002). The camera mouse: Visual tracking of body features to provide computer access for people with severe disabilities. *IEEE Transactions on Neural Systems and Rehabilitation Engineering, 10*(1), 1–10. doi:10.1109/TNSRE.2002.1021581 PMID:12173734

Brône, G., Oben, B., Van Beeck, K., & Goedemé, T. (2011). Towards a more effective method for analyzing mobile eye-tracking data: Integrating gaze data with object recognition algorithms. In *Proceedings of the 1st International Workshop on Pervasive Eye Tracking & Mobile Eye-based Interaction*, 53-56. New York: ACM Press.

Butterworth, G., & Itakura, S. (2000). How the eyes, head, and hand serve definite reference. *The British Journal of Developmental Psychology*, *18*, 25–50. doi:10.1348/026151000165553

Camera Mouse. (2002). *Camera mouse*. Retrieved from http://www.cameramouse.org.

CanAssist. (2008). *Dynamic keyboard*. Retrieved from http://www.canassist.ca/EN/main/programs/free-downloads/dynamic-keyboard/dynamic-keyboard-development.html.

COGAIN. (2012). *COGAIN: Communication by gaze interaction*. Retrieved from http://wiki.cogain.info.

Corkum, V., & Moore, C. (1998). The origins of joint visual attention in infants. *Developmental Psychology*, *34*(1), 28–38. doi:10.1037/0012-1649.34.1.28 PMID:9471002

De Beugher, S., Ichiche, Y., Brône, G., & Goedemé, T. (2012). Automatic analysis of eye-tracking data using object detection algorithms. In *Proceedings of the 2012 ACM Conference on Ubiquitous Computing*, 677-680. New York: ACM Press.

Ditchburn, R. W., & Ginsborg, B. L. (1953). Involuntary eye movements during fixation. *The Journal of Physiology*, *119*, 1–17. PMID:13035713

Drewes, H., De Luca, A., & Schmidt, A. (2007). Eye-gaze interaction for mobile phones. In *Proceedings of the 4th international Conference on Mobile Technology, Applications, and Systems and the 1st international Symposium on Computer Human interaction in Mobile Technology*, 364-371. Singapore: ACM Press.

Drewes, H., Hußmann, H., & Schmidt, A. (2007). Blickgesten als Fernbedienung. In T. Gross (Ed), Mensch & Computer 2007 (79-88). Berlin: Oldenburg-Verlag.

Duchowski, A. T. (2007). *Eye tracking methodology: Theory and practice*. London: Springer-Verlag.

EegleEyes. (1996). *EagleEyes project*. Retrieved from http://www.bc.edu/schools/csom/eagleeyes/.

Essig, K., Seifert, S., Sand, N., Künsemöller, J., Pfeiffer, T., Ritter, H., & Schack, T. (2011). JVideoGazer-Towards an automatic annotation of gaze videos from natural scenes. In *Proceedings of the World Congress on Engineering and Technology*, 1–4. IEEE Press.

EyeWriter. (2009). *EyeWriter*. Retrieved from http://eyewriter.org.

Gaze Tracker, I. T. U. (2012). *ITU Gaze Tracker*. Retrieved from http://www.gazegroup.org/downloads/23-gazetracker/.

Gips, J., & Olivieri, P. (1996). EagleEyes: An eye control system for persons with disabilities. In *Proceedings of the Eleventh International Conference on Technology and Persons with Disabilities*. MIT Press.

Hansen, D. W., Skovsgaard, H. H. T., Hansen, J. P., & Møllenbach, E. (2008). Noise tolerant selection by gaze-controlled pan and zoom in 3D. In *Proceedings of the 2008 Symposium on Eye Tracking Research & Applications*, 205-212. New York: ACM Press.

Harbusch, K., & Kühn, M. (2003). Towards an adaptive communication aid with text input from ambiguous keyboards. In *Proceedings of the Tenth Conference on European Chapter of the ACL: Vol 2*, 207-210. Stroudsburg, PA: Association for Computational Linguistics.

Hood, B., Willen, J. D., & Driver, J. (1998). Adults' eyes trigger shifts of visual attention in human infants. *Psychological Science*, *9*, 131–134. doi:10.1111/1467-9280.00024

Hornof, A. J., & Cavender, A. (2005). EyeDraw: Enabling children with severe motor impairments to draw with their eyes. In *Proceedings of CHI 2005: Eyes on Interaction*, 161-170. Portland, OR: ACM Press.

Huckauf, A., & Urbina, M. H. (2007). Gazing with pEYE: New concepts in eye typing. In *Proceedings of the 4th Symposium on Applied Perception in Graphics and Visualization*. New York: ACM Press.

Huckauf, A., & Urbina, M. H. (2008). On object selection in gaze controlled environments. *Journal of Eye Movement Research*, *2*(4), 1–7.

Hülsmann, F., Dankert, T., & Pfeiffer, T. (2011). Comparing gaze-based and manual interaction in a fast-paced gaming task in virtual reality. In C.-A. Bohn & S. Mostafawy (Eds.), Virtuelle & Erweiterte Realität, 8. Workshop der GI-Fachgruppe VR/AR (1-12). Aachen, Germany: Shaker Verlag.

Hutchinson, T., White, K. Jr, Martin, W., Reichert, K., & Frey, L. (1989). Human-computer interaction using eye-gaze input. *IEEE Transactions on Systems, Man, and Cybernetics*, *19*, 1527–1534. doi:10.1109/21.44068

Indra. (2012). *Head mouse*. Retrieved from http://www.tecnologiasaccesibles.com/en/headmouse.html.

Isokoski, P. (2000). Text input methods for eye trackers using off-screen targets. [New York: ACM Press.]. *Proceedings of the Eye Tracking Research & Applications*, *2000*, 15–22. doi:10.1145/355017.355020

ITU GazeGroup. (2007). *StarGazer*. Retrieved from http://www.gazegroup.org/research/14.

ITU GazeGroup. (2012). *GazeTalk 5*. Retrieved from http://www.gazegroup.org/research/15.

Jacob, R. J. K. (1993). What you look at is what you get. *Computer*, *26*(7), 65–66. doi:10.1109/MC.1993.274943

Karat, C.-M., Halverson, C., Horn, D., & Karat, J. (1999). Patterns of entry and correction in large vocabulary continuous speech recognition systems. In *Proceedings of CHI*, 568–575. New York: ACM Press.

Lake Software. (2001). *Click-N-Type*. Retrieved from http://cnt.lakefolks.com.

Larson, K., & Mowatt, D. (2003). Speech error correction: The story of the alternates list. *International Journal of Speech Technology*, 183–194. doi:10.1023/A:1022342732234

Li, D., Babcock, J., & Parkhurst, D. J. (2006). OpenEyes: A low-cost head-mounted eye-tracking solution. In *Proceedings of the ACM Eye Tracking Research and Applications Symposium*, 95-100. New York: ACM Press.

Mankoff, J., & Abowd, G. D. (1998). Cirrin: A word-level unistroke keyboard for pen input. In *Proceedings of the 11th Annual ACM Symposium on User Interface Software and Technology*, 213-214. New York: ACM Press.

MidasTouch. (2009). *Midas Touch*. Retrieved from http://www.midastouch.org/.

Norton, D., & Stark, L. (1971). Scanpaths in saccadic eyemovements during pattern perception. *Science*, 308–311. doi:10.1126/science.171.3968.308 PMID:5538847

OpenEyes. (2006). *OpenEyes–Tracking for the masses*. Retrieved from http://thirtysixthspan.com/openEyes/.

OpenGazer. (2012). *Opengazer: Open-source gaze tracker for ordinary webcams*. Retrieved from http://www.inference.phy.cam.ac.uk/opengazer/.

PETMEI. (2011). In *Proceedings of 1ˢᵗ International Workshop on Pervasive Eye Tracking and Mobile Eye-Based Interaction*. Retrieved from http://2011.petmei.org/home/.

Pfeiffer, T. (2008). Towards gaze interaction in immersive virtual reality: Evaluation of a monocular eye tracking set-up. In M. Schumann & T. Kuhlen (Eds.), Virtuelle und Erweiterte Realität-Fünfter Workshop der GI-Fachgruppe VR/AR (81–92). Aachen, Germany: Shaker Verlag.

Pfeiffer, T. (2011). *Understanding multimodal deixis with gaze and gesture in conversational interfaces*. Aachen, Germany: Shaker Verlag.

Pfeiffer, T. (2012). Measuring and visualizing attention in space with 3D attention volumes. In *Proceedings of the Symposium on Eye Tracking Research and Applications*, 29–36. New York: ACM Press.

Pfeiffer, T., Latoschik, M. E., & Wachsmuth, I. (2009). Evaluation of binocular eye trackers and algorithms for 3D gaze interaction in virtual reality environments. *Journal of Virtual Reality and Broadcasting*, 5(16).

Pfeiffer, T., & Mattar, N. (2009). Benefits of locating overt visual attention in space using binocular eye tracking for mixed reality applications. In S. Kain, D. Struve, & H. Wandke (Eds.), Workshop-Proceedings der Tagung Mensch & Computer 2009: Grenzenlos frei!? (272–274). Berlin, Germany: Logos.

Pfeiffer-Leßmann, N., Pfeiffer, T., & Wachsmuth, I. (2012). An operational model of joint attention-Timing of gaze patterns in interactions between humans and a virtual human. In N. Miyake, D. Peebles, & R. P. Cooper (Eds.), *Proceedings of the 34th Annual Meeting of the Cognitive Science Society* (851-856). Austin, TX: Cognitive Science Society.

Polital Enterprises, L. L. C. (2012). *Point-N-Click*. Retrieved from http://www.polital.com/pnc/.

Pomplun, M., Ritter, H., & Velichkovsky, B. (1996). Disambiguating complex visual information: Towards communication of personal views of a scene. *Perception*, 25, 931–948. doi:10.1068/p250931 PMID:8938007

Renner, P., Lüdike, N., Wittrowski, J., & Pfeiffer, T. (2011). Towards continuous gaze-based interaction in 3D environments-Unobtrusive calibration and accuracy monitoring. In C.-A. Bohn & S. Mostafawy (Eds.), Virtuelle & Erweiterte Realität, 8. Workshop der GI-Fachgruppe VR/AR (13-24). Aachen, Germany: Shaker Verlag.

Robinson, D. A. (1963). A method of measuring eye movement using a scieral search coil in a magnetic field. *IEEE Transactions on Bio-medical Electronics*, 10(4), 137–145. doi:10.1109/TBMEL.1963.4322822

Robinson, D. A. (1968). The oculomotor control system: A review. *Proceedings of the IEEE, 56*(6), 1032–1049. doi:10.1109/PROC.1968.6455

Sensory Software Ltd. (2012). *Dwell clicker 2*. Retrieved from http://www.sensorysoftware.com/dwell-clicker.html.

StaggeredSpeech. (2009). *Staggered Speech*. Retrieved from http://www.staggeredspeech.org/.

SueCenter. (2012). *Sue Center*. Retrieved from http://www.suecenter.org/.

Tchalenko, J. (2001). Free-eye drawing. *Point: Art and Design Research Journal, 11*, 36–41.

UbiComp. (2011). *ACM Conference on Ubiquitous Computing 2011*. Retrieved from http://www.ubicomp.org/ubicomp2011/.

Urbina, M., & Huckauf, A. (2007). Dwell-time free eye typing approaches. [ACM Press.]. *Proceedings of COGAIN, 2007*, 65–70.

Velichkovsky, B., Sprenger, A., & Pomplun, M. (1998). *On the way to look mouse: The effect of fixation duration by cognitive and communicative tasks software ergonomics*. Stuttgart, Germany: Teubner.

Vertanen, K., & MacKay, D. J. C. (2010). Speech Dasher: Fast writing using speech and gaze. In *Proceedings of the ACM Conference on Human Factors in Computing Systems*, 595—598. New York: ACM Press.

Ward, D. J., & MacKay, D. J. C. (2002). Fast hands-free writing by gaze direction. *Nature, 418*, 838. doi:10.1038/418838a PMID:12192400

Wobbrock, J. O., Myers, B. A., & Kembel, J. A. (2003). EdgeWrite: A stylus-based text entry method designed for high accuracy and stability of motion. In Proceedings of User Interface Software and Technology, 61-70. New York: ACM Press.

Wobbrock, J. O., Rubinstein, J., Sawyer, M. W., & Duchowski, A. T. (2008). Longitudinal evaluation of discrete consecutive gaze gestures for text entry. In *Proceedings of the Eye Tracking Research and Applications 2008*. New York: ACM Press.

Wooding, D. S. (2002). Fixation maps: Quantifying eye-movement traces. In *Proceedings of the 2002 Symposium on Eye Tracking Research & Applications*, 31-36. New York: ACM Press.

Yarbus, A. L. (1967). *Eye movements and vision*. New York: Plenum Press.

Young, L. R., & Sheena, D. (1975). Survey of eye movement recording methods. *Behavior Research Methods and Instrumentation, 7*(5), 397–429. doi:10.3758/BF03201553

ADDITIONAL READINGS

Bolt, R. (1981). Gaze-orchestrated dynamic windows. In *Proceedings of the 8th Annual Conference on Computer Graphics and Interactive Techniques*, 109-119. New York: ACM Press.

Holmqvist, K., Nyström, M., Andersson, R., Dewhurst, R., Halszka, J., & van de Weijer, J. (2011). *Eye tracking: A comprehensive guide to methods and measures*. New York: Oxford University Press.

Sibert, L. E., & Jacob, R. J. (2000). Evaluation of eye gaze interaction. In *Proceedings of the CHI 2000*, 281-288. New York: ACM Press.

Ten Kate, J. H., Frietman, E. E. E., Willems, W., Ter Haar Romeny, B. M., & Tenkink, E. (1979). Eye-switch controlled communication aids. In *Proceedings of the 12th International Conference on Medical & Biological Engineering*, 19-20. IEEE Press.

Vytautas, V., & Bulling, A. (2012). Eye gesture recognition on portable devices. In *Proceedings of the 2012 ACM Conference on Ubiquitous Computing*, 711-714. New York: ACM Press.

KEY TERMS AND DEFINITIONS

Eye Tracking: The detection and following of position and orientation of the (human) eye. This includes rotation and sometimes also torsion of the eye. Different phases of eye movements are of relevance: fixations, saccades and smooth pursuits. Eye tracking is often confused with gaze tracking, because in fixed settings, where head position and orientation remain stable in relation to the environment, the resulting measurements are essentially the same.

Fixation: The moment of rest in the eye movements when the peak of visual processing is done.

Gaze Tracking: The detection of the point of regard the eyes of an observer are targeted at. For this, eye tracking has to be coupled at least with a tracking of position and orientation of the head. An additional tracking of the environment could be necessary if this is dynamically changing. By integrating the information about the head and the eye, the line of sight into the environment can be reconstructed and the point of regard can be computed. This is rather trivial in settings with a fixed head in a static environment, typical examples are gaze-based interactions with a desktop computer.

Point of Regard: The external target of the overt visual attention; where the line of sight meets an object in the environment.

Saccade: The swift transitional movement between fixations to re-orient the eye towards a new point of regard. They are the fastest bodily movements and achieve up to 900°/sec.

Smooth Pursuit: Continuous eye movements when following a moving target, up to a speed of 30°/s. If the targets are faster, then catch-up saccades are triggered to keep up.

This research was previously published in Assistive Technologies and Computer Access for Motor Disabilities edited by Georgios Kouroupetroglou, pages 90-109, copyright year 2014 by Medical Information Science Reference (an imprint of IGI Global).

Chapter 4
Design and Evaluation of Vision–Based Head and Face Tracking Interfaces for Assistive Input

Chamin Morikawa
Motion Portrait Inc., Japan

Michael J. Lyons
Ritsumeikan University, Japan

ABSTRACT

Interaction methods based on computer-vision hold the potential to become the next powerful technology to support breakthroughs in the field of human-computer interaction. Non-invasive vision-based techniques permit unconventional interaction methods to be considered, including use of movements of the face and head for intentional gestural control of computer systems. Facial gesture interfaces open new possibilities for assistive input technologies. This chapter gives an overview of research aimed at developing vision-based head and face-tracking interfaces. This work has important implications for future assistive input devices. To illustrate this concretely the authors describe work from their own research in which they developed two vision-based facial feature tracking algorithms for human computer interaction and assistive input. Evaluation forms a critical component of this research and the authors provide examples of new quantitative evaluation tasks as well as the use of model real-world applications for the qualitative evaluation of new interaction styles.

INTRODUCTION

The past decade has witnessed dramatic change in the field of Human Computer Interaction (HCI). Interface technologies that were previously found only in the laboratory have started to show up in consumer devices. Tablet computers and smart phones allow smooth and nearly faultless tactile interaction that computer interface researchers of the past could only dream about. The use of digital devices is moving

DOI: 10.4018/978-1-5225-2589-9.ch004

beyond button, keyboard, and mouse, and towards more intuitive interaction styles better suited to the human brain and body.

Interaction methods based on computer-vision hold the potential to become the next powerful technology to support breakthroughs in HCI (Jaimes, 2007; Porta, 2002). Computer-vision algorithms can obtain real-time knowledge about the actions of a human user for use in HCI (Ahad 2008). Most research on vision-based HCI has naturally focused on movements of the arms and hands (Jaimes, 2007; Porta, 2002). However, it is also interesting to consider other parts of the body such as the head and features of the face, because these afford detailed and expressive movements (Lyons, 2004).

Action of the face plays an important role in many human behaviors including speech and facial expression. It is therefore not unreasonable to think that the actions of the face could play an important role in man-machine interactions. While there is a considerable body of prior research on automatic facial expression recognition and lip reading, there has been relatively little work examining the possibility of using these for intentional interactions with computers or other machines or, notably, for assistive input. This may be partly due to technological limitations: how can information about motor actions of the face be acquired in an unencumbering, non-invasive fashion? As we will show in this chapter, this is no longer a consideration: robust, real-time acquisition of facial movements makes only modest technological demands. The strangeness and novelty of the idea of using the face or features of the face for intentional interaction may be another factor in the relative dearth of precedent studies, however novelty should not be a deterrent to research. Furthermore we will discuss several of our recent applications which focus on using mouth movements for HCI, in which our studies with users show the concept to be quite natural and advantageous.

Adoption of new interface paradigms depends not only on the invention and development of novel technology, but on how the technology is used to create engaging interaction styles. Therefore we have concretely examined what kinds of interaction styles may be suitable for vision-based interfaces with systematic evaluation tasks and also in the context of potential applications. In the current chapter we apply standard human factors evaluation methodology that has evolved in the HCI field, to characterize a facial gesture UI developed in our group, which allows the user to provide input to a computer using movements of the head and mouth. To demonstrate the value of the standard evaluation methodology we show how it may be used to accurately predict performance with real-world applications.

An outline of the chapter is as follows: Section 2 reviews the state of the art in the relevant areas of human-computer interaction, computer vision, and more specifically in the specialized area of vision-based human-computer interaction; Section 3 concretely illustrates the concept of vision-based facial gesture interaction by describing in some detail algorithms we have studied in our own research projects. Specifically these systems (a) initialize the face tracking by blink detection and nostril detection (b) track the tip of the nose for pointing (c) detect mouth opening to allow the user to input click events and continuous data using the size and shape of the mouth cavity; Section 4 concretely illustrates how new vision-based interaction techniques can be evaluated with standard and newly developed methods from the field of human-computer interaction. After briefly introducing Fitts' law and standard methodology for measuring the information throughput of a pointing device, we then describe a measurement of the throughput of a user-interface, comparing it to that of a standard computer mouse; in some cases newly designed tasks are needed: this is concretely illustrated with a measurement of the accuracy and precision of input derived from the shape of the mouth; Section 5 illustrates the application of qualitative measures for usability assessment using user questionnaires; Section 6 contains a brief overview of examples of applications for vision-based facial gesture interfaces; after general observations, in Section 7, Section

8 concludes the chapter with reflections on the outstanding limitations of vision-based head and face tracking interfaces and proposals for the direction of future work in this field.

STATE OF THE ART

The research presented in this chapter belongs to two main researched areas; human-computer interaction, and computer vision. This section reviews the state of the art of these areas, with respect to the proposed topic. We will also briefly review speech recognition research related to assistive technology, due to its similarity to the proposed topic.

Human-Computer Interaction

A brief outline of the evolution of hardware devices for Human-computer Interaction can be found in Saffer (2007). The first few generations of computers were designed for scientific calculations, to be used by experts or trained users. Interactions with such devices were facilitated using switches and punched cards, and required special training. However, with the emergence of personal computers, interfaces that are easier to use were designed. Other reasons for the development of such devices are the availability of inexpensive semiconductor devices, and the increase in the processing speed of microprocessors, enabling them to receive and process inputs from more complex devices. At the current state, keyboards, mice, touch pads, and touch screens are primarily used as the input devices used to interact with a computer.

There is a growing interest in computer interfaces that go beyond the standard keyboard/mouse Human-Computer Interaction (HCI) paradigm. Microphones, combined with speech analysis, have been successfully used as input devices in several systems and applications (Anusya, 2011; Lewis, 2010; Yankelovich, 1995). Voice-based search engines such as Google Voice Search, and Interaction systems such as Apple Siri demonstrate that speech analysis technology has sufficiently matured to be used for human-computer interaction. Koppu, Viswanathan and Kamalakannan (2012) present a detailed survey on recent trends in human-computer interaction.

A few other types of data are used in specific applications of human-machine interaction, at the consumer level. Infra-red sources and sensors are widely used as interfaces for computer-like devices (Kratz, 2009). Nintendo Wii remote controller uses infra-red illumination recorded with a camera, to determine its orientation. This allows the remote controller to be used as a pointing device. Microsoft Kinect uses video with depth information through structured infra-red lighting, to facilitate richer interactions with games. Game consoles use other customized input devices, such as pressure pads and motion-sensitive controllers. The timing and locations on users' feet on pressure pads provide input to the game. Accelerometers and Gyro sensors on tablet devices and game controllers allow users to interact with the devices using motion and orientation. There has also been some research projects where researchers try to extend the use of these devices to other applications (Gallo, 2009; Jia, 2012).

There are a few important criteria that determine whether a given method of human-computer interaction is appropriate (Accot, 1999; Poppe, 2007). Accuracy is the most important of these criteria. To take an example, a touch-screen keyboard is not accurate if tapping on an edge of the virtual key "A" on the screen does not always result in a letter "A" being entered as text. For devices that facilitate continuous inputs, resolution is also important. A pointing device has a high resolution if it can enter a large number of distinct points on the screen. The smoothness of inputs is also important for interfaces with continuous input. The speed at the input device can accept users 'inputs is also important. A more specific, quantitative measure for this criterion is the information throughput, the amount of information one can enter using the input device within a given time (this will be discussed in more detail in a nest section).

However, there are other qualitative criteria that determines whether a user interface is suitable for its intended users. The effort required to operate the interface is one such criterion. Although the popular interfaces such as keyboard, mouse and touch-screen require little effort when used by ordinary users, they are quite challenging for users with disabilities. The ease of learning is another important criterion, especially when introducing an unconventional interface. While a user with a disability might be more willing to spend time and effort to learn to use a new interface, it is still desirable to make it easy to learn.

Computer Vision

In computer vision, images from one or more cameras at a given scene are analyzed to make decisions similar to those made by a human who observes the same scene. A digital image is divided into a large number of square shaped picture elements called "pixels". Each pixel can be represented by the luminance (in case of grayscale images) or chrominance value at the corresponding position. By analyzing the properties of these pixel values and comparing them with predefined models, a computer can recognize objects contained in the image. If the input is a video camera, image sequence analysis is performed on the sequence of image frames from the camera/s. Temporal relationships between frames are used for recognizing actions.

Research in computer vision covers a wide range of topics and applications such as medical image analysis, surveillance, human motion analysis, etc. For the scope of this chapter, computer vision research for human activity analysis (Moeslund, 2001), head-pose estimation (Chutorian, 2009) and human-computer interaction (Porta, 2002) are more relevant. Interested readers are encouraged to refer to the computer vision textbooks in the additional readings section, for a more general discussion of computer vision algorithms.

There are several advantages in using computer vision based systems for the above applications. Cameras are relatively non-invasive input devices, compared to the state of the art sensors such as accelerometers, gyro sensors, etc. They are also more versatile; systems for different applications can be implemented using standard hardware set-ups that consist of cameras and computers, instead of custom-made sensors. An image can also capture a much larger amount of information compared to other sensors. Due to such advantages, computer vision has been an active and growing research area for the past couple of decades.

Due to the large number of pixels present in a digital image (millions of pixels) and the high frame rate of video cameras (25 frames per second and above), computer vision algorithms demand substantial processing power and memory. However, the major challenge in using computer vision for practical applications is the relatively low accuracy of the state of the art algorithms. Due to the large amount of additional information and noise recorded in a digital image, recognition of an object or activity becomes much more difficult compared to a sensor that is designed for a specific purpose.

Vision-Based Head and Face Tracking Assistive Technologies

With the increase of the performance of head and face tracking algorithms, there has been some research on assistive technology applications based on head and face tracking. Automating wheelchair movement using head tracking is a relatively well-researched topic in this area. Berjon et al (2011) designed an automatic wheelchair that can be controlled using head pose. Similar systems based on head pose tracking, facial gesture tracking and eye tracking have been designed in several other researches(Yanco, 1998; Kuhlen, 1995; Bergasa 1999). Gaze tracking for text input is another popular research topic. A detailed review of research on this topic can be found in (Majaranta, 2002). Bala et al. (2010) developed a system that can help a visually impaired person during conversations. This system tracks the face of the person talking to the visually impaired person, and converts the head and facial gestures to vibro-tactile outputs. These outputs are conveyed to the visually impaired person via a glove.

The system proposed in this chapter presents another application of face tracking as an assistive technology: human computer interaction for disabled users. The following subsection reviews researches related to this topic in more detail.

Vision-Based Human-Computer Interaction

For computer vision to be used as a means of human computer interaction, a computer should be able to analyze a video of the user at a rate of 25-30 frames per second and make decisions on user actions. It should also be noted that the computer should still have sufficient resources for the user to execute the programs that he/she intends to use. Therefore, research on computer vision for human-computer interaction became possible only around 1995, when computers became sufficiently powerful. At the time of writing this chapter, these requirements can be met easily even by laptop computers.

For a computer vision system to be used for human-computer interaction, it should detect human actions/gestures that are appropriate for interacting with a computer. Such actions and gestures depend largely on the application domain. For assistive interfaces, hand gesture recognition for sign language interpretation has been widely researched (Caridakis, 2008; Starner, 1998; Wu, 2001). For computer users with motor limitations in their hands, head movement and facial gestures are useful as means of inputs. A computer vision-based interface using head movement and facial gestures should have the following basic functionality. First, it should detect a user intending to interact with the computer. This is performed using head/face detection. After detection, it should track the detected head/face in the sequence of image frames captured using the camera. It should also detect specific gestures and actions to be used as interactions. All these tasks have to be performed at sufficient speed with high accuracy, to facilitate human-computer interaction.

A review of the face-tracking literature is not the aim of the present communication, however suffice it to say that several groups have developed algorithms that are approaching the level of robustness needed for general use in real- world applications. Most of these works end with a successful demonstration of face- tracking functionality, and sometimes include a simple application of their method. Betke et al. (2002) used computer vision-based face tracking to provide computer access for people with severe disabilities. Grauman et al. (2003) utilized facial gestures such as blinks and brow raises to trigger mouse clicks. Gaze tracking has been successfully used for text entry for both English and Japanese text input (Hansen, 2004). Varona et al. (2008) demonstrated how nose-tip tracking combined with wink detection can replace a mouse device, for the benefit of disabled users.

Input methods which integrate information from several sensory modalities, including sight and sound, are being considered for use in perceptual user interfaces, or PUIs (Turk, 2000). Steady advances in CPU performance, the widespread availability of inexpensive plug-and-play cameras which capture video at full frame rate, and significant advances in computer vision research make vision-based methods one of the most promising areas for progress in PUI research. The importance of the face in human communication suggests that User Interfaces (UIs) which process facial information will be popular and, not surprisingly, numerous works have studied vision based methods for tracking the face-(Bradski, 1998; Crowley, 1997; Davis, 2001; Edwards, 1998; Oliver, 1997; De Silva, 1995; Toyama, 1998)-to list only a few. Some face tracking algorithms use nostrils as the tracked feature points (Bourel, 2000).

An important exception from the above applications is a study (Darrell, 2002) of the HCI aspects of using a face-tracking UI for dual-pointing tasks, which found that use of the head-based input stream was appropriate for asymmetric control tasks. Other than this recent study, there seems to have been relatively little effort to characterize the HCI aspects of vision-based UIs. Before vision-based UIs can be taken seriously as input methods, however, the human side of the interaction needs to be considered. A significant fraction of the HCI literature is concerned with systematic and reliable evaluation of input devices such as mouse, joystick, and trackball, beginning with the influential work of Card and colleagues (1978).

In most previous works, mouth/lip detection and tracking is used for automatic lip-reading and facial expression recognition. Petajan (1996) uses Luminance and skin color to detect facial features including eyes, nostrils and lips, for robust automatic speech reading. Mixture models of spatial and color distributions have been used for real-time tracking of face and lips (Oliver, 1997). Lip corners result in image features that are relatively robust and easier to detect. Yang (1998) demonstrated that lip corner tracking combined with a few other feature detectors can be used for real-time lip reading. Snakes and surface learning (Bregler, 1994), motion segmentation (Stork, 1996), and face detection (Palleja, 2009) are other, widely used techniques for tracking lips and mouth contours. The Viola-Jones face detector (Viola, 2004) is a robust, multi-scale face detector that is widely used for initializing face trackers. However, this is computationally intensive to be used as a real-time face tracker. Most of these works use features that are unnecessarily complex for our purposes. The LAFTER (Oliver, 1997) system uses a simple set of features, but requires the presence of the complete face in the image for mouth detection. Mouthbrush (Chan, 2007) is substantially different from the above systems. Using a head-worn camera, it can detect the shape of the user's mouth without complex image processing, and uses only the basic shape features.

Speech Analysis Related to Assistive Technology

Assistive technology applications based on audio/speech signal analysis is more common and better established, compared to computer vision-based assistive technologies. Speech signals have a relatively lower bandwidth when compared to video, and therefore can be captured and processed relatively easily. For persons who have motor disabilities but are able to talk, speech can be used for interaction with devices that support them. Recent surveys on speech analysis for supporting people with disabilities can be found in Mosbah (2006), Lopresti et al. (2004), and Noyes and Frankish (1998).

The most common application for speech analysis in assistive technology is speech-to-text conversion. This enables persons with dexterity limitations to enter text to a computer. It can also allow deaf persons to understand spoken messages. Several commercial applications such as IBM's Via Voice, Dragon Naturally Speaking by Nuance Inc., are available for this task. Another common application is to use verbal commands as an interface to control appliances used by a person with motor disabilities. Wheelchairs and household appliances can be controlled using voice commands. A recent survey on voice activated appliances for disabled persons can be found in (Suk & Kojima, 2008).

While assistive technologies based on speech recognition are widely used in selected applications such as speech to text conversion, they suffer from sensitivity to environmental audio noise. When the surrounds are noisy, it is difficult to accurately distinguish the intentional input from the background noise. By contrast, input systems relying on computer vision do not suffer from sensitivity to environmental audio noise, or indeed, many other uncontrollable variations in natural usage settings. While speech systems are omnidirectionally sensitive to noise, cameras naturally capture light from a restricted solid angle. Moreover the user's body itself occludes some background variability. Similar directionality of capture is difficult to achieve in the audio domain, especially with ordinarily available microphones. A further advantage of video is that it provides a potentially richer source of information due to the naturally higher bandwidth compared to audio.

In summary: With the availability of small and computationally powerful hardware at lower costs, methods and devices for human-computer interaction have evolved rapidly during the past decade. At the current state, keyboards, pointing devices and touch-screens are the most popular input devices for computers. However, these devices are hard to use for those with disabilities related to hands. Alternative methods of input, based on audio and infra-red are available in mobile and gaming platforms at consumer level. In parallel to the recent progress in computer vision research, there has been a steady growth in research on computer vision-based human-computer interaction.These researches have resulted in several working prototypes that can function as vision-based interfaces for specific tasks. However, detailed studies on the usability and performance of such interfaces are currently unavailable. The following sections of this chapter describe our work on systems for vision-based human-computer interaction, and their evaluations.

FACE TRACKING SYSTEM

We propose two face tracking algorithms that suit different hardware setups and applications. The first system is more appropriate for a desktop computer with a camera located above the monitor. This system adopts of a previous face-tracking system developed in our group, to explicitly track the location of the tip of the nose and use it for cursor control (a schematic is shown in Figure 1a). First the eyes are detected. Next, the location of the nose tip is estimated within a small region below the eyes. The nose tip is convex and usually only one point in the estimated region has this feature (Gorodnichy, 2002). This reduces the difficulty of detecting the nose tip, which may then be tracked using template matching, with an adaptive template that is updated each video frame.

The second system (Figure 1b) is proposed for interfaces such as handheld devices. For these, the camera is usually kept below the eye level. Images of the lower face region of the user are acquired as input. The system uses nostril detection and tracking followed by mouth region location, to segment the mouth cavity region of the image. Geometric features of this region are extracted and passed to applications. The following sub-sections describe these two systems in detail.

Detecting and Tracking the Eyes

Blink detection is used to detect the eyes (Kawato, 2002). In detection mode, differences the previous and current frames are calculated, and pixels where the luminance change exceeds a threshold are extracted. If blinking occurs, a pair of regions corresponding to eyelid movement areas are expected, having

Figure 1. Schematics of the face tracking interfaces; (a) with the camera above the monitor, (b) with the camera below the monitor

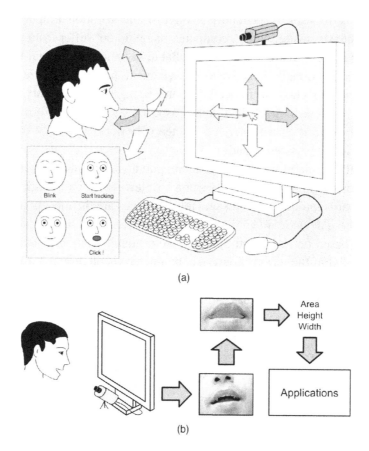

(a)

(b)

certain geometrical properties (size, distance, alignment). This is complicated by the fact that the head may move, hence thresholded pixels can include not only the eyelid regions but other parts of the face. To cope with this problem, head movement is estimated and used to cancel pixels where predicted and observed luminance change match. Subsequently, we apply labeling and connected component analysis and geometrical relation tests for candidate eye pair locations. Head movement estimation is not based on area patterns but only on pixels extracted from the frame difference image, which means the computation is not intensive and may be done in real-time (Kawato, 2002).

Subsequent to eye detection and location, the eyes are tracked. However, blinking causes rapid and drastic changes and even adaptive templates cannot follow these changes. Instead, a "Between-the-Eyes" template (Kawato, 2002b) is used to track the location of the face. Compared to other areas of the face its pattern is relatively stable for changes in facial expression. It has a relatively bright part at the nose bridge and relatively dark parts at the eyes like wedges on both sides. This is a very good feature for accurate location by template matching. After the detection of "Between the-Eyes," the eyes are searched again in very small areas, because their positions relative to the "Between-the- Eyes" template are known in the previous frame. In turn, the "Between-the-Eyes" template is updated each frame, based on the current eye positions (Kawato, 2002).

Detecting and Tracking the Nose Tip

After the eyes are located, it is relatively easy to detect the nose tip, which is convex shaped and somewhat specular, hence possesses a highlight. Although the precise location of the highlight depends on face orientation and lighting direction, it is located on the nose tip. Moreover, for fixed lighting, to extent that the nose tip approximates a sphere, the precise location of the highlight is not strongly affected by orientation of the face.

Figure 2a shows the search area for the nose tip relative to locations of the eyes. The brightest point in this area is taken as a candidate for the nose tip. If the distances from this point to the two eyes are nearly equal, we assume it is the nose tip, and begin tracking.

In tracking the nose tip, we also use a continuously updated template. A small rectangular pattern centered at the nose tip is saved as a template for the next frame. In the current frame, the best matching point with the template is searched around the previous position. Then the nose tip is registered again to the brightest point in a very small region around the matching point. Then, the nose tip template is updated. If it goes out of region shown in Figure 2a, we assume the nose tip is lost, and start again from detection. Figure 2b shows the results of the facial tracking algorithm, indicating positions of the detected eyes and nose tip.

Displacement/Angle Gain

Selection of a control movement to display output gain setting is important for pointing devices and head pointers are no exception (Schaab, 1996). Two possible measures of gain are (a) D/A: the ratio of D, the displacement on the display device (in centimeters) to the rotation angle A of the head (in degrees), and (b) A'/A, where the displacement on the display device is measured as a visual angle, A'. With 3D face tracking it is a simple matter to have a linear angular display displacement for angular head rotations, but it has been suggested that a constant D/A ratio is appropriate for head-controlled pointing (Schaab, 1996).

Figure 2. (a) Nose tip search area relative to the eyes; (b) results of face tracking

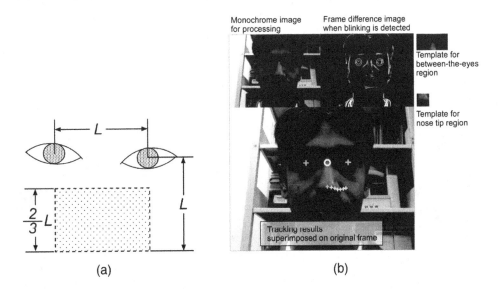

(a)   (b)

We track the nose in the 2D image, and map its displacement from the center of the image to displacement of the cursor from the center of the display. As a check, head rotation angle A was measured by setting gaze landmarks on a wall behind the computer display. For the range of angles needed to cover the display area the relation between D and A was found to be approximately linear. We adjusted the gain so that the entire horizontal display could be covered without uncomfortable movements resulting in a gain of 0.47 cm/deg, equivalent to an angular gain of about 4.35. This lies close to the gain found by earlier study (Schaab, 1996) to minimize cursor movement times. Rotation of the head (looking left and right) requires less effort than extension/flexion (looking up and down), so choose the gain to be anisotropic with a fixed ratio of vertical to horizontal D/A gain of 1.4. This allowed the vertical range of the display to be covered without uncomfortable movements.

Nostril Detection and Tracking

A computationally efficient method is used for nostril detection and tracking. This method, which is based on intensity gradient information, is a modified version of the algorithm used in (Petajan, 1996). Since nostrils are cavities, not surfaces, they appear darker relative to the surrounding face region under most lighting conditions. The pattern of intensity in a small window of the image containing the nostrils causes a characteristic profile across the horizontal and vertical directions (considering an upright face). This variation is prominent in the image intensity projections.

The system is initialized by positioning nostrils in a specific rectangular region of the image (as shown in Figure 3a) and clicking a mouse button. This region is 1/6th of the total area of the image. The initialization is nearly effortless since the requirement for initialization is satisfied when the lower part of the user's face is visible in the image.

The intensity information of the image region containing the nostrils is projected onto the horizontal axis and low pass filtered. The nostrils cause a pattern with two local minima in this projection (Fig. 3b). The horizontal coordinates of the centers of the nostrils, N1x and N2x, are estimated by locating the two minima. The vertical coordinates of the nostril centers, N1y and N2y, are located using the same approach (Figure 3c). Figure 3d presents the result of detection superimposed on the nostril region. The coordinates of the determined nostril centers N1=(N1x,N1y) and N2=(N2x,N2y) are used to determine the Euclidean distance between nostril centers, DN, the angle between the line between nostril centers and the horizontal axis, AN, and the mid-point between nostril centers, CN. Rectangular window to be

Figure 3. (a) Nostril detection and tracking; (a) initialization, (b) & (c) intensity projection for detecting nostril centers, (d) result of nostril detection

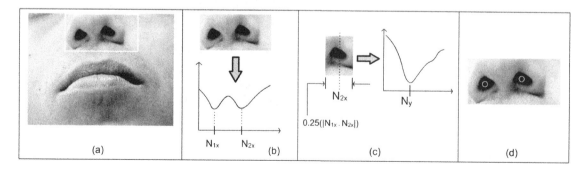

used for tracking in the next frame is estimated using these parameters (Fig.4b, upper rectangle). The tracking algorithm is slightly different from the detection algorithm. The window is rotated by angle -AN around CN before extracting the search region. DN and AN are smoothed by using a weighted sum of the previous value and current value. The position of is predicted assuming the motion with constant velocity within a duration of three frames, according to:

$$C_N(t+1) = C_N(t) + a\{C_N(t) - C_N(t-1)\}$$

where a is a constant between 0.1 and 1.

Mouth Segmentation

The region of the image where the mouth is contained is estimated using the detected facial feature locations. For detection of between-the eyes point and nose tip, this is shown in Figure 4a. This is refined based on the location of a local intensity minimum corresponding to the region just beneath the upper lip. For nostril detection, the lower rectangle of Figure 4b shows the search region. The window is rotated before the samples are extracted, so that the orientation dependent parameters of the mouth region (such as height and width) can be estimated easily. Portions of this region can be out of image bounds without affecting mouth region segmentation.

Since the mouth cavity appears as a dark, relatively red region in the image, we segment pixels having the red component above a certain threshold and the intensity component below another threshold. The thresholds can be adjusted by the user, observing the segmented mouth cavity region on the screen, to achieve a continuous region corresponding to the mouth cavity. This algorithm has been successfully employed with systems using a head-mounted camera (Lyons, 2001; Lyons, 2003).

Noise in the segmented region is reduced using a voting algorithm with a neighborhood of width 5 pixels and height 3 pixels. The neighborhood is longer than it is high because of the shape of the nearly closed mouth. Each segmented pixel is reset if there are less than 4 segmented pixels in its neighborhood. Non-segmented pixels in the mouth region having more than 4 segmented pixels as neighbors, are added to the segmented set of pixels. After smoothing, the largest segmented blob is selected as corresponding to the mouth cavity region.

Using the Mouth to Click

Intentional motion of the mouth is facile, hence we decided to use a mouth opening gesture for a "mouse click". An open mouth is identified by the size of the segmented mouth region exceeding a pre-set threshold. This procedure makes use of the fact that under a large range of lighting conditions the open mouth robustly exhibits a shadow area which is darker than surrounding teeth and skin areas. In this work, we mapped the opening of the mouth to a single click event. Closing the mouth, or keeping it open has no effect. In future work, we plan to study more elaborate mappings of mouth gestures, to allow, for example, double clicks, or clicking and dragging.

Figure 4. Detection of between-the eyes point and nose

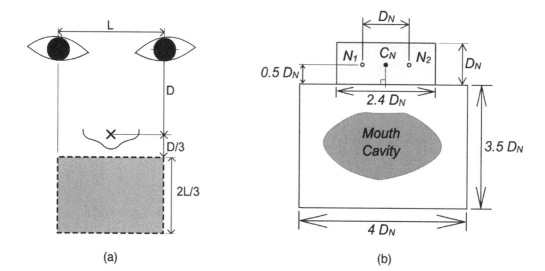

(a)   (b)

Mouth Shape Estimation

The following parameters are extracted using the geometric features of the selected blob. The number of pixels in the blob is proportional to the area, Am of the mouth cavity. The standard deviation of the pixels along the vertical axis of the blob is proportional to the height, Hm of the mouth cavity. The standard deviation of the pixels along the horizontal axis of the blob is proportional to the width, Wm of the mouth cavity. The aspect ratio, Rm of the mouth cavity is given by Rm=Hm/Wm. Estimates of Hm and Wm are based on the standard deviations, which are functions of all pixel positions, to minimize sensitivity to noise.

The parameters can change when the user moves his head, even if the mouth is opened to the same extent. We do not attempt to correct for the effects of pose, as the system is intended for interactive use so that users control the output directly by their actions.

PERFORMANCE EVALUATION

Fitts Law

Based on studies of the tradeoff between speed and accuracy in aimed movement tasks, Fitts (Fitts, 1954) proposed a linear relationship between the *difficulty*, $ID=\text{Log}_2(2D/W)$ (for a target of width W, at a distance D), of a task and the movement time, *MT*, taken for its completion. Numerous studies have used Fitts' law to compare input devices (Card, 1978). Fitts' law has evolved over the past few years and recent work (MacKenzie, 2001; ISO 9241-9:2000(E), 2000) uses the following form:

MT=ID$_e$/Throughput

The throughput, in bits/second, is an index of performance of the human- machine interface for an aimed target acquisition task, and an international standard method for measuring the information throughput of pointing devices, the ISO 9241-9 Standard (ISO 9241-9:2000(E), 2000) has developed. In the ISO standard (also see (MackKenzie, 2001)) the effective index of difficulty, Ide is an explicit function of the accuracy with which targets are selected:

$$ID_e = \text{Log}_2(D/W_e + 1) \text{ with } W_e = 4.133SD_x$$

where SD_x is the standard deviation of the target selection coordinate measured along the axis of approach to a target. The effective index of difficulty depends on the effective target width, which is based on the accuracy with which the task is performed.

Multi-Direction Tapping Task

Previous work using head-worn cursor control systems, has shown Fitts' law to hold for head movement tasks (Jagacinski, 1985). However, there seem to be no values in the published literature for the throughput of a vision-based face tracking pointer. Hence we decided to make a careful measurement of the information throughput of the pointing function of our UI, and at the same time a measurement of the performance of a standard mouse as a check of our methodology.

Figure 5a illustrates the ISO 9241-9 task as implemented in our experiments. A 240 pixel diameter circle was displayed at the center of a 640×480 pixel resolution monitor. Seventeen circular targets (each having a diameter of 21 pixels) were spaced equally around the perimeter of the circle. Subjects were required to move the cursor from one target to another, neighboring the diametrically opposite position, according to a pre-defined sequence indicated in the figure. Subjects pressed the space bar to indicate reaching a target, and the next target was highlighted by changing its color to red. The index of difficulty of each trial of this task, calculated using the above dimensions and is 3.4, without the correction for effective target width.

Experimental Procedure

Eight voluntary subjects participated in the experiment. All were regular computer users and familiar with use of the mouse, but none were involved in development of the face- tracking system, or had previously used it. None of the subjects had motor or other disabilities. Each subject was briefed about the task at the beginning of each experiment. Warm-up trials were not permitted in order to allow observation of the effect of learning. Each test subject performed a total of 20 repetitions of the multi-directional pointing task, alternating between using the mouse and the face-tracker to control the cursor, starting, in all cases with the mouse since the users are experienced mouse users. Breaks were allowed between blocks. Total time for completion of all 20 blocks was about 40 minutes. To calculate throughput values, pixel coordinates of the cursor at time of target selection were recorded, together with time taken to reach it. For further device characterization, coordinates of the cursor movement path were sampled at a rate of 32 samples/second and stored.

Figure 5. Evaluation of the face tracker as a pointing device; (a) ISO standard Multi-directional tapping task, (b) learning curves for the movement times, (c) sample trajectories for the multidirectional tracking task, (d) average movement time (sec) versus orientation (deg)

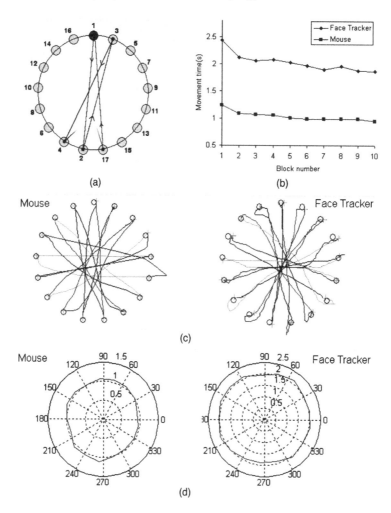

(a)   (b)

(c)

(d)

Results

Sample trajectories for one user completing one block of the experiment are shown in Figure 5c. The shakier movement of the cursor seen with the face tracker partially reflects jitter of the tracking system, but it is also a function of head movement behavior. As the mouse rests inertly on a flat surface its trajectories are not surprisingly smoother.

Figure 5b plots movement times, averaged over the eight subjects, for successive blocks. Movement times decrease with successive blocks for both devices, reflecting motor learning. The mouse resulted in generally faster interaction than the face tracker. With the face tracker, we observed a more rapid decrease of movement times, especially for the first three blocks. Since the subjects had little experience using a face tracking system to point, this may be the result of learning two skills, the ISO task and use of the vision based UI, at the same time. The mouse throughput, averaged over our last five trials, was 4.7 bits/

sec, which is similar to the value of 4.9 bits/sec measured recently also using the ISO task (MacKenzie, 2001). For the face tracking pointer, the average throughput was 2.0 bits/sec. This value exceeds the 1.8 bits/sec reported for a joystick, but is lower than the 3.0 bit/sec for a trackball and the 2.9 bit/sec for a touchpad, measured previously using the ISO task (MacKenzie, 2001).

Individual user mouse and nose pointer throughputs were not significantly correlated (Pearson r = -0.05; Spearman's $\rho = 0.05$), suggesting that there is no strong relationship between motor skills for using these pointing devices. In contrast to findings with a head-worn head tracking system (Radwin, 1990) the vision-based system we studied showed no significant dependence of throughput on movement direction orientation, as shown in the polar plot of throughput versus orientation, as may be seen in Figure 5d.

Evaluation Tasks for Input Using Mouth Shape

The accuracy and precision of the system as an input device was examined using an experiment based on 5 evaluation tasks. With the radius control task (Chan, 2003), the test subject adjusts the area of the open mouth to control the radius of a circle drawn on the screen until it is exactly tangent to a target square (Figure 6a). With the height control task the height of the opening of the mouth is adjusted to control the height of a rectangle drawn on the screen until it is tangent to a target rectangle (Figure 6b). With the width control task the width of the opening of the mouth is adjusted to vary the width of a rectangle until its edges meet those of a target rectangle (Figure 6c). The aspect ratio control task is similar to the height control task (Figure 6b). In this task, the aspect ratio of the mouth opening controls the height of a rectangle. Finally, with the ellipse control task the height and width of the mouth are varied to control the height and width of an ellipse until it is tangent to the edges of a target rectangle (Figure 6d).

Evaluation Experiment

The control parameters were determined from the parameters measured in the image according to:

$$P/P_{max} = gV_i$$

where P_{max} is the maximum value of the parameter P controlled in the experiment, V_i is the measured value in the image, and g, the control gain, is a dimensionless parameter between 0 and 1.

For the radius, height, width and aspect ratio control tasks, the half height and/or half width of the target rectangle took the values (5, 23, 42, 61, 80). The value of gain, g was used as an additional independent variable in these tasks. The values (0.25, 0.5, 0.8) were used for the experiment. Each combination of gain and target size was repeated three times, resulting in a total of 45 trials. For the ellipse control task, g was held constant at 0.25. The half sides of the rectangle took values (5, 30, 55, 80). Each combination of the height and the width was presented twice to the test subject, resulting in 32 trials altogether.

Three voluntary test subjects, with some prior experience using the mouth controller, participated in the experiments. Subjects sat comfortably at a distance of approximately 60 cm from a 19" LCD monitor with a resolution of 1152×864 pixels. The trials were presented in random order to each user during each task. In each trial, the test subject adjusted the radius/size of the circle/rectangle according to the target size and clicked the left mouse button. The computer recorded the radius/size of the circle/ rectangle at 67Hz for 3 seconds, before moving to the next trial. The users were allowed to rest between trials. The completion of each experiment took approximately 10 minutes.

For each experiment, the following were calculated. The mean absolute error, *E*, (difference between the target size and actual size) was calculated as a measure of the accuracy of control. The standard deviation from the mean size, *SD*, was calculated as a measure of precision of the input.

Results

Figures 6e, 6f, and 7 present the results obtained for the radius control task. Figure 6e plots the mean absolute error (*E*) averaged over all target sizes for each value of gain (g) while Figure 6f plots the standard deviation (*SD*) for the same. It is evident that both accuracy and precision are not strongly dependent on *g*, and have values close to 1 pixel. Figures 7a and 7b show the variation of *E* and *SD* respectively, over the target radius for different values of *g*. For all values of *g*, both the mean absolute error and average standard deviation increases with target radius. For the height, width and aspect ratio control tasks, the order of the values and the nature of their variation is similar to those for the radius control task. The overall results suggest that higher accuracy and precision is possible for smaller target

Figure 6. Evaluation of mouth shape input; (a) radius control task, (b) height and aspect ratio control task, (c) width control task, (d) ellipse control task, (e) accuracy with different gains, (f) precision with different gains

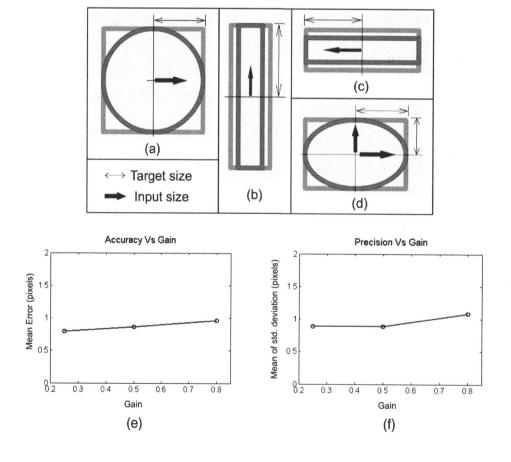

sizes while the accuracy does not depend significantly on the gain. The inputs have an accuracy and precision of about 1 pixel.

Figure 7c plots the results of the ellipse control task. The left and right graphs plot the mean absolute error in the width and the height inputs respectively, for different target heights and widths. It is evident that the accuracy is very low for small target widths. This reflects the difficulty of reaching these combinations of the heights and widths as mouth movements in these two directions are not completely independent. This is an anatomical limitation, not a limitation in the computer vision system. The mean standard deviation is approximately 2 pixels for both inputs - higher than those for the other tasks.

Despite the absence of a mechanism to normalize the inputs against variations due to head rotation and scaling, the results were comparable to those obtained with a head-worn Mouthesizer (Chan, 2003).

USABILITY ASSESSMENT

We conducted a preliminary assessment of usability and user comfort. Our greatest concern was for the possibility of neck fatigue through repetitive head movements. After completing the 20 blocks of the ISO task, the eight volunteers were asked to fill in a questionnaire adapted from the ISO 9241-9 document (ISO 9241-9:2000(E), 2000). Subjects rated the vision based user interface on eight criteria related to performance of the interface and comfort or fatigue of operation. A seven point response scale was

Figure 7. Accuracy and precision of mouth shape input; (a) accuracy with different target sizes, (b) precision with different target sizes, (c) accuracy of height and with in different directions

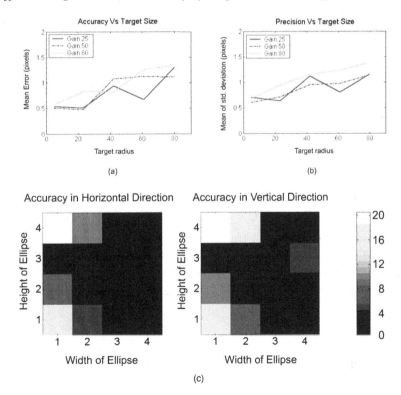

used with 1 being the worst rating (very poor performance or greatest discomfort) and 7 the best (very good performance or greatest comfort). Below we list the criterion descriptor, response mean, mode (in parentheses with more than one response number if the distribution is lat), and the range of responses:

- Strength required 4.5 (5) 3-6
- Smoothness 3.9 (2,3,6) 2-6
- Effort required 4.0 (3,5) 3-5
- Accuracy 3.5 (2,3,4,5) 2-5
- Speed 4.1 (2) 2-7
- Comfort 4.2 (4) 3-5
- Fatigue 4.0 (4) 2-6
- Overall 4.9 (6) 4-6

Overall neck effort was rated on Borg's 11 point scale [9], with 0 indicating no neck effort and 10 indicating very, very strong neck effort. Mean response was 3.7 (3=weak, 4 = moderate), the range of responses was 0-6 with a mode of 4.

In the list above we note that average responses lie close to the middle of the usability scale. The weakest points were smoothness and accuracy of cursor control and the strongest points were the overall usability and low demand on neck strength.

In addition to rating using independent usability scales, the ISO standard also recommends comparative ratings with different devices. Since our volunteers had much greater familiarity with the conventional mouse than with the nose pointer, we decided that it would be difficult to conduct a meaningful comparison in this case and decided not to pursue this experiment.

Descriptive User Feedback

The questionnaire concluded with two qualitative questions. Answers to the first question, "What are your suggestions for improvements?" are listed below (number of subjects responding this way is indicated in parentheses):

- Greater smoothness (3).
- Greater accuracy (2).
- More displacement gain (2).
- Less displacement gain (1).
- Velocity rather than position control (1).

Most users suggested improvements in smoothness and accuracy of the pointing device, in agreement with the results from the first part of the questionnaire, listed in the previous section.

Answers to the second question, "How would you imagine the system being used?", included:

- Interface for the disabled (5).
- For use as a dual pointer (2).
- Interface for computer games (2).

The absence of answers relating to mobile phone or palmtop computing may be a result of conducting the experiment with a desktop computer, rather than a strong indication that our users felt these were not desirable applications of the technology.

APPLICATIONS

Hands-Free Text Entry

Conventional keyboards are inconvenient for text-entry with mobile phones and PDAs, as well as for disabled computer users. Hence text-entry, is a potentially important application for vision-based interfaces. The Dasher system (Ward, 2000, 2002) allows for efficient text-entry by two-dimensional gestures. Figure 8 shows a screenshot from the Dasher text-entry interface. Letters automatically drift from right to left at a speed controlled by the horizontal position of the cursor. Letters are selected by the vertical position of the cursor. The size of the selection zone for each letter depends the probability that it will occur next in the typed sequence. This probability is estimated using a model trained on a large corpus of English text. This greatly improves the efficiency of text entry: after some practice time users feel they can easily steer the cursor along paths which follow correctly spelled English text.

Dasher has been tested with an eye tracking system (Ward, 2002), however this requires special hardware, calibration, and restriction of the user's head position. The face tracking system reported here, by contrast, requires no special hardware and only minor or no calibration adjustments.

For the language model used by Dasher, the estimated Shannon information per character is about 2 bits (Ward, 2000). So, ideally, with the measured throughput for the face tracker of 2 bits/sec, one should be able to type at a rate of 60 character/min. However, we can expect text entry with Dasher to be more difficult than the target selection task. Instead, we use the previously measured median (from a distribution of users) typing speed of 90 characters/min for Dasher operated with a mouse (Ward, 2000),

Figure 8. Operating the dasher text entry interface with head movements

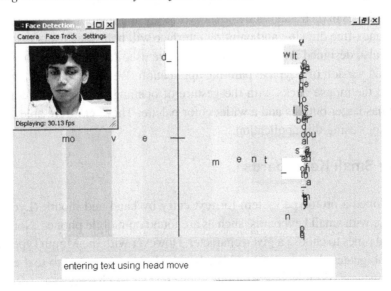

and our measured ratio of mouse to face tracker throughput of 2.35, to predict a typing speed of 38 char/min with the face tracker. To check this prediction, two subjects familiar with the use of the face tracker used Dasher to enter short excerpts from Hans Christian Andersen's story "The Little Match Girl", which is not contained in the corpus of texts used to train Dasher's language model. Eight excerpts of about 20 words in length were used, for a total of 160 words, or 819 characters. The average measured typing speed for the two subjects was 38 char/min (7.3 wpm), in excellent agreement with the above prediction. One of the authors, who has considerably more experience using Dasher than the two subjects above, averaged 61 char/min (12 wpm) on the same task, which is similar to the theoretical prediction based on the throughput. We note that faster rates should be possible with an improved language model or with adaptation to the user's writing style. As the information content of English text is estimated to be 1 bit/char (Shannon, 1993), this could be as great as a factor of 2, for a possible typing speed of 24 wpm, for users with some practice.

Musical Controller

We investigated the use of the shape of the mouth, as estimated using the proposed algorithms, as an interface for controlling music. Interested readers may refer to the course material at (Lyons, 2011) for a good general introduction to music-based applications of new interface technologies. Shape parameters of the mouth are converted to MIDI control change signals (Lyons, 2003). For example, the mouth was used to control audio effects such as wah-wah (resonant low pass filtering). It is intuitive to use the mouth to control such effects because of the role of the mouth in speech, singing, and facial expression. With the correct mapping of action to audio effect, the mouth is a very compelling way to play!

Drawing and Painting Interface

We have also implemented a drawing and painting system (Chan, 2003) which allows the user to control brush qualities such as size, hardness, opacity, and color, with their mouth, while the are drawing using a graphics tablet and stylus interface. Again some mappings, such as mouth size to brush size, result in a very natural interaction. Artists who used the system reported an interesting and expressive experience.

People with disabilities in their hands are known to draw by holding brushes with their toes, or mouth. We believe that a hands-free drawing and painting interface will help such users to create paintings using computers. We also designed an application that can be used for hands-free drawing and painting. This was a simplified version of a typical painting application. We controlled the mouse pointer using the face tracker and the mouse clicks with the gesture of opening the mouth. We also simplified the interface so that it has larger buttons and a wider color palette. The users were able to compose simple drawings and paintings using this application.

Text Entry With Small Key-Boards

We have also developed a prototype system for text entry by hand and mouth (Lyons, 2004). This is advantageous for use with small keyboards, such as are found on mobile phones. Normally the user has to push a key several times to choose a given character. However with the MouthType system, the shape of the mouth disambiguates the key press. This is particularly well suited to text entry with syllabic languages such as Japanese. With Japanese mobile phone text entry, characters corresponding to the five vowels are mapped to the same key, which corresponds to a consonant. Shaping the mouth as though pronouncing a given vowel selects the syllabic character corresponding to that vowel. Here we make use of the already existing expertise of the user in mapping mouth shape to vowel choice. This enables the user to enter Japanese syllabic characters with far fewer key presses and at a significantly higher speed than with previously existing Japanese text entry.

DISCUSSION

The face trackers proposed in this chapter use fairly simple image features and tracking algorithms. This allowed them to run fast, allowing users to have faster interaction. Both trackers could execute at more than 28 frames per second, with sufficient computing resources for the applications we demonstrated.

We also noted that the users were able to quickly adjust to the gain of the trackers, despite no prior calibration. This can be considered as one of the advantages in interactive systems. With continuous feedback from the mouse pointer and applications, the users were able to adjust themselves quickly.

The arrangement for the nostril tracker, where the camera is located below the computer monitor, is uncommon when compared to the usual arrangement of having the camera above the screen. However, none of the subjects who used the tracker during the user study mentioned that the positioning made it difficult to use it.

Our studies were conducted with subjects who had normal motor control. We feel this is justified because our major aim in the current study was to characterize the throughput of of the vision-based assistive input device. Because there greater variability is expected with physically challenged users, this would greatly increase the number of users needed to make a 'standard' measurement. Adaptation and customization of the interface will require further studies with users having specific physical abilities.

We observed that the users were more relaxed while using the musical controller, compared to the other applications. With the other applications, the users controlled text/graphics that appeared on a screen. This required more concentration as the users had to keep looking at the screen. Another reason for the high concentration required was the lack of a method to quickly disengage with the interface. While engaging with the interface is initiated by blinking, currently there is no method for stopping using the interface. This is different from conventional input devices such as mouse and keyboard, where a user can take the hand/s off the device to stop using it. Recognition of additional gestures can facilitate easier disengagement, and improving the smoothness of tracking can make the users require less concentration. We believe that when used as an assistive interface, the ability to be used as a hands-free interface will outweigh the requirement of concentration.

APPLICATION TO ASSISTIVE TECHNOLOGY

All of the systems described in the preceding sub-sections are functioning prototypes that could realistically be developed into usable products by adding some finishing touches such as a more friendly user interface for non-expert users. In general, any software application that involves pointing and clicking can be controlled using the methods we have demonstrated. Beyond this, the mouth controlled described in this chapter allows two or more mouth shape parameters to be input simultaneously in real-time, with excellent accuracy and speed. Hence, software applications requiring multiple continuous inputs (e.g. software for live musical performance) can be driven by our mouth controller.

The assistive systems we have described in this chapter should be usable by any user who retains some control of head and face movements, in spite of severe physical challenges accompanying loss of use of the limbs. This includes a broad range of injuries and diseases. Generally speaking, the muscles of the face are innervated via the cranial nerves which may not be affected by injuries to the spine, whereas limb movements rely on a healthy spinal cord. In many conditions, then, movement of the face may remain intact though there may be severe impairment of limb movements. More specifically, users with the potential to make head and face movements could make effective use of the head tracking system and mouth controller we have described, which could help them compensate for loss of limb movement control. On the other hand, users who could not more their limbs or head, could still benefit from using the mouth controller, for a condition which affected even the high spinal nerves but not the facial cranial nerves. For users who only retain eye movements or the ability to blink, a more specific system will be needed to perform multiple input functions in response to blinking movements.

Several of the prototypes we have described could be nearly directly adapted for use as assistive interfaces. For example, controlling the cursor location and clicking can be directly mapped to the windowing system of many personal computing devices. Take the highly versatile example of text entry. The text entry system we have prototyped and described in this chapter could be useful as a front end to several software applications, or even dedicated appliance interfaces, which often require text input. We have also given concrete examples of applications to artistic and musical expression, in which the mouth controller has been applied to create music, drawings, and other types of artworks. The ability to support artistic expression could greatly improve the enjoyment and quality of life for physically challenged users.

The interfaces and applications described above can be easily acquired and learned by users with disabilities. Almost all notebook computers and tablet devices made at the time of writing have a built-in front view camera. Therefore, the users do not have to purchase or set up additional hardware devices. A camera is less invasive compared to wearable sensors that can be used for head or face tracking. The proposed algorithms do not involve markers or calibration; this makes them easy to use and learn.

CONCLUSION

In this article, we have implemented a video-based interface that allows the user to provide input to the computer using head and mouth movements. The system is initialized in a hands-free manner, though minor calibration is sometimes needed for novice users. The information throughput of the system for cursor control was evaluated using the international standard methods for evaluating pointing devices and found it to be lower than a computer mouse but slightly higher than a joystick. The utility of measuring the throughput was shown by demonstrating reasonably accurate prediction of the typing rate of hands-free text entry with the Dasher software. With the ability to point with the nose and enter a single click with the mouth, Dasher may be operated in a completely hands-free manner and no special hardware beyond a USB or Firewire camera. This represents an application of the facial gesture interface with immediate usefulness.

The use of motor actions of the mouth for man-machine interaction was found to be natural and advantageous. The principle advantages of using the mouth for HCI are that it provides an input modality that is independent and distinct from the hands, which can therefore be used in parallel, and in conjunction with the hands. This is demonstrated by the success of Mouthesizer, Mouthbrush, and MouthType applications. Furthermore, as shown with Mouthesizer and Japanese text input with MouthType, where prior experience leads users to have existing expertise, the mouth is ideally suited for certain types of information input. Objective evaluation of the algorithm using several novel tasks showed that the system affords a high degree of accuracy and precision of control.

By using a low camera angle, we showed that it is possible to robustly track the lower region of the face in real-time with a simple and computationally efficient algorithm. The proposed method is ideally suited for desktop or palmtop computer vision systems. The low angle also implies that the relevant features (nostrils and mouth) are clearly visible and occupy a large percentage of the image pixels. By tracking the nostrils we avoided the need for a head-worn system, making this algorithm less encumbering than versions studied in our earlier work.

ACKNOWLEDGMENT

We thank the volunteers who took part in our HCI experiments.

REFERENCES

Accot, J., & Zhai, S. (1999). Performance evaluation of input devices in trajectory-based tasks: An application of the steering law. In *Proceedings of the SIGCHI Conference on Human Factors in Computing Systems*, 466-472. New York: ACM.

Aggarwal, J. K., & Cai, Q. (1997). Human motion analysis: A review. In *Proceedings of IEEE Nonrigid and Articulated Motion Workshop*, 90-102. IEEE Press.

Ahad, M., Tan, J. K., Kim, H. S., & Ishikawa, S. (2008). Human activity recognition: Various paradigms. In *Proceedings of* IEEE *International Conference on Control, Automation, and Systems*, 1896-1901. IEEE Press.

Anusuya, M. A., & Katti, S. K. (2011). Front end analysis of speech recognition: A review. *International Journal of Speech Technology*, *14*(2), 99–145. doi:10.1007/s10772-010-9088-7

Bala, S., Ramesh, V., Krishna, S., & Panchanathan, S. (2010). Dyadic interaction assistant for tracking head gestures and facial expressions. In *Proceedings of IEEE International Symposium on Haptic Audio-Visual Environments and Games*. IEEE Press.

Bergasa, L. M., Mazo, M., Gardel, A., Garcia, J. C., Ortuno, A. E. M. A., & Mendez, A. E. (1999). Guidance of a wheelchair for handicapped people by face tracking. In *Proceedings of 7th IEEE International Conference on Emerging Technologies and Factory Automation, 1*, 105 111. IEEE Press.

Berjón, R., Mateos, M., Barriuso, A., Muriel, I., & Villarrubia, G. (2011). Head tracking system for wheelchair movement control. Highlights in Practical Applications of Agents and Multiagent Systems, 307-315. Berlin: Springer.

Betke, M., Gips, J., & Fleming, P. (2002). The camera mouse:Visual tracking of body features to provide computer access for people with severe disabilities. *IEEE Transactions on Neural Systems and Rehabilitation Engineering*, *10*(1), 1–10. doi:10.1109/TNSRE.2002.1021581 PMID:12173734

Bourel, F., Chibelushi, C. C., & Low, A. A. (2000). Robust facial feature tracking. In *Proceedings of British Machine Vision Conference*, *1*, 232-241. Springer.

Bradski, G. R. (1998). Computer vision face tracking for use in a perceptual user interface. In *Proceedings of the Fourth IEEE Workshop on Applications of Computer Vision*. 214-219). IEEE Press.

Bregler, C., & Omohundro, S. M. (1994). Surface learning with applications to lipreading. In *Proceedings of the Conference on Neural Information Processing Systems*, 43-50. Boston: Morgan Kaufmann Publishers.

Card, S. K., English, W. K., & Burr, B. J. (1978). Evaluation of mouse, rate-controlled isometric joystick, step keys, and text keys for text selection on a CRT. *Ergonomics*, *21*(8), 601–613. doi:10.1080/00140137808931762

Caridakis, G., Diamanti, O., Karpouzis, K., & Maragos, P. (2008). Automatic sign language recognition: vision based feature extraction and probabilistic recognition scheme from multiple cues. In *Proceedings of the 1st International Conference on Pervasive Technologies Related to Assistive Environments*. ACM Press.

Chan, C., Lyons, M. J., & Tetsutani, N. (2003). Mouthbrush: Drawing and painting by hand and mouth. In *Proceedings of the 2003 International Conference on Multimodal Interfaces*, 277-280. ACM Press.

Chan, C.-H., & Lyons, M. J. (2007). Mouthbrush: A Multimodal Interface for Sketching and Painting. *International Journal of Computational Science*, *1*(1), 40–57.

Chauhan, V., & Morris, T. (2001). Face and feature tracking for cursor control. In *Proceedings of the Scandinavian Conference on Image Analysis*, 356-362. IEEE Press.

Chutorian, E. M., & Trivedi, M. M. (2009). Head pose estimation in computer vision: A survey. *IEEE Transactions on Pattern Analysis and Machine Intelligence*, *31*(4), 607–626. doi:10.1109/TPAMI.2008.106 PMID:19229078

Crowley, J. L., & Berard, F. (1997). Multi-modal tracking of faces for video communications. In *Proceedings of the IEEE Conference on Computer Vision and Pattern Recognition*, 640-645. IEEE Press.

Darrell, T., Checka, N., Oh, A., & Morency, L. P. (2002). *Exploring vision-based interfaces: How to use your head in dual pointing tasks*. Cambridge, MA: MIT Press.

Davis, J. W., & Vaks, S. (2001). A perceptual user interface for recognizing head gesture acknowledgements. In *Proceedings of the 2001 International Workshops on Perceptual/Perceptive User Interfaces*. IEEE Press.

De Silva, G. C., Lyons, M. J., Kawato, S., & Tetsutani, N. (2003). Human factors evaluation of a vision-based facial gesture interface. In *Proceedings of the 2003 International Conference on Computer Vision and Pattern Recognition.* IEEE Press.

De Silva, L. C., Tahara, M., Aizawa, K., & Hatori, M. (1995). Detection and tracking of facial features by using a facial feature model and deformable circular templates. *IEICE Transactions, (9),* 1195-1207.

Edwards, G. J., Taylor, C. J., & Cootes, T. (1998). Learning to identify and track faces in images sequences. In *Proceedings of the 1998 International Conference on Computer Vision, 317-322.*

Fitts, P. M. (1954). The information capacity of the human motor system in controlling the amplitude of movement. *Journal of Experimental Psychology, 47,* 381–391. doi:10.1037/h0055392 PMID:13174710

Gallo, L., & Ciampi, M. (2009). Wii Remote-enhanced hand-computer interaction for 3D medical image analysis. In *Proceedings of the International Conference on the Current Trends in Information Technology, 85-90.* CTIT Press.

Gorodnichy, D. O. (2002). On importance of nose for face tracking. In *Proceedings of the 2002 IEEE International Conference on Automatic Face and Gesture Recognition, 188-193.* IEEE Press.

Grauman, K., Betke, M., Lombardi, J., Gips, J., & Bradski, G. R. (2003). Communication via eye blinks and eyebrow raises: Video-based human-computer interfaces. Universal Access in the Information Society, 2-4. Berlin: Springer Verlag.

Hansen, J. P., Tørning, K., Johansen, A. S., Itoh, K., & Aoki, H. (2004). Gaze typing compared with input by head and hand. In *Proceedings of Symposium on Eye Tracking Research & Applications, 131-138.* ACM Press.

ISO 9241-9:2000(E). (2000). Ergonomic requirements for office work with visual display terminals (VDTs), Part 9. *Requirements for Non-Keyboard Input Devices.* London: International Standards Organization.

Jagacinski, R. J., & Monk, D. L. (1985). Fitts' law in two dimensions with hand and head movements. *Journal of Motor Behavior, 17,* 77–95. PMID:15140699

Jaimes, A., & Sebe, N. (2007). Multimodal human–computer interaction: A survey. *Computer Vision and Image Understanding, 108*(1), 116–134. doi:10.1016/j.cviu.2006.10.019

Jia, W., Yi, W., Saniie, J., & Oruklu, E. (2012). 3D image reconstruction and human body tracking using stereo vision and Kinect technology. [IEEE Press.]. *Proceedings of EIT, 2012,* 1–4.

Kawato, S., & Tetsutani, N. (2002a). Detection and tracking of eyes for gaze-camera control. In *Proceedings of the 15th International Conference on Vision Interfaces, 348-353.* ACM Press.

Kawato, S., & Tetsutani, N. (2002b). Real-time detection of between-the-eyes with a circle frequency filter. In *Proceedings of the 2002 Australian Conference on Computer Vision, 2,* 442-447.

Koppu, S., Viswanatham, V. M., & Kamalakannan, J. (2012). A survey on recent trends in human-computer interaction. *International Journal on Bioinformatics & Biosciences, 2*(3), 13–20. doi:10.5121/ijbb.2012.2302

Kratz, S., & Rohs, M. (2009). HoverFlow: Expanding the design space of around-device interaction. In *Proceedings of the 11th Conference on Human-computer Interaction with Mobile Devices and Services 2009*, 4-11.

Kuhlen, T., & Dohle, C. (1995). Virtual reality for physically disabled people. *Computers in Biology and Medicine*, 25(2), 205–211. doi:10.1016/0010-4825(94)00039-S PMID:7554838

Lewis, J. R. (2010). *Practical speech user interface design*. New York: Taylor & Francis Publications. doi:10.1201/b10461

LoPresti, E. F., Mihailidis, A., & Kirsch, N. (2004). Assistive technology for cognitive rehabilitation: State of the art. *Neuropsychological Rehabilitation*, 14(1-2), 5–39. doi:10.1080/09602010343000101

Lyons, M., & Fels, S. (2011). Advances in new interfaces for musical expression. In *Proceedings of ACM SIGGRAPH Asia 2011 Courses*, 2. ACM Press.

Lyons, M. J., Chan, C., & Tetsutani, N. (2004) MouthType: Text entry by hand and mouth. In *Proceedings of 2004 Conference on Human Factors in Computing Systems*. ACM Press.

Lyons, M. J., Haehnel, M., & Tetsutani, N. (2003). Designing, playing, and performing with a vision-based mouth interface. In *Proceedings of the 2003 Conference on New Interfaces for Musical Expression*, 116-121. NIME Press.

Lyons, M. J., & Tetsutani, N. (2001). Facing the music: A facial action controlled musical interface. In *Proceedings of the 2001 Conference on Human Factors in Computing Systems*, 309-310. ACM Press.

MacKenzie, I. S., Kauppinen, T., & Silfverberg, M. (2001). Accuracy measures for evaluating computer pointing devices. In *Proceedings of 2001 Conference on Human Factors in Computing Systems*, 9-16. ACM Press.

Majaranta, P., & Räihä, K. J. (2002). Twenty years of eye typing: Systems and design issues. In *Proceedings of the 2002 Symposium on Eye Tracking Research & Applications*, 15-22. ACM Press.

Matsumoto, Y., Ino, T., & Ogsawara, T. (2001). Development of intelligent wheelchair system with face and gaze based interface. In *Proceedings of 10th IEEE International Workshop on Robot and Human Interactive Communication*, 262-267. IEEE Press.

Moeslund, T. B., & Granum, E. (2001). A survey of computer vision-based human motion capture. *Computer Vision and Image Understanding*, 81(3), 231–268. doi:10.1006/cviu.2000.0897

Mosbah, B. (2006). Speech recognition for disabled people. In Information and Communication Technologies, 1, 864-869. IEEE Press.

Noyes, J., & Frankish, C. (1992). Speech recognition technology for individuals with disabilities. *Augmentative and Alternative Communication*, 8(4), 297–303. doi:10.1080/07434619212331276333

Oliver, N., Pentland, A. P., & Berard, F. (1997). LAFTER: Lips and face real time tracker. In *Proceedings of the 1997 International Conference on Computer Vision and Pattern Recognition*, 123-129. IEEE Press.

Palleja, T., Rubion, W., Teixido, M., Tresanchez, M., del Viso, A. F., Rebate, C., & Palacin, J. (2009). Using the optical flow to implement a relative virtual mouse controlled by head movements. *Journal of Universal Computer Science, 14*(19), 3127–3141.

Petajan, E., & Graf, H. P. (1996). Robust face feature analysis for automation speechreading and character animation. In *Proceedings of the International Conference on Automatic Face and Gesture Recognition*, 357-362. IEEE Press.

Poppe, R., Rienks, R., & van Dijk, B. (2007). Evaluating the future of HCI: Challenges for the evaluation of emerging applications. *Artificial Intelligence for Human Computing, 4451*, 234–250. doi:10.1007/978-3-540-72348-6_12

Porta, M. (2002). Vision-based user interfaces: Methods and applications. *International Journal of Human-Computer Studies, 57*(1), 27–73. doi:10.1006/ijhc.2002.1012

Radwin, R. G., Vanderheiden, G. C., & Lin, M. L. (1990). A method for evaluating head-controlled computer input devices using Fitts' law. *Human Factors, 32*, 423–438. PMID:2150065

Saffer, D. (2007). *Designing for interaction: Creating smart applications and clever devices*. Berkeley, CA: New Riders.

Schaab, J. A., Radwin, R. G., Vanderheiden, G. C., & Hansen, P. K. (1996). A comparison of two control-display gain measures for head-controlled computer input devices. *Human Factors: The Journal of the Human Factors and Ergonomics Society, 38*(3), 390–403. doi:10.1518/001872096778702042 PMID:8865765

Sloane, N. J. A., & Wyner, A. (1993). *Collected papers* (C. E. Shannon, Ed.). New York: IEEE Press.

Starner, T., Pentland, A., & Weaver, J. (1998). Real-time american sign language recognition using desk and wearable computer based video. *IEEE Transactions on Pattern Analysis and Machine Intelligence, 20*(12), 1371–1375. doi:10.1109/34.735811

Stork, D. G. (1996). *HAL's legacy: 2001's computer as dream and reality*. Cambridge, MA: MIT Press.

Suk, S. Y., & Kojima, H. (2008). Voice activated appliances for severely disabled persons. Speech Recognition, Technologies, and Applications, 527-538. Rijecka, Croatia: InTech.

Toyama, K. (1998). Look, ma-No hands! Hands-free cursor control with real-time 3d face tracking. In *Proceedings of PUI'98*, 49-54. ACM Press.

Turk, M., & Robertson, G. (2000). Perceptual user interfaces. *Communications of the ACM, 43*(3), 33–34. doi:10.1145/330534.330535

Varona, J., Manresa-Yee, C., & Perales López, F. J. (2008). Handsfree vision-based interface for computer accessibility. *Journal of Network and Computer Applications, 31*(4), 357–374. doi:10.1016/j.jnca.2008.03.003

Vezhnevets, V. (2002). Face and facial feature tracking for natural human-computer interface. [IEEE Press.]. *Proceedings of Graphicon, 2002*, 86–90.

Viola, P., & Jones, M. J. (2004). Robust real-time face detection. *International Journal of Computer Vision*, *57*(2), 137–154. doi:10.1023/B:VISI.0000013087.49260.fb

Ward, D. J., Blackwell, A. F., & MacKay, D. J. C. (2000). Dasher-A Data Entry Interface Using Continuous Gestures and Language Models. In *proceedings of the 13th Annual ACM Symposium on User Interface Software and Technology*, 129-137. ACM Press.

Ward, D. J., & MacKay, D. J. (2002). *Fast Hands-Free Writing by Gaze Direction.* (Master's Dissertation). Retrieved from arXiv preprint. (cs/0204030).

Wu, Y., & Huang, T. (2001). Hand modeling, analysis, and recognition for vision-based human computer interaction. *IEEE Signal Processing Magazine*, *18*, 51–60. doi:10.1109/79.924889

Yanco, H. (1998). Wheelesley: A robotic wheelchair system: Indoor navigation and user interface. *Assistive Technology and Artificial Intelligence*, *1458*, 256–268. doi:10.1007/BFb0055983

Yang, J., Stiefelhagen, R., Meier, U., & Waibel, A. (1998). Visual Tracking for multimodal human computer interaction. In *Proceedings of the 1998 Conference on Human Factors in Computing Systems*, 140-147. ACM Press.

Yankelovich, N., Levow, G., & Marx, M. (1995). Designing Speechacts: Issues in speech user interfaces. In *Proceedings of the SIGCHI Conference on Human Factors in Computing* Systems, 369-376. New York: ACM Press/Addison-Wesley Publishing Co.

ADDITIONAL READINGS

Ahad, M. A. R. (2011). *Computer vision and action recognition.* Berlin: Springer. doi:10.2991/978-94-91216-20-6

Bradski, G., & Kaehler, A. (2008). *Learning openCV: Computer vision with the openCV library.* Sabastapol, CA: Oreilly Media.

Buxton, B. (2012). *A directory of sources for input technologies.* Retrieved from http://www.billbuxton.com/InputSources.html.

Chin, J. P., Diehl, V. A., & Norman, K. L. (1988). Development of an instrument measuring user satisfaction of the human-computer interface. In *Proceedings of the SIGCHI Conference on Human Factors in Computing Systems*, 213-218. ACM Press.

Cipola, R., Battiato, S., & Farinella, G. M. (Eds.). (2010). *Computer Vision–Detection, Recognition, and Reconstruction.* Berlin: Springer.

Dix, A., Finlay, J., Abowd, G., & Beale, R. (2004). *Human-computer interaction* (3rd ed.). Upper Saddle River, NJ: Prentice Hall.

Fitts, P. M. (1954). The information capacity of the human motor system in controlling the amplitude of movement. *Journal of Experimental Psychology*, *47*, 381–391. doi:10.1037/h0055392 PMID:13174710

Hammoud, R. I. (2008). *Passive eye monitoring, algorithms, applications, and experiments*. New York: Springer. doi:10.1007/978-3-540-75412-1

Jaimes, A., & Sebe, N. (2007). Multimodal human–computer interaction: A survey. *Computer Vision and Image Understanding*, *108*(1), 116–134. doi:10.1016/j.cviu.2006.10.019

Lazar, J., Feng, J. H., & Hochheiser, H. (2010). *Research methods in human-computer interaction*. Hoboken, NJ: Wiley.

Lyons, M., & Fels, S. (2011). Advances in new interfaces for musical expression. In Proceedings of SIGGRAPH Asia 2011 Courses, 2. ACM Press.

Lyons, M. J., Haehnal, M., & Tetsutani, N. (2003). Designing, Playing, and Performing with a Vision-based Mouth Interface. In *Proceedings of the 2003 International Conference on New Interfaces for Musical Expression*, 116-121. NIME Press.

Lyons, M. L. (2004). Facial gesture interfaces for expression and communication. In *Proceedings of 2004 IEEE International Conference on Systems, Man, and Cybernetics, 1*, 598-603. IEEE Press.

Moggridge, B. (2006). *Designing interactions*. Cambridge, MA: MIT Press.

Overington, I. (1992). *Computer vision: A unified, biologically inspired approach*. Amsterdam: North Holland.

Sears, A., & Jacko, J. A. (Eds.). (2007). *The human-computer interaction handbook: Fundamentals, evolving technologies, and emerging applications*. New York: CRC. doi:10.1201/9781410615862

Shneiderman, B., & Plaisant, C. (2009). *Designing the user interface: Strategies for effective human-computer interaction* (5th ed.). Reading, MA: Addison-Wesley Publishing Co.

Szeliski, R. (2010). *Computer vision: Algorithms and applications*. New York: Springer.

Turk, M., Medioni, G., & Dickinson, S. (2010). *Visual perceptual interfaces–Synthesis lectures on computer vision*. New York: Morgan & Claypool Publishers.

KEY TERMS AND DEFINITIONS

Computer Vision: Technology that enables computers to analyze digitized images of a given scene, and extract meaningful information similar to what is perceived by a human observing the same scene.

Facial Gesture Interface: A user interface that takes head movements and facial gestures as the primary input.

Head-Tracking: The task of estimating the position of a human head and face that appears in a sequence of images.

Human-Computer Interaction: A multi-disciplinary field of research and development concerned with the systems and processes by which humans interact via computer systems.

Information Throughput: In general terms, the amount of information that can be transferred through a given channel, measured in bits per second. Within the context of human-computer interaction, information throughput is a quantitative measure useful when comparing the efficiency of input devices, such as pointing devices.

Pointing Device: An input device, such as a mouse, joystick, or trackball, which allows a user to precisely specify (or 'point to') a location on a display device. A pointing device therefore allows the user to move or manipulate a cursor on a windowing operating system.

User Interface: A device or mechanism useful in the context of human-computer interaction. Ideally a well designed user interface should facilitate intuitive and low-stress use of computer software and hardware systems.

This research was previously published in Assistive Technologies and Computer Access for Motor Disabilities edited by Georgios Kouroupetroglou, pages 180-205, copyright year 2014 by Medical Information Science Reference (an imprint of IGI Global).

Chapter 5
Next Wave of Tele-Medicine:
Virtual Presence of Medical Personnel

Kelvin J. Bwalya
University of Johannesburg, South Africa

ABSTRACT

Information and Communication Technologies (ICTs) are being embedded into healthcare system front-end and back-end platforms both in the developing and developing world contexts in ways unimaginable 20 years ago. This trend has brought about ubiquity culminating into spatial-temporal healthcare delivery models where health practitioners and patients do not need to be simultaneously in the same physical domain in order for healthcare to be delivered. This chapter presents a development projectile of healthcare systems and explores interventions and current trends in pervasive healthcare delivery systems and makes a prognosis of what is to come in future. The first parts of the chapter generally present formulaic concepts about telemedicine. The chapter is hinged on literature and document reviews focussing on innovations in telemedicine and gives a commentary on what needs to be done to achieve true ubiquity in healthcare delivery systems both in the developing and developed world contexts. The chapter posits that pervasiveness will be highly enshrined into healthcare systems to a point where physicians will not have to leave their working space to provide a service. The design of the Defibrillator Drone, for example, provides an opportunity for healthcare application developers to develop information system applications which do not only carry medical supplies from one place to the other, but are able to reason and prescribe medications. With acute advances in the science of robotics and ICTs in general, this is a reality in the foreseeable future.

INTRODUCTION

Because of ever emergence of new forms of diseases due to changing climate and lifestyles, there is need to continuous change healthcare systems so as to overcome new threats and challenges. One of the promising platforms for delivering responsive health care is through technology platforms (*deemed telemedicine*) which enshrines capabilities in healthcare able to overcome infrastructural, cultural and socio-economic challenges. Many of the developed world countries have adopted telemedicine as a

DOI: 10.4018/978-1-5225-2589-9.ch005

vehicle towards delivering contemporary healthcare. However, most of the developing world countries, especially African countries, are yet to jump onto the bandwagon. Africa lags behind the level of information systems development worldwide with a very poorly developed health sector. Luckily, this gloomy picture is slowly changing as many of the developing world countries are seriously investing in increasing their capacity to globally use technologies in their healthcare systems. This has seen a significant increase in mobile applications usage in developing countries. Worldwide, majority of mobile phone users (64%) are based in low and middle income countries which points to the likely acceptance of citizens in developing world to use mobile applications in different spheres of their lives. Therefore, chances are that telemedicine can be adopted in the developing world in the realm of mobile health (m-Health) given the proliferation of mobile gadget usage. Conclusively, telehealth and m-Health are potential game changers with regards to healthcare delivery in these countries.

The American Telemedicine Association defines telemedicine as the "*use of medical information exchanged from one site to another via electronic communications to improve a patient's clinical health status*" with communications taking the form of video conferences, e-mail messages, faxes, texts, voice-mail messages, and other applications through smartphones (Malasanos & Ramnitz, 2013). Telemedicine can be used within a wide array of the healthcare continuum: diagnosis, treatment, disease management, rehabilitation, palliative care, and aged care services. Further, telemedicine allows individuals to access healthcare without physically visiting the hospital/clinic. This enables people very far from medical facilities, remote rural areas, geographically disadvantaged areas, etc. to access health care ubiquitously. This possibility brings about convenience on the part of the patient and the medical personnel. Thus, it is without doubt that telemedicine is a good alternative to face-to-face traditional consultations especially in places with attributes described above and with large populations where queues to access medical care are unimaginable (Malasanos & Ramnitz, 2013). Evidently, with the huge potential of telemedicine, it is not surprising that it is becoming part of the business plan of many hospitals (Linkous, 2012). It can, therefore, be posited that telehealth and m-Health are potential game changers in developing world contexts as much as in developed countries.

Despite the perceived 'socio-goodness' of telemedicine, many countries still ignore to implement it and therefore pay a huge opportunity cost. In the contemporary societal setup worldwide, it is unimaginable that humans can ignore the benefits and Return-on-Investment (ROI) that are attributed to telemedicine in as far as improving healthcare is concerned. The break-even-point of national investments in telemedicine applications can be reached quickly although at face value, these investments are perceived as very expensive. It is worth noting that in the immediate short term, telemedicine interventions are not cost-effective owing to huge costs in technology installation and training. However, in the long term telemedicine is worth the cost as the cost of healthcare delivery and access is significantly reduced. The general reduction in overall cost is achieved by utilization of the newest telemedicine platforms and systems which are no longer built on expensive ISDN (phone) lines but on IEEE802.11 which can tap wireless networks through mobile devices.

There are different forms and types of telemedicine access platforms and solutions from the basic 'out-of-synch' applications such as e-mail to 'in-synch' applications such as video conferencing or chat systems. Traditional telemedine applications may involve taking a photo of the ailment, attaching the photo as an e-mail attachment to a physician who then downloads it from the e-mail and analyses it. Contemporary telemedicine applications are usually built on in-synch models offering two-way audio and visual interactions. Within the realm of 'in-synch' models, robotic applications have been used to replace the physical presence of a paramedic where healthcare service is desired. A medical robot should also emulate the physical presence of the remote health professional. The discovery of medical robots has opened opportunities for offering pervasive medical services by exploiting the virtual presence of medical personnel. Although telehealth is changing the delivery model of healthcare, its major concern is how to overcome barriers to its adoption so that a lot more individuals use it. Success of telemedicine depends on acceptance of the different telemedicine platforms by the patients, clinicians and the medical industry at large (Harper, 2004).

This chapter is hinged on literature and document review done with EBSCOhost database. Although it discusses the general trends in telemedicine, this chapter has a bias on discussing concepts and innovations with a special reference to the developing world. The chapter especially discusses the general concepts of telemedicine, takes a special look at the status of telemedicine in the developing world, provides the historical and current perspectives of telemedicine the world over, and concludes by discussing the likely further trends of technology use in the health sector. The major thesis of this chapter is that the metamorphosis of telemedicine will continue into different forms given the evolution of technology to a point where robots will be used extensively in the healthcare value chains providing virtual presence of medical personnel and further complementing capabilities of the healthcare system as a whole. In such a scenario, even the developing world will jump onto the bandwagon to increase access to healthcare among its citizens.

BACKGROUND

Telemedicine

Telemedicine is the delivery of healthcare services through the use of technology platforms such as desktop computers, mobile phones, i-pads, smart devices, sensors, etc., using simple/complex multimedia, videoconferencing or virtual reality. Further, telemedicine allows a multitude of modern technology platforms to transmit information via text, audio, video, etc. to a wide range of audience (Eccles, 2012). Users of telemedicine applications include minimally-trained community health workers, highly trained paramedics, and the general population (Scott, 2014). Application of telemedicine is loosely termed telecare.

Telecare is mostly implemented through two modes: Synchronous (real-time platform applications realising face-to-face virtuality via teleconferencing) and asynchronous (e-mail, mobile phones or other automated messaging platforms). The two modes of telemedicine implementation are coupled with two categories of interaction modules: Store and Forward Telemedicine (SF – to a physician or medical specialist at a convenient time for evaluation (essentially described as the 'out-of-synch' above); and Real Time Telemedicine - called 'in-synch'. Interactive telemedicine, can provide immediate advice to patients who live in remote areas and require medical attention (Hassibian & Hassibian, 2016). Telehealth projects fall into four distinct areas: (1) provider-to-provider communication with patient present; (2) provider-to-provider communication without patient present; (3) telemonitoring; and (4) health education – using technology platforms to provide medical information so as to educate the masses (Dixon, Hook & McGowan, 2008). Further, telehealth services can be divided into four major categories: Patient care (sharing of audio, video, and medical data between the patient and healthcare), medical education and mentoring (continuing education services for healthcare professionals and seminars for targeted groups on special topics or procedures), consumer and medical/health information (use of the Internet to provide consumers with specialized health information and/or peer-to-peer support groups), and remote patient monitoring (remotely collect and transmit data to a monitoring station of some type.) (NTT DATA, 2014).

Most common telemedicine applications include teleconsultation (where patients narrate their situation to medical personnel through a technology platform), telecardiology (transmission of electrocardiograms (ECGs)), teleradiology, and teledermatology (Scott, 2014). Some of the current telehealth solutions include: Observation of Daily Living (ODL) applications (observing daily routines of individuals obtaining data such as health information as eating habits, sleep behaviour, medication adherence, level of physical activity and weight – to form part of the Personal Health Record (PHR) replacing the traditional clinical health record); store-and-forward applications (digital images, video, audio, observations of daily living and clinical data are captured and stored on the client's computer or mobile device and then transmitted securely in a batch to another location where they are studied by relevant specialists); real-time applications (instantaneous interactions between patient and physician where two-way video and audio communication is required) and remote patient monitoring application (healthcare professionals can check a patient remotely) (NTT DATA, 2014). Other common applications include dermatology which is a very suitable medical practical for telemedicine and as such many of the telemedicine projects in the developing world are concentrating on dermatology (Kaddu, Kovarik, Gabler & Soyer, 2009).

Given the developing world context, the potential of m-Health in providing real-time access to health services, information and diagnosis in rural or any marginalised areas cannot be overemphasized. It is worth noting that given the limited bed spaces and healthcare systems infrastructure in developing and other resource-constrained countries and setups, m-Health ushers in a paradigmatic change where remote monitoring of patients is realised. Remote patient monitoring enables clinicians to virtually monitor medication adherence by patients – a capability critical in palliative care, and provides pervasive out-patient services to the convenience of the patient. In the realm of remote monitoring, depending on the type and make, on-body sensor and gardget applications can automatically communicate with a data console which can be accessed by a physician so that he/she monitor the health status of an individual pervasively. There are different types of on-body sensors/gadgets each with a specific focus. Figure 1 below shows some of the most common on-body sensors and gadgets.

Generally, although challenges and barriers for implementing telemedicine are unique in different developing countries, the following are some of the common issues: general high cost (because of general financial resource constraints, developing countries generally find the telemedicine agenda as a very expensive undertaking especially at the onset), cultural issues bordering on limited confidence by patients in telemedicine platforms (a lot of education has to be done in order for the general citizenry of most of the developing world to trust telemedicine systems with their personal health information. Most think the information supplied onto a telemedicine system may be used at a later stage to disadvantage them), and unreliable and low wideband internet and limited communications systems (Hassibian & Hassibian, 2016). On the softer side, the main hurdles for telemedicine penetration are: inconsistent state laws and regulations around its use; technology risk aversion and evidence of value (Economist Intelligence Unit, 2011). On the management side, some of the challenges include poor quality health information transmission and data security (many people are sceptical as they don't know where the health information they supply will end up to), organisational issues (lack of guidelines as such health practitioners and patients alike do not exactly know how to effectively use the telehealth systems), unwillingness to change, no adequate facilities through which telehealth solutions can be accessed, etc), patient issues, ethics, liability issues, inter-professional conflict, and older generation attitude towards telemedicine (Vital Wave Consulting, 2009). Other telemedicine bottlenecks include privacy issues

Figure 1. On-body e-Health applications
Source: Linkous, 2012

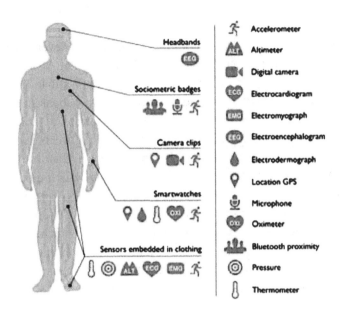

(degree of likelihood compromise in the storage and transmission channels especially in asynchronous transmission models, integrity of human being involved in the process, vulnerabilities in the software used, etc.). Other than privacy concerns, there are costs involved in the data management on the part of the patient (Malasanos & Ramnitz, 2013).

Developing Countries and Telehealth

In most of the developing world, there are acute challenges with regards to providing acceptable levels of quality healthcare delivery. For example, in Africa, the healthcare sector is battling with increasing capacity so that it can cope with broad range of communicable diseases – malaria, HIV/AIDS, tuberculosis etc. and the growing chronic conditions such as obesity and heart disease due to poor and unhealthy lifestyles. Africa lags behind the rest of the world on all indicators of health. Notably, Africa has inadequate skilled healthcare workers, insufficient healthcare delivery infrastructure and poor/corrupt procurement and medical supplies distribution systems contributing to unequal access to healthcare. Coupled with the above, Africa has a huge percentage of its roads impassable thereby further broadening the healthcare access divide for people in remote rural locations against those in the urban areas. With such contextual characteristics, alternative healthcare system delivered through anywhere, anytime technology applications is candidate to mitigate the glaring problems that the developing world faces. It is worth mentioning that even in the developed world, issues that the developing world grapple with are evident there. However, the good news is that mobile penetration is very high regardless of rural or urban setups providing an opportunity for individuals to access internet applications upon which many telemedicine application are based (Linkous, 2012; World Economic Forum, 2016). It cannot be overemphasized that in such an environment, telemedicine is a potential to mitigate the aforementioned inadequacies (Economist Intelligence Unit, 2011).

The genesis of telemedicine implementation in Africa was in Uganda through the Uganda Tele-Dermatology and e-Learning project which started in 2007 (Kaddu, Kovarik, Gabler & Soyer, 2009). After that, other countries in Africa started implementing telemedicine as an alternative and complement to traditional healthcare systems. Some of the common telemedicine developments in Africa include: the fundamental of modern telemedicine for Africa (FOMTA), the Pan-African e-network project and the Reseau en Africue Francophone pour la Telemedicine (RAFT) (Wamala & Augustine, 2013). With a population equally divided between the rural and urban areas, it was apparent that South Africa realise the need to explore the option of telemedicine in order to order to provide universal healthcare (Mars, 2009). South Africa realised the importance of telemedicine almost 20 years ago with their first national telemedicine system planned in 1998. A considerable effort has been done to develop the capability of telemedicine in South Africa. The strategy for improving capacity was hinged on the use of low-cost infrastructure and equipment such as the old telephone system (POTS) with 56K of integrated service digital network (ISDN) using a bandwidth of 128k or more (Fortuin & Molefi, 2006). Despite that being the case, there is is still low utilization of the system (Gulube & Wynchank, (2001). One of the key telemedicine programs in South Africa was implemented between Pretoria Academic Hospital (PAH) and Witbank Hospital. Teleradiology used between the PAH and Witbank Hospital to exchange radiological information for neurosurgical cases (stroke, motor vehicle accident, etc.) of patients, who in the past would have to be transported between the two hospitals (Fortuin & Molefi, 2006).

Developing countries such as India with about 70% of its population residing in rural areas and faced with limited medical care need to resort to telemedicine. Realising this need, India has seen over 57,000 teleconsultations in the last 10 years. In order to achieve this, a custom-made Web-based software (Medintegra) was designed to transmit electrocardiograms (ECGs), images (x-ray films, computed tomography [CT] scans, ultrasound pictures) (Ganapathy, 2009). In Pakistan, which has more than half of its population located in rural areas, it was deemed fit to implement m-Health (Burney, Abbas, Mahmood & Arifeen, 2013). Therefore, the likelihood that telemedicine will be a viable alternative to traditional healthcare systems in the public healthcare systems in the developing world cannot be overemphasised.

EARLIER AND CURRENT TRENDS OF TELEMEDICINE

Although not popular at that time, telemedicine started in the late 19th century when physicians used telephones to support their medical communications. Around 1970, STARPAHC (Space Technology Applied to Rural Papago Advanced Health), a product of 20 years work between NASA and the US Public Health Service, started providing medical services to the Indian reservation in Arizona (Vital Wave Consulting, 2009).

One of the main cornerstones of telemedicine is for automation to be widely used in the healthcare systems, other than the reasons articulated in the background section, to achieve unparalleled precision in health care. Precision was thought to be achievable by wider utilization of robotic applications in surgical procedures or other aspects of healthcare. The first well-known surgical robots, ROBODOC® (Kazanzides et al., 19920 and Acrobot (Davies et al., 1997) for orthopaedic surgery, and Probot (Harris et al., 1997) for prostate surgery, initiated from similar design considerations prior to evolving into customised surgical platforms. (UK-RAS, 2016). Medical revolution continued with the deployment of Acrobot (Active Constraint Robot) by Dr Brian Davies at Imperial College London started in 1992. These earlier innovations paved way for the development of contemporary medical robots.

After further research, and because of ergonomical difficulties encountered in the performing of laparoscopic surgery, augmentation of surgical skills was found in robotics because of their capabilities emanating from their hardware-based remote centres of motion (RCM). This development resulted in two innovative platforms: the Zeus by Computer Motion (Ghodoussi et al., 2002), and the legendary da Vinci® from Intuitive Surgical (Guthart and Salisbury, 2000). One such robot was the Zeus, also known as the AESOP (Automated Endoscopic System for Optimal Positioning) robotic system. The Zeus system was used to perform the first transatlantic telesurgery between Manhattan, New York, USA and Strasbourg, France (UK-RAS, 2016). This signalled the birth of contemporary telemedicine. Telemedicine may allow different ancillary healthcare services to take place: teleradiology (used for the last 60 years, uses direct digital capture of images and transmitting them to other geographic places and provides individuals in rural/remote areas with teleconsultation with a radiologist); telepathology (digitization of pathology slides); telepharmacology (computerised order entry, remote review and remote dispensing coupled with two way audio-video consultation) (World Economic Forum, 2016).

Telemedicine has been used in different contextual setups throughout the world demonstrating its potential for future global usage in healthcare systems. For example, the interdisciplinary telemedicine evaluations done in Iowa reported that parents of children with special needs reported consultations done through telemedicine platforms were as effective as those received on-site. Future studies should specifically investigate what type of clinical consultations (e.g., new evaluations, screening, care coordination, follow-up, and counselling) are more suitable for telemedicine in a given context ; they also need to investigate limits of telemedicine consultations Harper (2004). In another context, in the mobile industry, Samsung's Galaxy S4 and the later models are endowed with health sensors in the built-in app 'S-Health' which can track steps taken, food intake and even sleep patterns of individual users. In another part of the USA, a wearable device, called First Warning System is used to monitor changes in cellular structure over a period of time. This is an advancement/improvement and departure from the practice of only monitoring static mammogram which gave limited medical information. (NTT DATA, 2014). In Japan, wearable medical sensors and devices are used by the older population to transfer vital signs such as electrocardiogram (ECG and heart rate through satellite communications or 3G/4G mobile phones between remote sites (individuals) and base hospitals (clinicians) automatically without disturbing the lifestyle of the individual. The 3G/4G networks can be used to transmit video, medical images ECG signals (Gamasu, 2015).

Emerging in the use of telemedicine applications are consumer wearables. As shown in Figure 1, different technology/electronic gadgets can be put on the body of an individual to capture certain biomedic information. Consumer wearables provide individuals with personalised health data which can be used to inform them of how they need to change their behaviour in order to maintain a healthy lifestyle – providing a scenario where individuals are involved in managing their health (Piwek, Ellis, Andrews & Joinson, 2016). Further, other non-conventional open software such as iPath are used for building web and e-mail-based telemedicine applications. The software has a database component which makes it possible to store medical cases with images and other information. This software can be implemented in a closed-group setup where individual members can provide suggestions on diagnoses (Kaddu, Kovarik, Gabler & Soyer, 2009).

It is worth noting that the different telemedicine technology solutions have different functional and non-functional requirements depending on their context of use. The most definite requirement from a technology standpoint for success of telemedicine is the need for adequate broadband to handle huge information traffic and the need for technology gadgets embedded with an acceptable degree of reasoning. 'Reasoning' will be required for diagnostic and prescription capabilities desirably embedded into technology platforms and solutions. Given the short life-cycle of technologies, it is important to understand the design heuristics employed in the development of different telemedicine applications. Some of these include: natural language processing (NLP) and cognitive computing – used in text processing to understand, identity, record and extract information from diverse sources; speech recognition system – automatic translation of spoken language into text at either front-end or back-end of the clinical documentation process in the framework of Automatic Speech Recognition (ASR). The ASR uses back-end speech recognition (deferred) where a patient dictates into a digital dictation system, then the voice is routed through speech-recognition machine and further undergoes several processes before it can be discerned on the other end. ASR also uses the Computer-Assisted Physician Documentation (CAPD) which is an emerging speech recognition system; wearable sensing technology and remote monitoring – continuously captures physiological data for managing chronic diseases or patients post hospitalization (Impact Advisors, 2014).

ROBOTS AS HALLMARKS FOR VIRTUAL PRESENCE OF MEDICAL PERSONNEL

The robot is a surgical tool designed to improve the efficacy of a procedure. (Dr Paul - founder of Integrated Surgical Systems)

With the rapid development of technology, 'plug –and-play' technologies with video input, data storage components and man-machine interface such as ophthalmoscopes, electrocardiograms, and ultrasound machines have become available to be utilised in telemedicine scenarios (Malasanos & Ramnitz, 2013). Robots were first used in human surgery in 1985 for brain biopsy using a computed tomography (CT) image and a stereotactic frame. The Swiss Minerva robot (1991) was used to direct tools into the brain under real-time – but was discontinued in 1993 due to limitation of single dimensional incursions. Other robots such as the NuroMate, Pathfinder and Renaissance were developed after that (Beasley, 2012).

There are many advantages of using robots in healthcare some of which are: they extend clinicians' technical capabilities by cementing complementary strengths of humans and machines; robots have high degrees of precision and are generally geometrically accurate; can operate in hostile radiological environments; enhance ability of an average surgeon to perform extricate procedures; and promote surgical safety (World Economic Forum, 2016). The science of medical robots is growing and taking centre stage in e-Health research and practice and is generally going to revitalise healthcare delivery further by improving orthopaedic surgery. In order to increase the efficiency of medical robots in healthcare, their precision is improved by 'surgical navigation' which maps the position of instruments relative to reference markers on the patient (patient anatomy, medical images, etc.) using advanced electromechanical, optical, electromagnetic or sonic digitizers or more specialised computer vision techniques. Surgical navigation systems are endowed with simple versatility to explore surgeon's dexterity and perceived haptic sensitivity (Impact Advisors, 2014). Controlled by a clinician at a remote site using semi-autonomous, internet-enabled, real-time, two-way audio-visual communications platform, remote presence (RP) robots replace a clinician at the bedside. RP robots are used on patients who do not have face-to-face access to a clinician for various reasons or owing to their location (Simonyan, Gagnon, Duchesne & Roos-Weil, (2013). The RP robots enable the virtual presence of medical personnel in areas which are difficult for traditional care to reach. Virtual presence of medical personnel is made possible by the capability of medical robots to usher in remote monitoring of patients. Remote monitoring offers potential for the palliative management of HIV/AIDS or diabetes mellitus, and other conditions. Although currently used on a very small scale in developing countries, for example between Pretoria and Witbank Hospital in South Africa, there are chances that remote monitoring will become widespread in a few years to come.

Development is underway to increase the capabilities of the human being so as to closely bring about virtual presence of medical personnel. Notable innovations have been done in the drone technology; for example start-up Matternet uses a drone called One transporting up-to 1kg of medical stuff travelling up to 40mph (Piwek, Ellis, Andrews & Joinson, 2016). Apart from this, there are other innovations around the world currently being tested. Medical robotics are slowly being accepted for because of their degree of precise automation especially in sensitive surgical operations (UK-RAS, 2016). Remote monitoring is also made possible using unmanned aircraft systems (UAVs). UAVs have been used in many countries such as Haiti, Switzerland, etc., demonstrating the future potential of UAVs in telemedicine. One of the more prominent UAVs is the ambulance drone, Automated External Defibrillator (AED) which communicates through a two-way radio and video equipment realising a virtual conferencing scenario. The AED, with commercial name 'Defibrillator drone' was designed by scientists and innovators at a technology university in Delft, the Netherlands. The Defibrillator drone specifically intends to aid patients with cardiac arrest addressing the relatively slow response time for emergency services in most parts of the world. The drone able to reach a top speed of 20km/h in its prototype form can carry medical equipment and is able to perform first aid procedures.

FUTURE TRENDS

There are a lot of possibilities that can be pursued in the near future to bring about true virtual presence of medical personnel in remote situations. Such innovations will extend the usefulness of telemedicine regardless of context. Advancement in drone technology will enable the advancement of telemedicine for diagnostics, drug dispatch, transporting of lab samples or blood, medical supplies, prescriptions (Piwek, Ellis, Andrews & Joinson, 2016). In future, magnetic resonance imaging (MRI) which has an unmatched potential for guiding, monitoring, and controlling therapy, invoking intensive research on MRI compatible robotic systems will be used extensively for needle placement (Impact Advisors, 2014). Further, bluetooth enabled in-car applications will be built to monitor the vital signs of drivers and passengers and send the information straight to medical officers if danger is detected to place alarm so that unnecessary accidents can be avoided. Microsoft Corporation is already working on this (UK-RAS, 2016).

Miniaturized body-worn sensors such as Medical Body Area Network (MBAN) devices are already used to collect information on respiratory function. Advanced wearable devices will form some of the main telehealth gadgets in the future. These devices will be placed onto or inside a patient's body. Already, wearable devices such as Body Bugg, FitBit, Lose it, RunKeeper, and Nike Fuel are used on a large scale for fitness monitoring on persons' bodies and these are available even in the developing world contexts. Researchers at the University of California in Los Angeles (UCLA) are collaborating with other researchers/innovators in exploring the idea of developing a wearable bandage-system-on-chip powered by radio-frequency waves and other RF devices to monitor the gait of patients (NTT DATA, 2014). Such management of medical data will enable medical doctors to ubiquitously monitor the health of their patients timely and put in interventions if need be to save human life.

With intense research in medical robots currently underway, new capabilities will be harnessed for future commercial systems. Future robots include: Raven II and Micro-Surge which is a tele-operated laparoscopic system designed to maximize surgical performance (University of Washington and UC Santa Cruz); NeuroArm and MrBot – a two-armed, MRI-guided neurosurgical robot actuated via piezoelectric motors equipped with powerful optical force sensors (University of Calgary, MacDonald Dettwiler and Associates, IMRIS); TraumaPod – semi-autonomouse telerobotic surgical system; HeartLander – minimal invasive robot using suction to crawl around the surface of the heart; Robots In Vivo – aim to advance the capabilities of the earlier Da Vinci robot, etc. (Beasley, 2012). Further, flexible snake-like and micro-robotic platforms are emerging and are expected to further improve surgical outcomes and blur the boundaries between prevention and intervention (UK-RAS, 2016).

The popularity of on-body e-Health applications is fast gaining popularity – over 19% of smartphone owners use a health app. For example, hypertensive patients use blood pressure telemonitoring (BPT) which are linked to the primary physician further reducing/preventing cardiovascular consequences of high blood pressure (Omboni, Caserini & Coronetti, 2016). The future holds that individuals will detect ailments immediately as they occur and will not have to wait until they deteriorate beyond redemption. The author posits that melemedicine is the new norm in healthcare delivery systems and will overtake traditional healthcare delivery systems in popularity in not more than 30 years to come.

CONCLUSION

This chapter has discussed the development projectile of innovations in telemedicine and has articulated the future of telemedicine given recent developments. The chapter has not reviewed, to any sufficient detail, the different forms of telemedicine and has articulated the novel innovations that have pertain in the theory and practice of telemedicine.

Generally, it is evident that telemedicine is not integrated into the mainstream health care systems globally although there is enough evidence that it is growing beyond anybody's expectations. Despite this being the case, it is worth noting that telemedicine is beneficial to a health system because of the reduction in health care costs, reduction in patients' and physician's travel costs, etc. Implementation of telemedine requires well-thought strategic planning. One component for the successful deployment of telemedicine solutions is education and training on the system and designing telemedicine applications according to the local contextual characteristics.

In the near future, there are many potential telemedicine applications that will truly bring about the virtual presence of medical personnel in rural/remote locations to the benefit of both the patient and the medical personnel. It is true what Samsung says: 'The future is now' and practitioners and researchers/innovators have to take advantage to explore their imaginative capabilities to advance the different novel applications being designed in the realm of telemedicine applications.

REFERENCES

Beasley, R.A. (2012). Medical Robots: Current Systems and Research. *Journal of Robotics*. doi:10.1155/2012/401613

Burney, A., Abbas, Z., Mahmood, N., & Arifeen, Q. (2013). Prospects for Mobile Health in Pakistan and Other Developing Countries. *Advances in Internet of Things*, *3*(02), 27–32. doi:10.4236/ait.2013.32A004

Dixon, B. E., Hook, J. M., & McGowan, J. J. (2008). *Using Telehealth to Improve Quality and Safety: Findings from the AHRQ Portfolio (Prepared by the AHRQ National Resource Center for Health IT under Contract No. 290-04-0016)*. AHRQ Publication No. 09-0012-EF. Rockville, MD: Agency for Healthcare Research and Quality.

Eccles, N. (2012). *Telemedicine in Developing Countries: Challenges and Successes*. Retrieved June 6, 2016 from http://www.sciencedirect.com/science/refhub/S1350-9462(13)00069-4/sref33

Economist Intelligence Unit. (2011). *The future of healthcare in Africa, A report from the Economist Intelligence Unit sponsored by Janssen, 2011*. Retrieved 27 December 2016 from www.janssen-emea. com/.../The%20Future%20of%20Healthcare%20in%20Africa.pdf

Fortuin, J. B., & Molefi, M. (2006). *Telemedicine in South Africa*. Retrieved 26 December 2016 from http://www.aehti.eu/Advances_vol_1.pdf

Gamasu, R. (2015). Literature Review of Telemedicine System for Emergency Health Tribulations. *Journal of Electronic and Electrical Engineering*, *3*(2), 163–170.

Ganapathy, K. (2009). Telemedicine in India. *Telemedicine Journal and e-Health*, *2009*(July/August). doi:10.1089/tmj.2009.0066 PMID:19659414

Gulube, S. M., & Wynchank, S. (2001). Telemedicine in South Africa: Success or failure? *Journal of Telemedicine and Telecare*, *2*(2_suppl), 47–49. doi:10.1258/1357633011937100 PMID:11747657

Harper, D. C. (2004). Telemedicine for Children With Disabilities. *Childrens Health Care*, *35*(1), 11–27. doi:10.1207/s15326888chc3501_3

Hassibian, M. R., & Hassibian, S. (2016). *Telemedicine Acceptance and Implementation in Developing Countries: Benefits, Categories, and Barriers*. *Razavi Int J Med*. doi:10.17795/rijm38332

Impact Advisors. (2014). *Emerging Technologies in Healthcare*. A White Paper. Retrieved January 4, 2017 from https://www.scottsdaleinstitute.org/docs/sponsors/ImpactAdvisors/2014-May.Emerging-Technologies-in-HC.pdf

Kaddu, S., Kovarik, C., Gabler, G., & Soyer, H. P. (2009). Teledermatology in developing countries. In Telehealth in the Developing. IRDC & Royal Society of Medicine Press Ltd.

Linkous, J. (2012). *4 Challenges in Telehealth. Institute of Medicine. In The Role of Telehealth in an Evolving Health Care Environment: Workshop Summary*. Washington, DC: The National Academies Press. doi:10.17226/13466

Malasanos, T., & Ramnitz, M. S. (2013). Diabetes Clinic at a Distance: Telemedicine Bridges the Gap. *Diabetes Spectrum*, *26*(4), 226–231. doi:10.2337/diaspect.26.4.226

Mars, M. (2009). Telemedicine in South Africa. In Telehealth in the Developing. IRDC & Royal Society of Medicine Press Ltd.

NTT DATA. (2014). *Trends in Telehealth: Making healthcare more collaborative, affordable, and effective.* NTT Data White Paper. Retrieved January 2, 2017 from http://americas.nttdata.com/Industries/Industries/Healthcare/~/media/Documents/White-Papers/Trends-in-Telehealth-White-Paper.pdf

Omboni, S., Caserini, M., & Coronetti, C. (2016). *Telemedicine and M-Health in Hypertension Management: Technologies, Applications and Clinical Evidence.* Springer International Publishing Switzerland. Retrieved January 3, 2017 from https://www.ncbi.nlm.nih.gov/pubmed/27072129

Piwek L, Ellis DA, Andrews S, Joinson A (2016) *The Rise of Consumer Health Wearables: Promises and Barriers. PLoS Med, 13*(2), e1001953. doi:10.1371/journal.pmed.1001953

Scott, R. E. (2014). *Telehealth in the developing world: current status and future prospects.* Dove Medical Press Ltd. https://dx.doi.org/10.2147/SHTT.S75184

Simonyan, D., Gagnon, M.-P., Duchesne, T., & Roos-Weil, A. (2013). Effects of a tele-health programme using mobile data transmission on primary healthcare utilisation among children in Bamako, Mali. *Journal of Telemedicine and Telecare, 19*(6), 302–306. doi:10.1177/1357633X13503429 PMID:24163292

Taylor, R. H., Menciassi, A., Fichtinger, G., & Dario, P. (2003). *Medical Robotics and Computer-Integrated Surgery.* Retrieved December 26, 2016 from www.ieeexplore.ieee.org/iel5/70/27726/01236750.pdf

UK-RAS. (2016). Surgical Robotics: *The Next 25 Years Successes, Challenges, and the Road Ahead.* UK-RAS White papers©. Retrieved January 3, 2017 from http://hamlyn.doc.ic.ac.uk/uk-ras/sites/default/files/UK_RAS_WP_SR25yr_web.pdf

Vital Wave Consulting. (2009). mHealth for Development: The Opportunity of Mobile Technology for Healthcare in the Developing World. Washington, DC: UN Foundation-Vodafone Foundation Partnership.

Wamala, D. S., & Augustine, B. (2013). A meta-analysis of telemedicine success in Africa. *Journal of Pathological Information, 4*(1), 6. doi:10.4103/2153-3539.112686 PMID:23858382

World Economic Forum. (2016). *Digital Transformation of Industries: Healthcare.* World Economic Forum White Paper. Retrieved December 30, 2016 from http://reports.weforum.org/digital-transformation-of-industries/wp-content/blogs.dir/94/mp/files/pages/files/wef-dti-healthcarewhitepaper-final-january-2016.pdf

ADDITIONAL READING

Antezana, F. (1997). *Telehealth and telemedicine will henceforth be part of the strategy for health for all.* Retrieved 29 December 2016 from http://www.who.int/archives/int-pr-1997/en/pr97-98.html

Bauer, J. C., & Ringel, M. A. (1999). *Telemedicine and the reinvention of healthcare: The seventh revolution in company.* New York: McGraw-Hill.

Caumes, E., Le Bris, V., Couzigou, C., Menard, A., Janier, M., & Flahault, A. (2004). Dermatoses associated with travel to Burkina Faso and diagnosed by means of teledermatology. *The British Journal of Dermatology, 150*(2), 312–316. doi:10.1111/j.1365-2133.2004.05745.x PMID:14996103

Effertz, G., Beffort, S., Preston, A., Pullara, F., & Alverson, D. (2004). A model for persuading decision makers and finding new partners. In P. Whitten & D. Cook (Eds.), *Understanding health communication technologies* (pp. 46–58). San Francisco, CA: Jossey-Bass.

Glueckauf, R. L. (2002). Telehealth and chronic disabilities: New frontier for research and development. *Rehabilitation Psychology, 47*(1), 3–7. doi:10.1037/0090-5550.47.1.3

Rollason, J; Outtrim, J. & Mathur, R. (2014). A pilot study comparing the DuoFertility monitor with ultrasound in infertile women. *International Journal of Women's Health. 2014;p. 657.* doi:. pmid:2507520010.2147/IJWH.S59080

Schmid-Grendelmeier, P., Doe, P., & Pakenham-Walsh, N. (2003). Teledermatology in sub-Saharan Africa. *Current Problems in Dermatology, 32,* 233–246. PMID:12472018

Schmid-Grendelmeier, P., Masenga, E. J., Haeffner, A., & Burg, G. (2000). Teledermatology as a new tool in sub-saharan Africa: An experience from Tanzania. *Journal of the American Academy of Dermatology, 42*(5), 833–835. doi:10.1067/mjd.2000.104796 PMID:10775865

Williams, P. M. (2012). Integration of health and social care: A case of learning and knowledge management. *Health & Social Care in the Community, 20*(5), 550–560. doi:10.1111/j.1365-2524.2012.01076.x PMID:22741611

KEY TERMS AND DEFINITIONS

Developing Country: A country with limited developed human capital, industrial base or socio-economic infrastructure with a low Gross Domestic Product (GDP).

E-Health: Entails utilization of ICTs such as mobile phone, personal computers, laptops, PDAs and various communication gardgets/tools to access health services and information.

E-Healthcare: Provision of healthcare through different forms of ICTs without the patient and the paramedic enjoying the same physical space (face-to-face).

Information and Communication Technologies (ICTs): A set of technology platforms and tools used for facilitating the bringing together of the patient and paramedics into one environment so that medical procedures can take place without necessarily the two having to be in one space.

M-Health: A special form of e-Health where only gadgets allowing mobility such as PDAs and mobile phones are used to access health services and communication.

Telecare: Utilization of ICTs to transfer medical information for the delivery of health services anywhere at anytime.

Teleconsultation: A possibility brought about by the ICTs where patients are able to interact with paramedics to exchange medical information on how their given condition can be managed.

Videoconferencing: The use of ICT platforms for two people to see each other's physical being through a display device and exchanging information through voice (two-way video and audio communication).

This research was previously published in Health Information Systems and the Advancement of Medical Practice in Developing Countries edited by Kgomotso H. Moahi, Kelvin Joseph Bwalya, and Peter Mazebe II Sebina, pages 168-180, copyright year 2017 by Medical Information Science Reference (an imprint of IGI Global).

Chapter 6
Emerging Technologies for Dementia Patient Monitoring

Tarik Qassem
The University of Warwick, UK

ABSTRACT

In this chapter, the author explores the available technologies that can enhance the Quality of Life of individuals with dementia. He investigates the foundations of telemetry, different sensor technologies, Context-Aware Systems, and the use of the Internet of Thing in supporting those to live an independent life. The author reviews the use of Smart Homes in supporting individuals with dementia. He then discusses the role of social networking sites in keeping this group connected. In addition to that, the author examines the use of Global Poisoning System (GPS) technology in management of wandering behaviour and the possible use of the currently available technologies in the detection, diagnosing the cause, assessing the response to treatment, as well as prevention of Behavioural and Psychological Symptoms in Dementia (BPSD). This is followed by a brief discussion of the acceptability and the ethical issues that surround the use of these technologies.

INTRODUCTION

We live at a unique juncture of human history, with an aging population and a rapid spread of technology. This is a result of a growing body of scientific knowledge that has helped in increasing the average life span of citizens and the development of new technology. With more technology, there is a tendency for increasing prosperity, which in turn encourages states to invest more in science and its applications (Charness, 2003).

However, this increase in the elderly population comes with its own challenge, whether social, political, cultural, economic or health-related. The scope of such challenges has never been faced before in human history. Hence, it would be fairly reasonable to assume that such challenges need novel solutions.

Longevity comes with its drawbacks. One of these drawbacks is the increased risk of dementia. That in turn, incurs a huge burden on the economy. For example, in 2012 the financial cost of dementia in the UK was £23 billion a year. This cost will grow to £27 billion by 2018 (Lakey, Chandaria, Quince,

DOI: 10.4018/978-1-5225-2589-9.ch006

Kane, & Saunders, 2012). More than a 25% of that cost is the cost of unpaid care. The financial burden of dementia on the UK economy is more than what cancer and heart disease cost combined (Luengo-Fernandez, Leal, & Gray, 2010). In the whole of Europe, the total direct cost of dementia in 2010 was estimated to be above €105 billion per year, of which €88 billion is spent on care (Olesen, Gustavsson, Svensson, Wittchen, & Jönsson, 2012). Meanwhile in the USA, it was estimated that dementia would cost the economy $214 billion in 2014. That is in addition to 17.7 billion hours of unpaid care that is valued at more than $220 billion (Alzheimer's Association, 2014).

Though technology cannot be the solution to all the challenges dementia care faces, The Law of Accelerating Returns suggests that the exponential growth of technology will result in more effective and efficient ways that would increase productivity. That is then expected to change all aspects of individuals' lives in a more effective, efficient and personalised way, including how health and social care are conducted. This should then promote autonomy, independence, and safety and would enhance the quality of life of individuals with dementia (Fahy, West, Coles, & Harris, 2010; Peterson, Prasad, & Prasad, 2012)

CHAPTER ORGANISATION

This chapter will explore a number of subjects related to the use of emerging technologies in the care of individuals suffering with dementia. First, we will define the challenges associated with dementia that new technologies can help solving. Then, a review of literature will follow, studying the possible uses of ambulatory monitoring and telemetry. The use of big data combined with ubiquitous computing will be examined revealing how these can improve the quality of life for those who suffer with dementia. We will also discuss the concept of Internet of Things as a foundation for Smart Homes. We will then explore the role of Social Network Sites in keeping patients in contact with their loved ones.

Wandering is a common problem in dementia; therefore possible solutions like Global Positioning System (GPS) and non-GPS technologies will be examined and assessed in this chapter. The role of other currently available technologies will also be reviewed and how they can prevent and manage Behavioural and Psychological Symptoms of Dementia (BPSD). The chapter will end by discussing the attitude towards these new technologies and the ethical foundations that may have a role to play in the use of new technology in dementia.

PROBLEM UNDER STUDY

Dementia is a chronic progressive disease that affects an individual's ability to live independently. Hence, it is not surprising that it is the strongest predictor of living in institutional care (Andel, Hyer, & Slack, 2007). With no cure in the near future, the main focus for services is to keep patients in a safe environment while maintaining their freedom, ideally in their own home. Another focus is managing challenging behaviours that could happen at different stages of dementia. Though psychological and medical interventions like acetyl- cholinesterase inhibitors play a significant role in managing dementia, there is still a lack of effective solutions that enable individuals to live a fairly safe, independent and autonomous life while having a condition like dementia.

New and emerging technologies have the potential to enable those who suffer from dementia to enjoy life in their own homes. Moreover, using relatively new technologies such as the Internet of Things and wearable smart devices, a complex syndrome like BPSD could be managed in more effective and potentially less costly way.

REVIEW OF LITERATURE

In order to discuss solutions to the problem under study, we will review the use of telemetry and Big Data as technological foundation, and their applications in Smart Homes and GPS monitoring. We will also examine the use of Social Network Sites and their role in keeping this vulnerable group connected, the possible use of the current technology in future management of BPSD as well as the ethical issues associated with the use of these technologies in dementia care.

1. AMBULATORY MONITORING AND TELEMETRY

Ambulatory monitoring of behaviour in dementia depends on telemetry, which is automatic measurement and transmission of data from remote sources (Princeton University, 2014). These systems use portable, wearable and ubiquitous computing devices. They allow for monitoring of behavioural, cognitive, affective and physiological responses of individuals in various situations (Goodwin, Velicer, & Intille, 2008; Intille, 2007).

In 2006, Nusser et al made the assertion that with the technology available at that time it was not uncommon to create a comfortable device that records and transmits a stream of video data of what the person sees, audio data of what is being heard and said, accelerometer data of muscle activities, physiological data such as heart rate, GPS information on the subject's location and the feelings of the subject reported to a mobile computer device user interface. With such technology, all of the information collected can be chronologically stamped and synchronised so their relation to time and surrounding is recognised and confirmed (Goodwin et al., 2008; Nusser, Intille, & Maitra, 2006).

Like other tools used in psychometrics, telemetrics needs to be valid, reliable, and should not affect the behaviour that is measured. These are also referred to as ecological validity, repeated measurement, and reactivity to measurement.

Ecological validity means that the methods and the setting of the study must approximate the real-world that is being examined (Brewer, 2000), which would mean that the device makes observations in an environment where behaviour occurs naturally.

One of the challenges that is associated with repeated measurement is the inherent variability of individual's behaviours, as it tends to vary in response to situations and across time (Baltes, Reese, & Nesselroade, 2014). While the nomothetic approach of behavioural assessment relies on population averages captured at one or at a few time points, using a limited number of dependent variables (Lamiell, 2003), the idiographic approach aims to capture the uniqueness of individual behaviour through sampling behaviour that focuses on the prospective, multivariate, time-dependent variation within individuals (Molenaar, 2004). There are several advantages to the idiographic behaviour sampling technique. The first is the depth of data collection from different channels such as environmental, social, and historical contexts that could influence behaviour. Second, as time is sampled repeatedly, it is possible to detect temporal pattern changes over time. Thirdly, time-intensive sampling enables the capturing of the proximity of events to behaviours, which would help in causal inference (Goodwin et al., 2008). Reactivity to measurement refers to the effect of the act of measurement on the behaviour measured (Campbell, Stanley, & Gage, 1963). Behavioural psychologists have long advocated unobtrusive observation procedures to avoid reactivity to measurement (Goodwin et al., 2008).

In their review, (Goodwin et al., 2008) on the use of telemetric monitoring, they described two classes of telemetry: passive and active.

Passive telemetry does not need an active interaction between the individual and the device. They record behavioural, physiological, and environmental data automatically from sensors worn on the body or embedded discreetly in the environment. These two initiatives have led to what is now called wearable computing and ubiquitous computing (Goodwin et al., 2008).

Ubiquitous computing as a concept was introduced in 1991 by Mark Weiser, head of the Computer Science Laboratory at the Xerox Palo Alto Research who suggested that computer technologies could "weave themselves into the fabric of everyday life until they are indistinguishable from it" (Weiser, 1991). Since Weiser's declaration, researchers integrated ubiquitous sensing technologies in surrounding environment to create monitor rooms and smart laboratories where environmental and behavioural monitoring can be done wirelessly and passively (Abowd, Atkeson, & Bobick, 2000; Intille et al., 2005; Pentland, 1996). A single synchronised set of information can be obtained when all of these sensors continuously and automatically send out their recorded data to a nearby computer network (Goodwin et al., 2008).

Telemetric systems are able to capture data through the use of a wide range of sensors. In general, sensors are classified into hospital-based sensors and community-based sensors. The hospital-based sensors are of the level of technological sophistication that is expected of a specialist environment. These sensors range from MRI scanners, to digital thermometers (McGrath, Nafus, & Scanaill, 2013). For the

Figure 1. A typical example of obtrusive monitoring
Source: (Ouwerkerk, Pasveer, & Langereis, 2008).

purpose of this chapter we are not going to focus on hospital-based sensors. Meanwhile community-based sensors are of the standard that general practices, care homes and private households can make use of. These range from infrared thermometers, body fat analysers, radio-frequency identification, accelerometers, gyroscopes, and passive infrared sensors. These sensors are either wearable sensors or sensors distributed across the environment. The wearable sensors are usually used for capturing physiological measurements such as heart rate, electricity skin conduction, respiratory rate, or even electrical signals from the surface of the head (EEG). Environment-embedded sensors are usually used for capturing or measuring physical phenomena such as motion, degree of noise or intensity of light. Wearable computing are perception systems that can be embedded into wearable items like jewellery, gloves, clothes or shoes (Wilhelm, Roth, & Sackner, 2003). For example, discrete on-body wireless sensors have been developed to record cardiovascular, respiratory and muscle activity as well as skin conductivity of freely mobile individuals (Healey, 2000). Tiny accelerometers and actigraphs monitoring and quantifying physical activities have been embedded into wearable bracelets, wristbands and belts. They can objectively measure dynamic activities (including climbing stairs and walking) and body posturing (Bao & Intille, 2004). Unobtrusive recording microphones have also been integrated into wearable computing platforms where the client's voice and remarks are recorded together with ambient audio events in the surrounding environment (Mehl, Pennebaker, Crow, Dabbs, & Price, 2001). Miniature sensitive infra-red cameras are embedded into eye-glasses to detect where a user is looking and what they are looking at (Dickie et al., 2004; Vertegaal, Slagter, Van der Veer, & Nijholt, 2001).

There is now a growing market for consumer wearable sensorswearable sensors which range from wristbands that are able to measure heart rate, calories burned, depth of sleep to newly developed user interface devices that are able to remotely control other computer devices through brain electrical activity. There is merging evidence that commercial EEG headsets are able indeed to detect and differentiate emotions such as excitement or frustration in non-clinical population (Cernea, Kerren, & Ebert, 2011).

For comparing the different wearable consumer devices, please refer to Table 1.

In Ubiquitous computing a vast array of telemetric sensing technologies are integrated to record domestic conditions like temperature, humidity, light and barometric pressure. Unobservable microphones, video cameras and motion sensors are hidden to record activities people do. Even less obtrusive weight-sensitive load tiles can recognise the presence and location of people entirely based on footsteps (Kidd et al., 1999; Orr & Abowd, 2000). Radiofrequency identification tags (RFIDs) attached to common objects can detect a person's touch-object interaction (Fishkin, Jiang, Philipose, & Roy, 2004; Tapia, Intille, & Larson, 2004) and Global Positioning Systems (GPS) are used in identifying location and movement of people (Ashbrook & Starner, 2003).

In contrast to passive telemetry, active telemetry depends on the individual's interaction with smart phones and other handheld computer devices to relay their affective and cognitive experiences related to recent events through interactive software questionnaires on repeated instances (Barrett & Barrett, 2001; Goodwin et al., 2008; Shiffman, 2000).

2. BIG DATA

Nowadays, behavioural scientists are able to observe human behaviour on a scale that has never been achieved before and in the finest temporal granularity. That gives us the opportunity to assess the course of treatment and disease in a temporal continuum, instead of relying on glimpses (Markowetz, Błaszkiewicz,

Table 1. Activity tracker comparison

Product	Location	Measurements				
		Steps	**Calories**	**Distance**	**Heart Rate**	**Sleep**
Fitbit Force	Wrist	X	X	X		X
Fitbit Flex	Wrist	X	X	X		X
Fitbit One	Clip	X	X	X		X
Fitbit Zip	Clip	X	X	X		
Nike+ FuelBand SE	Wrist	X	X			
Withings Pulse	Clip	X	X	X	X	X
Garmin Vivofit	Wrist	X	X	X	X	X
BodyMedia LINK	Band	X	X			X
Jawbone UP 24	Wrist	X	X	X		X
Jawbone Up	Wrist	X	X	X		X
Polar Loop	Wrist	X	X		X	X
Misfit Shine	Wrist or Clip	X	X	X		X
LifeTrak Core C200	Wrist	X	X	X	X	
LifeTrak Move	Wrist	X	X	X	X	
LifeTrak Zone	Wrist	X	X	X	X	X
Sketcher GOWalk	Wrist	X	X	X		X
Basis (2013)	Wrist	X	X			X
Basis Carbon Steel (2014)	Wrist	X	X			X
Omron Activity Tracker	Clip	X	X	X		
Bowflex Boost	Wrist	X	X	X		X
Oregon Scientific Dynamo	Wrist	X	X	X		X
Beachborn	Wrist	X	X	X		X
Striiv	Clip	X	X			
FitBug Orb	Wrist	X	X	X		X

Source: "Activity Tracker Comparison Guide I Fitoop Blog," 2014. (Rodzon, 2014).

Montag, Switala, & Schläpfer, 2014). With the combined force of telemetry and Big Data, the care for those who suffer from dementia could be revolutionised.

Big Data refers to the process of extraction, collection, cleaning and transforming, storage, management, analyses, indexing and searching, as well as visualisation of complex data. The data is commonly described using the following parameters: velocity, volume, and variety. While velocity indicates the speed at which data arrive, the volume refers to the amount of data. The variety refers to the wide range of different data types and sources.

Data Mining and Machine Learning are the two main applications for Big Data. Data Mining paradigm is pattern recognition through the use of large datasets to recognise unnoticed patterns between different variables. Meanwhile, Machine Learning paradigm is the discovery of new properties about known entities, so future predictions are possible.

Both Data Mining and Machine Learning are heavily used in marketing to recognise shopping behaviour and in the banking sector for the purpose of making credit decisions. As an example of how mining of simple data, like web searches, can outperform the American Centres (CDC) for Disease Control and prevention, an outbreak of flu was predicted by Google two weeks earlier than the CDC when searches related to flu symptoms began to surge (Butler, 2008). Another example that illustrates how modern machine learning can outperform human observational powers. It was reported by Duhigg that a concerned American father has complained to a store for marketing products related to pregnancy to his teen-age daughter (Duhigg, 2012). The truth was that the marketing department of the store has actually used machine-learning algorithms to analyse the shopping behaviour of its users. The girl's shopping habits have shown subtle changes, such as the tendency to buy scent-free soap, which were analysed by the algorithms and classified as those of a second trimester pregnant lady, which turned out to be the case with this girl.

Of the different methods of data mining, temporal (Jakkula & Cook, 2008) and sensor (Avvenuti, Baker, Light, Tulpan, & Vecchio, 2010) data mining could be of particular interest in the case of monitoring of patients with dementia. Both temporal and sensory data mining make use of the dimension of time and the modality of sensory data respectively. With temporal data mining, the chronology of data is exploited and used to infer a possible causal relationship between events. For example, one could infer that a certain medication is the cause of a particular patient getting agitated if the agitation occurred following the intake of that medication. Meanwhile, sensor data mining uses the spatial orientation of sensors of different modalities to map an event in the space (Mainwaring, Culler, Polastre, Szewczyk, & Anderson, 2002). For example, combining motion data from multiple sensors and their location in the space could be an indication of wandering behaviour.

The fusion of multimodal sensor network and the analytic power of data mining and machine learning give us a potentially very effective way in improving the quality of life of individuals who suffer from dementia. Yet, still much research is needed to improve the adoption of these methods to the needs of patients with dementia. Also, the pervasive nature of these technologies requires a rigorous debate on different ethical aspects to their use.

3. SMART HOMES

As with all technologies, monitoring of individuals with dementia has seen vast advances since the use of community alarms. It is currently possible to group the different monitoring systems into three generations based on artificial intelligence and sophistication (Siotia & Simpson, 2008).

The first generation of patient monitoring systems is represented by social alarms. These equipment are worn by the person or installed in the home (such as wall-mounted call units or pull cords). The user must activate them and they raise an alarm at a help centre or let the individual speak to a responder (M. J. Fisk, 2003). It is roughly calculated that 1.3 million people in the UK utilise these alarms (Siotia & Simpson, 2008) and although they have been useful and are well accepted they are significantly limited because they need to be started off by the operator. This may not be achieved if the person has fallen or is unconscious, or if a cognitively impaired user may basically forget to start off the call.

Second-generation alarms are more 'intelligent' and 'proactive' as they can be switched on by detectors and do not require an operator to activate them. A good example is the systems designed to detect falls. An alternative fall sensor uses one or more detectors attached, for instance, to a belt or placed on the patient's body. The detectors are automatically activated when the patient falls and the call centre is notified. Thus, second-generation alarms depend on the event and not on the operator to initiate the alarm (Siotia & Simpson, 2008).

Third-generation systems are intelligent systems that use input from different sensors. The data from those sensors are then processed and an automatic action is triggered (Siotia & Simpson, 2008). The best example of third generation monitoring systems is Smart Homes.

A Smart Home refers to a residence augmented with sensors to monitor the environment and devices to provide proactive services with the goal to improve the residence's experience (Ding, Cooper, Pasquina, & Fici-Pasquina, 2011a). The term "Smart Homes" first appeared in medical literature in 2000, when (Tang & Venables, 2000) reviewed the possible use of sensors in helping elderly with care-needs to live independently. This concept of living in a "Smart Home" has evolved to include interconnectedness of sensors to monitor falls, mobility and the performance of activities of daily living such as dressing, cleaning and food preparation or regulating home temperature and the operating household appliances such as washing machines and ovens (Morris et al., 2012). The use of multimodal, interconnected sensors allows smart homes to acquire patterns possibly reflecting physical and mental health conditions and then recognise when the patterns begin to deviate from individualised norms and when atypical behaviour may indicate problems or requires intervention (Skubic, Alexander, Popescu, Rantz, & Keller, 2009).

Smart homes usually use a combination of both wearable and ubiquitous computing systems. They utilise set of sensors dispersed throughout the place of residence for detection of motion, light, sound, temperature and pressure (Boers et al., 2010). These sensors could be a part of the building infrastructure such as the electrical system (Patel, Reynolds, & Abowd, 2008). For those sensors to work they need a network to transfer data to a centralised monitoring system where data processing takes place (Boers et al., 2010).

Figure 2. Smart home
Source: (Morris et al., 2012).

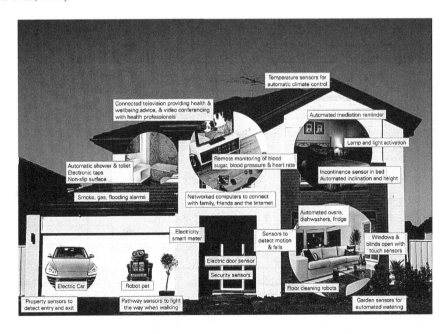

As an example of how this technology works, sensors such as simple binary (on/off) sensors that detect an event; motion, touch, pressure, or light, could be used to infer the behaviour of the inhabitant of the Smart Home. More sophisticated sensors are able to detect a range of physical phenomena, such as the temperature range to ensure safe and comfortable home environment. Radio frequency identification (RFID) is a technology that uses communication via radio waves to exchange data between a reader and an electronic tag. When interrogated by an RFID reader, the tags respond with a unique identifier (Ding, Cooper, Pasquina, & Fici-Pasquina, 2011b). That makes it able to trigger different responses accordingly. For example, RFID could be used in microwave based cooking system where an RFID reader situated under the countertop is made to determine which cooking instructions to be used from a database. The instructions are chosen according to the food packet scanned and are automatically programmed through the microwave (Russo, Sukojo, Helal, Davenport, & Mann, 2004).

Sensors' triggers are usually divided into event-based and clock-based parameters (Peterson et al., 2012). For example, motion detectors are triggered if the user has opened the front door, signalling an event. The system will interpret this as the user is leaving the house. Depending on the time of the day and other contextual parameters such as temperature outside, pattern recognition engine processes the data to interpret if there has been significant deviation from the normal daily pattern. Depending on the system interpretation of the event, it could trigger the appropriate response, such as telling the person that it is too late to go out. The precision of the responses of the system could be improved through machine learning algorithms (Peterson et al., 2012). Moreover, the technology used could be connected through the Internet to other services (Ding et al., 2011b), such as alerting the carer to check the cameras in the house or talk to the person who is trying to leave the house late at night.

As we see form the above example, for such systems to work, they need to be context-aware the ability of a system to take into account the users' present status and activity in addition to all the data surrounding the user, including user characteristics, as shown in figure (3.3) (Mokhtari et al., 2012).

Figure 3. Architecture of the context engine module
Source: (Mokhtari et al., 2012).

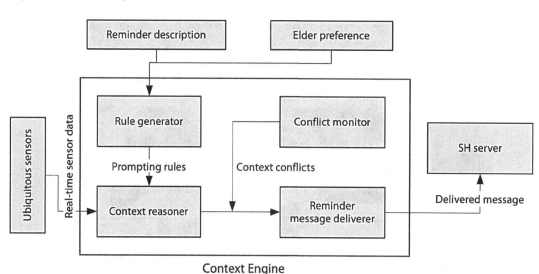

Acceptability

There are limited number of studies that addressed the acceptability of the technology used in Smart Homes. However, many of those studies (Larizza et al., 2014; Londei et al., 2009; Pot, Willemse, & Horjus, 2012) elicited favourable responses from both patients and carers. Patients reported that they felt more independent (Pot et al., 2012). However, some have expressed concerns about cost, privacy, security of the information obtained, system accuracy, and the ease of use (Larizza et al., 2014).

Efficacy

In a systematic review evaluating the efficacy of technologies used in Smart Homes, (Morris et al., 2012) found emerging evidence for the efficacy of this kind of technology in monitoring falls, mobility and the performance of activities of daily living such as dressing, cleaning and food preparation. They also found evidence to support their role in regulation of home entertainment systems, heating and cooling and the operation of household. In addition, the evidence also suggests that remote security systems, and remote sensors seem to be mainly useful for falls prevention and detection, incontinence management and mobility mapping.

4. INTERNET OF THINGS

One cannot talk about Smart Homes in a modern sense without mentioning the Internet of Things (IoT). In recent years, IoT technology has risen as a promising aid in tele-healthcare delivery to resolve health care problems (Jara, Moreno-Sanchez, Skarmeta, Varakliotis, & Kirstein, 2013; Yu, Zhang, Fang, & Yu, 2012; Zhang, Song, & Bai, 2013). The IoT is a complex cyber-physical system that assimilates all modules of sensing, communication, networking, and smart devices, and "seamlessly joins all the people and things upon interests, so that anybody, at any time and any place, through any device and media, can more efficiently access the information of any object and any service" (European Research Cluster on the Internet of Things, n.d.; Pang, 2013). "Ubiquitous" is the distinctive character of IoT technologies, so the IoT is often related to ubiquitous identification (Pang, 2013; Sheng, Zeadally, Luo, Chung, & Maamar, 2010), ubiquitous sensing (Pang, 2013; Report & February, 2008), ubiquitous computing (Friedewald & Raabe, 2011; Pang, 2013), and ubiquitous intelligence (Zheng et al., 2008).

Physiological parameters are collected from a patient and transmitted through Bluetooth to the patient's mobile terminal. It is further transmitted from the mobile device to the mIoT platform via WiFi or the third-forth generation (3G-4G) network. The platform software analyses data and yields results, which are stored in the system and transmitted to the physician's mobile terminals. Medical staff may then modify the results and provide feedback to patients. Patients, general practitioners in community hospitals, and specialists in medical centres may communicate via mobile terminals. Source: (Zhang et al., 2013)

Mobile- IoT (mIoT) provides interactive communication among clients and health care providers in medical centres and communities. Confronted with the need for large data processing in modern life, cloud computing is crucial to improve data processing efficiency (Zhang et al., 2013). Patients and carers can access the mIoT platform via their mobile terminals to obtain instant and personalised services. In addition to patient monitoring, these platforms could also offer health promotion advice (Zhang et al., 2013).

Figure 4. Overview of the mobile phone-based Internet of things (mIoT) platform

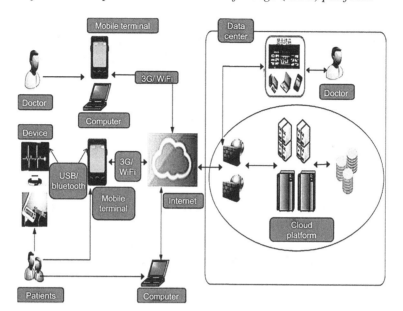

Health-IoT service will speed up the transformation of healthcare through ubiquitous and personalised patient-centric approach (Klasnja & Pratt, 2012; Liu, Zhu, Holroyd, & Seng, 2011; Pang, 2013). Typically, a Health-IoT solution includes the following functions (Pang, 2013):

1. **Tracking and Monitoring:** Powered by the ubiquitous identification, sensing, and communication capacity. All the objects (people, equipment, medicine, etc.) can be tracked and monitored by wearable sensors on a 24/7 basis (Alemdar & Ersoy, 2010).
2. **Remote Service:** Healthcare and assisted living services e.g. emergency detection and first aid, stroke rehabilitation and training, dietary and medication management, telemedicine and remote diagnosis, health social networking can all be delivered remotely through the internet and field devices (Klasnja & Pratt, 2012; Pang, 2013; Plaza, Martín, Martin, & Medrano, 2011).

Effective device and service integration is crucial for the success of Health-IoT solution. As a bridge between the service back-end and the patients at home, an In-Home Healthcare Station (IHHS) is needed to realise such service and device integration (Pang, 2013).

5. SOCIAL NETWORKING SITES AND OLDER USERS

Social networking sites (SNS), also known as "social media" is defined as an internet-based service that enables people to build an open or semi-open profile inside a contained system, setup a list of other individuals whom they could share a connection, view and browse their list of connections and those made by others within the system (Boyd, DM & Ellison, 2007).

The use of SNS by older generation was examined in a systematic review by (Nef, Ganea, Müri, & Mosimann, 2013). They examined the degree of use of SNS by older individuals, factors affecting this use, the experience of older user, attitude of older individuals towards SNS and relationship between SNS use to mental health in this age group.

Use of Social Networking Sites

In October 2012, Facebook announced that the number of its users had reached 1 billion (Dave Lee, 2012). Of these, 7% are older than 55 years (Johnson, 2012). The fastest-growing group is those above the age of 50 years and the number of older SNS users is projected to increase significantly in the years to come (Lovett, 2011). This age group use SNS mostly for communication and picture sharing (Joinson, 2008). It is reported that SNS does not require computer know-how (Cornejo, Favela, & Tentori, 2010), which could be a particularly attractive feature to elderly people.

(Farkas, Schrenk, & Hlauschek, 2010) presented the case for using SNS to reduce social isolation and loneliness, and to promote involvement of older people in their family life. Particularly for elderlies with mobility issues, SNS may help them to maintain contacts and connections (Erickson, 2011). Not only that, SNS may help in facilitating intergenerational communication for the benefit of both generations (Mesch, 2012; Williams, Kemper, & Hummert, 2004).

Among the SNS, Grouple is a special online social hub helping people share the responsibilities of caring for individuals with dementia. It enables carers to work collaboratively towards looking after their loved-one. It provides a platform where care activities could be logged, tracked and shared between carers (Grouple.cc, 2012).

Experience of Older Users of the SNS

In a field trial on the experience of elder individuals using Facebook, researchers found that this age group had some difficulties with using Facebook. This group had some difficulty using keyboard/mouse, especially with double-clicks. The layout of webpages did not particularly suite this group's needs. For example too many choices and too many text was a particular challenge to the group as in contrast to younger users, they read everything displayed on the screen (Chou, Lai, & Liu, 2010). This age group tends to do significantly better using touchscreen interface (Teixeira, 2011; Tsai, Chang, Wong, & Wu, 2011).

Attitude Towards SNS

Several studies (Chou et al., 2010; Gibson et al., 2010; Lehtinen, Näsänen, & Sarvas, 2009; Norval, 2012; Xie, Watkins, Golbeck, & Huang, 2012) have reported the tendency of older users to raise concerns on the issue of personal privacy on SNS. The other finding that was repeatedly reported was the belief of this age group that SNS had limited benefits. But, in spite of this negative attitude to SNS, (Xie et al., 2012) could show that with education, this negative perception could change to a more positive but cautious attitude. Even when older individuals could see the role SNS plays in supporting social relationships and helping in overcoming loneliness, face-to-face contact was significantly much more appealing (Eggermont, Vandebosch, & Steyaert, 2006). Staying in contact with geographically remote grandchildren was a major motivation for those who were willing to use SNS (Gibson et al., 2010).

User Interface Requirements

Increasingly, people between the ages of 55-74 are adapting digital and computer-based technologies (Australian Institute of Health and Welfare, 2007; Haukka, 2011). However, this group seem to have specific needs with regards to user-interface design. Among the things that need special attention, cognitive and perceptual deficits may hinder the use of digital technologies (Czaja et al., 2006; A. Fisk, Rogers, Charness, Czaja, & Sharit, 2012; Granata, Chetouani, Tapus, Bidaud, & Dupourqué, 2010). Having a limited computer experience constitutes an additional barrier for the adoption of these technologies (Czaja et al., 2006; A. Fisk et al., 2012).

As part of their study of graphical user interface for older adults with cognitive impairment, (Pino, Granata, Legouverneur, Boulay, & Rigaud, 2012) summarised the aspects where older users find it difficult when using some features of Graphical User Interfaces (GUIs). Among the elements that have been associated to accessibility problems in this population are (Brajnik, Yesilada, & Harper, 2011; Chadwick-Dias, McNulty, & Tullis, 2003; Hellman, 2012; Leung, McGrenere, & Graf, 2011; Savitch & Zaphiris, 2006):

1. Excessive use of links,
2. Icon comprehension,
3. Images used as titles,
4. Links/buttons that are too close to each other,
5. Links/buttons that are too small,
6. Moving contents,
7. Navigation menus,
8. Scrolling,
9. Text that cannot be resized, and
10. Visual contrast.

(Pino et al., 2012) found that older individuals tend to have less difficulty with icons that use graphical elements that are linked to real-life. For example, the use of an icon of syringe was correctly identified as a Medication Reminder. In contrast, this group found it difficult to connect the "@" sign with Email. They suggested to use metaphors involving familiar physical objects for icons that represent novel functionality (Marcus, 1998). Another possible suggested solution was to use text labels which has shown to improve icon comprehension (Leung et al., 2011).

Relationship of SNS Use to Mental Health

The effect of SNS use on mental health in this age group has not been thoroughly investigated. However, there is emerging evidence pointing to possible benefit of SNS on cognitive performance (Béland, Zunzunegui, Alvarado, Otero, & del Ser, 2005; Holtzman et al., 2004), mental health (Steffens et al., 2005; van Beek, Frijters, Wagner, Groenewegen, & Ribbe, 2011; van der Post et al., 2012; Voils et al., 2007), and quality of life (Litwin & Shiovitz-Ezra, 2011; Sun, Lucas, Meng, & Zhang, 2011).

As loneliness and social isolation have been directly linked to depression (Ayalon & Shiovitz-Ezra, 2011), one would assume the use of SNS would protect against depression in this age group. However, there is evidence that suggests that excessive use of SNS could contribute to depression or reduce the time for outdoor physical activity and the time for real social relationships (Pantic et al., 2012). In addition to that, it could significantly contribute to Internet Addiction in younger adults (Andreassen, Torsheim, Brunborg, & Pallesen, 2012; Kittinger, Correia, & Irons, 2012; Machold et al., 2012). However, it is not clear if SNS could lead to Internet Addiction in older users (Nef et al., 2013).

6. LOCALISATION TECHNOLOGIES IN DEMENTIA

Wandering around is one of the main reasons why dementia sufferers are admitted for a long time in care homes. Their safety is endangered simply because they just leave home without informing their carers(Coen, Swanwick, O'Boyle, & Coakley, 1997). Moreover, less than half of the individuals with dementia do wander with only a quarter of those wander on regular basis (Scarmeas et al., 2007). Wandering behaviour carries with it a risk of serious injury to the elderly and the distress caused to their carers who may spend hours searching, often aided by the police (Coen et al., 1997). Nevertheless, it is more likely that the patient will remain close to home, follow familiar routes and eventually go back home safe and sound (McKinstry & Sheikh, 2013).

Although wandering, as a non-cognitive aspect of dementia, can harm the elderly and cause distress to family (Scarmeas et al., 2007), it should be weighed up against the benefits of autonomy, independence and physical exercise when carried out safely (L. Robinson, Hutchings, Corner, et al., 2007). It is very useful for dementia sufferers with mild to moderate cognitive impairment to walk in nearby areas where there is a chance of exercise and good social contact, supervised by neighbours and local shopkeepers. But, the decision on how to support individuals who wander depends on many factors. Those factors range from the degree of cognitive impairment, awareness of patients of their surroundings, availability of family and carers and history of previous wandering and being lost (McKinstry & Sheikh, 2013).

In their review, (McKinstry & Sheikh, 2013) assessed the current technologies available to deal with wandering behaviour in individuals with dementia. The main focus of that review was the use of the Global Positioning System (GPS) in promoting freedom and safety for those who suffer from dementia.

Non-GPS Management of Wandering

For the least impaired, a mobile phone with prestored numbers to call when being lost is a fair solution for safe wandering as it provides peace of mind to them and their carers. Still they need to remember taking the phone with them and to know how to use it when lost. If they are able to do that, they may not be capable to recognise where they are. Asking strangers may also compound their risk of being harmed. Those with the least impairment mostly benefit from the GPS technologies.

For the most impaired dementia sufferers, wandering unaccompanied is almost always dangerous for them and nerve wrecking for their carers because they lack a general road sense and they can get injured. Discouraging them from wandering is usually obtained by making it hard through door locks or security coded keys. Downsides of those techniques are inability to escape in life endangering situations, like fire and the possible restriction of liberty, which could have legal implications.

Electronic devices installed to the doors are able to detect when doors get opened, link that to time of day or night, alert a carer or a nearby relative to respond, store a previously recorded message in an attempt to talk to and persuade the patient to stay at home giving an info about the time. The alert they provide can be connected to a call centre or to the social services. But, the drawback of such systems is that they cannot locate the elderly or confirm that they actually left the house; hence the need for long-term admission to care homes emerges.

Evidence for Non-Global Positioning System (GPS) Management of Wandering

The non-pharmacological prevention and management of wandering in dementia sufferers in domestic settings have been reviewed recently (L. Robinson, Hutchings, Dickinson, et al., 2007). However, the review could not find randomised control trials or high quality research demonstrating the effectiveness of interventions controlling the surrounding environment such as musical, touch, psychological, bright light or physical therapy. A Cochrane review concluded the need for high quality trials demonstrating the usefulness of non-pharmacological intervention in managing behavioural problems of dementia like in wandering (Hermans, Htay, & McShane, 2007).

Potentials of GPS Localisation

Against this background, GPS or global positioning system can be used to locate the position of the patient thus encouraging safe walking. This is achieved by a constellation of satellites capable of positioning any location on earth. It is based on a receiver, which transmits a mobile phone signal received by at least 4 satellites without obstruction. The distances between the different satellites and the receiver as well as the known location of these same satellites can be calculated and translated to a specific position of the receiver (with minimal error of a few meters) on an electronic map.

The elderly can wear the location device harbouring the receiver as a watch, pendant or carried as a mobile phone. Considerable effort is being carried out to miniature their size in recent years. The call for help is initiated whenever the user feels lost. Their location is pinpointed provided that they are outdoors and unobstructedly visible to the satellites. If they are indoors, the GPS stops working and an alternative triangulation signal technique is relied upon in some systems. A mixture of both is also used in modern smart phones. Apps for smart phones specifically aiming at finding lost people are on the rise (Sposaro, Danielson, & Tyson, 2010).

The GPS system can be used to reassure carers if, for example, the patient is late from shopping. They can contact an alarm call centre or log onto the computer system themselves. A mobile phone signal is sent to the device with the elderly starting an active satellite search, which can pinpoint their exact location on an electronic map. The main reason for selling these devices however is on-going monitoring rather than a one off check.

Another solution that is more actively monitored is the creation of geofences, with a detailed plan of where and when the client is allowed to use their usual route to nearby facilities, like a garden or a bus stop to a park. The boundaries of geofences are determined with the carers of the dementia sufferer. Once the patient exceeds the geofences or sets out at unusual times, the carers are alerted, the GPS receiver is activated and the user's position is located.

Monitoring wandering clients can be entirely managed by family members, carers or by personnel working in a call centre. Their duty is to monitor, alert family or carers and sometimes phone the lost elderly to reassure them or send people to find them and bring them home. GPS receivers are linked to smart mobile phones used by the clients and can send a picture of the patient to the call centre, their nick names they like to be called with or their closest family member names, such as son or daughter. Occasionally, the police maybe involved in search of lost wanderers when cognitively most impaired.

Assessment for Suitability to Use GPS

A lot of carers and less frequently patients approach social services or commercial companies to see if a specific GPS technology can help them. Many guidelines have been developed to help elderly and their carers decide and choose the proper device that suits them best (South-east Scotland GPS forum, 2010). Assessment of the clients and their carers is of utmost importance and includes many points, the previous times when the patient got lost, the frequency of wandering, the usual routine of the elderly's lifestyle so the device does not end up curtailing the useful exercise or socialisation activities, the risk of injury or harm to the patient as it is seen as trespassing the client's rights if a device is used for patients with low risk of getting lost as well as the capacity of the patient. If they have no capacity, then the device should be least restrictive. Some social service facilities provide the carers with a device for a trial period so they can see if it is useful. By all means, a review of the GPS device should be carried out after a few months of use.

GPS Technologies and Evidence

GPS technologies are already in use by dementia sufferers and their carers. Some manufacturing companies have inflated claims about the effectiveness of their devices helping patients to continue living at home. Although some pilot studies have shown that these devices achieve quick positioning of clients (Miskelly, 2005), there is a lack of high quality trials proving the safety of such devices on the elderly and their families. Little attention has been paid to the possibility of risk by encouraging walking using these devices. The more wandering cognitively impaired dementia sufferers do, the more likely accidents do happen because of their reduced sense of traffic awareness.

While many devices seem to be popular with carers (Landau, Werner, Auslander, Shoval, & Heinik, 2009), professionals tend to be the most reserved and concerned about civil liberties (Hughes & Louw, 2002) as well as privacy invasion. Civil liberties do not seem to bother particularly older family carers (McShane et al., 1998).

It has been suggested that about a quarter of individuals with dementia will actually benefit from GPS devices. Meanwhile, the use of those devices would bring no benefit for those where no level of safe unsupervised walking is possible. Such devices may even increase the risk of accidents (Miskelly, 2005). Patient groups suggest that these devices should be used by clients who choose to leave the house for a purpose and not to be used in order to confine elderly people in a secure environment (Alzheimer's Society & Hubbard-Green, 2011).

A qualitative study carried out by (White, Montgomery, & McShane, 2010) on a commercial product revealed that users and their carers perceive the product as a supplementary device rather than a primary mean of managing lost or wandered dementia sufferers. In spite of that, they all felt reassured when using the device and of the opinion that the device enhances independence.

Battery life could be another issue with these devices. As, the smaller the devices are the shorter battery life will be. Therefore, more frequent charging will be needed. Battery life is inversely proportionate to the frequency of location data upload. The more frequent the information is transmitted, the quicker the dementia sufferer is positioned, particularly when they trespass the geofences. System alerts can be programmed to appear when the GPS signal is lost or the battery dies. Speed detection algorithm can also be utilised to conclude that the patient is on a bus or a car (McKinstry & Sheikh, 2013).

Lighter devices can be integrated into a mobile phone or be worn as a removable pendant, watch or key chain by clients relied upon to put them on. For users with serious cognitive impairment, the device can be worn as a watch with secure fitting. These are bulky enough looking like action watches worn by children or sportsmen which put the potential clients off accepting them.

Indoors Positioning Solutions

As GPS have limited indoor use, other technologies have been used to detect indoor wandering behaviour. Current technologies that are used for indoor localisation depend on the RFID, especially Ultra Wide-Band (UWB) (Kearns, Algase, Moore, & Ahmed, 2008; Schwarz, Huber, & Tuchler, 2005), infrared and ultrasonic platforms (Beigl, 2005; D'Souza, Ros, & Karunanithi, 2012).

RFID has routinely been used to manage indoor wandering, as it is able to discriminate among individuals and selectively alarm or secure portals contingent on the presence of a specific individual (Kearns et al., 2008). RFID could be embedded in individual's wristwatch or shoes.

UWB is a variant of RFID. It has the capacity to detect the identity and precise locations of multiple individuals moving simultaneously, which makes it useful in care institutions, where there are many residents (Kearns et al., 2008).

Other systems use transducers that emit either infrared or ultrasonic beams on regular periods. Those transducers are usually embedded in a wristwatch like devices. The beams emitted may carry information on the identity of the person wearing that device (Koyuncu & Yang, 2010).

All of the above mentioned technologies depend on sensory network to operate. When a receiver is activated by the radio/infrared/ultrasonic wave, it is possible to identify the receiver position and hence determine the location and the identity of the individual (Koyuncu & Yang, 2010).

Wandering Behaviours Detection

Wandering behaviour in dementia is widely complex and diverse, thus making it difficult to capture in data modelling. The current work on capturing wandering behaviour depends on four models that are based on (Algase, Beattie, Bogue, & Yao, 2001), Frequency and extent of movement, locomotion pattern, transgression of boundaries (geofencing) and navigational deficit (Lin, Zhang, Huang, Ni, & Zhou, 2012).

Models based on frequency support the idea of direct relation between wandering and the excess, persistence and continuity of ambulation. Detection of wandering frequency is achieved by using bio-mechanical devices (Algase, Beattie, Leitsch, & Beel-Bates, 2003), such as counting the user's steps or measuring movement distances in 3D spaces using accelerometers. Due to individual variation of movement nature, it is hard to apply the same approach in real life situations. Currently available devices are still considered inaccurate in detection of wandering behaviour. Meanwhile models based on navigational deficit are aimed at detecting functional decline in dementia people when they navigate to find their way. Both are lacking accuracy or real life practicality.

Geofences is a way of reducing potential harm through confining wandering within a safety zone. Safety monitoring is implemented through examining the movement area of the subject using GPS devices. Through pre-setting of a safe area for wandering, an alarm is started when the monitored elderly is about to exceed its boundaries. (Ogawa, Yonezawa, Maki, Sato, & Caldwell, 2004) worked on safety support, where a wandering user was monitored via a mobile phone terminal. When the user approached the boundaries of the safe area, according to the terminal ID, an alarm was sent to the carer with an email-sent info about the user's location. Additional support is applied by using small microphones linked to the phone gathering sounds from the surrounding environment as in the Take Me Home-Service of COGKNOW project (Mulvenna et al., 2010) particularly used in disoriented users to find their way home using a GPS based digital device.

Another model is based on profiling of locomotion pattern. In that model there are movement patterns recognised (Martino-Saltzman, Blasch, Morris, & McNeal, 1991). These are direct travel, pacing, lapping and random wandering. Direct travel refers to moving from one place to another with no deviation. Random travel means visiting various locations within an area without repetition. Pacing is moving between limited locations back and forth while lapping is repeatedly traveling within a large circle of area. Generally speaking, pacing and lapping are considered wandering (Cohen-Mansfield, Marx, & Rosenthal, 1989; Dawson & Reid, 1987; Warren, Rosenblatt, & Lyketsos, 1999) and both are characterised by loop-like locomotion through frequent changes in direction throughout each move. Therefore wandering behaviour of the elderly can be conveniently monitored via GPS tracing, of their movement direction, embedded in many mobile phones nowadays. This later model of locomotion pattern showed promising accuracy of detecting wondering behaviour with false alarm rate that is less than 5% (Lin et al., 2012).

7. EMERGING TECHNOLOGIES AND BPSD

Behavioural and Psychological Symptoms of Dementia (BPSD) are a heterogeneous group of clinical phenomena that is characterised by disturbed emotions, mood, perception, thought, motor activity, diurnal rhythm and personality changes (Cerejeira, Lagarto, & Mukaetova-Ladinska, 2012; Finkel, Costa e Silva, Cohen, Miller, & Sartorius, 1997).

BPSD are a source of significant distress and poor quality of life (QoL) to both patients as well as their carers (Cerejeira et al., 2012; Ryu, Ha, Park, Yu, & Livingston, 2011). They are associated with increased mortality rate and rapid deterioration of cognition (Cerejeira et al., 2012; Russ, Batty, & Starr, 2012; Weamer et al., 2009). Moreover, BPSD have a profound physical and emotional toll on carers (Ballard et al., 2000). Furthermore, it is a major reason for early institutionalisation of patients (Chan, Kasper, Black, & Rabins, 2003), which in turn significantly increases the overall cost of dementia (Herrmann et al., 2006).

BPSD are common regardless of the type or the stage of dementia. Even in the early stages of cognitive impairment, BPSD are frequent with estimated rates of 35–85% in individual with mild cognitive impairment. While in community-dwelling patients, BPSD are generally more frequent (56–98%), it is almost universal in patients who are in hospital or live in a long-term care facility (91–96%) (Frisoni et al., 1999).

Causes of BPSD

In their review, (Krishnamoorthy & Anderson, 2011) reported that the causes of challenging behaviour in dementia fall under four main areas. These areas are physical disease, psychological/psychiatric disorders, environmental causes, and dysfunctional communication.

1. **Physical Problems:** Acute physical issues like pain, urinary tract infection, constipation, breathlessness or fatigue can affect behaviour whether directly or indirectly through causing delirium.

Individuals with dementia have a five times higher risk of developing delirium compared to normal old people (Cole, 2004). That delirium usually resolves when the underlying acute physical cause is treated. Delirium in dementia adds confusion to an already confused patient. The only manifestation noted maybe a change of behaviour, hardly if ever noticed. Delirium can be caused by any medical condition, the commonest are infections, dehydration and as a drug side effect. If the challenging behaviour coincides with the introduction of a drug, then it should be suspected as a possible cause. In severe dementia, delirium and distress can be triggered by quite minor physical causes leading to possible challenging behaviour. Unfortunately, at least 50% of patients with dementia in institutions who exhibit BPSD suffer from undiagnosed physical condition that could contribute to the development of their BPSD (Doraiswamy, Leon, Cummings, Marin, & Neumann, 2002; Larson, Reifler, Sumi, Canfield, & Chinn, 1985). In community-residing older adults with dementia the rate of undiagnosed relevant medical condition is 36% (Hodgson, Gitlin, Winter, & Czekanski, 2011).

2. **Psychological/Psychiatric Conditions:** The commonest psychiatric conditions associated with dementia are anxiety, depression and psychosis.

Depression is more likely to occur in dementia than in healthy elderly. Their behaviour becomes challenging in severe dementia as patients fail to communicate their symptoms. This manifests itself as aggression, anxiety, irritability, crying, calling for help, withdrawal, anorexia, poor sleep, reduced conversation, non-compliance or clinging to people for reassurance.

Anxiety is more likely to develop in people with premorbid anxious personalities. Patients with anxiety tend to startle easily, worry, seek reassurance, are fearful, restless, and hyper-vigilant. It is worth noting that anxiety can be a symptom of depression in elderly and can be the most manifest sign.

Psychosis usually manifest as two groups of symptoms, delusions or hallucinations. Delusions are usually persecutory. Hallucinations are often of people or animals that are usually threating or frightening but can also be pleasant.

Delusions of persecution can result in defensive behaviour such as aggression, room barricading, pushing people away, making accusations and non-compliance. Patients usually voice those delusions.

Threatening hallucinations result in similar behaviour as the patients usually feel that they are at risk. Hallucinations may be detected by what the person says or more often by observing them responding to things that are not there, for instance talking to air or empty chair, patting an imaginary animal or picking invisible things or clothes. Even in severe cases of dementia, patients retain some self-awareness, which can be a cause of psychological distress, for example embarrassment over incontinence or the need of personal assistance may lead to aggression. The absolute frustration over failure to communicate one's needs or to understand surrounding environment and the loss of control over one's life can result in aggression, anxiety, depression or rage. Other causes for challenging behaviour in dementia are feeling of loneliness and boredom.

3. **Environmental Causes:** Patients with dementia are quite sensitive to changes in the environment. That is due to their impaired ability for new learning, which leads to poor adaptation to environmental changes. The mere admission in a hospital or care-home can precipitate challenging behaviour. It can be a frightening experience especially when they don't know the reason for admission or the people around them.

When care-homes are under-lit or have no signage, patients seem to lose their way and wander with incidences of accidental urination or defecation in inappropriate places. Other challenging behaviour can emerge when helpers try to approach them.

Dementia sufferers need their own personal space and an environment where they can explore. Most of them show fewer problems when left to their own devices. Restrictive environment where people get in each other's way can raise conflicts and cause challenging behaviour. They may think that others have come to inhabit their home and so try to eject them. Other environmental conditions to consider are room temperature whether too hot or cold and constant noise that may cause distress and annoyance.

4. **Communication Difficulties:** Failing to express oneself through language is tremendously frustrating and the patient is only left with non-verbal communication as a way of interaction. This can result in depression. Deafness or inability to understand spoken or written words can cause misunderstandings and inappropriate or challenging behaviour. An example is a patient who doesn't understand speech perceiving help in washing or dressing as an attempted assault. High skill is needed to deliver care in these situations. When people can't understand language, they greatly rely on non-verbal communication delivered by carers they trust. This is achieved by kind and sincere facial expressions, clear visible movements and tasks performed slowly with the least physical contact. Aggression in care situations can simply be caused by the fact that patients are unhappy with the way they are handled or that they don't like the carers. The latter is identified when challenging behaviour is linked to a certain carer and it can be sorted out by basically changing the caregiver.

Assessment and Management

In clinical practice, assessment of BPSD requires a thorough clinical history taking, examining patient's subjective experience, and objective behaviour. Collateral history from a reliable family member or carer is essential to obtain adequate description of behavioural disturbances and their context. Though individuals with dementia may have difficulty in communication, it is essential to have an individual assessment with them. Whenever possible, patients should be encouraged to express their own concerns. That could give the clinician valuable insight to the patients' inner experience. In addition to that clinician usually rely on Functional Behaviour Assessment, also known as ABC approach, which is an acronym for Antecedent, Behaviour and Consequence.

Functional Behaviour Assessment requires clear specification of a problem behaviour ('B') that is understood in terms of the observed influence of events that precedes it (antecedents 'A'), and the events consequent ('C') upon it (Stokes, 2000). Traditional 'ABC' Functional Behavioural Assessment underlying hypothesis is that behaviour is always observable and follows a linear pattern. However, this is not necessarily true for the development and maintenance of challenging behaviour in dementia (Moniz-Cook, Woods, & Gardiner, 2000). Furthermore, a particular behaviour may have different functions for different individuals, or more than one function for a particular person for different occasions (Moniz-Cook, Stokes, & Agar, 2003). That makes the Functional Behaviour Assessment a complex task. In addition to the complexity of analysing a behaviour that could be contingent of an intricate array of factors, in some cases challenging behaviour is triggered by a purely physical condition, such as infection or electrolyte imbalance.

One of the problems in the methods used for assessing behaviour is recall bias, as informers could fail to report the frequency and severity of a challenging behaviour. Also, relying on a stressed caregiver as a source of information could carry the risk for reporting bias due to overestimation or underestimation of the behaviour in question. Instead, objective assessment of behaviour gives the opportunity to measure the severity, frequency and the nature of the challenging behaviour. With objective assessments, it is more possible to elicit the precedents and consequences of challenging behaviour. However, continuous observation itself is arduous due to the high resource costs. That is especially true in the case of behaviours that are not frequent or with behaviours with patterns that are not easily recognised. For example, a patient who suffers from constipation could get agitated every three or four days and this agitation could stop suddenly after he/she opens his/her bowel, but this agitation could build up again as they failed to open his/her bowel for the next three to four days to come. In short, data gathered by traditional means of capturing change in individual's condition is rather poor. It is too coarse to show temporal patterns, and lacks dynamics (Markowetz et al., 2014).

With the advance in artificial intelligence and machine learning, use of computer could aid in identifying recurrent patterns of behaviour. However, recognising complex behaviours remains a challenging and evolving area of research. As human behaviour is not a simple phenomenon, artificially intelligent systems face the following challenges recognising complex human behaviour, such as (Kim, Helal, & Cook, 2010):

- Recognising concurrent activities as an individual can do multiple activities at the same time. For example, a person could read and have a meal at the same time.
- Recognising interleaved activities as certain real life activities could interleave. For instance, while reading, a person could respond to a phone call and after finishing the call he/she could return to reading.
- Ambiguity of interpretation as the interpretation of similar activities may be different. For example, an activity such as opening a fridge could be interpreted as eating or cooking.
- Multiple residents, as it is usual for more than one person to live at the same place. The activities that are being performed by more than one person at the same time need to be recognised.

These challenges can be partially addressed by having a clear definition of individual behaviours, acquiring data using integrated and multimodal sensors (see Table 2), use of pervasive and ubiquitous computing along with the use of Big Data that could represent a wide repertoire of different varieties for individual human behaviours.

Behavioural and Psychological Symptoms of Dementia and the Use of Big Data

With the use of pervasive computing techniques such as wearable and ubiquitous computing, the data generated could be analysed in a large scale, and to extract meaningful indices (Markowetz et al., 2014), such as an ''agitation index'', or a ''distress index'', rather than depending on the report from carers. Clinicians can then track patients' symptoms in fine-granular temporal resolution. They can explore interdependencies between different factors that could affect those symptoms, such as social activities, medications, and psychical conditions. Machine Learning techniques could be able to alert early warning signs, so they could act proactively. In this case, they can intervene earlier. At the same time, regular

Table 2. Possible sensors to capture BPSD

Sensor	Behaviour
Motion Radar GPS tracking	Restlessness
	Tapping/Banging
	Wandering
Acoustic	Vocalisation
Pressure (bed)	Sleep disturbance
Video	Daily activities

Source (Yefimova & Woods, 2012).

appointments can be spaced further apart, which would be significantly cheaper for the health economy (Markowetz et al., 2014).

The use of data generated by pervasive computing gives a continuous temporal, but contemporary picture to patient's condition and what factors could be influencing any change. Mining patients' individual data through electronic health records, enables the system to recognise any anomaly in individuals' behaviours and possible risk factors, such as recent start of medication or recent infection. While, with Machine Learning, an intelligent system could classify patients according to risk score and predict patients' individual risk, for example falls or having an underlying infection as a cause of the BPSD. That needs integration of data from different sources including patients' health records as well as the ability to recognise patterns in the records of patients of the same characteristics.

Emerging Applications

There have been few applications in attempt to use ambulatory monitoring in the assessment of challenging behaviour. Of the symptoms of BPSD, wandering and agitation are the ones most studied. For monitoring wandering behaviour, please refer to GPS section.

The literature (Foo Siang Fook, Tay, Jayachandran, Biswas, & Zhang, 2006; Moore, Thomas, Tadros, Xhafa, & Barolli, 2013; Moore, Xhafa, Barolli, & Thomas, 2013) on monitoring of agitation and aggression in patients with dementia has focused on the use of Scale to assess Observed Agitation in Persons with Dementia of the Alzheimer Type (SOAPD) (Hurley et al., 1999). The SOAPD rates the following aspects of agitated behaviours:

1. Total body movements,
2. Up and down movements,
3. Repetitive motions in place,
4. Outward motions,
5. High pitched/loud words,
6. Repetitive vocalization,
7. Negative words.

This scale was adapted for the purpose of automatic monitoring of agitation in patients with dementia by (Foo Siang Fook et al., 2006). They also explored the use of the video recognition in assessment of agitated behaviour in patients with dementia. They reviewed the ontology of agitation in dementia, its determinants, its digital representation and how the pattern recognition system could identify early pre-cursor. Their work lays the theoretical foundation for future use of technology in assessment of agitated behaviour in dementia (Foo Siang Fook et al., 2006).

Another described method used for assessing challenging behaviour is wearable computing. (Plötz et al., 2012) described a system they developed to recognise challenging behaviour in children with developmental disorder. They examined three types of challenging behaviour: aggression, disruption, and self-injurious behaviour. They had three phases of the experiments. Phase 1 aimed at training the computer system to detect simulation of the challenging behaviour. They instructed experienced staff member to simulate the three types of behaviour. In this phase, Machine Learning could automatically detect the simulated challenging behaviour in 95% of time. It was also able to differentiate between the three types of behaviours with the precision of approximately 80%. In the second phase of the experiments, the researchers instructed the participants just to simulate taking part in normal daily routine activities. The aim of the second phase was to examine the rate of false positive detection in challenging behaviour. The system achieved negligible false positive results. In phase 3 of the experiments, the researchers tested the developed system on real patients with challenging behaviour and they achieved approximately 70% precision rate. The authors' explanation of the lower precision rates in the third phase was failure of one of the subjects to tolerate an ankle sensor, hence lowering the detection rate and real patients.

Possible Applications for Current Technology

Even the currently available sensors and computing technologies (Table 3) could hold the key for the future development in managing one of the difficult aspects of dementia, such as BPSD.

8. ATTITUDE TOWARDS THE USE OF NEW TECHNOLOGY

Despite the high expectations and interest in digital technology, the overall take up among clinicians hasn't been great (Davidson & Heslinga, 2006). In their review, (Boonstra & Broekhuis, 2010) examined available literature in order to identify the barriers perceived by clinicians hindering them from adopting new technology in clinical practice. Their review identified what they called primary barriers; which are impediments that clinicians have explicitly voiced. They also identified a more subtle and often unconscious obstacles to adopting new technologies.

Technical obstacles were one of the most cited reasons. Clinicians had several concerns that are related to technical aspects of new technologies. Examples of these concerns are skills of the staff, lack of technical training and support, complexity and lack of reliability. Another recurrent theme is a financial one, as clinicians might not see the return on investing in new technologies, not only that but also the high start-up and ongoing costs. Time has been also quoted as an obstacle to take up new technology, especially the time needed to train on a particular technology and how these technologies could increase the time spent with patients trying to operate new systems.

Table 3. Causes of BPSD and possible ways of detection using smart technologies

Select Triggering Factors in Behavioural and Psychological Symptoms of Dementia (Kapusta, Regier, Bareham, & Jensen, 2011)	How Monitoring Technology Could Help
Psychosocial	Emerging evidence that ambulatory monitoring could distinguish emotional from physical activation (Wilhelm, Pfaltz, Grossman, & Roth, 2006)
• Distress	
• Fear of danger	
• Misinterpretation	
• Feeling abandoned	
• Loss of autonomy	
• Paranoia	
Environmental	
• "Bad" company	
• Boredom	Quite environment detected by sensors that precedes the challenging behaviour
• Confusing surroundings	Detection of wandering pattern
• Excessive demands	
• Lack of routine	
• Inadequate lighting	Low lighting detected by sensors that precedes the challenging behaviour
• Loneliness	Quiet environment detected by sensors that precedes the challenging behaviour
• Noise	Excessive sounds detected by sensors that precede the challenging behaviour
Medical	
• B12 or folic acid deficiency	
• Hunger or thirst	
• Hypercalcemia	
• Hypothyroidism	
• Infection (e.g., urinary tract infection, pneumonia)	
• Metabolic	
• Nocturia	Nocturnal pattern of behaviour that is associated with incontinence or frequent visits to the toilet
• Pain	Automatic recognition of pain through facial expressions using Machine Learning is in development (Bartlett, Littlewort, Frank, & Lee, 2014; LeResche, 1984; Michel F Valstar & Pantic, 2012; Michel François Valstar, Mehu, Jiang, Pantic, & Scherer, 2012).
• Constipation	Recognition of the cyclic pattern of challenging behaviour that is associated with the cyclicity of bowel movements.
Medications (i.e., rule out drug-induced delirium)	
• Anticholinergic drugs	Detection of temporal relation to intake of medication though pattern recognition.
• Benzodiazepines	
• Cholinesterase inhibitors	
• Digoxin	
• Opioids	
• Substance abuse	

Less cited, yet influential factors that play a role for the lack of adoption of new technologies by clinicians are psychological, social, legal and organisational factors. The lack of belief in the new technology plays a central role in clinicians' hesitance to adopt new technologies (Lærum, Ellingsen, & Faxvaag, 2001). Other studies found that some clinicians are concerned that technology will lead to their loss of control over their work (Jha et al., 2009; Lærum et al., 2001). The uncertainty about how new technology would influence doctor-patient relationship and the lack of support from colleagues, as well as managers are often cited as social factors that hinder clinicians taking up those technologies (Lærum et al., 2001; Terry et al., 2008). Privacy or security concerns are often quoted among clinicians much more than among patients or relatives (Boonstra & Broekhuis, 2010). The size, and the culture of the health care organization play an important part in bringing new technology to practice or adopting a more conservative approach to innovation. The larger the size of the organization, the more the resources that need to be invested in what could be an expensive technology.

Research have shown that, in contrast to professionals (Cohen-Mansfield et al., 2005; Courtney, Demiris, Rantz, & Skubic, 2008; Melenhorst, Fisk, Mynatt, & Rogers, 2004; Mihailidis, Cockburn, Longley, & Boger, 2008; Steele, Lo, Secombe, & Wong, 2009; Wild, Boise, Lundell, & Foucek, 2008), older people are generally willing to adopt in-home monitoring technologies. These studies repeatedly reported that the importance of maintaining independence superseded concerns about privacy or security. Older people view these technologies as tools that could help in achieving the goal of independent living, getting help in emergencies and tracking of specific health conditions. However, they felt uncomfortable with technologies that used video monitoring.

9. ETHICAL ISSUES

In their review, (Siotia & Simpson, 2008) discussed how Beauchamp's and Childress' general bioethical principles apply to the use of assistive technology in dementia. These principles are widely accepted moral doctrines that govern clinical practice. These principles are respect for autonomy, beneficence, non-maleficence, and justice (Beauchamp & Childress, 2001). Though these principles are guidelines that govern clinical practice in general, Siotia & Simpson argued how the same principles are related to using these technologies in this vulnerable group. In this model, respect for autonomy translates into the individual's entitlement to make decisions that are related to their own treatment. In this context, professionals are not only required to obtain informed consent in relation to the use of assistive technologies, but they are also encouraged to empower patients to make informed decisions, especially as the use of these technologies could significantly affect the individual sense of privacy and entitlement to confidentiality. Meanwhile, the principle of beneficence refers to the commitment of healthcare professionals to be of benefit to the patient, in addition to taking positive steps to prevent and remove harm from the patient. While, non-maleficence refers to refraining from any act that could lead to patient's harm (Beauchamp & Childress, 2001). Whereas justice in that context indicates that, not all assistive technologies will be the justified solution for all patients.

Nevertheless, and in spite of the wide acceptance of Beauchamp & Childress bioethical approach, it mostly suits clinical situations that happen in junctures of patients' lives. However, in dementia, individuals' needs are ongoing in nature and frequently changing. Hence, Beauchamp & Childress approach may not be the most suitable model to address such ongoing changing care needs of individuals with dementia. For example, trading-off privacy for benefit is common in the medical practice, when a clinician physically examines a patient. Though this clinical examination could involve intimate contact with the patient, the trade-off is the possible benefit this examination could bring. In this case, trust between the clinician and a patient is central, though implicit. But, in the case of ongoing tracking and monitoring of sufferers with dementia, it could be complete strangers in remote control rooms who may be observing the individual's behaviour in his or her own home. That brings the issue of informed consent to question, as the individual consenting would not be able to give a consent based on the implicit trust mentioned earlier. In addition to that, Beauchamp & Childress principle of autonomy may bring with it greater isolation, especially in individuals with dementia (Frisby, 2000).

As seen from the Table 4, the sensors used in monitoring individual with dementia could have varying degrees of intrusion level. These varying degrees and the implications of intrusion on an individual's privacy need to be weighed up against any benefits the use of such sensors may bring.

Another issue with the use of monitoring and tracking technology, is the restriction or even the possibility of deprivation of liberty and privacy, especially as such technologies, could radically change the character of the home environment which has traditionally been regarded as a safe, secure, and private space (Twigg, 1999). This privacy is protected by Eighth article of the European Convention for the Protection of Human Rights and Fundamental Freedoms (Coblentz & Warshaw, 1956), which states the right to private life. That is in addition to England's Mental Capacity Act that gives a framework to safeguard against deprivation of liberty for individuals lacking the mental capacity to make welfare decisions (Department of Health, 2005).

Under the Deprivation of Liberty Safeguards (DoLS) (Ministry of Justice, 2008), there is a formal procedure to ensure that the deprivation of liberty is in the best interests of the individual. This best interests' decision is rarely straight forward, as care-needs play only a part of the overall needs of the individuals. For example, some older people value independence highly and might feel uncomfortable

Table 4. Some common sensors, their potential contexts and potential intrusion levels

Sensor	Environmental	Symptoms	Location	Emotion	Intrusion Level
Optical/scanning	X	X	X	X	H
Air quality	X	X		X	L
Room state	X	X	X	X	L
Hazardous gases	X	X		X	L
Speech recognition	X	X		X	M
Screens with GUIs	X	X	X	X	M
Accelerometers		X	X		M
Gyroscopes		X	X		M
Proximity			X		L
Wireless location			X		M
RFID and Barcodes			X	X	M
Simple sensors		X	X	X	L
Medical		X		X	H
Humans	X	X	X	X	M/L

Source: (Thomas et al., 2013).

being the recipient of care. Others, who feel socially isolated, might welcome human assistance. As human contact and technologically based care both serve different needs to different people, the superiority of one over the other cannot be argued (Pols & Moser, 2009). Best interests' decisions, would need to take into account the perspectives of patients along with individuals involved in patient's care, including other professionals, family and friends (Department of Health, 2005; Ministry of Justice, 2008).

Also, to justify the infringement of a patient's privacy using electronic tracking technology, it is often compared to alternative courses of action and is thought of as less intrusive when compared to the constant supervision by a carer. Surveillance undertaken by a carer, considered to be appropriate, is also seen as an intrusion on privacy (McShane, Hope, & Wilkinson, 1994). As an explicit way of surveillance, the nature of monitoring dementia sufferers by their carers is perceived as more invasive than electronic tagging, (McShane et al., 1994) justifying the breech of privacy by narrowing the outline of the definition of privacy. They argued that intrusion of privacy only applies if the patient under surveillance wants to hide. Hence, if a patient agrees on being monitored, concerns about privacy should not be an issue..

It is worth mentioning that even with 24-hour monitoring, the degree of intrusion on individual's privacy varies depending on what is being monitored and the way it is being monitored. While 24-hour video monitoring could be quite intrusive, a door sensor that alerts a carer when a door opens late at night could be considered much less intrusive.

In addition to the general biomedical ethical framework, system-generated data should undergo strict confidentiality recommendations. It should be clear who has the right to access sensitive information such as the tracking of data and whether it is always appropriate to access where a client is, unless it is threatening their safety. This access should be limited to trusted people using a log to access the location website (McKinstry & Sheikh, 2013). Nevertheless and as with any new technology, it is not the technology form that influences the ethics of its use, but how it is used in a particular case (Gillies, 2001).

Stigma is another issue that can worsen depersonalisation of the Individual (Innes, 2009). Association of electronic tracking with use in the criminal justice system has also been debated in the media (Smith, 2007). The stigma does not arise from the technology itself, but from society's perspective of its use. A proponent of that view are (McShane et al., 1994) who assert that electronic tracking is not humiliating or dehumanising in itself, but these associations rather emanate from the conditions within which the technology is used Furthermore, (Hughes & Louw, 2002) argued that using electronic tracking reduces the stigma of the disease by preventing experiences like "being lost and found half-dressed on a motorway".

The stigma of dementia is aggravated by the negative public impression of the disease and it being linked to loss of ability as well as the physical burden and emotional distress experienced by the caregivers (Innes, 2009). One study has linked stigma to the delay in the diagnosis of dementia in eight European countries (Vernooij-Dassen et al., 2005). This means that more care should be directed towards the visibility of the electronic tracking devices and involving individuals with dementia in the design of these devices (Louise Robinson, Brittain, Lindsay, Jackson, & Olivier, 2009).

Another related issue is public engagement, which is essential to avoid the stigma that could be associated with this technology. Hence, special attention should be paid to the use of language in that context. Locators is a more preferred term over trackers or tagging, which is primarily used for tagging criminals under curfew (McKinstry & Sheikh, 2013).

24/7 monitoring is reminiscent of George Orwell's novel "1984", where everyone was under surveillance by the Big Brother. Hence the potential for abuse cannot be overstated. While monitoring patients with dementia must follow a strict ethical code and must be in the patient's best interests, it could potentially be abused by unauthorised users. Similarly, it would be unethical to deny concerns about privacy. At the same time, the technology discussed has huge potential in enhancing the quality of lives of millions of individuals who suffer from dementia, and promoting a more independent and safer life. This would make it equally unethical to deny the use of new technology under privacy concerns.

Medicine has long held a tradition of balancing risks and benefits on a case-by-case basis. These benefits and risks could be examined using the questions in Table 5.

These guiding principles require taking active steps to ensure that the use of assistive technologies does not finally become an inappropriate substitute for human care and does not cause a patient to lose skills by being over reliant on such systems. Technology should be given as part of a person-centred comprehensive community care package, and not as an independent service (Siotia & Simpson, 2008).

CONCLUSION

Though the aim of this chapter is to review the use of new technology in management of dementia, one should not conclude that technology would be the answer to all the challenges that are associated with a complex condition like dementia. Nonetheless, technology could play an integral part, in most aspects of dementia care.

Pervasive computing is infiltrating our lives day by day, as it's becoming more accessible and cheaper. Although there has been growing interest in wearable computers and devices that could aid in maintaining our health and fitness, yet, there has been limited research in the use of pervasive and wearable computing in the dementia care. We believe there are huge opportunities for these technologies to be exploited in dementia care. However, for pervasive computing to work, it will need the use of mining Big Data sets in order to have a more efficient Machine Learning algorithms.

Smart Home technologies are gaining popularity among patients, carers and professionals. There is emerging evidence of their effectiveness in reducing falls, improving mobility and encouraging more independence. However, newer Smart Home technologies have to rely on the use of pervasive computing, where data obtained by pervasive sensors are mined in order to ensure that the individuals are safe and their needs are met appropriately. That would require development and use of the Internet of Things as an infrastructure that connects different devices in Smart Homes to servers where the data are processed and made sense of.

Table 5. Questions to ask to determine the ethical use of assistive technologies

14. Does the patient understand what the assistive technology is presumed to do?
15. Have they been provided with the full explanation of the choices?
16. Have they consented to trying assistive technologies?
17. Have their nearest friends and family been involved in these talks?
18. Have you considered how you will balance any dispute or tension between the risks and rights of all parties involved?
19. Have you utilised a suitable assessment tool to recognise needs?
20. Have you planned the way to introduce assistive technologies to the person?
21. Have you arranged how assistive technologies will be set up?
22. Do you have a system for its use?
23. Do you have members able to respond in case of crises, difficulties etc.?
24. How will you evaluate the system's immediate efficacy?
25. How will you judge its continued efficacy?
26. Do you have a withdrawal plan?

Source: (Siotia & Simpson, 2008) with modification.

In addition to the individual's safety and care needs, connection to other fellow human beings is essential for mental wellbeing. We think that SNS are an important way that can free individuals from the restriction of the boundaries of place and time. People are able now to contact loved ones thousands of miles away. They are able to follow their news in real time. That could be particularly liberating for older people with limited mobility, SNS may help maintain connections that would otherwise be difficultly kept (Erickson, 2011). Nevertheless, special attention should be directed to examine possible negative side effects, such as internet addiction and sedentary life style that could affect this age group (Nef et al., 2013).

GPS is another technology that has the potential of liberating individuals with dementia form remaining confined in an institution or in their own homes. It gives them the chance to live a normal and safe life. It also gives them the chance to maintain a good degree of physical activity, through allowing them to have safe outdoor walks. Yet, there is still work to be done in the area of wandering detection algorithms that are context aware.

A complex condition like BPSD needs novel approaches to tackle it. Collaboration between researchers, clinicians and Information Technology experts is essential to find innovative approaches for this debilitating condition. We envisage that the use of using Big Data and pervasive computing will eventually help in detection, diagnosing the cause, assessing the response to treatment and prevention of BPSD. However, this field is still in its infancy. The proposed methods of monitoring behaviour are yet to be refined and validated for the use in patients with dementia.

As with any technology, pervasive computing and the use of Big Data in management of dementia need establishing rigours safeguards to protect against their possible abuse. As violation to individual's privacy is a real threat, concerns need to be addressed through policies and regulations in addition to robust enforcement.

One cannot argue against using banks because they deal with private data every day. The same principle should apply to the use of technology for health care purposes. We believe that in spite of the reality of the threat to patient's privacy, denying the use of new technology under privacy concerns would be unethical.

In dementia care, the four principles of respect to autonomy, beneficence, non-maleficence, and justice could be interpreted in different ways. Each way could end up in a different decision to be made. For example, while one would argue that use of GPS could mount up to surveillance, others would argue that its use liberates individuals with dementia to lead a normal life. We do not think there is a straight answer to that, but it all depends on the individuals' capacity to make decisions and what is in their best interest.

We believe that the use of technology must not substitute human contact. It can put people in touch with their loved ones, but can never make them feel their touch.

REFERENCES

Abowd, G., Atkeson, C., & Bobick, A. (2000). Living laboratories: The future computing environments group at the Georgia Institute of Technology. *Factors in Computing*, 215. http://doi.acm.org/10.1145/633292.633416

Alemdar, H., & Ersoy, C. (2010). Wireless sensor networks for healthcare: A survey. *Computer Networks*, *54*(15), 2688–2710. doi:10.1016/j.comnet.2010.05.003

Algase, D. L., Beattie, E. R. A., Bogue, E.-L., & Yao, L. (2001). The Algase Wandering Scale: Initial psychometrics of a new caregiver reporting tool. *American Journal of Alzheimer's Disease and Other Dementias, 16*(3), 141–152. doi:10.1177/153331750101600301 PMID:11398562

Algase, D. L., Beattie, E. R. A., Leitsch, S. A., & Beel-Bates, C. A. (2003). Biomechanical activity devices to index wandering behaviour in dementia. *American Journal of Alzheimer's Disease and Other Dementias, 18*(2), 85–92. doi:10.1177/153331750301800202 PMID:12708223

Alzheimer's Association. (2014). 2014 Alzheimer's disease facts and figures. In *Alzheimer's & dementia* (pp. 1–46). Elsevier Ltd.

Alzheimer's Society, & Hubbard-Green, T. (2011). *Safer walking technology.* Retrieved from http://alzheimers.org.uk/site/scripts/documents_info.php?categoryID=200167&documentID=579&pagenumber=1

Andel, R., Hyer, K., & Slack, A. (2007). Risk factors for nursing home placement in older adults with and without dementia. *Journal of Aging and Health, 19*(2), 213–228. doi:10.1177/0898264307299359 PMID:17413132

Andreassen, C. S., Torsheim, T., Brunborg, G. S., & Pallesen, S. (2012). Development of a Facebook addiction scale 1, 2. *Psychological Reports, 110*(2), 501–517. doi:10.2466/02.09.18.PR0.110.2.501-517 PMID:22662404

Ashbrook, D., & Starner, T. (2003). Using GPS to learn significant locations and predict movement across multiple users. *Personal and Ubiquitous Computing, 7*(5), 275–286. doi:10.1007/s00779-003-0240-0

Australian Institute of Health and Welfare. (2007). *Older Australia at a glance.* AIHW Canberra.

Avvenuti, M., Baker, C., Light, J., Tulpan, D., & Vecchio, A. (2010). Non-intrusive patient monitoring of Alzheimer's disease subjects using wireless sensor networks. In *Proceedings of 2009 World Congress on Privacy, Security, Trust and the Management of e-Business.* Academic Press.

Ayalon, L., & Shiovitz-Ezra, S. (2011). The relationship between loneliness and passive death wishes in the second half of life. *International Psychogeriatrics, 23*(10), 1677–1685. doi:10.1017/S1041610211001384 PMID:21777504

Ballard, C., Neill, D., O'brien, J., McKeith, I. G., Ince, P., & Perry, R. (2000). Anxiety, depression and psychosis in vascular dementia: Prevalence and associations. *Journal of Affective Disorders, 59*(2), 97–106. doi:10.1016/S0165-0327(99)00057-9 PMID:10837878

Baltes, P. B., Reese, H. W., & Nesselroade, J. R. (2014). *Life-span developmental psychology: Introduction to research methods.* Psychology Press.

Bao, L., & Intille, S. S. (2004). Activity recognition from user-annotated acceleration data. In *Pervasive computing* (pp. 1–17). Springer. doi:10.1007/978-3-540-24646-6_1

Barrett, L. F., & Barrett, D. J. (2001). An introduction to computerized experience sampling in psychology. *Social Science Computer Review, 19*(2), 175–185. doi:10.1177/089443930101900204

Bartlett, M. S., Littlewort, G. C., Frank, M. G., & Lee, K. (2014). Automatic decoding of facial movements reveals deceptive pain expressions. *Current Biology*, *24*(7), 738–743. doi:10.1016/j.cub.2014.02.009 PMID:24656830

Beauchamp, T. L., & Childress, J. F. (2001). *Principles of biomedical ethics*. Oxford University Press.

Beigl, M. (2005). *Proceedings of the 7th International Conference, UbiComp 2005 (Vol. 3660)*. Springer.

Béland, F., Zunzunegui, M.-V., Alvarado, B., Otero, A., & del Ser, T. (2005). Trajectories of cognitive decline and social relations. *The Journals of Gerontology. Series B, Psychological Sciences and Social Sciences*, *60*(6), 320–P330. doi:10.1093/geronb/60.6.P320 PMID:16260706

Boers, N. M., Chodos, D., Gburzynski, P., Guirguis, L., Huang, J., Lederer, R., … Stroulia, E. (2010). The smart condo project: services for independent living. *E-Health, Assistive Technologies and Applications for Assisted Living: Challenges and Solutions*, 289.

Boonstra, A., & Broekhuis, M. (2010). Barriers to the acceptance of electronic medical records by physicians from systematic review to taxonomy and interventions. *BMC Health Services Research*, *10*(1), 231. doi:10.1186/1472-6963-10-231 PMID:20691097

Boyd, D. M., & Ellison, N. (2007). Social network sites: Definitions, history, and scholarship. *Journal of Computer-Mediated Communication*. Retrieved from http://jcmc.indiana.edu/vol13/issue1/boyd.ellison.html

Brajnik, G., Yesilada, Y., & Harper, S. (2011). Web accessibility guideline aggregation for older users and its validation. *Universal Access in the Information Society*, *10*(4), 403–423. doi:10.1007/s10209-011-0220-5

Brewer, M. B. (2000). Research design and issues of validity. In Handbook of research methods in social and personality psychology (pp. 3–16). Academic Press.

Butler, D. (2008). Web data predict flu. *Nature*, *456*(7220), 287–288. doi:10.1038/456287a PMID:19020578

Campbell, D. T., Stanley, J. C., & Gage, N. L. (1963). *Experimental and quasi-experimental designs for research*. Houghton Mifflin Boston.

Cerejeira, J., Lagarto, L., & Mukaetova-Ladinska, E. B. (2012). Behavioral and psychological symptoms of dementia. *Frontiers in Neurology, 3*.

Cernea, D., Kerren, A., & Ebert, A. (2011). Detecting insight and emotion in visualization applications with a commercial EEG headset. In *Proceedings of SIGRAD 2011 Conference on Evaluations of Graphics and Visualization-Efficiency, Usefulness, Accessibility, Usability* (pp. 53–60). Academic Press.

Chadwick-Dias, A., McNulty, M., & Tullis, T. (2003). Web usability and age: how design changes can improve performance. In *ACM SIGCAPH computers and the physically handicapped* (pp. 30–37). ACM.

Chan, D.-C., Kasper, J. D., Black, B. S., & Rabins, P. V. (2003). Presence of behavioral and psychological symptoms predicts nursing home placement in community-dwelling elders with cognitive impairment in univariate but not multivariate analysis. *The Journals of Gerontology. Series A, Biological Sciences and Medical Sciences*, *58*(6), M548–M554. doi:10.1093/gerona/58.6.M548 PMID:12807927

Charness, N. (2003). *Impact of technology on successful aging.* Springer Publishing Company.

Chou, W.-H., Lai, Y.-T., & Liu, K.-H. (2010). Decent digital social media for senior life: A practical design approach. In *Proceedings of Computer Science and Information Technology (ICCSIT)* (Vol. 4, pp. 249–253). IEEE.

Coblentz, W. K., & Warshaw, R. S. (1956). European convention for the protection of human rights and fundamental freedoms. *California Law Review, 44*(1), 94. doi:10.2307/3478312

Coen, R. F., Swanwick, G. R., O'Boyle, C. A., & Coakley, D. (1997). Behaviour disturbance and other predictors of carer burden in Alzheimer's disease. *International Journal of Geriatric Psychiatry, 12*(3), 331–336. doi:10.1002/(SICI)1099-1166(199703)12:3<331::AID-GPS495>3.0.CO;2-J PMID:9152717

Cohen-Mansfield, J., Creedon, M. A., Malone, T. B., Kirkpatrick, M. J., Dutra, L. A., & Herman, R. P. (2005). Electronic memory aids for community-dwelling elderly persons: Attitudes, preferences, and potential utilization. *Journal of Applied Gerontology, 24*(1), 3–20. doi:10.1177/0733464804271277

Cohen-Mansfield, J., Marx, M. S., & Rosenthal, A. S. (1989). A description of agitation in a nursing home. *Journal of Gerontology, 44*(3), M77–M84. doi:10.1093/geronj/44.3.M77 PMID:2715584

Cole, M. G. (2004). Delirium in elderly patients. *The American Journal of Geriatric Psychiatry, 12*(1), 7–21. doi:10.1097/00019442-200401000-00002 PMID:14729554

Cornejo, R., Favela, J., & Tentori, M. (2010). Ambient displays for integrating older adults into social networking sites. In. Proc. Collaboration and Technology (LNCS), (vol. 6257, pp. 321–336). CRIWG. doi:10.1007/978-3-642-15714-1_24

Courtney, K. L., Demiris, G., Rantz, M., & Skubic, M. (2008). Needing smart home technologies: The perspectives of older adults in continuing care retirement communities. *Informatics in Primary Care, 16*(3), 195–201. PMID:19094406

Czaja, S. J., Charness, N., Fisk, A. D., Hertzog, C., Nair, S. N., Rogers, W. A., & Sharit, J. (2006). Factors predicting the use of technology: Findings from the Center for Research and Education on Aging and Technology Enhancement (CREATE). *Psychology and Aging, 21*(2), 333–352. doi:10.1037/0882-7974.21.2.333 PMID:16768579

D'Souza, M., Ros, M., & Karunanithi, M. (2012). *An indoor localisation and motion monitoring system to determine behavioural activity in dementia afflicted patients in aged care.* Academic Press.

Davidson, E., & Heslinga, D. (2006). Bridging the IT adoption gap for small physician practices: An action research study on electronic health records. *Information Systems Management, 24*(1), 15–28. doi:10.1080/10580530601036786

Dawson, P., & Reid, D. W. (1987). Behavioral dimensions of patients at risk of wandering. *The Gerontologist, 27*(1), 104–107. doi:10.1093/geront/27.1.104 PMID:3557136

Department of Health. (2005). *Mental capacity act.* Author.

Dickie, C., Vertegaal, R., Shell, J. S., Sohn, C., Cheng, D., & Aoudeh, O. (2004). Eye contact sensing glasses for attention-sensitive wearable video blogging. In Proceedings of CHI'04 Extended Abstracts on Human Factors in Computing Systems (pp. 769–770). ACM. doi:10.1145/985921.985927

Ding, D., Cooper, R. A., Pasquina, P. F., & Fici-Pasquina, L. (2011a). Sensor technology for smart homes. *Maturitas*, *69*(2), 131–136. doi:10.1016/j.maturitas.2011.03.016 PMID:21531517

Ding, D., Cooper, R. A., Pasquina, P. F., & Fici-Pasquina, L. (2011b). Sensor technology for smart homes. *Maturitas*, *69*(2), 131–136. doi:10.1016/j.maturitas.2011.03.016 PMID:21531517

Doraiswamy, P. M., Leon, J., Cummings, J. L., Marin, D., & Neumann, P. J. (2002). Prevalence and impact of medical comorbidity in Alzheimer's disease. *The Journals of Gerontology. Series A, Biological Sciences and Medical Sciences*, *57*(3), M173–M177. doi:10.1093/gerona/57.3.M173 PMID:11867654

Duhigg, C. (2012). How companies learn your secrets. *The New York Times, 16.*

Eggermont, S., Vandebosch, H., & Steyaert, S. (2006). *Towards the desired future of the elderly and ICT: policy recommendations based on a dialogue with senior citizens.* Poiesis & Praxis. doi:10.1007/s10202-005-0017-9

Erickson, L. B. (2011). *Social media, social capital, and seniors: The impact of Facebook on bonding and bridging social capital of individuals over 65.* Academic Press.

European Research Cluster on the Internet of Things. (n.d.). *IERC-European research cluster on the internet of things.* Retrieved March 22, 2014, from http://www.internet-of-things-research.eu/about_iot.htm

Fahy, G. M., West, M. D., Coles, L. S., & Harris, S. B. (2010). *The future of aging: Pathways to human life extension.* Springer. doi:10.1007/978-90-481-3999-6

Farkas, P. A., Schrenk, M., & Hlauschek, W. (2010). Senior social platform–An application aimed to reduce the social and digital isolation of seniors. In *Proceedings of REAL CORP.* Academic Press.

Finkel, S. I., Costa e Silva, J., Cohen, G., Miller, S., & Sartorius, N. (1997). Behavioral and psychological signs and symptoms of dementia: A consensus statement on current knowledge and implications for research and treatment. *International Psychogeriatrics*, *8*(S3), 497–500. doi:10.1017/S1041610297003943 PMID:9154615

Fishkin, K. P., Jiang, B., Philipose, M., & Roy, S. (2004). *I sense a disturbance in the force: Unobtrusive detection of interactions with RFID-tagged objects.* UbiComp.

Fisk, A., Rogers, W., Charness, N., Czaja, S., & Sharit, J. (2012). *Designing for older adults: Principles and creative human factors approaches.* CRC Press.

Fisk, M. J. (2003). *Social alarms to telecare: Older people's services in transition.* The Policy Press.

Foo Siang Fook, V., Tay, S. C., Jayachandran, M., Biswas, J., & Zhang, D. (2006). An ontology-based context model in monitoring and handling agitation behavior for persons with dementia. In *Proceedings of Pervasive Computing and Communications Workshops.* IEEE. doi:10.1109/PERCOMW.2006.22

Friedewald, M., & Raabe, O. (2011). Ubiquitous computing: An overview of technology impacts. *Telematics and Informatics*, *28*(2), 55–65. doi:10.1016/j.tele.2010.09.001

Frisby, B. (2000). *ASTRID: A guide to using technology in dementia care.* London: Hawker.

Frisoni, G., Rozzini, L., Gozzetti, A., Binetti, G., Zanetti, O., Bianchetti, A., & Cummings, J. et al. (1999). Behavioral syndromes in Alzheimer's disease: Description and correlates. *Dementia and Geriatric Cognitive Disorders*, *10*(2), 130–138. doi:10.1159/000017113 PMID:10026387

Gibson, L., Moncur, W., Forbes, P., Arnott, J., Martin, C., & Bhachu, A. S. (2010). Designing social networking sites for older adults. In *Proceedings of the 24th BCS Interaction Specialist Group Conference* (pp. 186–194). British Computer Society.

Gillies, B. (2001). *Smart support at home: An evaluation of smart technology in dispersed housing.* Livingstone.

Goodwin, M. S., Velicer, W. F., & Intille, S. S. (2008). Telemetric monitoring in the behavior sciences. *Behavior Research Methods*, *40*(1), 328–341. doi:10.3758/BRM.40.1.328 PMID:18411557

Granata, C., Chetouani, M., Tapus, A., Bidaud, P., & Dupourqué, V. (2010). Voice and graphical-based interfaces for interaction with a robot dedicated to elderly and people with cognitive disorders. In Proceedings of RO-MAN, 2010 IEEE (pp. 785–790). IEEE. doi:10.1109/ROMAN.2010.5598698

Grouple.cc. (2012). *About us | Grouple.* Retrieved April 10, 2014, from http://www.grouple.cc/about-us

Haukka, S. (2011). *Older Australians and the internet.* Academic Press.

Healey, J. (2000). Future possibilities in electronic monitoring of physical activity. *Research Quarterly for Exercise and Sport*, *71*(2Suppl), S137–S145. Retrieved from http://eutils.ncbi.nlm.nih.gov/entrez/eutils/elink.fcgi?dbfrom=pubmed&id=10925836&retmode=ref&cmd=prlinks PMID:10925836

Hellman, R. (2012). Usable user interfaces for persons with memory impairments. In *Ambient assisted living* (pp. 167–176). Springer. doi:10.1007/978-3-642-27491-6_12

Hermans, D. G., Htay, U. H., & McShane, R. (2007). Non-pharmacological interventions for wandering of people with dementia in the domestic setting. *Cochrane Database of Systematic Reviews (Online)*, *CD005994*. doi:10.1002/14651858.CD005994.pub2 PMID:17253573

Herrmann, N., Lanctôt, K. L., Sambrook, R., Lesnikova, N., Hébert, R., McCracken, P., & Nguyen, E. et al. (2006). The contribution of neuropsychiatric symptoms to the cost of dementia care. *International Journal of Geriatric Psychiatry*, *21*(10), 972–976. doi:10.1002/gps.1594 PMID:16955429

Hodgson, N., Gitlin, L. N., Winter, L., & Czekanski, K. (2011). Undiagnosed illness and neuropsychiatric behaviors in community-residing older adults with dementia. *Alzheimer Disease and Associated Disorders*, *25*(2), 109–115. doi:10.1097/WAD.0b013e3181f8520a PMID:20921879

Holtzman, R. E., Rebok, G. W., Saczynski, J. S., Kouzis, A. C., Doyle, K. W., & Eaton, W. W. (2004). Social network characteristics and cognition in middle-aged and older adults. *The Journals of Gerontology. Series B, Psychological Sciences and Social Sciences*, *59*(6), 278–P284. doi:10.1093/geronb/59.6.P278 PMID:15576855

Hughes, J. C., & Louw, S. J. (2002). Electronic tagging of people with dementia who wander: Ethical considerations are possibly more important than practical benefits. *BMJ: British Medical Journal*, *325*(7369), 847–848. doi:10.1136/bmj.325.7369.847

Hurley, A. C., Volicer, L., Camberg, L., Ashley, J., Woods, P., Odenheimer, G., & Mahoney, E. et al. (1999). Measurement of Observed Agitation in Patients With Dementia of the Alzheimer Type. *Journal of Mental Health and Aging, 5*(2), 117–134.

Innes, A. (2009). Dementia studies: A social science perspective. *Sage (Atlanta, Ga.)*.

Intille, S. S. (2007). Technological innovations enabling automatic, context-sensitive ecological momentary assessment. In *The science of real-time data capture* (pp. 308–337). Self-Reports.

Intille, S. S., Larson, K., Beaudin, J. S., Nawyn, J., Tapia, E. M., & Kaushik, P. (2005). A living laboratory for the design and evaluation of ubiquitous computing technologies. In CHI'05 extended abstracts on Human factors in computing systems (pp. 1941–1944). ACM. doi:10.1145/1056808.1057062

Jakkula, V., & Cook, D. J. (2008). Anomaly detection using temporal data mining in a smart home environment. *Methods of Information in Medicine, 47*(1), 70–75. PMID:18213431

Jara, A. J., Moreno-Sanchez, P., Skarmeta, A. F., Varakliotis, S., & Kirstein, P. (2013). IPv6 addressing proxy: Mapping native addressing from legacy technologies and devices to the internet of things (IPv6). *Sensors (Basel, Switzerland), 13*(5), 6687–6712. doi:10.3390/s130506687 PMID:23686145

Jha, A. K., Bates, D. W., Jenter, C., Orav, E. J., Zheng, J., Cleary, P., & Simon, S. R. (2009). Electronic health records: Use, barriers and satisfaction among physicians who care for Black and Hispanic patients. *Journal of Evaluation in Clinical Practice, 15*(1), 158–163. doi:10.1111/j.1365-2753.2008.00975.x PMID:18759752

Johnson, J. (2012). Social networks broken down by demographic. *The Blog Herald*. Retrieved March 24, 2014, from http://www.blogherald.com/2012/06/07/social-networks-broken-down-by-demographic-infographic/

Joinson, A. N. (2008). Looking at, looking up or keeping up with people?: motives and use of facebook. In *Proceedings of the SIGCHI Conference on Human Factors in Computing Systems* (pp. 1027–1036). ACM. doi:10.1145/1357054.1357213

Kapusta, P., Regier, L., Bareham, J., & Jensen, B. (2011). Behaviour management in dementia. *Canadian Family Physician Medecin de Famille Canadien, 57*(12), 1420–1422. PMID:22170199

Kearns, W. D., Algase, D., Moore, D. H., & Ahmed, S. (2008). Ultra wideband radio: A novel method for measuring wandering in persons with dementia. *Gerontechnology (Valkenswaard), 7*(1), 48–57. doi:10.4017/gt.2008.07.01.005.00

Kidd, C. D., Orr, R., Abowd, G. D., Atkeson, C. G., Essa, I. A., MacIntyre, B. ... Newstetter, W. (1999). The aware home: A living laboratory for ubiquitous computing research. In Cooperative buildings: Integrating information, organizations, and architecture (pp. 191–198). Springer.

Kim, E., Helal, S., & Cook, D. (2010). Human activity recognition and pattern discovery. *Pervasive Computing, IEEE, 9*(1), 48–53. doi:10.1109/MPRV.2010.7 PMID:21258659

Kittinger, R., Correia, C. J., & Irons, J. G. (2012). Relationship between Facebook use and problematic Internet use among college students. *Cyberpsychology, Behavior, and Social Networking, 15*(6), 324–327. doi:10.1089/cyber.2010.0410 PMID:22703039

Klasnja, P., & Pratt, W. (2012). Healthcare in the pocket: Mapping the space of mobile-phone health interventions. *Journal of Biomedical Informatics*, *45*(1), 184–198. doi:10.1016/j.jbi.2011.08.017 PMID:21925288

Koyuncu, H., & Yang, S. H. (2010). A survey of indoor positioning and object locating systems. *IJCSNS International Journal of Computer Science and Network Security*, *10*(5), 121–128.

Krishnamoorthy, A., & Anderson, D. (2011). Managing challenging behaviour in older adults with dementia. *Progress in Neurology and Psychiatry*, *15*(3), 20–26. doi:10.1002/pnp.199

Lærum, H., Ellingsen, G., & Faxvaag, A. (2001). Doctors' use of electronic medical records systems in hospitals: Cross sectional survey. *BMJ (Clinical Research Ed.)*, *323*(7325), 1344–1348. doi:10.1136/bmj.323.7325.1344 PMID:11739222

Lakey, L., Chandaria, K., Quince, C., Kane, M., & Saunders, T. (2012). A national challenge. *Dementia (London)*, 2012.

Lamiell, J. T. (2003). Beyond individual and group differences: Human individuality, scientific psychology, and William Stern's critical personalism. *Sage (Atlanta, Ga.)*.

Landau, R., Werner, S., Auslander, G. K., Shoval, N., & Heinik, J. (2009). Attitudes of family and professional care-givers towards the use of GPS for tracking patients with dementia: An exploratory study. *British Journal of Social Work*, *39*(4), 670–692. doi:10.1093/bjsw/bcp037

Larizza, M. F., Zukerman, I., Bohnert, F., Busija, L., Bentley, S. A., Russell, R. A., & Rees, G. (2014). In-home monitoring of older adults with vision impairment: Exploring patients', caregivers' and professionals' views. *Journal of the American Medical Informatics Association*, *21*(1), 56–63. doi:10.1136/amiajnl-2012-001586 PMID:23676244

Larson, E. B., Reifler, B. V., Sumi, S. M., Canfield, C. G., & Chinn, N. M. (1985). Diagnostic evaluation of 200 elderly outpatients with suspected dementia. *Journal of Gerontology*, *40*(5), 536–543. doi:10.1093/geronj/40.5.536 PMID:4031401

Lee, D. (2012). *BBC News - Facebook surpasses one billion users as it tempts new markets*. Retrieved March 24, 2014, from http://www.bbc.co.uk/news/technology-19816709

Lehtinen, V., Näsänen, J., & Sarvas, R. (2009). A little silly and empty-headed: older adults' understandings of social networking sites. In *Proceedings of the 23rd British HCI Group Annual Conference on People and Computers: Celebrating People and Technology* (pp. 45–54). British Computer Society.

LeResche, L. (1984). Facial behaviors related to pain in the elderly. *Gerodontology*, *3*(1), 83–86. doi:10.1111/j.1741-2358.1984.tb00357.x

Leung, R., McGrenere, J., & Graf, P. (2011). Age-related differences in the initial usability of mobile device icons. *Behaviour & Information Technology*, *30*(5), 629–642. doi:10.1080/01449290903171308

Lin, Q., Zhang, D., Huang, X., Ni, H., & Zhou, X. (2012). Detecting wandering behavior based on GPS traces for elders with dementia. In *Proceedings of Control Automation Robotics & Vision (ICARCV)* (pp. 672–677). IEEE. doi:10.1109/ICARCV.2012.6485238

Litwin, H., & Shiovitz-Ezra, S. (2011). Social network type and subjective well-being in a national sample of older Americans. *The Gerontologist*, *51*(3), 379–388. doi:10.1093/geront/gnq094 PMID:21097553

Liu, C., Zhu, Q., Holroyd, K. A., & Seng, E. K. (2011). Status and trends of mobile-health applications for iOS devices: A developer's perspective. *Journal of Systems and Software*, *84*(11), 2022–2033. doi:10.1016/j.jss.2011.06.049

Londei, S. T., Rousseau, J., Ducharme, F., St-Arnaud, A., Meunier, J., Saint-Arnaud, J., & Giroux, F. (2009). An intelligent videomonitoring system for fall detection at home: Perceptions of elderly people. *Journal of Telemedicine and Telecare*, *15*(8), 383–390. doi:10.1258/jtt.2009.090107 PMID:19948704

Lovett, G. (2011). Over 50s drive Facebook growth, study says. *Marketing Week*. Retrieved March 24, 2014, from http://www.marketingweek.co.uk/over-50s-drive-facebook-growth-study-says/3027863.article

Luengo-Fernandez, R., Leal, J., & Gray, A. (2010). The economic burden of dementia and associated research funding in the United Kingdom. *Dementia (London)*, 2010.

Machold, C., Judge, G., Mavrinac, A., Elliott, J., Murphy, A. M., & Roche, E. (2012). *Social networking patterns/hazards among teenagers*. Academic Press.

Mainwaring, A., Culler, D., Polastre, J., Szewczyk, R., & Anderson, J. (2002). Wireless sensor networks for habitat monitoring. In *Proceedings of the 1st ACM international workshop on Wireless sensor networks and applications* (pp. 88–97). ACM. doi:10.1145/570738.570751

Marcus, A. (1998). Metaphor design for user interfaces. In CHI 98 Cconference Summary on Human Factors in Computing Systems (pp. 129–130). ACM.

Markowetz, A., Błaszkiewicz, K., Montag, C., Switala, C., & Schläpfer, T. (2014). Psycho-informatics: Big data shaping modern psychometrics. *Medical Hypotheses*, *82*(4), 405–411. doi:10.1016/j.mehy.2013.11.030 PMID:24529915

Martino-Saltzman, D., Blasch, B. B., Morris, R. D., & McNeal, L. W. (1991). Travel behavior of nursing home residents perceived as wanderers and nonwanderers. *The Gerontologist*, *31*(5), 666–672. doi:10.1093/geront/31.5.666 PMID:1778493

McGrath, M. J., Nafus, D., & Scanaill, C. N. (2013). *Sensor technologies: Healthcare, wellness and environmental applications*. Apress. doi:10.1007/978-1-4302-6014-1

McKinstry, B., & Sheikh, A. (2013). The use of global positioning systems in promoting safer walking for people with dementia. *Journal of Telemedicine and Telecare*, *19*(5), 288–292. doi:10.1177/1357633X13495481 PMID:24163239

McShane, R., Gedling, K., Kenward, B., Kenward, R., Hope, T., & Jacoby, R. (1998). The feasibility of electronic tracking devices in dementia: A telephone survey and case series. *International Journal of Geriatric Psychiatry*, *13*(8), 556–563. doi:10.1002/(SICI)1099-1166(199808)13:8<556::AID-GPS834>3.0.CO;2-6 PMID:9733337

McShane, R., Hope, T., & Wilkinson, J. (1994). Tracking patients who wander: Ethics and technology. *Lancet*, *343*(8908), 1274. doi:10.1016/S0140-6736(94)92159-8 PMID:7910283

Mehl, M. R., Pennebaker, J. W., Crow, D. M., Dabbs, J., & Price, J. H. (2001). The electronically activated recorder (EAR): A device for sampling naturalistic daily activities and conversations. *Behavior Research Methods, Instruments, & Computers*, *33*(4), 517–523. doi:10.3758/BF03195410 PMID:11816455

Melenhorst, A.-S., Fisk, A. D., Mynatt, E. D., & Rogers, W. A. (2004). Potential intrusiveness of aware home technology: Perceptions of older adults. In *Proceedings of the Human Factors and Ergonomics Society Annual Meeting* (Vol. 48, pp. 266–270). SAGE Publications. doi:10.1177/154193120404800209

Mesch, G. S. (2012). Technology and youth. *New Directions for Youth Development*, *2012*(135), 97–105. doi:10.1002/yd.20032 PMID:23097367

Mihailidis, A., Cockburn, A., Longley, C., & Boger, J. (2008). The acceptability of home monitoring technology among community-dwelling older adults and baby boomers. *Assistive Technology*, *20*(1), 1–12. doi:10.1080/10400435.2008.10131927 PMID:18751575

Ministry of Justice. (2008). *Deprivation of liberty safeguards: Code of practice to supplement the main mental capacity act 2005 code of practice*. The Stationery Office.

Miskelly, F. (2005). Electronic tracking of patients with dementia and wandering using mobile phone technology. *Age and Ageing*, *34*(5), 497–499. doi:10.1093/ageing/afi145 PMID:16107453

Mokhtari, M., Aloulou, H., Tiberghien, T., Biswas, J., Racoceanu, D., & Yap, P. (2012). New trends to support independence in persons with mild dementia – A mini-review. *Gerontology*, *58*(6), 554–563. doi:10.1159/000337827 PMID:22677914

Molenaar, P. C. M. (2004). A manifesto on psychology as idiographic science: Bringing the person back into scientific psychology, this time forever. *Measurement*, *2*(4), 201–218.

Moniz-Cook, E., Stokes, G., & Agar, S. (2003). Difficult behaviour and dementia in nursing homes: Five cases of psychosocial intervention. *Clinical Psychology & Psychotherapy*, *10*(3), 197–208. doi:10.1002/cpp.370

Moniz-Cook, E., Woods, R., & Gardiner, E. (2000). Staff factors associated with perception of behaviour as' challenging'in residential and nursing homes. *Aging & Mental Health*, *4*(1), 48–55. doi:10.1080/13607860055973

Moore, P., Thomas, A., Tadros, G., Xhafa, F., & Barolli, L. (2013). Detection of the onset of agitation in patients with dementia: Real–time monitoring and the application of big–data solutions. *International Journal of Space-Based and Situated Computing*, *3*(3), 136–154. doi:10.1504/IJSSC.2013.056405

Moore, P., Xhafa, F., Barolli, L., & Thomas, A. (2013). Monitoring and detection of agitation in dementia: Towards real-time and big-data solutions. In *Proceedings of P2P, Parallel, Grid, Cloud and Internet Computing (3PGCIC)* (pp. 128–135). IEEE.

Morris, M., Ozanne, E., Miller, K., Santamaria, N., Pearce, A., Said, C., & Adair, B. (2012). Smart technologies for older people: A systematic literature review of smart technologies that promote health and wellbeing of older people living at home. Institute for a Broadband-Enabled Society.

Mulvenna, M., Martin, S., Sävenstedt, S., Bengtsson, J., Meiland, F., Dröes, R. M., … Craig, D. (2010). Designing & evaluating a cognitive prosthetic for people with mild dementia. In *Proceedings of the 28th Annual European Conference on Cognitive Ergonomics* (pp. 11–18). ACM. doi:10.1145/1962300.1962306

Nef, T., Ganea, R. L., Müri, R. M., & Mosimann, U. P. (2013). Social networking sites and older users - a systematic review. *International Psychogeriatrics, 25*(7), 1041–53. doi:10.1017/S1041610213000355

Norval, C. (2012). Understanding the incentives of older adults' participation on social networking sites. *ACM SIGACCESS Accessibility and Computing*, (102), 25–29.

Nusser, S. M., Intille, S. S., & Maitra, R. (2006). Emerging technologies and next-generation intensive longitudinal data collection. *Models for Intensive Longitudinal Data*, 254–277.

Ogawa, H., Yonezawa, Y., Maki, H., Sato, H., & Caldwell, W. M. (2004). A mobile phone-based safety support system for wandering elderly persons. In *Proceedings of Engineering in Medicine and Biology Society* (Vol. 2, pp. 3316–3317). IEEE. doi:10.1109/IEMBS.2004.1403932

Olesen, J., Gustavsson, A., Svensson, M., Wittchen, H., & Jönsson, B. (2012). The economic cost of brain disorders in Europe. *European Journal of Neurology, 19*(1), 155–162. doi:10.1111/j.1468-1331.2011.03590.x PMID:22175760

Orr, R. J., & Abowd, G. D. (2000). The smart floor: A mechanism for natural user identification and tracking. In CHI'00 extended abstracts on Human factors in computing systems (pp. 275–276). ACM. doi:10.1145/633451.633453

Ouwerkerk, M., Pasveer, F., & Langereis, G. (2008). Unobtrusive sensing of psychophysiological parameters. In *Probing experience* (pp. 163–193). Springer. doi:10.1007/978-1-4020-6593-4_15

Pang, Z. (2013). *Technologies and architectures of the internet-of-things (IoT) for health and wellbeing*. Royal Institute of Technology. Retrieved from http://kth.diva-portal.org/smash/get/diva2:621384/FULLTEXT01.pdf

Pantic, I., Damjanovic, A., Todorovic, J., Topalovic, D., Bojovic-Jovic, D., Ristic, S., & Pantic, S. (2012). Association between online social networking and depression in high school students: behavioral physiology viewpoint. *Psychiatria Danubina, 24*(1), 90–93.

Patel, S. N., Reynolds, M. S., & Abowd, G. D. (2008). Detecting human movement by differential air pressure sensing in HVAC system ductwork: An exploration in infrastructure mediated sensing. *Pervasive Computing*, 1–18.

Pentland, A. P. (1996). Smart rooms. *Scientific American, 274*(4), 54–62. doi:10.1038/scientificamerican0496-68 PMID:8934646

Peterson, C. B., Prasad, N., & Prasad, R. (2012). The future of assistive technologies for dementia. In Proceedings of Workshop ISG-ISARC, 27. doi:10.4017/gt.2012.11.02.427.00

Pino, M., Granata, C., Legouverneur, G., Boulay, M., & Rigaud, A. S. (2012). Assessing design features of a graphical user interface for a social assistive robot for older adults with cognitive impairment. *Gerontechnology (Valkenswaard), 11*(2), 383.

Plaza, I., Martín, L., Martin, S., & Medrano, C. (2011). Mobile applications in an aging society: Status and trends. *Journal of Systems and Software, 84*(11), 1977–1988. doi:10.1016/j.jss.2011.05.035

Plötz, T., Hammerla, N. Y., Rozga, A., Reavis, A., Call, N., & Abowd, G. D. (2012). Automatic assessment of problem behavior in individuals with developmental disabilities. In *Proceedings of the 2012 ACM Conference on Ubiquitous Computing* (pp. 391–400). ACM. doi:10.1145/2370216.2370276

Pols, J., & Moser, I. (2009). Cold technologies versus warm care? On affective and social relations with and through care technologies. *ALTER-European Journal of Disability Research, 3*(2), 159–178.

Pot, A. M., Willemse, B. M., & Horjus, S. (2012). A pilot study on the use of tracking technology: Feasibility, acceptability, and benefits for people in early stages of dementia and their informal caregivers. *Aging & Mental Health, 16*(1), 127–134. doi:10.1080/13607863.2011.596810 PMID:21780960

Princeton University. (2014). *WordNet search - 3.1*. Retrieved April 05, 2014, from http://wordnetweb. princeton.edu/perl/webwn?s=telemetry

Report, B., & February, N. (2008). Ubiquitous sensor networks (USN). *Group, 4*, 1–10. Retrieved from http://www.itu.int/dms_pub/itu-t/oth/23/01/T23010000040001PDFE.pdf

Robinson, L., Brittain, K., Lindsay, S., Jackson, D., & Olivier, P. (2009). Keeping in touch everyday (KITE) project: Developing assistive technologies with people with dementia and their carers to promote independence. *International Psychogeriatrics, 21*, 494–502. doi:10.1017/S1041610209008448

Robinson, L., Hutchings, D., Corner, L., Finch, T., Hughes, J., Brittain, K., & Bond, J. (2007). Balancing rights and risks: Conflicting perspectives in the management of wandering in dementia. *Health Risk & Society, 9*(4), 389–406. doi:10.1080/13698570701612774

Robinson, L., Hutchings, D., Dickinson, H. O., Corner, L., Beyer, F., Finch, T., & Bond, J. et al. (2007). Effectiveness and acceptability of non-pharmacological interventions to reduce wandering in dementia: A systematic review. *International Journal of Geriatric Psychiatry, 22*(1), 9–22. doi:10.1002/gps.1643 PMID:17096455

Rodzon, K. (2014). Activity tracker comparison guide. *Fitoop Blog*. Retrieved April 12, 2014, from http://blog.fitoop.com/2014/01/15/activity-track-comparison-guide/

Russ, T. C., Batty, G. D., & Starr, J. M. (2012). Cognitive and behavioural predictors of survival in Alzheimer disease: Results from a sample of treated patients in a tertiary-referral memory clinic. *International Journal of Geriatric Psychiatry, 27*(8), 844–853. doi:10.1002/gps.2795 PMID:21956773

Russo, J., Sukojo, A., Helal, S., Davenport, R., & Mann, W. C. (2004). SmartWave – Intelligent meal preparation system to help older people live independently. In *Proceedings of the Second International Conference on Smart homes and health Telematics* (Vol. 14, pp. 122–135). Academic Press.

Ryu, S.-H., Ha, J. H., Park, D.-H., Yu, J., & Livingston, G. (2011). Persistence of neuropsychiatric symptoms over six months in mild cognitive impairment in community-dwelling Korean elderly. *International Psychogeriatrics, 23*(02), 214–220. doi:10.1017/S1041610210001766 PMID:20863423

Savitch, N., & Zaphiris, P. (2006). Accessible websites for people with dementia: A preliminary investigation into information architecture. In *Computers helping people with special needs* (pp. 144–151). Springer. doi:10.1007/11788713_22

Scarmeas, N., Brandt, J., Blacker, D., Albert, M., Hadjigeorgiou, G., Dubois, B., & Stern, Y. et al. (2007). Disruptive behavior as a predictor in Alzheimer disease. *Archives of Neurology, 64*(12), 1755–1761. doi:10.1001/archneur.64.12.1755 PMID:18071039

Schwarz, V., Huber, A., & Tuchler, M. (2005). Accuracy of a commercial UWB 3D location/tracking system and its impact on LT application scenarios. In *Proceedings of Ultra-Wideband* (pp. 599–603). IEEE.

Sheng, Q., Zeadally, S., Luo, Z., Chung, J.-Y., & Maamar, Z. (2010). Ubiquitous RFID: Where are we? *Information Systems Frontiers, 12*(5), 485–490. doi:10.1007/s10796-009-9212-x

Shiffman, S. (2000). Real-time self-report of momentary states in the natural environment: Computerized ecological momentary assessment. In The science of selfreport implications for research and practice (pp. 277–296). Academic Press.

Siotia, R., & Simpson, C. (2008). Applying telecare in dementia: What psychiatrists need to know. *Advances in Psychiatric Treatment, 14*(5), 382–388. doi:10.1192/apt.bp.107.003566

Skubic, M., Alexander, G., Popescu, M., Rantz, M., & Keller, J. (2009). A smart home application to eldercare: Current status and lessons learned. *Technology and Health Care : Official Journal of the European Society for Engineering and Medicine, 17,* 183–201. doi:10.3233/thc-2009-0551 PMID:19641257

Smith, R. (2007). *Plea to tag Alzheimer's patients.* Retrieved April 15, 2014, from http://www.telegraph.co.uk/news/uknews/1573776/Plea-to-tag-Alzheimers-patients.html

South-East Scotland GPS Forum. (2010). *Towards implementing safer walking with GPS technology.* Retrieved April 06, 2014, from http://www.jitscotland.org.uk/downloads/1315481589-Towards implementing a safer walking service with GPS technology-SE Scotland GPS Forum (2).pdf

Sposaro, F., Danielson, J., & Tyson, G. (2010). iWander: An Android application for dementia patients. In *Proceedings of Engineering in Medicine and Biology Society (EMBC)* (pp. 3875–3878). IEEE.

Steele, R., Lo, A., Secombe, C., & Wong, Y. K. (2009). Elderly persons' perception and acceptance of using wireless sensor networks to assist healthcare. *International Journal of Medical Informatics, 78*(12), 788–801. doi:10.1016/j.ijmedinf.2009.08.001 PMID:19717335

Steffens, D. C., Pieper, C. F., Bosworth, H. B., MacFall, J. R., Provenzale, J. M., Payne, M. E., & Krishnan, K. R. R. et al. (2005). Biological and social predictors of long-term geriatric depression outcome. *International Psychogeriatrics, 17*(01), 41–56. doi:10.1017/S1041610205000979 PMID:15948303

Stokes, G. (2000). *Challenging behaviour in dementia: A person-centred approach.* Speechmark.

Sun, X., Lucas, H., Meng, Q., & Zhang, Y. (2011). Associations between living arrangements and health-related quality of life of urban elderly people: A study from China. *Quality of Life Research: An International Journal of Quality of Life Aspects of Treatment, Care and Rehabilitation, 20*(3), 359–369. doi:10.1007/s11136-010-9752-z PMID:20878548

Tang, P., & Venables, T. (2000). "Smart" homes and telecare for independent living. *Journal of Telemedicine and Telecare, 6*(1), 8–14. doi:10.1258/1357633001933871 PMID:10824384

Tapia, E. M., Intille, S. S., & Larson, K. (2004). Activity recognition in the home using simple and ubiquitous sensors. *Pervasive Computing, 3001*, 158–175. doi:10.1007/978-3-540-24646-6_10

Teixeira, V. (2011). *Improving elderly access to audiovisual and social media, using a multimodal human-computer interface.* Faculdade de Engenharia, Universidade do Porto.

Terry, A. L., Thorpe, C. F., Giles, G., Brown, J. B., Harris, S. B., Reid, G. J., & Stewart, M. et al. (2008). Implementing electronic health records Key factors in primary care. *Canadian Family Physician Medecin de Famille Canadien, 54*(5), 730–736. PMID:18474707

Thomas, A. M., Moore, P., Shah, H., Evans, C., Sharma, M., Xhafa, F., & Patel, A. et al. (2013). Smart care spaces: Needs for intelligent at–home care. *International Journal of Space-Based and Situated Computing, 3*(1), 35–44. doi:10.1504/IJSSC.2013.051988

Tsai, T.-H., Chang, H.-T., Wong, A. M.-K., & Wu, T.-F. (2011). Connecting communities: designing a social media platform for older adults living in a senior village. In Universal access in human-computer interaction: Users diversity (pp. 224–233). Springer. doi:10.1007/978-3-642-21663-3_24

Twigg, J. (1999). The spatial ordering of care: Public and private in bathing support at home. *Sociology of Health & Illness, 21*(4), 381–400. doi:10.1111/1467-9566.00163

Valstar, M. F., Mehu, M., Jiang, B., Pantic, M., & Scherer, K. (2012). Meta-analysis of the first facial expression recognition challenge. *IEEE Transactions on Systems, Man, and Cybernetics. Part B, Cybernetics, 42*(4), 966–979.

Valstar, M. F., & Pantic, M. (2012). Fully automatic recognition of the temporal phases of facial actions. *IEEE Transactions on Systems, Man, and Cybernetics. Part B, Cybernetics, 42*(1), 28–43.

Van Beek, A., Frijters, D. H. M., Wagner, C., Groenewegen, P. P., & Ribbe, M. W. (2011). Social engagement and depressive symptoms of elderly residents with dementia: A cross-sectional study of 37 long-term care units. *International Psychogeriatrics, 23*(04), 625–633. doi:10.1017/S1041610210002061 PMID:21073769

Van der Post, L. F. M., Mulder, C. L., Peen, J., Visch, I., Dekker, J., & Beekman, A. T. F. (2012). Social support and risk of compulsory admission: Part IV of the Amsterdam study of acute psychiatry. *Psychiatric Services (Washington, D.C.), 63*(6), 577–583. doi:10.1176/appi.ps.201100080 PMID:22638005

Vernooij-Dassen, M. J. F. J., Moniz-Cook, E. D., Woods, R. T., Lepeleire, J., De, , Leuschner, A., & Zanetti, O. (2005). Factors affecting timely recognition and diagnosis of dementia across Europe: From awareness to stigma. *International Journal of Geriatric Psychiatry, 20*(4), 377–386. doi:10.1002/gps.1302 PMID:15799080

Vertegaal, R., Slagter, R., Van der Veer, G., & Nijholt, A. (2001). Eye gaze patterns in conversations: there is more to conversational agents than meets the eyes. In *Proceedings of the SIGCHI Conference on Human Factors in Computing Systems* (pp. 301–308). ACM. doi:10.1145/365024.365119

Voils, C. I., Allaire, J. C., Olsen, M. K., Steffens, D. C., Hoyle, R. H., & Bosworth, H. B. (2007). Five-year trajectories of social networks and social support in older adults with major depression. *International Psychogeriatrics, 19*(06), 1110–1124. doi:10.1017/S1041610207005303 PMID:17433120

Warren, A., Rosenblatt, A., & Lyketsos, C. G. (1999). Wandering behaviour in community-residing persons with dementia. *International Journal of Geriatric Psychiatry, 14*(4), 272–279. doi:10.1002/(SICI)1099-1166(199904)14:4<272::AID-GPS896>3.0.CO;2-P PMID:10340188

Weamer, E. A., Emanuel, J. E., Varon, D., Miyahara, S., Wilkosz, P. A., Lopez, O. L., & Sweet, R. A. et al. (2009). The relationship of excess cognitive impairment in MCI and early Alzheimer's disease to the subsequent emergence of psychosis. *International Psychogeriatrics, 21*(01), 78–85. doi:10.1017/S1041610208007734 PMID:18814807

Weiser, M. (1991). The computer for the 21st century. *Scientific American, 265*(3), 94–104. doi:10.1038/scientificamerican0991-94 PMID:1675486

White, E. B., Montgomery, P., & McShane, R. (2010). Electronic tracking for people with dementia who get lost outside the home: A study of the experience of familial carers. *British Journal of Occupational Therapy, 73*(4), 152–159. doi:10.4276/030802210X12706313443901

Wild, K., Boise, L., Lundell, J., & Foucek, A. (2008). Unobtrusive in-home monitoring of cognitive and physical health: Reactions and perceptions of older adults. *Journal of Applied Gerontology, 27*(2), 181–200. doi:10.1177/0733464807311435 PMID:19165352

Wilhelm, F. H., Pfaltz, M. C., Grossman, P., & Roth, W. T. (2006). Distinguishing emotional from physical activation in ambulatory psychophysiological monitoring. *Biomedical Sciences Instrumentation, 42*, 458–463. PMID:16817651

Wilhelm, F. H., Roth, W. T., & Sackner, M. A. (2003). The LifeShirt an advanced system for ambulatory measurement of respiratory and cardiac function. *Behavior Modification, 27*(5), 671–691. doi:10.1177/0145445503256321 PMID:14531161

Williams, K., Kemper, S., & Hummert, M. L. (2004). Enhancing communication with older adults: Overcoming elderspeak. *Journal of Gerontological Nursing, 30*(10), 17–25. doi:10.3928/0098-9134-20041001-08 PMID:15515441

Xie, B., Watkins, I., Golbeck, J., & Huang, M. (2012). Understanding and changing older adults' perceptions and learning of social media. *Educational Gerontology, 38*(4), 282–296. doi:10.1080/03601277.2010.544580 PMID:22639483

Yefimova, M., & Woods, D. L. (2012). Using sensor technology to monitor disruptive behavior of persons with dementia. In *2012 AAAI Fall Symposium Series.* AAAI.

Yu, H., Zhang, H., Fang, B., & Yu, X. (2012). A large scale code resolution service network in the internet of things. *Sensors (Basel, Switzerland), 12*(12), 15206–15243. doi:10.3390/s121115206 PMID:23202207

Zhang, J., Song, Y.-L., & Bai, C.-X. (2013). MIOTIC study: A prospective, multicenter, randomized study to evaluate the long-term efficacy of mobile phone-based Internet of Things in the management of patients with stable COPD. *International Journal of Chronic Obstructive Pulmonary Disease, 8*, 433–438. doi:10.2147/COPD.S50205 PMID:24082784

Zheng, L.-R. Z. L.-R., Nejad, M. B., Zou, Z. Z. Z., Mendoza, D. S., Zhang, Z. Z. Z., & Tenhunen, H. (2008). Future RFID and Wireless Sensors for Ubiquitous Intelligence. In *2008 NORCHIP*. doi:10.1109/NORCHP.2008.4738269

KEY TERMS AND DEFINITIONS

Big Data: Refers to the process of extraction, collection, cleaning and transforming, storage, management, analyses, indexing and searching, as well as visualisation of complex data.

Context-Aware System: A computer system that is able to sense the environment and any change in that environment and then adopt it behaviour in accordance to such change.

Data Mining: Computer pattern recognition through the use of large datasets to recognise unnoticed patterns between different variables.

Internet of Things: An infrastructure within the Internet that provides a mean of connecting different objects and devices together.

Machine Learning: Algorithmic discovery of new properties about known entities, so future predictions are possible.

Smart Home: A sensor rich living environment that helps the person to live safely and independently.

Social Networking Sites: An internet-based service that enables people to build an open or semi-open profile inside a contained system, setup a list of other individuals whom they could share a connection, view and browse their list of connections and those made by others within the system.

Telemetry: Automatic measurement and transmission of data from remote sources.

Ubiquitous Computing: When computers "weave themselves into the fabric of everyday life until they are indistinguishable from it".

This research was previously published in Advanced Technological Solutions for E-Health and Dementia Patient Monitoring edited by Fatos Xhafa, Philip Moore, and George Tadros, pages 62-104, copyright year 2015 by Medical Information Science Reference (an imprint of IGI Global).

APPENDIX

List of Index of Terms

Table 6. List of acronyms and glossary of terms

Definition	Abbreviation
Behavioural and Psychological Symptoms of Dementia	BPSD
Centers for Disease Control	CDC
Deprivation of Liberty Safeguards	DoLS
Electroencephalogram	EEG
Global Poisonings System	GPS
Graphical User Interface	GUI
In-Home Healthcare Station	IHHS
Internet of Things	IoT
Mobile Internet of Things	mIoT
Quality of Life	QoL
Radio-frequency identification	RFID
Social Network Site	SNS
Observed Agitation in Persons with Dementia	SOAPD
Ultra Wide-Band	UWB

Section 2
Corporate Innovation

Chapter 7
PRHOLO:
360° Interactive Public Relations

João Rodrigues
University of Algarve, Portugal

Ricardo Alves
University of Algarve, Portugal

Luís Sousa
University of Algarve, Portugal

Aldric Negrier
University of Algarve, Portugal

Jânio Monteiro
University of Algarve, Portugal

Pedro Cardoso
University of Algarve, Portugal

Paulo Felisberto
University of Algarve, Portugal

Mauro Figueiredo
University of Algarve, Portugal

Bruno Mendes da Silva
University of Algarve, Portugal

Roberto Lam
University of Algarve, Portugal

Jaime Carvalho Martins
University of Algarve, Portugal

Miguel Gomes
SPIC - Creative Solutions, Portugal

Paulo Bica
SPIC - Creative Solutions, Portugal

ABSTRACT

In the globalized world, possessing good products may not be enough to reach potential clients unless creative marketing strategies are well delineated. In this context, public relations are also important when it comes to capture the client's attention, making the first contact between the clients and the company's products, while being persuasive enough to make them confident that the company has the right products to fit their needs. Three virtual public relations installations were purposed in this chapter, combining technology with a human like public relations ability, capable of interacting with potential clients located in front of the installation, at angles of up to 57° (degrees), 180° and 360°, respectively. From one to several Microsoft Kinects were used to develop the three interaction models, which allows tracking and recognition of users' gestures and positions (heat map), sound sources, voice commands and face and body extraction of the user interacting with the installation.

DOI: 10.4018/978-1-5225-2589-9.ch007

INTRODUCTION

Customer acquisition is the most, or at least one of the most important parts of any company's marketing strategies. Today, the first contact with any company is probably the company's website, which should do its best to contain all the necessary information so that the customer can resolve unanswered questions. However, a website is one medium that in many cases may not be enough to capture the clients' attention and answer all their questions.

A Public Relation (PR) or a salesperson are normally responsible for the first personal contact with potential clients, helping the establishment of links between the customers' demand and the company's offers. New customers are most of the time unaware of all the details surrounding a company's products and services, and in an initial stage, have many unanswered questions. Many times, companies having several exhibitions, conferences, events, etc., need a number of human PRs, that is either not available or that they do not want or like to move or allocate. In such cases they might prefer a high tech creative digital PR to represent the company.

A real size human PR can be digitally represented using avatars or videos of a prerecorded person. There are several technics for projecting these digital representations, where three of the most common are: (a) Frontal projection, which is the most common technique used. The drawback of this technique is that the user in some situations can conceal the projection with his/her presence in front of the installation. (b) Rear projection, which usually uses an ultra-short throw projector, with the projection being made from the back of the projected area onto a retention film. The main advantages of this technique are to allow the projector to be hidden from the users that are in front of the display area, and of course, the lack of occlusion on the projection, which could occur due to the user's presence. (c) Holographic representation, which are alternative technique that uses a holographic images of the digital representation of the PR person. One of the techniques used to create this holographic representation is the Pepper's Ghost (see e.g., Figueiredo, Cardoso, Gonçalves, & Rodrigues, 2014). The main drawback of this technique is the requirement of a large space, while the advantage being the most likeness to capturing a client's attention due to its attractiveness and novelty.

In this Chapter three PR installations are presented. All these installations allow the interaction with a user, supporting several features like the track and recognizing of gestures, users' positions (heat map), sound sources, voice commands, and the extraction of the face and body of the user which is interacting with the installation. The first two installations are of real size persons (avatar or video), with the first using a holographic representation and the second a rear projection representation. The third is a prototype installation, combining a holographic representation of an object or face, with a screen where a menu is displayed. The area for the users' interaction with the PR changes in each of the three installations reaching, respectively, 57° (degrees), 180° and 360° in front of the installation.

The main contribution of this chapter is the development of a model that is capable of tracking users' sounds, position, and gestures inside the working range of the Microsoft Kinect sensors (Kinect, 2014) used in the installations. By installing several Microsoft Kinect sensors, all users are tracked on-the-fly, and the one closest to the installation is chosen to interact with it, by using the most appropriate sensor (depending on the installation). If no user is detected by the installation, the sensors search for a sound source, and when the location is fixed to the emitting sound source, the best-located sensor initiates voice command detection of small sentences or words.

A database is used to store the interactions, tracking data, user's extracted information (e.g., biometric information), allowing posterior statistical analysis, such as user's actions, favorite menus, etc. Currently, natural interaction (NI) is widely used for many different applications, but none of them have all the characteristics mentioned above.

The structure of the chapter is as follows: the present section introduces the subject and chapter goals. In the "Contextualization" section, the state of the art and the contextualization of the installations are presented. Section "Frontal Holographic Installation" presents the first of the three installations, which is a full sized holographic human PR installation, with all the necessary modules to support the interactions. Section "180° Rear Projection Installation" explains the advances between the frontal installation and the 180° installation, including the introduction of the rear projection. In Section "360° Interactive Public Relations" is again shown the advances from the 180° installation to a 360° Interactive PR. The final section summarizes the discussion, results and conclusion from all the installations.

CONTEXTUALIZATION

In the Time Machine movie (2002), directed by Simon Wells, the library scene features a hologram that hosts, communicates and interacts naturally with a time traveler. Amazingly, a product of this kind, operating in its fullness, does not yet exist, while the technology needed to develop it already does (Figueiredo et al., 2014). On the other hand, as mentioned in the introduction section, the markets are increasingly demanding these kind of products.

Holography is a technique for recording interference patterns of light that can generate or display images in three dimensions (António, Herrera, & Enriquez, 2013; Mihaylova, 2013). One of the most common technique to generate so called "holograms" is the Pepper's Ghost (Sprott, 2006), due to John Henry Pepper that popularized the effect. The Pepper's Ghost is an illusion technique used in theatre and in some magic tricks. In its basics, it is a combination of lighting techniques and a large piece of glass, forming a 45° angle with the audience, that present a combination of light passing through from behind the glass and light reflecting of the glass at a 90° angle from the line of sight of the viewers. The so-called "hologram" is actually an object or image hidden from the audience and reflected on a foil/glass. The best effect is achieved when using a dark background. An example applied to the theatre, illustrating the entire length technique, can be found in (Rennie, 2014). Another example is the D'Strict 3D Sensing Hologram Installation product (D'Strict, 2014), incorporating a hologram and a monitor in a small box, allowing interaction through gestures.

At the commercial level there are already some systems featuring, in some extend, the installations presented in this chapter, many of them reported on web sites, like Flyaway (Flyaway, 2015), where it is possible to find a Christie Digital film presenting a music concert by two hologram Musicians (based on Pepper's Ghost technique). This product consists on a projection system that lies between the stage and the audience and projects the characters to the stage, followed by a reflection through a mirror system, similar to the solution presented in Dimensional (2015). Another similar example, now at the level of airports, shows a hologram with human dimensions AVA (Advanced Virtual Avatar), used as a PR (AVA, 2015). However, none of the presented products follows the movement of the interlocutor (user) or allows the interaction with the hologram through its movements.

As already mentioned, the D'Strict has the "3D Sensing Hologram Installation" product (D'Strict, 2014), which includes a hologram and a small display box, where the gesture interaction is possible. However, the hologram is only visible frontally and dimensions are limited, roughly to 1.0×0.5 m (meters). The Active8-3D (2015) presents both medium and large holographic systems, where the holograms are only visible in front of the installation, with a limited interactivity, e.g., it uses a control to interact with the hologram. The same company introduced the 3D-holopyramid, an approach to the 360° hologram, but of reduced dimensions, with images ranging from 45×25 cm (centimeters) to 90×68 cm. The system does not allow interactivity and features angles where the hologram is not seen, losing the effect of a realistic 360° installation.

Also within the 360° projection there is the Litefast Magic Displays (Litefast, 2013). Although not visible when active, there is a mechanical system rotating at high speeds in a cylinder, limiting the product in terms of maintenance and particularly limiting the development of a full size PR. Also, no interactivity is present by the system. The Vizoo (2015), with its Cheoptics360 product, also presents a 360° and frontal solutions. In the 360° product, the object is projected onto a form of "Pyramid", implying again blind spots on the hologram (where you do not see the hologram correctly), with the product not presenting any interactivity. Paradigm (Rearpro, 2015) has a high number of products, several supporting interactivity. However, none of the solutions resembles the PRHOLO (PRHOLO-Holographic Public Relations) project desired effect, presented in this chapter, although the company is designated as one of the world's leaders in gesture-based systems and multi-touch interactivity. Canadian startup H+ Technology created a see-through tabletop box called Holus, presenting a tiny 3D digital world you can interact with (Holus, 2015), but is still a prototype under financing in Kickstarter.

There are also several solutions that use interactive systems with tables and screens. For instance, Vertigo (2015) has several solutions with a high level of interactivity. Other companies present solutions that incorporate some of features explained above. Examples are: Globalzepp (2015), Holodisplay (2015), AVconcepts (2015), Eonreality (2015), Xstage (2015), Holomedia (2015) and the Musion (2015) that present a set of solutions of holograms projected on various surfaces with various shapes and sizes, including 360°. It is possible to continue enumerating more examples of installations and companies that present products similar to the ones included in this chapter, but most of them are based on frontal holograms (Pepper's Ghost technique) or use the pyramid technique and none of those systems presents all the features developed in the installation introduced in this document.

While the Pepper's Ghost is one of the most commonly used techniques, there is also another technique that was proposed in 1908, by Professor Gabriel M. Lippmann from the French Academy of Sciences. It is based on a series of lenses placed on the surface of an image that creates a sense of depth called "La Photographie Integral" (Lippmann, 1908). This technique relies on recording of a full parallax image (including all the directions) using a spherical lens structure, known as fly's-eye lens, with both used to either capture or to represent pictures. The screen used was basically constituted by a large number of small convex lenses. In 1920, several scientists, including Herbert Ives, tried to simplify the solution proposed by Lippmann, introducing the sheet of lenticular lens solution. Each of these sheets are comprised of an array of fine, spherical lenses designed such that, when seeing from different angles, different pixels are displayed in a given image. To this end, on the opposite face of the sheet, which in use is rather flat, is placed an image specially constructed to fit the desired prospects. One of the first uses of these solutions, called lenticular printing, is widely known in the form of cards or other form of advertising in which, depending on the user's position, different images appear. Starting from the original solution, this technology has been used more recently to create 3D images on a flat screen.

The holodeck (Verge, 2015), a solution proposed by Microsoft, reuses the concept of "lenticular lens" to get a sense of depth and 3D. For this, multiple images are sent separated by a few degrees, allowing the reception of a "different image" in each eye. If different images are positioned according with the user's point of view then the holographic effect is obtained. Another example can be found in (Dick, Almeida, Soares, & Nunes, 2011).

There are still other solutions in research, such as TeleHuman (Kim, Bolton, Girouard, Cooperstock, & Vertegaal, 2012), which is a 3D videoconferencing system that supports 360° motion parallax, where a viewer moves around the cylinder and the projection follows him (Telehuman, 2013). However, this system has limitations when viewed by two or more observers, with one observer seeing the figure (avatar or video) and the remaining seeing the inverse of the picture or a "hole". In addition, the system does not follow the user who is interacting with the hologram. There are also mechanic systems, as the 360° system from the University of California (Jones, McDowall, Yamada, Bolas, & Debevec, 2007). Microsoft presents Vermeer (Butler et al., 2011), a display allowing visualization of 360° and interaction by touching on the display without the need of glasses or other instrumentation. However due to the small size and state of research, it seems that for now it is not applicable in real situations. Other applications are, for example, holographic desks for handling objects (Hilliges, Kim, Izadi, Weiss, & Wilson, 2012), and approaches that use computer graphics with interaction with holograms (Bimber, Zeidler, Rundhoefer, Wetzstein, & Moehring, 2005). More solutions exists, see e.g., the works of Lim and Kim (2014), Noor and Aras (2015), and Yamaguchi (2015).

In terms of user interaction, it can be done by using several different types of sensors and cameras. Usually it uses three-dimensional (3D) sensors, such as the Asus Xtion (Asus, 2014), the Microsoft Kinect (Kinect, 2014), or the Structure Sensor (Structure, 2014). All those sensors are very popular due to their hands free capability for controlling devices and graphical user interfaces, while tracking users' skeletons, recognizing joints and gestures of one or several users. Not all 3D sensors have this capability. The Leap Motion (Leap, 2014) sensor is also a 3D sensor, but it has only the capability to track hands and gestures (with finer details than the mentioned above). All these capabilities allow for what is now called natural interaction.

From the sensors mentioned above, the Microsoft's Kinect is one of the most famous 3D sensor on the market, popularized by the video gaming industry. In addition, this sensor is used in many applications, for example: in robotics (El-laithy, Huang, & Yeh, 2012), for head pose classification (Yun, Changrampadi, & Gu, 2014), enabling interaction with art installations (Alves et al., 2014; Weiss, Frid, Malin, & Ladijenski, 2015), applied in assistive technologies, such as enhancing visual performance skills on older adults (Chiang, Tsai, & Chen, 2012) or for the operation of wheelchairs (Kondori, Yousefi, Liu, & Li, 2014). More applications can be found, e.g., in (Cruz, Lucio, & Velho, 2012; Fong, Zhuang, Fister, & Fister, 2013; Kamizono, Abe, Baba, Takano, & Murakami, 2014; Cippitelli, Gasparrini, Gambi, & Spinsante, 2014; Rahman, Poon, Amin, & Yan, 2015; Gasparrini, Cippitelli, Spinsante, & Gambi, 2015). Interaction can also be achieved using other 3D sensors, like the Leap Motion, where the interaction with holograms for teaching technical drawings can be applied (Figueiredo et al., 2014). For the installations presented in this chapter up to eight Kinects were used.

FRONTAL HOLOGRAPHIC INSTALLATION

As mentioned briefly in the Introduction section, the frontal Public Relation installation consists of a human size holographic PR for an industrial (commercial) installation. The hologram can be represented by an avatar or a video from a real human PR, both allowing visualization of different contents (text, image, video, maps, etc.). The interactivity is achieved using a single Kinect sensor and based in very intuitive gestures. All interactions are recorded, creating and returning to the company key statistics about their main products, based on the attention given to each presented content, users' actions, favorite menus, viewing direction, face and body extraction, etc. (Alves et al., 2015a).

The holographic frontal installation uses the Pepper's Ghost technique for the hologram projection. As mentioned in the Contextualization section, this technique uses either a glass or a transparent acrylic, or also, for better results, a Mylar film in a 45° angle over the projected image, and the resulting holographic image appears in a 90° angle from the line of sight of the installation user/viewer. Figure 1 top row-left shows the illustration of this technique. More details on how to create the full sized holographic installation is out of the focus of this chapter, nevertheless, for more information about scaled installations see the works of Figueiredo et al. (2014) and Alves et al. (2015a). Also in Figure 1, in the middle is represented the position of the Kinect (necessary for the interaction) as well as the area it covers in front of the installation. On the second row-right is the illustration of the frontal installation.

Two main modules constitute the fontal installation: (a) Users Data Module, responsible for manipulating and handling the data received from the Kinect Sensor, creating statistics, reading gestures, head direction, body and face extraction, sound and RFID information. (b) Database and Interface Module,

Figure 1. Frontal installation, from top to bottom, left to right. Illustration of the holographic scheme using Pepper's Ghost technique. Representation of the position of the Kinect (necessary for the interaction, heat map, etc.) as well as the area it cover in from of the installation. Gestures representation ("pose" and "swipe"). The swipe gesture illustration. Example of a heat map and the user being mapped to matrix M. The illustration of the frontal installation. An illustration of a user looking to his right, center and left. Finally, the face and body extraction

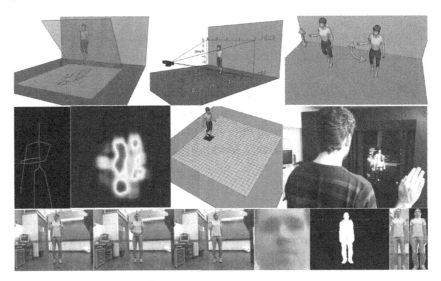

responsible for storing information gathered from the previous module, as well as the application configuration settings and interface options. In addition, it is responsible for displaying and processing the visual information, such as the virtual characters and menus. The following subsections will cover these modules in more detail.

Users Data Module

All the data from the Kinect sensor (Kinect, not Kinect 2) is handled and manipulated by the Users Data Module. For more details about Kinect, and how to program it see, e.g., Miles (2012). The sensor records sound using a four-microphone array, color (RGB), depth frames and the skeleton: 25 joints of 2 users and can track up to 6 individual users. The Kinect covers a space from about 0.8 m to 4 m, with 43° vertical by 57° horizontal field of view; as described in (Kinect, 2014; KinectSpec, 2014). All this data is handled and manipulated in 5 main phases: (a) Spatial information, (b) gestures recognition, (c) heat map, (d) user head direction, (e) body and face extraction, (f) sound extraction and (g) RFID module.

It is also important to stress that the initial implementation and tests of the user data modules were conducted with male subjects around 23 years old. Nevertheless, all the parameters presented in the phases described below were tested with male and female users, from 12 to 50 years, with heights from 1.40 to 1.90 meters. Interaction (user data module) tests are presented in (Alves et al., 2015c), which shows tests results for the 360° holographic installation (see below), which integrates results from the user data modules for all the installations presented here. No tests were done with elder persons or persons with any kind of motor deficiency.

Spatial Information

The frontal installation uses a single Kinect sensor ($i = 1$) in the top or bottom of the installation (in Figure 1 second row right, the sensor is near the floor). The user's spatial information (x, y, z) regarding theirs joints and their global position (P), are queued in two FIFO (First In, First Out) lists, one being used for the current detected users (Pc_i), and the other for the lost users (Pl_i). Every time new information is available, given by the Kinect sensor, three different scenarios may occur:

1. The *detection of a new user* is automatically added to the end of the current users list (Pc_i), as well as the information regarding all its joints, the time of entry (*t*) and an internal ID, which is incremented afterwards.
2. If the *detected new user already exists*, then the new information is stored with the previous information onto the current users list as well as the time of entry of the new information.
3. In the case where the *user is lost*, then all information regarding that user is updated to the database (see below, Section Database and Interface Module), and the user is added to the lost users list and removed from the current users list.

Gestures Recognition

The users can interact with the installation using gestures (Alves et al., 2015a; 2015b). The gestures are used as an input for the hands free system. After experimenting with several different gestures, the "swipe gesture" and the "pose gesture" were chosen because of their intuitive nature. Figure 1, first row right illustrates the two gestures, in the most left side the "pose", and on the most right the "swipe". The implementation consists in:

1. The *pose gesture* can be detected using a vector defined by the arm, $\overrightarrow{V_a}$, calculated by subtracting the *hand* (right/left) position (P_h), from the *elbow* (right/left) position (P_e), and using the user's body vector $\overrightarrow{V_b}$, that is calculated by subtracting the *shoulder center* position (P_{sc}), from the *spine* position (P_s) (Kinect, 2014). In order to validate a menu pose gesture, the following conditions have to be met:

   a. The user is considered doing the gesture only if the distance between the *elbow* and the Kinect must be approximately the same as the *hand* and the Kinect, $|z_h - z_e| \geq 0.6d(P_h, P_e)$, where d is the Euclidean distance, and z_h and z_e are the *z-axis* coordinates of the *hand* and *elbow* respectively. Also, of course, the user needs to be facing the Kinect.

   b. Plus, the angle between $\overrightarrow{V_a}$ and $\overrightarrow{V_b}$ has to be between $20° \leq \theta \leq 160°$, with $\theta = \text{acos}\left(\left(\overrightarrow{V_b}.\overrightarrow{V_a}\right) / \left(\left\|\overrightarrow{V_b}\right\|\left\|\overrightarrow{V_a}\right\|\right)\right)$.

   c. To increase the reliability of the pose gesture it is verified if at least 85% out of the previous detections made in the past 1 s (second) are according to the above conditions. If the user is performing the pose gesture, it is considered:
      i. up, if the angle θ is less than 90°;
      ii. down, otherwise.

2. The *swipe gesture* requires a minimum swipe speed velocity of $v_s = 200$ cm/s and a minimum swipe distance of $d_s = 30$ cm. These values were empirically chosen, after experimenting with different users. By analyzing only user information acquired from current instance t to $t - \Delta t_s$, with Δt_s a time window computed using $\Delta t_s = d_s / v_s$, a swipe was made if in any other sub-interval Δt_k (defined $[t, t - \Delta t_s]$), with k the latest instance of Δt_k, all *hand* positions (h) have the same signal along the whole interval Δt_k. The hand positions are computed using the current hand position subtracted by its previous hand position, taking only into account the x component for the horizontal swipe, or the y component for the vertical swipe ($|\sum_{j=k-\Delta t_k}^{k-1} \text{sgn}\left(h_{j+1,\{x,y\}} - h_{j,\{x,y\}}\right)| = k - 1$), and if the total distance travelled, taking only into account the *x/y* component respectively for the horizontal and vertical swipe, between the first and the last point of that sequence is greater or equals to $d_s \geq |h_{k,\{x,y\}} - h_{k-\Delta t_k,\{x,y\}}|$.

Figure 1, second row left illustrates a horizontal swipe movement, and in the same row right the user is doing a pose gesture.

Heat Map

The heat map (Alves et al., 2015a) can be useful for obtain statistics about the most active locations of a user or a group of users. The users' global position (*P*) returned by Kinect, represents the distance in each axis between the Kinect and the user, with the x and z axis constituting the horizontal and vertical distance respectively, as shown in Figure 1 top row middle. As mentioned before, it is assumed that the physical limits of the Kinect is 4 m in length and in width (Kinect, 2014; KinectSpec, 2014). A matrix M with size of $N \times N$ can be created, with $N = 26\,px$ (pixels), dividing the region in squares of approximately $4 / N \times 4 / N$ m, where each square has the area of approximately 0.024 m^2 (see Figure 1, second row and third column). A user position detected from Kinect on instance t is mapped to matrix M using $(x_t,\ y_t) = (-x_{k_t} \times (N / 4) + N / 2, z_{kt} \times (N / 4))$, with x_k and z_k the coordinates obtained from Kinect. Starting with M equal to the null matrix, every detection made at instance t increments the mapped entry value, as well as its 8 neighbours: $M\left(x_t + i,\ y_t + j\right) = M\left(x_{t-1} + i,\ y_{t-1} + j\right) + 1$, with $i, j = \{-1, 0, 1\}$. After this step, the matrix M holds estimated values for the positions of a user, or group of users. The matrix is then normalized and converted to a color map using JET color map. Figure 1, second row and column shows the heat map of a single user during the interaction with the installation for a period of more or less 15 minutes.

User's Head Direction

One of the installations' goals is to know whether the user is watching or not to it. In other words, an objective is to estimate the time spent by the user in interactive activities with the installation (e.g., doing gestures, reading the available information, and/or seeing images/videos). Due to the Kinect color resolution, getting the precise point the user is looking at, i.e., "eye-tracking" (Martins, Rodrigues, & Martins, 2015), is quite difficult and imprecise.

For that reason, the computation of where the user's head is facing to was implemented as an alternative. That estimation was achieved employing reference points (Alves et al., 2015a). First, the position of the user's eyes was obtained using the Kinects SDK, see Figure 1 bottom left (read dots). Those eyes' positions are then combined with the *shoulders'* (S) positions (left, center and right), marked with black dots (on the shoulders) in the same figure. Using the coordinates of this set of points, a vector $\vec{V_s} = \left(x_{Sl} - x_{Sr}, y_{Sl} - y_{Sr}\right)$ is obtained as well as its normal vector $\vec{V}' = \left(-V_{Sy}, V_{Sx}\right)$. Vector $\vec{V_s}$ defines the direction containing both shoulders' points and, in order to compute it, the positions of the *left shoulder* (*l*) and the *right shoulder* (*r*) are used, i.e., $\vec{S}_{l/r} = \left(x_{S_l/S_r}, y_{S_l/S_r}\right)$. In the same figure, the sketched vertical (or almost vertical) blue line corresponds to the "application" $\vec{V}'$ to the *shoulders' center* position (Kinect, 2014). Three different scenarios can happen, i.e., a user can have:

1. An eye on each side of the blue line (Figure 1 bottom left-center), meaning that the user is looking to the front.
2. Both eyes can be placed on the left side of the blue line (Figure 1 bottom left-left), thus the user is looking to the right.
3. Alternatively, the user can have both eyes placed on the right side of the blue line, (Figure 1 bottom left-right), determining that the user is looking left.

Depending on the user's position, extreme left and right directions where excluded and a timer was implemented in order to count the time a user spent looking at each direction.

Body and Face Extraction

One of the features of the installation allows face or body "selfies" which, for instance, can be used for "promotional gifts" or, under the user request, to be inserted in a social network. The face extraction is done directly by Kinect SDK (Kinect, 2014), see Figure 1 bottom row, 4th column. However, the full body photo is not directly achieved from the SDK, which is done as explained next.

Every time a new depth frame from the sensor is available, the first three bits represent which user that pixel belong to, from 1 to 6, with 0 representing the background. For each user a Boolean mask is constructed (Figure 1 bottom row, 5th column) and the contours are smoothed using a Gaussian filter ($\sigma = 2$). The next step determines the highest and lowest coordinates values, $x_{min/max}$ and $y_{min/max}$, of the Boolean mask, which are used to crop the color image and optionally applying the Boolean mask itself. The illustration of the resulting images is shown in Figure 1 bottom row, from the 5th to the 7th column.

Sound Extraction

Each Kinect is equipped with a built-in microphone array, composed of 4 microphones that enable sound extraction. With this setup the microphone array is capable of sound source location formally entitled beam forming, that is, the capacity of calculating differences between captured audio streams and estimating the sound source direction. For each Kinect, the audio beam angle range, covers 100° in front of itself, 50° from the center to each side (Kinect, 2014). The beam angle can be one of 11 different values, an integer multiple of 10 ranging from -50 to 50 including 0. Each of this values represent sound source directions, for each sound source located. In addition, the Kinect SDK also estimates a confidence level (Kinect, 2014) of that estimation, with values ranging from 0.0 to 1.0, where 0.0 represents no confidence and 1.0 maximum confidence. The Kinect SDK supports speech recognition in several languages, allowing the detection of words or sentences captured by the microphone array.

The installation saves the direction from where the sound appears, but more importantly, the system has a list of "keywords" and "key-phrases" (saved in a GRXML file) that when identified and confirmed (using the available functions in Kinect SDK) trigger a response using a stored answer, which uses an implemented text-to-speech functionality or, optionally, a ".wav" pre-recorder sentence. The keywords can also trigger actions similar to the gesture interaction.

In general, if during 30 s (configurable) there are no gesture, or user detected, but there are sounds which do not produce recognized words, then the installation returns an audio personalized message to call the attention to itself.

RFID Module

The RFID module was developed to allow Radio-Frequency Identification (RFID) interaction between the installation (RFID's passive reader) and users badges (RFID's passive tags), in the form of ID cards. An RFID receiver module (RFID, 2014) is attached to the installation and connected to the on-board computer. A user can pass his/her badge in front the installation's RFID receiver module to interact with the installation.

This interaction can be materialized in several different ways, e.g., to welcome guests in a special event by a vocal and a visual greeting from the installation. For instance, the guests' names can be previously stored in a database (see next section) and, when the RFID matches the ID from the RFID card, the system uses text-to-speech to greet the guest. This application is an integral part of the system as a hole, and can be activated and deactivated whenever necessary.

Database and Interface Module

In this section, the main features of the database will be will briefly explained. The database is supported on a relational database management system, namely MySQL. There are two types of information stored in the database module:

1. Statistics and
2. Menus and configurations, i.e., information for and from the interface module.

For the first case, statistics, the information stored in the database is been discussed along the chapter, i.e., the module stores the acquired data from all of the installation's inputs devices (e.g., user's ID, number of users, time present in front of the installation, time interacting with the installation and with each menu, time spend looking into the installation, user(s) positions, gestures, interactions, visualizations, and biometry).

For the second case, menus and configurations, the interface module is responsible for reading the information stored in the database and then uses it to generate graphical user interface layouts, and responses to the users' inputs. The layouts can be generated by the application supported on

1. Menu title contents which serve as links to other menus,
2. By fitting small text descriptions, or
3. Images, video and other media content, with the respective descriptions, in order to give the user a more appealing explanation.

Besides the contents, other configuration are also stored in the database, e.g., the orientation of the layouts with options like diagonal or vertical. An option for displaying only video or images is available. This data (layout and configurations data) is loaded from the database when the application starts. The use of the database provides easier modification, updates and synchronization between multiples installation.

In terms of the Interface Module, user's inputs generate responses from the PR avatar or video. For example, if a new user starts interacting with the installation, the video/avatar waves their hand (or any other predefined movement) and shows the user's photo on the display. In another example, if the user selects a menu option then avatar/video triggers the menu change by "touching" the menu.

It is important to reinforce, that all interaction data is saved on the database, such as the time spent interacting with menus, requests of content provided by the installation, etc. Finally, it is also important to recall that the installation presented in Figure 1 second row right is an holographic representation, in this case of an avatar of a lady, with 1.70 m height.

180° REAR PROJECTION INSTALLATION

In this section the modifications done to the frontal installation to cope with a set of Kinects will be explained. The system is illustrated using a rear projection installation, although the software development and interaction is exactly the same using a full human size rear projection or a holographic installation.

Two main problems were detected in some situations when using the previous installation (Frontal Holographic Installation), namely:

1. It occupies a considerable space to project a real size person, and
2. The interaction can only occur when the user is in front of the installation (due to the Kinect limitations).

Also the price of the installation is of some concern.

The first problem (as well as the installation price) can be solved by using a rear projection installation instead of a holographic installation. Although the rear projection installation is less impactful than the holographic one, this is an option that each company can take.

The second problem can easily be solved by making use of four Kinect sensors instead of using a single one. The use of four Kinetics, organized in a way that optimizes overlapping areas from their neighbor sensors (see Figure 2 first row left), allows to capture a 180° field of view. Figure 2 first row right shows a snapshot of real time data streaming obtained from the Kinects' system, with the RGB information in the top, the depth information (the whiter the closest to the Kinect sensor) in the middle, and the skeletons (in green) at the bottom. In the top of each image is shown the number of frames per second (fps) that each Kinect is acquiring at the moment.

Now, the application is composed by 3 modules (Alves et al., 2015b):

1. Users' Data Module, similar to the one in the frontal installation, is responsible for manipulating and handling data received from each of the Kinect Sensors (creating statistics, reading gestures and sounds, etc.);
2. Global Management Module (new module), responsible for converting the users' spatial information, obtained from each individual sensor, to a global reference system and disambiguate users that are detected by multiple Kinects; and
3. Database and Interface Module (similar to the frontal installation), responsible for storing information gathered from the set of sensors as well as the global information (retrieved by the Global Management Module).

Similar to the frontal installation, the Database and Interface Module has also at is charge the application's configuration settings and interface options, and is responsible for displaying and processing the visual information (texts and menus).

To implement the present solution, three physical properties are needed from the Kinects' system:

1. The Kinects relative position $C_i(x, y, z)$ in a global reference (red dot in Figure 2 second row left), where $i = 0..3$ represents the Kinect index,
2. Their horizontal rotation β_i, and

Figure 2. 180° installation. From left to right, and top to bottom: the physical installation layout. Real time data streaming from 4 Kinects: RGB, depth and skeletons. 180° Kinect coordinate system, the physical coordinates and angles relative to each Kinects. A real time sound source beams example from all 4 Kinects, in a polar plot. A map of 4 users in front of the installation and the respective heat map from the previous users (5 minutes) represented on a JET color map. Finally, examples of the installation working

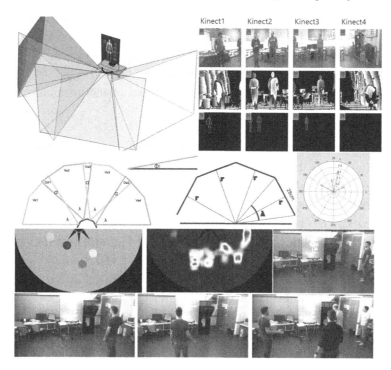

3. Their vertical angle ϕ_i. Parameter β_i and ϕ_i represent the frontal directions of each sensor.

The Kinects SDK has built in methods for retrieving the vertical angle. In order to determine the Kinect's position, C_i, the horizontal angle they are facing has to be calculated first. As already mentioned, the installation captures a 180° angle, visible in Figure 2 second row left, where the intersection angle (α) between Kinects' views can be obtained by solving equation $180 = 4 \times \lambda - 3 \times \alpha$, where $\lambda = 57°$ is the Kinect's horizontal field of view angle (Kinect, 2014), which gives $\alpha = 16°$. The horizontal angles β_i can be calculated, starting with the Kinect on the right and counter-clockwise (Figure 2 second row left): $\beta_0 = \lambda / 2 = 28.5°$ and $\beta_l = \beta_{l-1} + \lambda - \alpha$, with $l = 1..3$ returning $\beta_1 = 69.5°$, $\beta_2 = 110.5°$ and $\beta_3 = 151.5°$.

Positions C_i would ideally be the same for all Kinects, but because the Kinect's width is $w_{KS} = 28$ cm (Kinect, 2014) this is not physically possible. Therefore, the Kinect sensors need to be distanced from the center point by a distance r in the direction of the angle they are facing (Figure 2 second row middle). The distance can be calculated using $r = w_{KS} / \left(2 \times \tan\left((\beta_1 - \beta_0) / 2\right)\right)$, resulting in $r \approx 36$ cm. Position C_i can be calculated using $C_i(x,y,z) = (r \times \cos(\beta_i), 0, r \times \sin(\beta_i))$, thus $C_0(x,y,z) \approx (32, 0, 17)$ cm, $C_1(x,y,z) \approx (12, 0, 34)$ cm, $C_2(x,y,z) \approx (-12, 0, 34)$ cm and

$C_3\left(x,y,z\right) \approx \left(-32,0,17\right)$ cm. With all C_i values and r calculated for the positioning of the sensors, it is now possible to program the components of the NI model.

Global Management Module

The Global Management Module, as the name refers, is responsible of managing users, sounds detected by the Kinects, selecting the user that is interacting (gesture/sound) with the installation, creating a global reference, and solving inconsistencies when two Kinects detect the same user because of the overlapping areas on their field of view. Working similar as the Users Data Module, the Global Management consists of two FIFO lists: one containing the current detected users Gc and the other for lost users Gl.

Global Reference Conversion

Once the update of all the Users Data Modules are done, users from Pc_i, their values are transformed to a global reference and positioned onto an array of potential users, Uc. The coordinates returned by the Kinect are converted from the coordinates shown in Figure 1 top middle, to a global reference, that can be seen in Figure 2, third row left. In the figure aforementioned, the lighter area represents the interaction zone that starts from the center of the Kinect group, having a 4-meter radius.

On the same image, each user is represented by a circle, occupying approximately 50 cm. The conversion of the Kinects coordinates to a global reference system, where the x axis grows from left to right, the y axis grows from up to down, and the z axis is the depth distance, is necessary for the Kinects physical layouts, as well as the distances between each other and their rotation in the horizontal plane (β_i) and vertical plane (ϕ_i).

For each Kinect sensor a coordinate unitary vector is determined for each axis: $\overrightarrow{V_a}$ representing the vector of the axis the Kinect is facing, $\overrightarrow{V_b}$ representing the axis with an horizontal 90° to $\overrightarrow{V_a}$ and $\overrightarrow{V_c}$ representing the third axis with 90° to both $\overrightarrow{V_a}$ and $\overrightarrow{V_b}$ pointing upwards in relation to Kinect. The three vectors can be computed as

$$\overrightarrow{V_a}\left(x,y,z\right) = \left(\cos\left(\beta_i\right) \times \sin\left(\pi/2+\phi_i\right), \cos\left(\pi/2+\phi_i\right), \sin\left(\beta_i\right) \times \sin\left(\pi/2+\phi_i\right)\right),$$

$$\overrightarrow{V_b}\left(x,y,z\right) = \left(\cos\left(\beta_i+\pi/2\right) \times \sin\left(\pi/2+\phi_i\right), \cos\left(\pi/2+\phi_i\right), \sin\left(\beta_i+\pi/2\right) \times \sin\left(\pi/2+\phi_i\right)\right),$$

and

$$\overrightarrow{V_c}\left(x,y,z\right) = \left(\cos\left(\beta_i\right) \times \sin\left(\phi_i\right), \cos\left(\phi_i\right), \sin\left(\beta_i\right) \times \sin\left(\phi_i\right)\right).$$

The Kinect SDK returns a user's joint positions, $\dot{J}$, in meters. The new position in the global reference, Ig, can now be calculated, in meters, by $Ig = \left(J_x \times \overrightarrow{V_a} + J_y \times \overrightarrow{V_c} + J_z \times \overrightarrow{V_a} + C_i\right)/100$ m. Jg

represents the conversion of any joint or a user's global position from any sensor to the global reference system. By using this transformation, we denote Pg as the global position of the user and, finally, all users are mapped onto the same global reference system, see Figure 2 third row left (Alves et al., 2015b).

Detecting the Same User in Multiple Kinects

In a multiple Kinect configuration, the field of view of a Kinect overlaps the ones of the neighbor Kinects and vice versa (Figure 2 top left), which led to the implementation of a method to determine if the same user is being detected by two neighbor Kinects.

The method compares the users on Uc with each other to find if they might be the same user, using the following cumulative criteria:

1. The Euclidean distance between the global positions of the two compared users (for instance Pg_1 and Pg_2) is less than 50 cm and the two users were detected by different Kinects

2. Given the last $T = 5$ skeletons information, the global position variation on all axis are similar, i.e.,
$$(|\,Pg_{1/2,x}\left(\delta\right) - Pg_{1/2,x}\left(\delta - 1\right)| < 15\,\text{cm}) \wedge \qquad (|\,Pg_{1/2,y}\left(\delta\right) - Pg_{1/2,y}\left(\delta - 1\right)| < 15\,\text{cm}) \wedge$$
$(|\,Pg_{1/2,z}\left(\delta\right) - Pg_{1/2,z}\left(\delta - 1\right)| < 15\,\text{cm})$, with $\delta = \left\{t,...,t - T\right\}$ (then it is assumed that both users are in fact the same user).

If the relation between the users was found, the newest user will be forced to change his/her internal ID to the internal ID of the oldest detected user. If the two users have the same internal ID, then they are automatically associated as being the same user, meaning that the association was already established in a previous situation. In any of the cases, the closest user to its Kinect will be marked and added to the end of the Gc list, with the other removed from that list.

The threshold values mentioned in this subsection were determined empirically. Nevertheless, the above mentioned 50 cm were considered as the minimum space that a user/person occupies and the 15 cm, which is roughly 1/3 of that length, was considered the minimum value an user can slightly move but still be in the same place/be the same person (we can call it "personal space").

Updating, Adding and Removing Users

Upon completing the previous step, the marked users will be added to the current users' list, Gc, where a detected user can be either completely new in the list, or can be already an existing user of Gc, but with new information. The users marked as new (are stored in Uc, being represented by u_l, with l ranging from 0 to the size of array Uc), are compared to each user already on Gc (where the user is gc_j, with j ranging from 0 to size of list Gc). If both users u_l and gc_j have the same internal ID, then the user gc_j will be updated with the last skeleton (global reference) of the user u_l. On the other hand, if user u_l does not have the same ID with any user of G_c then u_l is a new user and will be inserted at the end of the list Gc.

An occlusion detection method was developed in order to recover lost users, necessary because sometimes users can block the Kinect's view. A verification in the lost users list Gl for Δt seconds is made when a new user is detected. For all of the last positions of all lost users (k) for the previous Δt

seconds, Gl_k, the current position of a detected user (u), Gu_c, is considered to belong to a previous user if the Euclidean distance $d_{i,u}$ between Gl_i and Gc_u is less than 50 cm. The closest distance d is chosen if more than one lost uses is closer than 50 cm to the position P_u, recovering all information to the current users list Gc (empirically it was used $\Delta t = 5$ s).

The user that will be selected to interact with the installation is the one in the Gc list that is close to the installation, and maintains this status until he leaves the 180° space analyzed by the system. However, if the user leaves the space or does not have any type of movement during 30 seconds then the selected user will correspond to the next element in the Gc list that is close to the installation.

180° Heat Map

As mentioned in the Heat Map in the frontal installation section, the users' heat map is one of the most important features, being very useful to obtain statistics about the installation surroundings, including most active locations (and the times spent on those locations) of a group of users or a single user. The heat map is calculated by using the user's global position (Pg). Furthermore, the heat map region has approximately 8 × 4 meters, given by the physical range limits of the Kinects (a little bellow 4 meters; (Kinect, 2014)). To be more precise, it is approximately a semi-circle with a 4 m radius and center in the middle of the Kinect sensor group (see Figure 2 third row right).

As in the frontal installation, the heat map is transformed now into a *HM* matrix with a $2N \times N$ size, creating a new map divided by small squares of approximately $(4/N) \times (4/N)$ m. Also similar to the frontal installation, the value of N was 26 px, resulting in a 0.024m² square area. The remaining process is exactly equal to the one done for the heat map in the frontal installation. Figure 2 third row middle shows the heat map where several users (4) are moving during 5 minutes in front of the installation.

Sound

The installation is capable of detecting sound source angles and interact with users even if they are not present in from of it. As mentioned before, the Kinect sensor is capable of speech recognition, however in a 4 Kinect configuration (180° installation), where 16 microphones are present (4 × 4), the Kinect that is most frontal do the sound source location must be selected to handle the speech recognition.

As mentioned, the Kinect has the capability of detecting the sound source location within a 100° angle. In a 4 Kinect configuration, where the sensors are positioned side by side and misaligned from each other, the total aggregated audio source range is calculated by summing the 100° angle from each Kinect minus the 3 overlapping areas (O_a), that exist due to the adjacent positioning of the multiple Kinect's close to each other. The total audio source range of this 4 Kinects configuration is given by S_d $\approx 223°$ ($S_d = 4 \times 100° - 3 \times O_a$), that is greater than the field of view of 180°.

Because of the wide angle of the audio range obtained from 4 Kinects, a transformation was applied to all individual audio beam angles, converting the 223° range into a 180° range, $\varphi_t = \varphi_o \times 180 / S_d$, where φ_t represents the transformed angle and φ_o the original audio beam angles. By doing this transformation, the resulting location of the sound source will become distorted from the real sound source location (i.e. captured), nevertheless, since the objective is just to select witch Kinect will be responsible for handling speech recognition this small distortion will not influence the selection. An alternative solution would be to clip all sound information from the audio source inside the range $[-(S_d - 180)/2, 0]$ and $[180, 180 + (S_d - 180)/2]$ degrees. To determine which Kinect will handle speech recognition when a user is interacting with the system using their voice or when environmental sound is detected, the following algorithm is applied:

1. Read the sound beam and confidence levels from all 4 Kinects microphones.
2. For each Kinect sum and store the result of the audio beam angles multiplied by the respective confidence levels.
3. For filtering isolated sounds and noise, step ii) is repeated several times (10 times).
4. After step iii) is done it is determined which of the sums has the greatest value.
5. If there is a tie or a close tie (between 5% of the highest value), the selection is done by selecting the value that has the sound beam closest to 0° (corresponding to the most frontal sound relative to the middle of the Kinect).
6. The Kinect associated to the maximum computed value will be chosen to process the speech recognition.

Figure 2 second row right displays a polar plot containing real time sound source beams from 4 Kinects. In this case the selected Kinect was the second from the right.

In terms of speech recognition, the process is similar to the frontal installation, after the selection of the active sensor. The Kinect captures sounds from the users words and sentences and compares them with the ones stored on the speech SDK, and then detects with a degree of certainty if the word is valid or not. If a keyword is detected and confirmed the application triggers a response using a pre-stored answer (using text-to-speech) using a synthesized voice or a pre-recorded voice. Actions can also be triggered by keywords similar to the gesture interaction (the same as the frontal installation). When the installation does not detect sound for 30 seconds, it emits a pre-recorded message through its speakers to call attention to itself (this is only done if no user is interacting with the installation).

Database and Interface Module

This module is exactly the same as the frontal installation. Figure 2 second row right and bottom row shows the prototype installation with several users interacting whit it.

360° INTERACTIVE HOLOGRAPHIC PUBLIC RELATIONS

The 360° holographic installation, is very similar in terms of development to the 180°. The main differences are: (a) is also a holographic installation (as the frontal installation), with a holographic projection that can, in this case, be seen from a 360° degree walk. (b) The interaction can be done by 4 or 8 Kinect sensors, which are put in a "circular" (hexagonal) disposition, where the center is the hologram.

In terms of the holographic installation, it continues to use the Pepper's Ghost technique, but now, the area of projection is divided in 8 slices, i.e., the holographic display is composed by an 8 sided prism made from acrylic. A short throw projector projects the image onto a special acrylic in a rear projection way, which is then reflected by an 8 sided prism, giving the ("illusion" of a) hologram fluting inside of the 8 prism structure. Each volume to be holographic projected object is also divided in 8 views. Each view will be projected in each slice of the holographic projection. Figure 3 first and second rows left, shows the representation of the installation, with the field of view of each Kinect sensor, bottom two rows show the installation working. More details about the technique of projection is out of the focus of this Chapter (Alves et al., 2015c).

In term of interaction (b) the installation can use from 4 to 8 Kinects. Figure 3 first row center, shows the RGB, depth and skeletons from the 8 installation Kinects. In the case of 4 Kinects they are organized in a cross "+" while in the case of 8 Kinects they are placed forming an octagon around the installation, as shown in see Figure 3, first and second row left, where the blue field of views represents the 4 Kinects and the blue plus the red the 8 Kinects. As already mentioned, in this installation, each Kinect sensor

Figure 3. 360° holographic installation. From Left to right, and top to bottom: The holographic representation of the installation with the 8 field of views of the Kinects sensors; RGB, depth and skeleton for each of the 8 sensors; Real time sound sources beams example, from the 8 Kinects configuration, in a polar plot; A second view of the holographic installation; the 360° Kinect coordinate system; the physical coordinates and angles relative to each Kinect; A map of users in front of the installation and the respective heat map represented on a JET color map for the 8 and 4 Kinects configuration; And examples of the installation working

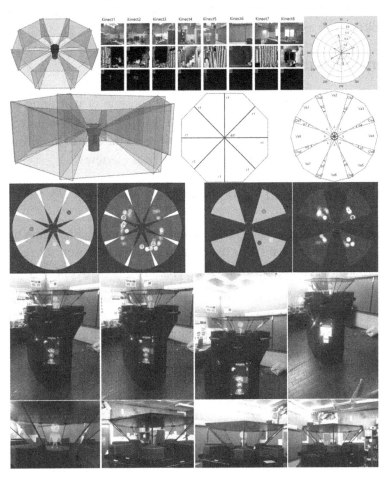

is positioned in a hexagonal way, side by side from each other, at the same distance to the center of the installation. Being $r1$ ($r1 = 60$ cm, for the present installation) the distance from the center of the hexagon where the holographic projection is shown to the Kinect. Each Kinect is positioned perpendicular to the line where the distance $r1$ is calculated, being their lines drawn with a 45° angle from each other (or 90° angle in the case of using only 4 Kinects); see Figure 3 second row and column.

Regarding the configuration of the 4 Kinects, four zones were considered. Each of these zones have a 33° angle that is not covered by the interaction ("dead zones"), i.e., as already mentioned, each Kinect can cover around a radius of 4 meters in front of it, with a 57° horizontal field of view (thus four Kinects can cover $4 \times 57° = 228°$). The uncovered angle is 132°, which divided by 4 parts results in a 33° angle (see Figure 3 third row and column). In the case of using 8 Kinects there is an overlap angle between to neighbor Kinects of 12°. Again, this angle can be obtained by multiplying the number of Kinect by their field of view ($4 \times 57° = 456°$), subtracting 360° and dividing the total overlap area by 8 (($456°-360°$) / $8 = 12°$), see Figure 3 second row right and third row left. The Kinect position C_i, for $i = 1..4$ and $i = 1..8$ (4 and 8 Kinects), can be calculated using $C_i\left(x, y, z\right)$ as shown in the 180° installation, but now using $r1$ and the angles mentioned above (see also Figure 3 second row right). In the following sections the differences between the 180° and 360° installation will be described in terms of interaction.

The application was developed as in the 180° installation, with three modules that have the same functionalities, namely: (a) Users Data Module, (b) Global Management Module and (c) Database and Interface Module. The first one is exactly the same as shown before. The other two modules are similar, nevertheless some differences exist.

Global Management Module

The 360° Global Management Module, as the 180°, is responsible of managing the users, the sound detected by each Kinect, selecting the user that is interacting with the installation, creating a global reference, and solving inconsistencies when 2 side-by-side Kinects (in the case of the 8 Kinects configuration) detect the same user due to the overlapping areas on their field of view.

Detecting, Updating, Adding and Removing Users

The process of detecting, updating, adding and removing users applies the same methods as the 180° installation: making use of two global FIFO lists, one for the current users Gc and other for the lost users Gl. Users are added or removed based on the separated FIFO lists of each Kinect Pc_i (current users) and Pl_i (lost users). However, the problem where adjacent Kinects detect two users only persists on the 8 Kinects configuration, since the 4 Kinects configuration has no overlapping areas. Therefore, the algorithm presented in Section "Detecting the Same User in Multiple Kinects" is applied to the 8 Kinect configuration, where the Gc and Gl FIFO lists will have the exact same users as the union of the Pc_i and Pl_i lists. In the case of the 4 Kinects configuration it is not possible to determine (with the algorithms shown in this Chapter) if a user/person is moving from one Kinect field of view to other Kinect field of view.

To solve this problem a solution was implemented that allows a user to leave the area of interaction with the installation and return to it a few minutes or hours later, and still be recognized as the same user. For details about this implementation, see the work of Alves et al. (2015c).

Sound

As mentioned, in a 4 Kinect configuration there are a total of 4 microphone arrays composed by and aggregate of 16 microphones. As stated before, each Kinect can capture 100° degrees of audio in front of it, resulting in 400° of audio source location. The 100° range from each Kinect was firstly normalized to a 90° range. This transformation allows a 360° audio source location. In the 8 Kinect configuration there are a total of 8 microphone arrays composed by and aggregate of 32 microphones, resulting in 800° of audio source location, and the normalization has done to 45°. This transformation also allows a 360° audio source location instead of the 800°. The above distortions does not significantly change the audio source locations, because the final resulting audio source location is extrapolated using the distorted audio source locations from several Kinects. The implemented algorithm for beam audio source was the same as 180° installation. Figure 3 first row right represents the real time audio beam angle sources captured and transformed in a polar plot. In this case, the Kinect sensor selected to do the sound functions, such as speech recognition, was the one corresponding to the longest vector (Kinect number 2, in the example).

360° Heat Map

In this installation the heat map has the shape of a ring, with the inner radius, of the inside circle, approximately equal to 0.6 m, and the outer radius approximately equal to 4.6 meters (both counting from the central point/middle of the 360° installation). The computation and update of the heat map is done as presented for the 180° installation. The second and fourth columns of Figure 3 third row shows, for a group of 4 persons moving around the installation for about 5 minutes, the heat maps represented as JET color map for the 360° installation with 8 and 4 Kinects, respectively. In this case, it was verified that in both configurations some persons were quite static in several locations, creating the red circular blogs presented in the images.

Database and Interface Module

This module is exactly the same as the one for the frontal and the 180° installations. The last two rows of Figure 3 show the prototype installation. Nevertheless, in this installation, due to its specification, the menu is presented in a LED screen (see also the illustration shown in Figure 3 second row left). Alternatively, 8 LED screens could be used with the menus duplicated in each screen, one for each view of the hologram which is located in the top of the installation. This allows the hologram (mainly with an avatar representation) to follow the user when he is moving inside the interaction region (see Figure 3, bottom row). The hologram will always be with its frontal representation turned to the field of view of the selected user, even when the user is not gesturally interacting with the installation, but continues moving inside the interaction region, or giving voice commands/demands, and the installation (hologram) is responding to him/her.

Another implemented functionality turns the frontal view of the hologram to the biggest sound source when no user is present, followed by a sound calling the attention of a possible future user to the installation.

CONCLUSION

In this chapter, three interactive complementary installations were presented, based on a model for natural interaction. A hologram (avatar or video) replaces a public relations person, establishing the first contact between a company and a potential client. The installations are capable of recognizing sound sources and voice commands while interacting with sound and gestures.

The fully customizable nature of the application is a major asset. The application is also capable of extracting statistics about the user's gestures and positions at any instance of time, the most requested contents, as well as the time spent by users in each of the contents. The installation works in a frontal (57°), 180° and 360° interaction environment. When a user is interacting with the installation, the gesture commands are obtained tracking his joints. Two main gestures were considered: (a) the swipe gestures and (b) pose gesture. Swipe gestures recognition can fail when the user does it with lack of speed or extend (distance). As for the pose gesture, it allows users' easy navigation through the menus. There were no noticeable failures in its recognition, except to the lack of speed or extend (distance), as previously.

Results regarding the recognition of multiple detections of a user have also shown good outcomes, even in complex environments, with errors susceptible of occurring in two situations.

1. In the case of the 180° installation and the 360° installation with 8 Kinect sensors, the users' tracking can fail if they abruptly change their positions (e.g., run) or are not facing the center of the installation. These errors result mainly from the small overlap area of the two neighbor Kinects. The possible incapability of tracing abrupt changes of position is due to one of the limitations of Kinect sensors, which does not detect well users when they are sideways to it. On the other hand, results on recovering users were satisfactory. If a Kinect is obstructed and a user does not move, then it works as expected, as long as the obstruction doesn't take too long. However, if the user moves to a different location, the results have shown not to be so reliable. In addition, if another user switches position with the obstructed user, then he/she will be recognized as the user that switched places with.
2. The second pitfall occurs in the case of the 360° installation with 4 Kinects, where it is not possible (at the moment) to track a user that "moves" from one Kinect to another. In these cases, the user is lost and a new user is created as he/she switch between Kinect areas.

Current work focuses in the solving of the above problem (Alves et al., 2015c), by improving obstruction and overlap difficulties, as well as users leaving the installation and returning back a few minutes/ hours later. To achieve this last feature, biometric information, such as distance between joints, color descriptors in each joint, and face recognition (when possible), is being used. Future work includes the prediction of user movements to increase certainty about the user position inside the interaction region.

ACKNOWLEDGMENT

This work was supported by projects PRHOLO QREN I&DT, nr. 33845 and FCT, LARSyS (UID/ EEA/50009/2013) and CIAC (PEstOE/ EAT/UI4019/2013). We also thank our project leader SPIC - Creative Solutions [www.spic.pt].

REFERENCES

Active8-3D (2015). 3D holographic projection displays. Retrieved from http://www.activ8-3d.co.uk/

Alves, R., Madeira, M., Ferrer, J., Costa, S., Lopes, D., Silva, B. M.,... Rodrigues, J. (2014). Fátima revisited: an interactive installation. *Proceedings of the SGEM2014 Conference on Arts, Performing Arts, Architecture & Design SGEM '14* (pp. 141-148).

Alves, R., Negrier, A., Sousa, L., Rodrigues, J. M. F., Felisberto, P., Gomes, M., & Bica, P. (2015b). Interactive 180° Rear projection public relations. *Procedia Computer Science, 51*(0), 592–601. doi:10.1016/j. procs.2015.05.327

Alves, R., Sousa, L., Negrier, A., Rodrigues, J. M. F., Cardoso, P. J. S., Monteiro, J.,... Bica, P. (2015a). PRHOLO: Interactive holographic public relations. *Proceedings of the 3rd International Conference on Advances in Computing, Communication and Information Technology* (pp. 124-128). doi:10.15224/978-1-63248-061-3-74

Alves, R., Sousa, L., Negrier, A., Rodrigues, J.M.F., Monteiro, J., Cardoso, P., Felisberto, P., Gomes, M., & Bica, P. (2015c). 360° Public relations, an interactive installation. *The Visual Computer.*

António, S., Herrera, R., & Enriquez, E. (2013). Projection's panel of models for touch screen. *International Journal of Innovative Research in Computer and Communication Engineering, 1*(9), 2057–2064.

Asus. (2014). Asus Xtion pro. Retrieved from http://goo.gl/HxQcli

AVA. (2015). AVA advanced virtual assistant. Retrieved from http://airportone.com/airportvirtualassistancesystem.htm

AVconcepts. (2015). Retrieved from http://www.avconcepts.com/

Bimber, O., Zeidler, T., Rundhoefer, A., Wetzstein, G. & Moehring, M. (2005). Interacting with augmented holograms, In SPIE, Practical Holography XIX: Materials and Applications, 41-54.

Butler, A., Hilliges, O., Izadi, S., Hodges, S., Molyneaux, D., Kim, D., & Kong, D. (2011). Vermeer: direct interaction with a 360° viewable 3D display. *Proceedings of the 24th Annual ACM Symposium on User Interface Software and Technology* (pp. 569-576). doi:10.1145/2047196.2047271

Chiang, I., Tsai, J. C., & Chen, S. T. (2012). Using Xbox 360 Kinect games on enhancing visual performance skills on institutionalized older adults with wheelchairs. Proceedings of the IEEE 4th International Conference on Digital Game and Intelligent Toy Enhanced Learning (DIGITEL) (pp. 263-267).

Cippitelli, E., Gasparrini, S., Gambi, E., & Spinsante, S. (2014). Depth stream compression for enhanced real time fall detection by multiple sensors. *Proceedings of the IEEE Fourth International Conference on Consumer Electronics, Berlin (ICCE-Berlin)* (pp. 29-30). doi:10.1109/ICCE-Berlin.2014.7034215

Cruz, L., Lucio, D., & Velho, L. (2012). Kinect and RGDB images: Challenges and applications. *Proceedings of the Conference on Graphics, Patterns and Images Tutorials (SIBGRAPI-T)* (pp. 36-49).

D'Strict. (2014). 3D sensing holographic installation. Retrieved from http://global.dstrict.com/projects/j4.php

Dick, J., Almeida, H., Soares, L. D., & Nunes, P. (2011) 3D Holoscopic video coding using MVC, In *IEEE International Conference on Computer as a Tool (EUROCON)*, 1-4. doi:10.1109/EUROCON.2011.5929394

El-laithy, R. A., Huang, J., & Yeh, M. (2012). Study on the use of Microsoft Kinect for robotics applications. Proceedings of the IEEE Position Location and Navigation Symposium (PLANS) (pp. 1280-1288). doi:10.1109/PLANS.2012.6236985

Eonreality (2015) Eonreality. Retrieved June 30, 2015, from http://eonreality.com/

Eyeliner 3D. (2015). Dimensional studios, musion setup: How it works. Retrieved from http://www.eyeliner3d.com/musion_eyeliner_setup_video.html

Figueiredo, M. J., Cardoso, P. J., Gonçalves, C. D., & Rodrigues, J. M. (2014). Augmented reality and holograms for the visualization of mechanical engineering parts. *Proceedings of the IEEE 18th International Conference on Information Visualisation* (pp. 368-373). doi:10.1109/IV.2014.17

Flyway. (2015). 3D holographic projection – the future of advertising? Retrieved from http://flyaways-imulation.com/news/3630/3d-holographic-projection-future-of-advertising/

Fong, S., Zhuang, Y., Fister, I., & Fister, I. Jr. (2013). A biometric authentication model using hand gesture images. *Biomedical Engineering Online, 12*(1), 111. doi:10.1186/1475-925X-12-111 PMID:24172288

Gasparrini, S., Cippitelli, E., Spinsante, S., & Gambi, E. (2015) Depth Cameras in AAL Environments: Technology and Realworld Applications. In L.B. Theng (Ed.), Assistive Technologies for Physical and Cognitive Disabilities (Ch. 2). Hershey, PA, USA: IGI Global. doi:10.4018/9781466673731

Globalzepp. (2015). Retrieved from http://www.globalzepp.com/

Hilliges, O., Kim, D., Izadi, S., Weiss, M., & Wilson, A. D. (2012). HoloDesk: Direct 3D interactions with a situated see-through display. *Proceedings of the SIGCHI Annual Conference on Human factors in computing systems* (pp. 2421 – 2430). doi:10.1145/2207676.2208405

Holodisplay. (2015). Retrieved from http://www.holodisplays.com/

Holomedia. (2015). 3D live interactive holographic. Retrieved from http://www.holomedia.co.uk/

Holus (2015) Holus: The interactive tabletop holographic display. Retrieved from http://www.digital-trends.com/cool-tech/holus-tabletop-hologram-kickstarter/

Jones, A., McDowall, I., Yamada, H., Bolas, M., & Debevec, P. (2007). Rendering for an interactive 360° light field display. In ACM SIGGRAPH 2007. doi:10.1145/1275808.1276427

Kamizono, T., Abe, H., Baba, K. I., Takano, S., & Murakami, K. (2014). Towards activity recognition of learners by Kinect. *Proceedings of the 3rd International Conference on Advanced Applied Informatics* (pp. 177-180). doi:10.1109/IIAI-AAI.2014.45

Kim, K., Bolton, J., Girouard, A., Cooperstock, J., & Vertegaal, R. (2012) TeleHuman: effects of 3D perspective on gaze and pose estimation with a life-size cylindrical telepresence pod. *Proceedings of the SIGCHI Conference on Human Factors in Computing Systems (CHI '12)* (pp. 2531-2540). doi:10.1145/2207676.2208640

KinectSpec. (2015). Kinect for Windows sensor components and specifications. Retrieved from https://msdn.microsoft.com/pt-pt/library/jj131033.aspx

Kondori, F., Yousefi, S., Liu, L., & Li, H. (2014). Head operated electric wheelchair. *Proceedings of the IEEE Southwest Symposium on Image Analysis and Interpretation (SSIAI)* (pp. 53-56).

Leap. (2014). Leap motion. Retrieved from https://www.leapmotion.com/

Lim, S., & Kim, S. (2014). Holographic projection system with 3D spatial interaction. Proceedings of the 5th International Conference on Advanced Data and Information Engineering (DaEng-2013) (pp. 409-416). doi:10.1007/978-981-4585-18-7_46

Lippmann, M. (1908). La photographie integral. *Compt. Rend. Acad. Sci., 146*, 446.

Litefast. (2013) Litefast MAGIC displays. Retrieved from http://www.litefast-display.com/products/litefast-products/litefast-magic/litefast-magic.html

Martins, J. M. S., Rodrigues, J. M. F., & Martins, J. C. (2015). Low-cost natural interface based on head movements. *Proceedings of the 6th International Conference on Software Development and Technologies for Enhancing*, Fraunhofer FIT, Sankt Augustin, Germany. doi:10.1016/j.procs.2015.09.275

Microsoft. (2014). Kinect for Windows. Retrieved from http://goo.gl/fGZT8X

Mihaylova, E. (Ed.). (2013). *Holography - Basic Principles and Contemporary Applications*. InTech. doi:10.5772/46111

Miles, R. (2012). *Start here! Learn the Kinect API*. Pearson Education.

Musion. (2015). Retrieved from http://www.musion.co.uk/

Noor, A. K., & Aras, R. (2015). Potential of multimodal and multiuser interaction with virtual holography. *Advances in Engineering Software, 81*, 1–6. doi:10.1016/j.advengsoft.2014.10.004

Rahman, M. M., Poon, B., Amin, M. A., & Yan, H. (2015). Support system using Microsoft Kinect and mobile phone for daily activity of visually impaired. In Transactions on Engineering Technologies (pp. 425-440). doi:10.1007/978-94-017-9588-3_32

Rearpro. (2015). Paradigm audio visual. Retrieved from http://www.rearpro.com/

Rennie, J. (2014). The Tupac hologram, virtual Ebert, and digital immortality. Retrieved from http://www.smartplanet.com/blog/thesavvy-scientist/the-tupac-hologram-virtual-ebert-anddigital-immortality/454

RFID. (2014). RFID Reader ID-12LA (125 kHz). Retrieved from https://www.sparkfun.com/products/11827

Sprott, J. C. (2006). Physics demonstrations: A sourcebook for teachers of physics. Univ of Wisconsin Press.

Structure. (2014). Structure sensor. Retrieved from http://structure.io/

Telehuman. (2013). Telehuman. Retrieved from http://www.hml.queensu.ca/telehuman

Verge. (2015). To build a holodeck: an exclusive look at Microsoft's Edison lab. Retrieved from http://www.theverge.com/2011/12/28/2665794/microsoft-edison-lab-holodeck-tour

Vertigo. (2013). Retrieved from http://www.vertigo-systems.com/

Vizoo. (2015). Vizoo, cheoptics. Retrieved from http://www.vizoo.com/flash/

Weiss, C. M., Frid, A., Malin, M., & Ladijenski, V. (2015). Generating 3D CAD art from human gestures using Kinect depth sensor. *Computer-Aided Design and Applications*, 12(5), 608-616.

Xstage. (2015). Retrieved from http://www.xstage.de/

Yamaguchi, M. (2015). Holographic 3D touch sensing display. In *Digital Holography and Three-Dimensional Imaging, DM3A-1*. Optical Society of America. doi:10.1364/DH.2015.DM3A.1

Yun, Y., Changrampadi, M. H., & Gu, I. Y. (2014). Head pose classification by multi-class AdaBoost with fusion of RGB and depth images. *Proceedings of the International Conference on Signal Processing and Integrated Networks* (pp. 174-177). doi:10.1109/SPIN.2014.6776943

KEY TERMS AND DEFINITIONS

3D Interaction: A form of human-computer interaction where users are able to move and perform interaction in a three-dimensional space.

Computer Vision: A scientific discipline concerned with the theory behind artificial systems that extract information from images. The image data can take many forms, such as video sequences, views from multiple cameras, or multi-dimensional data (including 3D data). As a technological discipline, computer vision seeks to apply its theories and models to the construction of systems based on (computer) vision.

Gesture Recognition: A topic in computer science and language technology with the goal of interpreting human gestures via mathematical algorithms, in the present case based on computer vision algorithms.

Hologram: A photographic recording of a light field, rather than of an image formed by a lens, and it is used to display a fully three-dimensional image of the holographed subject, which is seen without the aid of any intermediate optics.

Human-Computer Interaction: Also called human-machine interaction, is a researcher field related to the design and use of computer technology, focusing particularly on the interfaces between people (users) and computers; it can both observe the ways in which humans interact with computers as well as design technologies that let humans interact with computers in novel ways.

Interfaces: A shared boundary across which two separate components of a computer system, the exchange can be between software, computer hardware, peripheral devices, humans and combinations of these.

Natural Interaction: The common denomination used by designers and developers of human-computer interfaces to refer to a user interface that is effectively invisible, and remains invisible as the user continuously learns increasingly complex interactions.

Rear Projection: A projection technique where the projector is placed behind the screen, shooting straight towards the audience.

This research was previously published in Handbook of Research on Human-Computer Interfaces, Developments, and Applications edited by João Rodrigues, Pedro Cardoso, Jânio Monteiro, and Mauro Figueiredo, pages 162-187, copyright year 2016 by Information Science Reference (an imprint of IGI Global).

Chapter 8
Usability Evaluation of Dialogue Designs for Voiceprint Authentication in Automated Telephone Banking

Nancie Gunson
The University of Edinburgh, UK

Fergus McInnes
The University of Edinburgh, UK

Diarmid Marshall
The University of Edinburgh, UK

Hazel Morton
The University of Edinburgh, UK

Mervyn Jack
The University of Edinburgh, UK

ABSTRACT

This paper describes an empirical investigation of the usability of different dialogue designs for voiceprint authentication in automated telephone banking. Three strategies for voice authentication were evaluated in an experiment with 120 telephone banking end-users: 1-Factor (voiceprint authentication based on customers' utterances of their account number and sort code); 1-Factor with Challenge (1-Factor plus a randomly generated digit string); and 2-Factor (1-Factor plus secret information known only to the caller). The research suggests the 2-Factor approach is the most effective strategy in this context: results from a Likert questionnaire show it to be highly usable and it is rated highest in terms of both security and overall quality. Participants welcome the option to use voiceprint technology but the majority would prefer it to augment rather than replace existing security methods.

DOI: 10.4018/978-1-5225-2589-9.ch008

1. INTRODUCTION

Despite substantial research efforts devoted to the development of voiceprint authentication technology e.g. the NIST evaluation program (Martin, Przybocki, & Campbell Jr, 2005), surprisingly few studies have been reported which examine users' attitudes towards it (Gunson, Marshall, McInnes, & Jack, 2011; Tassabehji & Kamala, 2009; Toledano, Fernández Pozo, Hernández Trapote, & Hernández Gómez, 2006). This is important since the usability of new security measures is vital for customer cooperation and acceptance (O'Gorman, 2003). In this paper, an empirical study is described which provides a comprehensive usability evaluation of three different dialogue designs for voiceprint authentication in automated telephone banking. The three designs chosen offer different levels of security based on different levels of user input, with the aim of examining the relationship between security and usability. All are realistic options for deployment.

The rest of the paper is organised as follows. A review of the relevant literature is provided in Section 2. Section 3 details the three different dialogue designs for voiceprint authentication that were examined. Section 4 describes the research methodology, Section 5 the experiment design and Section 6 the participants. Results are presented in Section 7 with conclusions given in Section 8.

2. BACKGROUND

Although Internet banking is increasingly popular, with one survey reporting 47% of respondents used it in the previous month (Gartner, 2009), automated telephone banking continues to be an important service delivery channel for banking organisations around the world. The U.K. service on which the application in this research is based, for instance, has 4 million registered users, and receives 5.5 million calls per month. Its development is the subject of continued interest at the Bank.

The customer authentication process in the existing service is knowledge-based ("what you know"). Users must recall two digits selected at random from their Secret Number or 'PIN'. The service is not alone in this method - the use of a PIN or alphanumeric password (or some combination of the two) is the current *de facto* standard for customer verification in U.K. telephone banking.

When they are used correctly, such passwords and PINs play an important part in the security of automated services (O'Gorman, 2003). However, the ubiquity of their use across different applications means that users are typically required to have many, making it difficult to remember them all.

A common response to this problem is to write some of them down or to use the same one across a number of different services, both of which have inherent security risks (Adams & Sasse, 2005; Dhamija & Perrig, 2000; Gaw & Felten, 2006). In one study (Dhamija & Perrig, 2000), for example, it was found that participants had ranging from ten to fifty situations where passwords were required, but in practice used one to seven repeatedly. Users have also been shown to choose passwords and PINs that are easy to remember, and are therefore high risk (Adams & Sasse, 2005; Bishop, 2005; Yan, Blackwell, Anderson, & Grant, 2004).

Alternative and/or additional security measures are therefore increasingly being sought, particularly in the banking sector where remote fraud is on the increase (Hiltgen, Kramp, & Weigold, 2006). One possibility is 'two-factor' authentication using physical tokens such as card-readers ("what you have") in addition to memorised information. Here, any fraud depends on both knowing the secret information *and* physical possession of the device (Gunson, Marshall, Morton, & Jack, 2011; Weir, Douglas, Carruthers, & Jack, 2009). Another option is the use of *biometrics* ("who you are"). Biometrics are a range of technologies that use some distinguishing feature measured from the human body to authenticate an individual. Examples include voice, fingerprints and iris patterns (Arivazhagan, Ganesan, & Srividya, 2009; Naini, Homayounpour, & Samani, 2010; Yamagishi, Nishiuchi, & Yamanaka, 2008). A key advantage of biometrics is that, unlike physical tokens, they cannot be lost or forgotten. Moreover, they are relatively difficult to copy or falsify (Jain, Ross, & Pankanti, 2006). These factors have led to a considerable interest in biometrics from the banking industry e.g. (Coventry, De Angeli, & Johnson, 2003; Peevers, Williams, Douglas, & Jack, 2013). Importantly, several Banks have started to deploy voice verification in telephone banking (Business Wire, 2010; Flare-design, 2013; National Australia Bank Limited, 2013).

In the context of a telephone banking service voiceprints are an obvious choice of biometric. The user is not required to use any specialist equipment and capture of the biometric is physically non-intrusive (unlike, for example, fingerprinting systems). Moreover, the interaction is based on spoken conversation – of which all users already have experience.

The implementation of voiceprint authentication involves two stages: *enrolment* and *verification*. During enrolment, which is a one-off procedure, the true user provides speech samples with which to create a unique voiceprint. In subsequent verification speech input is then compared against this stored voiceprint to check for a match. Two types of voiceprint verification are available: *text dependent* and *text independent*. A detailed discussion of their relative merits is provided in Gunson, Marshall, McInnes, et al. (2011). The focus of this research is on the former, in which the user is required to speak a specific phrase or token during verification (one that was used during the enrolment process).

Previous research on voice authentication has tended to concentrate on technical aspects e.g. (Khan, Baig, & Youssef, 2010; Naini, et al., 2010; Snelick, Uludag, Mink, Indovina, & Jain, 2005). These studies, in line with the latest biometric evaluation standards (ISO/IEC JTC, 2012), focus primarily on *False Match Rates* or FMR (i.e. false acceptance of impostors), *False Non-Match Rates* or FNMR (i.e. false rejection of true users), and the trade-off between the two.

There are also some papers that discuss the pros and cons of biometric technology more generally (Coventry, 2005; Jain, et al., 2006; O'Gorman, 2003; Venkatraman & Delpachitra, 2008). Several European and UK government initiatives (BIOSECURE[1], Biometrics Working Group[2]) have sought to promote the use of biometrics. Some have highlighted the importance of a user-centred approach (BioVisioN[3]). However, even some of the most recent (BEAT[4]) remain focused on technical evaluation. Few studies exist that provide data on user reaction to voiceprint technology (or indeed the other types of biometric).

In one valuable exception (Toledano et al., 2006) the usability of three different types of biometric verification was investigated (fingerprint, voice and signature). Likert attitude scales (Likert, 1932) were used to evaluate user satisfaction. As part of the experiment, however, participants were asked to act as an impostor – an unusual experience for end-users. Moreover, the sole purpose of the (on-screen) application was to compare the different types of biometric.

Another study measured attitudes towards the use of biometrics in the more realistic context of Internet banking (Tassabehji & Kamala, 2009). Crucially, however, participants did not directly experience the service demonstrated. The paper also readily admits that participants were all students, chiefly young males.

Previous research by the authors (Gunson, Marshall, McInnes, et al., 2011) compared the usability of voiceprint authentication using digits with that of sentences. Here, importantly, the research was set in the context of a real-life automated telephone banking service. Also, participants were actual customers of the Bank. The results showed high customer acceptance of the technology. Usability was higher for digits and there was a majority preference for digits over sentences. There were, however, indications that customers would prefer to use voice authentication *in addition* to existing security procedures rather than as a replacement as experienced in the experiment.

As noted earlier, it is important to measure user attitudes towards new security measures in this way (O'Gorman, 2003) since if they are difficult to use, customers will avoid them or will not use them properly.

Usability and security, however, are often seen as competing goals in automated systems (Florêncio & Herley, 2010; Kainda, Flechais, & Roscoe, 2010; Sasse, 2005). There is a widespread belief that improvements in one aspect inevitably lead to a decline in the other. The evidence for this is somewhat limited however. It is true that a number of studies involving text-based passwords have shown that the more secure the password is, the harder it is to remember (Forget, Chiasson, & Biddle, 2007; Forget, Chiasson, van Oorschot, & Biddle, 2008; Kuo, Romanosky, & Cranor, 2006; Shay et al., 2010). However, in concentrating on particular measures such as password memorability these studies are limited in focus (particularly since this type of security measure places the onus of increased security entirely on the user).

Research investigating the impact of different security mechanisms on service usability as a whole has so far centred on the use of physical devices. Gunson, Marshall, Morton, et al. (2011) found that increased security in the form of a key fob *did* lead to a decrease in usability of the overall service. Weir, et al. (2009), and Weir, Douglas, Richardson, and Jack (2010), on the other hand, presented mixed data from two studies in Internet banking. Results from the first (Weir, et al., 2009) supported the idea that usability is sacrificed when security is improved (comparing passwords versus passwords plus a physical device). The second study on the other hand (Weir, et al., 2010) showed that the existing single-factor authentication procedure (two passwords) was significantly *less* usable than two different types of two-factor authentication; password plus digital token, and password plus SMS text message.

Data on this topic are therefore somewhat mixed. Commentators, moreover, have remarked on a lack of empirical work examining the usability of secure systems (Kainda et al., 2010; Sasse, 2005).

The research reported in this paper aims to address some of the gaps identified in the literature, firstly in the assessment of voiceprint technology from a user perspective; and secondly, in the broader field of usability and security. Three strategies for voiceprint authentication offering different levels of security were compared in an automated telephone banking system. Importantly, the research was carried out in the context of a real-world application, that of a major UK Bank, with participants who were actual customers of the Bank.

3. DIALOGUE DESIGNS

The three different strategies for voiceprint authentication were as follows:

1. **Factor Strategy:** Verification based on the caller's utterances of their 8-digit account number and 6-digit sort code, given during the identification stages;

2. **Factor With Challenge (Hereto Referred to as Challenge for Brevity):** Verification based on the account number and sort code utterances plus repetition of a randomly generated 6-digit string;

3. **Factor Strategy:** Verification based on the caller's utterances of their account number and sort code plus some 'secret' information: either two digits selected at random from their Secret Number; or their date of birth and 3-digit security code from the back of their debit card (also known as the 'Card Verification Value' or 'CVV') if no Secret Number held.

The difference in dialogue in the 2-Factor strategy reflects the customer groups that exist in real life. In the existing live service, customers with a Secret Number have access to the full range of banking services available. Those without are limited to account information services only e.g. balances.

The 1-Factor strategy represents a likely minimum in terms of the number and type of utterances on which voiceprint authentication might be based in a telephone banking service. The key advantage of this design is that it keeps the identification and verification procedure to a minimum, as both steps are carried out at once. Verification is performed on the identification tokens without requiring any further input from the caller e.g. recall of secret information, passwords etc. Of the three strategies described, however, it provides the lowest level of (actual) security. The use of fixed phrases as the verification tokens makes it vulnerable to fraud through recording and playback of the customer's speech (known as 'spoofing'). It also involves the smallest amount of speech data on which to carry out a voiceprint match.

Spoofing in this case can be guarded against using recordings of the previous N accepted verification utterances (listening for 'too good' a match). This form of protection is unlikely to be obvious to users however, who may feel this approach is vulnerable to this type of attack. Moreover, the other strategies examined can also employ this type of protection – but in addition offer other forms of defence against spoofing. (They also provide additional speech data for the voiceprint matching process.) The use of a randomly generated string which varies from one call to another in the Challenge strategy, for example, reduces the predictability of the interaction and therefore the likelihood of fraudsters' having the correct recording. The drawback of this approach is that it involves an extra stage in the dialogue, and one which may be both unfamiliar and unintuitive for users. To reduce the potential cognitive load associated with this stage, the 6-digit string requested consists of three digits repeated (Hébert, 2008). Digits were chosen as the challenge token based on previous research (Gunson, Marshall, McInnes, et al., 2011) which showed that these were more usable than sentences in this context.

The 2-Factor strategy increases security by combining information as to *who the caller is* (as determined by matching the caller's voice against the voiceprint) and *what the caller knows*. Unlike the Challenge strategy the caller is not prompted with the input they should speak. Instead, they must have prior knowledge of the information requested (or be in possession of the bank card in the case of the CVV). Moreover, in the case of a Secret Number the two digits requested are selected at random in each call. This reduces the predictability of the interaction, reducing the chances of successful spoofing.

A potential drawback of the 2-Factor approach is that it involves additional dialogue stages (two in comparison to the 1-Factor strategy, one compared to the Challenge strategy). Importantly also, in the case of the Secret Number it requires the caller to remember secret information. This is of particular interest since the argument for using biometrics is often for the sake of convenience, to avoid having to remember a password (O'Gorman, 2003). The dialogue is, however, potentially more intuitive for callers than the Challenge strategy, as this type of knowledge-based security procedure is common across a wide variety of services.

4. METHODOLOGY

The methodology employed in this research involves the use of a controlled experiment in a laboratory setting. Users directly experience two or more versions of the system under test. Participants are carefully selected to be target users of the service. They are given detailed fictitious personae to use during the experiment in order to encourage a sense of realism. Such user testing with real users has often been described as the gold standard in the usability evaluation of a new or modified interface (Lewis, 2001).

Following each experience of the services, participants are asked to complete a usability questionnaire (See Appendix). This questionnaire was developed and tested over a number of experiments (Dutton, Foster, Jack, & Stentiford, 1993; Jack, Foster, & Stentiford, 1993; Love, Dutton, Foster, & Jack, 1992). It has been frequently used and adapted since (Davidson, McInnes, & Jack, 2004; Larsen, 1999, 2003; Sturm & Boves, 2005). It is in Likert format (Likert, 1932) and consists of 20 short proposal statements, balanced for polarity, with 7 tick boxes ranging from "strongly agree" through neutral to "strongly disagree". On this 7-point scale, once the responses are normalised for statement polarity a score over 4.0 represents a positive attitude; scores below 4.0 represent a negative attitude, with 4.0 the neutral point. Each participant's overall attitude to the service can be measured by taking the mean of these numbers across all of the items in the questionnaire. A measure of the overall attitude to the service can then be obtained by averaging all the questionnaire results for participants who experienced that service.

At the end of the session participants take part in a structured interview, which provides qualitative as well as quantitative data on participants' preference between variants of the design.

5. EXPERIMENT DESIGN AND PROCEDURE

All participants had been identified by the Bank as having used the real-life telephone banking service at least once. During recruitment, they were asked how often they used the existing service, and whether they used a Secret Number. On the basis of this information they were then assigned to one of two experiment groups. The real-life Secret Number users were assigned to the *SN group*, the others to the *nonSN* group. This was important because in real life customers with and without a Secret Number would experience different verification procedures in the 2-Factor version of the service.

Each participant was supplied with a fictitious persona, including a replica debit card. Participants then made a total of seven telephone calls: one enrolment call, and then six further calls experiencing authentication by voiceprint – two to each version of the service. The order of presentation of the different versions was balanced across the group. The task in the enrolment call was simply to enrol a voiceprint. In the other calls it was to request a balance (this changed automatically in each call). A usability questionnaire was completed after each of the six balance calls. At the end of the session there was a structured de-briefing interview.

In the enrolment call participants were identified and verified using existing security procedures, plus additional security questions in the case of those without a Secret Number. In real life such procedures would be necessary in order to ensure the integrity of the enrolled voiceprint.

In a live service, the set of phrases requested in the enrolment call would reflect the verification strategy adopted. In the experiment however, rather than a separate enrolment call for each version, which would make the session too long, participants made a single enrolment call which included *all* of the phrases necessary for the experiment. i.e. account number, sort code, 'their' (persona's) date of birth, and the digits from zero to nine. Each phrase was repeated three times in the call.

As in previous research (Gunson, Marshall, McInnes, et al., 2011), the verification results were controlled to ensure a consistent outcome across all participants, with the aim of focusing participants' attention on the differences in the dialogue design. All participants experienced successful authentication (only), which provides a best-case comparison of the three different strategies for voiceprint authentication. In reality, in each strategy a small proportion of true customers would experience a false rejection (non-match) as a result of an error by the verification engine. However, in order to accurately measure the error rates involved, an extensive data capture and analysis would first be required in order to set the decision thresholds for each strategy that yield optimum performance. This type of analysis and tuning was not the focus of this research. Thus, given that the proportion of errors is likely to be low it was considered reasonable to focus on the majority case of successful authentication. Previous research found, for example, that verifying with four utterances (a membership number, an account number and two single PIN digits) resulted in an equal error rate (where the false match rate is the same as the false non-match rate) of just 1.2% (Morgen, 2012). Other research comparing three different commercial verification engines showed an equal error rate best performance of 0.91% on a single utterance of the digit sequence 1-9 (Wagner, Summerfield, Dunstone, Summerfield, & Moss, 2006).

6. PARTICIPANTS

A total of 120 customers of the Case Bank were recruited in the Bristol area, UK. Key participant data are summarised in Table 1.

A total of 62 participants were allocated to the SN experiment group. The remaining 58 were allocated to the nonSN group. A minority of participants call the existing service on a regular basis (25.0%); the majority however, call infrequently or no longer call. Participants who had a Secret Number in real life and were therefore allocated to the SN group tended to be more frequent callers - 38.7% of this group called the service at least once a month compared to 10.3% in the nonSN group. This is reasonable since those who call frequently are more likely to be offered (and to accept) the option to register a Secret Number. The majority of participants in both groups call a few times a year or less.

Table 1. Participant data

Demographic	Category	No. Participants
Age	18-44 yrs	71
	45+ yrs	49
Gender	Male	48
	Female	72
Call existing service	At least once a month	30
	A few times a year or less / stopped	90

7. RESULTS

7.1. Usability of the Service With Voice Authentication

The mean usability scores for the first and second uses of each version, and the overall mean for each version computed over both calls, are shown in Table 2. Scores are on a scale from 1 (least favourable) to 7 (most favourable), with 4 the neutral point.

All three versions were rated positively on the 7-point scale, indicating a usable service. A repeated measures ANOVA was run on the mean usability scores, with *service version* as the within-participants factor. The between-participants factors included were *order of presentation of versions* and *verification token* (Secret Number or the combination of date of birth and CVV – affecting only the calls to the 2-Factor version).

The ANOVA results are shown in Table 3. The main effect of service version was significant ($p=0.011$). Pair-wise tests showed significant differences between the Challenge strategy and each of the other two versions ($p=0.014$ in each case), but no significant difference between the 1-Factor and 2-Factor strategies. In each case the Challenge strategy was rated as significantly *less* usable.

The main effect of call number was very highly significant ($p<0.001$), with consistently higher scores on the second use of any particular version than on the first use, indicating a learning effect.

There were no significant interactions between the within- and between- subjects variables. The between-participants effect of verification token was moderately significant ($p=0.012$), with higher scores for all versions of the service in the SN group than in the nonSN group. This may be due to the fact that a higher proportion of participants in the SN group were frequent users of the existing telephone banking service; familiarity with parts of the service potentially improving their perceptions of usability across the board. Importantly, there was, however, no interaction between the effect of version and the

Table 2. Mean usability scores by service version and call number

Service Version	1-Factor	Challenge	2-Factor
First Call	5.65 (SD=0.77)	5.51 (SD=0.84)	5.65 (SD=0.79)
Second Call	5.77 (SD=0.71)	5.64 (SD=0.78)	5.72 (SD=0.73)
Mean	5.71 (SD=0.71)	5.58 (SD=0.78)	5.68 (SD=0.74)

Table 3. ANOVA results for mean usability scores

		Sum of Squares	df	Mean Square	F	Sig
Within subjects	Service version	2.369	1.733	1.368	4.944	0.011
	Call number	1.882	1	1.882	23.041	0.000
Between subjects	Version order	17.042	5	3.408	1.280	0.278
	Verification token	17.408	1	17.408	6.537	0.012
Interactions	Version * call number	0.168	1.956	0.086	1.223	0.296
	Version * token	0.048	1	0.048	0.586	0.446

verification token used i.e. participants rated the *relative* usability of the three versions similarly regardless of which group they were in.

Analyses similar to the first ANOVA on the mean usability scores were then run on the scores for all the individual usability attributes. Table 4 shows the effects of service version.

The 1-Factor strategy scored significantly higher than the Challenge strategy on six of the 20 attributes, predominantly those relating to cognitive aspects of the service e.g. *confusing* and *concentration* (the latter was a particularly strong result). While the results were almost all highly significant however, it is worth noting that both versions received positive ratings for these attributes and the actual differences in ratings were relatively small (ranging from 0.21 to 0.43 for the most significant result, *concentration*).

The 2-Factor approach scored significantly above the Challenge strategy on two attributes: degree of *concentration* required and not being *too fast*. Although again in practical terms the differences were relatively small, both were highly significant results ($p<0.01$).

The difference between the 1-Factor and 2-Factor strategy was significant for two attributes: *flustered* and *reliable*. These effects, however, were in different directions and were not highly significant. They could be due to chance, considering that on average one significant result ($p<0.05$) would be expected by chance in a set of 20 tests.

Table 4. ANOVA results for individual usability attributes (service version)

Attribute Name	1-Factor	Challenge	2-Factor	Main Effect	Pair-Wise Tests
Confusion	6.03	5.80	5.95	.009	1-F>Ch (.006)
Concentration	5.48	5.05	5.33	.000	1-F>Ch (.000) 2-F>Ch (.003)
Flustered	5.85	5.54	5.68	.003	1-F>Ch (.002) 1-F>2-F (.020)
Stress	5.86	5.65	5.75	.051	1-F>Ch (.027)
Frustration	5.90	5.67	5.81	.033	-
Complication	6.10	5.86	6.00	.004	1-F>Ch (.002)
Knew what to do	5.68	5.55	5.63	-	-
Control	5.58	5.46	5.60	-	-
Too fast	5.83	5.66	5.89	.013	2-F >Ch (.003)
Ease of use	6.07	5.85	5.98	.004	1-F>Ch (.002)
Clarity of voice	6.18	6.11	6.18	-	-
Prefer human	4.02	4.02	4.17	-	-
Use again	5.82	5.82	5.88	-	-
Reliable	5.63	5.75	5.78	(.076)	2-F>1-F (.027)
Efficient	5.93	5.88	5.95	-	-
Needs improvement	5.41	5.31	5.55	-	-
Friendly	5.77	5.77	5.71	-	-
Liked voice	5.63	5.56	5.58	-	-
Enjoyment	5.44	5.34	5.40	-	-
Polite	5.95	5.91	5.89	-	-

It appears therefore that the predicted additional cognitive load of the Challenge strategy did have a negative effect on user attitudes towards it. There was, however, very little difference in usability between the 1-Factor and 2-Factor strategies, despite the additional dialogue stages for the user to complete in the latter.

7.2. Ratings of Security

As part of the de-briefing interview participants were asked to rate the security of the three versions by placing markers on a scale from 0 (worst) to 30 (best). The mean ratings are shown in Table 5.

Overall, the 2-Factor version was rated as the most secure version by a considerable margin. This was followed by the Challenge strategy, with the 1-Factor version (voiceprint authentication of sort code and account number only) rated the least secure approach. The main effect of version was very highly significant (ANOVA $p<0.001$), with very highly significant pairwise differences for all pairs of versions ($p<0.001$ in each case).

There was a moderately significant interaction between version and verification token ($p=0.013$), suggesting a difference in perceptions of security between the two experiment groups (Figure 1).

Separate ANOVAs within the two verification token groups showed that all pairwise differences between versions were significant in both groups (at $p<0.01$). Participants in the nonSN group, however, rated the security of the 2-Factor approach significantly lower than those equipped with a Secret Number (independent samples t-test, $p=0.009$). This suggests that customers (rightly) consider date of birth and CVV to be a less secure form of verification token than a Secret Number. There were no significant differences in the two groups' attitude towards the other two versions.

Table 5. Mean ratings - Perceived security

Service Version	Security Rating
1-Factor	10.57
Challenge	18.45
2-Factor	25.14

Figure 1. Security rating by verification method and experiment group

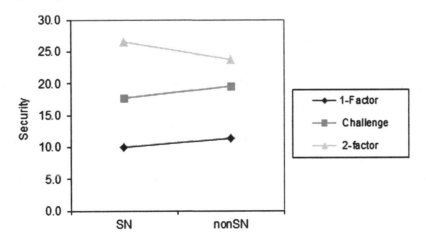

Table 6. Votes for most and least preferred versions (N=120)

Service Version	1-Factor	Challenge	2-Factor	No Preference
Preferred	37 (30.8%)	19 (15.8%)	49 (40.8%)	15 (12.5%)
Liked least	40 (33.3%)	34 (28.3%)	16 (13.3%)	30 (25.0%)

7.3. Explicit Preference

Participants were also asked which version of the service they preferred, and which they liked least. The results are summarised in Table 6.

The clearest result was an overall preference for the 2-Factor strategy. The 2-Factor version scored the largest number of preferences. It was also identified as the least liked version by considerably fewer participants than either the 1-Factor or Challenge strategy. The Challenge strategy had the fewest 'preferred' votes by a considerable margin - but interestingly was not 'liked least' by the largest number of participants. This was reserved for the 1-Factor strategy, which appeared to divide opinion in the group. Almost as many participants chose the 1-Factor strategy as their most preferred version (presumably on the grounds of ease of use / convenience) as chose it as their least preferred version (presumably because of its weaker security).

Pairwise preferences were derived from the responses for each participant. So, for example, 59 participants preferred the 2-Factor strategy over the 1-Factor version, 42 vice versa, and 19 had no preference between these two versions. Binomial tests omitting those with no preference showed that a majority preference for the 2-Factor approach over the Challenge strategy was very highly significant ($p<0.001$) but none of the other pairwise preferences were significant.

The SN group exhibited a stronger preference for the 2-Factor version, with 50% stating that this was their preferred method, compared to 31% in the nonSN group. Reasons for this are discussed in the following section.

Participants were asked to comment on their reasons for their preferences. The majority of comments from those who preferred the 2-Factor version were with regards to it being more secure. (Just two participants commented that it was similar to the current telephone banking service.) The most frequent reason given for disliking the 1-Factor version was that it was not as secure as the other versions. Reasons for disliking the Challenge version were mixed and included dislike of the random sequence of numbers, lack of security, and comments relating to the concentration / effort required.

7.4. Ratings of Overall Quality

Participants were asked to rate the overall quality of the three versions by placing markers on a scale from 0 (worst) to 30 (best). The mean ratings are shown in Table 7.

Reflecting the explicit preferences, the 2-Factor version scored highest of the three versions. The Challenge strategy was rated second and the 1-Factor strategy third. A repeated measures ANOVA showed the main effect of version was very highly significant ($p<0.001$), with significant pairwise differences between the 2-Factor version and each of the other two strategies (1-Factor, $p=0.001$; Challenge, $p<0.001$).

Table 7. Mean ratings: Overall quality

Service Version	Overall Quality
1-Factor	15.74
Challenge	16.20
2-Factor	20.84

There was a *marginally* significant interaction between version and verification token (p=0.043). The Secret Number group rated the 2-Factor strategy higher, and the 1-Factor version lower, than those using their date of birth and CVV (Figure 2). The Challenge strategy was rated very similarly in both subgroups.

In both subgroups the 2-Factor approach was rated the highest in terms of overall quality, in keeping with other results, with little difference between the other two versions. Separate ANOVAs performed for each group confirmed that in the SN group the difference between the 2-Factor strategy and each of the other two versions was significant (p<0.001 in each case) but there was no significant difference between the 1-Factor and Challenge strategies. In the nonSN group the trend was the same but the result was more dilute with no significant pairwise differences.

These results support those for Explicit Preference, further indicating that much of the overall preference for the 2-Factor approach emanates from those in the SN group. Possible reasons for this include greater experience of the existing service amongst customers in this group. More participants in the SN group were regular callers to the live service, which may have led them to prefer the version that most closely resembles it. However, this is unlikely to provide a full explanation, since regular callers (those who call at least once a month) accounted for less than 40% of participants in this group. Another possible reason relates to differences in perceptions of security between the two experiment groups. It was noted earlier that participants in the nonSN group rated the security of the 2-Factor version lower than those in the SN group. This suggests customers consider date of birth and CVV to be less secure verification tokens than a secret number. It is possible therefore that the perceived advantages of the 2-Factor approach are reduced for participants using these verification tokens, and that the relative simplicity of the 1-Factor approach is thus more appealing.

Figure 2. Overall quality rating by version and verification token

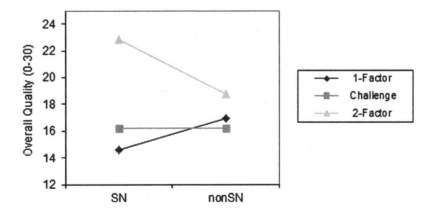

7.5. Qualitative Interview Data

A total of 72.3% of participants said they would be happy to speak their account number and sort code out loud. There were similar findings when the verification tokens were included - 64.1% in the SN group and 62.5% in the nonSN group. These results are encouraging, although it must be borne in mind that here participants' experience was in the relative privacy of the laboratory setting, using fictitious account details.

When explicitly asked, a majority of participants expressed some concern regarding the technology (75.8%): mostly that they did not know how secure it was or how it works (32). Others were more specific, commenting on the possibility that their voice could be mimicked by someone else (23) or that the system would not work if they had a cough or cold (14). These results highlight the importance of good customer communication in deploying the technology.

The majority of participants had no problem with the Bank storing their voiceprint data (69.2%). A further 16 (13.3%) said it would be fine as long as certain qualifications were met e.g. the Bank did not share the data with anyone else, and/or the voiceprint was destroyed if they left the Bank.

Participants in the SN group were asked whether they would prefer authentication to comprise digits from their Secret Number only, their voiceprint only, or digits from their Secret Number plus their voiceprint. A clear majority, 74.2%, said they would prefer the 2-Factor method; whilst 24.2% said that they would prefer to be authenticated using their voiceprint alone. Just one participant (1.6%) opted for the Secret Number without the voiceprint. These numbers confirm those found in a previous experiment (Gunson, Marshall, McInnes, et al., 2011); here, however participants had actually experienced the 2-Factor procedure.

The vast majority of participants, 88.1%, said that they would be happy to use voiceprints in real life when calling the Bank. Most of those who said they would not remarked that they would need more information on voiceprints prior to using them.

7.6. Summary of Main Results

Table 8 summarises the main results from the experiment. Note that in the "Significant Differences" column, ">" means 'significantly better than', and that for most of the metrics, larger values are better, but for *time taken* the opposite applies.

Table 8. Summary of main results

	1-Factor	Challenge	2-Factor	Significant Differences
ID&V Duration	27.0s	40.0s	46.0s	1-Factor > Challenge > 2-Factor
Usability Score	5.71	5.58	5.68	1-Factor, 2-Factor > Challenge
Security Rating	10.57	18.45	25.14	2-Factor > Challenge > 1-Factor
Preference Votes (*Votes Against*)	30.8% (*33.3%*)	15.8% (*28.3%*)	40.8% (*13.3%*)	2-Factor > Challenge
Quality Rating	15.74	16.20	20.84	2-Factor > 1-Factor, Challenge

8. CONCLUSION

The experiment revealed some interesting differences between the voiceprint authentication strategies examined. These data can aid decisions on the implementation of voiceprints in an automated telephone service. Moreover, they can inform the debate on the trade-off between usability and security in automated systems. Results from the experiment also revealed some variations in attitude between different customer groups, highlighting the importance of reflecting all user segments in research of this nature.

A common finding for most of the metrics was that the 2-Factor strategy was significantly better than the Challenge strategy; of the two it was perceived as both more usable and more secure, and was strongly preferred overall. Overall, the only metric on which the 2-Factor strategy scored less favourably than the Challenge version was the time taken to complete ID&V.

Compared with the 1-Factor strategy, the 2-Factor was rated similarly in terms of usability, despite the additional stages and use of secret/confidential information involved in the latter. It was also considered significantly more *secure* than the 1-Factor approach and was rated significantly higher in terms of overall quality. It did, however, yield significantly longer ID&V times. Perhaps because of this, the overall preference votes were split with almost as many participants choosing the 1-Factor strategy as their most preferred version (30.8%, presumably on the grounds of speed / convenience) as chose it as their least preferred version (33.3%, presumably because of its weaker security).

The Challenge strategy was rated second in terms of security, and was also second in terms of ID&V duration, but was rated the least usable of the three and was preferred by fewest participants.

When explicitly asked whether they would prefer to be verified using Secret Number digits, a voiceprint or both, 74.2% said both, 24.2% chose voiceprint only and just one (1.6%) chose Secret Number digits on their own. These results support the idea suggested by the results above that a minority of users are attracted to the possibility of greater convenience afforded by voiceprints, but that for the majority increased security is the priority. Further, they provide a strong vote for change from the existing system of authentication.

The main practical conclusion from the experiment therefore, is that voiceprint authentication should be used to augment rather than replace the existing security procedures. Where possible, moreover, the additional security should be based on secret information such as a secret number rather than confidential information such as date of birth. While the 1-Factor approach appeals to a minority of customers, largely amongst those who are verified using their date of birth and CVV, both customer groups agree the 2-Factor strategy is the most secure, and is highly usable. Moreover, there was a clear preference for the 2-Factor approach amongst customers with a Secret Number, who tended to be more frequent callers to the live service.

More generally, data from the experiment are positive in that they suggest a high degree of willingness amongst Bank customers to use voiceprint technology for telephone banking in real life (88.1% said they would happily do so). There were fewer objections to speaking what might be regarded as sensitive information than might be expected (72.3% said without qualification that they would be comfortable speaking their account number and sort code for example), although it should be borne in mind that participants' experience of this was in the laboratory setting. That said, the existing service already allows the spoken input of sort code and account number.

In addition, participants were largely unconcerned about the storage of their voice data by the Bank (69.2% said they had no concerns at all). Concerns over privacy are frequently mentioned as a potential barrier to the deployment of biometrics. In this context, however, it does not appear to be an issue. This is highly encouraging for practitioners in the field. Interview results did, however, highlight the value in explaining the technology to new users. In particular, communications should reassure customers of the technology's ability to resist mimics and tolerate variations in their own voice.

In terms of the alleged trade-off between usability and security in automated systems, the results present a somewhat complex picture. Indications from the experiment are that higher levels of security do not necessarily lead to lower usability. Equally, however, there is little evidence to suggest that the reverse is true and higher levels of security automatically lead to increased usability. The 2-Factor strategy was rated highest in terms of security but was also rated joint highest in terms of usability alongside the 1-Factor approach – which was considered to be the least secure.

Here, it appears that user attitudes may depend on the *form* the added security takes. On reflection, two of the three strategies examined (the 1-Factor and 2-Factor approaches) comprised for the most part elements likely to be familiar to the user i.e. the collection of sort code and account number, and of verification tokens (date of birth and CVV or digits from a secret number). While the majority of participants were infrequent callers to the existing service, procedures of this nature are typical across many services. Thus in the case of these two strategies, although voiceprint authentication is new, it largely takes place 'in the background' of familiar processes with little effect on the interaction itself. The prompts, for example, refer to using the customer's voiceprint, but do not require new or extra effort from the user. The Challenge strategy, on the other hand, involves a new dialogue stage that requires unfamiliar input unlikely to have been experienced in other services. The indications were that participants found this cognitively challenging, as reflected in the usability and preference results.

Thus, it may be that where additional security measures can be carried out alongside existing or familiar procedures, there is little negative impact on usability. Where, on the other hand, additional security measures involve extra, unfamiliar effort on the part of the user (as in the Challenge strategy) there is more likely to be a negative impact on users' attitude towards the service. In this sense, the use of voiceprint technology in an automated telephone service may be a special case in that it accommodates the possibility of background use more easily than other forms of additional security, albeit an initial enrolment process is required.

Attitudes towards the enrolment process were not specifically examined in this experiment, although all participants did experience an enrolment call. The scope of this experiment also did not extend to customers experiencing a false non-match due to an error by the verification engine. Errors of this type are not expected to be common but nevertheless may affect the results since their level of occurrence may vary between the different strategies.

Despite these limitations, the research presented in this paper provides a comprehensive evaluation of voiceprint authentication technology from the point of view of the user which is often missing from other research in this area. Its setting within the context of a real-life application makes it of particular value to organisations considering use of the technology, as it supplies practical data with which to inform design decisions.

Future work being considered includes a large-scale performance evaluation of the state-of-the-art in commercial voiceprint technologies, as would be available to the Bank. Other plans include research *directly* comparing the existing knowledge-based security procedure with the 2-Factor approach described here (comparing established procedures with new biometric verification modalities as suggested by Toledano et al., 2006).

REFERENCES

Adams, A., & Sasse, A. (2005). Users are not the enemy. In L. F. Cranor & S. Garfinkel (Eds.), *Security and usability* (1st ed., pp. 639–649). O'Reilly.

Arivazhagan, S., Ganesan, L., & Srividya, T. (2009). Iris recognition using multiresolution transforms. *International Journal of Biometrics*, *1*(3), 254–267. doi:10.1504/IJBM.2009.024273

Bishop, M. (2005). Psychological acceptability revisited. In L. F. Cranor & S. Garfinkel (Eds.), *Security and usability* (1st ed., pp. 1–11). O'Reilly.

Business Wire. (2010). *Top 3 Israeli banks roll out customer facing voice biometrics technology by Persay*. Retrieved April 9, 2013, from http://www.businesswire.com/news/home/20100415005768/en/Top-3-Israeli-Banks-Roll-Customer-Facing

Coventry, L. (2005). Usable biometrics. In L. F. Cranor & S. Garfinkel (Eds.), *Security and usability* (1st ed., pp. 175–198). O'Reilly.

Coventry, L., De Angeli, A., & Johnson, G. (2003, April 5-10). Usability and biometric verification at the ATM interface. In *Proceedings of the SIGCHI conference on Human factors in computing systems*, Fort Lauderdale, Florida. doi:10.1145/642637.642639

Davidson, N., McInnes, F., & Jack, M. A. (2004). Usability of dialogue design strategies for automated surname capture. *Speech Communication*, *43*(1), 55–70. doi:10.1016/j.specom.2004.02.002

Dhamija, R., & Perrig, A. (2000, August 14-17). Deja vu: A user study using images for authentication. In *Proceedings of the 9th USENIX Security Symposium*, Denver, CO.

Dutton, R., Foster, J. C., Jack, M. A., & Stentiford, F. (1993, September 22-25). *Identifying usability attributes of automated telephone services*. Paper presented at the Third European Conference on Speech Communication and Technology, Berlin, Germany.

Flare-design. (2013). *Voice biometrics at Barclays Bank*. Retrieved April 9, 2013, from http://flare-design.com.au/voice-biometrics-at-barclays-bank/

Florêncio, D., & Herley, C. (2010). Where do security policies come from? In *Proceedings of the Sixth Symposium On Usable Privacy and Security (SOUPS)*, Redmond, WA. doi:10.1145/1837110.1837124

Forget, A., Chiasson, S., & Biddle, R. (2007). Helping users create better passwords: is this the right approach? In *Proceedings of the third Symposium On Usable Privacy and Security (SOUPS)*, Pittsburgh, PA. doi:10.1145/1280680.1280703

Forget, A., Chiasson, S., van Oorschot, P., & Biddle, R. (2008). Improving text passwords through persuasion. In *Proceedings of the fourth Symposium On Usable Privacy and Security (SOUPS)*, Pittsburgh, PA. doi:10.1145/1408664.1408666

Gartner. (2009). *Gartner consumer survey shows that barriers to online banking use continue to fall*. Retrieved April 9, 2013, from http://www.gartner.com/newsroom/id/1020212

Gaw, S., & Felten, E. W. (2006). Password management strategies for online accounts. In *Proceedings of the second Symposium On Usable Privacy and Security (SOUPS)*, Pittsburgh, PA. doi:10.1145/1143120.1143127

Gunson, N., Marshall, D., McInnes, F., & Jack, M. (2011). Usability evaluation of voiceprint authentication in automated telephone banking: Sentences versus digits. *Interacting with Computers, 23*(1), 57–69. doi:10.1016/j.intcom.2010.10.001

Gunson, N., Marshall, D., Morton, H., & Jack, M. (2011). User perceptions of security and usability of single-factor and two-factor authentication in automated telephone banking. *Computers & Security, 30*(4), 208–220. doi:10.1016/j.cose.2010.12.001

Hébert, M. (2008). Text-dependent speaker recognition. In J. Benesty, M. M. Sondhi, & Y. Huang (Eds.), *Springer handbook of speech processing* (pp. 743–762). Springer Berlin Heidelberg. doi:10.1007/978-3-540-49127-9_37

Hiltgen, A., Kramp, T., & Weigold, T. (2006). Secure internet banking authentication. *Security & Privacy, IEEE, 4*(2), 21–29. doi:10.1109/MSP.2006.50

Jack, M. A., Foster, J., & Stentiford, F. (1993). *Usability analysis of intelligent dialogues for automated telephone services.* Paper presented at the Joint ESCA/NATO Workshop on Applications of Speech Technology.

Jain, A. K., Ross, A., & Pankanti, S. (2006). Biometrics: A tool for information security. *IEEE Transactions on Information Forensics and Security, 1*(2), 125–143. doi:10.1109/TIFS.2006.873653

Kainda, R., Flechais, I., & Roscoe, A. (2010). *Security and usability: Analysis and evaluation.* Paper presented at the International Conference on Availability, Reliability, and Security (ARES'10). doi:10.1109/ARES.2010.77

Khan, L., Baig, M., & Youssef, A. M. (2010). Speaker recognition from encrypted VoIP communications. *Digital Investigation, 7*(1), 65–73. doi:10.1016/j.diin.2009.10.001

Kuo, C., Romanosky, S., & Cranor, L. F. (2006). Human selection of mnemonic phrase-based passwords. In *Proceedings of the second Symposium On Usable Privacy and Security (SOUPS)*. doi:10.1145/1143120.1143129

Larsen, L. B. (1999). *Combining objective and subjective data in evaluation of spoken dialogues.* Paper presented at the ESCA Tutorial and Research Workshop (ETRW) on Interactive Dialogue in Multi-Modal Systems.

Larsen, L. B. (2003). *Assessment of spoken dialogue system usability-what are we really measuring?* Paper presented at the Eighth European Conference on Speech Communication and Technology.

Lewis, J. R. (2001). Introduction: Current issues in usability evaluation. *International Journal of Human-Computer Interaction, 13*(4), 343–349. doi:10.1207/S15327590IJHC1304_01

Likert, R. (1932). A technique for the measurement of attitudes. *Archives de Psychologie*, 140.

Love, S., Dutton, R., Foster, J., & Jack, M. (1992). *Towards a usability measure for automated telephone services*. Paper presented at the Institute of Acoustics Speech and Hearing Workshop.

Martin, A., Przybocki, M., & Campbell, J. P. Jr. (2005). *The NIST speaker recognition evaluation program. Biometric Systems* (pp. 241–262). Springer.

Morgen, B. (2012). Voice biometrics for customer authentication. *Biometric Technology Today, 2012*(2), 8-11.

Naini, A. S., Homayounpour, M. M., & Samani, A. (2010). A real-time trained system for robust speaker verification using relative space of anchor models. *Computer Speech & Language, 24*(4), 545–561. doi:10.1016/j.csl.2009.07.002

National Australia Bank Limited. (2013). *What is speech security?* Retrieved April 9, 2013, from http://www.nab.com.au/wps/wcm/connect/nab/nab/home/Personal_Finance/21/Speech+Security/?ncID=ZBA

O'Gorman, L. (2003). Comparing passwords, tokens, and biometrics for user authentication. *Proceedings of the IEEE, 91*(12), 2021–2040. doi:10.1109/JPROC.2003.819611

Peevers, G., Williams, R., Douglas, G., & Jack, M. A. (2013). Usability Study of Fingerprint and Palmvein Biometric Technologies at the ATM. [IJTHI]. *International Journal of Technology and Human Interaction, 9*(1), 78–95. doi:10.4018/jthi.2013010106

Sasse, A. (2005). Usability and trust in informations systems. In R. Mansell & B. S. Collins (Eds.), *Introduction: Trust and crime in information societies* (pp. 319–348). Edward Elgar.

Shay, R., Komanduri, S., Kelley, P. G., Leon, P. G., Mazurek, M. L., & Bauer, L. et al. (2010). Encountering stronger password requirements: User attitudes and behaviors. In *Proceedings of the sixth Symposium On Usable Privacy and Security (SOUPS)*. doi:10.1145/1837110.1837113

Snelick, R., Uludag, U., Mink, A., Indovina, M., & Jain, A. (2005). Large-scale evaluation of multimodal biometric authentication using state-of-the-art systems. *IEEE Transactions on Pattern Analysis and Machine Intelligence, 27*(3), 450–455. doi:10.1109/TPAMI.2005.57 PMID:15747798

Sturm, J., & Boves, L. (2005). Effective error recovery strategies for multimodal form-filling applications. *Speech Communication, 45*(3), 289–303. doi:10.1016/j.specom.2004.11.007

Tassabehji, R., & Kamala, M. (2009). *Improving e-banking security with biometrics: modelling user attitudes and acceptance*. Paper presented at the 2009 3rd International Conference on New Technologies, Mobility and Security (NTMS). doi:10.1109/NTMS.2009.5384806

Toledano, D. T., Fernández Pozo, R., Hernández Trapote, Á., & Hernández Gómez, L. (2006). Usability evaluation of multi-modal biometric verification systems. *Interacting with Computers, 18*(5), 1101–1122. doi:10.1016/j.intcom.2006.01.004

Venkatraman, S., & Delpachitra, I. (2008). Biometrics in banking security: A case study. *Information Management & Computer Security, 16*(4), 415–430. doi:10.1108/09685220810908813

Wagner, M., Summerfield, C., Dunstone, T., Summerfield, R., & Moss, J. (2006). *An evaluation of "commercial off-the-shelf" speaker verification systems*. Paper presented at the Odyssey Speaker Recognition Workshop.

Weir, C. S., Douglas, G., Carruthers, M., & Jack, M. (2009). User perceptions of security, convenience and usability for ebanking authentication tokens. *Computers & Security*, *28*(1), 47–62. doi:10.1016/j.cose.2008.09.008

Weir, C. S., Douglas, G., Richardson, T., & Jack, M. (2010). Usable security: User preferences for authentication methods in eBanking and the effects of experience. *Interacting with Computers*, *22*(3), 153–164. doi:10.1016/j.intcom.2009.10.001

Yamagishi, M., Nishiuchi, N., & Yamanaka, K. (2008). Hybrid fingerprint authentication using artifact-metrics. *International Journal of Biometrics*, *1*(2), 160–172. doi:10.1504/IJBM.2008.020142

Yan, J., Blackwell, A., Anderson, R., & Grant, A. (2004). Password memorability and security: Empirical results. *Security & Privacy, IEEE*, *2*(5), 25–31. doi:10.1109/MSP.2004.81

ENDNOTES

[1]   BIOSECURE. Biometrics for Secure Authentication (2004-2007). Retrieved April 8, 2013 from http://www.ist-world.org/ProjectDetails.aspx?ProjectId=83aa8f7b0a4b416fb19f61ed18ba7390

[2]   Biometrics Working Group. Retrieved April 8, 2013 from http://www.cesg.gov.uk/policyguidance/biometrics/Pages/index.aspx

[3]   BioVisioN. Roadmap to successful deployments from the user and system integrator perspective (2002-2003). Retrieved April 8, 2013 from http://www.ist-world.org/ProjectDetails.aspx?ProjectId=c73fc0f5692b4ef8a79a4e0644a0211f.

[4]   BEAT Biometrics Evaluation and Testing (2012- 2015). Retrieved April 8, 2013 from www.beat-eu.org

This research was previously published in the International Journal of Technology and Human Interaction (IJTHI), 10(2); edited by Anabela Mesquita and Chia-Wen Tsai, pages 59-77, copyright year 2014 by IGI Publishing (an imprint of IGI Global).

APPENDIX

Items in Usability Questionnaire

Statements were presented in a randomised order for each participant:

Q1: I thought the service was too complicated.
Q2: When I was using the service I always knew what I was expected to do.
Q3: I thought the service was efficient.
Q4: I liked the voice.
Q5: I would be happy to use the service again.
Q6: I found the service confusing to use.
Q7: The service was friendly.
Q8: I felt under stress when using the service.
Q9: The service was too fast for me.
Q10: I thought the service was polite.
Q11: I found the service frustrating to use.
Q12: I enjoyed using the service.
Q13: I felt flustered when using the service.
Q14: I think the service needs a lot of improvement.
Q15: I felt the service was easy to use.
Q16: I would prefer to talk to a human being.
Q17: I thought the voice was very clear.
Q18: I felt that the service was reliable.
Q19: I had to concentrate hard to use the service.
Q20: I did not feel in control when using the service.

Chapter 9
Technology–Enabled Experiential Marketing:
Promotional Strategies Towards New Service Opportunities

Thorben Haenel
Tongji University, China

Wilhelm Loibl
University of Chester, UK

Hui Wang
Birmingham City University, UK

ABSTRACT

In recent years, there has been an increased interest from both academia and practitioners in the topic of customer experience. Companies nowadays are transforming their attention and endeavour to focus on memorable or customer experiences rather than premium prices or superior quality of products and services. Importantly, the value generated by unique customer experiences has a significant impact upon business performance in terms of customer commitment and customer loyalty. Along with the rapid and continuous development of ICT, the travel experience is no longer limited to services encounters on-site but is extended and dynamically created in both physical and virtual experience spaces. With the continuous proliferation of smart technology, travel industry has seen a radical transformation from product and service orientation to a customer-experience driven approach.

INTRODUCTION

In recent years, there has been an increased interest from both academia and practitioners in the topic of customer experience. In fact, the emergence of experience economy is not accidental but rather an inevitable trend (Zhang, 2010). The services has inherent nature of being intangible are so are not seen or felt but only experienced with. Thus companies nowadays are transforming their attention and endea-

DOI: 10.4018/978-1-5225-2589-9.ch009

vour to focus on memorable or customer experiences rather than premium prices or superior quality of products and services. Importantly, the value generated by unique customer experiences has a significant impact upon business performance in terms of customer commitment and customer loyalty (Lemke, Clark and Wilson, 2011; Ferreira and Teixeira, 2013). This thinking has led to the creation of a new marketing management area, which is commonly referred to as "experiential marketing" (Schmitt and Zarantonello, 2013, p.26).

Defining the Concept of Experiential Marketing

The rise of experiential marketing during last decade shed some light on academic literature. It is noted that the rise of the concept has turned the understanding of consumption experience into a hot topic for market scholars and researchers (Caru and Cova, 2008). Many scholars from different scientific disciplines have defined experiential marketing from different angles, and various definitions are referred to in the academic literature. In the 1990s, the concept of experiential marketing is described as a process wherein experiences are generated for customers (Schmitt, 1999). Smilansky (2009, p.33) further defines experiential marketing as "the process of identifying and satisfying customer needs and aspirations profitably, engaging them through two-way communications that bring brand personalities to life and add value to the target audience". Similarly, Hauser (2011) advocates that experiential marketing is regarded as authentic experience customers possess which drive sales through brand images and awareness. "Experiential Marketing can be seen as a marketing tactic designed by a business to stage the entire physical environment and the operational processes for its customers to experience" (Yuan and Wu, 2008, p.388). Also from a strategic marketing perspective, You-Ming (2010, p.190) defines experiential marketing as "a marketing tactic designed as a kind of face-to-face communication method, which mainly raises customers' physical and emotional feelings, thereby making customers feel and experience wholehearted". In the same vein, Snakers and Zajdman (2010) view experiential marketing as a novel way by making the customers living an experience through creation of their emotional experiences. In other words, experiential marketing plays a key role of creating emotions which leads to the enjoyment of the brand from customers. It makes customers feel connected with the brand particularly helps them to feel the brand value (Lawler, 2013). Of this, investing in experiential marketing will serve as an effective tool for marketing products and services.

Dimensional Research of Experiential Marketing

The emerging market has ever increasing service industry, be it banking, telecom, tourism or education or any other. So, experiential marketing strategies have become a cornerstone of many recent advances in marketing with a great potential for its application in tourism marketing (McIntosh and Siggs, 2005). However, the experiential aspects of tourism remain relatively unexplored in developed as well as in emerging markets and therefore, research is called for on identifying the unique elements of the tourism experience. Over the past two decades academics have paid considerable attention to tourism and leisure experiences, examining its different dimensions (Schmitt, 1999; Cutler and Carmichael, 2010; Uriely, 2005; Walls, Okumus, Wang and Kwun, 2011). Schmitt (1999) presents five types of experiential marketing approaches, namely, "sense, feel, think, act, and relate" dimensions. Experiential marketing focuses on how customers sense, feel, think, act and relate their experiences to the environment and a sustainable world. For example, a traveller spends several times in visiting a particular tourist attraction, experiencing the attraction. In this context, the customer experience includes what the customer sees and feels as well as how he or she interacts with environment (Jahromi, Adibzadeh, & Nakhae, 2015).

The first is sense, which "appeals to the senses, with the objective of creating sensory experiences through sight, sound, touch, taste, and smell" (Schmitt, 1999, p.13). In fact, introducing sense dimension can help companies to differentiate their products and services from competitors. Importantly, this dimension highlights functionality and benefit of the products and services to keep customers interested (Grundey, 2008). The second dimension is feel, which is explained as "the understanding of stimuli that can trigger certain emotions" (Schmitt, 1999, p.13). The necessity of understanding is obvious because, companies endeavour to trigger particular emotions about their brand in order to greatly induce customer purchases. Think is the third dimension, and its objective is to "create cognitive, problem-solving experiences that engage customers creatively" (Schmitt, 1999, p.13). The fourth dimension is act, which is explained by Schmitt (1999, p.13) as "enrich customer's lives by targeting their physical experiences, showing them alternate ways of doing things, as well as alternate lifestyles and interactions". The purpose of introducing act is to "change long-term behaviour and habits in favour of a particular product or service" (Grundey, 2008, p.139). Relate is the fifth dimension of experiential marketing, which "digs deeper and targets that motivation for self-improvement and longing to be accepted by others and the society they live in" (Schmitt, 1999, p.13). Within the context of a brand experience, these five dimensions need to fully exploit "products, communications, and marketing campaigns to deliver an experience" (Schmitt, 1999, p.57). The brand should be as a "source of sensory, affective, and cognitive associations" that can produce "memorable and rewarding brand experiences" (Schmitt, 1999, p.57). The above five dimensions are individually different owing to different objectives and outcomes. In order to create and broaden experiential appeals, companies need to combine two or more dimensions (Schmitt, 1999, p.14). The experiential marketing is like a stage drama, where audiences themselves experience this drama by participating themselves as actors and watchers.

Technology Transfer and Innovation Within the Experiential Marketing Context

Besides the movement of investment capital technology transfer and innovation strategy have become an important topic in academic research and for practitioners in this context (Laafia, 2002; Hänel & Li-Hua, 2011). Brooks et al. (2004: 148) argue that technology has been 'the biggest story of the twentieth century [...]. The proliferation of technology [...] and the pace of technological change [and innovation]' have effected on any organization all over the world. In times of 'hyper-competition' (Sparrow, 2003: 371) organizations seek more than ever to achieve sustain competitive advantage by a long-term strategy (Porter, 2004; Barney, 1991). Thus, it is necessary to bring technology transfer and innovation into a strategic and experiential marketing context (Li-Hua, 2004) even though academics fail to agree on one definition (Hänel & Li-Hua, 2011). In general terms technology must be regarded in its wider context meaning the process of transferring skills, knowledge, technologies and innovation (Thomke, 2003). Furthermore, Li-Hua (2003: 2) states that the term technology transfer 'has matured from the early period of emphasis on the technology itself' to a wider understanding as 'types and patterns of activity, equipment and material, and knowledge or experience to perform tasks' (Gillespie & Mileti, 1977: 9).

According to Li-Hua (2004) nowadays technology transfer and innovation must be seen in a wider context, he points out 'the coherence of technology and knowledge, and that [strategic] technology transfer is not achievable without knowledge transfer'. Chen and Li-Hua (2011: 93) state that 'in the long term technology strategy encompasses technological capacity building through the acquisition of appropriate technologies [to build] [...] a strategic architecture' (2011: 94). Porter (2004: 231) goes beyond the previous definitions by stating that technological strategy is a 'vehicle for pursuing generic competitive strategies aiming at fundamentally different types of competitive advantage [and hence] business model and process innovation is an evolving consequence', Li-Hua (2004) adds technology and innovation strategy 'is but one element of an overall competitive strategy and thus must be consistent with and reinforced by the actions of other functional departments'. Chen and Li-Hua (2011:.94) conclude that 'technology transfer and innovation are strategic instruments in creating wealth and prosperity', which evidently can be applied to developed and emerging economies.

EXPERIENTIAL MARKETING IN TRAVEL INDUSTRY

Experience and Tourism

Owing to the rising demand in the travel industry, consumers nowadays seek to more engaging experiences. Travellers are no longer passive receivers of tourism products and services, instead, they are active experientialists, and may even assume the role of significant generators (O'Dell, 2007; Rahimi and Gunlu, 2016; Rahimi and Kozak, 2016). It is like consumers take the role of co-creators and consumers at the same time. Therefore, tourism operators along with Tourist should jointly construct diverse and innovative product offerings to strengthen consumer experiences. The concept of tourist experience is said to have been popularised as a notable topic in the tourism literature from early 1970s by social scientists (Barthes, 1972; MacCannell, 1973; Turner & Ash, 1975; Cohen, 1979; Mannell & Iso-Ahola, 1987; Feifer, 1985; Gronroos, 1996; Otto & Ritchie, 1996; Pine & Gilmore, 1999; Vargo & Lusch, 2004; Jennings, 2006; Jennings et al., 2009; Larsen, 2007; Gentile et al., 2007; Chen & Petrick, 2013; Walker & Moscardo, 2014; Campos, Mendes, Valle & Scott, 2015). Yet despite this level of attention, the concept remains relatively elusive (Jennings et al., 2009). Although a plethora of literature on testifying the significance of the concept, no consensus has been reached on probing the nature of tourist experiences. This ambiguity is that scholars and researchers propose different views which attribute to certain characteristics, from experimental to a conceptual manner. It is mainly because "different kinds of people may desire different modes of tourist experiences" (Cohen, 1979, p.180). In other words, different people perform different tourist activities. In that instance, the concept tends to be undervalued and under-researched (Larsen, 2007), which limits companies' ability to develop an effective experience strategy.

Applications of Experiential Marketing in Travel Industry

Tourism and experiential marketing are very tightly connected (Cuellar et al., 2015). Traditional marketing has proven successful for many companies across different industry sectors for the industrial age (Schmitt, 1999; Smith & Wheeler, 2002; Williams, 2006). However, along with the evolution of Information and Communication Technologies (ICT), a new way of thinking about marketing is called for. Experiential marketing has grown in importance to represent a fundamental shift from the traditional marketing concept with regard to segmentation (Jahromi, Adibzadeh, & Nakhae, 2015). Given this, companies in this new era of marketing must learn to develop a stronger bond with their customers. Smilansky (2009, p.12) suggests that companies need to "focus on a two-way interaction in real-time, a live brand experience and thereby a significantly deeper consumer bonding process". The technologies can enhance customer experiences and engagements with virtual reality and augmented reality applications.

Experiential marketing signifies point engagement between consumers and brands. Importantly it establishes emotional links to influence consumer behaviours in a very short time span (Robertson, 2007). A service marketing study by Yelkur (2000) indicates that customers' service experiences have a significant influence on customer attraction and retention. Similarly, Singh and Sirdeshmukh (2000) find that a strong bond exists between experiential marketing and consumer behavioural intentions. The use of experiential marketing creates those positive experiences for consumers and "fosters engagement" (Maurno, 2011, p.10). According to the study by Shaw and Ivens (2005), it receives increasingly recognition that merely making use of differentiation strategy in terms of uniqueness of product, price, and quality is no longer a sustainable competitive advantage. "What people really desire are not products, but satisfying experiences" (Holbrook, 2006, p.40). The nature of experiences is critical for the hospitality and tourism industry, because intangible experience is the core of the products and services offered by companies (Williams, 2006). Most recently, there has been a dramatic increase in terms of recognition of the value of experience (Ha and Perks, 2005; Alloza, 2008; Schmitt, 2009; Brakus et al., 2009). "Experience is the core element of experiential marketing" (Cuellar et al., 2015, p.501), and introducing experience factor is widely accepted as being very important to marketing professionals and employing the factor has been on agenda in the near future (Bigham, 2008). Lewis and Chambers (2000, p.46) define consumption experience as "the total outcome to the customers from the combination of environment, goods and services purchased". In fact, consumers are seeking to user experiences that "dazzle their senses, touch their hearts, and stimulate their minds" (Schmitt, 1999, p.57). The aim of experiential marketing is to create the stimulus to influence and actively engage consumers at the point of sale (Close et al., 2006). For examples, now many countries promote their destinations by using virtual reality. The tourists attraction like Madam Tusaid, provide tourist with opportunities to draw their own hands in wax or and experience 4 D pictures. The Musueam are using smart application to engage the tourists. The recent success of 'Pokemon Go' can be attributed to experiential marketing.

ICT and Tourism

The landscape for the Tourism experiences has continued to grow and diversify, and has become one of the largest and fastest growing economic sectors. According to UNWTO Tourism Highlights (2016), worldwide international tourist arrivals reached 1,184 million in 2015. By the end of 2030, international arrivals are expected to reach 1.8 billion (UNWTO, 2015).The fast development of ICT and the expansion of the Internet-based technologies have significantly revolutionised the Tourism Industry in the last decade. Tourism and ICT have had grown inseparably close and are transforming the way travel and tourism information is collected, and the way tourism products are purchased. According to Ramos and Rodrigues (2013), interest in the integration of ICT in the Tourism Industry is growing. Owing to its ability and utility, the Internet is being used to cope with the intangible nature of Tourism services through transforming marketing-mix variables to sustain a competitive edge for travel companies. Within the information intensive society, Tourism is ranked as the foremost industry in terms of volume of online transactions (Akehurst, 2009; Yuan et al., 2015).

With the help of an interactive platform, information can be accessed in a cost-effective way and importantly the online travel portals reduce cumbersome negotiations involved booking tickets and accommodation. This type of interactive platform is deemed as central to models of Internet marketing and

Electronic Commerce in Tourism Industry. Thereby the Internet has become a major source of information for travellers and an interactive platform for Tourism business transaction. Along with the rapid and continuous development of ICT, the travel experience is no longer limited to services encounters on-site but is extended and dynamically created in both physical and virtual experience spaces. With the continuous proliferation of smart technology, travel industry has seen a radical transformation from product and service orientation to a customer-experience driven approach. In fact, embracing innovation is an emerging trend being seen across the entire travel industry. ICT is transforming conventional experiences to a new type of travel experiences in terms of generating value-added experiences for travellers (Gretzel, 2011). More flexibility and technological integration are a few ways that travel operators today are evolving and managing to create experiential travel opportunities suitable for diverse travellers. Given this, travel industry need to pay close attention to the trend if they are to secure and maintain their realm. In the meanwhile, consumer engagement is turning out to be the winning formula. In other words, richer and enjoyable experiences need to be tailored to travellers' individual preferences. By using ICT, tourists are now able to connect and create new social experiences more than ever before. Beyond interactions with tourism operators, ICTs are now able to connect with locals for more social and localised tourism experiences.

For instance, introducing robot butlers is highly recommended in travel industry to greet customers and assist them during their journey. Hilton and IBM pilot "Connie", the world's Watson-enabled hotel concierge provides a recent example to greet travellers upon their arrivals and to answer questions about hotel amenities, services and hours of operation. Through interaction with the concierge, travellers can personalise and enhance their hotel experiences. Importantly, the entire travel experience will become smarter, easier and more enjoyable for travellers. Given this, one of the main challenges facing travel providers will thus be to understand how to use technology as a catalyst of change for the creation of successful, compelling and valuable travel experiences. Therefore, it is increasingly important for travel providers to keep up with the dynamics of travel market and adopt the most recent ICT applications to facilitate more personalised travel experiences.

Technology will give us many new ways to enjoy travel—from the planning phase to the actual trip. The future of travel will be driven by a complex and diverse set of converging forces and social trends will put increasing pressure on our available leisure time and driving the desire for personalisation of the experience. Smart tourism development is already under way and "How technology can reshape the travel experience?" is the question that we will have to be faced with. Thus, more investigation from management point of view has to be studied and has to empirically and conceptually investigate into economics of smart tourism concern. Travel companies need to take a fresh look at how they can use smart technology to enhance tourist experiences.

ICT TRENDS FOR TOURISM ORGANISATIONS

At the time of writing a simple app managed to motivate millions of people to visit many different sites. It also managed to make the company behind the software more valuable than Sony, although for just a very short time (Telegraph, 2016; The Verge, 2016). The global frenzy created by Pokemon Go (Bloomberg, 2016) shows two things very clearly. Firstly, customers are looking for new, unique experiences. Secondly, recent technological developments can deliver these experiences. Technological innovation does also foster change in the global tourism industry. Thereby, technology can either mean hardware which increasingly enables customers not only to passively consume content but also to create new content. This both personalises the experience and removes many of the limitations companies are facing like manpower. When the customer becomes the co-creator the resulting product potentially becomes limitless. Also some companies like Ricoh (Ricoh, 2016) already deliberately open their APIs (Application Programming Interfaces) allowing customers to adapt and extend the software tools for their hardware. This very short overview already gives an idea of the growing possibilities companies in the tourism sector have to engage their customers. The following section will explore these possibilities in more depth by explaining the underlying technology and providing best practice examples.

Real and Virtual Worlds

Augmented Reality

The success of Pokemon Go touches on two powerful concepts, Augmented Reality and gamification. Augmented Reality is "a technique that combines a live view in real-time with virtual computer-generated images, generating a real-time augmented experience of reality" (Kleef, Noltes, and Spoel, 2010, p. 1). This indicates that the real, physical environment is supplemented by computer-generated sounds, videos, graphics or location data (Taqvi, 2013).

Uses of AR in Tourism

Consequently, this has tremendous potential for the tourism industry as it allows the tourist to immerse him/herself in a virtually enhanced world which interacts with the real world. Such an enhanced visitor experience is especially important in tourism as tourists often have only limited knowledge of a destination (Cranmer et al., 2016). Using Augmented Reality applications visitors can explore unfamiliar surroundings, co-creating their own unique experience (Cranmer et al., 2016) which adds considerable value to tourism attractions (Timothy, 2011, p. 228). All this suggests that AR is the perfect tool to enhance all types of heritage sites (Tscheu and Buhalis. 2016: Jung et al. 2016; Hassan and Rahimi, 2016) or as tourist guides in destinations (Han, Jung and Gibson, 2013). Despite these clear advantages the success of any new technology depends on the acceptance of its users. Models like the Technology Acceptance Model (Davis, 1989) help analysing how and when users accept and use new technologies. The main constructs of the TAM are Perceived Usefulness and Perceived Ease of Use. While the usefulness for the tourist has already been outlined above, the Perceived Ease of Use identifies how the use of a particular system is seen as being free of effort (Davis, 1989).

The basic components of any AR system have not changed since the 1960s and contain displays, trackers, graphics computers and software (van Krevelen and Poelman, 2010). As these components can now be found in any smart phone the prospective user already has the necessary hardware and is also proficient in its use. As the AR application is handled just like any other mobile app it can be assumed that this increases the Perceived Ease of Use for the average user. This is supported by Chung, Han and Joun (2015) who discovered that Technology Readiness and visual appeal have a positive influence on Perceived Usefulness of AR while visual appeal and facilitating conditions (like prior knowledge of necessary devices) have a significant effect on Perceived Ease of Use. Yovcheva, Buhalis and Gratzidis

(2012) distinguish between three different types of AR applications in tourism. Augmented Reality browsers are similar to normal web browsers but enable content providers to publish their own thematic content. Dedicated AR applications build with a clear focus on AR functionality while AR view-enabled applications offer AR functionality but it is not their focus.

One such dedicated app is "Paris, Then and Now" by Mavilleavant. This app is available for iOS and Android and puts a layer showing historical images over physical surroundings allowing visitors to travel back in time and see the Paris of 100 years ago. For each of the more than 2,000 places of interest facts and anecdotes are provided. Push notifications and the interactive map can be used as a tour guide. Similar apps are available for Vancouver, Montreal, Barcelona and Tampa (Hutchings, 2013). A similar app to enhance the experience of a historical setting is the "Timetraveller Berlin Wall" app visually recreating the Berlin Wall (Vivion, 2014). An example for an AR-view enabled application would be Yelp Monocle. This feature inserts business addresses and reviews into the camera view. It also shows which businesses friends have checked in to, making it also a social media tool (Yelp, 2016). Layar offers an augmented reality guide to South Africa with over 5000 POIs like tourist attractions, monuments, museums, waterfalls or blue flag beaches (https://www.layar.com/layers/exploresa2/). Also Chinese Internet Search Giant Baidu has launched China's first AR platform. Although not specifically aimed at tourism applications it offers the possibility of turning 2D objects into 3D which was demonstrated using a map of Shanghai (Wang, 2016)

A concept which can be used very well together with Augmented Reality is gamification. Gamification is a relatively new term first used in the digital media industry in 2008 (Deterding et al., 2011a). Deterding et al. (2011b) define it as an "umbrella term for the use of video game elements in non-gaming systems to improve user experience (UX) and user engagement" whereby it just includes video game elements not full-fledged games (Deterding et al., 2011b). Gaming is a persuasive technology, meaning that it aims to change users' attitude or behaviour (Bogost, 2007, p. 59). Therefore, this cutting-edge concept is seen as a useful tool to help develop tourism experiences and support dynamic interactions, especially since the growing prevalence of smartphones and tables has empowered mobile gaming changing the whole gaming experience (Xu et al., 2015). According to Xu, Weber and Buhalis (2013) the main benefits of gamification for tourism businesses would be that it encourages tourist engagement, enhances the tourism experience, improve tourist loyalty and also increases brand awareness by placing advertisements in gaming apps. Any tourism company intending to use gaming apps should be aware though, that creating meaningful games is challenging and needs specialised knowledge. If not "gamifying" suitable tourism activities users might soon feel controlled and monitored or simply get bored (Xu, Weber and Buhalis, 2013).

Xu et al. (2015) distinguish between two types of games currently used in a tourism context. Social games are embedded within social media platforms like Facebook. Users usually play these games before they get to a holiday destination or attraction. The main focus of such games is on attracting potential customers and builds a certain company or destination image (Xu et al, 2015). Probably the best example was IrelandTown launched by Tourism Ireland in 2011. This game let the players create and run their own town encouraging the users to invite their friends. The concept tried to emulate the previous successes of Farmville and Cityville (May, 2011). Another more recent example is Norway's Holmenkollen Ski Jump game (http://holmenkollen.visitnorway.com/). Location-based mobile games are designed to engage players while visiting the destination or attraction. They are often combined with Augmented Reality elements to offer enhanced immersive on-site experiences. An example for such a game would be ExCORA which allows visitors to explore the natural environment and the hidden history of Urgull

Mountain in San Sebastian, Spain (Linaza et al., 2013). This implies that a good application of these concepts is the "treasure hunt" guiding visitors to various points of interest (Xu et al., 2015). A different approach is taken by Kerala Tourism which allows users to bid for a holiday on their gaming app (https://play.google.com/store/apps/details?id=oi.keralatourism.visitkerala).

360° Videos and 3D Virtual Worlds

A further step away from physical reality is Virtual Reality (VR). In contrast to Augmented Reality, Virtual Reality immerses the user in a completely digitally created environment (Guttentag, 2010). Over the last few years, head mounted displays such as Oculus Rift, Samsung Gear or even Google Cardboard have become affordable for the average user. An even easier way to implement virtual reality is the use of 3D virtual environments (VE). Such environments like Second Life (http://www.secondlife.com) can be ideal marketing platforms for tourism destinations because they allow potential visitor to experience the destination before they actually arrive there. Thus they can make better-informed decisions and have more realistic expectations. This in turn results in higher satisfaction. In addition these systems stimulate real visits (Pakanen and Arhippainen, 2014; Huang et al., 2016). An example for this would be Heidelberg3D (http://www.heidelberg-3d.de/start.en.htm) which provides a virtual city model of Heidelberg. Another showcase of the possibilities is the recreation of the Sistene Chapel in Second Life (http://www.vassar.edu/headlines/2007/sistine-chapel.html).

Producing such 3D models and creating entire cities and destinations in virtual environments takes time, effort and needs a lot of knowledge. An easier first step into 3D world creation is offered by 360° pictures and videos. Specialised cameras, often using fisheye lenses to make shots of the entire surrounding area, have become affordable for the average person within the last few years. Photos and videos taken from such cameras can be uploaded to websites or social media sites like Facebook (https://facebook360.fb.com/360-photos/) (Peltier, 2016). These pictures and videos can easily be used as a virtual tour around a hotel or a specific attraction. Such tours offer psychological relief to visitors suffering from travel anxiety (Guttentag, 2010). Examples for 360 degree videos for a destination can be seen on the Facebook page of seeAustralia (https://www.facebook.com/SeeAustralia/videos/10154049813445909/) while virtual walk trough's can be experienced at Incredible!India (http://incredibleindia.org/index.php/360-panoramic-walkthroughs). A less costly alternative is shown at the site of the Phoenix Ancient Town in China showing a series of 360-degree photos which nevertheless give a good impression of the destination (http://www.easypano.com/gallery/Tourweaver/780/html5/Phoenix-Ancient-Town/index.html).

Smart Tourism

The short overview above clearly shows that over the last few years advanced and cutting-edge technologies have become available even for smaller tourism businesses. It also shows that mobile technologies and social media platforms are gaining in importance when companies try to engage current and prospective customers. But a tourism marketer should never forget that motivating experiences can only be provided if the marketer understands the motivations, expectations and wishes of the customer. All the applications listed above provide a tremendous wealth of knowledge about their users. This knowledge can then be used to maximise tourist satisfaction. A system which analyses data from a wide variety of sources with the aim of improving the customer experience is called a smart tourism system.

Technological Foundations

"Smart" or "intelligent" systems sense their environment, learn from any actions in the environment, they then reason how to best achieve a particular goal from all the gathered information and finally act on the behalf of a user (Gretzel, 2011). For that purpose, smart systems draw on four core information technologies: mobile communication technology, cloud computing, artificial intelligence and the Internet of Things (IoT) (Guo et al. 2014). Mobile communication tools and cloud computing are already widely used in consumer products today. Therefore, of all these technologies, artificial intelligence and especially the Internet of Things need more explanation. Basically, machine learning uses statistics, computer science and engineering to turn raw data into information (Harrington 2012, p. 5). That means that large data sets are needed in which statistical methods and computational algorithms try to find useful patterns. To make these algorithms accessible to a wider professional audience they are implemented in software libraries like Apache Mahout (http://mahout.apache.org/). The necessary raw data is gathered through Internet of Things (IoT) technologies. According to Guinard and Trifa (2016, p. 3) the Internet of Things "is a system of physical objects that can be discovered, monitored and controlled, or interacted with by electronic devices that communicate over various networking interfaces and eventually can be connected to the wider internet". This definition suggests that at the core of this technology are physical objects (the "Things" in the term "Internet of Things") which offer one or more of the following features (Guinard and Trifa, 2016, p. 4):

- Sensors like motion, light, GPS, temperature, etc.
- Actuators like motors, displays, etc.
- Computational capabilities (ability to run programs)
- (Wired or wireless) Communication Interfaces

Using many different devices like smartphones, social media, electronic transit data or other useful "Things" allows tracing people and their activities forming digital footprints. Getting reliable real-time data from a wide variety of sources in specific locations help overcome the problems of sparsity and reliability which is important for Smart Systems to work properly (Groen, Meys and Veenstra, 2013). The Internet is used to enable other applications to access those "Things" through its existing infrastructure (Guinard and Trifa, 2016, p. 5) effectively bridging the real and the digital world (Buhalis and Amaranggana, 2013). The last critical component in the Internet of Things solves the problem of how a great variety of applications can use data from a great variety of smart devices. For this communication to work data has to be described in a machine-interpretable way using extensible vocabularies. The Resource Description Framework (RDF) is a standard which provides a data model for potentially describing any kind of information (Loibl, 2015, p. 4).

Smart Tourism Applications

As tourism has always heavily depended on ICT (Werthner and Klein, 1999) these new technologies create ample business opportunities by providing new services (Morandi et al. 2012). Therefore, it is only natural that the new developments in information technologies described above have led to smart tourism initiatives across the whole globe. Smart Tourism is defined by Gretzel et al. (2015) as "tourism supported by integrated efforts at a destination to collect and aggregate/harness data derived from physical infrastructure, social connections, government/organisational sources and human bodies/minds in combination with the use of advanced technologies to transform that data into on-site experiences and business value-propositions with a clear focus on efficiency, sustainability and experience enrichment". This definition suggests three main components of smart tourism: smart destinations, smart business ecosystems and smart experience (Gretzel et al. 2015). While currently some smart destination initiatives exist (Gretzel et al. 2015), especially in China (Wang et al. 2013), the uptake of these new technologies in individual tourism businesses has been quite conservative. Like tourism itself, smart tourism not a very homogenous field. Wang et al. (2016) tried to distinguish smart tourism into seven research areas. More geographically/organisationally oriented research focuses on smart cities, smart destinations or smart hotels. When looking at the underlying technology Wang et al. (2016) discriminated between smartphone applications for tourism, the use of smart cards in tourism, augmented reality and gamification in tourism as well as tourism recommenders. As the more technical topic about augmented and virtual realities have already been discussed above, the following sections outline the use of smart technologies within different organisational contexts.

Smart Destinations

Possibly the most challenging of all smart tourism areas are smart destinations. Making destinations smart requires all destination stakeholders like local governments, tourism organisations, local residents and tourists to interconnect and exchange information freely (Buhalis and Amaranggana, 2013). Most work about smart destinations seems to ultimately focus on smart cities though, leaving a clear research gap. So did Boes, Buhalis and Inversini (2015) analyse smart city cases to arrive at their smart tourism destination dimensions.

Smart Cities

The first dimension is leadership which can either be implemented in a top-down or bottom-up approach where the individual stakeholders are encouraged to contribute ideas. An example for the latter would be Amsterdam Smart City (Amsterdam Smart City, 2016). Other essential dimensions are entrepreneurship and innovation, social capital and human capital (Boes, Buhalis and Inversini, 2015). An overview of smart cities in Spain is provided by Jung (2011) although their smartness is not focussed on tourism. A more recent initiative is Smart City Wien, a long term initiative setting a framework strategy until 2050 including a wide array of different projects (https://smartcity.wien.gv.at/site/en/). These projects are based on requests and ideas by Viennese citizens who were invited to contribute in an early development stage of this initiative. Similar to this approach the Indian government launched its Smart Cities Mission in 2015 (http://smartcities.gov.in/#) with the aim of improving, renewing and extending a number of cities throughout the country (http://smartcities.gov.in/writereaddata/Strategy.pdf). A somewhat less positive example is Rio de Janeiro. In the course of its preparations for the FIFA World Cup Rio invested heavily in smart city technologies. Nevertheless, political and economic interests impeded their effective use. In addition, not all metropolitan areas seem to have benefited from technological improvements (Gaffner & Robertson, 2016).

Smart Attractions

Any tourism manager must never forget, that all the technological advances aim at improving the tourism experience for the visitor. For this purpose, Wang et al. (2016) researched the following list of items which are most important to tourists (importance in descending order):

1. Homepage of the tourist attraction.
2. Free WIFI.
3. Online information access.
4. Availability of a mobile application.
5. QR-codes.
6. Electronic touch screens.
7. Smart card (band).
8. Electronic entrance guard system.
9. Tourist-flow monitoring system.
10. Crowd handling.
11. Smart education.
12. Personal itinerary design.
13. Intelligent guide system.
14. Recommendation system.
15. E-Tour map.
16. Mobile payment.
17. Online coupons.
18. Online booking.
19. Intelligent environment monitoring.
20. Travel safety protection.
21. Smart emergency response system.
22. Smart vehicle scheduling.
23. Real-time traffic broadcast.
24. Tourist flow forecast.
25. Queueing forecast.
26. Weather forecast.
27. Virtual tourism experience.
28. Virtual travel community.

Surprisingly the more technologically sophisticated items like virtual experiences and virtual travel communities in social media are right at the bottom of this list. In this context it must be noted that Wang et al. (2016) used a convenience sample at Honshan Zoo in Nanjing, China to compile this list. Therefore, more research on what smart features are important at different types of attractions and within different contexts is needed.

Smart Hotels

On Friday 16th July 2015 the world's first hotel staffed by humanoid robots was opened in Nagasaki, Japan. Hideo Sawada, president of Huis Ten Bosch, the theme park where the Henn Na hotel is located, says that 90% of all hotel's services could be carried out by robots in the future (Telegraph, 2015).

CONCLUSION

This book chapter has contributed to the marketing and management literature from both academic and practical perspectives.

Theoretical Contributions

This chapter not only supports earlier literature and studies on experiential marketing, but more importantly, it fills a gap in the literature concerning experiential marketing as a promotional strategy and practice, and its impact in the service industry with the help of smart technology ('technology-enabled'). As such it can act as a basis to further conceptualise this emerging topic area by identifying related themes. It also allows making theoretical considerations as to how emerging markets should draw attention on new technologies to utilize existing potential and develop their economies further.

Practical Contributions

From a practical perspective, this chapter has provided useful information and knowledge about contribution of smart technologies. Specifically ICT and international technology transfer do present both challenges and opportunities with regard to smart technologies, however, if employed rightly to enhance customer experience it is undoubtedly a crucial chance for emerging economies to benefit even further and unlock further potential. The selected experiential marketing themes with regard to smart tourism delivered through smart technologies and applications do clearly support our argument that this is one of most contemporary trends, some countries anticipate this very well and our selected examples from emerging economies do prove that through the enhancement of the customer experience regional development and wealth can be at least supported. To this end, this study will furnish a set of guidelines for facilitating managerial decision-making and provides solutions for problems concerning the application of companies' smart technology and its impact on user experiences. For instance, marketers can use it for designing their marketing mix, smart technology developers and designers are able to improve business performance, and corporate managers can formulate their budgeting plan for promoting their businesses.

REFERENCES

Akehurst, G. (2009). User generated content: The use of blogs for tourism organisations and tourism consumers. *Service Business*, *3*(1), 51–61. doi:10.1007/s11628-008-0054-2

Alloza, A. (2008). Brand engagement and brand experience at BBVA, the transformation of a 150 years old company. *Corporate Reputation Review*, *11*(4), 371–379. doi:10.1057/crr.2008.31

Amsterdam Smart City. (2016). *Connect with Amsterdam's Smart City Innovators*. Retrieved from https://amsterdamsmartcity.com/

Barthes, R. (1973). *Mythologies* (A. Lavers, Trans.). London: Paladin.

Bigham, L. (2008). New survey: experiential spend to grow in 2008. *360° Newsletter*. Retrieved June 1, from http://360.jackmorton.com/articles/article012808.php

Boes, K., Buhalis, D., & Inversini, A. (2015). Conceptualising smart tourism destination dimensions. In *Information and communication technologies in tourism 2015* (pp. 391–403). Springer International Publishing.

Bogost, I. (2007). *Persuasive games: The expressive power of videogames*. MIT Press.

Brakus, J. J., Schmitt, B. H., & Zarantonello, L. (2009). Brand experience: What is it? How is it measured? Does it affect loyalty? *Journal of Marketing*, *73*(3), 52–68. doi:10.1509/jmkg.73.3.52

Buhalis, D., & Amaranggana, A. (2013). Smart tourism destinations. In *Information and Communication Technologies in Tourism 2014* (pp. 553–564). Springer International Publishing. doi:10.1007/978-3-319-03973-2_40

Campos, A. C., Mendes, J., Valle, P. O. D., & Scott, N. (2015). Co-creation of tourist experiences: A literature review. *Current Issues in Tourism*, 1–32. doi:10.1080/13683500.2015.1081158

Carù, A., & Cova, B. (2008). Small versus big stories in framing consumption experiences. *Qualitative Market Research: An International Journal*, *11*(2), 166–176. doi:10.1108/13522750810864422

Chen, C. C., & Petrick, J. F. (2013). Health and Wellness Benefits of Travel Experiences A Literature Review. *Journal of Travel Research*, *52*(6), 709–719. doi:10.1177/0047287513496477

Chung, N., Han, H., & Joun, Y. (2015). Tourists intention to visit a destination: The role of augmented reality (AR) application for a heritage site. *Computers in Human Behavior*, *50*, 588–599. doi:10.1016/j.chb.2015.02.068

Close, A. G., Finney, R. Z., Lacey, R. Z., & Sneath, J. Z. (2006). Engaging the consumer through event marketing: Linking attendees with the sponsor, community, and brand. *Journal of Advertising Research*, *46*(4), 420–433. doi:10.2501/S0021849906060430

Cohen, E. (1979). A phenomenology of tourist experiences. *Sociology*, *13*(2), 179–201. doi:10.1177/003803857901300203

Cranmer, E., Jung, T., tom Dieck, M. C., & Miller, A. (2016). Understanding the Acceptance of Augmented Reality at an Organisational Level: The Case of Geevor Tin Mine Museum. In *Information and Communication Technologies in Tourism 2016* (pp. 637–650). Springer International Publishing. doi:10.1007/978-3-319-28231-2_46

Cuellar, S. S., Eyler, R. C., & Fanti, R. (2015). Experiential Marketing and Long-Term Sales. *Journal of Travel & Tourism Marketing*, *32*(5), 534–553. doi:10.1080/10548408.2014.918925

Cutler, S. Q., & Carmichael, B. (2010). The dimensions of the tourist experience. In M. Morgan, P. Lugosi, & J. R. B. Ritchie (Eds.), *The tourism and leisure experience: Consumer and managerial perspectives* (pp. 3–26). Bristol: Channel View Publications.

Davis, F. D. (1989). Perceived usefulness, perceived ease of use, and user acceptance of information technology. *Management Information Systems Quarterly*, *13*(3), 319–340. doi:10.2307/249008

Deterding, S., Dixon, D., Khaled, R., & Nacke, L. (2011a, September). From game design elements to gamefulness: defining gamification. In *Proceedings of the 15th international academic MindTrek conference: Envisioning future media environments* (pp. 9-15). ACM. doi:10.1145/2181037.2181040

Deterding, S., Sicart, M., Nacke, L., O'Hara, K., & Dixon, D. (2011b, May). Gamification. using game-design elements in non-gaming contexts. In CHI'11 Extended Abstracts on Human Factors in Computing Systems (pp. 2425-2428). ACM.

Feifer, M. (1985). *Going places*. London: Macmillan.

Ferreira, H., & Teixeira, A. A. (2013). *'Welcome to the experience economy': Assessing the influence of customer experience literature through bibliometric analysis (No. 481)*. Universidade do Porto, Faculdade de Economia do Porto.

Gaffney, C., & Robertson, C. (2016). Smarter than Smart: Rio de Janeiros Flawed Emergence as a Smart City. *Journal of Urban Technology*, 1–18. doi:10.1080/10630732.2015.1102423

Gentile, C., Spiller, N., & Noci, G. (2007). How to sustain the customer experience: An overview of experience components that co-create value with the customer. *European Management Journal*, *25*(5), 395–410. doi:10.1016/j.emj.2007.08.005

Gretzel, U. (2011). Intelligent systems in tourism: A social science perspective. *Annals of Tourism Research*, *38*(3), 757–779. doi:10.1016/j.annals.2011.04.014

Gretzel, U., Sigala, M., Xiang, Z., & Koo, C. (2015). Smart tourism: Foundations and developments. *Electronic Markets*, *25*(3), 179–188. doi:10.1007/s12525-015-0196-8

Groen, M., Meys, W., & Veenstra, M. (2013, September). Creating smart information services for tourists by means of dynamic open data. In *Proceedings of the 2013 ACM conference on Pervasive and ubiquitous computing adjunct publication* (pp. 1329-1330). ACM. doi:10.1145/2494091.2499215

Grundey, D. (2008). Experiential Marketing vs. Traditional Marketing: Creating rational and emotional liaisons with consumers. *The Romanian Economic Journal*, *29*(3), 133–150.

Guinard, D. D., & Trifa, V. M. (2016). *Building the Web of Things*. Shelter Island: Manning.

Guo, Y., Liu, H., & Chai, Y. (2014). The embedding convergence of smart cities and tourism internet of things in China: An advance perspective. *Advances in Hospitality and Tourism Research*, *2*(1), 54–69.

Guttentag, D. A. (2010). Virtual reality: Applications and implications for tourism. *Tourism Management*, *31*(5), 637–651. doi:10.1016/j.tourman.2009.07.003

Ha, H. Y., & Perks, H. (2005). Effects of consumer perceptions of brand experience on the web: Brand familiarity, satisfaction and brand trust. *Journal of Consumer Behaviour*, *4*(6), 438–452. doi:10.1002/cb.29

Harrington, P. (2012). *Machine learning in action*. Shelter Island: Manning.

Hassan, A., & Rahimi, R. (2016). Consuming ''Innovation'': augmented reality as an innovation tool in digital tourism marketing. In P. Nikolaos & I. Bregoli (Eds.), *Global dynamics in travel, tourism, and hospitality* (pp. 130–147). Hershey, PA: IGI Global. doi:10.4018/978-1-5225-0201-2.ch008

Hauser, E. (2011). *Experiential Marketing Forum*. Retrieved May 18, 2016, from http://www.experientialforum.com

Holbrook, M. B. (2006). Consumption experience, customer value, and subjective personal introspection: An illustrative photographic essay. *Journal of Business Research*, *59*(6), 714–725. doi:10.1016/j.jbusres.2006.01.008

Huang, Y. C., Backman, K. F., Backman, S. J., & Chang, L. L. (2016). Exploring the Implications of Virtual Reality Technology in Tourism Marketing: An Integrated Research Framework. *International Journal of Tourism Research*, *18*(2), 116–128. doi:10.1002/jtr.2038

Hutchings, E. (2013). *Time Travel Through Paris With Augmented Reality App*. Retrieved from http://www.psfk.com/2013/07/paris-travel-augmented-reality-app.html

Jahromi, N. M., Adibzadeh, M., & Nakhae, S. (2015). Examination the interrelationships experiential marketing, experiential value, purchase behaviour and their impact on customers loyalty (Case Study: Customers of Hormoz Hotel in Bandar-e-Abbas). *Journal of Marketing and Consumer Research*, *12*, 73–87.

Jennings, G., Lee, Y. S., Ayling, A., Lunny, B., Cater, C., & Ollenburg, C. (2009). Quality tourism experiences: Reviews, reflections, research agendas. *Journal of Hospitality Marketing & Management*, *18*(2-3), 294–310. doi:10.1080/19368620802594169

Jennings, G. R. (2006). Quality tourism experiences – An introduction. In G. R. Jennings & N. Nickerson (Eds.), *Quality tourism experiences* (pp. 1–21). Burlington, MA: Elsevier. doi:10.1016/B978-0-7506-7811-7.50005-5

Jung, J. (2011). *The top five smartest cities in Spain and why the US should care*. Retrieved from http://www.forbes.com/sites/jaynejung/2011/10/24/the-top-five-smartest-city-in-spain-and-why-the-us-should-care/2/#55165c357cee

Jung, T., tom Dieck, M. C., Lee, H., & Chung, N. (2016). Effects of Virtual Reality and Augmented Reality on Visitor Experiences in Museum. In *Information and Communication Technologies in Tourism 2016* (pp. 621–635). Springer International Publishing. doi:10.1007/978-3-319-28231-2_45

Kleef, N., Noltes, J., & Spoel, S. (2010). *Success factors for augmented reality business models*. Enschede: University Twente.

Larsen, S. (2007). Aspects of a psychology of the tourist experience. *Scandinavian Journal of Hospitality and Tourism*, *7*(1), 7–18. doi:10.1080/15022250701226014

Lawler, E. (2013, November 18). The rise of experiential marketing. *Advertising Age*, pp. C1-C2.

Lemke, F., Clark, M., & Wilson, H. (2011). Customer experience quality: An exploration in business and consumer contexts using repertory grid technique. *Journal of the Academy of Marketing Science, 39*(6), 846–869. doi:10.1007/s11747-010-0219-0

Lewis, R. C., & Chambers, R. E. (1999). Marketing leadership in hospitality: foundations and practices (3rd ed.). John Wiley and Sons.

Linaza, M. T., Gutierrez, A., & García, A. (2013). Pervasive augmented reality games to experience tourism destinations. In *Information and Communication Technologies in Tourism 2014* (pp. 497–509). Springer International Publishing. doi:10.1007/978-3-319-03973-2_36

Loibl, W. (2015). *Semantics in Tourism* (Unpublished doctoral dissertation). Vienna University of Economics and Business.

MacCannell, D. (1973). Staged authenticity: Arrangements of social space in tourist settings. *American Journal of Sociology, 79*(3), 589–603. doi:10.1086/225585

Mannell, R. C., & Iso-Ahola, S. E. (1987). Psychological nature of leisure and tourism experience. *Annals of Tourism Research, 14*(3), 314–331. doi:10.1016/0160-7383(87)90105-8

Maurno, D. A. (2011, September). *New best practices in event marketing*. Retrieved May 23, 2016, from http://www.mpiweb.org/

May, K. (2011). *Tourism Ireland unveils Facebook game, on St. Patrick's Day of course*. Retrieved from https://www.tnooz.com/article/tourism-ireland-unveils-facebook-game-on-st-patricks-day-of-course/

Mcintosh, A. J., & Siggs, A. (2005). An exploration of the experiential nature of boutique accommodation. *Journal of Travel Research, 44*(1), 74–81. doi:10.1177/0047287505276593

Odell, T. (2007). Tourist experiences and academic junctures. *Scandinavian Journal of Hospitality and Tourism, 7*(1), 34–45. doi:10.1080/15022250701224001

Otto, J. E., & Ritchie, J. B. (1996). The service experience in tourism. *Tourism Management, 17*(3), 165–174. doi:10.1016/0261-5177(96)00003-9

Pakanen, M., & Arhippainen, L. (2014). User experiences with web-based 3D virtual travel destination marketing portals: the need for visual indication of interactive 3D elements. In *Proceedings of the 26th Australian Computer-Human Interaction Conference on Designing Futures: The Future of Design* (pp. 430-439). ACM. doi:10.1145/2686612.2686680

Peltier, D. (2016). *Facebook's 360-Degree Travel Videos Offer Destinations a New Path to Marketing*. Retrieved from https://skift.com/2016/04/05/facebooks-360-degree-travel-videos-offer-destinations-a-new-path-to-marketing/

Pine, B. J., & Gilmore, J. H. (1999). *The experience economy: work is theatre & every business a stage*. Harvard Business Press.

Rahimi, R., & Gunlu, E. (2016). Implementing Customer Relationship Management (CRM) in hotel industry from organisational culture perspective. *International Journal of Contemporary Hospitality Management., 28*(1), 89–112. doi:10.1108/IJCHM-04-2014-0176

Rahimi, R., & Kozak, M. (2016). Impact of Customer Relationship Management on Customer Satisfaction: The Case of a Budget Hotel Chain. *Journal of Travel & Tourism Marketing*, 1–12.

Ramos, C. M., & Rodrigues, P. M. (2013). The importance of ICT for Tourism demand: a dynamic panel data analysis. Quantitative Methods in Tourism Economics. In A. Matias, P. Nijkamp, & M. Sarmento (Eds.), *Quantitative Methods in Tourism Economics* (pp. 97–111). Physica-Verlag. doi:10.1007/978-3-7908-2879-5_6

Ravald, A., & Grönroos, C. (1996). The value concept and relationship marketing. *European Journal of Marketing*, *30*(2), 19–30. doi:10.1108/03090569610106626

Robertson, H. (2007, January 18). At last a definition of experiential marketing. *Marketing Week*, 21.

Schmitt, B. (1999). Experiential marketing. *Journal of Marketing Management, 15*(1-3), 53-67.

Schmitt, B. (2009). The concept of brand experience. *Journal of Brand Management, 16*(7), 417-419.

Schmitt, B., & Zarantonello, L. (2013). Consumer experience and experiential marketing: A critical review. *Review of Marketing Research, 10*, 25-61.

Shaw, C., & Ivens, J. (2005). *Building great customer experiences*. Basingstoke, UK: Palgrave Macmillan.

Singh, J., & Sirdeshmukh, D. (2000). Agency and trust mechanisms in consumer satisfaction and loyalty judgments. *Journal of the Academy of Marketing Science, 28*(1), 150–167. doi:10.1177/0092070300281014

Smilansky, S. (2009). *Experiential Marketing: A practical guide to interactive brand experiences*. Kogan Page Publishers.

Smith, S., & Wheeler, J. (2002). *Managing the customer experience: Turning customers into advocates*. Pearson Education.

Snakers, E., & Zajdman, E. (2010). *Does experiential marketing affect the behavior of luxury goods' consumers?* (Master Thesis). Umeå Universitet.

Taqvi, Z. (2013, December). Reality and perception: Utilization of many facets of augmented reality. In *Artificial Reality and Telexistence (ICAT), 2013 23rd International Conference on* (pp. 11-12). IEEE.

Timothy, D. J. (2011). *Cultural heritage and tourism* (Vol. 4). Channel View Publications.

Tscheu, F., & Buhalis, D. (2016). Augmented Reality at Cultural Heritage sites. In *Information and Communication Technologies in Tourism 2016* (pp. 607–619). Springer International Publishing. doi:10.1007/978-3-319-28231-2_44

Turner, L., & Ash, J. (1975). *"The" Golden Hordes: International Tourism and the Pleasure Periphery*. Constable Limited.

Uriely, N. (2005). The tourist experience: Conceptual developments. *Annals of Tourism Research, 32*(1), 199–216. doi:10.1016/j.annals.2004.07.008

Van Krevelen, D. W. F., & Poelman, R. (2010). A survey of augmented reality technologies, applications and limitations. *International Journal of Virtual Reality, 9*(2), 1.

Vargo, S. L., & Lusch, R. F. (2008). Service-dominant logic: Continuing the evolution. *Journal of the Academy of Marketing Science*, *36*(1), 1–10. doi:10.1007/s11747-007-0069-6

Vivion, N. (2014). *Time traveling app re-builds the Berlin Wall via augmented reality*. Retrieved from https://www.tnooz.com/article/time-traveling-app-re-builds-berlin-wall-via-augmented-reality/

Walker, K., & Moscardo, G. (2014). Encouraging sustainability beyond the tourist experience: Ecotourism, interpretation and values. *Journal of Sustainable Tourism*, *22*(8), 1175–1196. doi:10.1080/09669 582.2014.918134

Walls, A. R., Okumus, F., Wang, Y. R., & Kwun, D. J. W. (2011). An epistemological view of consumer experiences. *International Journal of Hospitality Management*, *30*(1), 10–21. doi:10.1016/j. ijhm.2010.03.008

Wang, D., Li, X. R., & Li, Y. (2013). Chinas smart tourism destination initiative: A taste of the service-dominant logic. *Journal of Destination Marketing & Management*, *2*(2), 59–61. doi:10.1016/j. jdmm.2013.05.004

Wang, X., Li, X. R., Zhen, F., & Zhang, J. (2016). How smart is your tourist attraction?: Measuring tourist preferences of smart tourism attractions via a FCEM-AHP and IPA approach. *Tourism Management*, *54*, 309–320. doi:10.1016/j.tourman.2015.12.003

Wang, Y. (2016). *Baidu Releases Augmented Reality Platform – Will It Be China's AR Leader?* Retrieved from http://www.forbes.com/sites/ywang/2016/08/05/baidu-releases-augmented-reality-platform-will-it-be-chinas-ar-leader/#5289d8c75770

Werthner, H., & Klein, S. (1999). *Information technology and tourism: a challenging ralationship*. Springer-Verlag Wien. doi:10.1007/978-3-7091-6363-4

Williams, A. (2006). Tourism and hospitality marketing: Fantasy, feeling and fun. *International Journal of Contemporary Hospitality Management*, *18*(6), 482–495. doi:10.1108/09596110610681520

World Tourism Organization (UNWTO). (2015). *UNWTO Tourism Highlights 2015 Edition*. Retrieved June 4, 2016, from http://tourlib.net/wto/WTO_highlights_2015.pdf

World Tourism Organization (UNWTO). (2016). *UNWTO World Tourism Barometer*. UNWTO.

Xu, F., Weber, J., & Buhalis, D. (2013). Gamification in tourism. In *Information and Communication Technologies in Tourism 2014* (pp. 525–537). Springer International Publishing. doi:10.1007/978-3-319-03973-2_38

Yelkur, R. (2000). Customer satisfaction and the services marketing mix. *Journal of Professional Services Marketing*, *21*(1), 105–115. doi:10.1300/J090v21n01_07

Yelp. (2016). *What is Yelp's Monocle feature?* Retrieved from http://www.yelp-support.com/article/What-is-Yelp-s-Monocle-feature?l=en_GB

You-Ming, C. (2010). Study on the impact of experiential marketing and customers' satisfaction based on relationship quality. *International Journal of Organisational Innovation*, *3*(1), 189–209.

Yovcheva, Z., Buhalis, D., & Gatzidis, C. (2012). Overview of smartphone augmented reality applications for tourism. *e-Review of Tourism Research (eRTR), 10*(2), 63-66.

Yuan, H., Xu, H., Ma, B., & Qian, Y. (2015). Where to go and what to play: Towards summarizing popular information from massive tourism blogs. *Journal of Information Science, 1*, 1–27.

Yuan, Y. H., & Wu, C. K. (2008). Relationships among experiential marketing, experiential value, and customer satisfaction. *Journal of Hospitality & Tourism Research (Washington, D.C.), 32*(3), 387–410. doi:10.1177/1096348008317392

Zhang, J. (2010, August). The Coming Era of Experience Economy and Breakthrough of Service Innovation Dilemma. In *Management and Service Science (MASS), 2010 International Conference on* (pp. 1-4). IEEE. doi:10.1109/ICMSS.2010.5577130

KEY TERMS AND DEFINITIONS

Augmented Reality: Augmented Reality (AR) is a technology which collects information from a variety of online sources to add to a user's view of the real world, thereby providing a composite view of reality.

Experiential Marketing: Experiential Marketing is a strategy which invites consumers to directly engage with marketing initiatives and participate in the evolution of brands.

Innovation: Innovation is the process of turning an idea into a product/service for which a customer is prepared to pay.

Smart Tourism: Smart Tourism reflects the growing reliance of tourism organisations on ICT, especially the transformation of large data streams into business opportunities.

Technology: In a business context technology can be defined as the application of knowledge to design, produce and utilise goods and services.

This research was previously published in Promotional Strategies and New Service Opportunities in Emerging Economies edited by Vipin Nadda, Sumesh Dadwal, and Roya Rahimi, pages 210-235, copyright year 2017 by Business Science Reference (an imprint of IGI Global).

Chapter 10
Emerging Technologies and Organizational Transformation

Albena Antonova
Sofia University, Bulgaria

ABSTRACT

Technologies continue to evolve and to largely transform business practices. In the near future, a few technologies, such as Internet of Things (IoT), Augmented Reality (AR), additive manufacturing (3D printing), and robots, can substantially influence businesses. The reason to focus specifically on these technologies as leading factors for organizational change is twofold: first, there already exist many prototypes and pilot experiments; and second, these technologies have the potential to provoke substantial breakthroughs, leading to substantial business changes. The chapter proposes an overall vision about the impact of these four emerging technologies on business practices and how they will fuel substantial business transformation. The chapter starts with a short analysis how IT influences the core business models and value formation. Then, the authors present the state of the art in e-business technologies and current emerging trends. Finally, the authors propose a detailed overview and discussion of the newly emerging bridge technologies, illustrating with examples their role and economic potential.

INTRODUCTION

Information technologies made the world closer, more interconnected and highly competitive. Due to sophisticated technologies, companies improved business efficiency and performance. Information technologies played an increasing economic role for reducing transaction costs and agency costs, providing the backbone infrastructure for value formation (Laudon & Laudon, 2007). Thus, they allowed many new business models to emerge, bringing additional sources for value-creation for customers. Moreover, e-business applications have largely transformed companies to become more flat, boundaryless, entrepreneurial, process- and project-oriented, developing complex and innovative global business models. Today, Internet is an essential and indispensable infrastructure for business transactions on many B2B and B2C levels, becoming a universal platform for services. In the recent "Global Wealth Report" (Credit Suisse, 2013), the global wealth is reaching a new high in 2013 with expectations for

DOI: 10.4018/978-1-5225-2589-9.ch010

a rise with another 40% for the next 5 years. In the same time unemployment data hits new records, especially among young workers (OECD, 2013). Experts and politicians are already discussing the threat of a "lost generation," reflecting many more social and economic problems. Technologies bring new and unexpected dynamics of economic and social processes. This will further threaten the social and community systems, education system and public priorities. For example, robots can replace not only repetitive tasks of blue-collar workers (as in automobile industries), but they can replace the work of highly-skilled staff (such as surgeons). Additive manufacturing and e-commerce advances will contribute for more custom-oriented production, exploring the long-tail models. In the same time many new smart technologies (for example smart driver-less car, "nurse" and home robots) will change the service sector employment. Thus with evolution of technologies we can further expect more working places to be replaced by automated systems and robots or to disappear.

Many researchers and practitioners anticipate that Internet technologies will soon leave the digital world in order to make "real world" objects and environments more smart, more operational and interconnected. The estimated impact of these newly emerging technologies will result in more change in the economic and social development, bringing many new challenges to businesses. These key "bridge" technologies are augmented reality (AR), additive manufacturing or 3D printing, robotics and the Internet of Things (IoT). The common issue for these technologically different applications is that all of them are closing the gap between the world of bytes and the world of objects. They lead to the development of new content- and context-rich connected environments and mobile objects, adding many Internet functions and services to "real world" objects, people and landscapes. The reason to focus specifically on these technologies as leading factors for organizational change is twofold: the first argument is that these technologies are expected to become widely implemented in the near future through the development of prototypes, proofs-of-concepts and pilot experiments as well as early-stage mass production. The second argument is that these technologies are expected to influence major business processes, leading to substantial change in organizations. With fast adoption of smart phones and tablets, interactive technologies, wireless Internet and portable devices (as AR glasses or head-mounted devices), this vision is gradually becoming reality not only for end-customers but also for companies and industries.

The present chapter aims to analyze the impact on business development and business transformation, due to some of the key emerging technologies. The methodology follows the bottom-up approach, focusing on case studies of innovative business practices and company changes. Case studies and best practices are admitted to serve as good source for research in information technologies business application (Benbasat, Goldstein, &Meat, 1987). The first part of the chapter provides a short introduction of organizational challenges and discusses the main sources of competitive advantages. The second part presents some of the main e-business applications implemented in business organizations, including, for example, company information systems such as ERP and CRM, supply-chain systems and networks, e-commerce and digital content, social web and marketing activity, and some related concepts such as tele-working and downsizing and crowd-sourcing. The third part of the chapter will focus on emerging technologies and expected organizational changes. It will provide a detailed overview of the main characteristics, challenges and opportunities of the new emerging technologies identified above: augmented reality, pervasive computing, Internet of Things, 3D printing and robotics. The chapter will present several examples of these technologies and discuss possible implementations of these emerging technologies in various organizational settings. Finally, the fourth part of the chapter will summarize the findings and will discuss the models and business approaches for organizations.

The main outcome of this chapter is to derive to a general business framework based on theoretical review and practical examples that will enable business organizations to better understand value creation models for emerging innovative technologies. The chapter will provide arguments and examples about how to adapt to the information technologies "outside" the computers, transforming further business practices and business models and increasing value for the customers and business competitiveness.

BACKGROUND

Business models are substantial part of any business. While traditional business models are simple and easy to understand, information technologies brought many new opportunities for organizational transformation. Ostenwalder, Pigneur, and Tucci (2005) identify that information and communication technologies and Internet are the main factors for business model differentiation and evolution. New technologies largely contributed for the emergence of complex business relationships, oriented to the end-customer. In result, many new business models evolved as for example the "long tail," crowd-sourcing, complex network business models and many others. Information technology implementations in organizations and introduction of new business models resulted in general reduction of costs, reduction of market prices and value chain optimization. The technologies changed as well the understanding of IT services as they often includes both products and service components. Technologies brought out the service dominant logic of the market, defined by Vargo and Luch (2004). Products are normally accompanied by some facilitating services, while services are often facilitated by products (Fitzsimmons & Fitzsimmons, 2006). Thus, the differentiation between products and services is increasingly blurring (Basole & Rouse, 2008). One of the key aspects of the business models evolution is the model of value creation. The understanding about value formation evolved significantly in the last years (Heinonen, Strandvik & Voima (2013). There emerged the concept of value-in-use (Ng, Nudurupati, & Tasker, 2010). The value as internal and residual part of the product is blurred. This means that the value of product nowadays depends more on how product are used, and not of their potential to be sold as an investment good. For example, the value of possessing a high-tech device such as laptop or smart phone is formed by the possibility to use it, and not by the potential from selling it further. Therefore, it is not economically justifiable for customers to invest in purchasing many high-tech products, but only to buy these that they can use immediately. Thus the value is realized when the service is used. The users are at the same time value co-creators and judges of the service value (Sandstrom, Edvardsson, Kristensson, & Magnusson, 2008). The value can be assessed only by customers (Levitt, 1983), while companies can make only value-offering (Vargo & Lusch, 2004). Thus the value formation is realized in the customer space, rather than in the producer space (Gronroos, 2011). Moreover, the customer is the key factor for value-creation, as usually the value is centered in the customer experience (Prahalad & Ramsey 2004).

Based on the findings about IT impact on the business model evolution, services and customer experience become the main factors for value formation (Vargo &Lusch, 2004). Allowing customers to better serve themselves, and providing better experience, based on improved knowledge and competences can lead to better value formation processes. That is why improved technology solutions have to be considered broadly not as "smart objects," but as infrastructure solutions for providing better self-services for end users.

E-Business Technologies in Companies

E-business technologies have already substantially changed the global business landscape. Today the use of technologies in organizations is imperative (Xu & Quaddus, 2010) as the business companies become more and more digital, globalized and competitive. The term E-business can be generally defined as applications of Internet and communication technologies for inter- and intra- organizational transactions. Nowadays it is not possible to figure out business companies and business transactions without ICT technologies. Some of the key factors for development of e-business technologies are the high rate of Internet usage across countries, the high potential of e-commerce adoption and expansion of available Internet services (Xu & Quaddus, 2010). E-business extends the technologies of e-commerce and can cover a wide range of standard and customized applications, automating the key business processes within the companies. E-business comprises 3 main stages (Kalakota & Robinson, 2001), including online corporate presence, adoption of e-commerce and Internet transactions, and finally front and back-office applications such as integrated ERP, CRM, SCM systems and others. The E-business navigator, proposed in Sigrist and Schubert (2004) covers the systematization of corporate e-business solutions in 3 main domains – e-procurement, e-commerce and e-organization. Thus, according to Schubert and Wölfle (2000), e-business supports the connections and processes within a business with its partners, clients, employees and staff by use of electronic media. E-business also covers different applications including security of transactions, methods for electronic payments, and e-government services. E-Commerce is the part of E-Business that is oriented toward the sales of products and services. The E-Organization is focused mainly on electronic support of communication between personnel and employees or between personnel/employees and business counterparts. Some of the popular e-business systems in companies today include the use of Content Management systems, mobile applications, Customer Relationship Management (for better engagement with customers) and Supply Chain Management (Schubert & Wölfle, 2000).

IT technologies and the Internet allowed the emergence of new business practices and processes, company flattening, outsourcing and downsizing. For example, the practice of teleworking was introduced based on the remote collaboration with employees and consultants. Management information systems improved the reporting capacity of the companies, so they can better control and understand business performance, which gives them the potential for processes and operations optimization. The CAD/CAM systems improved and facilitated the design and product-development processes, while decision support systems, business intelligence and knowledge management systems supported semi-structured decision making and business planning. Therefore, information technologies provide the opportunity for the emergence of the digital company (Laudon & Laudon, 2007) where business transactions are remote and no physical contact or exchange of goods or money is necessary. With the recent development of social media and mobile applications many new mobile applications emerge for marketing, finance, customer relationship and e-commerce.

NEW EMERGING TECHNOLOGIES

Ubiquitous Computing

Ubiquitous computing (UbiCom) was coined as a term by Mark Weiser in 1991. He stated that "the most profound technologies are those that will disappear. They will weave themselves into the fabric of everyday life until they are indistinguishable from it" (Ahmed, 2009 p3.). Therefore, ubiquitous computing was identified as a general vision for technology evolution, contributing for technology adoption of the fabric of everyday life. Ubiquitous computing consists of mobile devices, wireless networks and other advanced technologies and infrastructure. According to Poslad (2009), ubiquitous computing has 3 components - smart devices, smart environments and smart interaction. The author further states that smart devices are "mobile, personalized, planar, macro sized MTOS (Multi Task Operating System) devices, accessed remotely rather than on local services." Smart environments are environments in which static macro devices are embedded into it, or are environments that have micro and nano-sized devices, scattered into social and public spaces. Local interaction dominates the use of smart environments. Smart interaction aims to combine multiple individual smart devices and environments in order to interact in a flexible ways, such as supporting orchestrated, choreographed, competitive and cooperative interaction in dynamic virtual systems. Hybrid designs can also be used where systems combine smart devices, smart environments and smart interaction (Poslad, 2009). UbiCom systems cover a range of interaction: between two or more UbiCom devices (C2C or CCI); between devices and people (HCI); between devices and physical world (CPI). Some of CPI involves sensing the physical environment, performing tasks which are situated in it, affect it and may control it. Moreover, it can be defined that Ubiquitous computing encompasses a wide range of disparate technological areas brought together by a focus upon a common vision (Bell & Dourish, 2006).

Based on the general concept and vision of UbiCom, there can be enumerated some of its common characteristics. UbiCom technologies aim to facilitate connectivity and exchange of information in real time between objects, people and places, making the world context-aware, taking into account location and time. This way, UbiCom technologies will open many new opportunities for automation and further implementation of ICT into more business and social fields and practices, where companies can reach better business performance. Thus it can be expected the emergence of a new sensor-enabled digital world, where the objects have "senses" to collect and process information, accumulated through hearing, seeing, communicating, reacting, deciding, memorizing and storing. This can lead on one hand to minimizing resource usage and waste ("cost" oriented approach) and on the other hand, it can provide improved services, based on synergy of value networks for customers (becoming "profit-centers").

Overview of Ubiquitous Technologies

Augmented Reality

Augmented reality technologies form a class of solutions, aiming to extend and mix the real and virtual objects and its context. Augmented reality (AR) does not describe a specific technology, but a manner to virtually "extend" the reality. Augmented reality can be understood as a layer model that enriches reality with virtual levels to merge the real and the digital realms of experience. Therefore, some of the popular understandings are that AR takes part in the Mediated reality. Thus AR allows us to acquire simultaneously digital content, Internet and computational services to real life objects, to specific tasks, contexts, landscapes and people. Recognizing the real world objects and landscapes, and understanding location and time context dramatically increases the relevance of data and allow its better processing and further use. It can be expected that augmented reality will have a tremendous effect in the near future. For example, the first AR glasses are still in preparation, but many applications are already accessible through hand-held devices and smart phones. One of the most popular cases today is about AR applications in commerce and marketing (such as Homeplus®)[1]. Recently there emerged many new cases of AR implementation for improving the customer access to digital content, improving its self-service and service experience, as for example in advertising, in marketing, in co-production phase, in coordination and many others (such as the customer catalogue 2013 of Ikea®). Another example for AR is its ability to enhance product previews and customer experiences, allowing customer to view what is inside without opening product's packaging (Lego®). On the special kiosk, the Lego® clients can see the constructed three dimensional ready models before even opening the box. AR can also be used as an aid in selecting products from a catalog or through a virtual kiosk. Scanned images of products can activate views of additional content such as customization options and additional images of the product in its use. AR is used to integrate print and video marketing. Printed marketing material can be designed with certain "trigger" images that, when scanned by an AR enabled device using image recognition, activate a video version of the promotional material.

From the production point of view, there are a number of advantages for implementing AR to help industrial designers (or even customers) to experience a product's design and operations before final product completion. AR can be used to compare digital mock-ups with physical mock-ups for efficiently finding discrepancies between them. One example of the emerging applications is the Canon's MREAL® System[2], which is a design/production solution tool that merges the real world with virtual, computer-generated images in real time to create a new "mixed" reality. The system makes possible product evaluations early in the design process through the use of digital data, facilitating reduced development times and lower costs by lowering the number of prototypes required.

AR can help as well to facilitate collaboration, improving communication among distributed team members in a work force via conferences with real and virtual participants. AR can include brainstorming and discussion meetings utilizing common visualization via touch screen tables, interactive digital whiteboards, shared design spaces, and distributed control rooms.

Internet of Things

The Internet of Things (IoT) refers to the emerging trend of technologies, while augmenting physical objects and devices with sensing, computing, and communication capabilities, connecting them to form a network and making use of the collective effect of networked objects (Guo, Yu, Zhou, & Zhang, 2012). The term "Internet of Things" was coined as the title of a presentation by Kevin Ashton for Procter & Gamble in 1999. The Internet of Things (IoT) is an integrated part of the Future Internet and could be defined as a dynamic global network infrastructure with self configuring capabilities based on standard and interoperable communication protocols where physical and virtual 'things' have identities, physical attributes, and virtual personalities and use intelligent interfaces, and are seamlessly integrated into the information network.

The IoT requires any user to orchestrate its personal intelligent eco-system. It will provide a platform for knowledge acquisition and experimentation. It is expected that the Internet of objects would encode

50 to 100 trillion objects, and will be able to follow the movement of those objects. In the IoT paradigm, 'things' are expected to become active participants in business, information and social processes where they are enabled to interact and communicate among themselves and with the environment by exchanging data and information 'sensed' about the environment, while reacting autonomously to the 'real/physical world' events and influencing it by running processes that trigger actions and create services with or without direct human intervention. RFID and sensor technology enable computers to observe, to identify and understand objectivity without being biased from humans. Embedded systems are computer systems that are part of a larger system or product, from toys to trucks, from mobile phones to medical devices. Fields of applications include for example waste management, urban planning, sustainable urban environment, continuous care, emergency response, intelligent shopping, smart product management, smart meters, home automation and smart events. There emerged as well the concept of "Connected Home" which is considered as a social tool with the aim to allow people to connect, use, share and compose things, services and devices to create personalized applications in the field of the Internet of Things.

Robots and Robotics

A robot can be defined as a mechanical or virtual machine that is guided by a computer program or electronic circuitry. While the term "robot" was coined by Karel Tchapek in his theater piece "RUR" in 1920, today we still discuss how to differentiate robot systems. Robots still cannot be qualified as "artificial humans," but their role and functionality gradually expand. They can vary from autonomous or semi-autonomous systems and can range from humanoids to industrial robots, collectively programmed "swarm" robots, and even microscopic nano-robots or nano-bots. One of the common issues between these different machines is that usually they need to have some moveable parts. With increasing number of robots prototypes and applications, nowadays robots increasingly take different forms and functions.

In some recent reports, it was admitted that industrial robots should form an essential part of the manufacturing backbone of Europe, and will reach up to 18 Million globally in 2015 (EU, 2009). Robot-based production increases product quality, improves work conditions and leads to an optimized use of resources. Its large implementation is due not only in industry, but today more robots are implemented in surgery and medicine. According to the data of (World Robotics, 2013), in 2012 alone, about 160,000 robots were sold. Some of the main arguments for further expansion of industrial robots include the following (Nerseth, 2013) [3]:

- Growing consumer markets require expansion of production capacities.
- Decreasing life-cycles of products and increasing variety of products require flexible automation.
- Technical improvements of industrial robots will increase the use of robots in the general industry and in small and medium sized companies, e.g. easier to use robots for simple applications, collaboration of robots with human workers.
- Improved quality requires sophisticated high tech robot systems.

Robots improve the quality of work by taking over dangerous, tedious and dirty jobs that are not possible or safe for humans to perform. The evolution and wide implementation of robots is expected to bring many new opportunities and challenges to companies and management, but as well to the global society.

Additive Manufacturing or 3D Printing

Additive manufacturing or 3D printing is a newly emerging technology that allows users to turn any digital file into a three dimensional physical product. The objects are built up in many very thin layers. The pilot implementation of these technologies today cover a wide range of applications from food-production, to fashion and jewelry, to house-building, bio-printing of cells and organs and even to space missions. Thus many researchers and managers predict that 3D printing may soon do for manufacturing what computers and the Internet have already done for the creation, processing and storage of information. Current applications of 3D printing typically involve small quantity of highly customized production usually of complex items. 3D printing has been compared to disruptive technologies that enable consumers to order their selections online, allowing firms to profitably serve small market segments, and enabling companies to operate with little or no unsold finished goods inventory. In his paper, Berman (2012) makes an overview of 3D printing, highlighting his emerging economic value for companies. He makes an analysis, comparing 3D printing to other manufacturing methods, such as for example mass customization, injection molding or machining/subtractive technologies. In many cases, 3D printing proposes a cost effective solution, increasing the speed of production, limiting the wastage of raw materials and reducing the need for distributing workload in low-wage countries. 3D printing technologies are largely automated and based on CAD software that doesn't require further specialized work. Berman (2012) identifies 3 main phases for 3D printing implementation. The first stage includes rapid prototyping and bridge manufacturing, where 3D models are used to improve the design and development of mass products in companies. The second stage is for final product manufacturing, which is expected to reach about 50% of the market in 2020 ("3D Printing: The Printed World," 2010). The last stage consists of end-user manufacturing, where users will own and produce products in their homes, using pre-programmed or customized paid or open patterns. Berman states that when the price of the 3D printers becomes around USD 300, then it will enter the consumer market. Therefore, it can be expected that 3D printing can lead to a personal fabrication (Fab) revolution. It was defined by prof. Gershenfeld from MIT in his influential book "How to make almost everything". Fab Revolution describes the transfer of the digital revolution to the real world. This trend has been largely analyzed by Gershenfeld (2012).

Some of the main trends resulting from 3D printing evolution, identified by the recent reports of Explaining the future®, are as follows:

- **Decentralized Production:** Anyone can now become a producer or a part of production process.
- **Mass Customization:** Using the advantages of mass production and meeting the customers' growing needs for personalization of products.
- **Product Hacking:** The need to protect digital data and making systems that cannot simply be "hacked", and prevent products to be copied, modified and reproduced (as today - digital content).
- **Home Fadding:** 3D printers are becoming more and more affordable and thus product production is therefore shifted from factories to people's home desktops (desktop manufacturing).

Today, 3D printing continues to develop and to offer many advantages, as it allows the use of different materials in the same time from a wide variety of materials. During the last years there emerged many new applications and experiments with 3D printing, both for prototyping and for finished goods. There are many examples varying from fashion design, house building, customized consumer goods, printing 3D models and food, but as well there emerge a focused research on 3D printing for medical applications – such as bio-printing (organs and cells) to implants, bones, and many others (explaining the future.com). Other applications include bridge manufacturing, filling orders prior to product commercialization or filling emergency orders; custom manufacturing for jewelry and hobby applications; parts for machinery and aircraft, where strength is a major issue; emergency shipments of parts; and situations where inventory carrying costs are high relative to production costs. The website "explaining the future.com"[4] provides more interesting scenarios and applications of the coming 3D printing revolution.

New Models of Value Creation

Companies have to be prepared not only for new coming pervasive and UbiCom technologies, but they also have to respond on many of the challenges that new technologies will bring. New technologies will transform not only the way products are designed and produced, but they will influence the customers' expectations, the emergence of future professions and jobs. The companies have to reconsider their core competitive advantages in the overall value-added chain and to adopt new business models based on cooperation and value co-creation with end users. Birchnell and Urry (2013) discuss several scenarios based on the adoption of 3D printing technologies at home that range from total replacement of the production facilities with 3D devices, to the situation where these printers remain partially used as in rapid prototyping. In parallel, industrial robots are fast adopted in manufacturing, giving the increased possibility to automate different manufacturing and service processes, guaranteeing high quality, operability, adaptability and precision (EU, 2009). Smith (2012) further explained the potentials of IoT to transform business and social patterns. While today the main manufacturing business models are based on well coordinated distributed production chains in cheap labor countries, in the near future companies will have to reformulate the conception of mass production. These technology trends can influence not only the production and logistic processes but it can also lead to new political and economic distribution of power because it will focus on localization, adaptation and customization in local production-delivering facilities, based on universal raw materials. At the same time, the "dehumanization" of the service sector will increase, and thus customers will rarely be connected to real people – but increasingly to different types of vending machines, cash-management and universal service kiosks, specialized service robots or automated and computerized smart objects. In the vision of Microsoft Office labs® for the near future[5], it can be seen that the computers will disappear; replaced by new increasingly universal, interconnected and smarter devices and intelligent environments including walls, tables, intelligent surfaces, TV sets and mobile applications freely interconnecting and exchanging information.

1. **Changes in the Production Models:** It can be expected that the overall production costs will decrease because of the introduction of new technologies, improving quality, logistic models, inventory and resource usage (robotics, 3D printing, complex automated systems and others). For example, 3-D printing has many advantages comparing to other manufacturing methods, as for example mass customization, injection molding or machining/subtractive technologies (Berman, 2012). Therefore it will definitely change the life-cycle design, production and usage of products and services. As customers will be able to order their selections online, thus firms could profitably serve only small market segments ("long tail" business models), operating with little or no unsold finished goods and inventory. This will require better personalization and involvement of the end-users in the process of value-co-creation. That is why companies have to improve the production-chain logic, adapting its business processes and applications to the end-users preferences. For example, they

have to make possible for the end users to operate with CAD CAM design software, facilitating their choice and providing professional advices and expertise.

On the other hand, Berman (2012) points out that 3D printing could mean that low cost manufacturing centers would no longer possess the comparative advantage in manufacturing. Even if the oil is the basis of many powders used in such printing/manufacturing, there can be expected vast savings in transportation costs. Conversely there could be an intensification of transport due to the increased demand for raw materials for printing, added to the vast movements of manufactured objects by freight.

2. **Emerging Complex Systems for Experience-Oriented Services:** The ubiquitous technology development will lead to more automated and technology-based services. Improving customer experiences, participation and value co-creation will force companies to transform its value-adding mechanisms. The new emerging technologies as augmented reality and IoT will soon allow companies to provide much more context-based information and advices, depending on location, time, and customer preferences. In these realms the self-services will play an increasing role, as users will be able to customize their own experience by adding new digital layers to their activities. For example with the immersive technologies users can enrich their experience while playing a sport or travelling, by adding new landscape elements, information or exploring historical development of the site, or adding new challenges and displaying digital information. Moreover, new complex product-service packs will intensify the self-service model, exploring new ways of service use and conception. For example, the Autolib®[6] adopted an innovative business model for electric car sharing. They have extended the service of "renting a car" with additional economic, ecological and logistic layers by providing a complex service, including economic car use option, parking place and good infrastructure. With emerging Google driver-less car@ project, there can be anticipated further business models of car "owning". Thus one of the challenges for the companies in the future will be to overcome the need to "possess" a product. Thus they need to transform from selling a product, to selling a "service" model, by improving the service-product offering and extending it with new options for self-service and adaptation of experience design.

3. **New Challenges for Jobs and Professional Development:** The wide adoption of smart technology solutions will change the labor markets demands. Historically the implementation of new technologies and innovations initially results in a social price because of the changing labor needs. An example of this is the industrial revolution and the following artisans revolts (Ludditte) in 1811 due to the rising unemployment in the sectors because of the increased productivity of machines[7]. With new emerging technologies, smart devices and robots, the company performance will be further improved due to better understanding and optimization of internal processes and adaptability to market demands. However, sophisticated technologies cannot replace humans. Creativity, adaptability, knowledge and expertise, flexibility and dreaming make people a unique resource on the market. Even if the fast implementation of technologies can change the demands of specific jobs and expertise, only people can bring economic success to companies. As happened in the past, new professions will soon emerge, requiring new types of qualification and expertise. In the context of changing manufacturing models and automated services, we can expect a shift toward creative and art-focused professions, requiring high-order and out-of-the-box thinking, research skills, management and entrepreneurship competences and risk taking, working in complex systems and adaptability to change complex dominating paradigms. As educational and social systems adapt slowly

to the imposed market fluctuations, the society as a whole will have to pay the "price" for fuelling further economic growth. Neither politicians nor educational institutions will be able to overcome the gap on the labor market and the imposed social systems. Thus companies will have to lead the change to more flexible working patterns. Thus they should better prepare to turn technologies into business opportunities, jobs and business models, successfully overcoming and minimizing the imposed social price.

4. **New E-Business Architecture of Companies:** The tremendous transformation imposed by implementation of new technologies will require new ICT infrastructure and thus improved and scalable e-business architecture in companies. In the traditional e-business systems, company data base systems are accessed by different application software packages (as ERP, CRM, SCM, BI and others). The architecture of company information systems nowadays are based on 3 main layers – data bases, application layer, and user-interface (effectuated through browser). How will look the architecture of the transformed organization? The architecture of the companies have to propose better coordination of smart independent sub-systems, while extending the input/output of the applied IT models. It can be expected that the new realms of IoT and embedded technologies will provide multiple architecture layers and functions, providing better options for design and operations. In order to construct a complex architecture of multiple sub- and supper-systems, their operations and activities needs to be coordinated. For example, sub-systems need to check the priority and sequence of operations, should have different authorization models about specific autonomous activities and transactions and generally will be guided for further decision making. While more complex systems need to be interconnected, smooth operations need to be carefully designed and organized. It can be expected that companies will further reformulate the overall process of value formation and will further conceive revalorization of the value chain systems. The contact with customers will be increasingly automated and therefore, the points of value-formation should be better adapted for personal contact. The new emerging embedded systems will collect automatically much more context-related data through their sensors. These data will activate predefined patterns, such as activating new technologies to take autonomous decisions, applying functions in many context-related situations. New smart devices will be authorized to perform actions to "external" systems, for example to activate production processes, to send an order to supplier or to display information on client device.

A model of extended architecture in the context of improved e-business solutions is displayed on figure 1. One of its characteristics is the increased number and variety of input and output models. Moreover, it will result in more independent and autonomous systems.

Along the main processes of service/product delivery, customers can play an increasing role in the design and production process, highlighting some of the key issues in the service/product use.

CONCLUSION

While summarizing the current applications of e-business and organizational information systems, we can see that the main focus of technology implementation in companies today is to improve organizational processes and to optimize company transactions. Information technologies already transformed company structure and the company architecture, reduced the hierarchical levels and supported outsourcing, busi-

Figure 1. Transformation of traditional e-business model to complex IT ecosystem

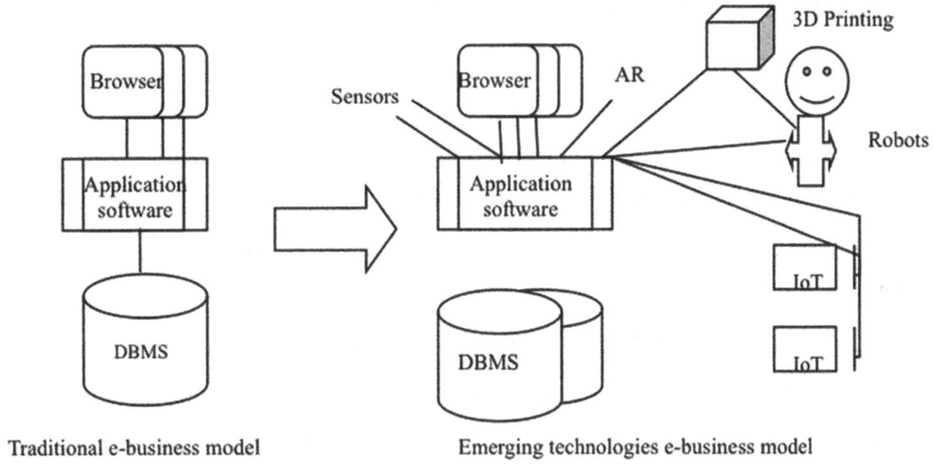

ness process reengineering, networking and alliances. However, information technologies today have only a small impact on the improved value co-creation mechanisms through the customized self-service of customers. The companies still work in the "mass-production" paradigm, offering pre-defined products and services to the market.

Due to new technology advances it can be expected another shift toward value-formation focused on customers and self-service improvement. Considering that the future is unpredictable, we can still anticipate that many social, political or technological circumstances can influence the implementation of the observed technology trends. Generally, many technology solutions are already available, but wait for appropriate business model, legislation push or social acceptance. For example, for wider implementation of Google driver-less car, there is a need for new road legislation, considering wider aspects as for example privacy and data protection of smart vehicles. Many other technologies (smart toilets) require legal and social considerations about data protection and data interchange.

Technologies are gradually changing the society and its business patterns. Companies need to adjust to these trends. On one side, many products will change, becoming more intelligent and smart, upgrading and modernized. On the other side, companies have to reorganize all additional services (including self-services). Thus new technologies propose many opportunities for company transformation as main center of value co-creation, improving customization and user involvement, enhancing value-in-use and self-service, increasing customer experiences and customer satisfaction.

REFERENCES

Ahmed, W. (2009) Marck Weiser – the father of Ubiquitous Computing. *TCG Software LP*. retrieved in 2013 from http://www.tcg- ai.com/documents/MarkWeiser,FatherOfUbiquitousComputing.pdf

Autolib and Bluecar. (2012). Retrieved in 2013 from https://media.autolib.eu/public/cms/550/Click%20 to%20download%20the%20press%20release_1.pdf

Basole, R., & Rouse, W. (2008). Complexity of service value networks, Conceptualization and empirical investigation. *IBM Systems Journal*, *47*(1), 53–70. doi:10.1147/sj.471.0053

Bell, G., & Dourish, P. (2006). *Yesterday's tomorrows: notes on ubiquitous computing's dominant vision*. London: Springer-Verlag.

Benbasat, I., Goldstein, D. K., & Mead, M. (1987). The Case: Research Strategy in Studies of Information Systems. *Management Information Systems Quarterly*, *11*(3), 369–386. doi:10.2307/248684

Berman, B. (2012). 3D printing: The new industrial revolution. *Business Horizons*, *55*(2), 155–162. doi:10.1016/j.bushor.2011.11.003

Birtchnell T., & Urry J., (2013). 3D SF and the future. *Futures*, *50*, 25-34.

Credit Swisse Research Institute. (2013). *Global Wealth Report 2013*. Retrieved in 2013 from http://thenextrecession.files.wordpress.com/2013/10/global-wealth-report.pdf

Duchene, V., Lykogianni, E., & Verbeek, A. (2009). *EU-R&D in Services Industries and the EU-US R&D Investment Gap* (IPTS Working Paper on Corporate R&D and Innovation, No4/2009). IPTS.

EU. (2009). *Strategic Research Agenda for robotics in Europe, 2009, Robotic visions to 2020 and beyond*. Retrieved from http://www.robotics-platform.eu/cms/upload/SRA/2010-06_SRA_A4_low.pdf

Explaining the Future. (n.d.). *3D Printing: The Next Industrial Revolution*. Retrieved in 2013 from www.explainingthefuture.com

Fitzsimmons, J., & Fitzsimmons, M. (2006). *Service management: operations, strategy and information technology* (5th ed.). London: McGraw -Hill.

Gershenfeld, N. (2012). How to Make Almost Anything: The Digital Fabrication Revolution. *Foreign Affairs, 91*(6). Retrieved in 2013 from http://cba.mit.edu/docs/papers/12.09.FA.pdf

Gronroos, C. A. (2011). A service perspective on business relationships. *Industrial Marketing Management*, *40*(2), 240–247. doi:10.1016/j.indmarman.2010.06.036

Guo, B., Yu, Z., Zhou, X., & Zhang, D. (2012). Opportunistic IoT: Exploring the social side of the internet of things. In L. Gao, W. Shen, J.-P. A. Barthès, J. Luo, J. Yong, W. Li, & W. Li (Eds.), CSCWD (pp. 925-929). IEEE.

Heinonen, K., Strandvik, T., & Voima, P. (2013). Customer dominant value formation in service. *European Business Review*, *25*(2), 104–123. doi:10.1108/09555341311302639

Kalakota, R., & Robinson, M. (2001). e-Business 2.0, Roadmap for Success. Addison-Wesley.

Laudon, K., & Laudon, L. (2007). *Management Information Systems* (7th ed.). Prentice Hall.

Levitt, T. (1983). *The marketing imagination*. New York: Free Press.

Lindgardt, Z., Reeves, M., Stalk, G., & Deimler, M. (2009). *Business Model innovation*. The Boston Consulting Group.

Masanell, R., & Ricart, J. (2007). *Competing through business models* (Working paper no 713). University of Navarra.

Nerseth, F. (2013). *Managers of the future.* Available at http://www.worldrobotics.org/index. php?id=home&news_id=267

Ng, I. C. L., Nudurupati, S. S., & Tasker, P. (2010). *Value co-creation in the delivery of outcome-based contracts for business-to-business service* (AIM working paper series, WP No 77 - May – 2010). Retrieved from http://www.aimresearch.org/index.php?page=wp-no-77

OECD. (2013). *OECD Employment Outlook 2013.* OECD Publishing. doi: 10.1787/empl_outlook-2013-en

Ostenwalder, A., Pigneur, P., & Tucci, C. L. (2005). Clarifying Business Models: Origins, Present, and Future of the Concept Communications of AIS. Springer.

PosladS. (2009). Ubiquitous Computing - Smart Devices, Smart Environments and Smart Interaction. Wiley.

Prahalad, C.K., &Ramsey, V. (2004). Co-creation experiences: The next practice in value creation. *Journal of Interactive Marketing, 18*(3), 5-14.

Sandstrom, S., Edvardsson, B., Kristensson, P., & Magnusson, P. (2008). Value in use through service experience. *Managing Service Quality, 18*(2), 112–126. doi:10.1108/09604520810859184

Schubert, P., & Wölfle, R. (Eds.). (2000). How to Successfully Plan and Implement E-Business: Case Studies of Future-Oriented Companies. München: Hanser Verlag.

Sigrist, B., & Shubert, P. (2004). The eBusiness Navigator: Implementing A Classification Scheme For The eDomain. In *Proceeding of 17th eGlobal Conference.* Bled. Available at https://domino.fov.uni-mb. si/proceedings.nsf/0/eac9b3cae72bc393c1256ee0002e7d70/$FILE/27Sigrist.pdf

Smith, E. (2012). Internet of Things 2012– New Horizons. *IERC Yearbook.* Retrieved in 2013 from http://www.internet-of-things-research.eu/pdf/IERC_Cluster_Book_2012_WEB.pdf

Vargo, S. L., & Luch, R. F. (2004). Evolving to a new dominant logic for marketing. *Journal of Marketing, 68*(January), 1–17. doi:10.1509/jmkg.68.1.1.24036

World Robotics. (2013). *Industrial and Service Robots.* Retrieved in 2013 from http://www.worldrobotics.org/index.php?id=downloads

Xu, J., & Quaddus, M. (2010). E-business in the 21st century - Realities, Challenges and Outlook, In *Foundation of E-Business and E-Business Technologies.* World Scientific Publishing Co. Pte. Ltd. Retrieved in 2013 from http://www.worldscibooks.com/business/7097.html

Zeithaml, V. (1988). Consumer perception of price, quality and value. *Journal of Marketing, 52*(July), 2–22. doi:10.2307/1251446

KEY TERMS AND DEFINITIONS

Additive Manufacturing: Additive manufacturing or 3D printing is a production method based on constructing 3 dimensional objects gradually, layer by layer. Thus any object can be built up in many very thin layers. This can allow users to turn any digital file into a three dimensional physical product. Experiments are made with different materials – metal, plastic, rubber, food (chocolate, pasta), concrete and others. There are applications in bio-printing.

Augmented Reality: Augmented reality technologies form a class of solutions complementing ordinary physical objects with real-time virtual information and extending its context and use. They allow users to access simultaneously digital content, Internet connection and computational services on real life objects. Recognizing the real world objects and landscapes, and understanding location and time context dramatically will increase the relevance of data and will allow its better processing and further use.

E-Business: The term e-business can be generally defined as applications of Internet and communication technologies for inter- and intra- organizational transactions.

Emerging Technologies: An emerging technology (as distinguished from a conventional technology) is a field of technology that broaches new territory in some significant way, with new technological developments. Emerging technologies are those technical innovations which represent progressive developments within a field for competitive advantage.

Internet of Things: The Internet of Things (IoT) can be defined as a dynamic global network infrastructure with self configuring capabilities based on standard and interoperable communication protocols where physical and virtual 'things' have identities, physical attributes, and virtual personalities and use intelligent interfaces, and are seamlessly integrated into the information network. In the IoT paradigm, 'things' are expected to become active participants in business, information and social processes where they are enabled to interact and communicate among themselves and with the environment by exchanging data and information 'sensed' about the environment, while reacting autonomously to the 'real/physical world' events.

Robot: A robot can be defined a mechanical or virtual machine that is guided by a computer program or electronic circuitry. With evolving technology it become harder to distinguish specific characteristics of robots, but one of the common issues is that usually they have some moveable parts. Robots still cannot be qualified as "artificial humans," but their role and functionality gradually expand. They can vary from autonomous or semi-autonomous systems and can range from humanoids to industrial robots, collectively programmed "swarm" robots, and even microscopic nano-robots or nano-bots.

Ubiquitous Computing: Ubiquitous computing (UbiCom) can be defined as a general vision for technology evolution, contributing for technology adoption in the fabric of everyday life. Ubiquitous computing consists of mobile devices, wireless networks and other advanced technologies and infrastructure, leading to smart devices, smart environments and smart interactions.

ENDNOTES

[1]   Homeplus is an e-commerce subsidiary of the International grocery company TESCO in South Korea, based on QR shopping business model. More information is available on: http://www.youtube.com/watch?v=fGaVFRzTTP4.

[2]   More information available on Canon official web site and http://www.canon.com/news/2012/jun18e.html.

[3]   http://www.worldrobotics.org/index.php?id=home&news_id=267.

[4]   Explaining the future.com.

[5]   Microsoft Office Labs Vision 2019, Official Video HD, available on http://www.youtube.com/watch?v=Zp-_oUwdSeY.

[6]   Autolib® is a PPP joint-venture between the Group Bollero and Community of Paris. More information about the service is available on: https://www.autolib.eu.

[7]   http://en.wikipedia.org/wiki/Luddite.

This research was previously published in Technology, Innovation, and Enterprise Transformation edited by Manish Wadhwa and Alan Harper, pages 20-34, copyright year 2015 by Business Science Reference (an imprint of IGI Global).

Chapter 11
Hybrid Intelligence for Smarter Networking Operations

Bassem Mahmoud Mokhtar
Alexandria University, Egypt

Mohamed Eltoweissy
Virginia Military Institute, USA

ABSTRACT

The ever-growing and ever-evolved Internet targets supporting billions of networked entities to provide a wide variety of services and resources. Such complexity results in network-data from different sources with special characteristics, such as widely diverse users, multiple media, high-dimensionality and various dynamic concerns. With huge amounts of network-data with such characteristics, there are significant challenges to a) recognize emergent and anomalous behavior in network-traffic and b) make intelligent decisions for efficient network operations. Endowing the semantically-oblivious Internet with Intelligence would advance the Internet capability to learn traffic behavior and to predict future events. In this chapter, the authors discuss and evaluate the hybridization of monolithic intelligence techniques in order to achieve smarter and enhanced networking operations. Additionally, the authors provide systematic application-agnostic semantics management methodology with efficient processes for extracting and classifying high-level features and reasoning about rich semantics.

1. INTRODUCTION

Due to semantically-oblivious networking operations, the current Internet cannot effectively or efficiently cope with the explosion in services with different requirements, number of users, resource heterogeneity, and widely varied user, application and system dynamics (Feldmann, 2007). This leads to increasing complexity in Internet management and operations, thus multiplying challenges to achieve better security, performance and Quality of Service (QoS) satisfaction. The current Internet largely lacks capabilities to extract network-semantics to efficiently build behavioral models of Internet elements at different levels of granularity and to pervasively observe and inspect network dynamics. For example, a network host might know the role of TCP; however, it might not know the behavior of TCP in a mobile *ad hoc* network.

DOI: 10.4018/978-1-5225-2589-9.ch011

We refer to the limited utilization of Internet traffic semantics in networking operations as the Internet semantic gap. Additionally, many evolutionary cross-layer networking enhancements and clean-slate architectures, see for example (Bouabene et al., 2010; Day, Matta, & Mattar, 2008; Hassan, Eltoweissy, & Youssef, 2009; Zafeiropoulos, Liakopoulos, Davy, & Chaparadza, 2010), did not consider capabilities for representing, managing, and utilizing the inherent multi-dimensional networking data patterns. Also, these architectures lack facilities to learn network-semantics and utilize them to dynamically allocate and predict "right-sized" services/resources on demand for example.

The current and future internetworks (for example, Internet of things (IoT) (Khan, Khan, Zaheer, & Khan, 2012; Zhiming, Qi, & Hong, 2011)) support a massive number of Internet elements with extensive amounts of data. Fortunately, these data generally exhibit multi-dimensional patterns (for example, patterns with dimensions such as time, space, and users) that can be learned in order to extract network-semantics (Srivastava, Cooley, Deshpande, & Tan, 2000). These semantics can help in learning normal and anomalous behavior of the different networking elements (for example, services, protocols, etc.) in the Internet, and in building behavior models for those elements accordingly. Recognizing and maintaining semantics as accessible concepts and behavior models related to various Internet elements will aid in possessing intelligence thus helping elements in predicting future events (for example, QoS degradation and attacks) that might occur and affect performance of networking operations. Furthermore, learning behavior of those elements will better support self-* properties such as awareness with unfamiliar services and also advance reasoning about their behavior. For instance, a router can classify a new running service in a network as a specific type of TCP-based file transfer service when it finds similarity between behavior of the new service and that of an already known service.

The lack of efficient methodology and capabilities for analyzing and learning patterns of high- and multi-dimensional big network-data and reasoning about network-semantics presents challenges including but not limited to the following:

- Recognizing emergent and abnormal behavior of various Internet elements;
- Making effective decisions for efficient network operations;
- Ensuring availability of resources on-demand; and
- Efficient utilization of networked entities' capabilities to store, access and process data and extract valuable network-semantics.

Many research works targeted intelligence-based solutions to enhance operation performance in different fields (e.g., networks, speech and image recognition). Those works present solutions either using monolithic or hybrid intelligence techniques for achieving intelligence in different areas, such as speech recognition, language modeling and networking. In this chapter, we discuss the hybridization of monolithic intelligence techniques in order to achieve smarter and enhanced operations, especially in the networking field. Endowing the semantically-oblivious Internet with Intelligence would advance the Internet capability to learn traffic behavior and to predict future events. Additionally, we present our proposed network-semantics reasoner which is designed via hybridizing hidden Markov models (HMM) and latent Dirichlet allocation (LDA) for enabling latent features extraction with semantics dependencies.

In literature, some works have targeted intelligence-based solutions to enhance operation performance in different fields (e.g., speech and image recognition). In (Willett & Rigoll, 1998), authors integrated HMM and Neural Networks (NN) to form a hybrid speech recognition system. They employed NN to extract discriminative speech features by processing multiple instances of the same feature vector.

Extracted features are then directed to HMM to model the acoustic behavior of speech. HMM helps overcome NN's limitations in extracting valuable information from highly-dynamic traffic data. Another system uses support vector machine (SVM) for data analysis, classification and pattern recognition plus Fuzzy rules (Nii, Nakai, Takahashi, Higuchi, & Maenaka, 2011) for discovering human behavior. The system performs abstraction of data using SVM-based classification into sequence of actions, and constructs Fuzzy rules for each behavior, defined by a sequence of actions. In (Griffiths, Steyvers, Blei, & Tenenbaum, 2004), the authors provided a system for language learning based on using LDA and HMM. They adopted the ability of LDA and HMM to simultaneously learn and find syntactic classes and semantic topics despite having no knowledge of syntax or semantics beyond statistical dependency.

Internet (or network) intelligence (referred to here as InetIntel) is defined in the literature as the capability of Internet elements to understand network-semantics to be able to make effective decisions and use resources efficiently (Li, Xiao, Han, Chen, & Liu, 2007). InetIntel has to support Internet elements with the capability for learning normal and dynamic/emergent behavior of various elements and in turn building dynamic behavior models of those elements. Consequently, this will enable elements to be conscious of surrounding contexts enabling them to enhance their performance, utilization of resources and QoS satisfaction.

InetIntel provides facilities to understand network traffic by identifying correlation among users, services, and protocols; and it might be able to represent acquired knowledge in a unified model. InetIntel is considered as a middleware where it forms an information layer with metadata from IP traffic. These data are fed to applications to enrich their information about network-based activity. Furthermore, InetIntel relates data from different traffics to enhance situational awareness and better cyber security and IP services. Here are some of the services that can be offered by InetIntel:

- Optimization for QoS of running services and applications and enhancing protocols operation based on end-to-end (e2e) and non e2e principles.
- Unified representation "metadata" for different types of traffic to be used by applications.
- Real-time traffic analysis and situational awareness.
- Behavior analysis based on statistics, for various Internet elements, such as users, services, applications and protocols.
- Accumulated and evolvable knowledge services within time for better decision making processes in different situations as anomaly discovery.

InetIntel can be achieved via employing intelligence techniques to design intelligence systems. InetIntel systems can employ monolithic and/or hybrid (or combinations of more than one monolithic technique) intelligence techniques. Each implemented monolithic technique for InetIntel has its mechanisms for learning data patterns, extracting features and reasoning about data semantics. The environment of Internet has tremendous and ever-growing scale. It is noisy and dynamic with dissimilar communicating networks and heterogeneous entities, running services and resources. Accordingly, generated and transmitted Internet data have special characteristics, such as massive volume with high- and multi-dimensionality. Those characteristics might affect negatively performance of monolithic intelligence techniques. Hybrid intelligence techniques (HIT) can mitigate that challenge (Abraham & Nath, 2000; Peddabachigari, Abraham, Grosan, & Thomas, 2007). HIT will integrate more than one monolithic intelligence technique. HIT can mitigate limitations of monolithic techniques that it can combine their significant capabilities to extract valuable information with good level of accuracy and timeliness. For example, in (Kumar, Kumar, & Sachdeva, 2010), comparisons among various InetIntel techniques-based intrusion detection systems showed the outperformance of HIT in achieving higher detection accuracy.

In the networking literature, monolithic- and hybrid intelligence-based solutions have been investigated to provide intelligence for networks and Internet to realize self-* properties, address intrusion detection and achieve improved network performance and operation. Kumar *et al.* in (Kumar et al., 2010) discussed artificial intelligence-based techniques that can help in enhancing intrusion detection in Internet. A classification for those techniques was provided. Machine leaning and genetic algorithm based techniques are examples of artificial intelligence-based techniques. In (Idris & Shanmugam, 2005), Idris *et al.* provided a software-based middleware solution via a HIT for intrusion detection system (IDS). The implemented HIT comprises Fuzzy logic and a data mining mechanism with the usage of neural networks (NN). The IDS system depended on extracting features or attributes from large sets of real network-data and applying those features over simple *if-then* Fuzzy rules. The proposed system combines: a) misuse detection (e.g., detect attacks based on learning patterns and matching with already known attack patterns); and b) anomaly detection (e.g., learning unfamiliar attacks or threats by applying statistical analysis methods over data and compare results with historical knowledge).

In this chapter, we discuss the importance of embedding Internet with Intelligence via employing monolithic and hybrid semantics reasoning techniques. We propose hybrid intelligence technique (HIT) integrating HMM and LDA for reasoning about network semantics and targeting intelligence-based networking operations. Additionally, we highlight the importance and impact of attaching Intelligence to operating and communicating Internet elements; such as hosts and routers, and show how this capability can aid in better and smarter networking operations like optimizing at runtime QoS of running applications and learning abnormal traffic and strengthening security. The chapter is organized as follows. Section 2 provides background of concepts underlying our work and explores some related work. Hybrid intelligence-based methodology for reasoning about network semantics is presented in Section 3. Also, Section 3 highlights the differences between utilizing monolithic and hybrid intelligence techniques for learning network semantics and having smarter networking operations. Section 4 evaluates via conducting simulation the performance analysis of the studied intelligence techniques. Future directions are presented in Section 5. Finally, Section 6 concludes the chapter.

2. BACKGROUND AND RELATED WORK

In this section, we first highlight some definitions related to network-semantics management methodology. Then, we survey some research work related to network-semantics management in literature.

2.1 Background

In this subsection, we present definitions related to the methodology, as shown in Figure 1, which we adopt to reasoning about and manage network-semantics. These definitions are as follows.

- **Big Network-Data:** Data generated from different sources (e.g., Internet traffic, offline databases, management information bases (MIB)) with special characteristics, such as massive volume, information diversity (e.g., text, audio, video, etc.), high- and multi-dimensionality (e.g., large sets of attributes related to different Internet elements) and various dynamics concerns (e.g., time-sensitive data). With big network-data, there are challenges regarding content, structure and behavior.

- **Big Network:** A network that generates big network-data and can benefit from big data management in their operations. Examples of big networks include the current Internet, the emerging Internet of Things (Khan et al., 2012) and social networks.

- **Data Virtualization:** Voluminous data are generated with different formats and representation modes from various sources in big networks. To have efficient data collection, data virtualization (DV) techniques ("[Online] "; IBM; informatica; queplix) should be used. This would enable data abstraction and federation from different sources employing unified data representation. We are inspired here by the sensory system in humans (Hawkins & Blakeslee, 2005), which collects huge amount of data from five senses and sends it to the brain via nerve signals in a unified representation.

- **Data Feature Selection:** Big network-data are high- and multi-dimensional. This requires huge storage and computation capabilities to analyze patterns of these data. To have efficient big network-data processing, dimensionality reduction algorithms with the capability of directive data feature selection process will be used. Inspired by functionalities of the human memory, capturing raw data from various sources can lead to retrieving some distinguished features which are already maintained in the memory. For example, seeing an unfamiliar restaurant across a road aids us in easily remembering and retrieving some known special restaurant features like the existence of dining tables, chairs, restrooms, etc. (not the locations of restrooms or number and color of chairs and tables).

- **Function-Behavior-Structure (FBS) Data Modeling:** Representing data uniformly, clarifying their functional, behavioral and structural aspects (Dorst & Vermaas, 2005; Gero, 1990) will facilitate data pattern learning. In the human memory, there are connectivity patterns established via synapses amongst neurons in different brain cortex areas. Those connectivity patterns refer to three different connectivity modes, namely, structural connectivity, functional connectively and effective connectivity between neurons. Structural connectivity gives information about the established links or synapses between neurons. Functional connectivity provides information about statistical dependencies and correlations between neurons. Effective connectivity refers to the information flow carried by electrochemical signals between neurons. The analysis of connectivity patterns using the previously discussed modes helps in learning the behavior and characteristics of neurons (e.g., specialized neurons) and related synapses and transferred electrochemical signals in different cortex areas.

- **Associative Storage:** To learn patterns, data will be maintained in warehouses, which will be extendible. That storage would be enabled with capabilities of identifying storage locations by their content or part of contents. This matches operations of short-term and long-term memories in human. Low or high levels of neurons fire in different cortex regions when they capture data, which indicate to different types of information. These groups of neurons are connected as sequences. They are referring to lots of detailed or abstracted data.

- **Pattern Sensing:** States the ability to discover big data patterns based on data attributes (or features) extraction and classification processes. In the human memory, sequences of neurons in certain cortex areas (e.g. visual and vocal areas) with certain connection pattern lead to identifying characteristics of that pattern. For instance, hearing and seeing a cat lead to a certain neurons pattern in our brain based on learned concepts (e.g., expectation of listening to cat *meow* voice).

- **Formal Reasoning:** A well-founded artificial intelligence functionality based on integrated statistical reasoning models to perform semantic reasoning and matching. Those models will be used to extract semantics from learned data patterns and already known semantics. Constructed chains of neurons in different cortex locations (e.g., vocal and visual cortex areas) of the human brain result in formation of high level neurons that will be fired along the human life. Capturing data via different senses (e.g., sight and hearing) result in having sequences of correlated fired neurons in various cortex areas.

2.2 Related Work

In this subsection, we compare various techniques that can be used in network-semantics reasoning and management. Table 1 shows a comparison between different schemes for implementing models for semantics reasoning, such as HMM (Rabiner & Juang, 1986), LDA (Blei, Ng, & Jordan, 2003), neural networks (Cross, Harrison, & Kennedy, 1995), Latent Semantics Analysis (LSA) (Landauer, Foltz, & Laham, 1998), Simulated Annealing (SA) (Van Laarhoven & Aarts, 1987) and Support Vector Machine (SVM) (Cristianini & Shawe-Taylor, 2000). The comparison highlights the advantages and the limitations of each technique.

3. HYBRID INTELLIGENCE TECHNIQUE-BASED REASONER FOR SMARTER NETWORKING

In this section, we discuss network-semantics management processes using monolithic and hybrid intelligence techniques. We will highlight three different monolithic intelligence techniques in literature for semantics reasoning where we show the operation and performance of each technique. Then, we present

Figure 1. Semantics management methodology

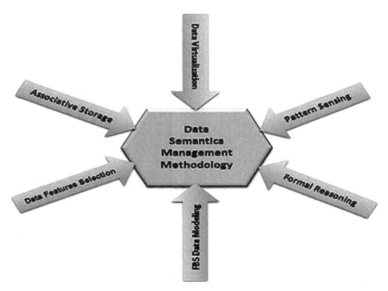

Table 1. Comparison between different schemes for network-semantics reasoning

Scheme	Description	Operation Technique	Application	Advantage	Limitation
HMM (Rabiner & Juang, 1986)	• HMM is a statistical Markov model for categorical sequence labeling (i.e., pattern recognition by statistical inference) based on using supervised/unsupervised learning algorithms (e.g., Baum-Welch algorithm (Baum, 1972)). • Sequence labeling can be treated as a set of independent classification tasks. • HMM is a structured architecture that is able to predict sequences of semantic topics based on hidden sequences of input data attributes or features.	Based on continuous input sequence with different Gaussian distributions then making distribution mixture for obtaining most likelihood output sequence.	• Labeling documents/ motions with certain tags or topics for information retrieval • Gesture imitation in robots	• HMM depends on a mathematical model with parameters) that can be adjusted for supporting different semantic topics in many contexts • HMM's statistical foundations are computationally efficient and well-suited to handle new data • HMM can support multi-dimensional data • HMM can be adjusted as prototype to extract spedific semanti topics	• The floating-point underflow problem. • discovering high-level features with long-range semantics dependencies • lot of HMM parameters to be calculated at large input states • require large sets of data to be trained • Low performance at operation with reduced-dimensional data
LDA (Blei et al., 2003)	• LDA is a generative probabilistic dynamic model that can be used for extracting hidden topics in group of observed unlabeled input data profiles and known words or attributes. • LDA has the capability to discover high-level features in data profiles where it has a well-defined inference methodology to associate a data profile with group of attributes with several semantic topics. • LDA is capable of extracting data semantics based on prior probabilities for data profile-semantic topic and attribute-semantic topic associations.	Based on supervised learning process and training data with prior probabilities that associate topics with words and documents and using sampling tech. (e.g., Gibbs)	• Modeling a mixture of topics with documents • Topic models for image and text recognition	• LDA models are extendible to support more associations amongst semantic topics and data attributes • Can be integrated with functionalities of other semantic reasoning models (e.g., HMMs) • discovering high-level latent features	• Randomization process for assigning parameters' values of attribute-topic • Probability for the overfitting problem at large number of training data sets • Big bag of attributes lead to topic misclassification process based on random topic sampling process
LDA-HMM (Hybrid) (Griffiths et al., 2004)	Probabilistic and Categorical sequence labeling supervised/ unsupervised algorithms for allocating latent topic and estimating semantics based on hidden sequence of input latent words	Based on sampling process for hidden topic bases on multinomial probability distribution and using Gaussian distributions with maximum likelihood estimation for outputting semantics	Topic modeling for many applications such as pattern and image recognition, and information retrieval	• Combine advantages of both LDA and HMM schemes • Number of input features or states to train the HMM is lower than operation with HMM alone • Mitigate the effect of topic misclassification and overfitting by LDA where final semantics output depends on group of syntactic states formed by extracted features by LDA	• The time complexity worsens to some extent compared to comprised monolithic schemes • The floating-point underflow problem. • Require large sets of data to be trained

continued on next page

Table 1. Continued

Scheme	Description	Operation Technique	Application	Advantage	Limitation
Simple statistical-analysis- based models	Models for learning statistics of input words and based on some defined rules, they can extract semantics	Collecting statistics about words, documents and using defined rules (e.g., Fuzzy rules) and thresholds that outputs depend on meeting those rules	Rule-based Reasoning (extraction of information related to specific semantic topics)	• Can be designed to be directed to specific types of semantic-topics or information ; achieving good performance • Low computation complexity	• Specific to certain semantic topics • Inefficient design lead to incorrect extracted information • No capability to extract high-level latent features
Neural network (Cross et al., 1995)	• Classification algorithms (supervised algorithms predicting categorical labels) • Learning is by training and used to model complex relationships between inputs and outputs, to find patterns in data, or to capture the statistical structure in an unknown joint probability distribution between observed variables	• Based on a hidden layer that relates group of input with other group of output via defined weights. • Connection weight based on relation between inputs and outputs and affect results (i.e. outputs) • Depending on composition of functions where components of each neural network layer are independent of each other	• System identification and control • Decision making • Pattern recognition • Data mining	• Flexibility: it can be applied to many applications • Robustness: it can work properly and mitigate the failure of some Internet elements • It can handle noisy data and analyze complex data patterns	• Design complexity: o Complicated group of neural units connected based on weighted inputs to outputs and passing thresholds o Long processing time in case of large neural network • More trainings is needed to operate efficiently • Its operation might face overfitting
Latent Semantic Analysis (LSA) (Landauer et al., 1998)	Probabilistic models which relates documents to topics based on weighted relationship specified by probabilities (mapping documents' words into concepts)	Building models for mixtures of topics and documents through training examples	Modeling a mixture of topics and concepts with documents and their words	Reduces dimensionality of documents for better representation, finding synonyms and minimizing computational complexity.	• Assuming Gaussian distribution for words in documents. • No directed capabilities for selecting efficient dimensions of reduced documents (based on heuristics)
Simulated Annealing (SA) (Van Laarhoven & Aarts, 1987)	Its name is inspired from annealing in metallurgy. It is a Probabilistic metaheuristic algorithm for searching for global optimum solutions of objective functions and with large search space.	Its operation methodology depends on a slow decreasing in probability for accepting worse solutions and moving from state to another state depending on a defined acceptance probability function, generated new solutions by mutation and a generated random number for making decision through number of iterations or until getting no more better solutions.	Optimizing operations of online information searching through massive number of Internet web pages and related information	• Capability to operate with arbitrary problems (e.g., combinatorial problems) and systems. • Easy to be coded and implemented for complex problems.	• Slow according to its sequential nature. • One candidate solution per iteration and capability for building quick overall view of search space. • Overstated for problems with few local minima.
Support Vector Machine (SVM) (Cristianini & Shawe-Taylor, 2000)	Machine learning models depending on supervised learning algorithms. SVM is used for analyzing data and learning patterns	Non-probabilistic binary linear and non-linear classifier using numerical quadratic programming It depends on a set of training examples via support vectors (to build an assignment model) and data input where it will classifies each input to one category	• Data classification • Anomaly detection • Regression analysis • Feature and online searching • Text and hypertext categorization	• Easy for training • No local minima • Versatile through using different kernel functions for modeling complex problems and decision making	• Poor performances at long feature dimensions compared with number of samples or support vectors • High complexity (long training time) with extensive memory requirements at large scale tasks • Selection of appropriate kernel functions to suit problems.

our hybrid intelligence techniques. Finally, we provide a qualitative comparison between the presented intelligence techniques for showing their capabilities and performance.

3.1 Introduction

Monolithic and hybrid intelligence techniques can be used to design reasoning models to manage network-semantics. The capability (e.g., latent features extraction ability, high prediction accuracy, etc.) of adopted reasoning model for learning rich semantics depends on the operation performance of the used intelligence techniques. In the following subsections, we discuss different semantics reasoning models, which can be implemented to reason about semantics related to various network concerns. Various monolithic intelligence techniques using Latent Dirichlet Allocation (LDA) (Blei et al., 2003) and Hidden Markov Models (HMM) (Rabiner & Juang, 1986) are presented for designing semantics reasoning models. Additionally, we propose hybrid intelligence technique (HIT)-based reasoning model integrating LDA and HMM to efficiently extract semantics and know high-level data features. We will show characteristics and capabilities of adopted reasoning models clarifying their advantages and limitations.

3.2 Monolithic Intelligence Technique-Based Reasoners

In this subsection, we discuss reasoning models implemented for extracting network-semantics using monolithic intelligence techniques.

3.2.1 Simple Statistical-Analysis-Based Reasoner

Characteristics of big data, such as massive volume and complexity, impede regular data monitoring and analysis tools to anticipate data contents and structure and to interpret patterns meaningfully. Construction of statistical models (Breiman, 2001; Vasconcelos & Lippman, 2000) can help in understanding patterns of big data. This would lead to a capability of extracting features and semantics. One of the problems with those models is that they are specific to certain semantic topics (i.e., those models have limitations in extracting latent features). Inefficient design (e.g., inadequate algorithmic model) for those models can lead to incorrect extracted information. There is a need for a data training phase to test accuracy of models. Some rules (e.g., Fuzzy rules) can be constructed to fit certain semantic topics. Adoption of classification techniques with rules can help statistical models to extract high level data features.

We provide a simple statistical-analysis-based model (via statistics and rules) for a network-semantics manager (SM) to extract semantics related to various Internet elements (e.g., behavior of TCP protocol or TCP hosts' storage memory). Figure 2 illustrates the algorithm of the proposed simple statistical-analysis-based model. Adopting this model, SM would learn patterns of N different data profiles represented in a related storage memory to derive semantics with higher levels of abstraction. There are K targeted attributes that can be extracted and classified from stored profiles. Using data pattern learning algorithms (e.g., ARL (Paul, 2010)) and a classification technique (e.g., FMF (Winter, 2007)), SM will learn group of attributes (A_p) per each data profile in the storage memory that match required K attributes. An assumption is made that attributes per profiles are independent with equal probabilities of existence at each analyzed profile (i.e., attributes have same weights per profile). SM searches every reasoning time period (t_R) for similar data profiles (N_{Pn}) of each (n) profile of total (N) profiles.

Figure 2. Simple statistical-analysis-based reasoning model

Input: *K*: targeted attributes, *A_p*: number of attributes per data profile, *P_n* : data profile which contains attributes, *N_{Pn}*: similar data profiles, *min_support*:: define the minimum number of data profiles that have common attributes (based on number of captured data profiles)
Operations:
For (n=2; $n \leq A_p$; n++) {
        Initialize *count*; counter for calculating number of data profiles' instances
        Generate candidate group **C_A** of *n* attributes;
        For N data profiles in the storage memory do {
            For all attributes in each P_n do {
                if (comprised attributes found in C_A) *count* ++;
            }

        }
        if (*count* ≥ **min_support)** K = C_A ; learn group of attributes that found in most data profiles
}
For N data profiles in the storage memory do {
        For all attributes in each P_n do {
            calculate attributes membership using FMFs
        }
        calculate profile weight W_{Pn}
        }
Learn group of N_{Pn}
For each N_{Pn} profiles do {
        calculate accuracy according to K, W_{Pn} , N, N_{Pn} and A_p
        apply defined Fuzzy rules for N_{Pn} with high accuracy
        generate semantics
}
Output: *Semantics that are maintained as concept classes*

Equations (1) and (2) describe the initial attribute weight and data profile weight, respectively. $I - A_{i,Pn}$ is the initial attribute i weight per data profile P_n where:

$$I - A_{i,Pn} = \frac{1}{K} \tag{1}$$

and $1 \leq n \leq N$, N number of profiles kept in the storage memory

$$Data\ profile\ P\ weight\left(W_{Pn}\right) = \sum_i \left(I - A_{i,Pn} \times M - A_{i,Pn}\right) \tag{2}$$

for each attribute i per data profile, where $1 \leq i \leq K$, where $M\_A_{i,Pn}$ is the membership value of the attribute i in a data profile P_n calculated by defined FMFs. The previous simple equations calculate group of low level features that can be used to extract semantics. SM has definitions for sets of fuzzy rules to aid in extracting semantics. Those rules can be used, for example, in determining normal behavior of the storage memory in TCP hosts. With Fuzzy rules, SM adopts a vector (T) of thresholds, which are determined by experts or via SM experience and history. Based on results from profiles analysis process and thresholds' values, SM can abstract semantics. Figure 3 depicts a trapezoidal FMF used for calculating membership values of the bandwidth attribute. The figure shows three different classes for the bandwidth attribute which are low; medium; and high based on the attribute's value. The accuracy for the semantics management processes executed in SM is calculated using (3).

$$SM\ Accuracy = W_{Pn} \times \left(\frac{A_p}{K}\right) \times \left(\frac{N_{Pn}}{N}\right) \tag{3}$$

Figure 3. Trapezoidal fuzzy membership function for the bandwidth attribute

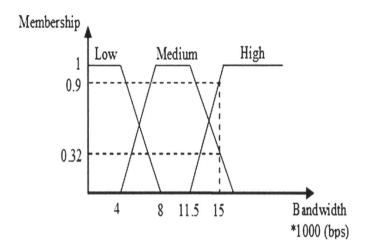

where $A_p \leq K$

Table 2 shows some statistics calculated using the above equations to learn patterns of 10 data profiles kept in the storage memory concerning a file transfer service operated by TCP protocol (Bassem Mokhtar, Eltoweissy, & El-Sayed, 2013). We assumed that three attributes, i.e., K=3, are considered in learning patterns by the ARL algorithm. Hence, SM will inspect data profiles in the storage memory and search for those attributes. Here, the problem is attribute extraction and classification (discrete target attributes) using discriminative functions, i.e., FMF. SM has definitions for Fuzzy rules which are used in, for example, determining normal behavior of the TCP communication protocol using an assigned vector (T) of thresholds, which are determined by experts or by SM via its experience and maintained history. Here is an example of a rule:

Table 2. Statistics of different TCP data profiles calculated by SM for learning TCP protocol patterns

Attributes (A_p) per the Service Data Profile			Number of Similar Profiles (N_{Pn})	Total Number of Profiles (N)	Data Profile Weight (W_{Pn})	Profile Rank (P_r)	SM Accuracy
Bandwidth (bps) Membership	**Buffer Size (Packets) Membership**	**Service Duration (Seconds) Membership**					
15000 0.9 (high)	7000 1 (high)	1000 1 (high)	5	10	1	1	48.33%
10000 1 (medium)	3000 1 (low)	200 1 (low)	1	10	1	2	10%
14000 0.82 (high)	6000 0.4(medium)	500 0.5(medium)	1	10	0.57276	4	5.7276%
---	6500 0.55 (high)	1000 1 (high)	1	10	0.51615	6	3.441%
15000 0.9 (high)	5000 1 (medium)	---	1	10	0.666	5	4.22%
12000 0.9(medium)	6000 0.4(medium)	1000 1 (high)	1	10	0.7659	3	7.659%

$$IF\left(\left(W_{Pn} > T_a\right) \& \&\left(N_{Pn} > T_b\right) \& \&\left(\left(N_{Pn} \, / \, N\right) \times t_R < T_c\right) \& \&\left(A_p == K\right)\right)$$

THEN normal behavior **ELSE** abnormal behavior

T_a, T_b and T_c are thresholds defined in T vector for profile weight, number, and arrival ratio, respectively. According to the above rule, SM will extract semantics for the TCP protocol as follows:

```
IF behavior = normal THEN develop semantics (S_normal);
S_normal = largeNumberOfProfiles,CompleteDataProfile, NormalProfileWeight.
IF behavior =abnormal THEN develop semantics (S_abnormal);
S_abnormal = SmallNumberOfProfiles,InCompleteDataProfile, AbnormalProfileWeight.
```

largeNumberOfProfiles means that N_{Pn} exceeds the threshold T_b, CompleteDataProfile means that the data profile maintains all interesting attributes, NormalProfileWeight means that W_{Pn} is above threshold T_a. The semantics for the abnormal behavior will reveal that profiles do not satisfy the above conditions.

3.2.2 Hidden Markov Models-Based Reasoner

Hidden Markov models (HMM) (Rabiner & Juang, 1986; Ramage, 2007) are a structured architecture that is able of predicting sequences of semantic-topics based on input sequences of extracted network attributes or features. Depending on input sequences or pattern of high discriminative network-data features, HMM with forward and backward algorithms can learn semantics efficiently. HMM is widely used in learning processes and extracting information (Jiten, Merialdo, & Huet, 2006; Seymore, McCallum, & Rosenfeld, 1999) in different fields, such as in image and speech recognition, detection of network attacks (Ourston, Matzner, Stump, & Hopkins, 2003), and robotics for gesture imitation (J. Yang & Xu, 1994). HMM is a statistical Markov model for categorical sequence labeling (i.e., pattern recognition by statistical inference) based on using supervised/unsupervised learning algorithms (e.g., Baum-Welch algorithm). Sequence labeling can be treated as a set of independent classification tasks. HMM depends on a mathematical model with parameters (i.e., initial (π), state transition (A), and observation (B) probabilities) that can be adjusted for supporting different semantic topics in many contexts. With sets of training data, Baum-Welch's forward-backward algorithm can be applied to HMM to discover unknown HMM parameters (i.e., unsupervised learning). HMM can support multi-dimensional data (e.g., big network-data with time-based, domain-based, and service-based features). Each input state in an HMM can be specific to an output semantics domain. Considering input states as Markovian processes might affect degree of accuracy for output data. This can be mitigated, to some extent, by adjusting parameters of HMM. For example, the forward and backward transition probabilities among specific states can have the same value. This will give equal weights for get certain semantic topics if transition occurs among those states.

HMM can extract low-level data features from variable length data attributes' sequence using unsupervised learning. HMM's statistical foundations are computationally efficient and well-suited to handle new data (Seymore et al., 1999). A single HMM can be built by combining a verity of knowledge sources (J. Yang & Xu, 1994) with the consideration of their properties. This enables an efficient design of an HMM to reason about semantics related to various Internet elements. One of HMM problems is the floating-point underflow problem. This can affect extracted correct semantics. It can be overcome by taking logarithm for values of probabilities and performing summation process instead of multiplication to calculate forward probabilities. HMM have limitations in discovering high-level features with long-range syntactic dependencies. Another limitation for HMM can be found if it is required to design an HMM with large input states. This means a lot of HMM parameters to be calculated. This might affect performance (e.g., timeliness) of a semantics reasoning model implemented with HMM. HMM can be combined to form a hybrid or multi-stage model constituting matrix of HMM models. This can aid in enhancing the performance if there is a need to separate of feeding large scale of parameters and/or focusing on specific set of parameters related to certain operation domains. HMM might require large sets of data to be trained. This can be found in case of big network-data if the system can sample some sets for training. Since HMM can be considered as static models or prototypes for semantic reasoning, HMM models face challenges at operation reduced-dimension data. This will affect accuracy of operations for obtaining right semantics. This can be mitigated via using an algorithm for latent features discovery from low and reduced dimension data. Then, those features can be supplied to HMM.

For instance, a semantic manager (SM) might employ HMM for semantics reasoning and extraction as shown in Figure 4 (B. Mokhtar & Eltoweissy, 2012). As shown in the figure, the HMM-based model depends on defining set of HMM parameters as will be discussed later. Then, a training phase is executed using sets of maintained data profiles to adjust the HMM parameters. After that, the operations of HMM-based model begin by calculating the probability of partial observation sequence according to his process will continue until reaching the whole input sequence length (i.e., the termination phase). Based on sequence and length of input attributes with stateless operation; calculated HMM parameters; and maximum likelihood estimation, HMM can extract features. These features will constitute associated semantics related to specific fields (e.g., behavior of Internet elements) or network concerns (application, communication, and resource).

1. The input to HMM-based models which is sequence of profiles' attributes;
2. The transition probability A among input attributes;
3. The observation probability B between each input attribute and each possible output feature.

Figure 4. HMM-based reasoning model

Input: Using HMM model $\lambda=(A,B,\pi)$ and the forward algorithm:
α: the probability of partial observation sequence at certain detection time t giving that there is a certain input state (i.e., feature or attribute) at that time
Operations:
a) Initialization:
$\alpha_1(i) = \pi_i B_i(concept(1))$, $1 \leq i \leq K$, where K: number of defined features, $B_i(concept(1))$ is the probability to have first concept from feature i
b) Induction:
$\alpha_{t+1}(j) = [\sum_i \alpha_t(i) A_{ij}] B_j(concept(t+1))$, $1 \leq i \leq K$, $1 \leq j \leq K$, $1 \leq t \leq T-1$
c) Termination:
$P(concept\ sequence/\lambda)= \sum_i \alpha_T(i)$, $1 \leq i \leq K$, considering accumulated value of α of T (length of sequence) states

HMM Performance Measure

A HMM is defined as $\lambda = (A, B, \pi)$ with the following notation:

π is the initial probability distribution for HMM states. For K discrete (feature) states and input sequence of T states, $\pi_i = p\left(state_{(t=1)} = i\right)$ where $1 \leq i \leq K$.

A is the state transition probability matrix, which is square matrix and it shows probabilities for transition from a state (i.e., feature) to another state. $A_{ij} = p\left[\dfrac{\left(state_{(t+1)} = j\right)}{\left(state_{(t)} = i\right)}\right]$ where $1 \leq i \leq K$ and $1 \leq t \leq T$.

B is the observable concept or semantic topic probability distribution. If there is a probability distribution over output concepts (i.e., observations) for each input feature (i.e., input state) that this distribution will show the probability to have a concept from a specific feature where there M discrete observations $\{1, 2, \ldots., M\}$. $B_j\left(concept(t)\right) = p\left[\dfrac{\left(concept_{(t)} = m\right)}{\left(state_{(t)} = j\right)}\right]$ where $1 \leq m \leq M, 1 \leq j \leq K$ and $1 \leq t \leq T$.

As mentioned in (Chatterjee & Russell, 2012), the time and space complexity of a HMM are $O(K^2T)$ and $O(K^2+KT)$, respectively.

3.2.3 Latent Dirichlet Allocation-Based Reasoner

Latent Dirichlet Allocation (LDA) is a generative probabilistic dynamic model that can be used for data semantics reasoning based on learned data attributes (Blei et al., 2003). LDA has the capability to discover high-level features of data profiles where it has a well-defined inference methodology to associate a data profile with group of attributes with several semantic topics. LDA is capable of extracting data semantics based on prior probabilities for data profile-semantic topic and attribute-semantic topic associations. For example, the operation of LDA to discover feature or semantic topics in M analyzed profiles is executed every defined reasoning window or through other criteria as initiating triggering signals. LDA samples a hidden semantic topic z for each m data profile through calculating sampled posterior probability vector θ of topic-data profile association which depends on prior association weight α, number of the mth profile's attributes related to a certain topic z, and N total number of attributes in the m profile. Also, LDA calculates sampled posterior probability φ of attribute-topic association based on prior attribute-topic association weight β, number of attribute instances assigned to topic z, and total number of attributes in all M profiles assigned to topic z.

Figure 5 shows LDA algorithm for semantics reasoning processes. Through certain number of iterations, the posterior probability to have a specific semantic topic assigned to data profiles and attributes is enforced. This is because that semantic topics with high association probabilities will have great chances to be assigned to data profiles and related attributes after finishing all iterations. For instance, assume a data profile which has prior association probabilities with four semantic topics (p(1)=0.1, p(2)=0.2,p(3)=0.3,p(4)=0.4). After using Gibbs sampling and choosing a random number (e.g., u) from the total summation of all probabilities (i.e., p_tot=1), u will be less than 1. So, the assigned topic to that data profile should be for a topic that its prior association probability greater than u.

Figure 5. LDA-based reasoning model

<u>*Initialization:*</u>
- Define Z semantic topics, input M profiles each has N attributes of total V attributes, α a real value Z-dimension vector (prior weight of topic z in a profile), β a real value V-dimension vector (prior weight of attribute v in a topic)
- Assign randomly a topic for each attribute in a data profile and build matrix z[M][N]

<u>*Definitions:*</u>
nw[i][j]: # of instance of attribute i assigned to topic j, nd[i][j] number of attributes in document i assigned to topic j, nwsum[j] total number of attributes assigned to topic j, ndsum[i] total number of attributes in document i

<u>*Generative Process:*</u>
For iter = 1:Iterations
    For m = 1: M (number of profiles)
        For n=1:N (number of attributes per each profile m)
            remove current state topic z from the count variables for each attribute n in profile m

            for z= 1 : Z (number of semantic topics)
                $p(topic\ z) = (nw[profiles[m][n]][z] + β)/(nwsum[z] + V * β) * (nd[m][z] + α)/(ndsum[m] + Z * α)$
            end
            sample topic z from p
            Add newly estimated topic z to count variables
        end
    end
end

LDA-based reasoning models provide semantic-topics models that enable discovery of hidden topic-based patterns through supervised learning process. LDA gives a systematic and well-defined way for inferring latent semantic topics in large scale of multi-dimensional data sets. LDA assign random values for prior probabilities semantic topics and related attributes based on data sampling (e.g., Gibbs sampling (Casella & George, 1992; Darling, 2011)), multivariate distribution (e.g., dirichlet distribution) and training data sets. LDA models have the capability of extracting latent features and semantics based on prior probabilities for data attribute- data profile and data attribute-semantic topic associations. LDA assumes that attributes of data are related to random chosen semantic topics. The selection of semantic topics is based on random values of multivariate probability distribution parameter. LDA executes semantic topic sampling for each data attribute in every data profile for all profiles, and the updating processes for profile-semantic topic and attribute-topic associations, which are iterated many times. LDA models have the ability to estimate semantics based on small scope of extracted features with long-range semantic dependencies. LDA supports semantic extraction from big data with high dimension. Semantic-topics selection parameters and prior probabilities can be directed to relate to specific attributes to group of topics (i.e., having specific distribution of semantic-topics over group of attributes). This enables LDA models to work with low-dimensional data, such as reduced-dimension data obtained through an LSH algorithm.

One of the main advantages for LDA models that these models are extendible (Bíró & Szabó, 2009) to support more associations amongst semantic topics and data attributes. LDA models can be used to enhance functionalities of other semantic reasoning models (e.g., HMM) to strengthen their capability of extracting latent features and semantics. Some limitations of LDA models can be found due to their randomization process for assigning parameters' values of attribute-topic associations. This can result in inaccurate predictions and semantic topics. LDA models, at large number of training data sets, can face the overfitting problem. LDA has some limitations (Newman, Asuncion, Smyth, & Welling, 2007), such as the bag of words or attributes assumption where there is a possibility of semantic topic sampling process to allow attributes, related to same semantic topics, to be assigned to other semantic topics. Furthermore, the LDA's probabilistic inference process for topics is computational complexity where that process takes polynomial time in case of inferring document's topics using a small number of semantic topics (Sontag & Roy, 2011).

LDA Performance Measure

Equations (4) and (5) is used to calculate the perplexity where that equation was derived based on the one mentioned at (Blei et al., 2003). Calculating perplexity helps in evaluating performance of the LDA models in detecting and categorizing attributes in data profiles based on learned parameters (e.g., prior profile-topic association weight or probabilities). A data profile is represented by a network-data storage model where it comprises data attributes related to traffic among Internet elements. So, based on *M* data profiles and their *N* related attributes and number of defined semantic topics *K*, we can get the value of perplexity.

$$Perplexity = \exp^{-\left(\frac{\left(\left|\sum_{m=1}^{M} \log\left(p\left(attribute_m\right)\right)\right|\right)}{\left(\sum_{m=1}^{M} N_m\right)}\right)}$$

(4)

where

$$p\left(attribute_m\right) = \prod_{n=1}^{N_m}\left(\sum_{j=1}^{K} p\left(\frac{attribute_n}{topic_j}\right) p\left(\frac{topic_j}{profile_m}\right)\right)$$

(5)

and N_m is the number of attributes per each data profile m.

In (Sontag & Roy, 2011), the authors investigated the inference problem, or the maximum a posteriori (MAP) problem, at LDA. That problem relates to the most likely assignment process of semantic topics to profile's attributes. Due to that problem, it was proved in (Sontag & Roy, 2011) that the time complexity of LDA is: a) *"polynomial"* $O((N_m K)^k (N_m + k)^3)$ in case of having small k topics appear in document (or data profile) where k << K; and b) non-deterministic polynomial (NP)-hard in case of LDA general settings with arbitrary topics per data profiles where each profile might have K topics in its MAP assignment. Henderson *et al.* in (Henderson & Eliassi-Rad), investigated the LDA inference using standard Gibbs sampling approach. Based on that approach, the runtime and space complexity of LDA with Gibbs sampling were $O(MKN_m)$ and $O(M(K+N_m))$, respectively.

3.3 Hybrid Intelligence Technique (HIT)-Based Reasoner

In this subsection, we discuss the proposed HIT-based reasoning methodology for reasoning about network-semantics.

3.3.1 HIT Overview

We propose and implement a HIT to build efficient reasoning model to reason about network-semantics based on learning patterns of full or reduced-dimensional data. The HIT integrates LDA (Blei et al., 2003) and HMM (Rabiner & Juang, 1986). Our HIT is designed to overcome limitations of the semantics reasoning operation with only adopting HMM. The hybridization of HMM and LDA enables latent features extraction with semantics dependencies not just based on learning features with syntax dependencies. On the one hand, LDA has the capability to discover high-level features of data profiles with full or reduced dimensionality. LDA possesses extendible operation (Bíró & Szabó, 2009) where it can support more associations amongst semantic topics and extracted high-level data features. LDA has a well-defined inference methodology to associate a data profile with groups of attributes with several semantic topics. However, adopting LDA alone in semantics reasoning might produce some shortcomings due to LDA's limitations, such as the bag of words assumption (Newman et al., 2007) that might result in semantic topics misclassification where there is a possibility of semantic topic sampling process to allow attributes, related to same semantic topics, to be assigned to other semantic topics. Furthermore, the LDA's probabilistic inference process for topics is computationally complex where that process has NP-hard complexity in case of inferring document's topics using a large number of semantic topics (Sontag & Roy, 2011). On the other hand, HMM can efficiently extract data semantics from variable-length input sequence of data features, extracted by LDA, using unsupervised learning algorithms (Jiang, 2009). HMM's statistical foundations are computationally efficient and well-suited to handle new data (Seymore et al., 1999). A single HMM can be built by combining a verity of knowledge sources (J. Yang & Xu, 1994) with the consideration of their properties. This enables an efficient design of an HMM to reason about semantics related to various Internet elements. However, utilizing HMM singularly for semantic reasoning might result in some deficiencies due to HMM incapability: a) to discover high-level features with long-term semantics dependencies due to the assumption about data using the Markovian process and the usage of maximum likelihood estimator (Merhav & Ephraim, 1991); and b) to work efficiently with reduced-dimension data since HMM needs large amounts of data for training and adjusting HMM's unstructured parameters.

We propose the HIT to overcome limitations of the operation with only HMM or LDA (Bassem Mokhtar & Eltoweissy, 2014). Integrating LDA with HMM enables latent features extraction with semantics dependencies not just based on learning features with syntax dependencies. Our proposed HIT can enhance the operation of LDA by assuming Markovianity of attribute sequences (Blei et al., 2003) which can mitigate the LDA limitation caused by the bag of words assumption (Newman et al., 2007). Also, the designed HIT will consider advantages of comprised intelligence techniques; HMM and LDA. We are motivated in our HIT design by the capability of LDA to discover latent high-level features from multi-dimensional network-data patterns with long-range semantics dependencies. Those features will be grouped as sequences that enable semantics reasoning operation via HMM with higher accuracy. LDA models are extendible (Bíró & Szabó, 2009) in that they can support more associations amongst semantic topics and extracted data features. Hence, HMM will be able to efficiently reason about data semantics related to input sequences of high-level data features. HMM (Rabiner & Juang, 1986) are structured architectures that are able to predicting sequences of semantic-topics based on input sequences of extracted network attributes or features. Depending on input sequences or pattern of high discriminative network-data features, HMM with forward and backward algorithms can learn semantics efficiently. The output from feature extraction process executed by LDA (i.e., input to HMM) is random based on analyzed data. This agrees with the characteristics of HMM to predict output based on hidden data sequences.

3.3.2 Semantics Reasoning Process Using the HIT

For instance, a semantic manager (SM) has tasks that depend on learning patterns of multi-dimensional dynamic network-data in a storage memory. Based on learned patterns, SM will reason about semantics and maintain them as associated and classified concepts. Figure 6 shows the pseudo code of the HIT-based semantics reasoning process which is executed by SM. SM learns group of attributes in data profiles kept in the storage memory through utilizing associative rule learning (Paul, 2010) and simple statistical-analysis-based models using FMF (Winter, 2007). Construction of statistical models (Breiman, 2001) can help in understanding patterns and analyzing low-level features of big data. SM adopts LDA for extracting and classifying high-level data features with long-range semantics dependencies. SM integrates the capabilities of LDA with HMM for semantics reasoning. Integration of LDA and HMM forms a hybrid model for semantics reasoning. LDA are extendible (Bíró & Szabó, 2009) that they can support more associations amongst semantic topics and extracted data features. Classified features by LDA are input to HMM as sequences.

Figure 7 describes the semantics extraction process implemented by the LDA-HMM-based reasoning model. Network-data characteristics include massive volume, high- and multi-dimensionality, dynamicity, complexity (variety in representation models and languages). In (Griffiths et al., 2004), authors proposed a generative model based on Latent Dirichlet Allocation (LDA) (Blei et al., 2003) and HMM for learning words with short-range syntax and long-range semantics dependencies. Consequently, this aids in forming richer ontology with more associated semantic topics and classes. There is similarity

Figure 6. Pseudo code of the HIT-based semantic reasoning model

```
Input: operation time t and reasoning period tR, LDA-parameters: Z hidden topics, K feature topics and
hyperparameters α & β, Gibbs sampling iterations J, HMM λ-model parameters (A,B,π) for N states & T
semantic topics
Operations:
1.1  Repeat every tR
1.2      Attribute corpus a = {a¹, a², ......., aᴸ} ← getAttributes()
1.3      Data/Concept Class Profiles corpus P = {P¹, P², ......, Pᴹ} ← captureDataConceptClassProfiles()
1.4      for j = 1:J do
1.5          for m = 1:M do
1.6              sample topic z of Z topics for the mᵗʰ data profile based on Gibbs sampling & prior probabilities
                 α & β
1.7          end for
1.8      end for
1.9          calculate  θᵐ = Dir(α) for Z feature topics in each data profile & calculate φᶻ = Dir(β)
             for attributes in each m profile
1.10     for m = 1:M do
1.11         draw zᵐ ~ multinomial(θᵐ)
1.12         for n = 1:N (where N of attributes per profiles & N ≤ L) do
1.13             sample feature topic fₙᵐ from K topics for each n attribute in the mᵗʰ data profile, draw fₙᵐ ~
                 multinomial(φᶻᵐ)
1.14         end for
1.15     end for
1.16     initialize HMM models and run Baum-Welch algorithm for learning models' parameters
1.17     for m = 1:M
1.18         for i = 1:T
1.19             calculate observation probability Bfₙᵐ(semantic-topicᵢ) for each n input state (i.e., classified
                 feature fₙ )
1.20         end for
1.21         get maximum likelihood semantic-topics sequence of length T with high probability for each
             implemented HMM
1.22     end for
1.23 until operation time
Output: set of semantic topics that are related to various concerns and represented as associated concept
classes
```

Figure 7. The LDA-HMM-based reasoning model

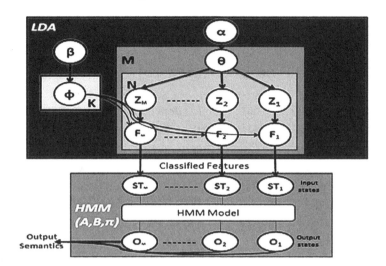

between characteristics (e.g., huge volume, high dimensionality, and complexity) of datasets in networks and language modeling. So, we provide the hybrid LDA-HMM-based reasoning model integrating LDA and HMM for combining the advantages of both algorithms in efficiently:

1. Learning patterns of big data with reduced-/high- and multi-dimensionality; and
2. Building dynamic network-concept ontology (DNCO) showing different and correlated concept classes (Rajpathak & Chougule, 2011).

We provide a semantic reasoning model for intelligent network entities using the proposed HIT in order to have highly abstracted and associated semantics at different levels of granularity and relate to various network concerns. At using HIT-based reasoning model, LDA is able to extract latent features with long-range semantics dependencies based on adopting inference models. Those models define correlations of semantic topics among data attributes and related data profiles. Relied on determined inference models, LDA can extract hidden semantic topics related to each data profile's attribute and also assign an overall topic to every data profile. HMM, as individual reasoning techniques, can be used to extract low-level features with short-range semantics dependencies (Jiang, 2009). Based on extracted semantic topics or features by LDA, HMM output depends on the sequence of input data features related to diverse network concerns. HMM can be designed and trained to get output based on sequences of data features, independent of features' order. In other words, the outcome from a HMM-based reasoning process can focus only on the existence of certain data features regardless of features' order.

We are motivated in our HIT design by the capability of LDA to discover latent high-level features from multi-dimensional network-data patterns with long-range semantics dependencies. Using correlations of semantic topics among data attributes, LDA can extract hidden semantic topics related to each data attribute and also assign an overall topic of a group of attributes. Those classified semantic topics of features will be sequenced to enable semantic reasoning via HMM with higher accuracy. HMM are structured architectures that are able to predict sequences of semantic topics (related to different network concerns) based on input sequences of extracted network features by LDA. Depending on input sequences or pattern of highly-discriminative network-data features, HMM with forward and backward algorithms can learn semantics efficiently showing their FBS aspects.

Some related work (e.g., (Idris & Shanmugam, 2005; Schuler, Bastos-Filho, & Oliveira, 2009; C. C. Yang, Yen, & Chen, 2000; Yao, 1999)) adopted monolithic and hybrid techniques for enhancing networking operations, such as intrusion detection and efficient routing. However, those works were application-specific and they did not provide a way for building ontology of associated concept classes related to various Internet elements (e.g., applications and services).

3.3.3 Operation of HIT-Based Reasoner

In our HIT-based reasoning model, LDA (Blei et al., 2003) is able to extract latent features with long-range semantics dependencies based on adopting inference models. Those models define correlations of semantic topics among data attributes and related data profiles. Relying upon determined inference models, LDA can extract hidden semantic topics related to each data profile's attribute and also assign an overall topic to every data profile. Based on extracted semantic topics or features by LDA, HMM (Rabiner & Juang, 1986) output depends on the sequence of input data features related to diverse network concerns. HMM can be designed and trained to get output based on sequences of data features, independent of features' order. Table 3 shows the parameters used within the HIT.

LDA Operation in HIT

LDA gives a systematic and well-defined way for inferring latent semantic topics in large scale of multi-dimensional data sets. LDA assigns random values for prior probabilities of semantic topics and related attributes based on data sampling (e.g., Gibbs sampling), multivariate distribution (e.g., dirichlet

Table 3. The LDA-HMM-based model's parameters

Symbol	Description
K	Number of feature topics
Z	Identity of hidden semantic topics
V	Number of attributes in all data profiles (or profiles)
N	Number of attributes per each data profiles, $N \leq V$
M	Number of data profiles
F	Identity of feature topics of all attributes
α	Prior feature topics/profile weight for feature topic-profile association
β	Prior attribute/topic weight for attribute-feature topic association
θ	Sampled posterior feature topics/profile weight vector of length Z for feature topic-profile association
φ	Sampled posterior attribute/profile weight vector of length V for profile attribute-feature topic association
π	Initial state probability vector of length N
A	State transition probability matrix of size N×N
B	Observation (or output semantics) probability matrix of size N×N
ST_i	Input HMM state i (or feature topic), $i \leq N$
O_i	Output semantics based on input state i

distribution) and training data sets. LDA has the capability of extracting latent features and semantics based on prior probabilities, using dirichlet distribution, for data-attribute data profile and data-attribute semantic topic associations. LDA assumes that attributes of data are related to randomly chosen semantic topics. The selection of semantic topics is based on random values of multivariate probability distribution parameters. LDA executes semantic topic sampling for each data attribute in every data profile for all profiles, and the updating processes for profile-semantic topic and attribute-topic associations, which are iterated many times. LDA looks at each data attribute and generates its related latent feature within each data profile (i.e., LDA makes semantic topic modeling for each data profile based on its comprised attributes). LDA randomly assigns a semantic topic for each attribute based on initially defined weights of topic-attribute associations. Accordingly, the weight of the assigned topic with respect to related attributes is increased. For certain number of iterations, the process repeats and LDA will provide posterior weights of topic-attributes association and accordingly profile-topic association.

Through a certain number of iterations and using Gibbs sampling (Casella & George, 1992), LDA extracts and classifies high-level features associated with each analyzed m data profile of total M profiles in the storage memory. LDA samples a hidden semantic topic z for each m data profile through calculating sampled posterior probability vector θ of topic-data profile association which depends on prior association weight α, number of the mth profile's attributes related to a certain topic z, and total number of attributes in the m profile. Also, LDA calculates sampled posterior probability φ of attribute-topic association based on prior attribute-topic association weight β, number of attribute instances assigned to topic z, and total number of attributes in all M profiles assigned to topic z. For example, three feature or semantic topics (i.e., $K=3$) are defined in LDA: ("normal TCP packet", "normal comm-flow", "TCP comm-protocol"). Ten data profiles ($M=10$) in the storage memory have the same three attributes (i.e., $N=V=3$). Each attribute and profile has a prior topic association weight vector. Based on the overall prior weight vectors *(α and β)* and number of semantic topics, a sampled topic association probability vector p_{assoc} of length equals the number of available semantic topics is calculated like p_{assoc}=p(semantic_topic_1)=0.75, p(s_2)=0.2, p(s_3)=0.05. In each LDA iteration, the current assigned topics for a data profile and comprised attributes are removed. Then, a random number u is sampled based on p_{assoc} and the summation of its contents. The higher p topic association value will be chosen and the related topic is assigned. For example, if u equals 0.6, number of attributes and related profiles assigned to the first semantic topic (i.e., the new topic) increases since p(s_1) which equals 0.75 is greater than 0.6. Thereafter, updates will be happened to posterior association weights θ and φ according to changes in number of attributes and profiles that relate to first semantic topic. Hence, the posterior association weight of the first topic with data profiles and comprised topic-related attributes increases.

HMM Operation in HIT

HMM comprises categorical sequence labeling supervised/unsupervised algorithms for estimating observations based on sequence of hidden input words (i.e, data attributes or features). Extracted and classified features, output from LDA, form a sequence and convey to parameters of HMM to generate semantics. The estimation process for HMM observations relies on continuous input sequence with different Gaussian distributions. Then, HMM performs distribution mixture for obtaining the most likelihood output sequence. HMM looks at the group and the sequence of data attributes or features. The order of states in an input sequence might change the output observations. In other words, the existence of the same data features, however, with different order might result in different outputs adopting the same HMM.

However, the HMM can be designed to have outputs based on having specific group of input states (or features) without considering their sequence order.

The HMM parameters (A, B, π), discussed shortly, are trained and assigned using the unsupervised Baum-welch learning algorithm (Baum, 1972). That algorithm depends on an initial developed HMM for finding the maximum likelihood HMM parameters through iteratively training the parameters of the initial model relied on the observed output sequence. The ability of input to HMM sequence of data features related to diverse network concerns enables getting output sequence with associated semantic topics or concept classes at different levels of abstraction. For example, an input sequence to HMM might be ("normal TCP packet size", "normal comm-flow", "TCP comm-protocol") with equal initial state probability π (i.e., $\pi = 1/3$) and state transition probabilities A (i.e., $A_{ij} = 1/2$ for $i \neq j$ and $A_{ij} = 0$ for $i=j$ where A_{ij} is the transition probability form state i to state j). The first feature can be classified as an application concern and the other two features as communication concerns. Accordingly, the expected HMM output observation based on the previous sequence with any feature order might be "normal TCP-based service". To get the previous output, the observation probability B matrix, which relates each input state with an output, regarding that concept class (i.e., output) will be high. For instance, B matrix might consist of three rows r and three columns c; and it might equal ((0.3,0.5,0.2),(0.2,0.8,0.0), (0.4,0.45,0.05)) where the number of r equals the number of input features and the number of c equals the number of output concept classes. According to the previous example, all input features have high observation probability with the "normal TCP-based service" concept.

3.4 HIT-Based vs. Monolithic Reasoners

We highlight in this subsection, via working example, the differences between semantics reasoning process using monolithic intelligence techniques, adopting HMM or LDA algorithms, and HIT (i.e., the hybrid LDA-HMM algorithm). The discussed example concerns reasoning about semantics of a TCP-based file transfer service based on capturing raw network-data related to TCP-based services and learning data patterns. Through a defined reasoning window, a semantic manager (SM), which adopts reasoning models, learns patterns of reduced-dimensional data profiles for recognizing and classifying attributes, respectively. SM recognizes the frequency of each data profile and its comprised attributes. For example, a captured profile might have multiple instances with the following attributes: P:={date, time, src_IP, dest_IP, packet_size, packet_type, service, protocol, port_number, sequence_number, MAC_address}. SM adopts locality sensitive hashing (LSH) algorithm to reduce the dimensionality of each profile (Mimaroglu & Simovici, 2008). The profile P after applying LSH for selecting specific attributes and with a hash function length equals five will be P_LSH:={packet_size, packet_type, service, protocol, port_number}. SM analyzes the data profile P_LSH and it gets the following information: 10000 profile's instances with the attributes vector Attr: {a^1= large_TCP-SYN_packet_size, a^2= TCP-SYN_packets, a^3= file_transfer_service, a^4=abnormal_ port_number}.

We show in the next paragraphs the operation technique for three implemented algorithms (HMM, LDA and HIT) for semantics reasoning based on processes of data representation and dimensionality reduction which are discussed in the last paragraph. Due to adopting different algorithms for semantics reasoning, various output semantics will be formed and kept.

Firstly, HMM-based reasoning model is used to extract semantics regarding the behavior of TCP-based file transfer services. The input states to HMM are described as sequences. Each input state represents one learned and classified data-attribute. For example, "large TCP-SYN packet size" is a learned and classified attribute based on captured values in the TCP *packet size* and *packet type fields* in a data profile. For HMM operation, we assume that we have four possible input states ST_1, ST_2, ST_3 and ST_4 to HMM for estimating the behavior of those services. Those input states represent the extracted and classified data attributes per each data profile. Those states are data attributes defined in the *Attr* vector. The estimated observation (or concept class) based on any sequence of the previously mentioned attributes is "O: *Abnormal TCP-based service*". HMM extracts that concept class based on its defined operation parameters. For instance, the observation probabilities B, using the maximum likelihood estimator, for the concept class O and the other concepts are high (e.g., 0.9) based on having any input attribute (i.e., state ST_i and $i \leq 4$) of the defined *Attr* attributes vector (a^1, a^2, a^3, a^4). Also, the transition probability A between any two input features (ST_i and ST_j, and $i \neq j$) has the same value. This increases the probability of having the targeted O based on using the trained HMM with the forward algorithm over sequences of interesting attributes.

Secondly, LDA-based reasoning model is used to reason about semantics for TCP-based file transfer services, LDA after 1000 iterations assigns attributes in P_LSH to the following feature topics: "Abnormal TCP-SYN packet size", "TCP-based File transfer service", "Abnormal TCP control packet", "Abnormal TCP-based file transfer service". LDA samples the feature topics as the following example. The classified attribute a^1, large_TCP-SYN_ packet_size, has high prior association weight β (e.g. $\beta > 0.75$) with the semantic topic, *Abnormal TCP-SYN packet size*. So, the updated attribute-topic posterior association weight ϕ for a^1 after 1000 iterations will be high with respect to the assigned feature topic. In addition, the prior association weight (α) of P_LSH with the feature topic "Abnormal TCP-based file transfer service" is high (e.g., $\alpha > 0.8$). Then, LDA samples P_LSH that specific topic based on the updated topic-profile posterior association weight θ taking into consideration the number of profile's attributes assigned to that topic (e.g., two attributes) and the total number of profiles' attributes (e.g., P_LSH has four attributes).

Finally, the hybrid LDA-HMM algorithm is designed to produce more meaningful information from analyzed data profiles and to form richer associations amongst extracted semantics. The hybrid algorithm extracts latent features of each data attribute in analyzed data profiles relying on learned and classified attributes in analyzed data profiles in the storage memory. Then, the hybrid algorithm outputs data semantics for each data profile based on a sequence of extracted latent features of the whole data profile. The LDA-HMM algorithm looks at both a) data attributes and related latent features within data profiles and b) the sequence of extracted latent features within each data profile. The implemented LDA algorithm performs semantic of feature topics modeling for analyzed data profiles and their comprised attributes. The output of that modeling process is a set of syntax states per each profile that is fed to HMM to reason about semantics concerning each profile. Utilizing simple feature classification techniques, e.g., using FMF, enables assignment of membership degrees for some extracted feature topics which have related designed FMF. These degrees enable SM to build and update DNCO. In the example of reasoning about TCP-based file transfer service semantics and using the same operation parameters of LDA in the previous semantics reasoning case, the latent feature topics T extracted by the LDA algorithm from P_LSH and its comprised attributes might be T:={ t^1= Abnormal TCP-SYN packet size, t^2= TCP-based File transfer service, t^3= Abnormal TCP control packet, t^4= Abnormal TCP-based file transfer service }. An input sequence comprised the previous latent feature topics (i.e., any sequence order of (t^1, t^2, t^3, t^4)) to a designed HMM might yield the following semantics or observations: O:={O_1=File_Transfer_Service_ Behavior, O_2=TCP_based_Service_Behavior, O_3=Abormal_TCP_based_Service_Operation, O_4=TCP_ SYN_Flood_Attack}Accordingly, a simple DNCO can be built via the obtained observations or concept classes. For instance, the top parent class will be O_1 and it will have three child classes O_2, O_3 and O_4. The concept class O_3 will be a child class for the parent class O_2 and so on. In addition, the four classified attributes in the *Attr* vector will be registered as FBS aspects for the lower child concept class O_4.

4. PERFORMANCE ANALYSIS

In this section, we discuss the effectiveness of semantics reasoning processes using monolithic and hybrid intelligence techniques-based reasoning models. We evaluate reasoning models via conducting a set of simulation scenarios. Semantics reasoning processes are implemented as an application written in Java including Java classes for the operations learning data patterns and extracting high-level latent features. We run simulation scenarios via integrating reasoning models' Java classes with java-based network simulator (J-Sim) (Sobeih, Viswanathan, Marinov, & Hou, 2007). A simulation scenario for a network of 50 nodes is conducted, with the aid of real offline KDD datasets (S. Hettich & S. D. Bay, 1999), to investigate the impact of learning concepts related to file transfer services and communication protocols over improving QoS of running services on top of TCP and UDP protocols. Our simulation studies include implementation of different semantics reasoning models (using simple statistical-analysis-based, LDA-based, HMM-based, and the hybrid LDA-HMM-based models).

4.1 Network Simulation Scenario Using Real Offline Datasets

In this scenario, we study the effectiveness of semantics reasoning operations using various reasoning models and adopting real offline datasets for learning patterns and extracting semantics of normal/abnormal flows of TCP- and UDP-based services and related attacks (e.g., TCP-SYN flood attacks). Extracted semantics are represented as accessible correlated concept classes and maintained in a shared database. Networking entities can access and learn those concept classes at runtime and on-demand to enhance QoS of their operations.

The simulation scenario is run at adopting various semantics reasoning models. The utilized semantics reasoning models are: LDA-based model, HMM-based model and the hybrid model (or the LDA-HMM model). We study the impact of employing those reasoning models by an intelligent network host on networking operations performance. Such host learns data traffic, analyzes data patterns and reasons about semantics accordingly. Also, the host accesses real offline datasets to learn other information and to update what it learnt before. Other network hosts in the scenario can learn extracted semantics, registered at shared database. Table 4 shows the addressed metrics for analyzing performance of the semantics reasoning process made by various models.

Our simulator is based on J-Sim. We adapted already existing java codes of HMM and LDA. We implemented a code for the LDA-HMM model and integrated it with J-Sim. Random fully-connected static network topologies were generated for 50 nodes using minimum degree proximity algorithm (Onat & Stojmenovic, 2007). TCP- and UDP-based file transfer services were run among nodes. Some nodes were chosen to send malicious and/or abnormal data (e.g., attacks like TCP SYN-flood attack and UDP flood attack). Exchanged data among hosts are represented and maintained in the intelligent host as profiles of attribute-value pairs with/without using LSH for dimensionality reduction. Those attributes give information about, for example, service type, packet type and packet size. KDD'99 dataset (S. Hettich & S. D. Bay, 1999) with 41 data attributes was used as offline dataset by the intelligent host to

Table 4. Performance analysis metrics of semantics reasoning techniques

Metric	Function	Equation	Unit
Average Throughput (Thp)	Describes data throughput at a current simulation time by the summation of current captured data packets' sizes (S_p) in a defined window divided by the window size (5 seconds)	$Thp = \sum (S_p)/(5 \text{ seconds window size})$.	bytes/sec
Network Latency (L)	Measures the consumed time from the beginning of simulation until learning all behavior classes of running file transfer services	$L = T_R + T_S$ where T_R is the time-overhead caused by the reasoning technique and T_S is the time period measured from simulation start	mseconds
Prediction Accuracy (A_c)	Calculates ratio of true positive (Tp) classes and true negative (Tn) classes that are learned with respect to all behavior classes (N_c) that should be learned	$A_c = (Tp+Tn) / N_c$	--
False Negative (Fn) Ratio	Calculates ratio of abnormal behavior classes that misclassified to normal classes according to N_c	Fn / N_c	--

learn semantics of normal TCP flows and some denial-of-service (DoS) attacks, such as TCP SYN-flood attack. The intelligent host learns patterns of registered data, recognizes their group of attributes and classifies those attributes utilizing a simple statistical-analysis-based model. SM extracts and classifies high-level latent features using the implemented semantics reasoning model. We tested three different semantics reasoning models which are

1. LDA-based model;
2. HMM-based model; and
3. The LDA-HMM or hybrid model.

We studied the capability of these models to learn data semantics and to know various concept classes related to normal/abnormal flows and attacks.

The intelligent host executes behavior classification for analyzed network flows of TCP- and UDP-based services. Extracted semantics concerning those flows will form ontology of concept classes which show for example classes for the normal_TCP-based_service, normal_UDP-based_service, attack_TCP-based_service and attack_UDP-based_service. An effective semantics reasoning model is the model which has the ability to discover all or most classes of concepts related to running services in the network. The intelligent host generates alerts when it detects matching between what it learns at real-time and maintained concept classes. A performance analysis was done for the operation of semantics reasoning process. Each implemented semantics reasoning model was evaluated based on the detected true positives (Tp) and negatives (Tn) besides false positives (Fp) and negatives (Fn). Table 5 shows simulation parameters and their default values.

Table 5. Simulation parameters of the network simulation scenario

Parameter	Default Value	Unit
Number of nodes	50	node
Number of attributes/KDD data set	41	attribute
Link data rate	1	Mbps
Router buffer size	7000	packet
TCP MSS (normal/abnormal)	512/1024,2048	byte
TCP MCWS	128	byte
TCP Time to Live	255	seconds
UDP packet size (normal/ abnormal)	512/512,2048	byte
UDP Client/Reply Timeout	30	seconds
Propagation model	Free space model	--
Propagation delay	100	mseconds
MAC protocol	IEEE 802.11	--
Routing protocol	AODV	--
Rate of database access by hosts	1	time/11 seconds
Rate of patterns learning	1	time/10 seconds
HMM approach/number of training sequences	Unsupervised with Baum-Welch algorithm/1000	--
LSH (L hash tables, K hash function length)	(L=6,K=3)	--
LDA (# of iterations)	20000	--
Simulation Time	100	seconds

For statistical validation for results, we repeated the experiment nine times for each implemented semantics reasoning model (LDA, HMM or LDA-HMM) and also when operation at different cases which are: a) without using LSH; b) using undirected LSH and c) using directed LSH. Directed LSH mechanism means that the implemented LSH algorithm adopts a specific attributes' group smaller than the one used by the undirected LSH and related to interesting file transfer services. Semantics reasoning models were designed to reason about data semantics clarifying the normal and abnormal behavior of TCP- and UDP-based service flows. Recognized semantics of abnormal service flows' behavior might refer to known attacks (e.g., TCP-SYN-flood attack and UDP-flood attack). We have 13 behavior concept classes which have to be learned. Five classes represent normal behavior and nine classes define abnormal behavior. The effectiveness of the adopted reasoning model by the intelligent host and its impact over networking operations was studied via measuring some network performance metrics such as average network throughput and latency. Figure 8 illustrates average network throughput measured at network destination with/without using LSH. The LDA-HMM model learned most data semantics (i.e., behavior concept classes) of normal/abnormal flows earlier, besides clarifying attacks in the network. This enabled intelligent host to generate early alerts that allowed nodes to recognize semantics and to subsequently suppress abnormal flows and attacks. Figure 9 illustrates the effectiveness of the implemented reasoning model to learn, in a timely manner, semantics of normal/abnormal flows and to

Figure 8. Average network throughput

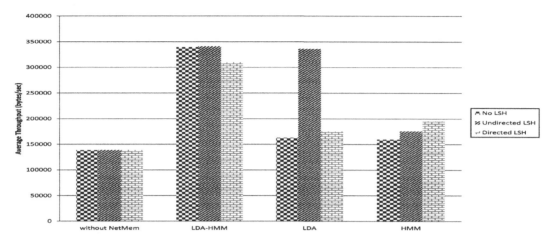

Figure 9. Network latency due to the usage of various reasoning models

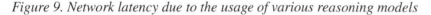
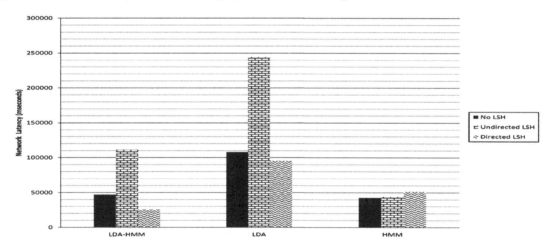

detect running malicious flows and attacks accordingly. Due to the time-overhead caused by semantics reasoning models to learn patterns and extract semantics, there was time delay experienced in the network to accomplish reasoning tasks.

In Figure 10, The LDA-HMM or the HIT model was able to learn semantics with higher level of accuracy through the simulation time compared with LDA and HMM. This showed the ability of the HIT to mitigate challenges faced by the HMM to work with reduced- dimensional data. Also, it can be concluded from obtained results that reasoning operations with the hybrid reasoning model achieved low false negative ratios compared with operations at adopting monolithic intelligence-based models. Figure 11 shows Fn ratio at using different semantics reasoning models. The hybrid model for semantics reasoning achieved better values compared with other models. This means that the HIT model was able to decrease the percentage of misclassified data profiles according to its internal capabilities of detecting successfully abnormal traffic with knowing small set of attributes.

Figure 10. Accuracy for learning semantics

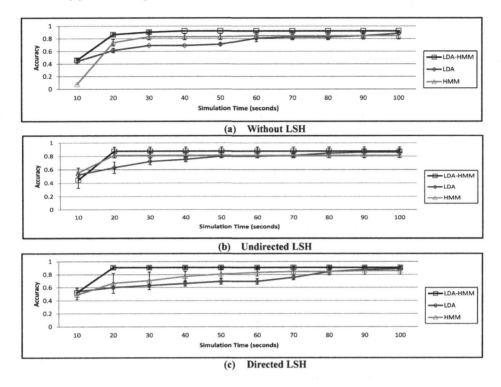

Figure 11. False negative (Fn) ratio for learning semantics

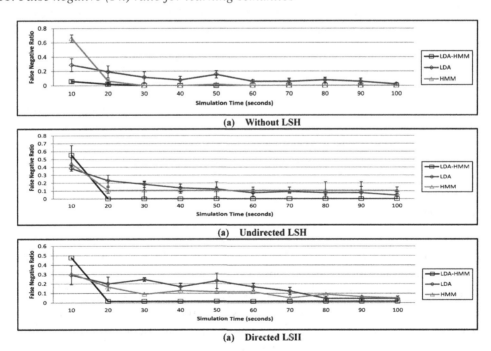

From the above results, we conclude the following:

1. The LDA-HMM-based model for semantics reasoning has overcome limitations of other models with individual intelligence techniques (LDA or HMM). Consequently, better performance (higher accuracy with low Fn ratio) of semantics reasoning process was achieved in case of using the LDA-HMM model; and

2. The LDA-HMM model was able to learn features in case of having full- or reduced-dimensional data profiles and reason about network-semantics. This led to recognize, in case of using or not using LSH, almost all behavior classes which are related to different Internet elements (normal file transfer services and attacks). Consequently, this aided in enhancing QoS of running services.

5. FUTURE RESEARCH DIRECTIONS

Today's and prospective coming technology-based applications are heterogeneous and related to various interesting fields such as healthcare, networking, food processing, renewable energy systems, etc. Those applications involve parameters of importance that can be captured and measured. Learning and analyzing set of correlated applications' parameters and extracting semantics (or high level information) accordingly will aid in enhancing applications' security, output and QoS and optimizing resource utilization. Easy measurements for application-specific parameters can be made with developing reliable small portable smart collaborative devices that minimize required implementation space and consumed energy resources. Capturing multi-dimensional application data with multi-sensors is needed for enabling combining data attributes related to various dimension. Also, there is a need to have a system with a means of coordinating and feeding the readouts of the sensors into sets of reasoning models' matrices to generate output from which efficient human decisions could be made. In other words, there will be intelligent processing unit that perform efficiently such roles.

For example, investigating real-life systems, such as smart grids, and implementing autonomous reconfigurable semantic reasoning capabilities for them would help in improving the performance of the system operations and jobs. Semantic reasoning processes can strengthen the security of state estimation processes in smart grids by providing dynamic models for state estimation which clarify the normal/abnormal behavior of multiple smart grid elements, like remote terminal units, power generation units, and network entities (e.g., routers) in communication networks of smart girds.

6. CONCLUSION

In this chapter, we have discussed network-semantics management methodology using monolithic and hybrid intelligence techniques for extracting semantics and building dynamic ontology of network concepts. The hybridization of more than one monolithic intelligence technique can help in integrating the capabilities of each technique when it is used separately. Additionally, we discussed the operations of semantics reasoning via designing multiple reasoning models using monolithic and hybrid intelligence techniques. We discussed the effectiveness of the implemented reasoning models via simulation over real Internet traffic data. Simulation results showed the capability of reasoning models to learn patterns of large-scale data with full or reduced dimensionality and reason about semantics that are used in a) enhancing QoS of running services; b) detection of anomalies and attacks; and c) learning normal/abnormal behavior classes of some Internet elements (e.g., services and attacks). The presented hybrid LDA-HMM-based reasoning model achieved higher effectiveness whether using full- or reduced data dimensionality compared with the other monolithic intelligence-based reasoning models.

REFERENCES

Abraham, A., & Nath, B. (2000). Hybrid intelligent systems design: A review of a decade of research. *IEEE Transactions on Systems, Man and Cybernetics (Part-C),* August.

Baum, L. E. (1972). An Inequality and Associated Maximization Technique in Statistical Estimation for Probabilistic Functions of a Markov Process. *Inequalities, 3.*

Bíró, I., & Szabó, J. (2009). *Latent dirichlet allocation for automatic document categorization.* Paper presented at the ECML PKDD '09 Proceedings of the European Conference on Machine Learning and Knowledge Discovery in Databases. doi:10.1007/978-3-642-04174-7_28

Blei, D. M., Ng, A. Y., & Jordan, M. I. (2003). Latent dirichlet allocation. *Journal of Machine Learning Research, 3*, 993-1022.

Bouabene, G., Jelger, C., Tschudin, C., Schmid, S., Keller, A., & May, M. (2010). The autonomic network architecture (ANA). *IEEE Journal on Selected Areas in Communications*, *28*(1), 4–14.

Breiman, L. (2001). Statistical modeling: The two cultures (with comments and a rejoinder by the author). *Statistical Science*, *16*(3), 199–231. doi:10.1214/ss/1009213726

Casella, G., & George, E. I. (1992). Explaining the Gibbs sampler. *The American Statistician*, *46*(3), 167–174.

Chatterjee, S., & Russell, S. (2012). A temporally abstracted Viterbi algorithm. *arXiv preprint arXiv:1202.3707.*

Cristianini, N., & Shawe-Taylor, J. (2000). *An introduction to support vector machines and other kernel-based learning methods.* Cambridge university press. doi:10.1017/CBO9780511801389

Cross, S. S., Harrison, R. F., & Kennedy, R. L. (1995). Introduction to neural networks. *Lancet*, *346*(8982), 1075–1079. doi:10.1016/S0140-6736(95)91746-2 PMID:7564791

Darling, W. M. (2011). *A Theoretical and Practical Implementation Tutorial on Topic Modeling and Gibbs Sampling.* Paper presented at the 49th Annual Meeting of the Association for Computational Linguistics: Human Language Technologies.

Data virtualization by denodo technologies. (2012, December). from http://www.denodo.com/en/solutions/technology/data_virtualization.php

Day, J., Matta, I., & Mattar, K. (2008). *Networking is IPC: A guiding principle to a better Internet.* Paper presented at the 2008 ACM CoNEXT Conference. doi:10.1145/1544012.1544079

Dorst, K., & Vermaas, P. E. (2005). John Gero's Function-Behaviour-Structure model of designing: A critical analysis. *Research in Engineering Design*, *16*(1), 17–26. doi:10.1007/s00163-005-0058-z

Dvb queplix, (2012, September). Retrieved from http://www.queplix.com

Feldmann, A. (2007). Internet clean-slate design: What and why? *Computer Communication Review*, *37*(3), 59–64. doi:10.1145/1273445.1273453

Gero, J. S. (1990). Design prototypes: A knowledge representation schema for design. *AI Magazine*, *11*(4), 26.

Griffiths, T. L., Steyvers, M., Blei, D. M., & Tenenbaum, J. B. (2004). *Integrating topics and syntax*. Paper presented at the Advances in Neural Information Processing Systems.

Hassan, H., Eltoweissy, M., & Youssef, M. (2009). *CellNet: a bottom-up approach to network design*. Paper presented at the 3rd International Conference on New Technologies, Mobility and Security (NTMS). doi:10.1109/NTMS.2009.5384680

Hawkins, J., & Blakeslee, S. (2005). On Intelligence: St. Martin's Press.

Henderson, K., & Eliassi-Rad, T. *Applying latent dirichlet allocation to group discovery in large graphs*. Paper presented at the 2009 ACM symposium on Applied Computing. doi:10.1145/1529282.1529607

Hettich, S., & Bay, S. D. (1999). *The UCI KDD Archive*. Irvine, CA: University of California, Department of Information and Computer Science.

IBM. (n. d.). Retrieved from http://www.ibm.com

Idris, N. B., & Shanmugam, B. (2005). *Artificial intelligence techniques applied to intrusion detection*. Paper presented at the IEEE INDICON '05.

informatica, D. v. b. (2013, January). Retrieved from http://www.informatica.com

Jiang, J. (2009). *Modeling syntactic structures of topics with a nested hmm-lda*. Paper presented at the 9th IEEE International Conference on Data Mining. doi:10.1109/ICDM.2009.144

Jiten, J., Merialdo, B., & Huet, B. (2006). *Semantic feature extraction with multidimensional hidden Markov model*. Paper presented at the Proceedings of SPIE. doi:10.1117/12.650590

Khan, R., Khan, S. U., Zaheer, R., & Khan, S. (2012). *Future Internet: The Internet of Things Architecture, Possible Applications and Key Challenges*. Paper presented at the 10th International Conference on Frontiers of Information Technology (FIT). doi:10.1109/FIT.2012.53

Kumar, G., Kumar, K., & Sachdeva, M. (2010). The use of artificial intelligence based techniques for intrusion detection: A review. *Artificial Intelligence Review*, *34*(4), 369–387. doi:10.1007/s10462-010-9179-5

Landauer, T. K., Foltz, P. W., & Laham, D. (1998). An introduction to latent semantic analysis. *Discourse Processes*, *25*(2-3), 259–284. doi:10.1080/01638539809545028

Li, D., Xiao, L., Han, Y., Chen, G., & Liu, K. (2007). Network Thinking and Network Intelligence. In N. Zhong, J. Liu, Y. Yao, J. Wu, S. Lu, & K. Li (Eds.), *Web Intelligence Meets Brain Informatics* (Vol. 4845, pp. 36–58). Springer Berlin Heidelberg. doi:10.1007/978-3-540-77028-2_3

Merhav, N., & Ephraim, Y. (1991). Maximum likelihood hidden Markov modeling using a dominant sequence of states. *IEEE Transactions on Signal Processing, 39*(9), 2111–2115. doi:10.1109/78.134449

Mimaroglu, S., & Simovici, D. A. (2008). *Approximate computation of object distances by locality-sensitive hashing.* Paper presented at the Proceedings of the 2008 International Conference on Data Mining, Washington, DC.

Mokhtar, B., & Eltoweissy, M. (2012). *Biologically-inspired network "memory" for smarter networking.* Paper presented at the 8th International Conference on Collaborative Computing: Networking, Applications and Worksharing (CollaborateCom).

Mokhtar, B., & Eltoweissy, M. (2014). *Hybrid Intelligence for Semantics-Enhanced Networking Operations.* Paper presented at the The Twenty-Seventh International Flairs Conference.

Mokhtar, B., Eltoweissy, M., & El-Sayed, H. (2013). *Network "memory" system for enhanced network services.* Paper presented at the 9th International Conference on Innovations in Information Technology (IIT).

Newman, D., Asuncion, A., Smyth, P., & Welling, M. (2007). Distributed inference for latent dirichlet allocation. Advances in Neural Information Processing Systems, 20(1081-1088), 17-24.

Nii, M., Nakai, K., Takahashi, Y., Higuchi, K., & Maenaka, K. (2011). *Behavior extraction from multiple sensors information for human activity monitoring.* Paper presented at the IEEE International Conference on Systems, Man, and Cybernetics (SMC). doi:10.1109/ICSMC.2011.6083831

Onat, F. A., & Stojmenovic, I. (2007). *Generating random graphs for wireless actuator networks.* Paper presented at the IEEE International Symposium on World of Wireless, Mobile and Multimedia Networks WoWMoM '07. doi:10.1109/WOWMOM.2007.4351712

Ourston, D., Matzner, S., Stump, W., & Hopkins, B. (2003). *Applications of hidden markov models to detecting multi-stage network attacks.* Paper presented at the 36th Annual International Conference on System Sciences, Hawaii. doi:10.1109/HICSS.2003.1174909

Paul, S. (2010). An Optimized distributed association rule mining algorithm in parallel and distributed data mining with xml data for improved response time. *International Journal of Computer Science and Information Technology, 2*(2), 90–103. doi:10.5121/ijcsit.2010.2208

Peddabachigari, S., Abraham, A., Grosan, C., & Thomas, J. (2007). Modeling intrusion detection system using hybrid intelligent systems. *Journal of Network and Computer Applications, 30*(1), 114–132. doi:10.1016/j.jnca.2005.06.003

Rabiner, L., & Juang, B. (1986). An introduction to hidden Markov models. *ASSP Magazine, IEEE, 3*(1), 4–16. doi:10.1109/MASSP.1986.1165342

Rajpathak, D., & Chougule, R. (2011). A generic ontology development framework for data integration and decision support in a distributed environment. *International Journal of Computer Integrated Manufacturing, 24*(2), 154–170. doi:10.1080/0951192X.2010.531291

Ramage, D. (2007). Hidden Markov Models Fundamentals. *CS229 Section Notes.*

Schuler, W., Bastos-Filho, C., & Oliveira, A. (2009). A novel hybrid training method for hopfield neural networks applied to routing in communications networks. *International Journal of Hybrid Intelligent Systems*, 6(1), 27–39.

Seymore, K., McCallum, A., & Rosenfeld, R. (1999). *Learning hidden Markov model structure for information extraction.* Paper presented at the AAAI-99 Workshop on Machine Learning for Information Extraction.

Sobeih, A., Viswanathan, M., Marinov, D., & Hou, J. C. (2007). *J-Sim: An integrated environment for simulation and model checking of network protocols.* Paper presented at the Parallel and Distributed Processing Symposium, 2007. IPDPS 2007. IEEE International. doi:10.1109/IPDPS.2007.370519

Sontag, D., & Roy, D. M. (2011). *Complexity of inference in latent dirichlet allocation.* Advances in Neural Information Processing Systems NIPS.

Srivastava, J., Cooley, R., Deshpande, M., & Tan, P.-N. (2000). Web usage mining: Discovery and applications of usage patterns from web data. *ACM SIGKDD Explorations Newsletter*, 1(2), 12–23. doi:10.1145/846183.846188

Van Laarhoven, P. J., & Aarts, E. H. (1987). *Simulated annealing.* Springer. doi:10.1007/978-94-015-7744-1

Vasconcelos, N., & Lippman, A. (2000). Statistical models of video structure for content analysis and characterization. *Image Processing. IEEE Transactions on*, 9(1), 3–19.

Willett, D., & Rigoll, G. (1998). Hybrid NN/HMM-based speech recognition with a discriminant neural feature extraction. *Advances in Neural Information Processing Systems*, 763–772.

Winter, M. (2007). *Goguen categories: a categorical approach to L-fuzzy relations.* Springer Publishing Company, Incorporated.

Yang, C. C., Yen, J., & Chen, H. (2000). Intelligent internet searching agent based on hybrid simulated annealing. *Decision Support Systems*, 28(3), 269–277. doi:10.1016/S0167-9236(99)00091-3

Yang, J., & Xu, Y. (1994). Hidden markov model for gesture recognition: *Tech. Report CMU-RI-TR-94-10.*

Yao, X. (1999). Evolving artificial neural networks. *Proceedings of the IEEE*, 87(9), 1423–1447. doi:10.1109/5.784219

Zafeiropoulos, A., Liakopoulos, A., Davy, A., & Chaparadza, R. (2010). *Monitoring within an autonomic network: a GANA based network monitoring framework.* Paper presented at the Service-Oriented Computing. ICSOC/ServiceWave 2009 Workshops. doi:10.1007/978-3-642-16132-2_29

Zhiming, D., Qi, Y., & Hong, W. (2011). *Massive Heterogeneous Sensor Data Management in the Internet of Things.* Paper presented at the 2011 International Conference on Internet of Things and 4th International Conference on Cyber, Physical and Social Computing (iThings/CPSCom).

This research was previously published in the Handbook of Research on Advanced Hybrid Intelligent Techniques and Applications edited by Siddhartha Bhattacharyya, Pinaki Banerjee, Dipankar Majumdar, and Paramartha Dutta, pages 253-286, copyright year 2016 by Information Science Reference (an imprint of IGI Global).

Section 3
Culture, Society, and the Arts

Chapter 12
Upgrading Society With Smart Government:
The Use of Smart Services Among Federal Offices of the UAE

Badreya Al-Jenaibi
United Arab Emirates University (UAEU), UAE

ABSTRACT

This paper aims to explore the goals and motives of electronic government utilization among the citizens, the motives of their preference as well as the extent of use of these smart applications in the UAE. Also, it investigates the basic element of Smart Government uses within the federal authorities, response times, and recommendations for improving smart government. This study answers the following questions: What is the purpose of creating smart government? What are the users' aims in using smart government and what level of satisfaction do they experience? To augment this research, 450 questionnaires were distributed among federal authorities' users in all 7 emirates in the UAE. In addition, 18 interviews were conducted with managers in the federal government. The users reported high levels of satisfaction using smart government technologies, indicating a high level of usage and trust. The results also show that higher service speed contributes to higher levels of satisfaction. Managers are very optimistic about Smart Government, but some challenges remain, such as the existence of a lack of information or guidelines for using smart government. There is currently no central government department for applying smart government, and no clear vision or philosophies regarding smart government.

1. INTRODUCTION

In *Introducing E-gov: History, Definitions, and Issues,* Horan (2005) outlined the history of Smart Government, pointing out that Smart Government was created in 1970 when the computer industry opened to the public, and then it was officially applied to government in 1990 to be used by customers. Horan (2005) points out that Internet technology helps set the basic rules in Smart Government; without the Internet, Smart Government applications would have never appeared. As our dependence and use of

DOI: 10.4018/978-1-5225-2589-9.ch012

technology grows, the connection between the public and government also deepens, to build an Smart Government that will help people's lives and future (Hsieh, Chen & Lo, 2015; As-Saber, Hossain & Srivastava, 2007). Computer science helps institute Smart Government and ensures its usability and fast service (Lake, 2013; Abecasis, 2012; ITU, 2009a). Smart Government is employed for political and governmental purposes and involves using technology to provide the citizenry with greater ease and convenience (Bwalya & Mutula, 2015).

From the mid-1990s, e-mails and websites became an intrinsic part of the regime transformation. The government used websites and e-mails to communicate with users and gain information for their campaigns (WideView, 2014). The types of online services needed are unclear (Bardach, 2002). It is not clear "the extent to which IT is transforming public administration and politics and who is benefiting from the changes that are occurring. Indeed, in contrast to those who proclaim that IT has transformed government, there are counterclaims that IT has largely been adapted to and reinforced by existing behaviors and practices" (Andersen, 2006, p.2). In this case, IT is simply one additional political tool for leaders (Danziger & Andersen 2002; Andersen, 1998). Scholl and Scholl (2014) and Beynon-Davies (2007) argued that using IT in administration, both internally and externally, allows direct and real-time communication with consumers. Scholl (2001) and Linnefell (2014), indicated that a portion of Smart Government will be extremely organized, reliable, and able to have immediate use, such as for online building permits and car registration renewal forms. "The major portion of Smart Government communication will not be within government and will be hard to predict when and where it will come from. The standard protocol for responding to correspondence and creating archives for storing communication is under investigation. The new generation of applications, such as SMS, chat, and virtual collaboration technologies, alters the way communication takes place" (Scholl (2001, p.3).

Hadi (2006) stated that governments all over the world are competing to create smart government. In all nations, from emerging countries to the developed manufacturing countries (Gil-Garcia, Helbig & Ojo, 2014), the administrations put nationwide directives and serious information online with devices used to modernize once-difficult actions to increase and improve interactions electronically with their citizens (Wang, Bretschneider, Gant, 2005). Zaki (2009) and Bhattacharya & Gupta (2012) believed that the significance of the accessibility of this smart government for persons and residents is that it had elevated the level of the United Arab Emirates in terms of the use of electronic services, as well as increased the rank of the publics' consciousness of the meaning of services, easing the work of the mission rapidly without struggle. Also, smart government is an expansion of Smart Government so that services are provided everywhere at any time using smart tools (mobile phone applications and laptops, PDAs, etc.) to facilitate the customer professionally and successfully (Andersen & Henriksen, 2005; Colesca, S. E. (2009). The Smart Government plan exemplifies a recreation of government, ensuring advanced methods of doing business (Abhichandani, 2008). Feldstein and Gower (2015) agreed that new platforms, smart technologies and data to enhance society understanding of people life like students in class and digital interactions, and apply this information to course enhancement. The smart government is not only for students but publics in general for example, Shen, Dai, Wang and Gou (2015) studied the impact of online additional reviews on consumer's purchase process and new online or smart technologies. They found that consumers could post their recommendations or comments again in several months by using and measuring new apps and technologies. Also, Hiziroglu (2015) observed customer segment stability using soft computing techniques and Markov Chains within data mining framework. His study matches Shen, Dai, Wang and Gou (2015) study. He agreed that providing practitioners a better understanding of segment stability over time is useful managerial implications by using the smart government and new technology.

In the UAE, the announcement of the initiative of His Highness Sheikh Mohammed bin Rashid Al Maktoum (2013), Vice President and Prime Minister of the UAE, launched "smart government" during a meeting organized by the UAE government with the participation of more than 1,000 government officials (p.1). The Smart Government Initiative aims to promote and raise awareness among government agencies to take advantage of mobile phone services and the application of the best technologies in the field of services (Burn & Robins, 2003). According to Bwalya & Healy (2010), The initiative of smart government includes cell phones, mobile devices, and other advanced technological tools to provide services and information to the public.

In summary, different scholars have studied the Smart Government impacts and their effects in various countries and found that Smart Government is a new direction for the government to serve users. As Maktoum (2013) indicated, Smart Government will change UAE's society in general, and it will serve users everywhere via technologies like smartphones.

Misra (2007) argued that Smart Government has been in operation for over a decade, but it failed to improve the lives of the citizenry. However, there are many definitions and interpretations of what Smart Government really means (Cournède, Goujard & Pina, 2013). This creates challenges for Smart Government policy-makers. Smart Government provides many benefits for users, such as saving time in queues by filling applications online from anywhere. Citizens need smart government more than other users, like stockholders or civil servants. Citizens are the general public residing in cities or towns. They can search and use smart government to meet their social needs, such as renewing national identities online or paying bills through smart applications. Stockholders, on the other hand, are interested in their specific needs of their business, like getting formal approval letters from different authorities online.

The definition of Smart Government (e-gov) differs from one scholar to another depending on the assumed purpose of e-gov. E-gov as a definition is discussed by many scholars, such as Heek (2008), who argued in his published article entitled "Government for Development Information Exchange" (p.1), that smart government terms like "smart city" or "smarter planet", have been in use over the years 2008 to 2010.With smart Smart Government in place, it follows the new vision or policies of each country to develop and become more economically, socially, and environmentally sustainable.

Due to numerous interpretations of the term "Smart Government", for the purpose of this article it will be considered the use of information technologies by government agencies to positively transform their relations with citizens, businesses, and other arms of government. "Smart Government" is best defined as "the use of information and communication technologies in government to provide public services, to improve managerial effectiveness, and to promote democratic values, as well as deliver a regulatory framework that facilitates information-intensive initiatives and fosters the knowledge society" (Gant, Jon P., 2008, p. 15). According to the World Bank, technologies such as Wide Area Networks, the Internet, and mobile computing have the capability to transform relations with citizens, businesses, and other arms of government (World Bank, 2011). "These technologies can serve a variety of different ends: better delivery of government services to citizens, improved interactions with business and industry, citizen empowerment through access to information, or more efficient government management" (World Bank, 2011, p.1). Some of the potential benefits of Smart Government include decreasing corruption by increasing government transparency, providing greater ease to the citizenry through online resources, creating revenue growth by creating jobs involving IT, and/or increasing cost reductions by simplifying older tasks that can now be performed online or by a computer (Al-Shafi, 2012). There are hundreds of other definitions in the current literature of what Smart Government stands for. Most definitions in the field of practice take a governance perspective (Grönlund & Horan, 2004). All in all, Smart Government globally is viewed to not only be about the computerization of a government system or a technological endeavor, but a belief in the ability of technology to achieve high levels of improvement in various areas of government (APT, 2012). As the world is evolving and developing, there are many countries who want to incorporate Smart Government into their country's infrastructure (Ambali, 2010).

The United Arab Emirates has been using and developing Smart Government for many years; however, in the last few years, the government is taking the first steps in changing the services provided by Smart Government. In 2013, His Highness Sheikh Mohammed bin Rashid Al Maktoum said, "we have to work hard to make the people satisfied with the services of the government; as the government starts to apply Smart Government, the UAE government must think creatively" (p.1). In general, the people in the UAE and Gulf countries are open to the use of social network services (Awan, 2003). They view Smart Government as a benefit because they can accomplish their tasks online without having to leave home.

The key objective of this study is to examine users' knowledge of and attitude toward electronic government establishments that have been applied in the United Arab Emirates in order to improve the efficacy of public sector organizations. The researcher selected this topic because these types of government are a new phenomenon in the UAE yet to be examined, and they have important consequences in terms of public service provisioning and relationships between the public and government. The study will explore what smart government means to users, how users adapt to it, and whether or not it will contribute to the strengthening of relationships between the government offices and their constituencies. Moreover, the study will investigate the new e-gov policies in light of the vision of the UAE Vice President, who indicated that it is to serve the people in the best way possible, to be implemented by 2020 regarding government performance. Research questions to be empirically tested include: What are the new changes in the UAE community in the E-gov age? What are the users' aims in using smart government and what level of satisfaction do they experience?

This research identifies the smart government services that have been applied recently in the United Arab Emirates and charts the response of users to these services. Smart Government is being widely adopted to improve the service of public sector organizations, yet many people are unfamiliar with the concept of Smart Government and its uses. This research contributes a critical lens on Smart Government as a new technology concept and its applications in the Arab world, while shedding light on how Smart Government adoption affects the development of an organization or company. The study will illuminate the development of Smart Government in UAE institutions, gain information about the strategies of the services, and chart public opinion toward Smart Government. The paper focuses on users or customers who use Smart Government, exploring their needs, satisfactions, and benefits concerning Smart Government usage. Research on Smart Government has been limited, especially in the UAE, and this study fills a void in the literature.

2. LITERATURE REVIEW

2.1. Government-to-Citizen and Smart Government Approach

Bonina & Cordella (2008) indicated that government-to-citizen Smart Government focuses on making information accessible to citizens online. It is referred to as a citizen-centric Smart Government when the administration takes further steps to provide online services organized around citizens' needs. Smart Government uses information and communication technology to provide public services, increase the accessible services in organizations, allow citizens to learn how to use these new technologies, and foster democratic values (Cairncross, 1997). E-governance improves how governments are administered, how they exchange information, and how they bring services to citizens (Gauld & Goldfinch, 2006; Backus, 2001). Information technologies utilized include Wide Area Networks, the Internet, and mobile computing (Bhatnagar, 2013). Smart government also contributes to a greater link between physical and social capital in cities, improving urban services and infrastructure (Hirschfeld, 2012). They bring technology, information, and political aspects into one coherent program and improve their services (Lane, 2000). Many cities have been striving to adopt smart governance, and the UAE has been on the front line; according to a UN Smart Government survey in 2012, UAE ranked seventh in the "online service index". In light of the positive survey results, Sheikh Mohammed bin Rashid Al Maktoum announced a new initiative in "mobile government" to further provide widespread services to people (Smart Government, 2013). Other statistics indicate that around 11,200 users are already registered in the Abu Dhabi Smart Government's researcher ID service (Abu Dhabi Smart Government, 2014).

2.2. Potential Benefits to Implementation

Information and Communications Technologies (ICT) have affected the ways in which people, governments, and businesses interact with each other. The rapid diffusion of the Internet, mobile technology, and broadband networks demonstrates how pervasive this technology has become (Lane, 2000; Karanasios, 2011). Today, ICT is considered one of the fundamental building blocks of modern societies and digital economies (Castells, 2009; Varian, et al, 2005). Smart Government in its simplest form is about the use of ICT to provide access to governmental information and deliver public services to citizens and business partners (Lazer, 2002; Atkinson & Castro, 2008). However, employees who used Smart Government have not figured out how to exploit its full benefits (Karlsson, Holgersson, Söderström & Hedström, 2012). There is an equilibrium problem with Smart Government applications and limitations arising from the difficulty to tangibly justify the gigantic investments in ICT systems for the past decade and a half. The average public expectations concerning governments' efforts are shaped according to the ability of the government to successfully improve citizens' quality of life. Governments need to ensure that their policies, regulations, and systems enable citizen participation and address the needs of improving the delivery of services. The service delivery lifecycle needs to be reengineered and redesigned so as to meet citizens' expectations of enhanced social security and quality of life.

According to Al-Khouri (2012) in a study of e-gov in the UAE, policies should enable governments to undertake radical organizational changes that: (1) foster growth in services, (2) reduce unnecessary costs and regulatory burdens on firms, (3) strengthen education and training systems, (4) encourage good management practices, (5) foster innovation and new applications, and (6) create economic growth in the market that promotes a productive economy. Smart Government is in a state of constant change and evolution in different countries (Al-Khouri & Bal, 2007). A discussion of international case studies of Smart Government adoption follows.

2.3. International Adoption of Smart Government

Smart Government has been successfully utilized in the United States (Al-khaleej Times, 2012). After the Internet development and the application of online governmental services during the Clinton, Bush, and Obama administrations, "people in the United States now have the ability to access any number of programs online, from e-voting and health care to tax returns, and even access governmental data that was not previously available, creating a more transparent and accountable face for the government" (Holden, Norris & Fletcher, 2003, p. 325). While the US has been at the forefront with Smart Government, ultimately the goals of Smart Government are determined based on the political leadership of each government. Furthermore, key institutional stakeholders influence these goals among many countries. The World Summit for the Information Society Plan of Action recommends for governments to "develop national Smart Government initiatives and services, at all levels, adapted to the needs of citizens and businesses, to achieve a more efficient allocation of resources and public goods" (WSIS, 2005, p.1). Asgarkhani (2005) argued that there are many benefits to the use of e-governance in the U.S., and encourages the participation of nations in the procedure.

Due to e-governance, data is more freely obtainable to citizens. Dawes (2008) stated that this permits many people to engage in the political process without leaving the comfort of their homes. This may encourage citizens to be more widely involved in government and civic life. Smart Government in the U.S. also sees the building of trust between citizens and the state, a trend that goes against the impression of declining trust and confidence in government over the past few decades. Considering its easy access for citizens to data, government databases, and bureaucrats, Smart Government delivers an ideal platform to rebuild loyalty between citizens and government.

According to the United Nations Survey 2012 assessment of progress, measurements indicate that:

"Smart Government is increasingly being viewed among countries in the vanguard as going beyond service delivery toward a framework for a smart, inclusive, and sustainable growth for future generations. In countries that follow that trend, a focus on institutional integration coupled with online citizen orientation in public service continues to be dominant. Both in terms of information and services, the citizen is increasingly viewed as 'an active customer of public services' with borrowed private sector concepts being applied to improve public sector governance systems. A key driver for this approach is the need to achieve efficiency in government at the same time that services are being expanded. Advances in technology, which allow data sharing and efficient streamlining of cross-agency governance systems, are forming the back end of integrated portals where citizens find a myriad of relevant information arranged by theme, life cycle or other preferred use" (Erwin, 2012, p. 1).

In general, Smart Government was used in the U.S. to support services for its citizens and to improve its governmental services for all residents. The Smart Government system in the U.S. is very simple and established a long time ago. People can use their phones and home phones to get the services rather than waiting in customer lines inside organizations or waiting on phones for a long time. Providing fast services is the main purposes of Smart Government in the U.S.

Australia is another country that has successfully instituted Smart Government. Halligan (2004) highlighted that there are social benefits to Smart Government in the Australian context, including: faster turnaround of service delivery through virtual access rather than in-person visits and 24-hour service delivery that allows people to pursue information outside of working hours (Australia, 2003). Other benefits are: increased self-service allowing for effective decision-making with more freedom, improved ability to find information, including locating special programs to suit needs, and a wider reach of information to all communities.

Kernaghan (2003) stated that combining different services is viewed as the rational objective of Smart Government. In Australia, as in other developed countries, there is a clear political commitment to the institution of Smart Government. For example, the government recognized a program to have "all suitable services online by 2001" (DIST, 1997). Halligan (2004) mentioned that the Australian government has more experience about causal requirements and challenges by studying people's needs and uses of e-gov, "and have seen that there are a range of deeper drivers behind ISD, including citizen ICT literacy (the digital divide), economic development, and government reform. These drivers augment the basic need to improve government service delivery in general" (p. 6).

According to the Smart Government Benefits Study (2003) in Australia, they found that when applying e-gov in Australia, there is an increase of and better communication with rural and remote communities—nowadays, secluded populations are at the same levels of access to information and government dealings as larger cities. So, people can access and get services everywhere.

One of the best examples pointed out by Halligan (2004) is the Australian Taxation Office (ATO) and how they engage their citizens through e-gov services. From the ground up, the public was involved in the planning and implementation of the online taxation system. This created a deeper relationship with the government and its citizenry.

Song (2006) analyzed South Korea's experiment with smart government adoption and suggests that it is most effective with an action plan that contains three phases: pre-implementation, implementation, and post-implementation. According to the government of the Republic of Korea (2014), Smart Government was enacted in order to "help Korean people access public services without constraints of space, time, or medium through fusing and integrating Korea's cutting-edge IT technology and public services. The strategy is also a part of continuous efforts of the government to solve the low birthrate, aging population, and other social issues and to proactively respond to social security, public welfare, and other future issues" (p.1). For example, transparency (efficiency) is a vital part of the Seoul Metropolitan Smart Government. Online services reduce face-to-face communication between public servants by giving out all community services over Smart Government and reducing straight communication among public servants and public service applicants (Seoul Institute for Transparency, 2008). Therefore, citizens are not required to go to the main offices to get theie needs met; they can do it online, decreasing the number of customers in crowded lines. Efficiency of government and saving time are two separate issues.

It is possible that by allowing the citizens to be more involved in the governmental processes, it will lead to increased trust in the government. In order to progress, it will also be necessary to provide levels of help for people of all ages and backgrounds, from the younger generations who are familiar with technology to the older generations who may need a lot more help for this to be beneficial for them. By providing different online services designed by the users, this will better satisfy users' needs. (Kim and Kim, 2003*).*

Kim (2009) finds that South Korea shows regionalization and a decision-making leader's obligation to government improvements are significant growth factors in Smart Government. "In terms of the impact of Smart Government, a majority of employees perceived positive impacts of Smart Government innovations on service quality, responsiveness, and transparency. However, many employees had reservations about the positive impact of Smart Government on cost-efficiency" (p. 188). In summary, international use of e-gov reveals successes in many big countries who experience strong communication with their publics.

The U.S., Australia, and South Korea all offer case studies of governments that have increased the availability and usage of Smart Government to respond to citizen's needs for data accessibility and time-saving. Each of these countries is committed to the vital role of the strong communications and links between citizens and government that Smart Government affords. As a new government, the UAE also encourages the implementation of new technologies to serve citizens. Smart government is an initiative implemented in Dubai, the second largest city in the UAE (Dubai eGovernment, 2013). This stage is based on the announcement of the use of e-gov by the UAE administration and the establishment of Smart Government services (Lootah & Geray, 2006). Its aim is to promote change to obtain better services for the public or private sectors, as well as meet the demands of using technologies in the everyday life of the UAE community (Dubai Smart Government Department, 2013). According to Al-Jenaibi (2012), the smart government of Dubai was labeled the Dubai Smart Government, but His Highness Sheikh Mohammed bin Rashid Al Maktoum, UAE Vice President and Prime Minister and Ruler of Dubai, changed the name to "Smart Government" in 2013. His Highness ordered the transition of government workplaces and electronic devices to Dubai Internet City in 2014.

2.4. The UAE and Emphases of Smart Government

From the beginning, Sheikh Mohammed bin Rashid Al Maktoum had the vision that "we have to work hard to make the people satisfied with the service of the government" (Mohammed bin Rashid Al Maktoum, 2013, p. 2). In 2013, WAM (Emirates News Agency) wrote about the basic steps creating smart government in the UAE. In 2014, the same news agency stated that Sheikh Mohammed understood that as technologies become increasingly advanced in everyday life, such as with mobile phone technology, the government must adapt alongside these changes. He said that to keep up with developing technologies the government must work to make access easy and efficient for the people.

The UAE started applying Smart Government two years ago and it was a new step and movement in the community. The aim of smart government in the UAE is to provide services through avenues such as mobile phone and the Internet to maximize efficiency (Al Suwaidi, 2012). Al Suwaidi (2012) also mentioned that there is a lot of competition among programmers due to recognition among UAE institutions to make the government create electronic services. The UAE government (2014) announced a new award for the best use of e-gov between public and private sectors, establishing that by the end of 2015 every institution in the UAE must use Smart Government. Al Khouri (2012) argues that the United Arab Emirates is competing against time to develop the future of the government to ensure people's satisfaction from the services made for them. Meena (2009) believed that the completion deadline and award should help institutions create the best services for the public.

Alston (2013) predicted that smart government will have a positive impact on the city. The smart government will achieve cost-reduction through direct savings and lower cost of delivery (Fan & Yan, 2010). With the creation of the smart government, society will have a lower cost using communication channels because Smart Government is free and there is no charge for filling applications online while increasing resource efficiency, allowing easy communication between government units and with users through electronic devices (Fields, 2005; Flak & Munkvoid, 2008). Piecowye (2008) added that the UAE, and Dubai in particular, are excellent examples of how Smart Government developed. The Smart Government in Dubai is improving rapidly. Also, Piecowye (2008) argued that "changing to Smart Government will provide and facilitate many issues for citizens in the UAE" (Piecowye, 2008, p 9). For example,

the purpose of the Smart Government is the provision of government services that are better for the citizen on the basis of fairness, equality and transparency, and that introduce means and mechanisms of information technology in the delivery of government services as part of a new agreement between government and citizens basis of transparency and mutual trust between the citizen and the service provider. The success of the application of Smart Government must have the availability of several introductions and foremost: the political administration, the availability of human and material resources, and the existence of a plan and measurement criteria for judging the service provided (Zoubi, 2001, p. 201).

Smart Government will facilitate citizens' use of government services, where they will be able to complete operations through electronic services while saving a lot of time and effort (Flanagan, 2011). According to a report by Abdel-Wahab (2008), "The use of information technology, especially Internet applications based on a network of websites, is to support and enhance citizens' access to services transparently" (p 70). Garson, D.G. (2006) believed that Smart Government will reduce corruption practices such as bribery and nepotism in the administration.

2.5. Benefits of Smart Government in the UAE

Smart government allows optimum public services and administration to spread quickly in the community (Goldkuhl, 2007). It also increases the transparency of the government through direct involvement of citizens in carrying out policies of the public (ITU, 2009; Goldkuhl, 2006). According to Holgersson, Söderström, Karlsson, & Hedström (2010), citizens can easily access the information and services provided by their government and engage with administrators. Citizens can obtain official information and assess information through participation without fear of their privacy being disrespected due to the advanced security features that protect them (Smart cities, 2013; Hung, Chang & Yu, 2006). Bhatnaga (2013) discusses how consumers can use self-service rather than services delivered through intermediary staff help. This allows 24/7 services instead of services being restricted to certain days and times (Heeks, 2005). Also, online delivery eliminates the potential complications in finding the correct location of services in any government building (Al-Jenaibi, 2011). Jivani (2014) stated that consumers can also engage in the governance process through interaction with the government and may be empowered by accessing knowledge and information.

Mishra (2013) predicted that with smart government, the quality of life for citizens will improve, as well as the efficiency of and quality of services provided by the governing entities. According to Noie (2003), apart from improved specialized opportunities received in online transactions, such as renewing internet services or national identity cards, people gain community skills and knowledge in addition to new business and work opportunities. Government information can be provided to everybody, anywhere, and anytime. As a result, people enjoy faster delivery of services that is round-the-clock through self-service, wider information availability, greater access, and better communication with people from remote areas (Weinzierl, A. (2014). Last, but not least, the survey showed that there is reduced complexity when people deal with their government online. A greater percentage claim that the information is easy or very easy to find (42%), and 43% claim it is acceptable or moderate to find. Only a small percentage of 14% claimed information was difficult to find (Noie, 2003, p.8).

Some scholars such as Rubel (2011.a) have written about the benefits of smart government to agencies through cost reductions via direct savings, low delivery costs, and improved processes that are either business or internal in nature. Noie (2003) added that there are also reduced costs for communication with citizens and businesses and improved resource efficiency. For example, "23% of business and intermediary respondents showed that they had an approximate savings of $25 per interaction" (Noie, 2003, p. 9).

Agencies need smart technology to coordinate and collaborate with each other. The working environment is made more efficient and effective with smart technology. There is improved transparency in decision-making, actions, rules, and procedures. This helps to quicken procedures that are directed toward people who are critically in need of such aids, rather than delaying service delivery through traditional means (ITU, 2009.b). In addition, a smart government supports democratization. This is because citizens are able to take part in consultations that are political in nature in real-time and in a less costly manner. This way, politicians are fully and immediately aware of the opinion of the public. The citizens can influence processes that are political in nature, thus improving transparency and the accountability of the government (ITU, 2009.a).

If the UAE in Dubai increases its use of smart government, then it will also benefit the environment by going paperless (ITU, 2009, p. 6). Cities can be linked through wireless sensors and processors, video telecommunications, mobile telecommunications, and geographic information systems (Al-Jenaibi, 2010). The result is a maximized management of urban congestion, energy efficiency, and improved security (Al-Shafi & Weerakkody, 2008). Scarce resources can also be allocated based on evidence that is in real-time. The citizenry can be educated through remote learning (Katz, 2011). Mishra (2013) stated that due to the advanced technologies and promotion of knowledge and innovations, cities will be more civilized, competitive, modernized, and functional. This is the reason that UAE's people will have a bigger technological capacity—there will be more entrepreneurship and innovation, more creativity, and information-availability. Areas of knowledge, technology, leadership, and partnerships will be developed (Mourtada & Alkhatib, 2014). Furthermore, using electronic means for transactions requires that a government makes its processes streamlined, which eventually improves efficiency and cuts costs, resulting in savings, since it reduces service fees. Savings can then be re-invested into further development of electronic applications and services (ITU, 2009.b).

3. UNIFIED THEORY OF ACCEPTANCE AND USE OF TECHNOLOGY (UTAUT)

The unified theory of acceptance and use of technology (UTAUT) was developed by Venkatesh, Morris, and Davis (2003), and it focuses on consequent usage of technology and behavioral intentions. The theory is a technology acceptance model introduced in "User Acceptance of Information Technology: Toward a Unified View" (Venkatesh, Morris; Davis, 2003, p. 425). Venkatesh, Morris, and Davis (2012) focused on understanding how individual acceptance and the use of information technology is one of the most mature and published streams of information systems research today. The UTAUT purposes are to clarify consumer intents to use data and follow usage performance, like using the guidelines of each online service. The theory holds that four key constructs are "direct determinants of usage intention and behavior" (Venkatesh, Morris; Davis, 2003, p.426). They are 1) performance expectancy, 2) effort expectancy, 3) social influence, and 4) facilitating conditions. Sex, age, knowledge, and voluntariness of usage are theorized to moderate the influence of the four strategic concepts on usage meaning and actions. The theory was established over an examination period and merging of the concepts of eight models that previous studies used to clarify facts and structures, including the "theory of reasoned action, the technology acceptance model, the motivational model, the theory of planned behavior, a combined theory of planned behavior/technology acceptance model, the model of personal computer use, a diffusion of innovations theory, and the social cognitive theory" (Verhoeven, Heerwegh, and Wit, p. 55). Venkatesh, Morris, and Davis (2012) adjust these concepts and meanings from UTAUT to the customer equipment receipt and include background.

"Performance expectancy" (p.159) is meant as the step to which consuming a technology will deliver benefits to customers in performance positive actions; "effort expectancy" (Venkatesh, Morris & Davis, p. 159) is the step of comfort related to public usage of technology; "social influence" (p. 159) is the degree to which customers observe that significant others (e.g., personal associates and groups) trust they must use a specific technology; and "facilitating conditions" (Venkatesh, Morris & Davis, p. 159) refer to customers' awareness of the resources and care obtainable to achieve a behavior (Brown and Venkatesh, 2005). "According to UTAUT, performance expectancy, effort expectancy, and social influence are theorized to influence behavioral intention to use a technology, while behavioral intention and facilitating conditions determine technology use. Also, individual difference variables, namely age, gender, and experience (note that voluntariness is dropped, which was part of the original UTAUT), are theorized to moderate various UTAUT relationships. The lighter lines in Figure 1 show the original UTAUT along with the one modification noted above that was necessary to make the theory applicable to this context" (Venkatesh, Morris, and Davis, 2012, p. 159).

Figure 1. UTAUT Model
From: SSRN: http://ssrn.com/abstract=2002388

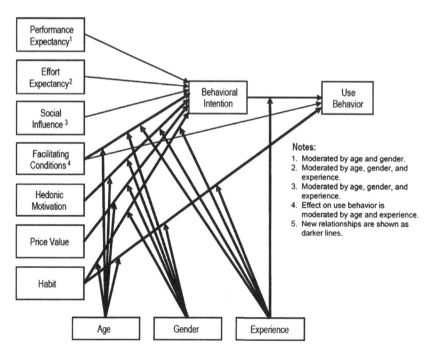

This study focuses on consumers and their usage of Smart Government like what Venkatesh, Morris, and Davis (2003) studied and tested in the UTAUT theory. The theory is linked to this study because one of the main objectives of this research is to discover the consumers' usage, awareness, social influence, and awareness of Smart Government in the UAE. The main objective of this research is to see how people's knowledge of electronic governmental bodies has been able to satisfy the needs of the citizenry through online services.

4. METHODOLOGY

Hesse-Biber (2010) validates the power of combining qualitative and quantitative research methods to ensure that extensive information about the sample to be accessed and searched. In this study, the researcher used the questionnaire and interviews together. Combining these methods allows the researcher to "permit the evaluator to enter into and understand the situation/context" (Frechtling & Sharp, 1997, p. 97). Mixed methods are used to create clear, different philosophical positions. These positions "bridge post-positivist and social constructivist worldviews, pragmatic perspectives, and transformative perspectives" (Greene, 2007, p. 4). Where the questionnaire provides statistics to measure, the test of the hypotheses and the use of mutual relations for the study of relational relations between the multiple variables are not available in the interviews (Mertens, 2009).

While a questionnaire gives clear results from the use of smart public services by clients, the interviewing approach differs by including employees of the federal authorities. Federal authorities were selected because Smart Government is a new system imposed on them by the government, and all federal agencies at the end of 2015 must apply and use smart government without exception. This ensures the researcher uses the correct target sample of those currently involved in smart government. In addition, the researcher examines the advantages and obstacles to the use of smart government by employees and the public. Interviews allow the researcher to collect in-depth information about managers, their thinking, and their opinions about smart government. Managers were chosen because they are the people who first deal with the directions, policies, and implementation of smart government.

Morse & Niehaus (2009) stated that the advantage of the combination of qualitative and quantitative methods is being able to attain a low-cost data collection that allows the researcher access to the largest possible number of the targeted sample, which includes the clients in the UAE and users of smart services. "Face-to-face interviews can no doubt capture an interviewee's emotions and behaviors. Similar to not being able to capture verbal and non-verbal cues, online and mobile surveys also do not capture raw emotions and behavior" (Wyse, 2014, p.1). In addition, questionnaires allow the person to express their opinions freely and without restrictions, encouraging a high response rate. (McQuerrey (2015) indicated that "qualitative interviews give the interviewer the advantage of using a non-traditional line of questioning to glean first-person assessments of a situation" (McQuerrey, 2015, p. 2).Therefore, interviews were conducted with a number of managers in the following federal authorities: (3) Emirate's Red Crescent, (1) Insurance Authority, (4) Emirate's Identity Authority, (1) Federal Authority for Government Human Resources, (2) Federal Electricity and Water Authority, (1) Telecommunication Regulatory Authority, (3) General Authority of Islamic Affairs and Endowments, (2) Federal Transport Authority, and the (1) Federal Customs Authority, for a total of 18 managers. There are 18 federal authorities in the UAE. The researcher tried to reach a larger number of them; however, some managers are very busy and research assistants failed to reach all of them. The researcher appointed five students from the University of United

Arab Emirates and paid them to gather information and conduct interviews after intensive training on how to perform interviews in workshops within the university.

Of the interviews, eight were face to face and ten were performed through the telephone. Among the employees successfully interviewed were two females and the rest males, and their ages were between 38 and 55. Three have master's degrees and fifteen have bachelor's degrees. All interviews were in the main authorities in Abu Dhabi (including Alain City) and Dubai, the biggest cities that have the main offices of the federal authorities. The length of interviews ranged from 15 to 20 minutes. There were no recorded interviews, but all information was written down. The data was collected in March and April of 2015. A structured interview was used with similar about: aims, advantages, struggles, and recommendations to improve the smart government. All interviews were conducted in Arabic and translated to the English language. The interviews were analyzed using themes and coding managers.

To determine user responses, 450 questionnaires were distributed among local clients who used the smart government in the UAE. Of them, 391 questionnaires were collected and returned in two months from January 2014 to February 2015. Questionnaires were distributed in all federal authorities and emirates in the UAE, including the Federal Authority for Government Human Resources, Federal Customs Authority, Federal Electricity and Water Authority, Telecommunication Regulatory Authority, General Authority for Youth and Sports Welfare, General Authority of Islamic Affairs and Endowments, General Civil Aviation Authority, General Authority for Pensions and Social Security, Federal Transport Authority, Emirates' Identity Authority, Securities and Commodities Authority, Insurance Authority, Emirates' Red Crescent, and the National HR Development and Employment Authority. Out of 18 federal authorities existing in the UAE, only 14 authorities were selected because the others were too difficult to communicate with due to limited customers and services.

The selected Federal Authorities all use smart government or Smart Government in the UAE, which is a new policy required for all federal authorities. The researcher divided questionnaires equally between the authorities; customers, around 33 to 35 left in each authority. The respondents were given a choice of response on the 5-point Likert scale, asking respondents to select (1) Strongly agree; (2) Agree; (3) Neutral; (4) Disagree; (5) Strongly disagree. The Likert scale instrument is best suited to a matrix questionnaire format that allows researchers to effectively gauge attitudes and gather large sets of data more efficiently.

Two professors in the business and communication fields reviewed the settings of the questions provided on the questionnaire. A total of 50 pilot questionnaires were tested and 43 were returned; only one unclear question was fixed. The reliability coefficient (Cronbach) for the total of 50 pilot questionnaires was.96. The questionnaire of this research is both descriptive and analytical. It is descriptive for the reason that it is aimed to classify the physical characteristics of a specified selected group—users of smart government by federal authorities. It is also analytical because it pursues clarifications for different levels of satisfaction of the same users. The demographic information for participants is analyzed in the data analysis. Both quantitative and qualitative data have been composed for the study from a mixture of primary and secondary kinds of data. Secondary data was gained over the web via literature searches, by online theoretical and academics indices such as SSRN, ProQuest, Emerald, and EBSCO, and by several online and libraries sources.

Questionnaires were selected as the primary data-gathering tool in order to classify users' approaches and views supplemented by content qualitative analysis of textual data that will discover these approaches and assess Smart Government service excellence in the UAE. The main reasons for choosing questionnaires in this study are the following: they are inexpensive and save time; they are more manageable than interviews; they can be provided to a large number of users; participants are free to explain their beliefs; questionnaires provide quantifiable answers and are relatively easy to analyze. The researcher chose questionnaires because of the need of statistical results, the greater number of respondents, and because of the sensitive information that would be asked. Interviews were not preferred for the Smart Government user profiles because of the limited time for the study, the distance among the seven emirates in the UAE, and to the difficulty managing the information. The quantitative method allowed researchers to measure variables to validate current concepts or theories. Statistics is frequently used to make new theories founded on the consequences of information collected about multiple variables. Questionnaires frequently appear as a rational and easy choice of gathering data from people (Wisker, 2008). According to Amora (2010), the questionnaire can be "descriptive and analytical and the purpose of questionnaire is to obtain reliable and valid data on the investigated subject" (p. 1). A questionnaire is a good method because it is time effective and efficient in obtaining answers. Pratt (2006) agreed that researchers can get a great answer rate with valid answers.

4.1. Statistical Analysis of Questionnaires

The study tool known as the questionnaire is one of the methods used to collect basic raw data directly from the selected sample of all the research community by directing a set of specific questions in advance (Hussein, 2011). Validity of the questionnaire instrument was tested by reviewing the questionnaire with two evaluators and modifying questions by deleting or adding new questions after distributing and testing a 50-question pilot survey. The questionnaire was divided into:

- **Unit One:** General features of the study sample to include sex, age, place of work, citizenship, marital status, and educational level.
- **Unit Two:** Goals, motives of the use of electronic government, motives of preference as well as the extent of use of these smart applications.
- **Unit Three:** Basic element of Smart Government uses in federal authorities, response times, and recommendations for improving smart government.

Questionnaire variables include:

- **Demographic Variables:** Age, sex, educational level, available smart devices, nationality, social status.
- **Independent Variables:** Employment, confidence, smart content services, satisfaction, and speed of services.

After gathering and testing the study data entered to version 22 "SPSS", the computer mediated the program in order to conduct the analysis of questions and retrieve the frequency tables: the correlation is used to test the degree of association between variables. The statistical analyses used were: Frequencies, mean and standard deviation, and factor analysis, and Pearson and Spearman-rho correlations were run to test the correlation between variables and the testing hypothesis.

4.2. Descriptive Analyses

4.2.1 Introduction

This study aimed to identify the use of smart government clients for applications in local institutions, to determine the extent of customer services of governmental bodies (e) of the newly applied smart government program, and how they responded to communicating with those bodies.

4.2.2 Research Questions

The main research questions are: What is the purpose of creating smart government? What are the users' aims when they use it?

4.2.3 Research Hypotheses

From the theoretical framework and related previous studies, the researcher found that:

1. There were statistically significant relationships between the multiplicity of services provided by institutions and customer satisfaction for smart services. Accepted
2. There is a relationship between the higher the degree of clarity and speed to find smart government, and the higher readiness and increased use of the client to use smart government. Accepted
3. There is a correlation between the spread of the E-gov concept and the use of E-gov. Accepted
4. There is a correlation between the importance of E-gov and the use of E-gov. Accepted

4.2.4 Descriptive Results (Demographic Information)

In terms of respondents' profiles, they were asked to answer questions regarding their gender, age, marital, nationality, and level of education (Table 1).

Results show that more than half of respondents were male (68%) and 32% of them were female. Among respondents, 57% are between 18 to 25 years old, followed by 26 to 35 years old (36%), and 36 years and older (7%). The nationalities of the respondents were UAE (84.4%), Gulf (6.6%), and Arab (9%). In terms of education levels, more than half of the respondents hold a bachelor's as their highest level of education (52%), 45% have the equivalent of a high school diploma, and 3% hold a master's.

Respondents were asked what channels they prefer to use to learn about Smart Government services; 33% answered the website, 21.5% a social networking page, 15.6% radio and TV, and 7.4% the daily newspaper (Table 2).

The highest-frequency reason given for using electronic services was money and easy to use (53%), easy to use (16%), and effortlessness (12%) (Table 3).

The most frequently given reason for the use of applications to request access to electronic services for respondents was quality (33%), application (29%), and trust (18%) (Table 4).

In terms of frequency of use of the government services during the year, 63% of respondents used it less than 5 times, and 22% used smart government 6 to 10 times (Table 5).

Table 1. Respondents' profiles

	Frequency	Percent
What's Your Gender?		
Female	126	32.2
Male	265	67.8
What's Your Age?		
18 to 25	223	57.0
26 to 35	141	36.1
36 and older	27	6.9
What's Your Status?		
Single	245	62.7
Married	142	36.3
Divorce	4	1.0
What's Your Nationality?		
UAE	330	84.4
Gulf	26	6.6
Arab	35	9.0
What's Your Education?		
High school	175	44.8
Bachelor	203	51.9
MA	13	3.3

Table 2. Channels where you prefer to learn about Smart Government services and updates

Channels	Frequency	Percent
Website	128	32.7
Social networking page	84	21.5
Radio and TV	61	15.6
Daily newspaper	29	7.4
News + social networks	18	4.6
Web + radio	14	3.6
Web + news	12	3.1
Web + radio + news + social networks	9	2.3
Radio + news + social networks	8	2.0
Web + news + social networks	8	2.0
Radio + news	6	1.5
Radio + social networks	6	1.5
Web + radio+ social networks	5	1.3
Web + radio + news	2	.5
Total	391	100.0

Table 3. What is the main reason for the use of electronic services?

Reason	Frequency	Percent
Money + easy	209	53.5
Easy use	63	16.1
Effort	48	12.3
Money	30	7.7
Time + money + effort + easy	16	4.1
Time + money + effort	8	2.0
Time + money	8	2.0
Effort + easy	6	1.5
Money + effort + easy	2	.5
Time	1	.3
Total	391	100.0

Table 4. Reasons for the use of applications to request access to electronic services?

	Frequency	Percent
Quality of e-gov application	129	33.0
Application	115	29.4
Trust	70	17.9
Others	50	12.8
Quality + app	16	4.1
Quality + app + trust	5	1.3
Quality + trust	4	1.0
Trust + other	1	.3
Total	391	100.0

Table 5. Frequency of use of government services in the past year?

Frequency of Use	Frequency	Percent
Less than 5 times	247	63.2
6 to 10 times	89	22.8
more than 20 times	28	7.2
11 to 20 times	27	6.9
Total	391	100.0

Table 6. What are the basic elements necessary for any application of smart government?

Basic Element	Frequency	Percent
Secret (privacy)	228	58.3
Ensure (continued use)	87	22.3
Ensure +secret	39	10.0
Battery (rate of consumption)	14	3.6
Ensure + secret + battery	12	3.1
Secret + battery	8	2.0
Ensure + battery	2	.5
Total	391	100.0

Respondents were asked to circle one or more than one choice regarding the necessary elements of smart government elements. Most of the respondents agreed that secret or privacy is the main element for application in the smart government and the lowest agreements come from the ensure and battery (Table 6).

A proportion of 50% of respondents reported that the duration of an authority to respond to them is between1 to 20 minutes (Table 7).

Respondents were asked what services they suggested to be improved upon regarding smart organizations/government, and 55% answered education, employment, and health, and 10% called for tourism or electronic payments (10%) (Table 8).

4.3 Descriptive Results (Variables)

All variables and its constructs, together with questions measuring the variables, are presented in Table 9.

In the following section, descriptive analyses for seven variables have been presented. Clients' uses of E-gov services, Clients' trust of E-gov services, and Content of smart services were measured using a four-point scale of confirmation (1: Yes to 2: no). Internet and smart services speed, Client satisfaction, Pros of smart government, and cons of smart government were measured using a five-point scale of agreement (1: strongly agree to 5: strongly disagree). All items are sorted based on highest to lowest mean.

Table 7. Times taken to respond

Respond Time	Frequency	Percent
1 min to 20 mins	196	50.1
21 mins to 40 mins	121	30.9
41 mins to 60 mins	50	12.8
more than 60 mins	23	5.9
Total	391	100.0

Table 8. Recommendations for improving smart government

Recommendation	Frequency	Percent
Education, employment, health	215	55.0
Tourism	40	10.2
Electronic payment	39	10.0
Phone application	27	6.9
Education + payment	22	5.6
Education + tourism	18	4.6
Education + tourism + payment + phone app	10	2.6
Education + tourisim + payment	10	2.6
Education + payment + phone app	4	1.0
Payment + phone app	2	.5
Education + tourism + phone app	2	.5
Tourism + payment+ phone app	1	.3
Tourism + phone app	1	.3
Total	391	100.0

In terms of clients' uses of e-gov services, a majority of respondents are ready to put their personal information in the e-gov applications (mean: 1.7) based on the scale defined as (1) Yes; (2) Sometimes; (3) Don't know; (4) No (Table 10).

Meanwhile, a majority of them answered "don't know (mean: 2.8) to questions that asked if they dealt with their bank through its website.

In terms of clients' trust of E-gov services, the majority of respondents thinks Smart Government services are necessary, and a majority of them sometimes agree that the e-gov concept is clear for them (mean: 1.8) based on the four-point scale defined as (1) Yes; (2) Sometimes; (3) Don't know; (4) No (Table 11).

In terms of content of smart services, a majority of respondents own smartphones, and they think that online services will contribute to the delivery of government services to simplify and facilitate transactions (mean:1.42) based on the four-point scale defined as (1) Yes; (2) Sometimes; (3) Don't know; (4) No (Table 12).

Respondents were asked to answer about their opinions of internet and smart services speed. As a result, a majority of them agree that the form of electronics is ease to browse (mean: 1.9). The lowest mean was for "the number of clicks you make until you reach what you want is minimal" (mean: 2.19) (Table 13).

Respondents were asked about their satisfaction regarding e-service. The majority of them are satisfied with SMS messaging services associated with electronic smart (mean: 1.8) as well as the quality of service (mean 1.9) (Table 14).

In terms of the pros of smart government, a majority of respondents agree that smart government's electronic services will save a lot of time and effort (mean: 1.8), and smart use of government in the UAE will be highly efficient and effective (1.8) based on an agreement five-point scale fromm 1: strongly

Table 9. Details of Questions Measuring Variables

Variables	Questions
Clients' Uses of e-gov Services	
5 Are you ready to put your personal information in the e-gov applications? 6 Do you feel assured to put your personal information in the e-gov applications? 7 Do you use the Internet to pay your bills? 8 Do you deal with your bank through its website?	
Clients' Trust of e-gov Services	
4 Do you think it is necessary? 5 Are the e-gov services easy to use electronically? 6 Is the e-gov concept clear for you?	
Content of Smart Services	
5 Do you currently own a smartphone? 6 Do you think that online services will contribute to the delivery of government services to simplify and facilitate transactions? 7 Do you think that the smart electronic services have succeeded in being a key requirement for the completion of the transactions of government at the state level? 8 Did you know that electronic forms (new) are available through the printing offices accredited at the state level?	
Internet and Smart Services Speed	
6 Form of electronic is ease to browse 7 Form of electronic search engine easy to use 8 Form of electronic content is accurate 9 Form of electronic has high speed of loading pages 10 Form of electronic number of clicks made until you reach what you want is minimal	
Client Satisfaction	
6 Are you satisfied with SMS messaging services associated with smart government? 7 Is your level of electronic services within the state continuing to improve, the quality of service meeting the needs of distinct dealers, and registration procedures easily successful? 8 Do you think electronic services in the printing offices are convenient and make it easier for dealers and customers? 9 Are you satisfied with the presence of representatives and their interaction through various media channels of communication for smart government? 10 Are you satisfied with the media content for e-services?	
Pros of Smart Government	
9 Electronic services help to save a lot of time and effort 10 Smart use of government in the UAE will be highly efficient and effective 11 Electronic transactions in the state will be smoother 12 Smart use of government in the UAE reduces administrative corruption (bribes, favoritism, etc.) 13 Website of the registration centers contributes to the provision of quality services and outstanding dealers and reviewers 14 Smart use of government in the UAE to reduce congestion in career advancement 15 Information entered will be valid through smart government 16 Reduction of bureaucracy in transactions	
Cons of Smart Government	
3 Will be negative in terms of possible leaks in some information systems by hackers in electronic services 4 Will have a negative impact on society in terms of the difficulty of dealing with electronic services	

Table 10. Clients' uses of e-gov services

Questions	Mean	Std. Deviation
Are you ready to put your personal information in the e-gov applications?	1.69	.939
Do you feel assured to put your personal information in the e-gov applications?	2.13	1.036
Do you use the internet to pay your bills?	2.61	1.193
Do you deal with your bank through its website?	2.78	1.212

Note: (1) Yes; (2) Sometimes; (3) Don't know; (4) No

Table 11. Clients' trust of E-gov services

Questions	Mean	Std. Deviation
Do you think it is necessary?	1.39	.693
Are the e-gov services easy to use electronically?	1.50	.730
Is the e-gov concept clear for you?	1.81	.989

Note: (1) Yes; (2) Sometimes; (3) Don't know; (4) No

Table 12. Content of smart services

Questions	Mean	Std. Deviation
Do you currently own a smartphone?	1.18	.570
Do you think that online services will contribute to the delivery of government services to simplify and facilitate transactions?	1.42	.674
Do you think that the smart electronic services have succeeded in being a key requirement for the completion of the transactions of government at the state level?	1.82	.881
Did you know that electronic forms (new) are available through the printing offices accredited at the state level?	2.34	1.175

Note: (1) Yes; (2) Sometimes; (3) Don't know; (4) No

Table 13. Internet and smart services speed

Questions	Mean	Std. Deviation
Form of electronic is ease to browse	1.91	.745
Form of electronic search engine easy to use	2.02	.797
Form of electronic content is accurate	2.03	.712
Form of electronic has high speed of loading pages	2.04	.809
Form of electronic number of clicks you make until you reach what you want is minimal	2.19	.817

Note: (1) Strongly agree; (2) Agree; (3) Neutral; (4) Disagree; (5) Strongly disagree

Table 14. Client satisfaction

Questions	Mean	Std. Deviation
Are you satisfied with SMS messaging services associated with smart government?	1.85	.782
Is your level of satisfaction of electronic services within the state continuing to improve, the quality of service meeting the needs of distinct dealers, and the registration procedures easily successful?	1.93	.780
Do you think electronic services in the offices of the printing convenient and made easier for dealers and customers?	2.03	.800
Are you satisfied with the presence of representatives and their interactions through various media channels of communication for smart government?	2.08	.862
Are you satisfied with the media content for e services?	2.10	.836

Note: (1) Strongly agree; (2) Agree; (3) Neutral; (4) Disagree; (5) Strongly disagree

Table 15. Pros of smart government

Questions	Mean	Std. Deviation
Electronic services help to save a lot of time and effort	1.78	.690
Smart use of government in the UAE will be highly efficient and effective	1.81	.660
Electronic transactions in the state will be smoother	1.85	.673
Smart use of government in the UAE will reduce administrative corruption (bribes, favoritism, etc.)	1.87	.855
The websites of the registration centers will contribute to the provision of quality services and outstanding dealers and reviewers	2.01	.597
Smart use of government in the UAE will reduce career congestion	2.06	.848
Information entered will be valid through smart government	2.17	.772
Reduction of bureaucracy in transactions	2.19	.800

Note: (1) Strongly agree; (2) Agree; (3) Neutral; (4) Disagree; (5) Strongly disagree

agree to 5: strongly disagree. Respondents are less agreeable about the reduction of bureaucracy in transactions (based on highest and lowest mean) (Table 15).

In terms of the cons of smart government, there is agreement that smart government will be negative in terms of possible leaks within some information systems by hackers in electronic services (mean: 2.2), as well as smart government having a negative impact on society in terms of the difficulty of dealing with electronic services (mean: 2.6). (Table 16).

4.4 Overall Level

Table 17 and 18 show the overall mean for all constructs. The overall mean for "Clients' uses of e-gov services", "Clients' trust of e-gov services", and "Content of smart services" ranged between 1.5 to 2.5, with the four-point scale *(1) Yes; (2) Sometimes; (3) Don't know; (4) No)*.

This shows the majority of respondents believe they are ready for adopting Smart Government and Smart Government is simple challenging.

Table 16. Cons of smart government

Questions	Mean	Std. Deviation
Will be negative in terms of leaks in some information systems by hackers in electronic services	2.25	.943
Will have a negative impact on society in terms of the difficulty of dealing with electronic services	2.59	1.011

Note: (1) Strongly agree; (2) Agree; (3) Neutral; (4) Disagree; (5) Strongly disagree

Table 17. Overall mean for e-gov use

Constructs	Mean	Std. Deviation
Trust	1.57	.60
Smartphone	1.69	.54
Use	2.30	.86

Overall mean for "Internet and smart services speed", "Client satisfaction", and the "Pros and cons of smart Gov" ranged between 2 and 2.6 using the five-point scale of agreement (1) Strongly agree; (2) Agree; (3) Neutral; (4) Disagree; (5) Strongly disagree. It shows the majority of respondents are satisfied about the services (Table 18).

4.4.1. Testing Hypothesis

4.4.1.1. Reliability

In order to test the reliability of measurement, Cronbach's coefficient alpha was determined. The Cronbach alpha-coefficient is recommended to be above 0.7 (Pallant, 2011). Table 19 shows the reliability of each constructs. The result shows that the value of Cronbach's alpha for all constructs ranged between 0.7 to 0.85, indicating the high inter-correlation between items in each construct. This result shows that the questions statistically measure its constructs, and items in each constructs have high internal consistency.

4.4.2. Testing the Hypothesis

4.4.2.1. Correlation

The Spearman-rho correlation was run to test the correlation between variables (Table 20).

Table 18. Overall mean for e-gov satisfaction

Constructs	Mean	Std. Deviation
Pros	1.97	.44
Satisfaction	2	.62
Service speed	2	.58
Hackers	2.25	.94
Difficulty of dealing with electronic services	2.6	1.01

Table 19. Reliability of constructs

Constructs	N	r
Clients' uses of E-gov services	4	0.78
Clients' trust of E-gov services	3	0.6
Content of smart services	4	0.5
Internet and smart services speed	5	0.8
Client satisfaction	5	0.8
Pros of smart government	8	0.75

Note: n = number of questions; r = Cronbach's Alpha

Table 20. Correlation matrix

	1	2	3	4	5	6	7	8
Use	1							
Trust	.307sig							
Smartphone	.419sig	.474sig						
Service Speed	.209sig	.310sig	.387sig					
Satisfaction	.220sig	.279sig	.436sig	.695sig				
Pros	.163sig	.103*	.215 sig	.231 sig	.275 sig			
Cons (electronic services)	.110sig	-.140**	.037	.061	.001	.051		
Cons (hackers)	-.021	-.029	.009	.018	-.026	.172sig	.379sig	1.0

There was a positive and significant correlation between "Clients' use of e-gov services" and "Clients' trust of e-gov services" [$r = 0.307$, $p = .00 < 0.05$]; "Content of smart services" [$r = 0.42$, $p = .00 < 0.05$]; "Internet and smart services speed" [$r = 0.21$, $p = .00 < 0.05$]; "Client satisfaction" [$r = 0.22$, $p = .00 < 0.05$]; and "Pros of smart government [$r = 0.16$, $p = .00 < 0.05$]. The results indicate that customers who have the highest level of trust in Smart Government use more Smart Government services. The result also shows that the higher the services' speed, the higher the usage of Smart Government services by clients. However, the highest correlation is between internet and smart services speed and satisfaction [$r = 0.7$, $p = .00 < 0.05$], meaning there is a strong relationship between these two constructs. The higher the speed of smart services, the highest satisfaction the clients have.

The correlation between the cons (electronic services) of e-gov and trust in the services [$r = 0.14$, $p = .00 < 0.05$] is negative and significant. This result shows that those who believe that they have difficulty dealing with electronic services are less likely to trust in Smart Government services.

5. SUMMARY

The aim of this study was to identify client readiness to use e-gov services and their level of satisfaction when using those services. Among the respondents, 68% were male and 32% of them female between the ages of 18 to 25 years old (57%), with a lesser amount 26 to 35 years (36%) and 36 and older (7%). The nationalities of the respondents were UAE (84.4%), Gulf (6.6%), and Arab (9%). More than half of the respondents hold a bachelor's degree as their highest level of reduction, while 45% completed high school and 3% hold a master's degree. Respondents were asked what channels they prefer to learn through regarding government information, 33% answered websites, 21.5% social networking pages, 15.6% radio and TV, and 7.4% the daily newspaper. The highest main reasons for the use of electronic services was to save money and it was easy to use (53%), ease of use (16%), and affordability (12%). Most respondents use applications to request access to electronic services because of quality (33%), application (29%), and trust (18%). In terms of the frequency of use of government services during the year, 63% of respondents used it less than five times in a year, and 22% used the services six to ten times. A proportion of 50% of respondents reported that duration of time waiting for somebody to respond to them was between 1 to 20 minutes. The services most respondents suggested to be improved via smart organization was education, employment, and health services (55%), tourism (10%), and electronic payments (10%). In terms of clients' uses of e-gov services, the majority of respondents are ready to put their personal information in e-gov applications and believe that e-gov services are necessary. Moreover, a majority only somewhat agree that the e-gov concept is clear for them. Most respondents own smartphones. They think that online services will contribute to the delivery of government services to simplify and facilitate transactions. As a result, a majority of them are agree that electronic service is easy to browse and they are satisfied with SMS messaging services associated with electronic government as well as their quality of service. In terms of the pros of smart gov, a majority of respondents agree that smart government's electronic services help save a lot of time and effort, and smart government in the UAE will be efficient and effective. Respondents are less likely to agree that electronic services help to reduce bureaucracy in transactions. In terms of the cons of smart government, many agree that smart government will be negative in terms of possible leaks of information by hackers in electronic services, and smart government will have a negative impact on society in terms of the difficulty of dealing with electronic services.

Overall, a majority of respondents believe they are ready for adopting Smart Government and are satisfied about the services. The results indicate that the customer who has the highest level of trust in Smart Government uses more Smart Government services. The results also show that the higher the services' speed, the higher the client's satisfaction as well as the more the client uses e-gov services. However, the highest correlation is between Internet and smart services speed and the level of satisfaction. This result also shows that those who believed that they were having difficulty dealing with electronic services were less likely to trust in e-gov services. The advantage of using smart government is the speed of service performance. With computers replacing the traditional manual systems, information is gathered and processed in a much faster time than what users had to endure before. Also, smart government reduces costs because performance of administrative work in the traditional way consumed large amounts of paperwork, documents, and stationery, which is significantly reduced due to the use of computers and smartphones providing paperless tools and reducing the number of staff resulting in an increased speed of service. In addition, Smart Government eliminates administrative corruption. As the system of Smart Government focuses on the completion of transactions electronically, where the owner can access the website of the administration region to determine the required service, stages, and procedures, the cost to get them, and does not face a direct interaction with an employee or student service, there is less chance of offenses such as bribery, corruption, and so on.

5.1 Qualitative Data Analysis

The interviews are analyzed using particular themes: aims of applying methods of smart government, assessment of applying smart government, and the optimistic comments and recommendations for increasing the use of smart government. All managers are coded by numbers because all employees preferred to be anonymous.

5.2. Aims of Applying Methods of Smart Government in the Authorities

Interviewees indicated that "the authority was trying its best to facilitate the easiest ways and means of modern technology available to all dealers, such as the Red Crescent Authority, which facilitates the process of charitable donations by entering special programme donors of the Authority over the phone at home or anywhere" (Interviewee #1, 2015). Interviewees #5 and #7 added that "in the Authority we change the methods and the user techniques so the access is preferred by customers; it is the easiest method to suit all customers in every place and time." By using smart government, smart applications are included in plans and schedules that must be followed in every authority's body of employees. The authority creates a specialist task team to work and follow-up on progress, thus supporting the public interest before applying Smart Government services. Regarding the shift and changes in the authorities, most of the interviewees stated that:

1. The process is an important shift; it is the evolution of new technologies in any federal body because they save time and reduce the number of employees in customer service and the congestion of the public in the main public buildings.
2. To meet all the customer needs and provide rapid response to their queries, the application and process is offered online all the time; it is a quick start of a fast and smart browsing of program and services.

3. Smart government is considered one of the most important and the latest modern technologies, especially when it used in developed countries such as the UAE. It has succeeded with the public and served the role of the authorities, its impact for clientele very high last year. Compared with other countries like the U.S. and Singapore, the UAE moved very fast in services changes and serving methods.

4. It has a positive impact inside and outside the authority, for both clients and workers, reducing printing papers and accumulation in offices, reducing congestion, shortening time and effort for the customers and the employees.

All interviewees agreed that it is a governmental new policy announced to be in place by end of this year; "we are compelled to take it seriously by creating new roles for clients and I think it's a very positive way". It serves the community as a whole, including different groups and nationalities in both Arabic and English. Also, it is in the initiative stage, which is good; a new movement in the society that leads to other movements and uses of new technologies, such as applying Smart Government for educational and learning purposes. Certainly it will be followed by other future initiatives. "We are in a changing world of technology and there is a need to use new smart inventions". It facilitates the task of the government: "we follow the orders issued by our government to apply better things; the government is studying what it takes to serve customers and we are following these roles" (Interviewee #9, 2015). Interviewee # 11 mentioned that most of the customers now have experienced applications through smart devices: "some of them have more background than employees, and we need services to suit their needs and experiences. He added "the community is changing; you can see kids with iPads and they know how to access and download programs". Four of the managers—interviewees 12, 13, 14, and 18—believed that, present requirements of society need to keep pace with technological changes, because most of the people have smartphones and PCs or laptops and they know how to use them. "If it is not applied now, we will face a problem. Every day we have new technology and we will be too far from future new applications" (Interviewee #18). It helps to get creative and innovative. "Most of the fans have smartphones and fast access to these applications; therefore, they need it" (Interviewee #13). In general, all the managers agreed that the authorities are trying hard to win customer satisfaction. It is easy to use when there are simple instructions for use to guide the large number of customers.

5.3 Assessment of Applying the Smart Government in the Authorities

The assessment varied among the authorities, including different methods and thoughts. All of the authorities used internal and external encouragement for the use of smart applications through public ads, websites, banners, and brochures. "Unfortunately, there are people with experience in the field of smart applications, but their role is marginalized; we need to get their experiences" (Interviewee #16, 2015). Also, there is a lack of awareness, experience, and staff. "The ignorance of the importance of smart applications is apparent for some people, whether clients or employees, who prefer the old style and face-to-face services inside the authority" (Interviewee #10, 2015). Interviewee #7 indicated there is a lack of experience in the use of smart services, "which, although a new style of practice, should be everyone's responsibility of learning and training on the use of techniques".

Age is another struggle; most managers agreed that the older staff, over 50 or 55 years, don't know how to use smart technology, but there are those who accept training and those who refuse. "One of the challenges is there is no clear philosophy about the use and application of smart government from the government itself" (Interviewee #11, 2015). So far, all managers offered positive comments, believing smart government is easy to use and that the training of employees and customers needs time. Also, they agreed that an increase in positive initiatives helps to facilitate tasks among employees. Some of the main points raised in these interviews are:

- There are no clear objectives and no centralized management about smart applications to contact in times of need.
- "We share the opinion of all the proposals and the introduction of the smart government" (Interviewee #14, 2015).
- There is a limited number of experts and interested people regarding smart government.
- There is not enough awareness of the importance of the extent of smart government; people and employees think it is exotic, complex, and difficult to use.
- "There is no political strategy or a clear plan about smart government from the government" (Interviewee #1, 2015).
- There is a lack of information from the government about modern applications and techniques used and projects of interest to the government.
- There is a lack of explanatory guide and clear instructions about the use of smart government.
- "We want to know the actual pros and services that must be worked out clearly" (Interviewee #17, 2015)

Eleven of the interviewees agreed that there is a need of involvement of the private and public sectors, and a unification of national goals and vision of smart services. In conclusion, all interviewees have a positive agreement about applying and assessing the smart government, but while trying hard to apply it they have suffered struggles that must be fixed from the government.

5.4. The Optimistic Comments About Smart Government

Employees indicated many advantages of smart government. The majority of managers stated that they need a central government department for inquiries. They already use applications in the UAE society and accept the idea of Smart Government because it saves time, effort, the securities used, and the preservation of the environment from a reduction of printing papers. In addition, there is an increased achievement at work and speed. They share similar views and work to get a clear inside plan in the authority to follow the government orders and apply the new approach. "There is a common interest between the public and private sectors and the need for private sector participation with us" (Interviewee #3, 2015). In general, Smart Government is faster and reduces congestion, but the Internet should be made available to all the public regardless of location or situation. Also, it is not only official communications and applications, but all information that should be documented electronically. On suggestion is to "Rehabilitate staff to use applications through ongoing workshops" (Interviewee #4, 2015). Interviewee # 5 believed that the diversity of the services available to the customer is increased online when compared to driving a car to see employees face to face and waste the time in the authority. Three interviewees, #15, #17, and #18 stated that Smart Government:

- Defines a clear plan that includes certain deadlines and follows the events of the applications to be applied.

- Downloads the applications needed for a few minutes only and so access to information is very guileless.
- Becomes the portal and storage of official documents or information that can be accessed very easily and quickly.

5.5. Recommendations for Increasing the Use of Smart Government

Employees suggested the following:

1. Link the official information by creating a center or a special government department as a reference for all authorities.
2. Clarify the policies and strategies from the government about smart applications.
3. Set up special smart government laws.
4. Find a unified system that links government bodies and institutions by state.
5. Provide experts to train staff.
6. Allocate clear government vision, goals, and standardization among the various government entities.
7. Organize and coordinate with all relevant public organizations.
8. "We need a plan of action and a clear formulation of objectives and implementation" (Interviewee #5, 2015).
9. "Provide us with sufficient information with a clear schedule" (Interviewee # 14, 2015).
10. Provide employees with the latest updated programs.
11. Provide courses and conferences for employees in the government.
12. Determine the budget of the government, especially smart government.
13. Link information and data, and consolidate it all with the Government of Abu Dhabi.
14. Supply staff who work outside the office with phones and programs for the application of smart government from remote locations.
15. Provide a comprehensive global study and benefit from the experiences of other countries.

6. DISCUSSION

The study shows that smart government provides significant benefits to consumers, agencies, society as a whole, and many government objectives. Consumers benefit by having reduced costs because access to services and convenience are improved. There are also direct-service cost reductions and clients gain improved quality of services and improved access to services. The findings mirror the suggestions of Katz (2011) that smart government saves time and effort (mean: 1.8), and smart government in the UAE will be highly efficient and effective (1.8). There is also indicated growth in business and work opportunities. Smart government has a faster turn-around of data requests and easy access to documents and forms, which increases the efficiency of transactions, supporting NOIE (2003) and Mishra (2013). Therefore, Gant (2008) and Andersen (2006) believe that smart government increases the communication between users and government. The researcher finds that their studies are similar to this study's findings because smart government improves the communication between citizens and their government agencies and thus creates a more customer-friendly culture. Users can now apply for anything electronically and this has increased the number of offers and deliveries in a given time. In fact, not only do customers benefit from this exchange, but the government as a whole benefits since so many transactions can be planned, executed, and implemented online, as indicated in the ITU (2009.a). Furthermore, establishing a smart government ensures services and programs of high quality are provided to the citizens. Rubel (2011.b) stated users need technology to interact with their government, and also the users stated that it brings better responses regarding the performance of governmental agencies to improve on services delivery.

In connecting with the Unified Theory of Acceptance and Use of Technology (UTAUT), the emphasis on significant uses of technology, such as the smart government in this study, accentuates the social intention that comes from the customers (Venkatesh, Morris, Davis, 2003, p. 425). The researcher finds that with increased ease of using e-gov, the more the number of users spread in the community. The interaction between the government, technologies, and people are applied according to what Venkatesh, Morris, and Davis mentioned in their theory (UTAUT). Most of the respondents accept the new technologies through computers, iPads, and smartphones. The UTAUT explores the consumer aims to use data following usage performance, such as 1) performance expectancy, 2) effort expectancy, 3) social influence, and 4) facilitation, which can be found in the hypothesis test; there was a positive and significant correlation between "Clients' use of e-gov services" and "Clients' trust of e-gov services" [$r = 0.307$, $p = .00 < 0.05$]; "Content of smart services" [$r = 0.42$, $p = .00 < 0.05$]; "Internet and smart services speed" [$r = 0.21$, $p = .00 < 0.05$]; "Client satisfaction" [$r = 0.22$, $p = .00 < 0.05$]; and "Pros of smart government (speed)" [$r = 0.16$, $p = .00 < 0.05$]. The result indicated that customers with the highest levels of trust used more Smart Government services. The theory is related to this study for the reason that one of the key objectives is to find out consumers' usage, awareness, and social influence of Smart Government in the UAE. The study found that most of the managers agreed about the positive effect of the smart government, because clients already started using the new smart applications in the authorities and so it has a social influence, as Brown and Venkatesh (2005) indicated.

In answering the research questions (What is the purpose of creating smart government? What are the users' aims in using smart government and what level of satisfaction do they experience?), the researcher finds that the importance of the availability of this smart government for the individuals and citizens raised the level of the United Arab Emirates in terms of the use of electronic services, as well as raised the level of people's awareness of the importance of services and facilitated the work quickly without effort. Also, smart government is an extension of Smart Government, so that government services are provided from any place and at any time through smart tools (mobile phone applications and laptops, PDAs, etc.) to service clients efficiently and effectively. From here, it is clear that smart devices are multitalented. All managers believed that the Smart Government project represents a major re-creation of a new government, following innovative ways of doing business away from methods that were previously used. The most important results of Smart Government in a lot of states is the focus of development and progress in customer service. Smart services are considered an integral part of the transformation of the public sector and play a role in communications technology information and the provision of many modern services to citizens and businesses. Smart Government encourages information transference, corporate community profitability, and non-dividend transformation of papers written, as well as reviews. It puts pressure on government policy, preparing them for the future and training staff on smart services and how to use them. At present, many countries are trying to find the best and fastest smart services to offer customers, but unfortunately many users face the problem of a lack of adequate familiarity with smart government and how it is used, and many users have noted that the information and method of use needs to have a better strategy and information such as how to use the applications as well to the need for free online access for the use of smart services. That helps citizens participate in the development of the public sector and the provision of high quality and efficient public services. It is worth mentioning that the presence of a comprehensive approach to smart services is not enough without constant involvement in the drafting of a resolution and determination of the public's opinions. Consequently, managers indicate there are a lot of challenges facing smart government, such as lack of information, absence of a central department, and no clear philosophy and visions established. In the end, however, smart government is a key tool for ensuring the implementation of services that focus on the user. In conclusion, the limitation of this study comes from an inadequacy of published related studies. However, this study covers the UAE citizens and users of smart government not in the Gulf area. Very limited studies were published about smart government, such as the Al-Khouri's studies in 2012 and 2013 that focus on the National Identity services, not general uses of Smart Government. This study is unique in the UAE and the Gulf area because it measures the use of clients of smart government in the federal authorities, which have not been studied before by any scholar. Also, it covers 18 interviews with managers of those federal authorities, surveyed 391 users among the different authorities, and includes suggestions for a new strategy and policy. Scholars, students, and authorities will benefit from this study because they can study the respondents' answers about online services and can improve them in the future. Further studies can focus on the public or private sectors' employees' readiness of using smart government. Also, there is a significant need to further study employee satisfaction about smart government.

6.1. Research Suggestions and Recommendations

- Training for the employees and individuals on how to use applications in smart government.
- Providing free WIFI widely in public places.
- Providing instructions and educational courses and workshops for clients and employees.
- Facilitating online services such as hospital appointments and the payment of traffic fines, and improving the exchange of information between government agencies.
- Getting clear vision to get helpful documentation, ease handling, and assure high quality.

Understand that Smart Government was the result of multiple transfers. The implementation of this project requires the provision of a basic infrastructure for carrying out the series of requirements, such as providing network communications, computing, the Internet and the proliferation of specialized legislation in this area, and qualified human resources among others. The government needs to mobilize the citizens regarding the benefits and advantages of these techniques and provide them with the necessary facilities. They need to increase free WIFI availability everywhere, because people need the internet to use the Smart Government. Most importantly, the government needs to solve the problem of lack of responsiveness to customers.

REFERENCES

Abhichandani, T. (2008). *Evaluation of Initiatives for Citizen-Centric Delivery: Analysis of Online Public Transit Information Services*. Germany: VDM Verlag Publishing.

Al-Jenaibi, B. (2012). The scope and impact of workplace diversity in the United Arab Emirates–A preliminary study. *Malaysia Journal of Society and Space*, 8(1), 1–14.

Al-Jenaibi, B. (2011). The practice of Public Relations Departments in increasing social support in the diverse workplaces of the United Arab Emirates. *Cross-Cultural Communication, 7*(3), 41–54.

Al-Jenaibi, B. (2010). Differences between gender treatments in the Work Force. *Cross-Cultural Communication, 6*(2), 63–74.

Al-Khouri, A. M. (2013). Technological and Mobility Trends in E-Government, www.id.gov.ae/assets/zbOAvc6B.pdf.aspx

Al-Khouri, A. M (2012). E-Government Strategies The Case of the United Arab Emirates (UAE). *European Journal of ePractice,* 2012, 135-140

Al-Khouri, A. M., & Bal, J. (2007). 'Electronic Government in the GCC Countries,' International. *Journal Of Social Sciences, 1*(2), 83–98.

Al-khaleej Times. (2012). UAE among emerging e-Government leaders. Retrieved from http://www.khaleejtimes.com/mobile/inside.asp?xfile=/data/todayevent/2012/September/todayevent_September18.xml&section=todayevent

Al-Shafi, S. (2012). Free Wireless Internet park Services: An Investigation of Technology Adoption in Qatar from a Citizens Perspective. *Journal of Cases on Information Technology, 10*(3), 21–34. doi:10.4018/jcit.2008070103

Al-Shafi, S., & Weerakkody, V. (2008). The Use Of Wireless Internet Parks To Facilitate Adoption And Diffusion Of E-Government Services: An Empirical Study In Qatar. *Proceedings of the 14th Americas Conference on Information Systems (AMCIS 2008),* Toronto, Ontario.

As-Saber, S., Hossain, K., & Srivastava, A. (2007). Technology, society and government: In search of an eclectic framework. *Electronic Government. International Journal (Toronto, Ont.), 4*(2), 156–178.

Atkinson, R. D., & Castro, D. D. (2008). Digital Quality of Life: Understanding the Personal and Social Benefits of the Information Technology Revolution. *Proceedings of the Information Technology and Innovation Foundation* (pp. 137–145). Retrieved from www.itif.org/files/DQOL.pdf

Australia (2003). An Over Review of the E-government Benefits Study. Retrieved April 20, 2015 from: www.finance.gov.au/agimo-archive/__data/assets/file/.../benefits.pdf

Backus, M. (2001). E-Governance and Developing Countries, Introduction and examples. Retrieved from www.iicd.org/files/report3. doc

Beynon-Davies, P. (2007). Models for Smart Government, Transforming Government. *People Process Policy, 1*(1), 7–28.

Bhattacharya, D., Gulla, U., & Gupta, M. P. (2012). E-service quality model for Indian government portals: Citizens' perspective. *Journal of Enterprise Information Management, 25*(3), 246–271. doi:10.1108/17410391211224408

Burn, J. & Robins, G. (2003). Moving towards e-government: a case study of organizational change processes. *Logistics Information Management, 3*(2), 25-35.

Bwalya, K. J. (2015). *E-Government in Emerging Economies: Adoption, E-Participation, and Legal Frameworks*. Hershey, PA: IGI Global Publishing.

Bwalya, K. J., & Healy, M. (2010). Harnessing e-government adoption in the SADC region: a conceptual underpinning. *Electronic journal of e-government,8*(1), 23-32.

Castells, M. (2009). *The Rise of the Network Society: The Information Age - Economy, Society, and Culture* (2nd ed., Vol. I). Chichester: John Wiley & Sons. doi:10.1002/9781444319514

Colesca, S. E. (2009). Understanding Trust in e-Government, Inzinerine Ekonomika – Engineering Economics, 3, 7–15.

Cournède, B., Goujard, A., & Pina, Á. (2013). How to Achieve Growth-and Equity-friendly Fiscal Consolidation?.

Dubai eGovernment. (2013). eGovernment to 24/7 smart government. Retrieved from http://www.dsg.gov.ae/SiteCollectionImages/Content/DeG%20Documents/June-2013-en.pdf

Fan, W., & Yan, Z. (2010). Factors affecting response rates of the web survey: A systematic review. *Computers in Human Behavior, 26*(2), 132–139. doi:10.1016/j.chb.2009.10.015

Feldstein, A., & Gower, K. (2015). Using Social Network Analysis to Explore Digital Student Interactions and Business Competency Learning in a Web-based Educational Platform. *International Journal of Information Systems and Social Change, 6*(1), 1–23. doi:10.4018/ijissc.2015010101

Fields, A. (2005). *Discovering statistics using SPSS*. Beverly Hills: Sage Publications.

Flak, L., Nordheim, S., & Munkvold, B. (2008). Analyzing Stakeholder Diversity in G2G Efforts: Combining Descriptive Stakeholder Theory and Dialectic Process Theory e-. *e-Service Journal, 6*(2), 6. doi:10.2979/ESJ.2008.6.2.3

Flanagan, B. (2011). UAE is most high-tech country in Mena region. Retrieved from http://www.thenational.ae/business/technology/uae-is-most-high-tech-country-in-mena-region

Garson, D. G. (2006). *Public Information Technology and E-Governance*. Sudbury, MA: Jones and Bartlett Publishers.

Goldkuhl, G. (2007). What does it mean to serve the citizen in e-services?-Towards a practical theory founded in socio-instrumental pragmatism. *International Journal of Public Information Systems, 3*(3), 135–159.

Goldkuhl, G. (2006). What does it mean to serve the citizen?–Towards a practical theory on public e-services founded in socio-instrumental pragmatism. In K. Axelsson, & G. Goldkuhl (Eds.), *Proceedings of the International Workshop on E-services in Public Administration* (pp. 27-47).

Hirschfeld, B. (2012). Global Thesis Update: Technology and the Arab Spring. Retrieved from http://worldperspectivesprogram.org/2012/04/12/global-thesis-update-technology-and-the-arab-spring/

Hiziroglu, A. (2015). Observing Customer Segment Stability Using Soft Computing Techniques and Markov Chains within Data Mining Framework. *International Journal of Information Systems and Social Change, 6*(1), 59–75. doi:10.4018/ijissc.2015010104

Holgersson, J., Söderström, E., Karlsson, F., & Hedström, K. (2010). Towards a roadmap for user involvement in e-government service development. In Electronic Government (pp. 251-262). Springer Berlin Heidelberg. doi:10.1007/978-3-642-14799-9_22

Hung, S.-Y., Chang, C.-M., & Yu, T.-Y. (2006, July 6-7). Determinants of user acceptance of the... agent: a research note. *Proceedings of the European and Mediterranean Conference on Information Systems (EMCIS)*, Costa Blanca, Alicante, Spain.

Hussein, R., Mohamed, N., Rahman Ahlan, A., & Mahmud, M. (2011). E-government application: an integrated model on G2C adoption of online tax. *Transforming Government: People, Process and Policy*, 5(3), 225–248.

Heeks, R. (2005). *Implementing and Managing E-Government: An International Text*. Sage Publishers.

Jivani, M. (2014). UAE government launches world's first store for smart government application. Retrieved from http://techview.me/2014/03/uagovernment-launches-worlds-first-store-smart-government-application/

Karanasios, S. (2011). New and Emergent ICTs and Climate Change in Developing Countries (R. Heeks & A. Ospina, Eds.). Manchester: Centre for Development Informatics, Institute for Development Policy and Management, SED, International Development Research Centre. Retrieved from http://www.niccd.org/KaranasiosClimateChangeEmergentICTs.pdf

Karlsson, F., Holgersson, J., Söderström, E., & Hedström, K. (2012). Exploring user participation approaches in public e-service development. *Government Information Quarterly*, 29(2), 158–168. doi:10.1016/j.giq.2011.07.009

Linnefell, W. (2014).E-government Policy Formation, Retrieved from www.ejeg.com/issue/download.html?idArticle=348

Lootah, R., & Geray, O. (2006). Dubai eGovernment Case Study. Retrieved from http://www.oecd.org/dataoecd/4/40/36986277.pdf

Meena, R. S. (2009). Environmental-informatics---A solution for long term environmental research. *Global Journal of Enterprise Information System*, 1.

Mohammed bin Rashid. (2013). HH launches Mobile Government, ICT Fund offers AED 200m in support of the initiative: Emirates News Agency. Retrieved from http://www.wam.org.ae/servlet/Satellite?c=WamLocEnews&cid=1290004835681&pagename=WAM%2FWAM_E_Layout&parent=Collection&parentid=1135099399983&rendermode=preview-admin-1135099398363

Mourtada, R., & Alkhatib, F. (2014). 2014 UAE Social Media Outlook: Increasing Connectivity Between Government and Criticizes. Retrieved from www.mbrsg.ae/.../2014-UAE-Socual-Media-Outlook-Increasing-coneections

GCAA strategic Plan. (n. d.). Retrieved from https://www.gcaa.gov.ae/

Pallant, J. (2011). SPSS Survival Manual (4th ed.). Crow's Nest, Australia: Allen & Unwin.

United Nations Survey. (2014). E-government for the Future we Want. Retrieved from http://www2. unpan.org/egovkb/documents/2010/E_Gov_2010_Complete.pdf

UAE government. (2014). EGovernment in the United Arab Emirates 2014. Retrieved from government. ae/.../eGov...E.../22b5703a-d8d5-4fd4-ad1f-5d2c2bcde8cc

Shen, T., Dai, Q., Wang, R., & Gou, Q. (2015). The Impact of Online Additional Reviews on Consumer's Purchase Process. *International Journal of Information Systems and Social Change*, 6(1), 24–40. doi:10.4018/ijissc.2015010102

Varian, H. R., Farrell, J., & Shapiro, C. (2005). *The Economics of Information Technology*. New York: Cambridge University Press.

Weinzierl, A. (2014). Global Agenda Council Launches Guide to Good Government and Trust-Building. Retrieved from www.oecd.org/governance/WEF_NR_FutureOfGovernmentSmartToolb

This research was previously published in the International Journal of Information Systems and Social Change (IJISSC), 7(4); edited by John Wang, pages 20-51, copyright year 2016 by IGI Publishing (an imprint of IGI Global).

Chapter 13
Societal Implications of Current and Emerging "Smart" Technologies

Octavian Mihai Machidon
Transilvania University of Brasov, Romania

ABSTRACT

While every new technology brings along the expected "blessings" for its users, there is also the thick end of the stick, namely the potential hazards and undesired effects that it might cause. Today, smart technologies are being integrated in all social environments, at home, school or work, shaping a new world in which there is a closer interaction and interdependence between human and machine than ever before. This paper identifies the social and ethical concerns that have emerged as a consequence of such changes, and it has been put together after research reviewing literature from various research domains. It addresses the potential implications of smart technologies: the psychological and physical effects on their users, the social changes that they generate, and the concerns of privacy and security.

INTRODUCTION

In today's society "smart" things are in the center of attention: smartphones, smart grids, smart meters, smart cars, smart homes, smart cities, and so on, are just a few examples of (until yesterday) ordinary devices and technologies that turned "smart" in the past decade, becoming connected to the Internet, more attractive to customers, and also more pervasive with regard to the user's everyday life. Smart technologies are gaining more and more presence in the user's everyday life; they even enter highly sensitive environments, such as the home. This leads to the emergence of specific ethical issues concerning these new smart socio-technical systems.

Being based on the concept of ambient intelligence (which describes electronic environments that are sensitive and responsive to the presence of people), smart devices are developed by integrating microprocessors and sensors into ordinary objects, making them able to respond to the environment and interact with humans and other smart objects. Today's technology makes it possible for computers to surround

DOI: 10.4018/978-1-5225-2589-9.ch013

and serve humans in every-day life by working non-intrusively in the background. This is referred to as "ubiquitous computing", a concept that has long been foreseen by scientists and researchers (Weiser, 1993). Ubiquitous computing is a method of achieving the most efficient technology that interacts with and surrounds its users while remaining effectively invisible to them. Research in ubiquitous computing has focused on three main topics: natural interfaces (a diversity of communication capabilities between humans and machines), context-aware applications (the application's capability to adapt its behavior based on information from the physical and computational environment), and automated capture and access (for recording and rendering live experiences) (Abowd & Mynatt, 2000). The European Union 1999 IST Programme Advisory Group (ISTAG) vision statement for Framework Programme 5 describes a scenario where "people will be surrounded by intelligent and intuitive interfaces embedded in everyday objects around us and an environment recognizing and responding to the presence of individuals in an invisible way" (Ahola, 2001). This 1999 vision has become today's reality.

A common feature of all smart technologies and devices is the focus on existential experience, the capability of a particular item to provide situation and context-aware services to the users in real time. For example, a smartphone weather application knows how to update the weather forecast based on the user's location (location-awareness). A smart car navigation system can adapt its route based on real-time traffic and weather analysis. A smart grid provides real-time detection and understanding of conditions in order to get a timely response in emergency situations. All these smart products and services are being designed to co-exist in the emerging global Internet-based information architecture named the "Internet of Things" (IoT). The IoT is considered as the ideal backbone for ubiquitous computing by enabling objects to be easily identifiable in smart environments, easing the retrieval of information from the Internet, thus facilitating their adaptive functionality (Fabian, 2008). IoT enables ordinary objects to communicate and interact, therefore becoming smart and providing smart services.

The research presented in this paper pertains to the field of technoethics. This is an interdisciplinary field that emerged in the 1970's highlighting the moral and social responsibilities that engineers and technologists have for the outcomes of the technological progress and development (Bunge, 1977). Such an approach makes perfect sense given that technology cannot be viewed as a segregated part of society, but a complex, integrated component that influences life on a variety of levels.

Technoethics is defined as an interdisciplinary field concerned with all ethical aspects of technology within a society shaped by technology (Luppicini, 2009). Given the variety and heterogeneity of technologies, and the multitude of fields where they are being used, technoethics brings on the mandatory inter-disciplinary approach needed in order to properly deal with all the technological processes embedded within all the spheres of life.

This paper aims, using a technoethical perspective, to identify the specific ethical challenges and concerns that have been raised by the emergence of new smart technologies and to provide specific ideas on how to properly address them in order to benefit safely from the advantages and strongpoints of these technologies, while limiting the potential unintended consequences.

SMART TECHNOLOGY-SMART USERS?

The smart devices of today are tending to become extensions of the human brain. Latest generation smartphones offer a variety of features and functions that perform tasks which were normally done by the user's brain. For example, now the user doesn't have to remember important facts, because he can always tap into Google and the search engine offers him within seconds the answer he was looking for. Memory is thus one of the first functions of the brain that can be affected by the usage of smart devices.

The voice of the critics that yearn for a less technical age is getting louder, being amplified by studies that show how the offloading of mental functions to smart electronic devices could cause the brain to become less focused and less reliable. A 2010 study by McGill University researchers reports that depending on GPS to navigate may have a negative effect on the brain function, and especially on the hippocampus (the part involved in memory and navigation process). The study also states that participants who relied on their own to get around had better spatial memory, and a greater hippocampus volume than those using GPS navigation (Konishi & Bohbot, 2010).

One can apply the same judgment to smartphones. By storing phone numbers, appointments, context and location-based information, it gives the user's memory one less important exercise to work on. What was before accomplished using the brain's neurons has now been taken over by technology. So the problem is not with technology itself; the problem comes when a device takes over a function that the human brain was perfectly capable of performing on its own.

An important subject that is of great interest to researchers worldwide is the use of technology in the classroom. It was assumed that technological advances may help students learn better. This includes the use of laptops, tablets and smartphones by students while in class. However, despite this good intent, there seems to be troubling unintended consequences with many of these devices when used in the process of learning. Smart devices are ideally supposed to be used during class for taking notes or accessing useful academic information on the Internet, however students tend to multitask and use the social media, surf the web, chat, or email. Having all these temptations at hand makes it hard to resist. The sad outcome is that by doing two things or more at once, students are not able to fully attend to any of them. In the United States, where technology has been present in the classrooms for several years now, more and more voices of academics are asking for it to be banned.

Recent research has identified serious consequences that the use of technology in class has on the students, the level of laptop use being negatively related to the understanding of course material and overall course performance (Fried, 2008). However, there are also many educational advantages: being used wisely, the laptop can facilitate active learning and problem solving by providing a hands-on approach (Barak et al., 2006). A balanced approach is necessary in order to benefit from the advantages that a laptop or other technological device can provide while reducing the negative impacts generated by inappropriate use that disturb the learning process. Faculty should control and limit the use of technology, allowing it only in classes where it is integrated into the course and needed for specific practical applications.

Technology is not distractive only for students. The effects that the introduction of new communication technologies in workplaces has produced with regard to the workers' concentration level have been the subject of several recent studies (Rennecker & Godwin, 2003; Cameron & Webster, 2005). Productivity is directly influenced by the ability of the worker to stay focused and uninterrupted in a quiet work environment. Research has revealed that with the introduction of new technology, the sources of interruption have increased, and also that the main sources today for such interruptions at the workplace are the new communication technologies like e-mail and instant messaging (Röcker, 2010). As they are more attractive and are offering a diverse set of applications and services, smart devices have led to an increase in unwanted interruptions (Cameron & Webster, 2005). Employers might have to carefully control or limit the use of such devices and technologies (like instant messaging, smartphones or tablets) at the workplace in order to maintain an efficient and quiet working environment in cases where productivity or the relationships between coworkers are suffering from technology misuse.

The newly introduced smart technologies are very popular and attractive because they offer high quality sensorial stimulation (high definition video/audio), context and location-aware feedback and the "secure" feeling that everything is under control, anything the user needs to know is only a click away. While these technologies are getting smarter, concerns arise with regard to their effect on the mental capabilities of the user. By offloading cognitive functions that the brain was previously performing to such smart devices, there is the risk of a decrease in the reliability and responsiveness of the brain. Particularly in the case of children, intensive exposure to such devices and technologies might interfere with their development of social skills and intelligence, and with their overall psychological and emotional stability (Healy, 2011).

Given the concerns stated by various research studies, like the ones mentioned above, a deeper understanding of the effects that smart technology has on its users is needed. It is also clear that such a technology brings a lot of assets and has a great potential if used wisely. Further research should focus on identifying the areas and situations that can benefit from using this type of devices, while underscoring control and limitation measures which can be applied to reduce the negative impacts mentioned above. The users and potential beneficiaries of smart technologies, whether students, employees or parents, should be informed on how to properly make use of such smart devices so that they can maximize the benefits and avoid unwanted consequences.

HEALTH RISKS

Another implication of the development of smart devices and technologies is the effect of radiation, since all electrical devices that communicate with each other or the Internet are mainly wireless. As these gadgets are wearable computers, they increase the electromagnetic exposure, the distance between the device and the body influencing intensity. Also, these devices will have a part of their equipment permanently powered on and communicating, in order to maintain their functionality. This will cause a constant exposure to radiation over a long period of time, and on a daily basis – whether at home, in the car, at work or shopping - which affects everyone, both users and non-users of these technologies.

To this date, the way electromagnetic radiation affects physical health is still a subject open to debate for scientists. Several studies were conducted, and many voices point out the potential health hazards that EM (Electromagnetic) radiation could cause in the case of intensive exposure; this environmental effect might have an important impact on the smart object users' lives (Hardell & Sage, 2008; Khurana et al., 2010). There are also concerns about the possibility that RF (Radio frequency) field exposure from cellphones could affect people's health (Blackman, 2009). The World Health Organization (WHO) is conducting an ongoing project named "The International EMF Project" that has been established in order to assess health and environmental effects of exposure to static and time varying electromagnetic fields. In the past decade, the world has known a huge growth in mobile telecommunications, and according to an ITU (International Telecommunication Union) 2013 study there are 6.8 billion mobile-cellular subscriptions worldwide (ITU, 2013). The results of studies of mobile phone risks to human health have been brought to public attention, but many have been criticized due to reported methodological difficulties. However, there are several studies that point out specific hazards that mobile phone radiation causes to different tissues or biological functions (Repacholi, 2001; Khurana et al., 2009; Lönn et al., 2004). While not enough to provide an exhaustive analysis of the subject, these studies should be a strong motivation for deeper research.

A recent and interesting case of a wearable smart device with potential implications on the user's health is the announced Google smart contact lens, which was designed to help people suffering from diabetes monitor their sugar level (Tsukayama, 2014). The device, currently under test, is a soft contact lens integrating a sensor for measuring the glucose level in tears. It also contains a miniature antenna and controller for a wireless transfer of the information gathered by the lens to a device – a computer or monitor – so that the data can be read. Though credited as being of great help to people suffering from diabetes, this device raises important issues regarding the exposure to wireless radiation, since the lens is in permanent contact with the eye and situated in such close proximity to the brain. Extensive medical research is needed for analyzing the implications of the radiation levels for these parts of the body before such a device becomes available, in order to have guarantees that the device can help improve the person's health condition and not worsen it.

Due to the potential health hazards identified by the research quoted above, extensive further research is needed for a complete and objective evaluation of the health and environmental effects of EM and RF radiation, especially given the current technological trends and the speed of pervasive computing devices in penetrating public and private spaces. Already in many countries "electromagnetic hypersensitivity" has become a social issue, with many people claiming to have medical problems due to exposure to nearby electronic devices. Even though it is still weakly defined and not a recognized medical condition due to its variety of symptoms and health reactions, it is being considered by the WHO as an existing issue that affects many people around the world that are more sensitive to EM fields than others (Leitgeb, 2009). As the public and private spaces become more and more embedded with computing devices and wireless networks, all the parties involved (government agencies, employers, electric companies, electronic device manufacturers and network providers) should provide detailed information on EMF radiation in such spaces in order to properly inform the general population on the exposure to such fields, and should also work on optimizing the environmental factor, taking into consideration the implications of these technologies for human health.

SOCIAL PERSPECTIVE

The smart technology, regardless of its particular implementation, has become a part of the users' social life, being considered as an enhancement of everyday life. This raises a series of questions about the social and behavioral consequences, as well as issues with regard to the privacy and security of the people using such technologies (Nixon et al., 2004).

While it has become one of the most powerful forces in our lives today, one cannot predict how the technology and most of all the innovations regarding it will impact the society and the individual. Many people cannot conceive modern life without computers or technology. More and more every-day objects are turning "smart", being equipped with ambient-intelligence technology, which leads to an increase in the degree of dependency on these devices. Today one can still choose whether or not to rely on a technological device, but given the current trend, the future is seen as predictably a world full of smart objects, where escaping from this technological dependence might not be possible. Such a high dependence on technology could lead to a transfer of control from the individual user to the respective technological device with regard to a specific task or function (Coroama et al., 2004); it also poses the risk that eventual system failures could lead the user to a perceived feeling of helplessness if relying too heavily on smart technology for everyday tasks (Mattern, 2005). A relevant example is the 1987 crash of the stock markets worldwide (also known as "Black Monday") due to malfunctions in the automated program trading – a mechanism that started to be used on Wall Street to make trade easier when computers became highly available, and in which human decision-making is taken out of the equation, buy or sell orders being generated automatically (Bozzo, 2007).

The "computerization" of the world actually re-shapes many of its attributes, changing the social actions and creating new types of interaction between people. The analysis of the unintended consequences of this evolving technology is very relevant for the influence of the Internet and other technological breakthroughs on peoples' lives. Speed and complexity describe the 21st century society, and the technological progress has moved too fast to have been able to cogently consider what impact one innovation or another might have, before they were introduced. However, more recently the evolution has been more incremental (Karlgaard, 2011; Hilbert & Lopez, 2011) and questions have been raised on what technology has brought to peoples' lives.

In a 2012 study, researchers at Tel-Aviv University (TAU) examined how smartphones have impacted the social behavior of their users. They have found that smartphone users changed their behavior with regard to the phone use in public spaces, being 50 percent less likely than regular cell phone users to be bothered by others using their phone and 20 percent less likely to believe that their private phone conversations were irritating to those around them. Also, the study showed that smartphone users were more "attached" to their devices, feeling lost or tense without their phones, while the regular phone users claimed to be feeling free or quiet (Hatuka & Toch, 2012).

Given the fact that enhanced proactivity is one of the capabilities of smart devices (due to their context-awareness) one of the directions of research is using these technologies to assist elderly people and special groups (small children, people with various disabilities). Nevertheless, this target group confronts both developers and policy makers with a series of sensitive issues and challenges because such technologies may also have opposite effects. They could potentially increase isolation and decrease social interaction since family members or caregivers are no longer needed to be in direct contact with the respective person; they also tend to limit the autonomy of the patient, who becomes more tied to his home and potentially deprived of the community and interactions with places such as assisted living facilities (Kaplan & Litewka, 2008).

For example, monitoring blood pressure and heart rate, performing an ECG (electrocardiography) or measuring oxygen saturation can be performed remotely with such technologies, while the elderly patient is in his home, by devices linked to a central system that sends the measurements to a hospital. Despite improving the patient monitoring process, such a scenario deprives the patient of interaction with another person – a nurse for example, who could drop by to see how he is feeling and monitor his health condition.

All these issues, together with others that regard infringement on personal dignity due to invasive surveillance and lack of privacy make the use of enhanced proactive technologies for assisting special groups a sensitive matter still open for debates (Mäyrä & Vadén, 2013). The design process of such enhanced proactive systems should take into consideration social, psychological and physiological aspects, and should have an integrated approach, leading to a strengthening of human relations and interactions while protecting personal dignity and privacy.

PRIVACY AND SECURITY

The privacy issue is specific to all types of smart technologies, since in order to offer context-aware services, they need to collect personal information. From the tasks and functions performed by the smart devices, one can easily determine personal behavior patterns of the user. Also, because of the location-aware feature of most smart gadgets, the user can be tracked and localized in real time. The presence of smart things in the environment creates an invisible surveillance network with serious implications for public and private life, which leads critics to view this "transformation of the surroundings into responsive artifacts and surveillable objects" as "an attempt at a violent penetration of everyday life" (Araya, 1995). Being embedded into the users' surroundings, the activity of smart devices of scanning and storing data can go unnoticed by the persons concerned.

The smartphone, one of the most popular smart devices, stores information about almost everything the user does. Some of it is transmitted to the service provider (incoming/outgoing calls, text messages, how often the user checks his e-mail or browses the Internet, and his location), other is just stored in the device's memory (photos, videos, contacts, passwords, financial information etc…). Also, the smartphone can continuously track the user's location and keep a detailed profile of his current and recent whereabouts. There are also applications and services that while running in the background, collect and transmit data on the Internet. With the smartphone, the distinction between offline and online is no longer possible, as the device is permanently connected. This is a big change compared to the classic systems that people were used to, which collected and exchanged data only during the time the person was using them.

In the same TAU 2012 study, researchers state that smartphone users change their concept of privacy in public spaces; these users are 70 percent more likely than regular cellphone users to believe their phones offer a high degree of privacy, and are more willing to reveal private information while in public spaces. The researchers also show that smartphones create the illusion of a "private bubble" around their users, so that even if they use their smartphone while in public meeting spaces – like parks, city squares, transportation – the users are more caught up in their technology-based communication than their immediate surroundings (Hatuka & Toch, 2012). The smartphone is able to connect its user through the Internet to other people, having a range of features from live video-calls, interactive multiplayer games, and so on. Therefore, the smartphone turn into a "gateway" to another world, either virtual or real, and its user becomes a person that, while physically in a specific location, is simultaneously immersed into other activities – reading a book, chatting, checking the map or the Internet, thus having his attention and psychosomatic functions split between two parallel levels of existence. This explains the "private bubble" effect and also poses high risks for both the smartphone user and the people around him, since it could lead to accidents or other undesirable problems due to diminishing the user's attention and focus on his immediate surroundings.

Another emerging "smart" system that has the potential to intrude into the users' private life is the smart grid. This is a modernized electricity network that uses an intelligent monitoring system to track all electricity flow, integrate alternative sources of electricity (green power), to reduce cost, save energy and increase transparency. Every consumer is monitored by a smart meter that identifies consumption in detail and communicates the information via a network to the central node for monitoring and billing. This new power grid is being promoted and implemented by many governments; its implementation is also a priority in the EU's energy policy plan for the next decade (Giglioli et al., 2010).

Despite of its advantages, the smart grid is being questioned because of its potential to undermine users' privacy, and also because having such a complex architecture and offering remote access to the home power networks of millions of users, any security flaw could be very dangerous (Hadley et al., 2010). By turning "smart", the power grid will increase the amount of personal information available about the users. Infrastructure components together with the consumer devices will acquire data and send it on the network. The new smart meters will provide measurements of the energy use not only at the end of the billing period, but at much shorter intervals, as short as every few minutes.

These periodic readings can offer intimate details about what's going on inside the home: the approximate number of people living there, when they are present, when they are awake or asleep. Also, taking into consideration the fact that the energy fluctuations of many home appliances are somewhat unique, the readings could also reveal what type of appliance was on at a certain moment of the day, and maybe even its make and model (Quinn, 2009). Thus, such a detailed power usage data collection could lead to a potential abusive surveillance. Recent research has proved the ability of extracting even more detailed information from the energy consumption readings, such as the TV channel that is on at a certain moment (Greveler et al., 2012). Since the identifiable information gathered by the smart meters is enough to provide such a detailed perspective of one's intimate life inside his home, special care should be taken by legislators and researchers in charge with implementing the smart grid. A solution needs to be reached that offers household and industrial consumers strong guarantees regarding their privacy. This requires a clear distinction between data needed for billing purposes, which can be collected at a low frequency (once or twice a month) and needs to be linked to a particular individual, and high frequency data (collected every few minutes) that should be anonymized, thus protecting the individual's privacy while maintaining the grid's functionality.

Another concept that has been the subject of many publications and conferences in recent years is the smart Home. This is a house or other living environment that embeds technology for allowing devices and systems to be controlled automatically. Such a home can thus automatically adjust the temperature, level of security and other features by operating a Home Area Network (HAN) than connects the various home devices and communicates with the outside world over the Internet (Networking, 2002). It is considered that this enhancement will allow isolated and passive units like ordinary houses or office buildings to achieve an improved energy-efficiency level, and with this stated goal there is an increasing number of such projects under way, many of them being funded by the European Union's Seventh Framework Programme (EU FP7) (Karnouskos et al., 2011).

An important step in the design and implementation of smart Homes is the development of smart appliances. These are interconnected by means of machine-to-machine (M2M) communications, a concept describing various network protocols that enable connecting and remote-controlling machines with low-cost, scalable and reliable technologies (Niyato et al., 2011); this makes home appliances accessible and controllable through the Internet. They also take advantage of the smart grid's bidirectional communication interface and send detailed individual power usage information to a central data office where it is accessible to the utility provider or the user.

According to a 2013 Research and Markets report (Research and Markets, 2013), the leading vendors of the household appliances market like Whirlpool, Electrolux, Samsung and LG are increasing R&D (research and development) investments in the design and development of smart appliances. The same report states that the mentioned vendors consider this market to have huge potential, with its main driver being the increasing need for power-efficient appliances. However, the cost of smart appliances is still higher than that of their classical counterparts. Even so, according to the same report, analysts have forecasted the smart appliances market to grow at a CAGR (Compounded Annual Growth Rate) of 11.9 percent over the period 2012-2016.

Having in the intimacy of one's home various interconnected sensors and smart devices raises further issues regarding the risks of privacy breaches. Such a scenario changes the way personal data is collected – not by filling a form or taking part in a survey, but while cooking, sleeping or doing ordinary household activities. The information collected in this way can be exposed over a public network and other people can have access to it. Even if the personal data gathered by one smart device might look harmless at a first glance, combined with other information gathered by other devices it might lead to the creation of a digital copy of one's life (Korff, 2013). With such an increased attention from the major worldwide vendors, R&D in smart appliances should take into consideration security and privacy aspects, since it is much easier to ensure high privacy and security levels for systems in the design and development stages, than to have to deal with these sensitive and important issues afterwards, when resolving them could prove to be a greater engineering challenge.

In trying to protect personal data when dealing with the issues described above, both legal and technological approaches are necessary in order to develop "smarter" privacy and security mechanisms. Lawmakers must enact special laws regarding data protection that should stipulate clearly what types of information can and cannot be collected and sent by electronic devices with regard to user privacy, and what type of data is considered personal. Also, manufacturers and utility/network providers should be required to explicitly mention if the specific device/service collects personal data, what type and in what amount so that the users are informed about potential privacy risks.

Alongside the legal protection, the smart devices and services mentioned above should adapt and implement privacy-enhancing technologies (PET), an approach to protecting personal data conceived by engineers and supported by privacy activists (Korff, 2013) that involves data anonymization and identity management among other privacy protection mechanisms. Such a joint effort uniting lawmakers, researchers and engineers is needed in order to properly deal with the privacy threats raised by these new enhanced proactive technologies.

CONCLUSION

In today's world, technology has entered all the environments, whether public or private, bringing along a series of challenges derived from the close bond that has been established between these new devices and the people using them or being near them.

Being "smart", and thus offering context-aware feedback, and a multitude of functions meant to ease the owner's life, these devices raise concerns due to the risk of over-relying on technology at the expense of using the natural cognitive functions as before.

Smart devices tend to become items of wearable computing, they raise important issues regarding the exposure to electromagnetic and radiofrequency radiation; non-users are also affected, since almost every public or private space is technologized, and devices communicate with one another or the Internet through wireless networks.

Also, the constant information flow (containing personal data regarding location, decisions, contacts, preferences) from such devices towards the operators or the Internet (social networks) makes the privacy and the security of the users more vulnerable than ever before.

As shown in this paper, such technologies, together with their many assets and potential applications, have ethical and societal implications in various domains and this means that future research in this direction must have a broadened perspective, with various sources of information, an interdisciplinary view and, most of all, a preemptive approach. Future research on any new smart technology should try to find out how and to what degree that particular technology changes and affects the user. Since the technology is getting smarter, the privacy and security mechanisms that protect the users and non-users of these technologies must also adapt and become smart, in order to cope with the newly emerged challenges. Both legal and technical actions should be taken in order to properly regulate the use of the newly enhanced proactive systems and services.

A major challenge for the future is coping with the dynamic behavior of these technologies; the design and release of new smart devices and services are happening constantly and at a very high rate, thus generating new concerns in many directions. Future research should be proactive, taking into consideration all these implications while showing flexibility and creativity in order to anticipate the challenges and issues of these technologies and prevent potential dangerous consequences before they can occur.

ACKNOWLEDGMENT

This paper is supported by the Sectoral Operational Programme Human Resources Development (SOP HRD), ID134378 financed from the European Social Fund and by the Romanian Government.

REFERENCES

Abowd, G. D., & Mynatt, E. D. (2000). Charting past, present, and future research in ubiquitous computing. [TOCHI]. *ACM Transactions on Computer-Human Interaction, 7*(1), 29–58. doi:10.1145/344949.344988

Ahola, J., (2001). Ambient Intelligence, *ERCIM News*, No. 47.

Araya, A. A. (1995). Questioning ubiquitous computing. In *Proceedings of the 1995 ACM 23rd annual conference on Computer science* (pp. 230-237). ACM. doi:10.1145/259526.259560

Barak, M., Lipson, A., & Lerman, S. (2006). Wireless Laptops as Means For Promoting Active Learning In Large Lecture Halls. *Journal of Research on Technology in Education, 38*(3), 245–263. doi:10.1080/15391523.2006.10782459

Blackman, C. (2009). Cell phone radiation: Evidence from ELF and RF studies supporting more inclusive risk identification and assessment. *Pathophysiology, 16*(2), 205–216. doi:10.1016/j.pathophys.2009.02.001 PMID:19264460

Bozzo, A. (2007). Players Replay the Crash. *CNBC*. Retrieved February 18, 2014, from http://www.cnbc.com/id/21136884

Bunge, M. (1977). Towards a technoethics. *The Monist, 60*(1), 96–107. doi:10.5840/monist197760134

Cameron, A. F., & Webster, J. (2005). Unintended consequences of emerging communication technologies: Instant messaging in the workplace. *Computers in Human Behavior*, *21*(1), 85–103. doi:10.1016/j.chb.2003.12.001

Coroama, V., Bohn, J., & Mattern, F. (2004, October). Living in a smart environment - implications for the coming ubiquitous information society. In Proceedings of the 2004 IEEE International Conference on Systems, *Man and Cybernetics* (Vol. 6, pp. 5633-5638).

Fabian, B. (2008). *Secure name services for the Internet of Things*. Unpublished doctoral dissertation, Humboldt-Universität zu Berlin, Wirtschaftswissenschaftliche Fakultät.

Fried, C. B. (2008). In-class laptop use and its effects on student learning. *Computers & Education*, *50*(3), 906–914. doi:10.1016/j.compedu.2006.09.006

Giglioli, E., Panzacchi, C., & Senni, L. (2010). How Europe is approaching the smart grid. *McKinsey on Smart Grid report, McKinsey & Company*. Retrieved November 13, 2014, from http://www.mckinsey.com/client_service/electric_power_and_natural_gas/latest_thinking/mckinsey_on_smart_grid

Greveler, U., Justus, B., & Loehr, D. (2012). *Multimedia content identification through smart meter power usage profiles*. Computers, Privacy and Data Protection.

Hadley, M., Lu, N., & Deborah, A. (2010). Smart-grid security issues. *IEEE Security and Privacy*, *8*(1), 81–85. doi:10.1109/MSP.2010.49

Hardell, L., & Sage, C. (2008). Biological effects from electromagnetic field exposure and public exposure standards. *Biomedicine and Pharmacotherapy*, *62*(2), 104–109. doi:10.1016/j.biopha.2007.12.004 PMID:18242044

Hatuka, T., & Toch, E. (2012). Smart-Spaces: Smartphone's Influence on Perceptions of the Public Space. *Toch Research Group, Tel-Aviv University*. Retrieved October 29, 2013, from http://www.aftau.org/site/News2?page=NewsArticle&id=16519

Healy, J. M. (2011). *Endangered Minds: Why Children Dont Think And What We Can Do About I*. New York, NY: Simon and Schuster.

Hilbert, M., & López, P. (2011). The world's technological capacity to store, communicate, and compute information. *Science*, *332*(6025), 60–65. doi:10.1126/science.1200970 PMID:21310967

ITU (International Telecommunication Union). (2013). ICT Facts and Figures –. *WORLD (Oakland, Calif.)*, *2013*, http://www.itu.int/en/ITU-D/Statistics/Documents/facts/ICTFactsFigures2013-e.pdf Retrieved February 24, 2014

Kaplan, B., & Litewka, S. (2008). Ethical challenges of telemedicine and telehealth. *Cambridge Quarterly of Healthcare Ethics*, *17*(04), 401–416. doi:10.1017/S0963180108080535 PMID:18724880

Karlgaard, R. (2011). Is Technological Progress Slowing Down? *Forbes Magazine*. Retrieved February 15, 2014, from http://www.forbes.com/sites/richkarlgaard/2011/12/21/is-technological-progress-slowing-down/

Karnouskos, S., Weidlich, A., Kok, K., & Warmer, C. et al.. (2011). Field trials towards integrating smart houses with the smart grid. In *Energy-Efficient Computing and Networking* (pp. 114–123). Springer Berlin Heidelberg. doi:10.1007/978-3-642-19322-4_13

Khurana, V. G., Hardell, L., Everaert, J., Bortkiewicz, A., Carlberg, M., & Ahonen, M. (2010). Epidemiological evidence for a health risk from mobile phone base stations. *International Journal of Occupational and Environmental Health*, *16*(3), 263–267. doi:10.1179/oeh.2010.16.3.263 PMID:20662418

Khurana, V. G., Teo, C., Kundi, M., Hardell, L., & Carlberg, M. (2009). Cell phones and brain tumors: A review including the long-term epidemiologic data. *Surgical Neurology*, *72*(3), 205–214. doi:10.1016/j.surneu.2009.01.019 PMID:19328536

Konishi, K., & Bohbot, V. D. (2010). Grey matter in the hippocampus correlates with spatial memory strategies in human older adults tested on a virtual navigation task. In *Proceedings of the 40th Society for Neuroscience annual meeting*, San Diego.

Korff, S. (2013). PETs in Your Home – How Smart is That? *Symposium on Usable Privacy and Security (SOUPS)*, Newcastle, UK

Leitgeb, N. (2009). Electromagnetic hypersensitivity. In *Advances in electromagnetic fields in living systems* (pp. 167–197). Springer New York. doi:10.1007/978-0-387-92736-7_5

Lönn, S., Ahlbom, A., Hall, P., & Feychting, M. (2004). Mobile phone use and the risk of acoustic neuroma. *Epidemiology (Cambridge, Mass.)*, *15*(6), 653–659. doi:10.1097/01.ede.0000142519.00772.bf PMID:15475713

Luppicini, R. (2008). The emerging field of technoethics. In R. Luppicini & R. Adell (Eds.), *Handbook of Research on Technoethics* (pp. 1–19). Hershey, PA: Information Science Reference. doi:10.4018/978-1-60566-022-6.ch001

Mattern, F. (2005). Leben und Lernen in einer von Informationstechnologie durchdrungenen Welt – Visionen und Erwartungen. In M. Franzen (Ed.), *Lernplattformen (Web-Based Training 2005)* (pp. 39–61). Dübendorf, Switzerland: EMPA-Akademie.

Mäyrä, F., & Vadén, T. (2013). Ethics of Living Technology: Design Principles for Proactive Home Environments. *Human IT. Journal for Information Technology Studies as a Human Science*, *7*(2).

Nixon, P. A., Wagealla, W., English, C., & Terzis, S. (2004). *Security, privacy and trust issues in smart environments. Technical report of the Global and Pervasive Computing Group. Department of Computer and Information Sciences.* Glasgow, Scotland: University of Strathclyde.

Niyato, D., Xiao, L., & Wang, P. (2011). Machine-to-machine communications for home energy management system in smart grid. *IEEE Communications Magazine*, *49*(4), 53–59. doi:10.1109/MCOM.2011.5741146

Quinn, E. (2009). Privacy and the new energy infrastructure. *SSRN eLibrary*.

Rennecker, J., & Godwin, L. (2003). Theorizing the unintended consequences of instant messaging for worker productivity. *Sprouts: Working Papers on Information Environments. Systems and Organizations*, 3. Retrieved January 30, 2014, from: http://sprouts.aisnet.org/190/1/030307.pdf

Repacholi, M. H. (2001). Health risks from the use of mobile phones. *Toxicology Letters*, *120*(1), 323–331. doi:10.1016/S0378-4274(01)00285-5 PMID:11323191

Research and Markets. (2013). Global Smart Appliances Market 2012-2016. Retrieved February 24, 2014, from http://www.researchandmarkets.com/research/xdchz5/global_smart

Röcker, C. (2010). Social and technological concerns associated with the usage of ubiquitous computing technologies. *Issues in Information Systems*, *11*(1)

Tsukayama, H. (2014). Google's smart contact lens: What it does and how it works. *The Washington Post*. Retrieved February 20, 2014 from http://www.washingtonpost.com/business/technology/googles-smart-contact-lens-what-it-does-and-how-it-works/2014/01/17/96b938ec-7f80-11e3-93c1-0e888170b723_story.html

Valtchev, D., & Frankov, I. (2002). Service gateway architecture for a smart home. *IEEE Communications Magazine*, *40*(4), 126–132. doi:10.1109/35.995862

Weiser, M. (1993). Some computer science issues in ubiquitous computing. *Communications of the ACM*, *36*(7), 75–84. doi:10.1145/159544.159617

This research was previously published in the International Journal of Technoethics (IJT), 6(1); edited by Rocci Luppicini, pages 60-70, copyright year 2015 by IGI Publishing (an imprint of IGI Global).

Chapter 14
ZatLab Gesture Recognition Framework:
Machine Learning Results

André Baltazar
Catholic University of Portugal, Portugal

ABSTRACT

The main problem this work addresses is the real-time recognition of gestures, particularly in the complex domain of artistic performance. By recognizing the performer gestures, one is able to map them to diverse controls, from lightning control to the creation of visuals, sound control or even music creation, thus allowing performers real-time manipulation of creative events. The work presented here takes this challenge, using a multidisciplinary approach to the problem, based in some of the known principles of how humans recognize gesture, together with the computer science methods to successfully complete the task. This paper is a consequence of previous publications and presents in detail the Gesture Recognition Module of the ZatLab Framework and results obtained by its Machine Learning (ML) algorithms. One will provide a brief review the previous works done in the area, followed by the description of the framework design and the results of the recognition algorithms.

INTRODUCTION

Gestures are the principal non-verbal, cross-modal communication channel, and they rely on movements for different domains of communication (Volpe, 2005). Children start to communicate by gestures (around 10 months' age) even before they start speaking. There is also an ample evidence that by the age of 12 months children are able to understand the gestures other people produce (Rowe & Goldin-meadow, 2009). For the most part gestures are considered an auxiliary way of communication to speech, though there are also studies that focus on the role of gestures in making interactions work (Roth, 2001). We use our hands constantly to interact with things. Pick them up, move them, transform their shape, or activate them in some way. In the same unconscious way we gesticulate in communicating fundamental

DOI: 10.4018/978-1-5225-2589-9.ch014

ideas: stop; come closer; go there; no; yes; and so on. Gestures are thus a natural and intuitive form of both interaction and communication (Watson, 1993).

There is so much information contained in a gesture that is natural to think about using it besides simple human-to-human communication. However, the use of technology to understand gestures is still somehow vaguely explored, it has moved beyond its first steps but the way towards systems fully capable of analyzing gestures is still long and difficult (Volpe, 2005). Probably because if in one hand, the recognition of gestures is somehow a trivial task for humans, in other, the endeavor of translating gestures to the virtual world, with a digital encoding is a difficult and ill-defined task. It is necessary to somehow bridge this gap, stimulating a constructive interaction between gestures and technology, culture and science, performance and communication. Opening thus, new and unexplored frontiers in the design of a novel generation of multimodal interactive systems.

In this case one developed a framework to recognize human gestures automatically and use its information to enhance an artistic performance. This paper describes briefly the ZatLab Framework (for more detailed description please see (Baltazar & Martins, 2015)) and will focus on the empirical results of the Gesture Recognition Module that sustain it.

First one will review the literature on gesture research, followed by the framework proposal, implementation and results.

BACKGROUND

The field of human movements and gesture analysis has, for a long time now, attracted the interest of many researchers, choreographers and dancers. Thus, since the end of the last century, a significant corpus of work has been conducted relating movement perception with music (Fraisse, 1982).

Among the research community on this subject, there are works that stand out as important references on how video analysis technologies have provided interesting ways of movement-music interaction. Early works of composers Todd Winkler (Winkler, 1995) and Richard Povall (Povall, 1998), or the choreographer Robert Weschler work with Palindrome[1]. Also, Mark Coniglio continued development of his Isadora[2] programming environment, plus the groundbreaking work Troika Ranch[3] has done in interactive dance.

Other example of research in this field is the seminal work of Camurri, with several studies published, including an approach for the recognition of acted emotional states based on the analysis of body movement and gesture expressivity (Castellano, Villalba, & Camurri, 2007) and one of the most remarkable and recognized works, the EyesWeb software (Camurri et al., 2000).

Also, Bevilacqua, at IRCAM-France worked on projects that used unfettered gestural motion for expressive musical purposes (Bevilacqua, Müller, & Schnell, 2005; Bevilacqua & Muller, 2005; Dobrian & Bevilacqua, 2003). Chronologic speaking first development consisted of software to receive data from a Vicon motion capture system, translate and map it into music controls and other media controls such as lighting (Dobrian & Bevilacqua, 2003). Then this evolved to the development of the toolbox "Mapping is not Music" for Max/MSP, dedicated to mapping between gesture and sound (Bevilacqua et al., 2005). And in parallel (Bevilacqua & Muller, 2005) presents the work of the a gesture follower for performing arts, which indicates in real-time the time correspondences between an observed gesture sequence and a fixed reference gesture sequence.

Likewise, Nort and Wanderley (Nort, Wanderley, & Van Nort, 2006) presented the LoM toolbox. This allowed artists and researchers access to tools for experimenting with different complex mappings that would be difficult to build from scratch (or from within Max/MSP) and which can be combined to create many different control possibilities. This includes rapid experimentation of mapping in the dual sense of choosing what parameters to associate between control and sound space as well as the mapping of entire regions of these spaces through interpolation.

Another important work, published in 2011, is the one of Gillian (Gillian, Knapp, & O'Modhrain, 2011). He presented a machine learning toolbox that has been specifically developed for musician-computer interaction. His toolbox features a large number of machine learning algorithms that can be used in real-time to recognize static postures, perform regression and classify multivariate temporal gestures.

Also in 2009, the author made part of the project "Kinetic controller driven adaptive and dynamic music composition systems"[4]. One of the aims of the project was to utilize video cameras as gestural controllers for real-time music generation. The project included the development of new techniques and strategies for computer-assisted composition in the context of real-time user control with non-standard human interface devices. The research team designed and implemented real-time software that provided tools and resources for music, dance, theatre, installation artists, interactive kiosks, computer games, and internet/web information systems. The accurate segmentation of the human body was an important issue for increased gestural control using video cameras. In the International Computer Music Conference (ICMC) of 2010 the author published a paper (Baltazar, Guedes, Gouyon, & Pennycook, 2010), presenting an algorithm for real-time human body skeletonization for Max/MSP. This external object for Max/MSP was developed for the technology available at that time, a computer webcam capturing video in two dimensions. The algorithm was inspired by existing approaches and added some important improvements, such as means to acquire a better representation of the human skeleton in real-time.

The output of the algorithm could be used to analyze in real-time the variation of the angles of the arms and legs of the skeleton, as well as the variation of the mass center position. This information could be used to enable humans to generate rhythms using different body parts for applications involving interactive music systems and automatic music generation. Nevertheless, the common CV problems of image segmentation using a two-dimensional webcam, reduced the applications of the algorithm.

By the end of 2010 a new sensor was launched, with three-dimension video capture technology, that changed the way the human body could be tracked, the Microsoft Kinect camera (Zeng & Zhang, 2012). The Kinect impact has extended far beyond the gaming industry. Being a relatively cheap technology, many researchers and practitioners in computer science, electronic engineering, robotics, and even artists are leveraging the sensing technology to develop creative new ways to interact with machines. Being for health, security or just entertainment purposes.

For instance, Yoo (Yoo, Beak, & Lee, 2011) described the use of a Microsoft Kinect to directly map human joint movement information to MIDI.

Also, using a Kinect, the author published a first version of the framework in ARTECH 2012 conference (Baltazar, Martins, & Cardoso, 2012). The paper described a modular system that allows the capture and analysis of human movements in an unintrusive manner (using a custom application for video feature extraction and analysis developed using openFrameworks). The extracted gesture features are subsequently interpreted in a machine learning environment (provided by Wekinator (Fiebrink, Trueman, & Cook, 2009)) that continuously modifies several input parameters in a computer music algorithm (implemented in ChucK~ (Wang, Cook, & others, 2003). That paper was one of the first steps for the framework presented in the following section. The development of the aforementioned ZatLab Framework led to other publications describing it, such as (Baltazar & Martins, 2014), (Baltazar & Martins, 2015). This paper will go into further details, describing the machine learning recognition algorithms that were used and its results.

THE ZATLAB (ZtS) FRAMEWORK

The framework will take the view that perception primarily depends on the previous knowledge or learning. Just like humans do, first the framework will have to "learn" gestures and their main features so that later it can identify them. It is however planned to be flexible enough to allow learning gestures on the fly. In this particular case, while developing a framework to be used on a stage, by a dancer or performer, one wanted to allow as much freedom of movements as possible without being intrusive on the scene. The less the performer had to change is routine (by wearing sensors, markers or specific clothes) the better. That, together with the low cost of the technology (that allows the framework to reach to a broader number of performers), led to the decision of using the optical Motion Capture (MOCAP) option instead of others. The challenge of choosing this path resides on the development of sensor and Computer Vision (CV) solutions, and their respective computational algorithms.

Designed to be efficient, the resulting system can be used to recognize gestures in the complex environment of a performance, as well as in "real-world" situations.

An overview of the proposed gesture recognition framework is presented in Figure 1. The ZtS is a modular framework that allows the capture and analysis of human movements and the further recognition of gestures present in those movements.

Thus, using an optical approach, the Data Acquisition Module will process data from a Microsoft Kinect or a Vicon Blade MoCap. However, it can be easily modified to have input from any type of data acquisition hardware. The data acquired will go through the Data Processing Module. Here, it is processed in terms of movement analysis and feature extraction. This module has also access to the database where it can record or load files. These can include: gestures, an entire captured performance, or features extracted from the movements. Once the features are extracted, these are processed by the Gesture Recognition Module using two types of Machine Learning (ML) algorithms: Dynamic Time Warping (DTW) and Hidden Markov Models (HMM) (explained in the following section). If a gesture is detected, it is passed to the Processing Module and this will store it, represent it or pass it to the Trigger Output Module.

In the Trigger Output Module, the selected movement features or the detected gestures are mapped into triggers. These triggers can be continuous or discrete and can be sent to any program that supports the OSC communication protocol (Wright, Freed, Lee, Madden, & Momeni, 2001). Next section describes in detail the Gesture Recognition Module. If the reader wants to know more about the framework, this was presented in more detail at a previous publication (Baltazar & Martins, 2015).

Gesture Recognition Module

The gesture recognition in Human-Computer Interaction (HCI) has many similarities with other areas of research. Being encompassed in a more general area of pattern recognition, stand out, in particular, the similarities with speech or handwriting recognition. Being these areas already more developed in

Figure 1. The ZatLab framework architecture diagram

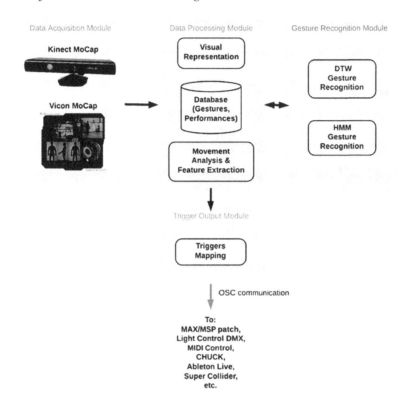

scientific terms, it is natural to try to mirror the various techniques applied in these areas to gesture recognition (Corradini, 2001).

Considering a gesture G can be described as a sequence of feature vectors, it can be assumed that the best way to describe it is to gather N sequences (prototypes) of that gesture (performed in different ways). Therefore, when in recognition mode, an unknown input can be compared against each one of these N prototypes and, taking into account the measures and criteria chosen, a degree of similarity can be assigned.

Although it has a high computational cost, a large set of reference patterns N should be used for this comparison, representing each gesture G. The biggest problem with this approach is the choice of a suitable distance measure. The simplest way to define it is by calculating the distances between the corresponding samples of the reference and the unknown input sequences and accumulate the result. Unfortunately, gestures have a variable spatial-temporal structure. They vary when performed by different people and even the same user is not able to perform a gesture exactly the same way several times in a row. This means that, depending on both the speed of the movement performance and the user, the recorded gesture signals can be stretched or compressed.

Therefore, to compare two signals permitting them to have different lengths requires dynamic programming. Learning from speech recognition, since speech shares the varying temporal structure of gestures, an algorithm often used in that field is the Dynamic Time Warping (DTW) (Lawrence Rabiner & Juang, 1993). The DTW algorithm performs a time alignment and normalization by computing a temporal transformation allowing two signals of different lengths to be matched.

Another alternative of dynamic programming is the statistical and probabilistic approach, such as Hidden Markov Model (HMM). It is a rich tool used for gesture recognition in diverse application domains. Probably, the first publication addressing the problem of hand gesture recognition is the seminal paper by Yamato (Yamato, Ohya, & Ishii, 1992). In his approach, a discrete HMM and a sequence of vector-quantized (VQ)-labels have been used to recognize six different types of tennis strokes.

In the following sections, one will discuss briefly the principles of both Machine Learning algorithms working on the Gesture Recognition Module, the DTW and the HMM.

Dynamic Time Warping

When two signals with temporal variance must be compared, or when looking for a pattern in a data stream, the signals may be stretched or shrunk along its time axis in order to fit into each other. A comparison made after these operations can give false results because we may be comparing different relative parts of the signals. The DTW is one of the methods to solve this problem (Ten Holt, Reinders, & Hendriks, 2007). The algorithm calculates the distances between each possible pair of the two signals taking into account their associated feature values. With these measured distances, it builds a matrix of accumulated distances and finds the path that guarantees the minimum distance possible between signals. This path represents the best synchronization of both signals and thus, the minimum feature distance between their synchronized points.

Consequently, the DTW has become popular by being extremely efficient as the time-series similarity measure which minimizes the effects of shifting and distortion in time, allowing ``elastic'' transformation of time series in order to detect similar shapes with different phases. It has been used in various fields, such as speech recognition (Lawrence Rabiner & Juang, 1993), data mining (Keogh & Ratanamahatana, 2005), and movement recognition (Corradini, 2001; Gillian et al., 2011).

Hidden Markov Models

HMM (LR Rabiner, 1989; Yamato et al., 1992) are powerful statistical models for representing sequential or time-series data, and have been successfully used in many tasks such as speech recognition, protein/DNA sequence analysis, robot control, and information extraction from text data. HMM have also been applied to hand and face recognition (Nefian & Hayes III, 1998).

The HMM is rich in mathematical structures and has been found to efficiently model spatial-temporal information in a natural way. The model is termed "hidden" because all that can be seen is only a sequence of observations (symbols). It also involves elegant and efficient algorithms, such as Baum-Welch and Viterbi (Viterbi, 1967) for evaluation, learning and decoding.

Formally, an HMM is defined as a quintuple (S, V, Π, A, B) (LR Rabiner, 1989) where $S = \{s_1, ..., s_N\}$ is a finite set of N hidden states (that model a gesture); $V = \{v_1, ..., v_M\}$ is a set of M possible symbols (e.g. features of the gesture) in a vocabulary; $\Pi = \{\pi_i\}$ are the initial state probabilities; $A = \{a_{ij}\}$ are the state transition probabilities; $B = \{b_i(v_k)\}$ are the output or emission probabilities.

Therefore, each HMM is modeled and expressed as $\lambda = (\Pi, A, B)$ where the parameters are:

- π_i - the probability that the system starts at state i at the beginning;
- a_{ij} - the probability of going from state i to state j;

- $b_i\left(v_k\right)$ - the probability of generating symbol v_k at state i.

The generalized topology of an HMM is a fully connected structure, know as an ergodic model, where any state can be reached from any other state. When employed in dynamic gesture recognition, the state index transits only from left to right with time.

EVALUATION AND RESULTS

A challenge when working with ML algorithms is collecting enough real-world data to partition the samples into three substantial sets: training, validation, and testing. The training set is used to fit the models. For model selection, the validation set is used in tuning the model parameters to yield the best results. For model assessment, the chosen model prediction recognition rate is estimated using the previously unseen testing set (Hastie, Tibshirani, & Friedman, 2003)

Regarding the evaluation of both recognition algorithms, one of the main differences, already known, between HMM and DTW is on their training.

In one hand, the DTW is an algorithm that is able to do pairwise comparison of signals, therefore it only needs one example of a ground-truth signal to instantly start looking for a similar. This brings the benefit of simple, immediate training and recognition, which in the purpose of an artistic performance can be a key feature (e.g. for live improvisation). Nevertheless, this simplicity of training has some disadvantages, in particular depending on the signal complexity, as will be reviewed in the next section.

In the other hand, the HMM relies on statistics and probabilities to do a correct recognition. Thus, the more data is used to train it, the better results will be achieved. This implies the gathering of more data until one can start the recognition process. Therefore, one will need more time until accomplish the training (and probably this training should be done immediately before a performance), but the achieved recognition results can compensate the work.

Another key aspect of the evaluation one have to consider, is if the training is done by the same person that is going to use the system or by someone else. This will influence the results of the recognition. Consequently, there are two approaches for testing: the "first-person" and the "third-person" methods. The former consists on using different samples of the same data set (same user) for training, refining and testing (one data set divided for the three functions). The latter comprises the use of different data sets (different users) to train, refine and then test (one different data set for each function).

For the evaluation of these algorithms an experiment was laid out, where 29 users of the framework were asked to execute 10 samples of each of the 5 gestures depicted in Figure 2. This generated a database of 290 samples for each gesture and a total of 1450 gesture samples. Having in mind the enormous variety of gestures a person can perform, this database can be classified as small, nevertheless this can be considered a base test, knowing that if the recognition algorithms perform well enough with this database, then one is on the right track and can expand it in the future.

The next sections describe the evaluations and results made for each recognition algorithm using the recorded gesture database.

Figure 2. Alphanumeric gestures the users were asked to perform

DTW Evaluation and Results

For the DTW evaluation, since it only requires one gesture sample to start the recognition process, it is very difficult to determine one gesture sample that will represent the majority of that gesture database.

Therefore, the first approach taken, using the "third-person" method, was on choosing a random example of each gesture, train the 5 gesture DTW and then testing the models against 90 unknown samples of each gesture (450 test samples total). The second approach, using the "first-person" method, was to go to each data set (50 samples - 10 for each gesture), use one of the samples of each gesture to train the 5 gesture DTW and then testing this against the other 45 samples. Repeat this 10 times to get the 450 sample test for comparison.

The results are depicted in the confusion matrices (Table 1 and Table 2).

Table 1. Confusion matrix of the 450 samples DTW test of each gesture with the "third-person" method

	Gesture	Prediction					Recognition Rate
		0	1	Z	3	8	
Actual	0	44	12	5	7	22	49%
	1	1	86	0	0	3	96%
	Z	2	6	45	14	23	50%
	3	17	0	2	66	5	73%
	8	28	5	2	7	48	53%
							Average Recognition: 64%

Table 2. Confusion matrix of the 450 samples DTW test of each gesture with the "first-person" method

	Gesture	Prediction					Recognition Rate
		0	1	Z	3	8	
Actual	0	51	18	8	12	1	57%
	1	2	86	0	0	2	96%
	Z	0	6	71	12	1	79%
	3	1	5	4	80	0	89%
	8	3	6	13	5	63	70%
							Average Recognition: 78%

It can be perceived an improvement of the results when using the "first-person" method. This may be explained by the fact of each subject executes the gestures in different ways, so when using one of their own gestures as a training set, obviously, this will provide better results. Nevertheless, the results of the "third-person" method are good, in particular for the Gesture "1", which did not change the recognition rate (96%). This may serve as an indicator on the simpler kind of gestures that work best with this recognition method.

The overall recognition rate of the DTW for the five distinct gestures was of 78%. Therefore, one is led to conclude its advantage for real-time improvisation, has the downside of limiting its recognition rate to simple gestures, such as the Gesture "1" (96% recognition rate). One assumes it will perform well distinguishing simple one-direction gestures (e.g. vertical top to bottom gesture, or horizontal left to right gesture).

HMM Evaluation and Results

For this evaluation, the methodology consisted in training one HMM for each gesture (using 130 samples), and refine it using the 70 samples of validation. Once, the best description models are found, these are tested against the 90 remaining samples ("third person" method).

The main refinements made were in respect to the number of hidden states that best suit each gesture description. Therefore, each gesture HMM was trained with 3, 5, 7, 9 and 11 hidden states, then they were analyzed in terms of accuracy rate against the 70 samples. The results are depicted in Table 3.

Regarding Table 3, one can realize that when using 11 hidden states to describe the gestures, their respective performance of recognition decreases. This is probably due to the elevated number of hidden states used, when compared to the number of observable symbols (one is using 12 different observable symbols in this case). Table 3 presents results only up to 11 hidden states, hence from there up the results were getting worse.

The best results, for each gesture, are achieved using the following combination of hidden states:

- Gesture "0" - 9 hidden states - 86%.
- Gesture "1" - 5 hidden states - 100%.
- Gesture "Z" - 9 hidden states - 96%.
- Gesture "3" - 5 hidden states - 96%.
- Gesture "8" - 5 hidden states - 100%.

Table 3. Recognition rate of HMM using different number of hidden states (testing against the 70 refinement samples)

Hidden States	Gestures Recognition Rate (%)					Avg. Recog
	0	**1**	**Z**	**3**	**8**	
3	76%	94%	91%	90%	97%	90%
5	73%	**100%**	91%	**96%**	**100%**	92%
7	79%	100%	91%	96%	100%	93%
9	**86%**	100%	**96%**	91%	100%	**95%**
11	84%	96%	94%	91%	96%	92%

The maximum overall average recognition is obtained when using 9 hidden states for every gesture (95%). Following these results, the HMMs were trained again and tested against the last 90 samples, using two approaches:

1. This approach consisted in training the HMM with the number of hidden states that achieved better results in the refinement test, for each gesture. Thus, considering the former results, the Gesture "0" was trained with 9 hidden states, Gesture "1" with 5, Gesture "Z" with 9, Gesture "3" with 5 and Gesture "8" with 5. The results achieved with this setup are displayed in the confusion matrix present in Table 4.
2. This approach consisted in training every HMM with 9 hidden states, to see if accordingly to the former evaluation, the overall recognition would improve. The confusion matrix is represented in Table 5.

Analyzing both Tables one can observe that the main difference is on the Gesture "3" recognition. When using 5 hidden states (the suitable number of states accordingly to Table 3) this has a 70% recognition rate and when using 9 hidden states, for all gestures, this achieved 90% recognition rate. One is able to realize also that the main confusion made on the Gesture "3" recognition was against Gesture "0".

Table 4. The confusion matrix using different number of hidden states in the training of each HMM

		Prediction					Recognition Rate
	Gesture	0	1	Z	3	8	
	0	83	0	1	1	5	92%
	1	1	89	0	0	0	99%
Actual	Z	0	0	85	3	2	94%
	3	26	0	0	63	1	70%
	8	1	0	0	0	89	99%
	Hidden States	9	5	9	5	5	
						Average Recognition: 91%	

Table 5. The recognition rate using 9 hidden states for every gesture HMM

		Prediction					Recognition Rate
	Gesture	0	1	Z	3	8	
	0	77	1	0	5	7	86%
	1	0	89	0	0	1	99%
Actual	Z	1	0	87	2	0	97%
	3	8	0	0	81	1	90%
	8	0	0	0	0	90	100%
	Hidden States	9	9	9	9	9	
						Average Recognition: 94%	

The performance of the remainder gestures stood almost the same between both tests. Gesture "0" decreased shortly, Gestures "Z" and "8" increased and Gesture "1" remained equal. Overall the recognition rate improved from 91% on the former test to 94% on this, mainly because the aforementioned confusion amongst Gesture "3" and "0" achieved better results.

This leads to the conclusion that the fact of using different number of hidden states to describe different gestures influences the recognition rates, and that in the particular case of this set of gestures, defining a single good number of hidden states for all, provides the best results.

Although there are not implementations exactly like this in the literature, when comparing this recognition rates to similar HMM experiments (Kim, 1999), (Elmezain & Al-Hamadi, 2009) one is able to conclude the results match the former, and are in some cases better.

CONCLUSION

The goal of this research is to foster the use of gestures, in an artistic context, for the creation of new ways of expression. Therefore, this paper proposes a flexible and extensible computer framework for recognition of gestures in real-time. The main advantage of this framework against other works developed in this area is to have a fully functional pipeline of integrated modules, allowing the human movement capture, movement feature extraction, gesture training and its recognition, all in a single application. Consequently, enabling a more straightforward use (specially by the artistic community).

The proposed system is based in a relatively cheap MOCAP system (Microsoft Kinect) and is developed to work without any third-party installations besides the respective capture device drivers. Although this provides a very straightforward use of the framework, it also has some constraints hence the Kinect has limitations in its field of view (with a practical range of capture between 0,8 and 2,5 m) and in its frame rate of 60fps that can compromise the recognition in case of very sudden movements.

The recognition process is based in ML algorithms, namely DTW and HMM. The different training processes and recognition rates achieved justify the use of both methods.

Although, there is not a system working like this, described in the state of art, the experimental validation shown the methods presented in this paper (in particular, the ML algorithms) provide results that compare satisfactorily to other state of the art implementations.

The gestures used for the quantitative evaluation are only a small representative sample of the enormous variety possible of human gestures, nevertheless this experiment can be considered a successful test case, showing the framework is on the right track for the recognition of a broader range of gestures.

A software implementation of the system described in this thesis was also made available as free and open source software. Together with the belief that this work showed the potential of gesture recognition, it is expected that the software implementation may stimulate further research in this area as it can have significant impact in many HCI applications such as interactive installations, performances and Human-Computer Interaction per se.

Regarding future work, one of the main improvements that can be accomplished is the further development of the GUI in order to make the framework even more intuitive and easy to work with.

Also, the current version still requires the prior specification of the number states to train each new HMM. This is a limitation of the current implementation, but the framework is flexible enough to include new approaches to an automatic estimation of the number of hidden states for each HMM.

Moreover, the latency measured by either capture systems should be further studied and research methods to overcome it, either by using anticipatory methods (Rett and Dias, 2007) or new MoCap approaches (e.g. Kinect 2).

It would be also interesting to integrate human movement feature analysis methods previously developed (when there were no 3D cameras available). Works like the human movement rhythm determination done by Guedes (Guedes, 2005) or explore further the emotion contained in the gesture has Camurri intended (Camurri, 2004).

The motivation for this research was drawn from the performative art domain. However, it was always kept in mind that the proposed concepts and methods could be used in other domains. Thus, interesting opportunities for future research comes from extending this framework to other domains and requirements. For instance, one has the future goal of applying these methods in benefit of the earing impaired community.

REFERENCES

Baltazar, A., Guedes, C., Gouyon, F., & Pennycook, B. (2010). *A Real-Time Human Body Skeletonization Algorithm For Max*. Msp / Jitter. In ICMC.

Baltazar, A., Martins, L., & Cardoso, J. (2012). ZATLAB: A Gesture Analysis System to Music Interaction. *Proceedings of the 6th International Conference on Digital Arts (ARTECH '12)*. Retrieved from http://www.inescporto.pt/~jsc/publications/conferences/2012ABaltazarARTECH.pdf

Baltazar, A., Martins, L., & Cardoso, J. (2014). ZatLab: A Framework for Gesture Recognition and Performance Interaction. In *Innovative Teaching Strategies and New Learning Paradigms in Computer Programming*. Hershey, PA: IGI Global

Baltazar, A., Martins, L., & Cardoso, J. (2015). ZatLab: A Framework for Gesture Recognition and Performance Interaction. *Proceedings of the 7th International Conference on Digital Arts (ARTECH '15)*. doi:10.4018/978-1-4666-7304-5.ch011

Bevilacqua, F., & Muller, R. (2005). A gesture follower for performing arts. *Proceedings of the International Gesture conference*. Retrieved from http://www.sdela.dds.nl/cinedebate/gesturalfollower.pdf

Bevilacqua, F., Müller, R., & Schnell, N. (2005). MnM: a Max/MSP mapping toolbox. In *Proceedings of the 2005 conference on New interfaces for musical expression* (pp. 85–88).

Camurri, A., Hashimoto, S., Ricchetti, M., Ricci, A., Suzuki, K., Trocca, R., & Volpe, G. (2000). EyesWeb: Toward Gesture and Affect Recognition in Interactive Dance and Music Systems. *Computer Music Journal*, *24*(1), 57–69. doi:10.1162/014892600559182

Camurri, A., Mazzarino, B., and Ricchetti, M. (2004). Multimodal analysis of expressive gesture in music and dance performances.

Castellano, G., Villalba, S., & Camurri, A. (2007). Recognising human emotions from body movement and gesture dynamics. Affective Computing and Intelligent Interaction (pp. 71-82). Springer. Retrieved from http://link.springer.com/chapter/10.1007/978-3-540-74889-2_7

Corradini, A. (2001). Dynamic time warping for off-line recognition of a small gesture vocabulary. Proceedings of the IEEE ICCV Workshop on Recognition, Analysis, and Tracking of Faces and Gestures in Real-Time Systems (pp. 82–89). doi:10.1109/RATFG.2001.938914

Dobrian, C., & Bevilacqua, F. (2003). Gestural control of music: using the vicon 8 motion capture system. Proceedings of the 2003 conference on New interfaces for musical expression (pp. 161–163). National University of Singapore. Retrieved from http://dl.acm.org/citation.cfm?id=1085753

Elmezain, M., & Al-Hamadi, A. (2009). A Hidden Markov Model-Based Isolated and Meaningful Hand Gesture Recognition. International Journal of Electrical, Computer, and Systems Engineering, 3(3), 156–163. Retrieved from http://www.researchgate.net/publication/228863941_A_Hidden_Markov_Model-Based_Isolated_and_Meaningful_Hand_Gesture_Recognition/file/9fcfd50eaa0bc7fc5f.pdf

Fiebrink, R., Trueman, D., & Cook, P. R. (2009). A metainstrument for interactive, on-the-fly machine learning. NIME. Retrieved from http://www.cs.dartmouth.edu/~cs104/BodyPartRecognition.pdf

Fraisse, P. (1982). Rhythm and Tempo. In D. Deutsch (Ed.), *The Psychology of Music* (pp. 149–180). Academic Press; doi:10.1016/B978-0-12-213562-0.50010-3

Gillian, N., Knapp, R. B., & O'Modhrain, S. (2011). A machine learning toolbox for musician computer interaction. *Proceedings of the 2011 International Conference on New Interfaces for Musical Expression (NIME11)*.

Guedes, C. (2005). The M-Objects: A Small Library For Musical Rhythm Generation And Musical Tempo Control From Dance Movement In Real Time. In Proceedings Of ICMC 2005

Hastie, T., Tibshirani, R., & Friedman, J. (2003). *The Elements of Statistical Learning: Data Mining, Inference, and Prediction.* Springer. Retrieved from http://amazon.com/o/ASIN/0387952845/

Keogh, E., & Ratanamahatana, C. A. (2005). Exact indexing of dynamic time warping. *Knowledge and Information Systems, 7*(3), 358–386. doi:10.1007/s10115-004-0154-9

Kim, J. H. (1999). An HMM-based threshold model approach for gesture recognition. *IEEE Transactions on Pattern Analysis and Machine Intelligence, 21*(10), 961–973. doi:10.1109/34.799904

Nefian, A. V., & Hayes, M. H., III. (1998). Hidden Markov models for face recognition. *Proceedings of the 1998 IEEE International Conference on Acoustics, Speech and Signal Processing (Vol. 5, pp. 2721–2724).*

Povall, R. (1998). Technology is with us. *Dance Research Journal, 30*(1), 1–4. Retrieved from http://www.jstor.org/stable/1477887 doi:10.2307/1477887

Rabiner, L. (1989). Tutorial on Hidden Markov Models and Selected Applications in speech Recognition. *Proceedings of the IEEE.* Retrieved from http://ieeexplore.ieee.org/xpls/abs_all.jsp?arnumber=18626

Rabiner, L., & Juang, B.-H. (1993). Fundamentals of Speech Recognition (1st ed.). Prentice Hall. Retrieved from http://amazon.com/o/ASIN/0130151572/

Rett, J., & Dias, J. (2007). Human-robot interface with anticipatory characteristics based on laban movement analysis and Bayesian models. *Proceedings of the IEEE 10th International Conference on Rehabilitation Robotics ICORR '07* (pp. 257–268). IEEE. doi:10.1109/ICORR.2007.4428436

Roth, W.-M. (2001). Gestures: Their Role in Teaching and Learning. *Review of Educational Research, 71*(3), 365–392. doi:10.3102/00346543071003365

Rowe, M. L., & Goldin-meadow, S. (2009). development. *First Language, 28*(2), 182–199. doi:10.1177/0142723707088310 PMID:19763249

Ten Holt, G. A., Reinders, M. J. T., & Hendriks, E. A. (2007). Multi-dimensional dynamic time warping for gesture recognition. *Proceedings of the Thirteenth annual conference of the Advanced School for Computing and Imaging (Vol. 119)*.

Van Nort, D., Wanderley, M. M., & Van Nort, D. (2006). The LoM Mapping Toolbox for Max/MSP/Jitter. *Proceedings of the International Computer Music Conference*, New Orleans, USA.

Viterbi, A. J. (1967). Error bounds for convolutional codes and an asymptotically optimum decoding algorithm. *IEEE Transactions on* Information Theory, *13*(2), 260–269. doi:10.1109/TIT.1967.1054010

Volpe, G. (2005). Expressive Gesture in Performing Arts and New Media: The Present and the Future. *Journal of New Music Research, 34*(1), 1–3. doi:10.1080/09298210500123820

Wang, G., Cook, P., & Associates. (2003). ChucK: A concurrent, on-the-fly audio programming language. *Proceedings of International Computer Music Conference* (pp. 219–226). Retrieved from http://nagasm.org/ASL/icmc2003/closed/CR1055.PDF

Watson, R. (1993). A survey of gesture recognition techniques (technical report tcd-cs-93-11). Trinity College. Retrieved from http://citeseerx.ist.psu.edu/viewdoc/download?doi=10.1.1.51.9838&rep=rep1&type=pdf

Winkler, T. (1995). Making motion musical: Gesture mapping strategies for interactive computer music. In *ICMC Proceedings* (pp. 261–264).

Wright, M., Freed, A., Lee, A., Madden, T., & Momeni, A. (2001). Managing complexity with explicit mapping of gestures to sound control with osc. *Proceedings of the International Computer Music Conference* (pp. 314–317).

Yamato, J., Ohya, J., & Ishii, K. (1992). Recognizing Human action in Time-sequential Images using Hidden Markov Model. *Proceeding of the 1992 IEEE Computer Society Conference on Computer Vision and Pattern Recognition CVPR '92*. Retrieved from http://ieeexplore.ieee.org/xpls/abs_all.jsp?arnumber=223161

Yoo, M. J., Beak, J. W., & Lee, I. K. (2011). Creating Musical Expression using Kinect. *Visualcomputing*. Retrieved from http://visualcomputing.yonsei.ac.kr/papers/2011/nime2011.pdf

Zeng, W., & Zhang, Z. (2012). Multimedia at Work Microsoft Kinect Sensor and Its Effect.

ENDNOTES

[1]   http://www.palindrome.de
[2]   http://www.troikatronix.com/isadora.html
[3]   http://www.troikaranch.org/
[4]   http://smc.inescporto.pt/kinetic/

This research was previously published in the International Journal of Creative Interfaces and Computer Graphics (IJCICG), 7(2); edited by Ben Falchuk and Adérito Fernandes-Marcos, pages 11-24, copyright year 2016 by IGI Publishing (an imprint of IGI Global).

Chapter 15

ZatLab:
Programming a Framework for Gesture Recognition and Performance Interaction

André Baltazar
Catholic University of Portugal, Portugal

Luís Gustavo Martins
Catholic University of Portugal, Portugal

ABSTRACT

Computer programming is not an easy task, and as with all difficult tasks, it can be faced as tedious, impossible to do, or as a challenge. Therefore, learning to program with a purpose enables that "challenge mindset" and encourages the student to apply himself in overcoming his handicaps and exploring different theories and methods to achieve his goal. This chapter describes the process of programming a framework with the purpose of achieving real time human gesture recognition. Just this is already a good challenge, but the ultimate goal is to enable new ways of Human-Computer Interaction through expressive gestures and to allow a performer the possibility of controlling (with his gestures), in real time, creative artistic events. The chapter starts with a review on human gesture recognition. Then it presents the framework architecture, its main modules, and algorithms. It closes with the description of two artistic applications using the ZatLab framework.

INTRODUCTION

There is so much information in a simple gesture. Why not use it to enhance a performance? We use our hands constantly to interact with things. Pick them up, move them, transform their shape, or activate them in some way. In the same unconscious way we gesticulate in communicating fundamental ideas: stop; come closer; go there; no; yes; and so on. Gestures are thus a natural and intuitive form of both interaction and communication (Watson, 1993). Children start to communicate by gestures (around 10 months age) even before they start speaking. There is also ample evidence that by the age of 12 months children are able to understand the gestures other people produce (Rowe & Goldin-meadow, 2009). For

DOI: 10.4018/978-1-5225-2589-9.ch015

the most part gestures are considered an auxiliary way of communication to speech, tough there are also studies that focus on the role of gestures in making interactions work (Roth, 2001).

It is also important to understand that whereas all gestures derive from a chain of movements, not all movements can be considered gestures (Kendon, 1994). Gestures are the principal non-verbal, cross-modal communication channel, and they rely on movements for different domains of communication (Volpe, 2005). Looking at the Merriam-Webster dictionary[1], one will find the word "gesture" means a movement usually of the body or limbs that expresses or emphasizes an idea, sentiment, or attitude, as well as the use of motions of the limbs or body as a means of expression.

Gestures and expressive communication are therefore intrinsically connected, and being intimately attached to our own daily existence, both have a central position in our (nowadays) technological society.

However, the use of technology to understand gestures is still somehow vaguely explored, it has moved beyond its first steps but the way towards systems fully capable of analyzing gestures is still long and difficult (Volpe, 2005). Probably because if in one hand, the recognition of gestures is somehow a trivial task for humans, in other, the endeavor of translating gestures to the virtual world, with a digital encoding is a difficult and ill-defined task. It is necessary to somehow bridge this gap, stimulating a constructive interaction between gestures and technology, culture and science, performance and communication. Opening thus, new and unexplored frontiers in the design of a novel generation of multimodal interactive systems.

This chapter describes the entire process of learning how to program and implement a framework that enables the recognition of gestures in real-time and their use for artistic purposes. Therefore, first one will review the literature on gesture research, followed by the framework proposal, implementation and application.

BACKGROUND

Introduction

As Godoy (Godøy & Leman, 2009) refers, there is no clear definition of what a gesture is: "Given the different contexts in which gestures appear, and their close relationship to movement and meaning, one may be tempted to say that the notion of gesture is too broad, ill-defined, and perhaps too vague." This framework is focused on gesture recognition, so there is intrinsically a demand for the explanation and definition of the terms that are not well clarified.

This section is dedicated to the understanding and definition of a gesture and how it can be captured and recognized. It will also discuss the previous works published on this research field and present a review and technologically comparison of the different Motion Capture (MoCap) systems available nowadays. This section will provide valuable input for the development of the proposed framework.

Gestures

The human movement (Zhao & Badler, 2001) can be involuntary, subconscious, that occurs for biological or physiological purposes (e.g. blinking, breathing, balancing), or voluntary, conscious like those task-driven actions such as speaking or running to get somewhere. There is also a wide class of movements that fall in between these two, having both the voluntary and involuntary qualities. Such movements are the ones that occur in an artistic performance or music concert and perhaps unconsciously with other activities. These can range from leg and foot coordination enabling walking, till the communicative gestures, such as facial expressions, expressive limb gestures and postural attitude. The communicative gestures are the focus of this work and thus, their definition is of central importance.

A good perspective on how to distinguish movement from gesture is given by Kurtenbach and Hulteen (Wachsmuth & Fröhlich, 1998), they state that "A gesture is a motion of the body that contains information. Waving goodbye is a gesture. Pressing a key on keyboard is not a gesture because the motion of a finger on its way to hitting a key is neither observed nor significant. All that matters is which key was pressed. Pressing the key is highlighted as the meaning-bearing component, while the rest of the movement of the person is considered irrelevant.".

Actually, there is no single universally accepted definition of what a gesture actually is. Depending on the domain of research one will find different meanings (Zhao & Badler, 2001). These domains can range from the psychological-linguistic, to the cognitive science or the performative arts. In the following subsections the different approaches are explained.

Gestures in the Psychological-Linguistic Domain

In psychological-linguistic domain, there are three authors that have made significant contributions, following the seminal work David Efron started in the 40s (re-issued later (Efron, 1972)). They are Kendon (Kendon, 1970, 1980, 1994), McNeill & Levy (D McNeill & Levy, 1982; David McNeill, 1985, 1992), and Rimé & Schiaratura (Feldman & Rimé, 1991; Rimé, 1982).

Kendon, presented the following definition: "...for an action to be treated as a gesture it must have features which make it stand out as such". Although this is not clearly a definition, it suggests the analysis of features as classification characteristics. Observing the relations between speech and gesture, he proposed his gesticulation theory. A gesture is the "nucleus of movement with definite form and enhanced dynamic qualities (...) preceded by a preparatory movement and succeeded by a movement which either moves the limb back to is rest position or repositions it for the beginning of a new gesture phrase." ((Kendon, 1980) pp.34).

Gestures in the Cognitive Science Domain

The cognitive science domain is a research area also related to psychology but with a strong branch on Artificial Intelligence. The research consists in building cognitive models in order to understand human behavior. If the model can reproduce human behavior under certain assumptions, it will also provide answer about human behavior in different assumptions. By changing these assumptions one can achieve different explorations and thus, different results. The speech and gesture relation has been broadly studied in the cognitive science context (Feyereisen & de Lannoy, 1991), but yielded contradictory hypotheses. These still need to be further investigated and reviewed. Maybe with different approaches from psychology, neurophysiology and even pathology, some day one will be able to delineate the functioning of communicative gesture.

Gestures in the Performing Arts Domain

Gestures are seen as the most appropriate mean of expression for theater and dance. Performers use gestures to communicate to an audience, either if is a comedy or a tragedy, either if a character is good or evil. Thus, through gestures, actors enhance the emotional content of their stories and characters.

For the contemporary dance and avant-garde theater the gesture is not simply a complement or a decoration. It is yes, the source, the cause and the conductor thread (Royce, 1984).

In this performative domain, gestures can have different interpretations due to culture specifications. In ballet, the gesture is based in Greco-Roman ideals of posture and movement. Standing straight, with slow, expansive and gracious movements will portray an elegant and graceful ballerina, while narrow, clumsy and rough movements will be seen as ugly and poor. Also in a play, the director must plan the combined movement of the cast, treating the movement as an extension of the line, mass and form. The actors themselves must be aware the quantity of movement used in a gesture, and how much space they are occupying in a stage, in order to transmit energy or weakness. The length of a gesture, either short or long, its intensity, either strong or soft, everything will add and convey emotional content. One wrong gesture can ruin a character or all the stage dynamics.

Thus, adequately planned, chosen and executed, gestures can create a mood, or a state of mind and arouse an emotional response from the audience (Dietrich, 1983).

Also in the music research field, body movement has been often related to the notion of gesture. The reason is that many musical activities (performance, conducting, dancing) involve body movements that evoke meanings, and therefore these movements are called gestures (Godøy & Leman, 2009).

To summarize, the study of gesture is a broad research field, with long branches extending from the rather philosophical, theoretical approaches, till the more technological, experimental areas. This gives a cross-disciplinary nature to the research (what is good) but also adds to the difficulty on defining precisely what is a gesture. What is common with the different approaches is that a gesture implies expression, communication and a purpose. Is the voluntary act of synthesizing movements to achieve a goal, fulfill an intention.

Recognizing Gestures

Gesture recognition consists in recognizing meaningful expressions of motion by a human, either to communicate or to interact with the environment.

Typically, the meaning of a gesture can be dependent on:

- **The Spatial Information:** Where it occurs;
- **The Temporal Information:** When and how fast it occurs;
- **Pathic Information:** The path it takes;
- **Symbolic Information:** The sign it makes; and
- **Affective Information:** Its emotional quality.

Indeed, gestures can involve the hands, arms, face, or even the entire body. They can be static, where the user assumes a certain pose, or dynamic, where the user treads a set of poses through time. Some gestures can also have both static and dynamic elements.

To detect and recognize all this range of gestures one needs to specify where it begins and where it ends in terms of frames of movement, both in time and space. So the automatic recognition of gestures implies the temporal or spatial segmentation of the movement.

Besides, in order to determine the relevant aspects of a gesture, the human body position, the angles and rotations of its joints as well as their kinetic information (velocities, accelerations) need to be determined. This can be done, either by using sensing devices attached to the user, or using cameras and Computer Vision (CV) techniques.

Next section will provide a review of previous works developed in the area of gesture recognition, with particular emphasis for the performative arts.

Previous Works

The field of human movements and gesture analysis has, for a long time now, attracted the interest of many researchers, choreographers and dancers. Thus, since the end of the last century, a significant corpus of work has been conducted relating movement perception with music (Fraisse, 1982). The important role of the human body in complex processes such as action and perception, and the interaction of mind and physical environment has been acknowledged originating new concepts such as embodiment (the argument that the motor system influences our cognition, just as the mind influences bodily actions) and enactive (the human mind organizes itself through interaction with the environment) (Varela, Thompson, & Rosch, 1993). Along with these relatively new concepts, many approaches have been proposed to translate the human physical movement and gesture into digital signals for further observation, study or plainly so that one can use them to control musical parameters in algorithmic music composition systems.

Already in the 90s, Axel Mulder (Mulder, 1994) characterized three techniques for tracking/capturing human movements that still remains an important reference. Accordingly to him, the human movement tracking systems can be classified as inside-in, inside-out and outside-in systems.

Inside-in systems are defined as those that employ sensors and sources that are both on the body (e.g. a glove with piezo-resistive flex sensors). The sensors generally have small form-factors and are therefore especially suitable for tracking small body parts. Whilst these systems allow for capture of any body movement and allow for an unlimited workspace, they are also considered obtrusive and generally do not provide 3D world based information.

Inside-out systems employ sensors on the body that sense artificial external sources (e.g. a coil moving in a externally generated electromagnetic field), or natural external sources (e.g. a mechanical head tracker using a wall or ceiling as a reference or an accelerometer moving in the earth gravitational field). Although these systems provide 3D world-based information, their workspace and accuracy is generally limited due to use of the external source and their form factor restricts use to medium and larger sized body parts.

Outside-in systems employ an external sensor that senses artificial sources or markers on the body, e.g. an electro-optical system that tracks reflective markers, or natural sources on the body (e.g. a video camera based system that tracks the pupil and cornea). These systems may suffer from occlusion, and a limited workspace, but they are considered the least obtrusive. Due to the occlusion it is hard or impossible to track small body parts unless the workspace is severely restricted (e.g. eye movement tracking systems). The optical or image based systems require sophisticated hardware and software and may be therefore expensive.

Following this least obtrusive Outside-In technique, several projects with the purpose of creating and controlling electronic music have been developed since the mid 1990s. Early works of composers Todd Winkler (Winkler, 1995) and Richard Povall (Povall, 1998), or the choreographer Robert Weschler work with Palindrome[2]. Also, Mark Coniglio continued development of his Isadora[3] programming environment, plus the groundbreaking work Troika Ranch[4] has done in interactive dance, stand out as important references on how video analysis technologies have provided interesting ways of movement-music interaction.

Other example of research in this field is the seminal work of Camurri, with several studies published, including:

- An approach for the recognition of acted emotional states based on the analysis of body movement and gesture expressivity (Castellano, Villalba, & Camurri, 2007). By using non-propositional movement qualities (e.g. amplitude, speed and fluidity of movement) to infer emotions, rather than trying to recognize different gesture shapes expressing specific emotions, they proposed a method for the analysis of emotional behavior based on both direct classification of time series and a model that provides indicators describing the dynamics of expressive motion cues;
- The Multisensory Integrated Expressive Environments (a. Camurri, Volpe, Poli, & Leman, 2005), a framework for mixed reality applications in the performing arts such as interactive dance, music, or video installations, addressing the expressive aspects of nonverbal human communication;
- The research on the modeling of expressive gesture in multimodal interaction and on the development of multimodal interactive systems, explicitly taking into account the role of non-verbal expressive gesture in the communication process (A. Camurri, Mazzarino, & Ricchetti, 2004). In this perspective, a particular focus is on dance and music as first-class conveyors of expressive and emotional content;
- The Eyesweb software (A. Camurri et al., 2000), one of the most remarkable and recognized works, used toward gestures and affect recognition in interactive dance and music systems.

Also Bevilacqua, at IRCAM-France worked on projects that used unfettered gestural motion for expressive musical purposes (Bevilacqua, Müller, & Schnell, 2005; Bevilacqua & Muller, 2005; Dobrian & Bevilacqua, 2003). The first involved the development of software to receive data from a Vicon motion capture system and to translate and map it into music controls and other media controls such as lighting (Dobrian & Bevilacqua, 2003). The second (Bevilacqua et al., 2005) consisted in the development of the toolbox "Mapping is not Music" (MnM) for Max/MSP, dedicated to mapping between gesture and sound. And the third (Bevilacqua & Muller, 2005) presents the work of the a gesture follower for performing arts, which indicates in real-time the time correspondences between an observed gesture sequence and a fixed reference gesture sequence.

Likewise, Nort and Wanderley (Nort, Wanderley, & Van Nort, 2006) presented the LoM toolbox. This allowed artists and researchers access to tools for experimenting with different complex mappings that would be difficult to build from scratch (or from within Max/MSP) and which can be combined to create many different control possibilities. This includes rapid experimentation of mapping in the dual sense of choosing what parameters to associate between control and sound space as well as the mapping of entire regions of these spaces through interpolation.

Schacher (Schacher, 2010) searched answers for questions related to the perception and expression of gestures in contrast to pure motion-detection and analysis. Presented a discussion about a specific interactive dance project, in which two complementary sensing modes were integrated to obtain higher-level expressive gestures. Polloti (Polotti & Goina, 2011) studied both sound as a means for gesture representation and gesture as embodiment of sound and Bokowiec (Bokowiec, 2011) proposed a new term, "Kinaesonics", to describe the coding of real-time one-to-one mapping of movement to sound and its expression in terms of hardware and software design.

Another important work, also published in 2011, is the one of Gillian (Gillian, Knapp, & O'Modhrain, 2011). He presented a machine learning toolbox that has been specifically developed for musician-computer interaction. His toolbox features a large number of machine learning algorithms that can be used in real-time to recognize static postures, perform regression and classify multivariate temporal gestures.

Also in 2009, the author made part of the project "Kinetic controller driven adaptive and dynamic music composition systems"[5]. One of the aims of the project was to utilize video cameras as gestural controllers for real-time music generation. The project included the development of new techniques and strategies for computer-assisted composition in the context of real-time user control with non-standard human interface devices. The research team designed and implemented real-time software that provided tools and resources for music, dance, theatre, installation artists, interactive kiosks, computer games, and internet/web information systems. The accurate segmentation of the human body was an important issue for increased gestural control using video cameras. In the International Computer Music Conference (ICMC) of 2010 the author published a paper (Baltazar, Guedes, Gouyon, & Pennycook, 2010), presenting an algorithm for real-time human body skeletonization for Max/MSP. This external object for Max/MSP was developed to be used with the technology available at that time, a computer webcam capturing video in two dimensions. The algorithm was inspired by existing approaches and added some important improvements, such as means to acquire a better representation of the human skeleton in real-time.

The output of the algorithm could be used to analyze in real-time the variation of the angles of the arms and legs of the skeleton, as well as the variation of the mass center position. This information could be used to enable humans to generate rhythms using different body parts for applications involving interactive music systems and automatic music generation. Nevertheless, the common CV problems of image segmentation using a two dimensional webcam, reduced the applications of the algorithm.

By the end of 2010 a new sensor was launched with three dimensions video capture technology, that changed the way the human body could be tracked, the Microsoft Kinect camera (Zeng & Zhang, 2012). The Kinect impact has extended far beyond the gaming industry. Being a relatively cheap technology, many researchers and practitioners in computer science, electronic engineering, robotics, and even artists are leveraging the sensing technology to develop creative new ways to interact with machines. Being for health, security or just entertainment purposes. For instance, Yoo (Yoo, Beak, & Lee, 2011) described the use of a Microsoft Kinect to directly map human joint movement information to MIDI.

Also, using a Kinect, the author published a first version of the framework in ARTECH 2012 conference (Baltazar, Martins, & Cardoso, 2012). The paper described a modular system that allows the capture and analysis of human movements in an unintrusive manner (using a custom application for video feature extraction and analysis developed using openFrameworks). The extracted gesture features are subsequently interpreted in a machine learning environment (provided by Wekinator (Fiebrink, Trueman, & Cook, 2009)) that continuously modifies several input parameters in a computer music algorithm (implemented in ChucK~ (Wang, Cook, & others, 2003). The paper published at ARTECH was one of the steps for the framework presented in the following section of this chapter.

ZATLAB: A FRAMEWORK FOR GESTURE RECOGNITION

The research on the topic of gesture recognition poses challenging demands on the development of software modules and tools so that any proposed hypothesis and algorithms can be objectively implemented and evaluated. The prototypes developed are also important to establish a starting point for future research, therefore enabling the further improvement and validation of the algorithms implemented.

Inevitably, during the development of this project a great deal of work has been invested into software development. Therefore, this section presents the main design requirements and the implementation strategies taken towards the development of a software framework for the analysis of gestures. It also describes in detail the major software contributions.

The framework described in this chapter will take the view that perception primarily depends on the previous knowledge or learning. Just like humans do, the framework will have to learn gestures and their main features so that later it can identify them. It is however planned to be flexible enough to allow learning gestures on the fly. In this particular case, while developing a framework to be used on a stage, by a dancer or performer, one wanted to allow as much freedom of movements as possible without being intrusive on the scene. The less the performer had to change is routine (by wearing sensors, markers or specific clothes) the better. That, together with the low cost of the technology (that allows the framework to reach to a broader number of performers), lead to the decision of using the optical \ac{MOCAP} option instead of others. The challenge of choosing this path resides on the development of sensor and \ac{CV} solutions, and their respective computational algorithms.

Designed to be efficient, the resulting system can be used to recognize gestures in the complex environment of a performance, as well as in "real-world" situations.

An overview of the proposed gesture recognition framework is presented in Figure 1. Summarized descriptions of the main blocks that constitute the proposed system are presented in this section. More detailed discussions about each of the processing stages will appear in the subsequent sections.

The ZtS is a modular framework that allows the capture and analysis of human movements and the further recognition of gestures present in those movements.

Thus, using the optical approach, the Data Acquisition Module will process data from a Microsoft Kinect or a Vicon Blade MoCap. However it can be easily modified to have input from any type of data acquisition hardware. The data acquired will go through the Data Processing Module. Here, it is processed in terms of movement analysis and feature extraction. This will allow providing a visual representation of the skeleton captured and its respective movements features. This module has also access to the database where it can record or load files. These can include: gestures, an entire captured performance, or features extracted from the movements. Once the features are extracted, these are processed by the Gesture Recognition Module using two types of Machine Learning (ML) algorithms: DTW and HMM (explained in the following sections). If a gesture is detected, it is passed to the Processing Module and this will store it, represent it or pass it to the Trigger Output Module.

In the Trigger Output Module the selected movement features or the detected gestures are mapped into triggers. These triggers can be continuous or discrete and can be sent to any program that supports the OSC communication protocol (Wright, Freed, Lee, Madden, & Momeni, 2001).

In the next sections the different modules are presented in detail.

Figure 1. The ZatLab framework architecture diagram

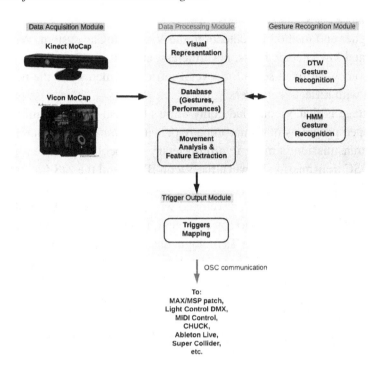

Data Acquisition Module

The human body tracking is one of the key elements of this system. The acquisition of human movements should be as accurate as possible, to ensure a proper analysis of their features and a correct gesture recognition. But the technology chosen must also be available and affordable to a broad range of performers. Also it should be the least intrusive possible. This arises some issues to solve and decisions to make. In a previous research, the author developed a similar module using a 2D webcam, whose output was then analyzed using image segmentation algorithms (as described in the Section 'Previous Works' (Baltazar et al., 2010)). Not being as accurate as one intended, another solution had to be taken.

More recently, with the Microsoft Kinect, it became possible to obtain a full-body detection using the depth information combined with the video signal. When compared with the previous webcam version, it can be said that it becomes simpler to detect and track a foreground object/person. The "traditional" CV tracking problems, such as light constraints or background/foreground separation can be solved using this new hardware.

Another advantage, that is very important in the scope of this framework, it is its portability. Not only it can be used in almost every environment imaginable (indoors, outdoors, good or bad light conditions, crowded places) but also, this sensor can be considered (almost) a Plug & Play technology. After some drivers and software installations, and computer teaks to make it work native, one just needs to plug it to the USB port and start working with it. To users/performers that are not keen to informatics, there is also the alternative to download applications that already have the drivers and software packages embedded, which will work instantly, such as the Synapse[6].

Altogether the Kinect provides a good solution for the framework: it is portable, reasonably cheap, and has high performance tracking capabilities.

There is also a higher end method for detection, the Vicon MoCap system. With the advantages of remarkable tracking and low latency. It has, nevertheless, explicit disadvantages, such as: the cost, the rather complex and somewhat fixed setup for several infrared cameras and the necessity of wearing a special suit equipped with reflective markers.

Another disadvantage is that Vicon Blade only allows the real-time transmission of data to other commercially developed programs of their company or with companies that have established sharing protocols. Also, the transmission is made in a proprietary protocol. Consequently, in the case of this work, the real-time OSC transmission between the Vicon Blade and the ZtS (or any other external program) had to be developed.

This application, named ofxViconOSC, developed within the scope of this project, that can stream, in real-time the data from a Vicon system to any computer, is now available to the scientific community at the Centro de Investigação em Ciência e Tecnologia das Artes (CITAR) website[7].

Having these two technologies available at CITAR, the framework developed should allow working with both.

In summary, this module consists on the acquisition of the real-world data to the virtual-world. It is independent of the hardware chosen to acquire the human movements, but is preset to work with a Microsoft Kinect and a Vicon Blade. In this module the hardware messages are decoded into human body joints to feed the Data Processing Module, presented next.

Data Processing Module

This module is the core of the framework, it will process and redirect the data to other modules keeping the framework functioning properly and effectively.

This receives the skeleton joints data from the aforementioned Data Acquisition Module and processes it for three different purposes:

1. **Visual Representation:** The GUI provides a real-time, intricate but intuitive visual feedback to the user. Not only displays the skeleton of the user as if he was in front of a mirror (a virtual mirror in this case), but it can also display different panels of information. These range from the gestures previously recorded (with velocity and acceleration information attached), the gesture that was recognized, what triggers are setup and if a movement trigger was activated or not. The Figures 2 and 3 present different views of the ZtS GUI.
2. **Database Management:** The database allows the user to record and load several types of files. It is organized in the following folders:
   a. **Performances:** The user can record an entire performance (e.g. a dance, a presentation, etc). It records the several skeleton joints data sequence in a text file. It allows reproducing exactly what was done by the user, thus enabling the review, setup and adjustment of triggers in offline mode (for instance, can be used to record a dance rehearsal, review it and setup some gesture triggers to use on the next rehearsal or in the presentation of the dance performance).
   b. **Gestures:** The user can record a set of gestures for training the recognition algorithms or for gesture notation purposes. Different from the performance recording, hence will be record-

Figure 2. The GUI in development mode and the respective control panel; on the control panel one can see the DTW Mode is activated and the triggers are being sent to "localhost" and port 12345. Next to the gesture is presented its index and some statistics about it, in this case its average speed and acceleration. On the top right corner one can see the algorithm just recognized gesture "1".

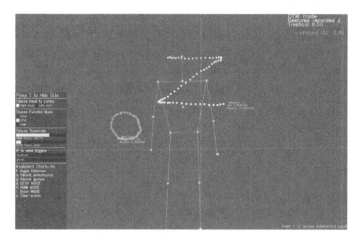

Figure 3. The application of the framework in FestivalIN (further described in next section); the different color particles indicate triggers have been activated (in this case sound triggers).

ing only the segment of data that represent the gesture and its main features (for instance, the circles presented in Figure 2 can be recorded in the database for future use).

c. **Gesture Models:** When the user trains the gesture recognition algorithms, he is creating a gesture model. This model contains the features of the recognition algorithms, necessary for the recognition of a similar gesture. This folder stores the model files.

d. **Drawings:** The user can use the framework in a more lateral purpose for free drawing (like for instance, a virtual board). In this folder the user can store the drawings. The files are stored with a single identifier name consisting on the data and time of the start of recording.

3. **Movement Analysis and Feature Extraction:** Having in mind the results of previous researches (Al-Hamadi, Elmezain, & Michaelis, 2010), the movement features chosen to compute are the ones provided by the Physics kinematic equations[8] to describe movement along with the orientation angle of the gesture path, described next.

From the data acquired one already has the information of the coordinates and the respective time-stamp t for each joint of the human body. Therefore, the following features can be computed.

    a. **Time:** For a given movement segment, its total time can be easily computed by subtracting the first sample time-stamp t_1 from the last sample time-stamp t_n:

$$T = t_n - t_1$$

    b. **Displacement:** Knowing all the coordinates of the movement segment, the total displacement D can be calculated by summing the relative difference among coord_i and the previous coord_{i-1}, from the first sample (i = 1) till the last (n).

$$D = \sum_{i=1}^{n} \left\| \text{coord}_i - \text{coord}_{i-1} \right\|$$

    c. **Velocity:** Also, the velocity and acceleration can be computed. The average velocity will be defined as the quotient of the displacement Δd and the interval time Δt. In the case of consecutive frames (where the Δt is very small) we can assume this is the instantaneous velocity v_i.

$$v_i = \frac{\left| \text{coord}_i - \text{coord}_{i-1} \right|}{t_i - t_{i-1}}$$

And the average velocity can be computed as the sum off all the v_i divided by the number of samples n:

$$v_{avg} = \frac{\sum_{i=1}^{n} \left\| v_i \right\|}{n}$$

    d. **Acceleration:** Similarly, the instantaneous acceleration can be approximated by the average acceleration over a small interval Δt.

$$a_i = \frac{v_i - v_{i-1}}{t_i - t_{i-1}}$$

And the average acceleration can be computed as:

$$a_{avg} = \frac{\sum_{i=1}^{n} \|a_i\|}{n}$$

All the features are extracted within a motion segment. These features are very important to describe the joint movements. Although with these features one is already able to visualize and extract relevant information from the data, the direction of movement the joint takes at each frame is also a key feature for the ML algorithms (explained in the next section). This feature will allow not only to detect immediately if the movement is done from left to right, but also if it is a simple line or something more complex like a circle or a square.

e. **Direction of Movement:** The angle or direction of movement can be calculated using the known coordinates at consecutive frames and applying the arc-tangent function. This is given by the following equation and the result is given in degrees (in this case computed only in two dimensions: Δx is the displacement along the x axis and Δy is the displacement along the y axis).

$$\phi = \arctan \frac{\Delta y}{\Delta x}$$

ϕ ranges from 0° till 360°. This would create a tremendous range of data to be analyzed, in real-time, by the ML algorithms (Al-Hamadi et al., 2010). Also, measuring the direction of the movement in single unit degrees could lead to additional noise in the data. Therefore, it is necessary to normalize the data to an observable "codeword". This can be done by dividing the total range of the angles in 12 equally separated spaces (12 spaces allow to understand differences in increments of 30°). So, the direction of movements is classified accordingly to the degrees belonging to a determined interval. The framework is setup to work with these 12 symbols, but it can be easily adapted to work with more or less. See Table 1 and Figure 4 for better understanding this angle based "codeword".

Having all the features extracted, these are passed to the Gesture Recognition Module, explained next.

Table 1. Angles codeword table

Angle	Codeword Value	Angle	Codeword Value
[0°, 30°]	0	[181°, 210°]	6
[31°, 60°]	1	[211°, 240°]	7
[61°, 90°]	2	[241°, 270°]	8
[91°, 120°]	3	[271°, 300°]	9
[121°, 150°]	4	[301°, 330°]	10
[151°, 180°]	5	[331°, 359°]	11

Figure 4. Examples of gestures recorded and their associated angle orientation codeword; in the case of the circle all the orientation values are present, but the timestamped sequence will reveal if it was executed in clockwise or counter-clockwise motion.

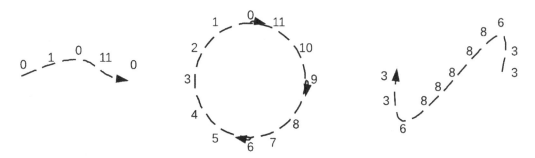

Gesture Recognition Module

The gesture recognition in Human-Computer Interaction (HCI) has many similarities with other areas of research. Being encompassed in a more general area of pattern recognition, stand out, in particular, the similarities with speech or handwriting recognition. Being these areas already more developed in scientific terms, it is natural to try to mirror the various techniques applied in these areas to gesture recognition (Corradini, 2001).

Considering a gesture G can be described as a sequence of feature vectors, it can be assumed that the best way to describe it is to gather N sequences (prototypes) of that gesture (performed in different ways). Therefore, when in recognition mode, an unknown input can be compared against each one of these N prototypes and, taking into account the measures and criteria chosen, a degree of similarity can be assigned.

Although it has a high computational cost, a large set of reference patterns N should be used for this comparison, representing each gesture G. The biggest problem with this approach is the choice of a suitable distance measure. The simplest way to define it is by calculating the distances between the corresponding samples of the reference and the unknown input sequences and accumulate the result. Unfortunately, gestures have a variable spatio-temporal structure. They vary when performed by different people and even the same user is not able to perform a gesture exactly the same way several times in a row. This means that, depending on both the speed of the movement performance and the user, the recorded gesture signals can be stretched or compressed.

Therefore, to compare two signals permitting them to have different lengths requires dynamic programming. Learning from speech recognition, since speech shares the varying temporal structure of gestures, an algorithm often used in that field is the Dynamic Time Warping (DTW) (Lawrence Rabiner & Juang, 1993). The DTW algorithm performs a time alignment and normalization by computing a temporal transformation allowing two signals of different lengths to be matched.

Another alternative of dynamic programming is the statistical and probabilistic approach, such as Hidden Markov Model (HMM). It is a rich tool used for gesture recognition in diverse application domains. Probably, the first publication addressing the problem of hand gesture recognition is the seminal paper by Yamato (Yamato, Ohya, & Ishii, 1992). In his approach, a discrete HMM and a sequence of vector-quantized (VQ)-labels have been used to recognize six different types of tennis strokes.

In this section, one will discuss the principles of both the algorithms working on the Gesture Recognition Module, the DTW and the HMM.

The DTW

When two signals with temporal variance must be compared, or when looking for a pattern in a data stream, the signals may be stretched or shrunk along its time axis in order to fit into each other. A comparison made after these operations can give false results because we may be comparing different relative parts of the signals. The DTW is one of the methods to solve this problem (Ten Holt, Reinders, & Hendriks, 2007). The algorithm calculates the distances between each possible pair of the two signals taking into account their associated feature values. With these measured distances it builds a matrix of accumulated distances and finds the path that guarantees the minimum distance between signals. This path represents the best synchronization of both signals and thus, the minimum feature distance between their synchronized points.

Consequently, the DTW has become popular by being extremely efficient as the time-series similarity measure which minimizes the effects of shifting and distortion in time, allowing "elastic" transformation of time series in order to detect similar shapes with different phases. It has been used in various fields, such as speech recognition (Lawrence Rabiner & Juang, 1993), data mining (Keogh & Ratanamahatana, 2005), and movement recognition (Corradini, 2001; Gillian et al., 2011).

To explain this implementation, first it is important to realize how to proceed in order to recognize a gesture. Regarding a case-study example of an user using his right hand to record and test gesture recognition. This relies in two main procedures:

1. **Recording Gestures:** When recording a gesture, a **vector_of_features** is incremented, at each frame, with several feature values, for instance x, y, z, ϕ where x, y, z are the coordinates and ϕ is the orientation angle of the hand movement. So when the user decides to record a gesture he will really be recording the sequence of movement features he is performing. The user can record as many gestures he wants, thus creating a database of several of these **vector_of_features** stored in a **vector_of_gestures**. This database will be the reference to which the forthcoming "test" gestures will be compared. Refer to Figure 5 to a graphical explanation of the recording procedure.
2. **Recognizing:** Having at least one gesture recorded on the database, the system enters in recognition mode. At each frame the **vector_of_test** will be fed with the same features the previous **vector_of_features**. This vector stores the data, keeping thus a real-time array of features (with size N - the double of space the biggest gesture recorded).

Once it gets *N* feature samples, the system will cyclically divide the movement input at regular intervals creating several **vector_of_test** that will keep charging (**vector_to_dtw**). The system performs the DTW distance of each one of this **vector_of_test** against each **vector_of_features** stored in the **vector_of_gestures**. When the DTW distance to one of the gestures recorded is lower than a determined threshold, the input sequence is recognized as a gesture. Refer to Figure 6 to a graphical explanation of the procedure.

In this case, you can realize the signal being tested in slightly bigger than **Gesture 1** (in Figure 4), nevertheless, is the same gesture in shape. Therefore, despite some distance between both signals, the DTW algorithm will detect it as being similar to Gesture 1 (as intended).

Figure 5. The sequence of gesture features are accumulated in a vector. When the user records the gesture, this sequence will be stored as a new gesture in the vector_of_gestures.

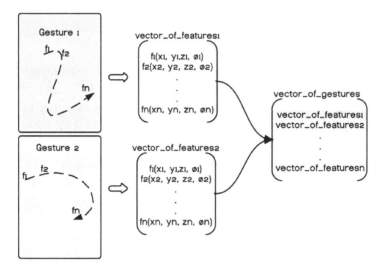

Figure 6. A movement is tested through the DTW distance in order to find if it is present in the Gestures Database. Relating to the previous Figure 5 when testing the entire movement (in blue) it would result in finding the stored Gesture 1 (vector_of_features1).

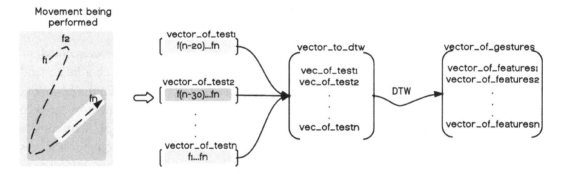

The key point of this algorithm is the construction of the DTW cost matrix. This is built by iteratively finding the minimum Euclidean Distance amongst the components of both vector signals, hence finding the optimal warping path, also named minimum warping distance.

Breaking down into a detailed description each component of **vector_of_test** will be tested against each component of **vector_of_features**. Once the minimum pair-wise distance is found, this distance will be stored in the cost matrix, and proceed to the next component. This cycle repeats until all the components have been analyzed and the cost matrix built. By summing all these minimum distance values along the cost matrix, one will have the shortest warping path, or the minimum distance of the signals. The implementation code was done based on Lemire (Lemire, 2009) approach to DTW algorithm.

The HMM

HMM (LR Rabiner, 1989; Yamato et al., 1992) are powerful statistical models for representing sequential or time-series data, and have been successfully used in many tasks such as speech recognition, protein/DNA sequence analysis, robot control, and information extraction from text data. HMM have also been applied to hand and face recognition (Nefian & Hayes III, 1998).

The HMM is rich in mathematical structures and has been found to efficiently model spatio-temporal information in a natural way. The model is termed "hidden" because all that can be seen is only a sequence of observations (symbols). It also involves elegant and efficient algorithms, such as Baum-Welch and Viterbi (Viterbi, 1967) for evaluation, learning and decoding.

Formally, an HMM is defined as a quintuple S, V, Π, A, B (LR Rabiner, 1989) where $S = \left\{ s_1, ..., s_N \right\}$ is a finite set of N hidden states (that model a gesture); $V = \left\{ v_1, ..., v_M \right\}$ is a set of M possible symbols (e.g. features of the gesture) in a vocabulary; $\Pi = \left\{ \pi_i \right\}$ are the initial state probabilities; $A = \left\{ a_{ij} \right\}$ are the state transition probabilities; $B = \left\{ b_i \left(v_k \right) \right\}$ are the output or emission probabilities.

Therefore, each HMM is modeled and expressed as $\lambda = \left(\Pi, A, B \right)$ where the parameters are:

- π_i: The probability that the system starts at state i at the beginning;
- a_{ij}: The probability of going from state i to state j;
- $b_i \left(v_k \right)$: The probability of generating symbol v_k at state i.

The generalized topology of an HMM is a fully connected structure, know as an *ergodic* model, where any state can be reached from any other state. When employed in dynamic gesture recognition, the state index transits only from left to right with time.

The global structure of the HMM recognition is constructed by training of each HMM $\left(\lambda_1, \lambda_2, ..., \lambda_M \right)$, whereby insertion (or deletion) of a new (or existing) HMM is easily accomplished. λ corresponds to a constructed HMM model for each gesture and M is the total number of gestures being recognized.

When working with HMM there are three basic problems to solve:

1. **Evaluation:** Given a model and a sequence of observations, how do we compute the probability that the observed sequence was produced by the model? Namely, one has to evaluate the probability of an observed sequence of symbols $O = o_1, o_2, ..., o_t$ (where $o_i \in V$) given a particular HMM (λ), e.g. $p \left(O | \lambda \right)$. This is extremely useful, in this case having several competing "models" of gestures, this will allow to find which gesture "model" best matches the observations (of the gesture being performed live).

2. **Decoding:** This is to uncover the hidden part of the model, i.e. to find the state sequence that illustrates best the model. In other words, to find the most likely state transition path associated with an observed sequence. Having a sequence of states $q = q_1, q_2, ..., q_t$ we will want to find $q^* = \arg \max_q p \left(q \char`\^ O | \lambda \right)$.

3.   **Training:** Is the crucial part of HMM, since it will allow adapting the model parameters to the observed training sequence, hence creating the best models for the gestures performed. In other words, is to adjust all the parameters of our model λ to maximize the probability of generating an observed set of sequences O, this is, to find $\lambda^* = \arg \max_\lambda p\left(O|\lambda\right)$.

These three problems already have solutions. The first is solved by implementing part of the Forward-Backward iterative algorithm. The second by using the Viterbi algorithm, and the third by using the Baum-Welch algorithm, which uses the Forward and Backward probabilities calculated previously to update the parameters iteratively.

Although the algorithms are elegant and sophisticated, their implementation is not very straightforward. Consequently, the next paragraphs will explain how these work together in gesture recognition. Specifically the *HMM class* was developed with 3 modes of operation: Train, Evaluate, Test (decode). These are called by using the pointer to the class and choosing the operation mode wanted (1-for testing, 2 - for evaluating, 3- for training). This implementation was based in (Liu, 2009) and (LR Rabiner, 1989).

Again, for a gesture to be recognized, first one will have to "teach" the algorithm how the gesture look like and how it is executed. In the previous DTW approach, one is able to do direct and immediate comparison of signals. In the case of HMM, being a probabilistic model build upon statistics, the "teaching" is not so forthcoming. It will involve the creation of a training set of gestures for each one we wish to detect. Recalling the same case-study proposed before, imagine a user using his right hand to record and test gesture recognition. In order to do so, this module operates in the following fashion.

1.   **Record Gesture Samples:** To train a HMM of a gesture first one needs to create several instances of the same gesture. Thus, using a similar method to the one explained before (Figure 4) one will be recording, at each frame, several feature values of the user movement (kept in **vector_of_features**). The user will record several identical samples of the same gesture being each one stored in a **vector_of_gestures**.
2.   **Create a New HMM:** Having a reasonable amount of examples of the same gesture (defined by the user), when the order to train a new HMM is made, this has to be created and initialized.

For each new HMM the user can dynamically choose the number of hidden states (N_{states}). For instance to create a new HMM with a **vector_of_gestures** and N_{states} one would do:

a.   **vec_hmm_models.push_back(new HMM(vector_of_gestures, N_{states}));**

This creates a new instance of **HMM class** with a new position in the pointer **vec_hmm_models** to it. The matrices of this new HMM are initiated following the next rules:

a.   The initial states probability (matrix N_{states} x 1) is initiated as $1/N_{states}$ to give an equal probability distribution amongst the states.
b.   Considering the gesture is done in one continuous, fluid movement, the transition probability between states should have more weight between the adjacent ones, thus the state transition probability matrix (a_{ij} of size N_{states} x N_{states}) is initiated as exemplified on Table 2.

Table 2. The state transition probability matrix initialization example; the probability is divided amongst adjacent states. The N -ish state is connected to the first, closing thus the probabilities loop.

State	0	1	2	N
0	0, 5	0, 5	0	0
1	0	0, 5	0, 5	0
2	0	0	0, 5	0, 5
N	0, 5	0	0	0, 5

    c.   At last, the state output matrix ($N_{observations}$ x N_{states}), that allows to relate the observed output data ($N_{observations}$) to the state transition, is initiated by distributing equally the probabilities of the output: $1/N_{observations}$.

3.   **Train a HMM:** Having the new HMM created, the system will train it using the samples provided. To do so, the **vector_of_gestures** will be passed to the Baum-Welch algorithm by calling the HMM class with the respective operation mode (mode 3, for training):

    a.   **vec_hmm_models[last]->RunHMM(3, vector_of_gestures);** the train routine will breakdown the **vector_of_gestures** in its constituents (**vector_of_features**). These features are the observed data and with it the algorithm performs a statistical evaluation of the data sequence that will lead to the update of the emission and transition probabilities matrices, modeling thus the hidden states for the gesture performed.

Computing the Baum-Welch

The algorithm takes sequences of observations as input and estimates the new values of transition matrix (a_{ij}) and emission matrix ($b_i(v_k)$) that maximize the probability for the given observations. It runs iterations over the input data and terminate when convergence or certain threshold condition is met, for instance: number of iterations, difference in parameter changes.

The algorithm takes two passes over the data. In the first pass, it uses forward algorithm to construct α probabilities (the pseudo-code for this algorithm is explained in the following section (Computing the Likelihood). In addition to the α probabilities, the algorithm runs a similar backward algorithm to construct β probabilities. The backward probability $\beta(t,i)$ is the probability of seeing observation from o_{t+1} to the end, given that we are in state j at time t .

Based on the α and β probabilities, one can compute the expected number (counts) of transitions ($\xi(i,j)$) from state i to state j at a given observation t ($\gamma(t,i)$).

Part of the pseudo-code for Baum-Welch algorithm is presented in Listing 1. The α probabilities are updated after calling the forward function at line 2. The remaining code computes $\xi(i,j)$ and $\gamma(t,i)$ counts.

With $\xi(i,j)$ and $\gamma(t,i)$ computed, the a_{ij} and $b_i(v_k)$ matrices are updated.

4.   **Verify the Model:** Having the model constructed with its respective emission and transition matrices one can verify if the training was done properly. This is accomplished using the Viterbi algorithm

Listing 1. The pseudo-code for the Baum-Welch algorithm

```
1  initialize all cells of α, β, γ, ξ to 0
2  calculate likelihood ← Forward(o)
3  β(o_T, 1) = 1  // base case t = T, end of sequence
4  for t = o_T to o_1  // cycle to compute the Backward algorithm
5    for i = 1 to N
6      do γ(t,i) = γ(t,i) + (α((t,i) · β(t,i)/likelihood)))
7          for j = 1 to N
8            do β(t,i) = β(t,i) + β(t+1,i)α_{ji}b_{it}
9                ξ(j,i) = ξ(j,i) + (α(t,j)β(t+1,i)α_{ji}b_{it}/likelihood)
```

(computer implementation explained next). This algorithm will provide the sequence of hidden states in respect to the HMM built:

a.   vec_hmm_models[last]->RunHMM(2, 0);

Computing the Viterbi

The Viterbi algorithm finds the most likely path of states that generate the observations. Instead of summing over all α probabilities (like Baum-Welch algorithm does), Viterbi algorithm finds the maximum one and keeps a pointer to trace the state that leads to the maximum probability. The pseudo-code for Viterbi algorithm is given in Listing 2. The input to the algorithm is a sequence of observations and output is a sequence of the most likely states that generate the observation.

Listing 2. The pseudo-code for the Viterbi algorithm

```
1   initialize all cells of α to 0
2   α(o_1, s) = 1  // base case t=1, there are no preceding states
3   for t = o_2 to o_T  // cycle to compute the Viterbi algorithm
4     for i = 1 to N
5       for j = 1 to N
6         if α(t-1,j)a_{ij}b_{it} > αMax(t,i)
7           then αMax(t,i) = α(t-1,j)a_{ij}b_{it}
8               MaxPointer(t,i) = j
9   Seq_of_states = sequence(MaxPointer)
10  return Seq_of_states
```

5.   **Recognizing:** Once having a trained HMM the system can enter in test mode. Again, like in the DTW case (Section ofxDTW) the **vector_of_test** will be fed with the same features of the previous samples used to train the model. In this case the vector will be continuously tested against the trained HMM:

a.   **vec_hmm_models[last]->RunHMM(1, vector_of_test);**

If there are more than one HMM trained, the **vector_of_test** is iteratively tested against all the models N of the **vec_hmm_models[M]**. The highest likelihood HMM is returned by the Forward Algorithm (computer implementation next).

This test is done in regard to each trained model emission and transition probabilities matrices. If the observed test sequence matches the probabilities previously calculated for the model matrices, the likelihood of that sequence will be maximized. Therefore, if that returned likelihood is high enough to surpass a user-defined threshold, the gesture is recognized as belonging to that respective model.

Computing the Likelihood

To compute the likelihood, the Forward algorithm computes the α for the sequence of O observations and N hidden states. This can be viewed as a matrix, where each cell $\alpha\left(o_t, i\right)$ is the probability of being in state i while seeing the observations until t.

An overview of Forward algorithm is shown in the pseudo-code below (Listing 3). The input to the algorithm is a sequence of observations O. The output is the likelihood probability for the observation. The algorithm makes the assumption the first observation in sequence is the start state, and the last observation is the end state.

The Gesture Recognition Module is of paramount importance for this framework. The recognition algorithms (DTW and HMM) can be used in simultaneous or individually, providing different modes of training and recognition.

When a gesture is recognized, this is communicated to the Processing Module that will redirect the information to the Triggers Output Module. Next is the description of this module.

Listing 3. The pseudo-code for the Forward algorithm

```
1  initialize all cells of α to 0
2  α(o₁,s) = 1  //base case t=1, there are no preceding states
3  for t = o₂ to oT  //cycle to compute the Forward algorithm
4      for i = 1 to N
5          for j = 1 to N
6              do α(t,i) = α(t,i) + α(t-1,j)aᵢⱼbᵢₜ
7  likelihood = α(oT,N)
8  return likelihood
```

Triggers Output Module

Paraphrasing Newton third law of movement, "For every action, there is an equal and opposite reaction". This module is responsible for the reaction. It may not be opposing neither equal, but it is definitely a reaction, in this case to a gesture performed.

This module has the setup of what will be the framework reaction to a gesture recognized. This can be internal or external. Internally it can react by generating visual contents on the GUI such as images, information or drawings. And externally it can control anything that directly assumes OSC communication protocol, what nowadays is pretty common.

OSC (Wright et al., 2001) was originally developed to facilitate the distribution of control structure computations to small arrays of loosely coupled heterogeneous computer systems. A common application of OSC is to communicate control structure computations from one client machine to an array of synthesis servers. OSC is a 'transport-independent' network protocol, meaning that OSC data can be carried by any general-purpose network technology. Today most implementations use the main Internet protocols (UDP and TCP/IP) via Ethernet or wireless network connections. Thus, most of the programs used in the performative arts domain (and other domains) allow communication through \ac{OSC}, these range from sound and music control programs, video or light setup and display tables, till computers and robotic hardware.

Therefore, is possible to control a vast amount of events with a gesture. One just have to decide on the trigger mapping and respective OSC syntax.

For each gesture trained in the framework a trigger is assigned. It can be discrete (triggering only events each time gesture is recognized) or continuous (controlling events such as sound pitch or modulation accordingly to a velocity or coordinate value). The triggers can be further customized by the user, but are preset to work in the following fashion:

1. **Discrete Triggering:** Each gesture trained for recognition is associated with a single identifier trigger, matching the gesture index (e.g. Gesture 1, Gesture 2, etc.). When a gesture is recognized a trigger message is sent through OSC, using the following syntax:

```
Gesture index, joint, coord_X, coord_Y, coord_Z, Avg. Velocity, Avg. Acceleration
```

2. **Continuous Triggering:** The default configuration for continuous triggering consists on maintaining a constant communication of the joints kinematic features. For instance, the left hand OSC message will be:

```
HandL, coord_X, coord_Y, coord_Z, Inst. Velocity, Inst. Acceleration
```

In order to create an interesting result one needs to map the triggers to the respective events. As reviewed in Background Section, there are several strategies to do the mapping of the triggers to expressive events. The choice of which to apply is done by the users of the framework. This is, the framework allows the association of triggers to gestures, therefore when the gesture is performed and recognized the trigger is sent. What the user does with that trigger is depends on his creativity or purpose. For instance, on the applications described on the following Section, the triggers were mapped internally to the emission of visual particles and externally to the control of sound events.

This section discussed some of the requirements, choices and the major contributions towards the development of an open source software platform for the computational analysis of gestures.

Some implementation details about the main building blocks of the framework proposed were described, where the efficiency, flexibility and code reusability aspects taken into consideration during the software development, were highlighted. Next section presents two artistic uses of the framework.

FRAMEWORK APPLICATIONS

Introduction

This section presents the artistic applications of the framework. Namely its use in an Interactive Opera, in collaboration with Miso Music Portugal, and the use of the framework as a public interactive installation in the Festival of Creativity and Innovation, in Lisbon, 2013.

Using ZtS in an Artistic Performance

MisoMusic Portugal[9] was commissioned to create an interactive multimedia Opera (to debut in September 2013), by the renown Polish Festival *Warsaw Autumn*[10] (Warszawska Jesień).

Knowing the work developed in the scope of this project, MisoMusic proposed the use of the ZtS framework in the Opera to control real-time audio samples and the direct sound input of the voice of one performer. But before entering on further details about the developments made, the following section will describe briefly the Opera, named "A Laugh to Cry". This will set the benchmark for the work developed in the ZtS framework.

About the Opera "A Laugh to Cry"

A *Laugh to Cry* explores some primary concerns, which have always haunted human beings, and reveals them from the perspective of our contemporary globalized world. The opera is shaped like a meditation on the hegemonic power of the destruction of memory, the devastation of the Earth and even the collapse of humanity. It evolves in the fringes between dream and reality, between the visible and invisible, being divided in several acts where five characters, two sopranos, one bass and two narrators (a female and a male voice), live and dwell constantly between these two parallels. The opera also involves seven acoustic instruments: flute, clarinet, percussion, piano, violin, viola, cello, as well as live electronics and extended video scenography.

A *Laugh to Cry* pursues Miguel Azguime goal, as poet and composer, to grasp an ideal balance between language and music, to merge the language semantic and metaphorical components with its sonic values, in order to achieve his concept of "speech as music and music as speech". A *Laugh to Cry* extends Miguel Azguime research on voice analysis, re-synthesis and processing, aiming at creating a dynamic continuum between timbre, harmony, rhythm and voice spectra.

System Requirements

The framework had to be tailored to the composer/performer (Miguel Azguime) needs. Specifically, he wanted to control sound samples and live voice input with his movements and gestures. In this case, the framework was adapted with several triggers that controlled sounds in a MAX/MSP[11] patch (this patch was developed by a fellow researcher, André Perrotta).

The framework went through a series of tests and refinements, in particular to respond to the composer choices and performer abilities.

In the end the ZtS framework enabled several types of sound control:

- The trigger of sound samples with the movement velocity of the hands of the performer;
- The cycle through eight banks of sound samples by performing a gesture;
- The trigger of capturing a sound action (sound sample or live voice input). The performer was able to freeze a sound when he performed a holding hands pose. This enabled the performer to control the captured sound in terms of pitch, reverb, feedback and loudness. When he wanted he just needed to do a more sudden movement with both hands (exceeding a pre-determined hand movement velocity threshold) to release the sound.

In Figure 7 one can see the hardware setup.

A Microsoft Kinect was used to capture the human body and an Apple MacMini running the ZtS was hidden under a black cloth. The framework was sending the control triggers to the sound computer on the technical regie at 25 meters of distance. One setup a Local Area Network to enable the triggers

Figure 7. The setup used for the opera "A Laugh to Cry"; on the top left image is the view from the technical sound area. The top right and left bottom images present the view of the ZtS setup. The last photo illustrates the view Miguel had when using the system.

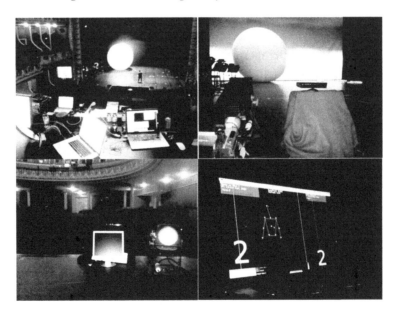

transmission. Also, in this case, the performer wanted the visual feedback to make sure he was in the right position, so there was a 15 inch LCD on stage (also hidden from the audience).

The framework ended up being used for the solo of one of the main Opera characters, performed by Miguel Azguime himself. The ZtS framework travelled with the Opera throughout the entire tour. In the first performances the setup was done by the author of the framework, which also supervised its function during the Opera. Since everything ran smoothly on the first three performances of the Opera (two in Lisbon and one in Poland), for the Sweden leg of the tour (four more presentations) one of the Opera technicians received a brief formation on how to do the setup and execute the ZtS. Important to realize that he did the setup alone and operated the framework on those four shows without any problem, thus revealing the usability of the framework.

In sum, the result of the developments made especially for the Opera use was very interesting. The relation between human movement/gestures and sound manipulation was immediately perceived by the audience, therefore creating a particular arouse during that part of the piece. Of course the principal credit goes to the performer, in this case Miguel, which learned very quickly to interact and get exactly what he wanted from the framework, when he wanted, thus enabling him to add extra layers of emotion and enhancement to the solo he performed.

In the following section is the statement Miguel gave regarding the use of the framework.

Evaluation

Once the Opera presentations were finished, one asked Miguel Azguime, the author/performer and main user of the ZtS framework, to answer a few questions about the system and to transmit his opinion about it. Here is a literal quote of the text he sent.

Since the beginning, in the design of the opera "The Laugh to Cry", were implicit certain technological aspects and modes of interaction, which had not been possible to research, develop and use in previous works. In particular the relationship sound - gesture took this project a clear role that was intended to develop and the Zatlab System developed by André Baltazar came precisely to meet this desire, having been adapted to respond to musical, performative and expressive purpose I intended for a crucial moment of the opera and true climax of the symbolic and narrative discourse thereof.}

Playwright and musical composition itself for this decisive moment in the opera were designed to take advantage of the interaction with the system and conditioned by the type of gestural control offered by the same.

A clear perception to the public that the gesture is that of inducing sound, responsiveness of the system to allow clarification of musical and expressive speech, effectively ensuring the alternation between sudden, rapid, violent gestures, sounds on the one hand and modular suspensions by gesture in total control of the sound processing parameters on the other, constituted a clear enrichment both in terms of communication (a rare cause and effect approach in the context of electronic music and it certainly is one of its shortcomings compared with music acoustic instruments) and in terms of expression by the ability of the system to translate the language and plastic body expression.

Clearly, as efficient as the system may be, the results thereof and eventual artistic validation, are always dependent on composite music and the way these same gestures are translated into sound (or other interaction parameters) and therefore is in crossing gesture with the sound and the intersection of performance with the musical composition (in this case) that is the crux of the appreciation of Zatlab. However, regardless of the quality of the final result, the system has enormous potential as a tool sufficiently open and malleable in order to be suitable for different aesthetic, modes of operation and different uses.

Using ZtS in a Public Interactive Installation

Another application of the system consisted in making it as an interactive installation at FestivalIN[12], Lisbon. The FestivalIN was announced as the biggest innovation and creativity aggregating event being held in Portugal, precisely in Lisbon at the International Fair of Lisbon. It is described as a unique event that integrates, in a practical, dynamic and consistent way, the core concepts associated to Creativity and Innovation.

It presents itself as an absolutely innovative event, anchoring sensorial experiences (physical and virtual interactions), crossing different areas of the Creative Industries. It is a space, which involves people, ideas and experiences and promotes, both nationally and internationally, Portugal most creative possessions, boosting its authors, creators and entrepreneurs in a worldwide scale.

System Requirements

Departing from the developments made to the Opera, the framework was adapted to be more responsive and easy to interact with. The users were able to trigger and control sound samples, much like Miguel did on the Opera, however they did not had the same level of control.

Since the purpose was to install the application at a kiosk and leave it there for people to interact with, the visuals were further developed to create some curiosity and attract users. The human body detection algorithm was also customized in order to filtrate the control, amongst the crowd, to only the person closer and centered to the system.

Figure 8. presents the setup and some interactions with the system. The closet was provided by CITAR. This stored inside a MacMini running the ZtS and had a custom fit opening for a Microsoft Kinect. Outside the visuals were displayed in a 32 inch LCD and the sound was provided by a stereo setup provided by the FestivalIn organization.

Evaluation

The response to the system was very good, in particular amongst the children. All day long there was someone playing with it. The fact that the people were detected immediately either if they were just passing by or really wanted to interact was a key factor to the system popularity. The persons saw their skeleton mirrored on the screen and wave at it, therefore triggering sounds and building up the users' curiosity. Soon enough they understand the system response to their gestures and were engaged, interacting and creating musical expressions.

Figure 8. The setup used for FestivalIn; on the left, the cabinet provided by CITAR, you can notice the Kinect bellow the LCD TV. On the right top, the visuals when someone interacted and left bottom a kid playing with the system.

CONCLUSION

The goal of this research is to foster the use of gestures, in an artistic context, for the creation of new ways of expression. Consequently, the approach taken envisioned the study of the gesture: its understanding, how to capture it (in a non intrusive way) and how to recognize it (in real-time).

Following this study, one concluded the gesture recognition is a rather simple task for the average person, but its automatically recognition, by a machine, is a much more complex task. Therefore, this chapter proposes a flexible and extensible computer framework for recognition of gestures in real-time.

Designed to be causal and efficient, the resulting system can be used to capture and recognize human body gestures, in real-time, paving the way to applications such as interactive installations, computer music interaction, performance events controlling, amongst others.

The main advantage of this framework against other works developed in this area is to have a fully functional pipeline of integrated modules, allowing the human movement capture, movement feature extraction, gesture training and its recognition, all in a single application. Consequently, enabling a more straightforward use (especially by the artistic community).

The proposed system is based in a relatively cheap MoCap system (Microsoft Kinect) and is developed to work without any third party installations besides the respective capture device drivers.

The recognition process is then based in ML algorithms, namely DTW and HMM.

This chapter also described two artistic applications of the framework. One was an interactive artistic installation and the other was its use in an interactive Opera. These applications sustain the artistic relevance of the framework.

In particular regarding its application in the Opera, one can conclude the framework was successfully applied in performance context, recognizing the performer gestures, in real-time, and triggering events. Being the performers the ultimate users of the framework, one reckons their opinion is very important.

Therefore the fact that Miguel Azguime (the Opera performer) considers the use of the framework "constituted a clear enrichment (to the performance) both in terms of communication and in terms of expression" leads to the conclusion the main goal one proposed to achieve (using gestures, in an artistic context, for the creation of new ways of expression) was accomplished.

A software implementation of the system described in this chapter was also made available as free and open source software. Together with the belief that this work showed the potential of gesture recognition, it is expected that the software implementation may stimulate further research in this area as it can have significant impact in many HCI applications such as interactive installations, performances and Human-Computer Interaction *per se*.

FUTURE WORK

After a great deal of investment in the area of algorithm development, which has given rise to the implementation of the framework proposed, there are nevertheless several lines of future work that are now possible to anticipate.

In regard to the present software implementation one of the main improvements that can be accomplished is the further development of the GUI in order to make the framework even more intuitive and easy to work with.

Also, the current version still requires the prior specification of the number states to train each new HMM. This is a limitation of the current implementation, but the framework is flexible enough to include new approaches to an automatic estimation of the number of hidden states for each HMM.

It would be also interesting to apply it on works previous made (when there were not 3D cameras available) and incorporate some of the features analysis into the framework, works like the human movement rhythm analysis done by Guedes or explore the emotion contained in the gesture has Camurri intended.

The motivation for this research was drawn from performative art domain. However, it was always kept in mind that the proposed concepts and methods could be used in other domains. Thus, the main opportunity for future research comes from extending this framework to other domains and requirements. For instance, one has the future goal of applying these methods in benefit to the hearing impaired community.

REFERENCES

Al-Hamadi, A., Elmezain, M., & Michaelis, B. (2010). Hand Gesture Recognition Based on Combined Features Extraction. *International Journal (Toronto, Ont.)*, 1–6. Retrieved from http://www.academia.edu/download/30613967/v6-1-1.pdf

Baltazar, A., Guedes, C., Gouyon, F., & Pennycook, B. (2010). *A Real-time human body skeletonization algorithm for MAX / MSP / JITTER*. ICMC.

Baltazar, A., Martins, L., & Cardoso, J. (2012). ZATLAB: A Gesture Analysis System to Music Interaction. In *Proceedings of 6th International Conference on Digital Arts (ARTECH 2012)*. Retrieved from http://www.inescporto.pt/~jsc/publications/conferences/2012ABaltazarARTECH.pdf

Bevilacqua, F., & Muller, R. (2005). A gesture follower for performing arts. In *Proceedings of the International Gestur*, (pp. 3–4). Academic Press. Retrieved from http://www.sdela.dds.nl/cinedebate/gesturalfollower.pdf

Bevilacqua, F., Müller, R., & Schnell, N. (2005). MnM: a Max/MSP mapping toolbox. In *Proceedings of the 2005 conference on New interfaces for musical expression* (pp. 85–88). Academic Press.

Bokowiec, M. A. (2011). V! OCT (Ritual): An Interactive Vocal Work for Bodycoder System and 8 Channel Spatialization. In Proceedings of NIME 2011 (pp. 40–43). NIME.

Camurri, A., Hashimoto, S., Ricchetti, M., Ricci, A., Suzuki, K., Trocca, R., & Volpe, G. (2000). EyesWeb: Toward Gesture and Affect Recognition in Interactive Dance and Music Systems. *Computer Music Journal*, 24(1), 57–69. doi:10.1162/014892600559182

Camurri, A., Mazzarino, B., & Ricchetti, M. (2004). Multimodal analysis of expressive gesture in music and dance performances. *Gesture-Based*. Retrieved from http://link.springer.com/chapter/10.1007/978-3-540-24598-8_3

Camurri, a., Volpe, G., Poli, G. De, & Leman, M. (2005). Communicating expressiveness and affect in multimodal interactive systems. *IEEE Multimedia, 12*(1), 43–53. doi:10.1109/MMUL.2005.2

Castellano, G., Villalba, S., & Camurri, A. (2007). Recognising human emotions from body movement and gesture dynamics. *Affective Computing and Intelligent*, 71–82. Retrieved from http://link.springer.com/chapter/10.1007/978-3-540-74889-2_7

Corradini, A. (2001). Dynamic time warping for off-line recognition of a small gesture vocabulary. In *Proceedings of Recognition, Analysis, and Tracking of Faces and Gestures in Real-Time Systems,* (pp. 82–89). IEEE. doi:10.1109/RATFG.2001.938914

Dietrich, J. E. (1983). Play Direction (2nd ed.). Prentice Hall. Retrieved from http://amazon.com/o/ASIN/0136833349/

Dobrian, C., & Bevilacqua, F. (2003). Gestural control of music: using the vicon 8 motion capture system. In Proceedings of the 2003 conference on New interfaces for musical expression (pp. 161–163). National University of Singapore. Retrieved from http://dl.acm.org/citation.cfm?id=1085753

Efron, D. (1972). *Gesture, Race and Culture*. Mouton and Co.

Feldman, R. S., & Rimé, B. (Eds.). (1991). Fundamentals of Nonverbal Behavior (Studies in Emotion and Social Interaction). Cambridge University Press. Retrieved from http://amazon.com/o/ASIN/052136700X/

Feyereisen, P., & de Lannoy, J.-D. (1991). Gestures and Speech: Psychological Investigations (Studies in Emotion and Social Interaction). Cambridge University Press. Retrieved from http://amazon.com/o/ASIN/0521377625/

Fiebrink, R., Trueman, D., & Cook, P. R. (2009). A metainstrument for interactive, on-the-fly machine learning. In Proc. NIME (Vol. 2, p. 3). Retrieved from http://www.cs.dartmouth.edu/~cs104/BodyPartRecognition.pdf

Fraisse, P. (1982). Rhythm and Tempo. In D. Deutsch (Ed.), *The Psychology of Music* (pp. 149–180). Academic Press. doi:10.1016/B978-0-12-213562-0.50010-3

Gillian, N., Knapp, R. B., & O'Modhrain, S. (2011). A machine learning toolbox for musician computer interaction. In *Proceedings of the 2011 International Coference on New Interfaces for Musical Expression (NIME11)*. NIME.

Godøy, R. I., & Leman, M. (2009). *Musical Gestures: Sound, Movement, and Meaning*. In R. I. Godøy & M. Leman (Eds.), *Musical Gestures Sound Movement and Meaning* (p. 320). Routledge. Retrieved from http://www.amazon.jp/dp/0415998875

Kendon, A. (1970). Movement coordination in social interaction: Some examples described. *Acta Psychologica*, *32*(0), 101–125. doi:10.1016/0001-6918(70)90094-6 PMID:5444439

Kendon, A. (1980). Gesticulation and speech: two aspects of the process of utterance. In M. R. Key (Ed.), *The Relationship of Verbal and Nonverbal Communication* (pp. 207–227). The Hague: Mouton.

Kendon, A. (1994). Do Gestures Communicate? A Review. *Research on Language and Social Interaction*, *27*(3), 175–200. doi:10.1207/s15327973rlsi2703_2

Keogh, E., & Ratanamahatana, C. A. (2005). Exact indexing of dynamic time warping. *Knowledge and Information Systems*, *7*(3), 358–386. doi:10.1007/s10115-004-0154-9

Lemire, D. (2009, June). Faster Retrieval with a Two-Pass Dynamic-time-warping lower bound. *Pattern Recognition*, 1–26. Retrieved from http://www.sciencedirect.com/science/article/pii/S0031320308004925

Liu, C. (2009). cuHMM: A CUDA implementation of hidden Markov model training and classification. *The Chronicle of Higher Education*.

McNeill, D. (1985). So you think gestures are nonverbal? *Psychological Review*, *92*(3), 350–371. doi:10.1037/0033-295X.92.3.350

McNeill, D. (1992). *Hand and {Mind}: What {Gestures} {Reveal} about {Thought}*. Chicago: University of Chicago Press.

McNeill, D., & Levy, E. (1982). Conceptual Representations in Language Activity and Gesture. In R. J. Jarvella & W. Klein (Eds.), *Speech, Place, and Action* (pp. 271–295). Chichester, UK: Wiley.

Mulder, A. (1994, July). Human movement tracking technology. *Hand*, 1–16.

Nefian, A. V., & Hayes, M. H., III. (1998). Hidden Markov models for face recognition. In *Proceedings of Acoustics, Speech and Signal Processing,* (Vol. 5, pp. 2721–2724). IEEE.

Polotti, P., & Goina, M. (2011). *EGGS in Action*. NIME.

Povall, R. (1998). Technology is with us. *Dance Research Journal*, *30*(1), 1–4. doi:10.2307/1477887

Rabiner, L. (1989). Tutorial on Hidden Markov Models and Selected Applications in speech Recognition. *Proceedings of the IEEE*. Retrieved from http://ieeexplore.ieee.org/xpls/abs_all.jsp?arnumber=18626

Rabiner, L., & Juang, B.-H. (1993). Fundamentals of Speech Recognition. Prentice Hall. Retrieved from http://amazon.com/o/ASIN/0130151572/

Rimé, B. (1982). The elimination of visible behaviour from social interactions: Effects on verbal, nonverbal and interpersonal variables. *European Journal of Social Psychology*, *12*(2), 113–129. doi:10.1002/ejsp.2420120201

Roth, W.-M. (2001). Gestures: Their Role in Teaching and Learning. *Review of Educational Research*, *71*(3), 365–392. doi:10.3102/00346543071003365

Rowe, M. L., & Goldin-meadow, S. (2009). development. *First Language*, *28*(2), 182–199. doi:10.1177/0142723707088310 PMID:19763249

Royce, A. P. (1984). *Movement and Meaning: Creativity and Interpretation in Ballet and Mime*. Indiana Univ Pr. Retrieved from http://amazon.com/o/ASIN/0253338883/

Schacher, J. C. (2010). Motion To Gesture To Sound : Mapping For Interactive Dance. Academic Press.

Ten Holt, G. A., Reinders, M. J. T., & Hendriks, E. A. (2007). Multi-dimensional dynamic time warping for gesture recognition. In *Proceedings of Thirteenth Annual Conference of the Advanced School for Computing and Imaging* (Vol. 119). Academic Press.

Van Nort, D., Wanderley, M. M., & Van Nort, D. (2006). The LoM Mapping Toolbox for Max/MSP/Jitter. In *Proceedings of the International Computer Music Conference*. Academic Press.

Varela, F. J., Thompson, E., & Rosch, E. (1993). *The Embodied Mind: Cognitive Science and Human Experience*. MIT Press. Retrieved from http://books.google.pt/books?id=QY4RoH2z5DoC

Viterbi, A. J. (1967). Error bounds for convolutional codes and an asymptotically optimum decoding algorithm. *IEEE Transactions on* Information Theory, *13*(2), 260–269. doi:10.1109/TIT.1967.1054010

Volpe, G. (2005). Expressive Gesture in Performing Arts and New Media: The Present and the Future. *Journal of New Music Research*, *34*(1), 1–3. doi:10.1080/09298210500123820

Wachsmuth, I., & Fröhlich, M. (Eds.). (1998). Gesture and Sign Language in Human-Computer Interaction. In *Proceedings of International Gesture Workshop*, (*Vol. 1371*, p. 198). Springer.

Wang, G., Cook, P., & Associates. (2003). ChucK: A concurrent, on-the-fly audio programming language. In *Proceedings of International Computer Music Conference* (pp. 219–226). Academic Press. Retrieved from http://nagasm.org/ASL/icmc2003/closed/CR1055.PDF

Watson, R. (1993). A survey of gesture recognition techniques technical report tcd-cs-93-11. *Department of Computer Science, Trinity College*. Retrieved from http://citeseerx.ist.psu.edu/viewdoc/download?doi=10.1.1.51.9838&rep=rep1&type=pdf

Winkler, T. (1995). Making motion musical: Gesture mapping strategies for interactive computer music. In *Proceedings of ICMC* (pp. 261–264). ICMC.

Wright, M., Freed, A., Lee, A., Madden, T., & Momeni, A. (2001). Managing complexity with explicit mapping of gestures to sound control with osc. In *Proceedings of International Computer Music Conference* (pp. 314–317). ICMC.

Wu, Y., & Huang, T. (1999). Vision-based gesture recognition: A review. *Urbana*, 103–115. Retrieved from http://link.springer.com/content/pdf/10.1007/3-540-46616-9_10.pdf

Yamato, J., Ohya, J., & Ishii, K. (1992). Recognizing Human action in Time-sequential Images using Hidden Markov Model. *Computer Vision and Pattern*. Retrieved from http://ieeexplore.ieee.org/xpls/abs_all.jsp?arnumber=223161

Yoo, M. J., Beak, J. W., & Lee, I. K. (2011, June). Creating Musical Expression using Kinect. *Visual Computing*, 324–325. Retrieved from http://visualcomputing.yonsei.ac.kr/papers/2011/nime2011.pdf

Zeng, W., & Zhang, Z. (2012). *Multimedia at Work Microsoft Kinect Sensor and Its Effect*. Academic Press.

Zhao, L., & Badler, N. (2001). *Synthesis and acquisition of laban movement analysis qualitative parameters for communicative gestures*. Retrieved from http://repository.upenn.edu/cis_reports/116/

KEY TERMS AND DEFINITIONS

Computer Vision: Consists in the estimation of several properties of physical objects, based on their two dimensional (projection) images through the use of computers and cameras. With its beginnings in the early 1960s, it was thought to be an easy problem with a solution probably possible over a short time period. However, it revealed to be a task far more difficult. Since those early days CV has matured from a small research topic to a complete field of research and application (Aggarwal, 2011).

Human Computer Interaction: A discipline concerned with the design, evaluation and implementation of interactive computing systems for human use and with the study of major phenomena surrounding them. Because HCI studies a human and a machine in communication, it draws from supporting knowledge on both the machine and the human side. On the machine side, techniques in computer graphics, operating systems, programming languages, and development environments are relevant. On the human side, communication theory, graphic and industrial design disciplines, linguistics, social sciences, cognitive psychology, and human performance are relevant (Chairman-Hewett, 1992).

Machine Learning (ML): Derives from the artificial intelligence field. It is concerned with the study of building computer programs that automatically improve and/or adapt their performance through experience. ML can be thought of as "programming by example" and has many common aspects with other domains such as statistics and probability theory (understanding the phenomena that have generated the data), data mining (finding patterns in the data that are understandable by people) and cognitive sciences. Instead of the human programming a computer to solve a task directly, the goal of ML is to devise methods by which a computer program is able of come up with is own solution to the task, based only on examples provided (Grosan & Abraham, 2011).

ENDNOTES

Some CV techniques are described in this chapter, including some algorithms developed and published by the author, e.g. (Baltazar et al., 2010).

[1]   http://www.merriam-webster.com/dictionary/gesture?show=0&t=1384961916

[2]   http://www.palindrome.de

[3]   http://www.troikatronix.com/isadora.html

[4]   http://www.troikaranch.org/

[5]   http://smc.inescporto.pt/kinetic/

[6]   http://synapsekinect.tumblr.com

[7]   http://artes.ucp.pt/citar/

[8]   http://www.physicsclassroom.com/class/1dkin/u1l6a.cfm

[9]   Music Portugal Cultural Association, which has the status of Portuguese Public Utility Institution, was born as an extension of Miso Ensemble, to develop and promote contemporary musical creation in Portugal and Worldwide. Its founders are Paula and Miguel Azguime, composers, performers and directors that since the foundation of the Miso Ensemble in 1985, develop their work tirelessly in the field of new music, contributing actively to expand the contemporary way.

[10]   http://warszawska-jesien.art.pl/en/wj2013/home

[11]   http://cycling74.com/products/max/

[12]   http://www.festivalin.pt

This research was previously published in Innovative Teaching Strategies and New Learning Paradigms in Computer Programming edited by Ricardo Queirós, pages 224-254, copyright year 2015 by Information Science Reference (an imprint of IGI Global).

Section 4
Educational Technology

Chapter 16
Second Language Learners' Spoken Discourse:
Practice and Corrective Feedback Through Automatic Speech Recognition

Catia Cucchiarini
Radboud University, The Netherlands

Helmer Strik
Radboud University, The Netherlands

ABSTRACT

This chapter examines the use of Automatic Speech Recognition (ASR) technology in the context of Computer Assisted Language Learning (CALL) and language learning and teaching research. A brief introduction to ASR is first provided, to make it clear why and how this technology can be used to the benefit of learning and development in second language (L2) spoken discourse. This is followed by an overview of the state of the art in research on ASR-based CALL. Subsequently, a number of relevant projects on ASR-based CALL conducted at the Centre for Language and Speech Technology of the Radboud University in Nijmegen (the Netherlands) are presented. Possible solutions and recommendations are discussed given the current state of the technology with an explanation of how such systems can be used to the benefit of Discourse Analysis research. The chapter concludes with a discussion of possible perspectives for future research and development.

INTRODUCTION

Research on L2 learning has indicated that although exposure to the target language and usage-based learning are essential elements in the learning process, these are not always sufficient to guarantee target-like proficiency (Ellis, 2008; Ellis & Bogart, 2007). Focus on linguistic form provided through corrective feedback may help improve form accuracy in L2 spoken discourse. Unfortunately, in tradi-

DOI: 10.4018/978-1-5225-2589-9.ch016

tional teacher-fronted lessons there is generally not enough time for sufficient practice and feedback on speaking performance.

In this setting, the interest in applying ASR technology to L2 learning has been growing considerably in recent years (Eskenazi, 2009). ASR-based CALL systems would make it possible to offer sufficient amounts of practice in L2 speaking and to provide automatic feedback on different aspects of L2 spoken discourse. In this sense, ASR-based CALL systems would constitute an interesting supplement to traditional L2 classes. In addition, such systems can provide speaking practice in a private environment, which is a considerable advantage as speaking tasks are known to cause anxiety in L2 learners (Young, 1990). Moreover, L2 learners can practice at their own pace whenever they want.

In light of these advantages, research and development in this field have increased in recent years, and many systems have been developed that provide different forms of feedback on a variety of aspects of L2 spoken discourse. The majority of systems with a speech interactive nature address L2 pronunciation, which is considered a particularly challenging skill in L2 learning. A comprehensive overview of ASR-based commercial systems for L2 pronunciation is provided by Witt (2012). Many of these systems, however, do not contain important and desirable features of feedback on L2 pronunciation, such as immediate, detailed feedback on individual segments in the context of meaningful communicative tasks involving connected speech. In addition, CALL systems that are intended for practicing grammar skills and for improving accuracy in general do not support spoken interaction, but tend to resort to drag-and-drop exercises and typing (Bodnar, Cucchiarini, & Strik, 2011).

Against this background a number of projects were started at our lab which were aimed at conducting research and developing technology that would be conducive to the realization of ASR-based CALL systems that support practice and automatic feedback on L2 spoken discourse in line with insights from L2 learning research and L2 learners' requirements.

The aim of this chapter is to inform the reader about recent developments in the field of ASR-based CALL research and to indicate how these can lead to new methods and paradigms for the acquisition of spoken discourse in a second language. We first provide a brief introduction to ASR, to make it clear for the reader why and how this technology can be used to the benefit of learning and development in L2 spoken discourse. We then go on to provide an overview of the state of the art in research on ASR-based CALL. Subsequently, we present a number of relevant projects conducted at our lab and discuss possible solutions and recommendations for the development of ASR-based CALL systems and for the use of such systems to the benefit of Discourse Analysis. We then conclude with a discussion of possible perspectives for future research and development.

BACKGROUND: AUTOMATIC SPEECH RECOGNITION (ASR)

Standard ASR systems are generally employed to recognize words. The ASR system consists of a decoder (the search algorithm) and three 'knowledge sources': the language model, the lexicon, and the acoustic models. The language model (LM) contains probabilities of words and sequences of words. Acoustic models are models of how the sounds of a language are pronounced; in most cases so-called hidden Markov models (HMMs) are used, but it is also possible to use artificial neural networks (ANNs). The lexicon is the connection between the language model and the acoustic models. It contains information on how the words are pronounced, in terms of sequences of speech sounds. Therefore, the lexicon contains two representations for every entry: an orthographic transcription representing how a word is written and a phonological transcription representing how a word is pronounced. Since words can be pronounced in different ways, lexicons often contain more than one entry for some words, i.e. the pronunciation variants, which indicate possible pronunciations of one and the same word.

ASR is a probabilistic procedure. In a nutshell, ASR (with HMMs) works as follows. The LM defines which sequences of words are possible, for each word the possible pronunciation variants and their transcriptions (sequences of speech sounds) are retrieved from the lexicon, and for each speech sound in these transcriptions the appropriate acoustic model (HMM) is retrieved. Everything is represented by means of a huge probabilistic network: an LM is a network of words, each word is a network of pronunciation variants and their transcriptions (sequences of speech sounds), and for each of the speech sounds in these transcriptions the corresponding HMM is a network of its own. In this huge complex network paths have probabilities attached to them. For a given (incoming, unknown) speech signal the task of the decoder is to find the optimal global path in this network, using all the probabilistic information. In standard word recognition the output then consists of the labels of the words on this optimal path: the recognized words. However, the optimal path can contain more information than just that concerning the word labels, such as information on pronunciation variants, the phone symbols in these pronunciation variants, and even the segmentation at phone level.

STATE-OF-THE-ART IN ASR-BASED COMPUTER ASSISTED LANGUAGE LEARNING (CALL) RESEARCH AND APPLICATIONS

Research on L2 acquisition underlines the importance of usage-based learning and skill-specific practice (Ellis, 2008; DeKeyser & Sokalski, 1996; DeKeyser, 2007) when it comes to learning to speak and write a second language: if learners want to speak a second language fluently and accurately, it is necessary for them to practice speaking it. Relevant in this respect are Swain's output hypothesis (Swain, 1985) which emphasizes the role of output in L2 learning and Schmidt's (1990) 'noticing hypothesis' which underlines that awareness of discrepancies between the learner's output and the L2 is necessary for the acquisition of a specific linguistic item. To achieve this kind of awareness exposure to the L2 and L2 output are not always sufficient (Ellis & Bogart, 2007) and corrective feedback is often required to help learners focus on formal aspects of their L2 speech production and stimulate them to attempt self-improvement (Havranek, 2002).

However, various studies on the use of corrective feedback in the classroom have indicated that the feedback provided by L2 teachers is often inconsistent, ambiguous, arbitrary, and idiosyncratic (Carroll & Swain, 1993; Iwashita, 2003; Sheen, 2004). Many of the studies on corrective feedback have produced mixed results (Norris & Ortega, 2000; Lyster & Saito, 2010), but there are indications that explicit feedback is more effective than implicit, potentially ambiguous feedback (Lyster, 1998; Bigelow, delMas, Hansen, & Tarone, 2006), that feedback does not work when it is erratic and inconsistent (Chaudron, 1988), that feedback should be intensive (Han, 2002), that it should be appropriate to learners' readiness (Mackey & Philp, 1998), and that it should provide opportunities for self-repair and modified output because these induce learners to revise their hypotheses about the target language (Lyster & Ranta, 1997; Panova & Lyster, 2002; Havranek, 2002).

For L2 spoken discourse achieving a sufficient amount of practice and feedback in the classroom can be difficult, mainly owing to lack of time. The emergence of CALL systems that make use of ASR has opened up possibilities of developing language learning environments that offer sufficient practice and corrective feedback that is intensive, consistent, personalized and that offers opportunities for self-repair and modified output. This has spawned a considerable amount of research and development in this field.

One of the issues to be addressed in this line of research is the automatic recognition of L2 speech. In the section on ASR we tried to explain the complexity of this procedure, assuming that it is native speech that has to be recognized. When it comes to recognizing the speech of people who are no native speakers of the language in question, the problem to be solved becomes much more complex, especially if these non-native speakers are still in the process of learning the target language. This is because L2 speech can deviate from native speech at the level of the individual sounds, the prosody, the word forms and the word order. Deviations in individual sounds, word forms and word order may thus affect the main components of a speech recognizer mentioned in the previous section: the acoustic models, the lexicon and the language model. Furthermore, L2 speech tends to contain more disfluencies and hesitation phenomena than native speech, which also pose problems to ASR.

Many of the first studies that considered employing ASR technology in the context of L2 learning focused primarily on the automatic assessment of different aspects of L2 oral proficiency, in particular L2 pronunciation (Coniam, 1999; Bernstein, Cohen, Murveit, Rtischev, & Weintraub, 1990; Neumeyer, Franco, Weintraub, & Price, 1996; Eskenazi, 1996; Cucchiarini, Strik, & Boves, 1997; Witt & Young, 1997). The results showed that automatic testing of certain aspects of oral proficiency was feasible: the scores obtained by means of ASR technology were strongly correlated with human judgments of oral proficiency (Franco, Neumeyer, Digalakis, & Ronen, 2000; Neumeyer, Franco, Digalakis, & Weintraub, 2000; Cucchiarini, Strik, & Boves, 2000a; 2000b; 2002).

This technology was also adapted and employed to realize systems and products for L2 language instruction and practice such as EduSpeak (Franco et al., 2000), Tell me More (www.tellmemore.com/), the Tactical Language Training System (Johnson et al., 2004), Carnegie Speech NativeAccent (Eskenazi, Kennedy, Ketchum, Olszewski, & Pelton, 2007), SpeakESL (http://www.speakesl.com/), Saybot (Chevalier & Cao, 2008; www.saybot.com), and Rosetta Stone (www.rosettastone.com). A comprehensive overview of ASR-based commercial systems for L2 pronunciation is provided by Witt (2012). Most of these products have the advantage that they stimulate L2 spoken output and in this sense they comply with Swain's view on language learning (Swain, 1985). Some of them, however, appear to be less satisfactory when it comes to pinpointing discrepancies between the learner's output and the target utterance, as is emphasized in Schmidt's requirements concerning noticing (Schmidt, 1990). The limitations of these systems in detecting and diagnosing errors in L2 spoken discourse may lead to corrective feedback that is unsatisfactory in various respects: not detailed enough, not always comprehensible, not personalized (Menzel, Herron, Bonaventura, & Morton, 2000; Neri, Cucchiarini, Strik, & Boves, 2002).

In addition, most of the systems that employ ASR to support spoken interaction and provide corrective feedback address L2 pronunciation, while CALL systems that are aimed at practicing grammar skills in general offer training through typing or drag and drop and do not employ ASR to support spoken interaction, to detect grammatical inaccuracies in the learners' spoken discourse and eventually provide specific feedback on grammatical discrepancies between the learners' spoken discourse and the target language (Bodnar et al., 2011).

Possible alternatives to practice a second or foreign language are provided by communities which offer the opportunity of interacting with other learners or native speakers through Computer Mediated Communication. (CMC). CMC has been shown to contribute to a comfortable interactional context that favors language learning (Payne & Whitney, 2002; Payne & Ross, 2005; Dickinson, Eom, Kang, Lee, & Sachs, 2008), but has received criticism with respect to the provision of corrective feedback. One of the shortcomings of CMC seems indeed to be that the interlocutors are not always capable of providing feedback that is relevant and accurate (Dickinson et al., 2008).

PRACTICE AND CORRECTIVE FEEDBACK IN L2 SPOKEN DISCOURSE: THE CONTRIBUTION OF ASR TECHNOLOGY

After the first studies that addressed automatic assessment of oral proficiency (Cucchiarini et al., 2000a; 2000b; 2002), research at our lab subsequently focused mainly on automatic error detection in L2 oral proficiency, with a view to developing and improving systems that could be used for independent practice and corrective feedback in L2 spoken discourse and for conducting research on different aspects of language learning.

An ASR-based CALL system that has to provide corrective feedback on speech utterances will first of all have to determine what the learner is trying to say (speech recognition) before proceeding to an analysis of the form of the utterance (error detection). As mentioned above, this first step of speech recognition may be very difficult in the case of non-native speakers, in particular those that are still in the process of learning a second or foreign language. Once an incoming utterance has been recognized as being an acceptable attempt at producing the response required, additional analyses may be required depending on the types of errors that have to be detected. For this purpose we employed a two-step procedure in which (1) first the content of the utterance is determined (what was said, speech recognition), and (2) subsequently the form of the utterance is analyzed (how it was said, error detection).

A common approach to limit the difficulties in speech recognition consists in applying techniques that restrict the search space and make the task easier. In line with this approach, we combined strategies aimed at constraining the output of the learner so that the speech becomes more predictable with techniques aimed at improving the decoding of non-native speech. The former is done by using elicitation techniques that direct the learners to certain responses. In the case of pronunciation this can be easily realized by asking students to read sentences out loud from the screen. In the case of grammar, it is more challenging to design tasks that allow the students enough freedom to be able to show whether they master a given construction, and that, at the same time, produce constrained, predictable output (see below). For the latter, i.e. improving decoding, we resorted to the use of predefined lists of possible (correct and incorrect) responses for each exercise.

Since learners thus have some freedom in formulating their responses, it first has to be determined which utterance (of the predefined list) was spoken, which is done by means of utterance selection. There is always the possibility that the learner's response is not present in the predefined list or that utterance selection does not select the correct utterance from the list. To check this, utterance verification is carried out. In the first step of the two-step procedure, two phases can thus be distinguished, (1a) utterance selection, and (1b) utterance verification (UV). Experiments conducted so far indicated that reasonable levels of accuracy could be obtained at the stage of (1a) utterance selection (about 8-10%) and (1b) utterance verification (10%) (van Doremalen, Strik, & Cucchiarini, 2009).

ASR TECHNOLOGY AND ERROR DETECTION IN L2 PRONUNCIATION

The algorithms used for automatic assessment of oral proficiency were generally aimed at calculating automatic scores that were maximally correlated with human scores of oral proficiency and could thus be considered to reflect how human raters valued L2 speech (Franco et al., 2000; Neumeyer et al., 2000; Cucchiarini et al., 2000a; 2000b; 2002). In general, such automatic scores were calculated at a rather global level, for instance for several utterances by the same speaker, because in this way more reliable measures could be obtained (Kim, Franco, & Neumeyer, 1997). Such measures might be suitable, and in certain cases even preferable, for testing purposes, for assessing the problems of individual speakers, for providing overviews of words or phonemes that appear to be difficult and suggesting remedial exercises for the problematic cases. However, such overall measures are generally not specific enough for practice and feedback purposes.

Research on corrective feedback in L2 learning has indicated that one of the drawbacks of feedback by L2 teachers is that it is often ambiguous, while L2 learners could profit from more explicit and informative feedback (Lyster, 1998; Bigelow et al., 2006). For these reasons research on the use of ASR in the context of L2 learning was directed at error detection by developing suitable techniques for calculating scores at a more local level such as the word or the phoneme, which could be used as a basis for providing feedback on an individual basis, for instance in the context of remedial exercises. For pronunciation error detection we studied different approaches.

As explained above, once the learner's utterance has been recognized as being an acceptable attempt at producing the response required, additional analyses may be required. In the case of pronunciation error detection, the speech recognizer has to go through the same utterance and carry out a stricter analysis to determine whether the sounds have been pronounced correctly. For this purpose, we applied different methods.

ASR-based metrics such as posterior probabilities and (log) likelihood ratios (Franco et al., 2000; ISLE 1.4, 1999; Menzel et al., 2000) are often employed. Research has shown that these confidence measures can be used for detecting pronunciation errors (Franco et al., 2000; ISLE 1.4, 1999; Menzel et al., 2000; Witt, 1999). One of these measures is the so-called goodness of pronunciation (GOP) metric (Witt, 1999). Detailed studies conducted on the GOP algorithm (van Doremalen, Cucchiarini, & Strik, 2010; Kanters, Cucchiarini, & Strik, 2009; Strik, Truong, de Wet, & Cucchiarini, 2007; 2009) have revealed that, if properly trained, GOP works satisfactorily; e.g. in the Dutch-CAPT system (see Figure 1) 80-95% of the sounds were classified correctly. However, there are large variations between individuals and sounds. If specific settings (thresholds) could be used for each person-sound combination, better results could be achieved (Kanters et al., 2009), but in practice this is not possible. And since the GOP algorithm has some other limitations, we studied possible alternative measures (e.g. van Doremalen et al., 2010).

Another approach we experimented with is based on acoustic phonetic features. Using these features classifiers were trained to carry out pronunciation error detection. For certain problematic sounds acoustic phonetic classifiers produced better performance than the GOP algorithm (Strik et al., 2007; 2009).

In a third approach we used phonetic information in a different way. Since sounds are often not distributed uniformly in the acoustic space (e.g. the Dutch vowels), it is better to use a variant of the GOP in which different weights are employed for the different sounds. The resulting measure, called wGOP, yielded better results than the standard GOP (van Doremalen et al., 2010).

Finally, in another approach it is also possible to generate pronunciation networks for the different sounds. For instance, learners of Dutch often realize the/x/as/k/, or the/a/as/A/(Neri, Cucchiarini, & Strik, 2006). Such known, frequent errors can then be included in the pronunciation network of that sound. The ASR then has to find the best path in these pronunciation networks. In this way, it is not only possible to detect whether a sound was pronounced correctly or not, but also which error was made. However, a disadvantage of this method is that only errors that have been included in the pronunciation networks can eventually be detected.

The different approaches described above can also be combined. The challenge then is to find the proper combination of approaches and settings that yields the best results. Most approaches, such as the often applied (supervised) machine learning approach, require large amounts of annotated data in order to train the classifiers. Since obtaining annotated data is laborious, we have been studying other ways to carry out pronunciation detection. The acoustic-phonetic approach mentioned above is already a first step in that direction. Another approach we studied consists in introducing plausible, artificial errors (Kanters et al., 2009) in already existing corpora. In this method, we first obtained overviews of errors that L2 learners frequently make. We then artificially introduced these errors in native speech corpora that were then employed as training material to develop error detectors we eventually implemented in the Dutch-CAPT system. Language learners then used the Dutch-CAPT system; their interactions were recorded and annotated afterwards. Analyses of these annotations showed that the performance of the error detectors trained on artificially introduced pronunciation errors in real use was comparable to the performance during development. This is remarkable given that speech technology performance in real use is often lower than performance during development. This particularly applies when there is a training-testing mismatch, which was the case here as training was based on errors artificially introduced in native speech, while testing was based on actually made errors in non-native speech. A possible explanation for this finding is that we carefully introduced artificial errors according to substitution patterns we had derived from analyses of actually occurring errors (Kanters et al., 2009).

In the 'Dutch Computer-Assisted Pronunciation Training' (Dutch-CAPT) project (http://hstrik.ruhosting.nl/Dutch-CAPT/) a pronunciation training program was developed to provide automatic feedback on segmental (phoneme) errors (see Figure 1). We evaluated this system by comparing production data by an experimental group of adult Dutch L2 learners with different L1s and proficiency levels who used the Dutch-CAPT system, with those of a control group that did similar exercises, but did not get feedback on pronunciation errors. The learners in the two groups had been living in the Netherlands and had followed DL2 lessons. Already after two short sessions of about 30-60 minutes, we could observe that the decrease in the number of pronunciation errors was significantly larger for the experimental group compared to the control group that did not receive feedback (Cucchiarini, Neri, & Strik, 2009; Neri, Cucchiarini, & Strik, 2008).

Before developing a CALL system, we generally try to obtain an overview of frequent errors made by language learners by combining information found in the literature, expertise of language teachers, and analysis of data. Even if the artificial error procedure described above is used, such an overview is essential to carefully introduce plausible errors in the right context. We have already derived overviews of frequent segmental errors for different combinations of first (L1) and target (L2) languages: many L1s - Dutch (Neri et al., 2006), Spanish - Dutch (Burgos, Cucchiarini, van Hout, & Strik, 2013), and Dutch - English (Cucchiarini, van den Heuvel, Sanders, & Strik, 2011).

Figure 1. Screenshot of the Dutch-CAPT system. The user first watches a video, then plays a role in a dialogue and gets feedback on pronunciation errors.

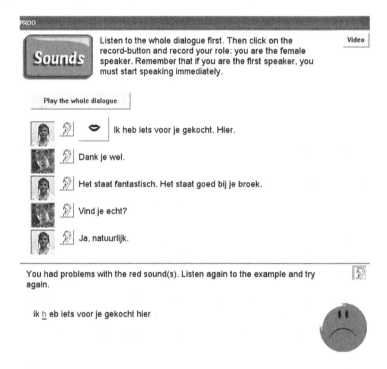

ASR TECHNOLOGY AND ERROR DETECTION IN L2 SYNTAX AND MORPHOLOGY

Based on the promising results we obtained with the Dutch-CAPT system on pronunciation, we decided to extend our approach to other aspects of L2 spoken discourse such as morphology and syntax.

This work was carried out within the framework of the DISCO project ('Development and Integration of Speech technology into Courseware for language learning,' see Figures 2-4), which was aimed at developing the prototype of an ASR-based CALL system for practice and feedback in Dutch L2 speaking performance (Strik, Cornillie, Colpaert, van Doremalen, & Cucchiarini, 2009; Strik, Colpaert, van Doremalen, & Cucchiarini, 2012; http://hstrik.ruhosting.nl/DISCO/). The system is intended for adult learners with different L1s at the A2 proficiency level of the Common European Framework of Reference.

Within the dialogues of the DISCO system there are three different types of exercises: pronunciation, morphology, and syntax. The user engages in a dialogue with a character on the screen (see Figures 3 and 4) and can choose from a list of two or three utterances (see Figure 4). Depending on the choice, the dialogue can proceed in different ways. In the pronunciation exercises the user speaks one of the utterances and gets feedback indicating whether the sounds are pronounced correctly or incorrectly (the corresponding graphemes are colored green or red, respectively). In the morphology exercises, different options are presented in brackets (see Figure 4), the user has to select the correct one and speak it up. If it is not correct, the word chosen is colored red. Finally, in the syntax exercises, words are presented in groups which the user has to put in the right order when speaking up the utterance. If the order is not correct, the groups of words are colored red (see Figure 3).

Figure 2. A screenshot of the DISCO system. The user can choose an interlocutor ('spraakmakker' – 'speech buddy') to speak to. The topics vary: a train journey, choosing a course, and going to the shop with a broken DVD player, respectively.

Figure 3. A screenshot of the DISCO system. It concerns a syntax exercise: words were presented in groups, and the user had to put them in the right order. In this example the spoken utterance was incorrect, and this is why the last three word groups (in 'blocks') are colored red. In the bottom-right corner (below the waveform of the recorded utterance) three options are provided: 1. listen to utterance spoken by the learner again, 2. listen to a pre-recorded correct (native) example, 3. proceed to the next exercise. In addition, there is a 4th option: the user can click on the microphone on the left, and try again.

For each grammar exercise a language model is built based on the prompts shown on the screen. The language model contains the possible responses by the user. For a spoken utterance, the ASR system then tries to determine what was said by finding the most likely path in the language model. In this way it is possible to determine whether the spoken utterance was correct or not, and what kind of feedback should be provided.

Figure 4. A screenshot of the DISCO system. It concerns a morphology exercise: the user can select one of the three utterances, and has to speak the words in the correct way.

However, to be able to perform automatic error detection at the level of morphology and syntax, it was necessary to have overviews of such grammatical errors in L2 spoken discourse. For this purpose, we developed novel procedures to obtain information on L2 grammatical errors from L2 speech data (Strik, van de Loo, van Doremalen, & Cucchiarini, 2010; Strik, van Doremalen, van de Loo, & Cucchiarini, 2011).

Several evaluation tests have been carried out to assess different aspects of the system. The results show satisfactory performance in detecting morphology and syntax errors, while user tests indicate that students are very positive about the system and consider it useful for improving their oral skills in Dutch L2 (Cucchiarini, van Doremalen, & Strik, 2012).

ASR TECHNOLOGY AND CORRECTIVE FEEDBACK ON L2 SPOKEN DISCOURSE

In addition to developing appropriate techniques for error detection, realizing suitable ASR-based systems for L2 speaking practice requires knowledge of how corrective feedback can best be provided. Many of the studies on the effect of corrective feedback on L2 development do not agree on which feedback forms best contribute to increasing linguistic competence in which learners (Lyster & Saito, 2010). Implicit feedback forms like recasts are particularly preferred in communicative contexts because they are discrete and do not interrupt the communication flow, but, for the same reason they are not always perceived as corrective feedback and often go unnoticed (Nicholas, Lightbown, & Spada, 2001; Lyster, 2004; Ellis & Sheen, 2006; Ellis, Loewen, & Erlam, 2006; Loewen & Philp, 2006). The effectiveness of recasts also appears to be related to the learner's degree of schooling, with more educated learners profiting more from recasts than less educated learners (Bigelow et al., 2006). Prompts are so-called negotiation of form techniques which are considered to be effective because they induce learners to reprocess their output (Lyster, 1998; 2004) and to produce "pushed output" (Swain, 1985; de Bot, 1996), but which have been criticized because they would contribute to linguistic knowledge and not to competence (Ellis & Sheen, 2006). Moreover, in so far as prompts appeal to metalinguistic skills, they are also likely to have a differential effect on learners with differing educational levels.

The evidence accumulated so far seems to suggest that the uncertainty that still exists as to how corrective feedback on L2 spoken discourse can best be provided is mainly due to the impossibility so far to create appropriate research conditions to offer feedback that is systematic, consistent, intensive, and clear enough to be perceived as such, and that provides opportunity for self-repair and modified output (El Tatawi, 2002). The use of ASR technology in the context of CALL offers the opportunity of providing corrective feedback on L2 spoken discourse under near-optimal conditions (Penning de Vries, Cucchiarini, Strik, & Van Hout, 2011). Within the framework of the project 'Feedback and the Acquisition of Syntax in Oral Proficiency' (FASOP) (http://hstrik.ruhosting.nl/FASOP/), an ASR-based CALL system is used to conduct experiments on the effect of different forms of corrective feedback on oral syntax practice and acquisition (see Figure 5). Dutch L2 learners are pre-tested before undergoing specific training in L2 syntax through different versions of the CALL system that provide different forms of feedback. The ASR-based CALL system also logs all interactions between the learner and the system. Post-tests are then administered to determine the effects of the feedback (see Figure 6). In addition, detailed analyses of the logs also provide useful information which can be employed to get a more complete picture of the learning process. The first results are encouraging (Bodnar, Penning de Vries, Cucchiarini, Strik, & van Hout, 2011).

Figure 5. A screenshot of the FASOP system. Learners first watch a video clip and then answer questions. In this example, the tutor is asking 'What does it say on the box that Melvin has packed his things in ?' To answer, learners compose an utterance using the prompt and word groups presented on the screen. All (='Allemaal') the word groups in the blue box have to be used, and only one ('Eentje') word group from the box in green.

Figure 6. Overview of the FASOP experiment: 'QNAIRE' – questionnaire, GJT – grammatical judgment test, DCT – discourse completion test.

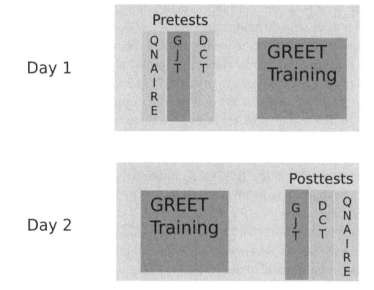

SOLUTIONS AND RECOMMENDATIONS

In the previous sections we have presented some of the issues that have to be addressed in developing systems for L2 learning that employ ASR for providing practice and feedback in L2 spoken discourse. This overview has made it clear that these issues are not trivial and that research is still required to optimize the technology. On the other hand, the research presented already indicates that the technology is mature enough to be employed in innovative learning methods for L2 spoken discourse and innovative research in Discourse Analysis. In this section we pay attention to what can already be realized with the current technology (solutions and recommendations). In the following section, we consider what kind of research should be conducted not only to improve the technology, but also to obtain better ASR-based CALL systems and to allow more innovative research in the field of Discourse Analysis.

First, the issue of L2 speech recognition still constitutes a challenge and research on how to achieve better performance is still a priority for many applications. However, there are strategies for circumventing the existing problems and still develop useful applications with acceptable performance (van Doremalen, Cucchiarini, & Strik, 2010). One of these strategies consists in reducing the search space by having the learners perform highly constrained tasks. We have seen above that this approach works satisfactorily even for morphology and syntax exercises, in which learners need to be given a certain amount of freedom in speech performance to be able to show whether they master certain grammatical constructions or not.

Second, with respect to error detection various approaches have been proposed which achieve varying levels of performance. Also in this respect further research is required to improve the algorithms and obtain higher levels of detection accuracy for different components of L2 spoken discourse. In the meantime, it is also important to consider what can already be realized with the present levels of accuracy, which, for certain aspects of L2 spoken discourse, may be already satisfactory. As we have seen in the Dutch-CAPT and DISCO projects, even systems that do not achieve 100% accuracy can still be useful for language learners.

Third, it is well-known that the traditional classroom is limited in its ability to stimulate the development of communicative competences in language learners (e.g. Demo, 2001). By using ASR-based CALL systems learners can participate in (simulated) dialogues, providing many opportunities for (practicing and studying) interaction. Since such CALL systems can be available 24/7, they allow for many contact hours and considerable amounts of exposure.

Fourth, in addition to the advantages ASR-based CALL systems can offer for L2 learning, there are also important research benefits for Discourse Analysis. For instance, an ASR-based CALL system can be used for acquiring data on L2 learning. These data are in the form of speech recordings collected in realistic situations that can subsequently be employed for different types of Discourse Analysis research such as phonetic and phonological research (McCarthy, 1992), for research on individual differences in second language learning and for "research" by the learners' themselves (Demo, 2001; Celce-Murcia & Olshtain, 2000; McCarthy & Carter, 1994; Riggenbach, 1999) to make them aware of possibly problematic features. The special advantage of these data is that they come with the relevant information for further automatic processing such as alignments between the speech signals and the orthographic and phonemic representations, and confidence measures.

Furthermore, ASR-based CALL systems can be designed and developed in such a way that it is possible to log details regarding the interactions with the users, as was the case in the DISCO project. By way of illustration, this logbook can contain the following information: what appeared on the screen, how the user responded, how long the user waited, what was done (speak an utterance, move the mouse and click on an item, use the keyboard, etc.), the feedback provided by the system, how the user reacted on this feedback (listen to example (or not), try again, ask for additional, e.g. meta-linguistic, feedback, etc.). So when language learners use an ASR-based CALL system to practice oral skills all their utterances can be recorded in such a way that it is possible to know exactly in which context the utterance was spoken, i.e. it can be related to all the information in the logbook mentioned above.

Such a corpus and the corresponding log-files can be useful for various types of Discourse Analysis: for research on language acquisition and second language learning, for studying the effect of various types of feedback on individual learners, for research on various aspects of man-machine interaction.

ASR-based CALL systems also open up new avenues of research, because they allow research conditions that were hitherto impossible to create. As mentioned above, in the FASOP project the impact of corrective feedback on the acquisition of syntax in oral proficiency (http://hstrik.ruhosting.nl/FASOP/) is studied through an ASR-based CALL system that makes it possible to investigate how individual learners process corrective feedback on oral skills on-line.

FUTURE RESEARCH DIRECTIONS

In the previous sections we have presented research aimed at developing and improving ASR-based CALL systems that can offer practice in L2 spoken discourse and can provide appropriate, individualized feedback to L2 learners. One of the issues we mentioned is relatively poorer performance of ASR technology on L2 speech. We have seen that creative solutions can be adopted that make it possible to develop pedagogically interesting applications, in spite of the limitations of the technology. However, improving ASR technology for L2 speech remains one of the chief priorities. Especially because by improving the technology it would be possible to realize applications that allow less constrained interactions between the learner and the system. In turn this would make these applications more realistic and pedagogically more interesting

Similarly, error detection algorithms also need to be improved to allow for more reliable applications that provide learners with the feedback they need to improve their L2 spoken discourse. Research should address the improvement of algorithms and metrics for both pronunciation error detection and grammar error detection in L2 spoken discourse. With respect to pronunciation error detection, one of the problems in studies addressing error detection accuracy concerns the need for appropriate corpora and test materials for benchmarking. In general, the accuracy of automatic error detection is determined through comparisons with human performance on the same tasks (Cucchiarini et al., 2009). However, the enormous effort required in obtaining the human annotations that are necessary for this purpose constitutes a serious problem in this type of research. This calls for new research paradigms that rely less on manually annotated corpora while still making it possible to gauge the accuracy of error detection algorithms in a reliable and valid manner. In our research we resorted to artificially created annotations of L2 speech errors that plausibly reflect the errors that are actually made by L2 learners. Along similar lines new approaches need to be proposed.

In addition to these more technological priorities for further research are of course research agendas that address pedagogical and usability issues. While it is important that the ASR technology employed in ASR-based CALL systems works properly, it is equally important to pay attention to how learners experience and perceive such systems, to how ASR-based CALL systems contribute to boosting motivation and enhancing learner autonomy. Such data can be easily collected through questionnaires, as is usually done in research on motivation in L2 learning, and can subsequently be employed in learner modeling to develop CALL systems that are tailored to individual learners in terms of communication, feedback, learning strategies and preferences.

In the previous section, we mentioned a number of examples of how ASR-based CALL systems could provide new data and paradigms for research in Discourse Analysis. However, there are also other directions that could be pursued and that could provide new insights in Discourse Analysis. For instance, the fact that ASR-based CALL systems provide easy access to realistic speech data could be exploited by studying these speech data from different perspectives. Recent developments in language and speech technology make it possible, for example, to investigate emotions and affective state in language learners through language and speech. In turn, such information could be employed to get a better understanding of the language learning process and of how learners experience it, which could eventually lead to more advanced and more dynamic approaches to motivation and learner modeling. With respect to systems that employ questionnaires to collect data on motivation and individual preferences, systems that rely on automatic analyses of emotions and affective state through language and speech have the advantage that they can automatically adapt to their users and their mood, status, and changing preferences.

In relation to the topics addressed in the present volume, it is also relevant to find out how ASR-based CALL systems can be employed in connection with computer-mediated discourse and synchronous computer-mediated communication (CMC) technologies and how they can be used to the benefit of Discourse Analysis. We saw above that with respect to L2 learning and feedback CMC technologies do not always provide the appropriate solutions (Dickinson et al., 2008), which makes it interesting to investigate whether combining these different technologies might lead to more flexible, reliable, and adequate learning environments.

Finally, it seems that different lines of research could address the issue of adaptivity, which has not been explicitly addressed in the present chapter, but which looms large in ASR-based research (van Doremalen, Cucchiarini, & Strik, 2011). Adaptivity should not be limited to the different components of ASR, but should also extend to other aspects of the CALL systems, such as adapting exercises to the proficiency level of the learner, or adapting the type of feedback provided to the preferences of individual learners. These different forms of adaptation can be realized through student modeling and are likely to improve user satisfaction and motivation.

CONCLUSION

Research has shown that if learners want to speak a language fluently and accurately, it is necessary for them to practice speaking. However, currently there are generally not enough possibilities to do so. ASR-based CALL systems do offer these possibilities, and this explains the recent interest in deploying ASR technology in the context of language learning.

Developing CALL systems for practice and feedback in L2 spoken discourse is complex and challenging because L2 speech is highly variable and substantially differs from standard speech. Still, with current state-of-the-art technology it is possible to develop useful CALL systems, but this clearly requires a combination of expertise. So far the focus has been on pronunciation. Our research has shown that it is also possible to develop systems for practicing grammar in spoken discourse and providing useful feedback.

Although it is already possible to build useful CALL systems, there is much room for improvement. With improved speech technology it will be possible to relax the constraints, improve the performance, and use the technology for different goals, in more natural, intuitive, and pedagogically sound ways. Furthermore, besides pronunciation and grammar, ASR-based CALL systems could also be developed for other aspects such as prosody, vocabulary, and formulaic language. Finally, more insights and expertise are required on how to optimally design, develop, and use these systems. ASR-based CALL systems can be combined with other types of learning, e.g. classical teacher-fronted classrooms, CMC, collaborative learning, and we need to study how these different approaches can be optimally combined. Different combinations of methods should be tested in practice for different types of learners, to study aspects such as user satisfaction, motivation, and effectiveness.

In any case, ASR-based CALL systems offer new and exciting possibilities; they will be used more and more, and will gradually improve. It is also likely that they will develop in new directions, e.g. CALL systems for mobile devices, which will really make it possible to learn everywhere 24/7, game like elements might be added, teachers and learners might have more possibilities to influence the content, and systems will become increasingly adaptive.

REFERENCES

Bernstein, J., Cohen, M., Murveit, H., Rtischev, D., & Weintraub, M. (1990). Automatic evaluation and training in English pronunciation. [Kobe, Japan.]. *Proceedings ICSLP, 90*, 1185–1188.

Bigelow, M., delMas, R., Hansen, K., & Tarone, E. (2006). Literacy and the processing of oral recasts in SLA. *TESOL Quarterly, 40*(4), 665–685. doi:10.2307/40264303

Bodnar, S., Cucchiarini, C., & Strik, H. (2011). Computer-assisted grammar practice for oral communication. *Proceedings of the 3rd International Conference on Computer Supported Education* (*CSEDU*) (pp. 355-361). Noordwijkerhout, The Netherlands.

Bodnar, S., Penning de Vries, B., Cucchiarini, C., Strik, H., & van Hout, R. (2011). Feedback in an ASR-based CALL system for L2 syntax: A feasibility study. *Proceedings of the SLaTE-2011 workshop* (pp. 1-4). Venice, Italy.

Burgos, P., Cucchiarini, C., van Hout, R., Strik, H. (in press). *Phonology acquisition in Spanish learners of Dutch: Error patterns in pronunciation.*

Carroll, S., & Swain, M. (1993). Explicit and implicit negative feedback: An empirical study of the learning of linguistic generalizations. *Studies in Second Language Acquisition*, *15*, 357–386. doi:10.1017/S0272263100012158

Celce-Murcia, M., & Olshtain, E. (2000). *Discourse and context in language teaching*. New York: Cambridge University Press.

Chaudron, C. (1988). *Second language classrooms*. New York: Cambridge University Press. doi:10.1017/CBO9781139524469

Chevalier, S., & Cao, Z. (2008). Application and evaluation of speech technologies in language learning: Experiments with the Saybot Player. [Brisbane, Australia.]. *Proceedings of Interspeech*, *2008*, 2811–2814.

Coniam, D. (1999). Voice recognition software accuracy with second language speakers of English. *System*, *27*, 49–64. doi:10.1016/S0346-251X(98)00049-9

Cucchiarini, C., Neri, A., & Strik, H. (2009). Oral proficiency training in Dutch L2: The contribution of ASR-based corrective feedback. *Speech Communication*, *51*(10), 853–863. doi:10.1016/j.specom.2009.03.003

Cucchiarini, C., Strik, H., & Boves, L. (1997). Automatic assessment of foreign speakers' pronunciation of Dutch. [Rhodes, Greece.]. *Proceedings Eurospeech*, *1997*, 713–716.

Cucchiarini, C., Strik, H., & Boves, L. (2000a). Different aspects of expert pronunciation quality ratings and their relation to scores produced by speech recognition algorithm. *Speech Communication*, *30*(2-3), 109–119. doi:10.1016/S0167-6393(99)00040-0

Cucchiarini, C., Strik, H., & Boves, L. (2000b). Quantitative assessment of second language learners' fluency. *The Journal of the Acoustical Society of America*, *107*(2), 989–999. doi:10.1121/1.428279 PMID:10687708

Cucchiarini, C., Strik, H., & Boves, L. (2002). Quantitative assessment of second language learners' fluency: Comparisons between read and spontaneous speech. *The Journal of the Acoustical Society of America*, *111*(6), 2862–2873. doi:10.1121/1.1471894 PMID:12083220

Cucchiarini, C., van den Heuvel, H., Sanders, E., & Strik, H. (2011). Error selection for ASR-based English pronunciation training in 'My Pronunciation Coach.' [Florence, Italy.]. *Proceedings Interspeech*, *2011*, 1165–1168.

Cucchiarini, C., van Doremalen, J., & Strik, H. (2012). *Practice and feedback in L2 speaking: An evaluation of the DISCO CALL system*. Paper presented at Interspeech 2012. Portland, Oregon.

Day, E. M., & Shapson, M. (2001). Integrating formal and functional approaches to language teaching in French immersion: An experimental study. *Language Learning, 51,* 47–80. doi:10.1111/j.1467-1770.2001.tb00014.x

De Bot, K. (1996). The psycholinguistics of the output hypothesis. *Language Learning, 46,* 529–555. doi:10.1111/j.1467-1770.1996.tb01246.x

DeKeyser, R. (2007). *Practice in a second language. Perspectives from applied linguistics and cognitive psychology*. UK: Cambridge University Press.

DeKeyser, R. M., & Sokalski, K. J. (1996). The differential role of comprehension and production practice. *Language Learning, 46*(4), 613–642. doi:10.1111/j.1467-1770.1996.tb01354.x

Demo, D. (2001). *Discourse analysis for language teachers. ERIC Digest. ERIC Clearinghouse on Languages and linguistics*. Washington, DC: Center for Applied Linguistics.

Derwing, T. M., Munro, M. J., & Carbonaro, M. (2000). Does popular speech recognition software work with ESL speech? *TESOL Quarterly, 34,* 592–603. doi:10.2307/3587748

Dickinson, M., Eom, S., Kang, Y., Lee, C. M., & Sachs, R. (2008). A balancing act: How can intelligent computer-generated feedback be provided in learner-to-learner interactions? *Computer Assisted Language Learning, 21*(4), 369–382. doi:10.1080/09588220802343702

Dlaska, A., & Krekeler, C. (2008). Self-assessment of pronunciation. *System, 36,* 506–516. doi:10.1016/j.system.2008.03.003

Doughty, C. J., & Long, M. H. (2003). Optimal psycholinguistic environments for distance foreign language learning. *Language Learning & Technology, 7*(3), 50–80.

El Tatawi, M. (2002). Corrective feedback in second language acquisition. *Working papers in TESOL and Applied Linguistics, 2,* 1-19.

Ellis, N., & Larsen-Freeman, D. (2006). Language emergence: Implications for applied Linguistics. *Applied Linguistics, 27*(4), 558–589. doi:10.1093/applin/aml028

Ellis, N. C. (2008). Optimizing the input: Frequency and sampling in usage-based and form-focused learning. In M. H. Long & C. Doughty (Eds.), *Handbook of language teaching* (pp. 139–158). Oxford: Blackwell.

Ellis, N. C., & Bogart, P. S. H. (2007). Speech and language technology in education: The perspective from SLA research and practice. *Proceedings SLaTE* (pp. 1-8). Farmington, PA.

Ellis, R., Loewen, S., & Erlam, R. (2006). Implicit and explicit corrective feedback and the acquisition of L2 grammar. *Studies in Second Language Acquisition, 28,* 339–368. doi:10.1017/S0272263106060141

Ellis, R., & Sheen, Y. (2006). Reexamining the role of recasts in second language acquisition. *Studies in Second Language Acquisition, 28,* 575–601. doi:10.1017/S027226310606027X

Eskenazi, M. (1996). Detection of foreign speakers' pronunciation errors for second language training – preliminary results. [Philadelphia, Pennsylvania.]. *Proceedings ICSLP*, *96*, 1465–1468.

Eskenazi, M. (2009). An overview of spoken language technology for education. *Speech Communication*, *51*, 832–844. doi:10.1016/j.specom.2009.04.005

Eskenazi, M., Kennedy, A., Ketchum, C., Olszewski, R., & Pelton, G. (2007). The NativeaccentTM pronunciation tutor: Measuring success in the real world. *Proceedings of the SLaTE-2007 workshop, Farmington* (pp. 124-127). PA, USA.

Franco, H., Abrash, V., Precoda, K., Bratt, H., Rao, R., & Butzberger, J. et al. (2000). The SRI Eduspeak system: Recognition and pronunciation scoring for language learning. [Dundee Scotland.]. *Proceedings ESCA ETRW INSTi*, *L2000*, 123–128.

Franco, H., Neumeyer, L., Digalakis, V., & Ronen, O. (2000). Combination of machine scores for automatic grading of pronunciation quality. *Speech Communication*, *30*, 121–130. doi:10.1016/S0167-6393(99)00045-X

Han, Z. (2002). A study of the impact of recasts on tense consistency in L2 output. *TESOL Quarterly*, *36*, 542–572. doi:10.2307/3588240

Havranek, G. (2002). When is corrective feedback most likely to succeed? *International Journal of Educational Research*, *37*, 255–270. doi:10.1016/S0883-0355(03)00004-1

Heift, T., & Schulze, M. (2007). *Errors and intelligence in computer-assisted language learning: Parsers and pedagogues*. New York: Routledge.

Hulstijn, J. (2002). Towards a unified account of the representation, processing and acquisition of second language knowledge. *Second Language Research*, *18*(3), 193–223. doi:10.1191/0267658302sr207oa

ISLE 1.4. (1999). Pronunciation training: Requirements and solutions. ISLE Deliverable 1.4. Retrieved February 27, 2002, from http://nats-www.informatik.uni-hamburg.de/~isle/public/D14/D14.html

Iwashita, N. (2003). Negative feedback and positive evidence in task-based interaction: Differential, effects on L2 development. *Studies in Second Language Acquisition*, *25*, 1–36. doi:10.1017/S0272263103000019

Johnson, W. L., Beal, C. R., Fowles-Winkler, A., Lauper, U., Marsella, S., Narayanan, S., & Papachristou, D. (2004). Tactical language training system: An interim report. *Intelligent Tutoring Systems*, 336-345.

Kanters, S., Cucchiarini, C., & Strik, H. (2009). The goodness of pronunciation algorithm: A detailed performance study. *Proceedings SLaTE-2009 workshop* (pp. 1-4). Warwickshire, England.

Kim, Y., Franco, H., & Neumeyer, L. (1997). *Automatic pronunciation scoring of specific phone segments for language instruction. Proceedings of Eurospeech* (pp. 645–648). Greece: Rhodes.

Larsen-Freeman, D., & Cameron, L. (2008). Research methodology on language development from a complex systems perspective. *Modern Language Journal*, *92*, 200–213. doi:10.1111/j.1540-4781.2008.00714.x

Loewen, S., & Philp, J. (2006). Recasts in the adult English L2 classroom: Characteristics, explicitness, and effectiveness. *Modern Language Journal*, *90*, 536–556. doi:10.1111/j.1540-4781.2006.00465.x

Lyster, R. (1998). Negotiation of form, recasts, and explicit correction in relation to error types and learner repair in immersion classrooms. *Language Learning*, *48*, 183–218. doi:10.1111/1467-9922.00039

Lyster, R., & Ranta, L. (1997). Corrective feedback and learner uptake. *Studies in Second Language Acquisition*, *19*, 37–66. doi:10.1017/S0272263197001034

Lyster, R., & Saito, K. (2010). Oral feedback in classroom SLA: A meta-analysis. *Studies in Second Language Acquisition*, *32*, 265–302. doi:10.1017/S0272263109990520

Mackey, A., & Philp, J. (1998). Conversational interaction and second language development: Recasts, responses, and red herrings. *Modern Language Journal*, *82*, 338–356. doi:10.1111/j.1540-4781.1998.tb01211.x

Mak, B., Siu, M., Ng, M., Tam, Y.-C., Chan, Y.-C., & Chan, K.-W. (2003). PLASER: Pronunciation learning via automatic speech recognition. *Proceedings of the HLT-NAACL 2003 Workshop on Building Educational Applications using Natural Language Processing* (pp. 23-29). Edmonton, Canada.

McCarthy, M. (1992). *Discourse analysis for language teachers*. New York: Cambridge University Press.

McCarthy, M., & Carter, R. (1994). *Language as discourse: Perspectives for language teachers*. New York: Longman.

Menzel, W., Herron, D., Bonaventura, P., & Morton, R. (2000). Automatic detection and correction of non-native English pronunciations. [Dundee, Scotland.]. *Proceedings of InSTIL*, *L2000*, 49–56.

Neri, A., Cucchiarini, C., & Strik, H. (2006). Selecting segmental errors in L2 Dutch for optimal pronunciation training. *IRAL -*. *International Review of Applied Linguistics in Language Teaching*, *44*, 357–404. doi:10.1515/IRAL.2006.016

Neri, A., Cucchiarini, C., & Strik, H. (2008). The effectiveness of computer-based speech corrective feedback for improving segmental quality in L2 Dutch. *ReCALL*, *20*(2), 225–243. doi:10.1017/S0958344008000724

Neri, A., Cucchiarini, C., Strik, H., & Boves, L. (2002). The pedagogy technology interface in computer assisted pronunciation training. *Computer Assisted Language Learning*, *15*, 441–467. doi:10.1076/call.15.5.441.13473

Neumeyer, L., Franco, H., Digalakis, V., & Weintraub, M. (2000). Automatic scoring of pronunciation quality. *Speech Communication*, *30*(2), 83–93. doi:10.1016/S0167-6393(99)00046-1

Neumeyer, L., Franco, H., Weintraub, M., & Price, P. (1996). Automatic text independent pronunciation scoring of foreign language student speech. [Philadelphia, Pennsylvania.]. *Proceedings ICSLP*, *96*, 1457–1460.

Nicholas, H., Lightbown, P. M., & Spada, N. (2001). Recasts as feedback to language learners. *Language Learning*, *51*, 719–758. doi:10.1111/0023-8333.00172

Norris, J. M., & Ortega, L. (2000). Effectiveness of L2 instruction: A research synthesis and quantitative meta-analysis. *Language Learning*, *50*, 417–528. doi:10.1111/0023-8333.00136

Panova, I., & Lyster, R. (2002). Patterns of corrective feedback and uptake in an adult ESL classroom. *TESOL Quarterly*, *36*, 573–595. doi:10.2307/3588241

Payne, J. S., & Ross, B. M. (2005). Synchronous CMC, working memory, and L2 oral proficiency development. *Language Learning & Technology*, *9*(3), 35–54.

Payne, J. S., & Whitney, P. J. (2002). Developing L2 oral proficiency through synchronous CMC: Output, working memory, and interlanguage development. *CALICO Journal*, *20*(1), 7–32.

Penning de Vries, B., Cucchiarini, C., Strik, H., & Van Hout, R. (2011). Adaptive corrective feedback in second language learning. In S. De Wannemacker, G. Clarebout, & P. De Causmaecker (Eds.), *Interdisciplinary approaches to adaptive learning. A look at the neighbors, Communications in Computer and Information Science series* (pp. 1–14). Heidelberg: Springer Verlag. doi:10.1007/978-3-642-20074-8_1

Riggenbach, H. (1999). Discourse analysis in the language classroom: Vol. 1. *The spoken language*. Ann Arbor, MI: University of Michigan Press.

Rohde, D., & Plaut, D. (1999). Language acquisition in the absence of explicit negative evidence: How important is starting small? *Cognition*, *72*, 67–109. doi:10.1016/S0010-0277(99)00031-1 PMID:10520565

Russel, J., & Spada, N. (2006). The effectiveness of corrective feedback for second language acquisition: A meta-analysis of the research. In J. Norris & L. Ortega (Eds.), *Synthesizing research on language learning and teaching* (pp. 131–164). Amsterdam: John Benjamins Publishing Company.

Schmidt, R. W. (1990). The role of consciousness in second language learning. *Applied Linguistics*, *11*, 129–158. doi:10.1093/applin/11.2.129

Sheen, Y. (2004). Corrective feedback and learner uptake in communicative classrooms across instructional settings. *Language Teaching Research*, *8*, 263–300. doi:10.1191/1362168804lr146oa

Strik, H., Colpaert, J., van Doremalen, J., & Cucchiarini, C. (2012). The DISCO ASR-based CALL system: Practicing L2 oral skills and beyond. *Proceedings of the Conference on International Language Resources and Evaluation (LREC 2012)* (pp. 2702-2707). Istanbul, Turkey.

Strik, H., Cornillie, F., Colpaert, J., van Doremalen, J., & Cucchiarini, C. (2009). Developing a CALL system for practicing oral proficiency: How to design for speech technology, pedagogy and learners. *Proceedings of the SLaTE-2009 workshop* (pp.1-4). Warwickshire, England.

Strik, H., Truong, K., de Wet, F., & Cucchiarini, C. (2007). Comparing classifiers for pronunciation error detection. [Antwerp, Belgium.]. *Proceedings of Interspeech*, *2007*, 1837–1840.

Strik, H., Truong, K., de Wet, F., & Cucchiarini, C. (2009). Comparing different approaches for automatic pronunciation error detection. *Speech Communication*, *51*(10), 845–852. doi:10.1016/j.specom.2009.05.007

Strik, H., van de Loo, J., van Doremalen, J., & Cucchiarini, C. (2010). Practicing syntax in spoken interaction: Automatic detection of syntactic errors in non-native utterances. *Proceedings of the SLaTE-2010 workshop* (pp.1-4). Tokyo, Japan.

Strik, H., van Doremalen, J., van de Loo, J., & Cucchiarini, C. (2011). Improving ASR processing of ungrammatical utterances through grammatical error modeling. *Proceedings of the SLaTE-2011 workshop* (pp.1-4). Venice, Italy.

Swain, M. (1985). Communicative competence: Some roles of comprehensible input and comprehensible output in its development. In M. A. Gass & C. G. Madden (Eds.), *Input in second language acquisition* (pp. 235–253). Rowley, MA: Newbury House.

van Doremalen, J., Cucchiarini, C., & Strik, H. (2010). Using non-native error patterns to improve pronunciation verification. [Tokyo, Japan.]. *Proceedings of Interspeech, 2010*, 1–4.

van Doremalen, J., Cucchiarini, C., & Strik, H. (2010). Optimizing automatic speech recognition for low-proficient non-native speakers. *EURASIP Journal on Audio, Speech, and Music Processing, 2010*, 1–13. doi:10.1155/2010/973954

van Doremalen, J., Cucchiarini, C., & Strik, H. (2011). Speech technology in CALL: The essential role of adaptation. In S. De Wannemacker, G. Clarebout, & P. De Causmaecker (Eds.), *Interdisciplinary approaches to adaptive learning. A look at the neighbors, Communications in Computer and Information Science series, 26* (pp. 56–69). Heidelberg: Springer Verlag. doi:10.1007/978-3-642-20074-8_5

van Doremalen, J., Strik, H., & Cucchiarini, C. (2009). Utterance verification in language learning applications. *Proceedings of the SLaTE-2009 workshop* (pp.1-4). Warwickshire, England.

Witt, S. (1999). *Use of speech recognition in computer assisted language learning.* (Unpublished doctoral dissertation). University of Cambridge, UK.

Witt, S. (2012). Automatic error detection in pronunciation training: Where we are and where we need to go. *Proceedings IS ADEPT* (pp. 1-8). Stockholm, Sweden.

Witt, S., & Young, S. (1997). Language learning based on non-native speech recognition. [Rhodes, Greece.]. *Proceedings Eurospeech, 1997*, 633–636.

Young, D. J. (1990). An investigation of students' perspectives on anxiety and speaking. *Foreign Language Annals, 23*, 539–553. doi:10.1111/j.1944-9720.1990.tb00424.x

ADDITIONAL READING

Benzeghiba, M., Mori, R. D., Deroo, O., Dupont, S., Erbes, T., & Jouvet, D. et al. (2007). Automatic speech recognition and speech variability: A review. *Speech Communication, 49*(10-11), 763–786. doi:10.1016/j.specom.2007.02.006

Chapelle, C. A. (2007). Technology and second language acquisition. *Annual Review of Applied Linguistics, 27*, 98–114. doi:10.1017/S0267190508070050

D'Mello, S., & Graesser, A. (2006). Affect detection from human-computer dialogue with an intelligent tutoring system. In J. Gratch, M. Young, R. Aylett, D. Ballin, & P. Olivier (Eds.), *Proceedings of the 6th International Conference on Intelligent Virtual Agents (IVA 2006)* (pp. 54-67). Marina del Rey, California, USA.

DeKeyser, R. (2005). What makes learning second-language grammar difficult? A review of issues. *Language Learning, 55*, 1–25. doi:10.1111/j.0023-8333.2005.00294.x

Delmonte, R. (2011). Exploring speech technologies for language learning. Retrieved February 6, 2013, from http://www.intechopen.com/books/speech-and-language-technologies

Dörnyei, Z., & Ushioda, E. (2009). *Motivation, language identity and the L2 self*. Bristol: Multilingual Matters.

Doughty, C. J., & Long, M. H. (2003). Optimal psycholinguistic environments for distance foreign language learning. *Language Learning & Technology, 7*(3), 50–80.

Egan, K. (1999). Speaking: A critical skill and challenge. *CALICO Journal, 16*, 277–293.

Ehsani, F., & Knodt, E. (1998). Speech technology in computer-aided learning: Strengths and limitations of a new CALL paradigm. *Language Learning & Technology, 2*, 45–60.

Ellis, R., & Barkhuizen, G. (2005). *Analyzing learner language*. Oxford: Oxford University Press.

Engwall, O., & Balter, O. (2007). Pronunciation feedback from real and virtual language teachers. *Computer Assisted Language Learning, 20*, 235–262. doi:10.1080/09588220701489507

Flege, J. (1995). Second-language speech learning: Theory, findings and problems. In W. Strange (Ed.), *Speech perception and linguistic experience* (pp. 229–273). Timonium, MD: York Press Inc.

Gass, S. M., & Selinker, L. (2008). *Second language acquisition*. New York: Routledge.

Hincks, R. (2005). Measures and perceptions of liveliness in student oral presentation speech: A proposal for an automatic feedback mechanism. *System, 33*, 575–591. doi:10.1016/j.system.2005.04.002

Housen, A., & Kuiken, F. (2009). Complexity, accuracy, and fluency in second language acquisition. *Applied Linguistics, 30*, 461–473. doi:10.1093/applin/amp048

Kapoor, A., & Picard, R. W. (2005). Multimodal affect recognition in learning environments. *Proceedings of the 13th Annual ACM International Conference on Multimedia MULTIMEDIA '05* (pp. 677-682). New York: ACM Press.

Levis, J. (2007). Computer technology in teaching and researching pronunciation. *Annual Review of Applied Linguistics, 27*, 184–202. doi:10.1017/S0267190508070098

Long, M. (1990). Maturational constraints on language development. *Studies in Second Language Acquisition, 12*, 251–285. doi:10.1017/S0272263100009165

Markowitz, J. (1996). *Using speech recognition*. NJ: Prentice Hall.

Neri, A. (2007). *The pedagogical effectiveness of ASR-based computer assisted pronunciation training*. (Unpublished doctoral dissertation). Radboud University Nijmegen.

Price, P. (1998). How can speech technology replicate and complement good language teachers to help people learn language? [Marholmen, Sweden.]. *Proceedings STiLL, 98*, 103–106.

Strange, W. (1995). Cross-language studies of speech perception and production in second-language learning. In W. Strange (Ed.), *Speech perception and linguistic experience* (pp. 3–45). Timonium, MD: York Press Inc.

Tomokiyo, L. (2001). *Recognizing non-native speech: Characterizing and adapting to non-native usage in speech recognition.* (Unpublished doctoral dissertation). Carnegie Mellon University.

Witt, S., & Young, S. (2000). Phone-level pronunciation scoring and assessment for interactive language learning. *Speech Communication, 30*, 95–108. doi:10.1016/S0167-6393(99)00044-8

Zechner, K., Higgins, D., Xi, X., & Williamson, D. (2009). Automatic scoring of non-native spontaneous speech in tests of spoken English. *Speech Communication, 51*(10), 883–895. doi:10.1016/j.specom.2009.04.009

KEY TERMS AND DEFINITIONS

ASR: Automatic speech recognition.

CALL: Computer Assisted Language Learning.

Corrective Feedback: Any indication to the learners that their use of the target language is incorrect (Lightbown, P.M., & Spada, N. (1999). *How languages are learned* (pp. 171-172). Oxford, UK: Oxford University Press.).

Error Detection: The process by which errors are found (detected) in an utterance.

Grammatical: Pertaining to the grammar of a language and its rules.

L2: Second language.

Morphology: The science and study of forms and formation of words.

Output: Language produced by an L2 learner, either oral or written.

Syntax: The study and rules of the relation of words to one another as parts of the structures of sentences.

This research was previously published in Innovative Methods and Technologies for Electronic Discourse Analysis edited by Hwee Ling Lim and Fay Sudweeks, pages 169-189, copyright year 2014 by Information Science Reference (an imprint of IGI Global).

Chapter 17

Speech Recognition Software Contributes to Reading Development for Young Learners of English

Kenneth Reeder
University of British Columbia, Canada

Jane Wakefield
University of British Columbia, Canada

Jon Shapiro
University of British Columbia, Canada

Reg D'Silva
University of British Columbia, Canada

ABSTRACT

Thirty-six English language learners aged 6;8 to 12;6 years received practice with The Reading Tutor, which uses speech recognition to listen to oral reading and provides context-sensitive feedback. A crossover research design controlled effects of classroom instruction. The first subgroup worked with the software for 3.5 months, and following a week's crossover period, the second subgroup worked for a subsequent 3.5 months. Both groups were assessed to obtain comparable gains both in regular classroom with English as an Additional Language (EAL) support and in the classroom condition with EAL support plus the Reading Tutor. Oral reading fluency was assessed by the DIBELS measure. Fluency was also calculated by the program, and grade level of materials mastered was assessed by the software's logs. Both groups made significant gains in oral reading fluency and grade level of materials mastered, according to measures internal to the software. For one period, gains in fluency following experience with the program appeared to have been slightly larger than gains with regular classroom instruction and EAL support only.

INTRODUCTION

Disproportionate numbers of adult Canadian immigrants are reported to have poor literacy abilities (Statistics Canada, 2005) and this constitutes an obstacle to their acquiring the full range of skills in one of the two official languages of Canada, French or English, as an additional language. A steady increase

DOI: 10.4018/978-1-5225-2589-9.ch017

in the numbers of children with diverse language and cultural backgrounds in hitherto English-dominant centres in Canada mean that well over 50% of the school populations in Vancouver and Toronto have for some years grown up with languages other than English at home (Gunderson & Clarke, 1998), suggesting an increasing proportion of young Canadian learners may potentially experience similar obstacles to acquiring English literacy. This is underlined by results of reading comprehension testing of 41,962 grade 4 students in British Columbia showing that 32% of students designated as learners of English as an Additional Language (henceforth referred to as EAL learners, and their tailored instruction as "EAL support") were reading at levels 'below expectations', compared to 19% of non-EAL students tested (British Columbia Ministry of Education, 2002). At the same time, the long-term educational importance of effective early reading and writing instruction has been long acknowledged (Strickland, 2002).

A useful approach to promoting reading literacy for EAL learners is to customize instruction by integrating technology into classroom teaching (Reeder, Shapiro, Early, Kendrick, & Wakefield, 2008) and leverage the time efficiencies of automation so as to add individualized reading practice to standard group classroom instruction, which has inherent constraints on instructional time that can be devoted to individuals. One limitation of earlier reading software has been its inability to 'hear' readers (D'Silva, 2011; Rasinki, 2013). Recently, prototype software from Project LISTEN, Carnegie Mellon University, entitled The Reading Tutor, (abbreviated to (the) RT throughout) addressed this limitation by using automated speech recognition (ASR) to assist children with oral reading (Mostow, 2001; Project LISTEN, 2007). The RT listens to children read aloud age-graded texts displayed on screen, and offers to read key words or whole sentences aloud, or provide word meanings when children click on a word for help or when the program senses that they are experiencing difficulty as indicated by unusual pauses or otherwise-dysfluent oral performance. Project LISTEN's study with 178 students, Grades 1-4 from schools in the Pittsburgh area found significant fluency and comprehension gains in RT users when the Sustained Silent Reading (SSR) method of instruction was compared to the use of the RT in classrooms (Mostow, Aist, Burkhead, Corbett, Cuneo, Rossbach, et al., 2002). SSR is an instructional method for schools in which all students and teachers devote a set time to leisure reading of their own choice. Studies with EAL learners have also shown similar results. Thirty-four EAL learners in Grades 2-4 whose home language was Spanish in a Chicago suburban school were part of a study that compared SSR instruction in the classroom with the RT and claimed significantly better gains in reading fluency among children using the RT (Poulsen, Wiemer-Hastings, & Allbritton, 2007). Because the RT had not been assessed using young second language learners at the outset of the present project, its potential as an effective literacy intervention for a major population of North American urban children remained unknown. Successful trials of the RT have also been conducted with English language learners in Ghana (Korsah, Mostow, Dias, Sweet, Belousov, Dias, & Gong, 2010) and India (Weber & Bali, 2010).

Technology to Support the Acquisition of Reading

Technologies such as digital audio, Internet technologies and software programs have become popular in the last decade as viable tools in reading instruction in English language contexts. A Statistics Canada report on Information and Communication Technology (ICT) integration in Canadian elementary and secondary schools claims that governments have recognized the importance of integrating ICT in learning and teaching and have put efforts into installing hardware and software in Canadian secondary schools (Plante & Beattie, 2004). Digital technologies also offer the potential of enhancing oral reading fluency (Rasinski, 2013), which the author notes is a critical element of overall reading proficiency. The

National Reading Panel report concluded that "computer technology can be used to deliver a variety of types of reading instruction successfully" (NICHD, 2000, pp.6-9). A number of digital technology tools have been identified by D'Silva (2011) to support classroom fluency and comprehension instruction in meaningful ways and are summarized below.

Simple audio recording of learners' oral reading were found to have improved prosodic performance (i.e., pitch, stress and timing variations) in oral reading (Hudson, Lane, & Pullen, 2005). Talking books and computer-based versions of print books have been assessed as independent reading and repeated reading activities in classrooms. These are merely print books that are augmented with audio recordings. Students could have access to fluency practice "without inordinate demands on classroom teachers and without provoking self-consciousness and frustration on the part of students" according to McKenna, Reinking, and Labbo, (1997, p.185).

Commercially-available interactive multimedia computer software programs are appearing frequently as reading fluency tools. 'Academy of Reading' designed for secondary schools, is proving to be successful in the USA (Loh, 2005). Moreover, reading program packages that consist of a set of graded-readings and activities for the classroom have augmented or replaced their print-based materials with CD- ROM, web-based or software versions. For instance 'Read Naturally', a program that was designed to improve fluency in beginning and older readers with print materials now has a software version (Hasbrouck, Ihnot, & Rogers, 1999; Hudson, et al., 2005). The program claims to use oral reading and repeated reading to promote reading fluency. Interactive singing software technologies like Carry-a-Tune8 (CAT) appeared to be useful in promoting reading skills with 24 struggling readers from grades 7 and 8 (Biggs, Homan, Dedrick, Minick, & Rasinski, 2008).

Automated speech recognition (ASR) software appears to be one of the more promising digital technologies to promote reading proficiency (Rasinski, 2013). In addition to the Reading Tutor (RT) speech recognition software that is reviewed in detail above, the Reading Assistant program, a commercial ASR software program, is designed to improve reading fluency and comprehension in youth and young adults. While its publisher reports upon nine school-based case study trials claiming promising results in reading gains (Scientific Learning, 2015), only one of these (Adams, 2006) was designed as a controlled efficacy study allowing researchers to attribute reported reading gains to the Reading Assistant intervention. Clearly there is a need for further well-designed efficacy studies that can attempt to disentangle the relative impacts upon reading development of real-world variables including traditional classroom instruction, additional instructional programming, and the simple effects of time or learning history, from the specific instructional interventions that are the object of an efficacy study.

Previous Findings of the Vancouver Reading Tutor Project

In previous descriptive studies of the RT, the authors collaborated with colleagues leading Project LISTEN to form the Vancouver Reading Tutor project. We implemented the RT software in schools rich in urban English language learners, contributing three useful discoveries about the appropriateness of the RT for multilingual English language learners.

First, Reeder, Shapiro and Wakefield, (2007, August) and Reeder *et al.*, (2008) in a study of 77 participants aged 7-12 years old, included 14 children from Hindi/Urdu speaking households, 21 Mandarin, 21 Spanish, and 21 native English speaking children 11 of whom completed the RT experience and 10 of whom served as a comparison group. The aim was to determine whether home language background played a role in determining any reading gains yielded by 20 minutes' daily experience on the RT over a 10-week period. All children had been designated to also receive regular EAL pullout instruction, and had been assessed by their school district on a locally developed measure as falling in its 'low intermediate' to 'high intermediate' English proficiency levels. Woodcock Reading Mastery Tests-Revised with the Normative Update (Woodcock, 1998) provided that study's dependent measures of reading, and they were administered in a pretest-posttest design. Analyses of covariance (controlling for age) of mean gain scores for four reading subtests (Word Attack, Word Identification, Word Comprehension, Passage Comprehension) by home language groups showed robust main effects of time for all four home language groups, indicating that participants taken as a whole made significant gains on all four measures over the 10-week period of treatment. The Spanish home language group initially appeared to have made relatively lower mean gains than the three other home language groups on all four reading measures, but that finding was discounted when it was discovered upon closer investigation that the majority of the Spanish speaking participants were recent refugee claimants whose educational history had been badly disrupted over the preceding years to the study. Teachers' reports to that effect are also borne out in a large-scale independent study of immigrant learners in the school district (Gunderson, 2006).

Second, the same study revealed that the lowest of three English language proficiency groups in the sample made greater gains than the higher proficiency groups and native speakers, outgaining the three other groups on Word Identification and Passage Comprehension measures. Their gains compared favourably to those of children in the sample who spoke English as their native language.

Third, in an analysis of the effectiveness of 20 minutes per day with the RT when compared to 30 minutes or more per day of human tutoring over the same six-week span, the two small groups (n=11 and n=10 in RT and Volunteer Tutor groups respectively) of native English-speaking participants were compared on the four reading outcome measures (Reeder, Shapiro, & Wakefield, 2009, July). Analyses of covariance of mean gains revealed main effects of time for all measures for both treatment groups, while paired comparisons analyses revealed that the Volunteer Tutoring group's mean gains were superior to those of the RT group for the Word Comprehension subtest. We tentatively concluded that the RT treatment offered some time efficiencies over conventional human tutoring for at least three of the four reading parameters we studied.

It remained to be seen whether a successful intervention like the RT was inherently superior to classroom instruction with EAL support. The present study extends the Vancouver Reading Tutor Project, and is designed to address the related questions:

1.   Is the Reading Tutor superior to classroom instruction with EAL support in improving English reading fluency for EAL learners? and more specifically;
2.   In the context of the types of urban schools that this project took place at, are any gains in reading fluency in EAL learners using the RT with EAL support superior to any gains of EAL learners taking only classroom instruction with EAL support?

METHOD

Participants and School Context

Thirty-six students were identified by classroom teachers to take part, (14 female, 22 male,) from one medium sized public elementary school serving a low income, multilingual neighbourhood in Vancouver,

Canada. Children were drawn from Grades 2-7, and ranged in age from 6;8-12;6 years. All participants were receiving what we judged to have been expert EAL pullout support for approximately 45 minutes several days per week from a highly experienced EAL specialist teacher, and had been provincially designated for funding for that purpose. The EAL program mandated in the province of British Columbia is designed to transition learners into the mainstream curriculum, which is delivered in English. Participants' English proficiency on the Woodcock Muñoz test ranged from 17 – 33, placing them nominally as beginners to low intermediates in English proficiency at the outset. Children's home languages were roughly representative of the school's catchment area in which the vast majority of households used a language other than English for everyday communication (Figure 1). None of the children's homes reported using English as their principal language.

Dependent Measures

As our primary measure of reading proficiency, we decided to use a widely employed curriculum-based assessment of reading, the DIBELS Oral Reading Fluency (ORF) 6th Edition. Children read a standardized set of passages prescribed for their grade level for one minute. Words omitted, replaced, as well as hesitations for three seconds or longer are scored as errors, while self-corrections within three seconds are accepted as accurately read. The number of words read correctly per minute yields the test score. Its publishers, The Center on Teaching and Learning, University of Oregon, claim that DIBELS assesses "accuracy and fluency with connected text" (Center on Teaching and Learning, University of Oregon, 2015, "Description of the ORF and RTF Measures," para 1). This external measure was not dependent upon administration of the RT and therefore could be administered at the beginning and end of each of the two treatment periods scheduled into the study's design.

As secondary measures of reading proficiency, we employed two measures that are embedded into the logging structure of the RT: reading fluency and grade levels of reading passages successfully read. The embedded reading fluency measure counted words recognized by the RT's speech analyzer per minute, averaged over one month intervals, thus it had the advantage of being a repeated measurement. It had the disadvantage that it was administered by an intelligent system that was itself in the process of learning each user's vocal patterns, particularly for the earlier measurements, and hence might have

Figure 1. Home languages of the study's 36 participants

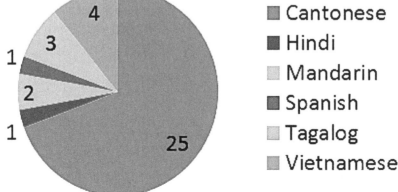

been subject to systematic underestimation of early reading fluency and consequent overestimation of gains over time. The grade level assessments were generated by the RT's internal routine for assignment of reading passage to users dependent upon the internally-measured fluency scores, so they were not strictly independent of that fluency measure. We report gains in grade level of materials mastered from the beginning to the end of the RT treatment periods.

The Crossover Research Design

Crossover research designs (Mills, Chan, Wu, Vail, Guyatt, & Altman, 2009) use participants as their own controls longitudinally, as illustrated in Table 1. Instead of structuring a control group and a treatment group in a two-group design, the design assigns each of two participant groups to a treatment condition as well as a control condition, comparing groups' performance under both conditions. The crossover design allowed us to look at the potential impact of the RT intervention twice, and offered the advantage of adding some control over the simple impact of time, while not denying any participants an educational experience that had independently been shown to be promising and associated with gains in reading proficiency. The design also allowed us to conduct both between- and within-group comparisons. Note that testing occurs at the beginning and end of each of the two 3.5-month treatment periods for both groups in the DIBELS Oral Reading Fluency outcome measure but only before and after the RT treatment (not regular instruction) for those measures that were internal to the RT itself, i.e., fluency with RT materials, grade level of RT materials selected. Hence it is the findings for the DIBELS Oral Reading Fluency measure that would allow us to test more rigorously the efficacy of the RT in comparison to regular classroom instruction with EAL support.

Table 1 also describes the assignment of the study's two subgroups to treatment and control conditions across the study's two 3.5-month treatment periods over the school year, and illustrates the crossover period of one week's duration in mid-February of the year at which point each group would switch treatment conditions. The standardized DIBELS Oral Reading Fluency measure was administered to all participants (regardless of their treatment assignment) at the beginning of October, in February during the crossover week, and in June at the conclusion of the study. Data from the two internal reading measures (fluency and grade level) were harvested from the RT software's logs with the cooperation of Project LISTEN at the beginning and end of each of the two RT treatment phases only for the group assigned to the RT. Gain scores were calculated for all measures.

Assignment to the two subgroups required for the crossover design was carried out by the participants' own classroom teachers, using timetabling constraints as the main consideration. Table 2 illustrates the composition of each subgroup in terms of some relevant variables that might bear upon reading development. In terms of similarity, groups came close to providing us with a matched sampling design for the study, but children were teacher-assigned, not randomly assigned, to groups, since this was an ordinary

Table 1. The study's crossover research design

October	Treatment (3.5 Months)	February	Treatment (3.5 Months)	June
Group 1	Classroom + RT		Classroom Only	
START		CROSSOVER		FINISH
Group 2	Classroom Only		Classroom + RT	

Table 2. Composition of the two subgroups used in the study's crossover design

	GROUP 1, n=18	GROUP 2, n=18
Age on entry	8.7 yrs (6;8-11;4)	8.6 yrs (7;0 – 12;6)
Gender	F=6 M=12	F=8 M=10
English Proficiency	26.7 (19-33)	25.0 (17-30)
Initial Reading fluency	60.3 words/min (16-108)	51.7 words/min (9-120)
Initial Reading comprehension	23.5 (6-40)	23.2 (6-37)

school with fixed timetables and the usual constraints rather than a laboratory. Thus, the design is quasi-experimental, not a fully randomized experiment. That limitation was, we believe, offset to a degree by the ecological validity of using intact school groups in more naturalistic groupings and normal timetabling.

Procedure

Two Reading Tutor systems were installed centrally in the school library under a Teacher Librarian's supervision (see Figure 2), who volunteered to deal with startup and shutdown at beginning and end of each school day, and to alert the research team of any technical difficulties encountered in the daily operation of the program or the hardware. Teachers worked with the research team to schedule each child for 20 minutes' practice with the software daily for the 3.5 months in either the first or second treatment period according to the design.

The investigators' RT treatment objective was 20 minutes' daily practice, over 4 days per week on The Reading Tutor for just over 3 months. The actual values achieved by participants slightly exceeded this objective and demonstrated good standardization of treatment on RT given the similarity of their profiles of participation:

Figure 2. The study's configuration of The Reading Tutor in its school setting

Photo credit: Lei Hong. Used with permission.

- Group 1 mean (range) participation:
  - 52.0 days (min 40 days, max 61 days);
  - 19.9 hours (min 14.0 hours, max 29.8 hours);
- Group 2 mean (range) participation:
  - 51.3 days (min 32 days, max 64 days);
  - 19.3 hours (min 11.0 hours, max 28.3 hours).

The working hypothesis for our comparison of the two treatment conditions was that if the RT treatment was indeed more effective in promoting oral reading fluency than classroom experience with EAL pullout support alone, then marginal mean reading fluency gain scores should resemble the idealization illustrated in Figure 3. In that idealization, students experiencing classroom teaching plus the RT would outperform students experiencing only classroom teaching, and further, each group would attain higher reading fluency gains under the RT treatment condition than under the classroom only condition. The idealized performance curves would thus resemble a diamond-shaped figure.

FINDINGS

We begin by presenting results gained from the two internal measures we accessed from Reading Tutor's user logs, its reading fluency measure, and its grade level measures, recorded at the start and finish of each group's assignment to the RT treatment. We then turn to the findings from the DIBELS Oral Reading Fluency test which was administered before and after all treatment conditions, offering us the possibility of comparing the efficacy of the two conditions in promoting oral reading fluency.

Figure 4 displays the mean gains in internally-assessed reading fluency from start to finish of the RT treatment for each group. We found a main effect of time ($F=4.92$ (1,34), $p=.03$) with an effect size of .126. We found no between group effect, in the sense of order of treatment advantage (fall vs. spring) for this measure, indicating that all students made strong gains in reading fluency on this measure, regardless of treatment order.

Figure 3. Idealized curves assuming greater efficacy of RT treatment condition

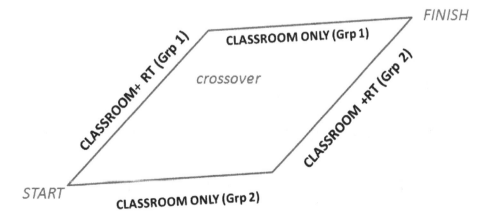

Figure 4. Internally measured fluency gains, start to finish of each RT treatment

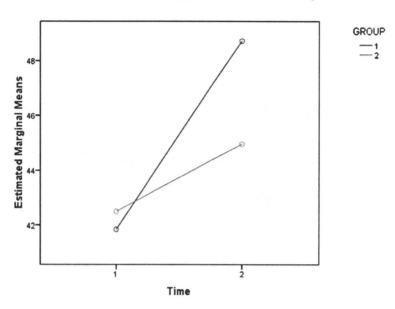

Figure 5 presents mean grade level gains with RT materials, assessed at the start and finish of each RT treatment phase. Again, there was a main effect of time found (F=72.55 (1,34), *p*=.000) with a substantial effect size of .681. And again, there was no group effect, in the sense that there appeared to have been no treatment order advantage, suggesting that all students made strong gains in grade level of materials fluently read, roughly a one-year's gain over the 3.5 months of treatment, regardless of treatment order.

Figure 5. Mean grade level gains from start to finish of each RT treatment period

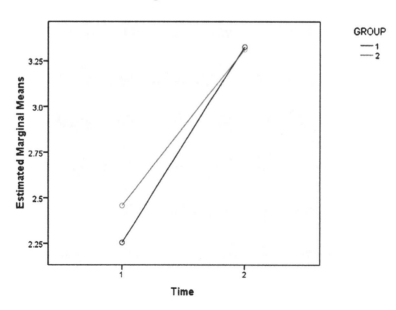

These findings derived only for the RT intervention are naturally descriptive only, since there was a confounding variable during the RT treatment periods, i.e., regular classroom experience together with expert EAL support. Would our standardized assessment of oral reading fluency administered not only before and after the RT treatments, but also before and after the classroom conditions provide comparative findings that might shed light upon the efficacy of the Reading Tutor treatment?

Figure 6 compares mean gains on the standardized DIBELS Oral Reading Fluency measure for the two subgroups before and after both treatment conditions. There was a substantial main effect of time, (F=33.23 (2,66), p=.000) with an effect size of .412. We also found a potential but non-significant effect of group, in which Group 1's mean gain score was slightly superior to that of Group 2 (F=1.195 (1,33), p=.282) with a very small effect size, .035. Similarly, we found a potential but non-significant treatment difference, suggesting that the RT group's mean gains were slightly superior to those of the classroom treatment group's in the October through February phase of the study (F=1.47 (1, 34), p=.23) again with a very small effect size, .043. This is noted by means of a vertical green arrow superimposed upon Figure 6, since this is the only suggestion in the findings that the RT in itself is potentially more effective than regular classroom instruction at enabling students to increase their oral reading fluency. While Figure 6 does indeed illustrate curves that move somewhat in the direction of Figure 3's idealized confirmation of the RT's efficacy when tested under the realistic conditions of good classroom instruction together with high quality EAL pullout support for English language learners, only in one of this study's two parallel trials was there a suggestion of the RT's superiority in promoting oral reading fluency, and that indicated a very small effect size. And this is not to diminish the role that the RT very probably played in contributing to the substantial reading gains achieved by both groups in our study, as we discuss below.

Figure 6. Mean gains on the DIBELS oral reading fluency measure for the two subgroups before and after treatment conditions

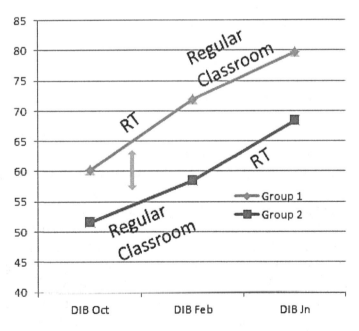

DISCUSSION AND LIMITATIONS OF THE STUDY

We need to consider why those fluency increases specifically associated with the use of The Reading Tutor were so modest (effect sizes.035 and.043) despite the impressive gains made by all students over the school year (effect size.412). We believe there are three reasons for these findings, and these relate to inherent limitations posed by the study's design and field implementation.

Effect of Short Crossover Period on Phase 2 Findings

It is conceivable that the oral reading fluency improvement associated with Group 1's experience on The Reading Tutor was cumulative, and continued to affect reading after the very short crossover or 'wash-out' period, only one week in length. Those early gains probably contributed to subsequent performance under regular classroom conditions without the RT, decreasing the within-group contrast by treatment for that group. Mills et al. (2009) note that crossover designs are most appropriate for studies whose treatment effects are short-lived and reversible. Clearly, early reading practice is not such an experience but is regarded by educators as continuing in its benefits, providing a foundation for later learning across the curriculum (Strickland, 2002).

Moderating Effect of Good Quality Classroom Instruction With Strong EAL Support for All Groups

This study took place in a well-run, reasonably well-funded school system that made a priority of supporting its majority population, who were English language learners from lower-income, multilingual homes. The investigators observed a good level of staff morale and experienced enthusiastic cooperation from teachers and school leadership alike. It might well have been that the large, main effects of time over the school year were exactly the findings that an independent assessment of reading development should have found, in the light of the relatively short exposure to the sophisticated ASR program that the RT represents: its impact was simply overwhelmed by good teaching and high quality support for English Language Learners. Quality classroom instruction – in its absence - may well have been the reason for the very promising results for a much shorter crossover classroom trial of the RT found by Poulsen, Wiemer-Hastings, and Allbritton (2007). That study reported difficulties at the school level in recruitment and cooperation, which suggested that its school setting was less than optimum, whereas the present study was carried out under optimal instructional conditions in our view.

Did the RT Contribute to Participants' English Language Development?

It is arguable, to the extent that reading is a language process rather than a disembodied cognitive skill, that the RT could have made a positive contribution to the fundamental English Language learning that all participants were undergoing during the school year. This is because the RT appears to promote one of the essential elements of good English language instruction itself. Second language acquisition research tells us that 'noticing errors' is crucial in promoting language error correction and learning more generally (Schmidt, 2012). Does the feedback provided by the RT promote language development in that respect? We would argue that the RT promotes noticing effectively because of three key design features:

- The feedback provided by the RT is subtle: It merely does not highlight incorrectly read text as the reader proceeds; further, it signals that the program is waiting for improved input only if there is a major delay or error;
- Feedback provided by the RT is imperfect in the sense that its ASR technology does not catch every single reading error and stop to offer help (Mostow & Aist, 1999). Consequently, discourse flow is not frequently interrupted, thus helping to balance contending fluency and accuracy performance goals. The RT offers more human-sounding, less robotic discourse interaction;
- Because feedback from the RT occurs in private, with no public failures or distractions, noticing an error is less stressful and potentially more easily undertaken.

For these reasons, we believe that the RT, for all its demonstrated benefits, did not differentiate itself sufficiently from the strong baseline of classroom instruction and language support that was in place in the present study for it to contrast greatly in its contribution to oral reading fluency development.

CONCLUSION

This crossover-design study was able to demonstrate gains in oral reading fluency for English language learners while undertaking several months' practice with The Reading Tutor. The first measure, internal to the RT software's logging system, showed significant gains for participants from beginning to end of their 3.5 months of RT use with an effect size of .126. The second measure, also internal to the RT's software, showed that participants by the end of their 3.5 months of RT practice were tackling reading materials one full year's reading level in advance of the materials they had begun with, showing a substantial effect size of .681. An independent, standardized procedure (DIBELS) for assessing gains in oral reading fluency revealed fluency gains following the RT treatment that were slightly larger than gains following regular classroom instruction and EAL support only for one of the administration periods of the study, the fall term. Although the effect sizes for the two group's gains under the RT condition, .035 and .043 were modest, we found a very strong overall gain in fluency for the two groups combined across the school year, with a substantial effect size of .412. In terms of the study's related research questions that concerned the superiority of the RT experience over the benefits of good classroom instruction coupled with expert English language support, our findings should be treated as cautious affirmations of our working hypothesis, given the modest effect sizes of our comparative data.

It is nonetheless safe to conclude that the RT was clearly associated with the observed strong gains in oral reading fluency when measured independently or within the intervention's own assessment tools, and with significant grade level gains in passages mastered. As such, the present study showed that it is a worthwhile addition to even optimal instruction and language support, and that it may indeed have contributed to the strong main effects of time our study revealed. Only replications of this work, ideally with a larger sample size and longer treatment periods, potentially more robust approaches to the assessment of reading including comprehension (cf. Fuchs, Fuchs, Hosp, & Jenkins, 2001) and perhaps even deployment in less optimal school settings can resolve more definitively the question of the relative efficacy of the RT in relation to 'regular' classroom teaching.

ACKNOWLEDGMENT

An earlier version of this paper was presented as: Reeder, Shapiro, & Wakefield (2014, August). The authors wish to thank Lei Hong for her contribution to data collection for the study reported here, and acknowledge the kind support of the Vancouver School Board, and the Social Sciences & Humanities Research Council, Canada, in its grant support to Kenneth Reeder and co-investigators.

REFERENCES

Adams, M. J. (2006). The promise of automatic speech recognition for fostering literacy growth in children and adults. In M. C. McKenna, L. D. Labbo, R. D. Kieffer, & D. Reinking (Eds.), *International Handbook of Literacy and Technology* (Vol. 2, pp. 109–128). Mahwah, NJ: Erlbaum.

Biggs, M. C., Homan, S. P., Dedrick, R., Minick, V., & Rasinski, T. (2008). Using an interactive singing software program: A comparative study of struggling middle school readers. *Reading Psychology*, *29*(3), 195–213. doi:10.1080/02702710802073438

British Columbia Ministry of Education. (2002). BC performance standards: Reading. Victoria, BC, Canada.

Center on Teaching and Learning, University of Oregon. (2015). *DIBELS Data System*. Retrieved fromhttps://dibels.uoregon.edu/market/assessment/measures/orf.php

D'Silva, R. A. (2011). *Promoting reading skills of young adult EAL learners through voice recognition software*. Unpublished doctoral dissertation, The University of British Columbia, Vancouver, BC.

Fuchs, L., Fuchs, D., Hosp, M., & Jenkins, J. (2001). Oral reading fluency as an indicator of reading competence: A theoretical, empirical, and historical analysis. *Scientific Studies of Reading*, *5*(3), 239–256. doi:10.1207/S1532799XSSR0503_3

Gunderson, L. (2006). *English-only instruction and immigrant studies in secondary schools: A critical examination*. Mahwah, NJ: Erlbaum.

Gunderson, L., & Clarke, D. (1998). An exploration of the relationship between ESL students' backgrounds and their English and academic achievement. In T.Shanahan, F. V.Rodriguez-Brown, C.Worthman, J. C.Burnison, & A.Cheung (Eds.), 47th yearbook of the National Reading Conference (pp. 264–273). Chicago, IL: National Reading Conference.

Hasbrouck, J. E., Ihnot, C., & Rogers, G. H. (1999). Read Naturally: A strategy to increase oral reading fluency. *Reading Research and Instruction*, *39*(1), 27–37. doi:10.1080/19388079909558310

Hudson, R., Lane, H. B., & Pullen, P. C. (2005). Reading fluency assessment and instruction: What, why, and how? *The Reading Teacher*, *58*(8), 702–714. doi:10.1598/RT.58.8.1

Korsah, G. A., Mostow, J., Dias, M. B., Sweet, T. M., Belousov, S. M., Dias, M. F., & Gong, H. (2010). Improving Child Literacy in Africa: Experiments with an automated reading tutor. *Information Technologies and International Development*, *6*(2), 1–19.

Loh, E. (2005). *Building reading proficiency in high school students: Examining the effectiveness of the academy of READING for striving readers.* Retrieved January 31, 2008, from http://www.autoskill. com/pdf/HS_metastudy2005.pdf

McKenna, M., Reinking, D., & Labbo, L. D. (1997). Using talking books with reading-disabled students. *Reading & Writing Quarterly, 13*(2), 185–190. doi:10.1080/1057356970130206

Mills, E., Chan, A., Wu, P., Vail, A., Guyatt, G., & Altman, D. (2009). Design, analysis, and presentation of crossover trials. *Trials, 10*(1), 27. doi:10.1186/1745-6215-10-27 PMID:19405975

Mostow, J., & Aist, G. (1999). Giving help and praise in a reading tutor with imperfect listening – because automated speech recognition means never being able to say you're certain. *CALICO Journal, 16*(3), 407–424.

Mostow, J., & Aist, G. (2001). Evaluating tutors that listen: An overview of Project LISTEN. In K. Forbus & P. Feltovich (Eds.), *Smart Machines in Education* (pp. 169–234). Palo Alto, CA: MIT/AAAI Press.

Mostow, J., Aist, G., Burkhead, P., Corbett, A., Cuneo, A., Rossbach, S.,.... (2002). *Independent practice versus computer-guided oral reading: Equal-time comparison of sustained silent reading to an automated reading tutor that listens.* Paper presented at the Ninth Annual Meeting of the Society for the Scientific Study of Reading, June 27-30, Chicago, IL.

NICHD. (2000). *Report of the National Reading Panel. Teaching children to read: an evidence-based assessment of the scientific research literature on reading and its implications for reading instruction: Report on the subgroups (No. NIH Pub. No. 00-4754).* Rockville, MD: National Institute of Child Health and Human Development.

Plante, J., & Beattie, D. (2004). *First results from the Information and Communications Technologies in schools survey, 2003-2004.* Retrieved from http://www.statcan.ca/english/research/81-595-MIE/81-595-MIE2004017.pdf

Poulsen, R., Wiemer-Hastings, P., & Allbritton, D. (2007). Tutoring bilingual students with an automated reading tutor that listens. *Journal of Educational Computing Research, 36*(2), 191–221. doi:10.2190/A007-367T-5474-8383

Project Listen. (2007). *Project Listen Summary.* Retrieved from http://www-2.cs.cmu.edu/~listen/

Rasinski, T. (2013). *Supportive fluency instruction: The key to reading success (especially for students who struggle). A white paper for Scientific Learning.* Scientific Learning, Oakland, CA. Retrieved from http://www.scilearn.com

Reeder, K., Shapiro, J., Early, M., Kendrick, M., & Wakefield, J. (2008). Listening to diverse learners: The effectiveness and appropriateness of a computer-based reading tutor for young Canadian language learners. In F. Zhang & B. Barber (Eds.), *Handbook of research on computer-enhanced language learning* (pp. 159–188). Hershey, PA: IGI. doi:10.4018/978-1-59904-895-6.ch010

Reeder, K., Shapiro, J., & Wakefield, J. (2007, August). The effectiveness of speech recognition technology in promoting reading proficiency and attitudes for Canadian immigrant children. Paper presented at the 15th European Conference on Reading, Berlin, Germany.

Reeder, K., Shapiro, J., & Wakefield, J. (2009, July). A computer based reading tutor for young English language learners: Recent research on proficiency gains and affective response. Paper presented at the 16th European Conference on Reading and 1st Ibero-American Forum on Literacies, Braga, Portugal.

Reeder, K., Shapiro, J., & Wakefield, J. (2014, August). *Advanced speech recognition supports reading development for young EAL learners.* Paper presented at the World Congress 2014, International Association of Applied Linguistics, Brisbane, Australia.

Schmidt, R. (2012). Attention, awareness, and individual differences in foreign language learning. In W. Chan, K. Chin, G. Bhatt, & I. Walker (Eds.), *Perspectives on individual characteristics and foreign language education* (pp. 27–50). Boston, MA: Walter de Gruyter. doi:10.1515/9781614510932.27

Scientific Learning Inc. (2015). *Reading Assistant ™ Results.* Retrieved from http://www.scilearn.com/results/reading-assistant-results

Statistics Canada. (2005). *Adult Literacy and Life Skills Survey.* Retrieved from http://www.statcan.gc.ca/daily-quotidien/050511/dq050511b-eng.htm

Strickland, D. (2002). The importance of early intervention. In A. Farstrup & S. J. Samuels (Eds.), *What research has to say about reading instruction* (3rd ed., pp. 69–86). Newark, DE: International Reading Association.

Weber, F., & Bali, K. (2010). Enhancing ESL education in India with a reading tutor that listens. In *Proceedings of the First ACM Symposium on Computing for Development* (20: pp. 1–9). New York, NY, USA: ACM. doi.org/ doi:10.1145/1926180.1926205

Woodcock, R. (1998). *Woodcock reading mastery tests – Revised/normative update.* Circle Pines, MN: American Guidance Service.

This research was previously published in the International Journal of Computer-Assisted Language Learning and Teaching (IJCALLT), 5(3); edited by Bin Zou, pages 60-74, copyright year 2015 by IGI Publishing (an imprint of IGI Global).

Chapter 18
Integration of Wireless Technologies in Smart University Campus Environment:
Framework Architecture

Yaser Khamayseh
Jordan University of Science and Technology, Jordan

Shadi Aljawarneh
Jordan University of Science and Technology, Jordan

Wail Mardini
Jordan University of Science and Technology, Jordan

Muneer Bani Yassein
Jordan University of Science and Technology, Jordan

ABSTRACT

In this paper, the authors are particularly interested in enhancing the education process by integrating new tools to the teaching environments. This enhancement is part of an emerging concept, called smart campus. Smart University Campus will come up with a new ubiquitous computing and communication field and change people's lives radically by providing systems and devices supported with smart technologies that have the capabilities of rapid respond to changes and circumstances without human interference, and it will be able to learn from these circumstances. This paper presents framework architecture for integrating various types of wireless networks into a smart university campus to enhance communication among students, instructors, and administration. Moreover, the authors study two possible applications to utilize the proposed networking framework: smart identification and social collaboration applications. An essential part to achieve the main principles of smart university campus is the deployment and usage of smart card technologies for identification and payment. Nowadays, there are several

DOI: 10.4018/978-1-5225-2589-9.ch018

types of smart identification cards that support wireless technologies such as RFIDs and NFC. In both types, a card reader can read the card information from a distance. Moreover, in NFC cards, the card is integrated with the user's cellular phone. Social networking services (such as Facebook) facilitate online communication and provide a suitable environment for collaboration among students. As a part of future work, the proposed framework is deployed in the authors' university campus to find out the end-end performance and system usability.

INTRODUCTION

The widespread of mobile devices with pervasive information appliances allows for the development of new information environments. Researchers and market needs realize a ubiquitous university campus information system by automatically combining mobile devices interaction with environment in an intelligent way.

Smart Campus will come up with a new ubiquitous computing and communication field and change people's life radically, by providing systems and devices supported with smart technologies that have the capabilities of rapid respond to changes and circumstances without human interference, and it will be able to learn from these circumstances. In this paper we propose a framework for integrating several emerging wireless technologies for smart campus. The proposed framework is intended to improve the social networking aspects among students, instructors, and administration. Several applications can be built to utilize the underlying proposed framework.

Social networking is an emerging and important concept in young students' daily activities. Students shares their daily life experiences and thoughts with their colleagues and friends, they chat and communicate all the time. Students spend a great amount of time on social networking sites. This trend has several social challenges as it limits real life interaction among young generations and it limits such interaction to computers and other electronic devices. However, and despite its challenging nature, these social networks can be utilized as educational tools and expand the horizons for the new generations of student to access and share knowledge related to their studies. An example of such usage, currently, in software development disciplines, where students learn how to write computer codes, a new generation of developing environment called Collaborative Development Environments (CDV) (Booch & Brown, 2003) and Social Development Environment (SDE) (Lanubile, 2009) are implemented such that software developers can share their ideas and codes.

The rest of this paper is organized as follows: Section 2 reviews some of these technologies, namely, Bluetooth, and ZigBee. Section 3 discusses some of the recent works on smart campus. Section 4 proposes the networking framework; it presents the 4 tires of communications using emerging wireless technologies Section 5 describes two applications for smart campus initiative: smart identification and social collaboration. Finally the conclusions and future works are drawn in Section 6.

WIRELESS TECHNOLOGIES IN SMART UNIVERSITY CAMPUS ENVIRONMENT

Bluetooth Networks

Bluetooth is an enabling communication technology that connects electrical devices wirelessly. It operates in the 2.4 GHz ISM (license free) frequency band. Devices (such as smart phones, headsets, tablets, and portable computers) communicate and send data to each other without the need for cables. The main attracting features of Bluetooth are: low cost, low size, and low power.

The Main Features of Bluetooth are:

- It can be operated in the free 2.4GHz frequency band;
- Transmission range between 10-100m;
- Supports both point-to-point and point-to-multipoint connections to enable both infrastructure ad hoc local wireless modes.

ZigBee Networks

ZigBee is a standard designed for sensor networks based on the IEEE 802.15.4 standard and created by the ZigBee Alliance (Specification, 2008), which incorporates hundreds of technological companies. ZigBee standard protocol was introduced by the ZigBee Alliance In 2002. ZigBee adopted IEEE 802.15.4 standards for its Physical Layer (PHY) and Medium Access Control (MAC) protocols. Moreover it defines the network layer specifications and provides the framework for the application layer (Farahani, 2008).

ZigBee work in Personal Area Networks (PAN's) and device – to – device network, connectivity between small packet devices and control in many of applications such as light, switches, etc. ZigBee is originally designed o target battery power applications with low data rate, low cost, low power consummation and long battery life. ZigBee-based wireless devices operate in 868 MHz, 915 MHz, and 2.4 GHz frequency bands. The maximum data rate is 250 K bits per second.

WLAN Networks

Wireless Local Area Networks (WLANs) are medium range wireless personal network technology; it supports data transmissions up to few hundred meters. It requires an access points to coordinate and mange communications between the network users. It is very common access technology to the Internet from homes and universities. For a user to communicate with other users or with the Internet, it first needs to connect to an access point, and the access point mange the connection for the user.

A common commercial WLAN network is WiFI with its various versions. The careful distribution of the access network in the environment (such as university campus) can enable the users to reach other users that are few hundred meters apart. Moreover, WLAN connections can carry data with large sizes, few Megabytes.

RELATED WORKS

We identify that the smart university campus initiatives has several domains and it is mainly concerned about adapting new set of intelligent services into the campus to replace old manual service. Smart University Campus will come up with a new ubiquitous computing and communication field and change people's life radically, by providing systems and devices supported with smart technologies that have the capabilities of rapid respond to changes and circumstances without human interference, and it will be able to learn from these circumstances. Sensors play an important role linking the physical world with the information world. Sensors collect data from their environments to raise awareness and helps in making informed decisions. Nanotechnology and miniaturization can embed intelligence in things which called smart devices. They can process information, self-configure. In this section, we present some of the recent works in the smart campus.

Zhao (2010) Identified authentication systems are designed by the convenience of accessing servers in the campus in this research, which can be integrated securely with the application server. The user accesses the system using his intelligent card, firstly, it need to identify the user's fingerprint when they access the system, and get the ticket. As the user got the ticket, he can access all application services without further authentication in the campus network.

Ting and Tai (2010) expected to provide a preliminary understanding, and an idea about how the adoption of a technology in students' life may be conducted in school and achieved success, by exploring new patterns of teaching and learning. By adopting new technologies teaching process changes its orientation from teaching students every single idea to teaching students different ways how to search and explore this idea and finding things out by themselves, which enhances their creativity.

The quality of live videos and video transfer via public networks is limited by the bandwidth of 3G cellular networks causing many dropped connections. Hence, the services provided are limited to sending the captured videos from mobile phones to the server in the background and providing video-on-demand rather than live video service. In Nurminen, Karonen, Farkas, and Partala (2009), the authors examine the practical operations, technical feasibility and user perception for mobile video services. The study focused on the capability of mobile phones to capture and share the events using both real time and stored video services. Furthermore, it studied the social relationships between events' shooter and viewers.

In Ng et al. (2010), a new approach of thinking about holistic intelligent campus (iCampus) environment is proposed to improve the end-to-end learning lifecycle of a knowledge ecosystem. This paper presented a scheme for iCampus digital nervous ecosystem, combined with a framework depicting the various domains (iHealth, iLearning, iManagement, iGovernance, iGreen, iSocial) required to set up a holistic intelligent campus environment.

In Han et al. (2004), anyone within the U-Campus can access the available campus services using image-based sensors (e.g., Bar codes, 2D codes, and ColorCode) and mobile devices (e.g., cellular phones and smart phones). U-Campus aims to provide a context-aware environment using available devices in the public sector and the marketplace. Ubiquitous computing provides a new conceptual computing environment by its orientation of combining with real physical space and virtual electronic space. U-Campus comes as a part from larger project named UTOPIA (Ubiquitous computing TOwn Project: Intelligent context Awareness) was recognized to construct the test bed to evaluate various new services. In this research, they produce the implementation of new services, such as the U-Profile, U-Messaging and UCampus Tour Guide services that support ubiquitous computing in campus life.

In Al Takrouri et al. (2007), the authors present a smart campus eyeJOT as a new context-aware information system joining surrounding wall-sized displays with location-aware, context-sensitive information sharing on mobile devices. eyeJOT provides an intelligent view of the many events, activities and information in the campus to the users to better guide them. It supports navigation using proximity detection and information posting for news, activities and schedules using Bluetooth and SMS.

Internet is a main communication between humans; it is predictable to be a communication with things, too. Tan and Wang (2010) present a new ubiquitous computing and communication field and change people's life radically. One of the common techniques that will be adopted to accomplish the internet of things (IOT) is Radio Frequency Identification (RFID); which has the ability to identify and track objects in real-time to get important information about their location and status. Things will have IDs and virtual personalities function in smart spaces using intellectual interfaces to connect and communicate within environment, and user contexts. Internet of Things combines both the physical world and information world. Sensors play a crucial role linking both worlds. Sensors collect data from their locations, generating information raising awareness about context.

PROPOSED GENERIC FRAMEWORK

In this context, we identify four levels of communications among entities in a smart campus environment. Collectively, four-tier architectures are Hardware/software models that enable the distribution of application functionality across independent systems. As shown in Figure 1, the four levels are listed and explained next as follows:

- **Tier 1 (Device Tier):** In this tier, the web gateway represents the main key that will bridge variety kinds of sensors, actuators and other Smart Devices into the Intranet, or Internet. Note that all data and capabilities of Smart Devices might be abstracted as Web resources and activated as Web services APIs. This means that it is not necessary to directly connect to the Web, and therefore these devices can be connected to the Web through web gateway. At this tier, the Smart Devices have completely Web interface that might reduce the underlying heterogeneity of devices;
- **Tier 2 (Service Tier):** This tier presents the important services that provided in the smart campus. The service architecture includes a number of basic functions such as emergency call to security guard for addressing any concern that might be occurred. As well as this tier supports other services such as security alarm service to notify for any fires, flooding and others among the buildings of the campus. This kind of tier requires wireless sensors, actuators and GPS- the wireless sensors will be spread out in some locations in the campus to detect and notify the real-time system in case of concern happened. In case any concern, the sensors will signal the actuator to take very fast response;
- **Tier 3 (Body-Devices Tier):** This tier concerns about the communication among the various wireless devices used by end users such as students, instructors and others. For example, a student may have several devices such as personal computer (laptop), cellular phone, and wireless microphone and speakers. The communication range for this tier is within centimeters to few meters. We propose to use the star topology for communication in this tier, as depicted in Figure 2. In this topology, each student wireless devices transmits to a central (master) point that is responsible to collect the data. The master point should satisfy the following criteria:

◦ It should support multiple wireless interfaces, at least two interfaces are required. One interface to communicate with all nearby devices. The second interface is to communicate with other students' mater points; this interface should be able to cover longer distances than the first one;

◦ It should have greater power, memory, processing and storage capabilities than the other devices.

As mentioned before, communication in this tier are light weighted and the amount of data transmitted between the devices is minimal, therefore, a low powered and low data rate technology is sufficient for this tier. Thus, we propose to use NFC and/or ZigBee technologies:

• **Tier 4 (Students Tier):** This tier facilitates communications among individuals in a limited geographical area such as lecture halls and students lounges. The communication range for this level is within few meters to 100 meter. For this tier we propose to provide fully communication among end users on an ad-hoc network (Schiller, 2003). It should be noted that an ad-hoc network does not require an existing infrastructure, which reduces the cost for spreading the network and make it easier to set up the network on unordinary environments. However, establishing ad-hoc network requires particular care as the users\devices need to work together and self-organize and self-manage themselves. No central point or base station is available to control the network.

For further explanation, Figure 3 depicts the setup for the proposed ad-hoc network in a smart campus environment. It is assumed that there are 5 users in this network; it can be easily expanded to include more users. Each user may have multiple devices of Tier 4. End devices of different users cannot com-

Figure 1. Proposed communication model in smart campus

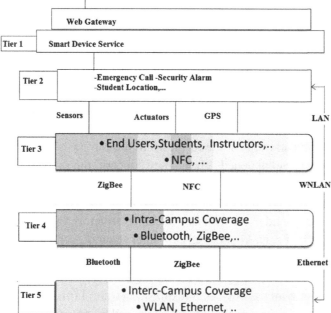

Figure 2. A star topology for tier 2 of communications

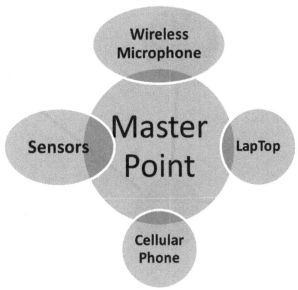

municate directly. In this configuration, the master points of the end users communicate with each other. If a device in user A wants to talk with another device in user B, the communication must be carried through the master points of each user.

All users in this network communicate either directly or through another user, therefore, each node must act as a data source and as a router. The routing task involves finding the best path from one source to a destination as well as routing the data between the source and the destination. To implement the communications in this tier, nodes require higher data rate and higher power technology than the one used in Tier 3. We proposed to use either Bluetooth or Wireless Local Area Network (WLAN) technologies for communication in this tier. We note that, in case of Bluetooth it is required to alter its design to support multi hop routing:

- **Tier 5 (Campus Tier):** This tier provides connections between various geographical locations in the campus. For example, it may connect the library with the cafeteria and so on. The communication range for this tier is within hundreds meter. And the amount of data transmitted is relatively larger than the amount of data transmitted in the other two tiers. Technology that can support long distances and large amount of data is required. Therefore, we propose to use Local Area Network (LAN) technologies such as Ethernet or/and WiFi to support communications in this tier. Moreover, both 3G and 4G cellular technologies can be used in this tier. This tier might be connected to the Internet (usually through the campus computer center) using a proxy servers. Figure 4 depicts the proposed architecture for tier 5;
- **Communication Among Tiers:** All four tiers must communicate with each other. Open, standard protocols and exposed APIs simplify this communication. In the first tier, we can use client components in any programming language (such as Java or C++) to represent the required services by the smart campus. These services run on any operating system, by speaking with the application logic layer in Tier1 and connected directly with Teir2. As well as, Tier2 connects with Tier3 and this can be of any design and this is similar to the connection between Tier3, Tier4 and Tier 5.

Figure 3. Ad-hoc topology for tier 4 of communications

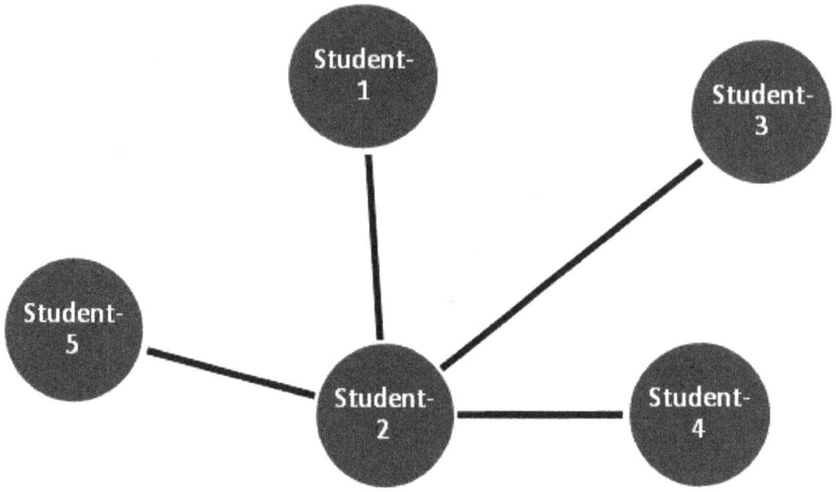

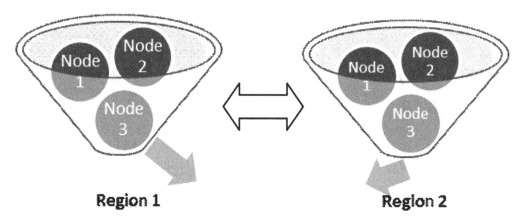

Figure 4. Network architecture for tier 5 of communications

Now, we present a brief introduction about the possible wireless technologies that can be used to setup the proposed framework and provide a constructive investigation on the challenges and benefits of using such technologies. It also provides a possible structure on how to integrate these technologies in the proposed framework.

PROPOSED CASE STUDIES

In a smart university campus, it is essential to provide state of art solutions to enhance the educational process and optimize the services provided to the students and faculty members by the administration. Universities provide several services to the faculty and students. These services can be classified in two types: (1) Academic services, related to the teaching process such as our library services; and (2) Business services, such as food services.

Today, business services are provided in a manual fashion and consumes considerable amount of time from the university administration and the students. There is a critical need to restructure and remodel these services as Smarter Services to be more intelligent and more efficient. Automating these services is an essential component of our Smarter Campus Initiative.

Moreover, wireless technologies have emerged as key components in our daily life activities as they offer wide range of services and applications to the users. In this paper we are particularly interested in enhancing the education process by integrating new tools to the teaching environments. This goal is part of our emerging direction called Smart Campus. Smart Campus will provide a new ubiquitous computing and communication infrastructure (i.e. instrument, interconnect, and intelligent) that can change people's life radically, by providing systems and devices supported with Smart technologies that have the capabilities to rapidly respond to changes and circumstances without human interference, and it will be able to learn from these circumstances.

Now, we present two possible case studies to utilize the proposed framework in section 4. The first application is the smart identification system. The second application is a smart collaboration system.

Smart Identification

Important components of the smart university campus are the e-identification and the e-payments system. Several technologies exist to facilitate these aspects such as smart cards. As, the world is moving toward wireless and mobile applications, there is a need for wireless-enabled smart cards. Students can use the card in many services. For example it can be used for identification, it can be used for lecture attendances and to access authorized locations. Moreover, it can be used for e-payment to certain service such as food service and copying service inside the campus. To increase the integrity of the cards usage, it can be connected to a central cloud service provider to monitor and provide the required business and technology services.

The system will be designed using business process modeling and optimization tools (such as Business Process Modeler) to build a Service Oriented Framework. Such design will enables us to dynamically add more features to the system easily. The system will support multiple wireless smart cards technologies such as RFID and NFC. In both types, a card reader can read the card information from a distance. Moreover, in NFC cards, the card is integrated with the user's cellular phone.

Identification devices can be used to enhance the performance in many sectors such as food services, campus threat response services, and identification theft. For example, it is possible for authorized personnel in case of emergency to locate and position any campus member once the card is activated. Moreover, campus purchases transactions can be handled efficiently to reducing the waiting times per individual. The implementation of smart cards will lead to both a higher services' efficiency and a higher return of profit. These features shall be integrated into a Radio Assisted Identification Device (RAID) (Kukkala, Adechoubou, Negrin, Dinh, & Capayachi, 2009).

The main goals of this system are:

- Incorporation of wireless smart identification cards (sID) into the campus fabric. The SIDs will store the student information. Examples of stored information are student name, number, address, degree major and debit balance;
- Provision of basic cloud services to the students in an efficient and intelligent manner. Using technology should speed the process of service providing. For example, today manual service

provided at the student cafeteria is inefficient and costly. This process can be automated and accelerated using intelligent payment methods, i.e. using the sID;

- Data collection and recording information about the students' use of business and academic services. All student transactions can be stored in cloud storage and analyzed to continually optimize the business process. The data can be later utilized to derive relations and certain patterns to enhance the services provided by the university. For example, in the food service section, the system can derive relations about the types, quantities and qualities of the meals provided to the students. Moreover, it can predict what meals to provide in the coming days.

Smart Collaboration

Social networking is an emerging and important concept in young students' daily activities. Students shares their daily life experiences and thoughts with their colleagues and friends, they chat and communicate all the time. Students spend a great amount of time on social networking sites. This trend has several social challenges as it limits real life interaction among young generations and it limits such interaction to computers and other electronic devices. However, and despite its challenging nature, these social networks can be utilized as educational tools and expand the horizons for the new generations of student to access and share knowledge related to their studies.

Several technologies exist to facilitate communication among students, instructors and administration. Most of these systems do not support collaborative behaviors as well as they are usually troublesome to access and use. As, the world is moving toward wireless and mobile applications, there is a need for wireless-enabled e-learning systems. The existing e-learning systems does not provide social networking services for the students, moreover, it is not easy to access using mobile devices. In the proposed smart e-learning system, students can share their ideas, notes and thought with each other and with their instructors. Overall, the system should increase collaboration between students and suggest and monitor this collaboration in a smart fashion.

The main goals of this application are:

- Incorporation of wireless smart devices into the campus fabric. It provides a gateway to access the smart e-learning system that stores important data about the courses, courses materials and discussion boards;
- Enhance the services provided by the e-learning system to support more services in an intelligent manner, such as suggesting team members for courses' projects, and sharing courses' material;
- Provide basic cloud services to the students in an efficient and intelligent manner. Using technology should speed the process of service providing. For example, service provided to the student using the existing e-learning system is insufficient and inefficient. This process can be accelerated and optimized using intelligent e-learning system;
- Collect data and record information about the students' use of business and academic services. All student transactions can be stored, analyzed and optimized in the cloud. For example, the system can identify certain relation to help forming groups among students to work on a particular project.

CONCLUSION AND FUTURE WORK

Emerging technologies play an increasingly important role in our daily activities, as it provide wide range of services and applications. Smart university campus initiative is an example of such applications. Wireless networks are an example of the technological advancements in the recent years. The advancement of wireless technologies faces many challenges, however, it provide a suitable arena for the development of new set of applications and services. This paper proposes an underlying framework for utilizing various types of wireless technologies to better support and realizes the smart campus initiative. To demonstrate the strength of the proposed framework, two possible applications were proposed as part of the smart university campus.

The proposed framework is flexible such that it can be further extended in the future to support higher levels of communications and more demanding applications such as video conferencing.

REFERENCES

Al Takrouri, C., Gongora, J., & Toader, S. (2007). eyeJOT - A ubiquitous context-aware campus information system. In *Proceedings of the 2nd International Conference on Pervasive Computing and Applications, 2007. ICPCA 2007*, (pp. 122-127). doi:10.1109/ICPCA.2007.4365424

Booch, G., & Brown, A. (2003). Collaborative development environments. Advances in Computers, 59.

Calvagna, M., & La Corte. (2010). WiFi bridge: Wireless mobility framework supporting session continuity. In *Proceedings of the First IEEE International Conference on Pervasive Computing and Communications* (PerCom 2003) (pp. 79-86). IEEE.

Erasala & Yen. (2002). *Bluetooth technology: A strategic analysis of its role in global 3G wireless communication era*. Academic Press.

Farahani, S. (2008). *ZigBee wireless networks and transceivers*. Elsevier.

Han, C., Ann, K., Yoon, L., Shin, L., Yook, J., & Choi, L. et al. (2004, May). Implementation of new services to support ubiquitous computing for campus life. In *Proceedings of the Second IEEE Workshop on Software Technologies for Future Embedded and Ubiquitous Systems*. IEEE.

Howitt, I., & Gutierrez, J. (2003). *IEEE802.15.4 low rate- Wireless personal area coexistence issues*. Academic Press.

Kukkala, A., & Negrin, D. C. (2009). Radio assisted identification device: A universal card. In *Proceedings of the Systems and Information Engineering Design Symposium*, (pp. 90-94). Academic Press.

Lanubile, F. (2009). Collaboration in distributed software development. In A. De Lucia & F. Ferrucci (Eds.), *Software engineering, (LNCS), (vol. 5413*, pp. 174–193). Springer-Verlag Berlin Heidelberg.

Muller, N. J. (n.d.). *Bluetooth demystified*. Academic Press.

Ng, A., Leida, S., & Afzal, Y. (2010), "The Intelligent Campus (iCampus): End-to-End Learning Lifecycle of a Knowledge Ecosystem", 2010 Sixth International Conference on Intelligent Environments (IE), pp.332-337, July 2010 doi:10.1109/IE.2010.68

Nurminen, K., & Farkas, P. (2009). Sharing the experience with mobile video: A student community trial. In *Proceedings of the Consumer Communications and Networking Conference*. IEEE. doi:10.1109/CCNC.2009.4784951

Persson, Manivannan, & Singhal. (2004). *Bluetooth scatternets: Criteria, models and classification*. Academic Press.

Schiller, J. (2003). *Mobile communications* (2nd ed.). Pearson Education.

Specification, Z. (2008). *ZigBee specification* (ZigBee Document 053474r06 version, 1(2), 378). ZigBee Alliance. Retrieved from http://scholar.google.com/scholar?hl=en&btnG=Search&q=intitle:ZigBee#0

Sriskanthan, N., Tan, F., & Karande, A. (2002). *Bluetooth based home automation system*. Academic Press.

Tan, W. (2010). Future internet: The internet of things. In *Proceedings of the 3rd International Conference on Advanced Computer Theory and Engineering* (ICACTE), (vol. 5, pp. 376-380). ICACTE.

Ting, Y. T. (2010). Teachers' view upon today's technology tool: Living or learning. In *Proceedings of the 2nd International Conference on Education Technology and Computer* (ICETC), (vol. 1, pp. 417-420). Academic Press.

Whitaker, R. M., Hodge, L., & Chlamtac, I. (2004). *Bluetooth scatternet formation: A survey*. Academic Press.

Zhao, M. Q. (2010). The design of security authentication system based on campus network. In *Proceedings of the 2010 International Conference on Electrical and Control Engineering* (ICECE), (pp. 3070-3073). ICECE.

This research was previously published in the International Journal of Information and Communication Technology Education (IJICTE), 11(1); edited by Lawrence A. Tomei, pages 60-74, copyright year 2015 by IGI Publishing (an imprint of IGI Global).

Chapter 19
A Kinect–Based Assessment System for Smart Classroom

W. G. C. W. Kumara
National Central University, Taiwan

Batbaatar Battulga
National Central University, Taiwan

Kanoksak Wattanachote
National Central University, Taiwan

Timothy K. Shih
National Central University, Taiwan

Wu-Yuin Hwang
National Central University, Taiwan

ABSTRACT

With the advancements of the human computer interaction field, nowadays it is possible for the users to use their body motions, such as swiping, pushing and moving, to interact with the content of computers or smart phones without traditional input devices like mouse and keyboard. With the introduction of gesture-based interface Kinect from Microsoft it creates promising opportunities for educators to offer students easier and intuitive ways to interact with the learning systems. The integration of Kinect based applications into classroom make students' learning experience very active and joyful. In this context, this paper proposes a system for assessment in a smart classroom environment. An interactive framework is designed using Microsoft Kinect sensor for virtual learning environment with new gesture-based questions supporting QTI-based assessment, and further a rich set of gesture commands are also introduced for practical usage in the classroom. Proposed system was experimented with teachers and students then collected feedback of the users using a usability questionnaire. The results show that the participants are satisfied with the system and it demonstrates that the proposed system is simple to use, provides better functionality and motivates student learning by assessment.

1. INTRODUCTION

With the time, the types of user interfaces people use to operate their digital tools are changing. Handheld devices, retinal trackers, speech recognition and gestural interfaces are becoming popular and famous, and are starting to become widely adapted for students' learning. These advanced tools are now challenging content developers to take advantage of new levels of interactivity between students and teachers.

DOI: 10.4018/978-1-5225-2589-9.ch019

Microsoft Kinect is a highly versatile, mobile, and accessible learning tool with numerous applications (Microsoft, 2013). Teachers and program coordinators can tap a fast-growing portfolio of games that spans across academic disciplines, sports, and adventure scenarios to energize classroom and after-school activities. Educators can also take advantage of Avatar Kinect to pursue unique opportunities for intra-school competitions, distance learning, and collaboration with colleagues, students, and parents.

Another important concept of automatic tests is the assessment, the process of documenting, usually in measurable terms, knowledge, skills, attitudes, and beliefs. Assessment can focus on the individual learner, the learning community (class, workshop, or other organized group of learners), the institution, or the educational system as a whole. However, despite the benefits of automatic tests using traditional types of questions (e.g., multiple choices, multiple response or fill in the blank) it is difficult to assess higher-order skills such as, problem solving, problem exploration, collaboration, creativity, discovering rules, developing effective strategies, spatial or time perception, among others. IMS Global provides specifications for assessment, named IMS question and test interoperability (QTI) (IMS Global Learning Consortium, 2013). The benefits of QTI are its easy manageability since it is built on XML, and its support in reusability, adaptability, scalability, and interoperability with other languages and systems. The aim of QTI is to provide an interoperable data model for the representation of questions, their aggregation in tests, and the definition of sophisticated ways of producing outcome reports for the whole test. These tests can be created and realized by compliant systems. A QTI compliant editor (used by a teacher) will turn the test and questions into a set of XML files containing all their information. Similarly, the students' interactions and answers can be visualized with a QTI compliant player.

Standing on the aforementioned background, the proposed research here has three major components, which are, QTI based assessment system, virtual learning environment, and gesture detective mechanism. The developed system aims to provide a friendly way for kids to answer questions in an interesting way. Although there is no much evidence in the literature on how to combine QTI into the gesture-based answering system, by doing this work, we believe the proposed system will be useful and appreciated by the users. Our system is different from the main stream researches in the game-based learning (GBL), from GBL's usual goal of sophisticated instructional design principals inside the game; rather, we try to provide a complete system to let instructors to design simple tests. With respect to the research stream of using gesture-based training supports in physical exercises, the proposed system, instead, is for general users to answer interactive questions. The developed system does not replace any existing assessment systems; instead, it encourages younger students to play with the system, and to answer the questions in an intuitive way. The system can be used in some unofficial situations, such as in a general customer reception area, or in a playground for kids. We believe complex assessment can still be used in traditional tests, which cannot be replaced by our method. Rather than focusing on new educational theory, existing general learning and testing theories can also be justified by using our mechanisms, which is planned in future works. Further, the demonstrated tool is a practical system for public to use, with no limitation in the usage to fit any existing learning or assessment theory.

In summary, this paper presents, discusses and analyses several evidences that shows how innovative technologies can be used in QTI system, in different scenarios, and analyzes the suitability of using QTI at the end. In this context we developed new tools and implemented real scenarios for smart classroom with Kinect. To use the proposed system for assessment with Kinect, first, the teacher creates course content and questions, then, the student can use own hand gestures to answer the questions provided by the teacher in smart virtual classroom with Kinect based interface. This global aim is divided into a set of specific objectives as, teacher's authoring tool to create and edit course and questionnaires, monitor and manage student's work and result of questionnaires in classroom in real time; design of gesture based assessment with Kinect with extended IMS QTI support in student's learning; and a smart classroom which supports more than two students use of our system to answer the question using the hand gestures in same time, with the capability of monitoring and managing the student's work in real time by the teacher.

The rest of the paper is organized as follows. Section 2 introduces background concepts of IMS QTI and Kinect. Then Section 3 explains our system design and implementation including the system architecture. Section 4 undertakes the evaluation of the experiments and implementations carried out following the proposals presented in Section 3 and discuss the main conclusions. Section 5 summarizes the main contributions of this paper. Appendix A provides user guide for use Kinect and interactions with proposed system.

2. RELATED WORKS

2.1. QTI

Educational technology specifications for assessment provide formalizations to computationally represent assessment methods and resources. The main aim of assessment specifications is to facilitate the creation, sharing and transfer of assessment data (questions, tests and results). The latest QTI versions are the 2.0 and the 2.1, whereas QTI 2.0 focuses on the representation of individual questions categorized by their types of interaction, and contains a set of graphic interactions to deal with images. QTI 2.1 extends QTI 2.0 by considering the aggregation of questions in tests organized in sections, and defines sophisticated ways of producing outcome reports for the whole test. It further defines a data model to represent assessment scenarios with a group of elements including, questions (assessment items), types of interactions (simple, text-based, graphical and miscellaneous interactions), tests (assessment tests) and their corresponding results reports (scores and outcome variables). QTI research team (Navarrete, T. et al., 2011) presented the QTIMaps model, which combined the IMS QTI standard with web maps services enabling the computational assessment of geographical skills. QTIMaps is a conceptual model enabling the creation of new types of questions, which integrate the interaction possibilities of web maps.

2.2. Gesture and Speech Recognition With Kinect

The Kinect sensor from Microsoft contains an infrared projector, two cameras, and four microphones in an array as shown in Figure 1. The color camera supports a maximum resolution of 1280×960 pixels and the depth camera supports a maximum resolution of 640×480 pixels while supporting depth recognition between 0.8 and 4 meters. On the underside of Kinect is the microphone array which is composed of four different microphones.

A gesture, within the context of user interfaces, is used to express a simple command. Further, a gesture is arbitrary in nature, based on convention, and can be misunderstood. A manipulation is any movement that is not a gesture. In the case of gesture detection, the result is binary whereas a gesture is either performed or not performed. Using algorithms to detect gestures is the most basic approach because it is easy to code, maintain, and straightforward to debug. But, the simplistic nature of algorithms can limit the types of gestures they can detect. Kinect for Windows SDK already supports and provides basic gestures such as push, gripping and hover. Further we want to recognize other gestures that may be

Figure 1. Components of Microsoft Kinect sensor (Webb, J. & Ashley, J., 2012)

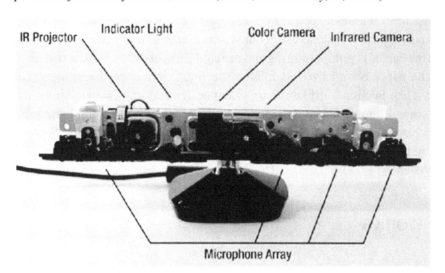

useful in our application which can be implemented using algorithmic method or template based search. The main challenge is to choose the most appropriate method. Neural networks or hidden Markov model (Wobbrock, J. O. et al., 2007) are very sophisticated, however, they require a training (learning) time on the form wanted before being served. This makes these types of algorithms less convenient for prototyping, in which, the user or developer wants to define its own recognizable recordable forms. In addition, this level of sophistication leads to a difficulty in both debugging and programming. However, other algorithms such as the one Dollar (Wobbrock, J. O. et al., 2007) and N Dollar recognizers (Anthony, L. & Wobbrock, J. O., 2012) can be implemented in any environment, even in a context of fast prototyping.

Speech recognition is broken down into two different categories: recognition of commands and recognition of free-form dictation. Free-form dictation requires that one training software to recognize a particular voice in order to improve accuracy. This is done by having speakers repeat a series of scripts out loud so the software comes to recognize the speaker's particular vocal patterns. Command recognition which also called command and control, applies another strategy to improve accuracy. Rather than attempt to recognize anything a speaker might say, command recognition constrains the vocabulary that it expects any given speaker to vocalize. Based on a limited set of expectations, command recognition is able to formulate hypotheses about what a speaker is trying to say without having to be familiar with the speaker ahead of time.

2.3. Smart Classroom Cutting Edge Components

Virtual learning environments (VLE) (Dillenbourg, P. et al., 2002) utilize virtual classrooms and meetings which often use a mix of communication technologies. Virtual classrooms enable students and instructors to communicate with each other via webcam, microphone, and real-time chatting in a group setting. The virtual classroom provides the opportunity for students to receive direct instruction from a qualified teacher in an interactive environment and students have direct and immediate access to their instructor for instant feedback and direction. The virtual classroom also provides a structured schedule of classes, which can be helpful for students who may find the freedom of asynchronous learning to be overwhelming.

This paper presents a real-time interactive virtual classroom (Deshpande, S. G., & Hwang, J. N., 2001) called smart classroom and combine with a Kinect based assessment system. In building smart classroom, cutting edge technologies such as, Helix 3D toolkit, ASP.Net SignalR, entity framework (EF), and language-integrated query (LINQ) were used. Helix 3D toolkit is a collection of custom controls and helper classes for Windows presentation foundation 3D, whereas Helix 3D is based on DirectX and is written in C# programming language. ASP.NET SignalR is a framework that facilitates building interactive, multiuser and real-time web applications, making extensive use of asynchrony techniques to achieve immediacy and maximum performance. The EF is a set of technologies in ADO.NET that support the development of data-oriented software applications. LINQ is a set of features introduced in Visual Studio 2008 that extends powerful query capabilities to the language syntax of C# and Visual Basic.

2.4. QTI, Kinect and VLE in Learning

To validate the fitness-for-purpose of the QTIMaps from the point of view of educational benefits and usability, Martinez et al. in 2003 used two authentic learning situations with real users by using several quantitative and qualitative techniques. A formal assessment scenario was carried out based on QTIMaps involving a Geography class with 23 students aged between 14 and 16 years. Further, QTIMaps was used in a mini case, an informal open workshop, Science Week at the Pompeu Fabra University (UPF). Students from different secondary schools visited an exhibition at UPF premises during a week, where, 23 students completed a test based on QTIMaps with 8 questions related to the UPF building locations using 6 different interaction types. Another good example is the use of the Wonderland-QTI platform-specific models which was designed in collaboration by a third party institution, the GAST research team (GAST, 2011) and the GTI team (GTI, 2011) in the Learn3 research project (Learn3, 2011). In the virtual world, questions can be represented using the interaction context of the 3D space (objects and avatars). Students can do actions over this space in order to answer the distributed questions and can complete the given test. Ibanez, M. B et al. in 2011 explained how the virtual world Wonderland can be used in a hypothetical educational scenario for assessing Spanish as a second language. Their goal was to create the scenario for developing the skills, reading, writing, listening and speaking. In this context, students have to interact with the different objects in order to demonstrate their language skills in the way they would have to do so in the real world. Yang, H. C. et al. in 2007 proposed an on-line adaptive testing system which provides the QTI standardized item and adaptive assessment mechanism. This system is adaptive for the learners with different learning abilities using the item response theory. Further, users can use this on-line assessment system to attend the examinations and browse the item bank to reference the solutions from author society. Chang, H. B. et al. in 2008 developed a QTI based assessment platform compliant with multimedia home platform (MHP) standard on digital TV. By this framework, users can examine how much they have learned by tests on TV and discover subjects which they are not familiar.

Homer, B. D. et al. in 2014 published their research finding about a reading supporting system for children in age group of 5 to 7 years with the functionality of story reading by a character in a Kinect game plus in-game activities, and their findings indicated that reading books on a gesture-based digital system can be an interesting, engaging activity for children, and with the addition of well-designed activities, it can further support children's acquisition of language and literacy.

Another example use of Kinect and virtual environments for learning purposes is presented by Hall, L. et al. in 2012. They presented an Kinect based virtual environment, TRAVELLER, a technology enhanced learning application that aims to provide 18-25 year olds with improved cultural understanding and sensitivity, where the players can virtually travel around the given virtual environment provided based on different cultures and can experience cultural differences during the virtual interaction with those characters. Going forward, Yang, M. T. & Liao W. C. in 2014, researched about the use of Kinect and VLEs in supporting students English and cultural learning incorporating the latest augmented reality and computer vision algorithms into a virtual English classroom, called VECAR, to promote immersive and interactive language learning. Their results show that the VECAR improved the cultural learning effectiveness and promoted interpersonal communication between teachers and students. A work in progress by Vermun, K. et al. in 2013, presented a work to determine some of the user's empathic states through her gestures using Kinect, and proposed to create an accurate system for cognitive state and affective gesture recognition by first developing a database of gestures signifying user's emotional and affected states related to e-learning context, and then by calibrating the system for accurate detection of emotions and allied states through gestures. This can be used independently or with other multimedia inputs for accurate feedback in e-learning environments. A framework for presentation and assessment in Holodeck classroom was presented by Sommool, W. et al. in 2013, using Microsoft Kinect sensor for e-learning, with new items of gesture-based questions in supporting QTI-based assessment, and a rich set of gesture commands for practical usage in classroom.

In summary, IMS QTI is an educational technology specification for assessment and to facilitate the creation, sharing and transfer of assessment data. The main elements of QTI are questions, types of interactions, tests, and their corresponding results reports. Extension of QTI mainly considers design of a new type of assessment and solving the special issue such as QTIMaps (Navarrete, T. et al., 2011). QTIMaps is a Google map based assessment which focuses on spatial and geographic information, its representation and helps develop student's skills related to spatial and geographic. Wonderland-QTI (Arroyo, D. M. et al., 2010) is further talking to the students and help to find correct answer. In recent researches students are enabled to access and control learning systems using Kinect, which is capable of recognizing student's voice, gesture and interaction, making the system as effective and joyful for the users. Smart classroom is an enhanced virtual classroom that enables students and instructors to communicate with each other via Kinect which allows real-time interactions in a group setting.

3. DESIGN AND IMPLEMENTATION

Proposed solution is discussed here in two sub sections as, system design and architecture, and implementation and experiments.

3.1. System Design and Architecture

This part was designed as a Kinect based assessment system for classroom to enhance the use of the traditional QTI. Kinect enables to use human pose making it easy to control for the interaction with the computer without traditional input devices like keyboard and mouse. The system consists of three major objects as, use of the Kinect and designed gesture for system interfacing and assessments; VLE; and real time multi-user asynchrony and interaction. A 3D virtual environment is created entirely from a computer database consisting of objects modeled in 3D. These objects are programmed to behave in certain ways as the user interacts with them. A 3D virtual environment is special because of the mixture of software and hardware gives the user an illusion of being immersed in a 3D space and the ability to interact with the 3D space. As shown in Figure 2 the proposed system have two views as, student view and teacher view, each loads from aforementioned 3D models, then Helix 3D toolkit was used to load and manage the 3D model.

Proposed system is an application that combines internet, asynchrony, and multi user cooperation and interaction at the same time. Our system is divided into four major parts (Figure 3) as authoring tool, web app, monitoring tool, and smart classroom where each part connects with others using the synchronization tool and exchanges information in real time. We use the ASP.Net SignalR technology for the synchronization which is a framework that facilitates building interactive, multiuser and real-time web applications, making extensive use of asynchrony techniques to achieve immediacy and maximum performance.

Our system uses two authoring tools to provide inputs into our system as course authoring tool and assessment authoring tool as shown in Figure 4 (a). Both authoring tools developed in WPF application and do not have any local database, because they are directly connected to webserver and sync data in real-time. Course authoring tool helps designing and creating the course with the main goal of helping teacher to create course content with 3D content such us 3D models, source code and help students to

Figure 2. (a) Teacher view: virtual classroom, (b) student view: classroom mapping

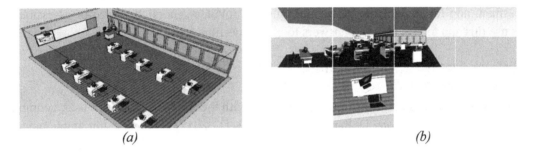

(a) *(b)*

Figure 3. System architecture

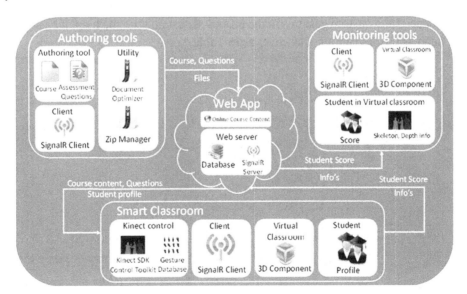

write code in 3D environments such as OpenGL, XNA etc. Main features of this tool are capability of teacher to attach lecture presentation and each slide of presentation with additional note, attaching files, such as a 3D model, source code, image and more. Assessment authoring tool is to make questionnaires of course for student which supports 10 types of questions. Utility library is a part of authoring tools section which helps to optimize course documents such as presentation files by converting into images, resizing images and archiving into zip file.

Web app (Figure 4 (b)) divides into course online content and SignalR based server. OAuth tool uses an open protocol to allow secure authorization in a simple and standard method from web, mobile and desktop applications. The main feature of OAuth tool is it enables students to access our system using their own accounts such as Facebook, Twitter, or Google. Course online content is an ASP.NET web application, which provides course content to students. It includes features, multiple content support (HTML, 3D model, course slide and source code), multiple interface support (mobile phone, smart device, PC or laptop), and real time synchronization. Database used is a MS SQL based database.

Figure 5 shows the architecture of the teacher's monitoring tool. Monitoring tools divide into two parts based on the platform, as web app and windows app. Monitoring tools receive students' information in real time using SignalR client component by XAML.

Smart classroom provides a VLE similar to a real classroom. Figure 6 shows a general architecture of a smart classroom. Our smart classroom consists of two agents as, student and teacher agent.

Assessment app for students as shown in Figure 7 provides general structure of assessment app. Students use this app to provide their answers to given questionnaires.

3.2. Implementation and Experiments

For the gesture recognition, we used a toolbox included with the Kinect SDK which uses a combination of golden section search and one Dollar method (Catuhe, D., 2012). Therefore, the implementation is able to recognize some other gestures as an example a circle. The algorithm is based on standardizing the gestures and then matching them to gestures in the database. The basics of the matching algorithm is that if no matching gesture was found at first, try to rotate the gesture a bit around the axis and see if a match will be found. Finally we recognize several basic geometric primitive as in Table 7. We have implemented enhanced and custom gestures in the proposed system with the help of basic gestures available in Kinect such as push, gripping and hover as in Table 1.

Figure 4. (a) Authoring tools, (b) web app

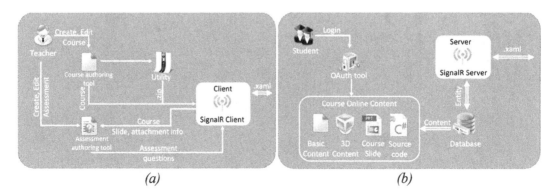

(a)   *(b)*

Figure 5. Teacher's monitoring tool of smart classroom

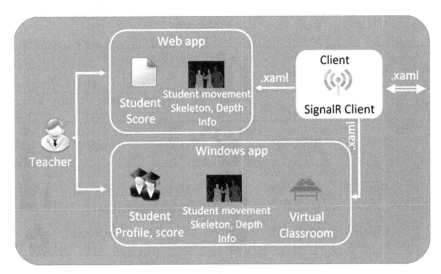

Figure 6. Smart classroom architecture

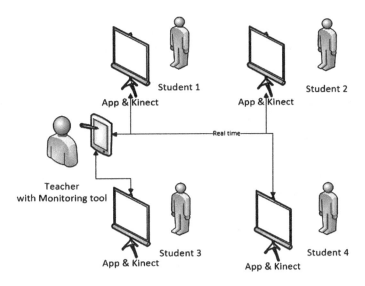

Figure 7. (a) Assessment app of smart classroom, (b) kinect control

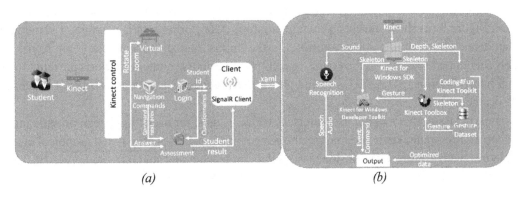

Table 1. Gesture implementation

Gesture type	Gesture	Basic gesture	User's interaction	Gesture	Basic gesture	User's interaction
Enhanced	Drag/Drop	[Gripping]				

Gesture type	Gesture	Basic gesture	User's interaction	Gesture	Basic gesture	User's interaction
Custom	True	[Gripping]		False	[Gripping]	
	Next	[Gripping]		Prev	[Gripping]	
	Drawing	[Gripping]		Rotate	[Gripping]	
	Zoom In/Out	[Gripping]		Drawing angle	[Gripping]	

Under the assessment item there are 20 types of quizzes as defined in QTI. We used several major items such as true or false, single choice, multiple choices, fill in blank, and pattern match. Table 2 shows the gestures used in those major items in the proposed system.

User interface in the proposed system divides into three types of interfaces as authoring tool interface, web interface and smart classroom interface. Figure 8 (1) shows the main screen of the course editor. The screen is divided into three sections as, inquiry which shows all courses by list and allows user to select and edit; command bar which executes commands such as save, delete, new and cancel; detail which shows the all information of selected course which the user is enabled to create, edit and delete. Assessment authoring tool is used to make questionnaires of course for students which supports 10 types of questions. Figure 8 (2) shows the main screen of the assessment editor. The screen divides into three sections as, command bar which executes commands; question which allows to edit general information of question such as question, title, difficulty coefficient and any required attachments such as optional video, audio, image, source code and 3D model; answers which contains the prompting answers to the question. For example Figure 8 (2) shows controls of single response question and the choices added by the teacher.

In the proposed system two types of web interfaces are designed as online course and teacher's monitoring tool. Figure 9 (a) shows teacher's monitoring tool. Monitoring tool is capable of showing more than 10 students who is online at a given time. In the online course, students can login to the system using their account and can access the course content. Online course content supports presentation slide, additional notes for slide, 3D model, source code, and also enables chat with teacher if the teacher is available online.

In the smart classroom a graphic user interface (GUI) is used for users. Users can provide inputs via devices such as a computer keyboard, mouse and Kinect and it provides articulated graphical output as a 3D model virtual environment. We designed two GUIs for teacher and student as in Figure 10. Teacher's

Table 2. Representation of assessment with Kinect

Assessment item	Gesture	User's interaction
1. True/False	[Gripping] [True] [False] [Both hand]	
2. Single response	[Push] [Single hand]	
3. Multiple response	[Push] [Both hand]	
4. Fill in blank	[Gripping] [Single hand]	
5. Pattern match	[Gripping] [Both hand]	
Custom gesture		
6. Kinect Angle *Student's use their right arm to draw an angle*	[Hand wave] [Both, Single hand]	
7. Voice *Student's use their sound to answer*	[Speech]	
8. Drawing *Student's use their right hand to draw given character or symbol*	[Drawing] [Single hand] [Gripping]	

Figure 8. (1) Course authoring tool: a) inquiry of course, b) toolbox of command, c) detail of selected course; (2) Assessment authoring tool: a) toolbox of command, b) question detail, c) possible answers.

(1)   *(2)*

Figure 9. (a) Monitoring tool, (b) online course

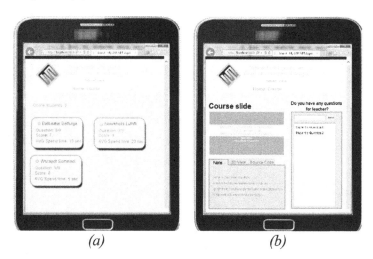

(a)   (b)

interface supports input via computer keyboard and mouse. Teacher enables to manipulate classroom model using a computer mouse. Basically student interacts with system via Microsoft Kinect sensor, a computer keyboard or mouse can be used if Kinect is unavailable.

4. EXPERIMENT AND EVALUATION

In this section the experiment carried out to evaluate the performance of the system is discussed. Two use cases were used as two different subject modules as details are given later. In demonstrating the suitability and usability of the proposed system and its functionalities, three different kinds of evaluations were performed. First, for the functionality the proposed system was compared with other five related systems and results are presented later in this chapter, then, the system was used in real two classroom scenarios and tested for the performance of each parameter, finally, for usability a questionnaire was used to evaluate the experience of the system with selected personals in the domain.

4.1. Use Cases and Performance Evaluation

Two learning scenarios were used to evaluate Kinect interaction features and user feedback with the proposed system. Used scenarios are an English learning class for primary school students and interactive computer graphics in game design for under-graduate students. For each scenario we designed and created a new assessment item type to achieve the goal.

In the first use case of helping primary school students to learn English two scenarios were provided as, understanding mathematical demonstration and learning angle related terms in English, and pronunciation of English letters words correctly providing related words starting with that letter and pronunciation of words. In the first scenario Kinect angle helps to provide input in respect to the item types in English such as angles, percentages, fractions, decimals, time and bearing. As an example in response to the question "demonstrate 90°" student can use his hand to show the angle relevant to the 90°. Then, the system recognizes his answer with the Kinect sensor and evaluates whether the answer

Figure 10. (1) Teacher's view in virtual environment, (2) student's screen interface: a) start, b) question, c) virtual classroom

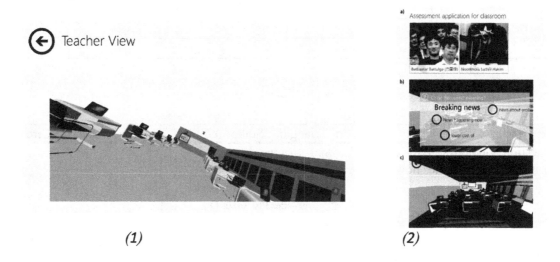

(1)   *(2)*

is correct or wrong and provides the feedback to the student, as well as stores for the later reporting purposes. Angle related example question types and one example use of Kinect in responding to the given question with hand gestures are tabulated in Table 3. In the second scenario speech recognition is used in the system to help students learn spelling and pronunciation of English words as an example given in Table 4. As an example for the use of speech recognition in Kinect, in response to the question "pronounce the letter shown" student speaks out the correct pronunciation for the letter. Then system recognizes users voice input through Kinect and evaluate whether the answer is correct or not by comparing to the stored sample answers.

Second use case was an undergraduate level computer graphics course named Interactive computer graphic in game design (ICGGD). The topics are filled with interesting images and animations related to the course and there is a wealth of support materials available, and students are motivated to express creativity in projects. Our major goal is help student to programming interactive computer graphics applications in OpenGL. Table 5 represents one example of learning OpenGL programming to draw

Table 3. Kinect angle based assessment

Item type	Angle	Percentages	Fractions	Decimals	Time	Bearing Direction
Question: Demonstrate	90°	25%	1/8	0.5	7:45	Northeast
Answer						
Gesture: *Draw angle*						

Table 4. Speech recognition based assessment

Item Type	Alphabet (26 Letter)	Vowel Sounds (Basic 15, Diphthongs Reached 27)	Vocabulary
Question: Please Spell	A	A	Apple
Result	Evaluate accuracy rate		

Table 5. Drawing based assessment and recognize primitive

Item Type	Triangle	Square	Line	Polygon	Quads	Circle

Question: Demonstrate the correct primitive based on the shown source	glBegin(GL_POLYGON)
	  glVertex3f(0.0, 0.0, 0.0);
	  glVertex3f(0.0, 1.0, 0.0);
	  glVertex3f(0.0, 0.0, 1.0);
	glEnd( )					

Answer						
Gesture: *drawing symbol*						

several basic primitives. As shown in the example, a part of the OpenGL code is shown in the student's screen as part of the assessment and student is asked to provide the relevant shape. Then student can demonstrate the relevant shape in front of the Kinect sensor, so that system can detect the gesture shown and outputs the recognized shape and the correctness of the provided answer. Table 6 shows another example of using OpenGL programming to learn about handling interactions. Here as per the given example, interaction related code which is written in OpenGL, is prompted to the student's screen and asked to demonstrate the relevant shape. Then system evaluates his answer against the sample answer in the system and provides the result.

Finally we recognize several basic geometric primitive as in Table 7. It further shows recognized shape with respect to the six types of primitive shapes and the recognition rate using the one Dollar algorithm (Wobbrock, J. O. et al., 2007). Average recognition rate is 83.1%. It indicates that circle and line gestures are with highest recognition rate, and square, polygon had lowest recognition rate, because of their drawing shape action really similar each other which makes it difficult to differentiate.

Then we tested our system and tried to evaluate the time spent by the user in answering the questions using Kinect based interactions and the results. We conducted the test by performing each of gesture interaction for 30 times per gesture. As we can see in Table 8, average accuracy rate is 85% and 5.5 seconds has spent to answer the question in average. If different interaction types are frequently used accuracy rate is decreased and takes more time comparatively because, then it becomes more complicate to answer the question. Kinect feature based assessment such as Kinect angle and drawing has higher accuracy. During this testing, we did not integrate evaluation of difficulty coefficient of the question, whereas only interaction considered.

Table 6. Custom gesture based assessment

Item Type	Click		Push	Zoom	Swipe	Rotate	Drawing

Question: Demonstrate the correct interaction for the source code shown	`void processMouse(int button, int state, int x, int y) {`
	`    specialKey = glutGetModifiers();`
	`    // if a mouse button and the ALT key are pressed then`
	`    if ((state == GLUT_DOWN) &&`
	`                (specialKey == GLUT_ACTIVE_ALT)) {`
	`        // set the color to pure red for the left button`
	`        if (button == GLUT_LEFT_BUTTON) {`
	`            red = 1.0; green = 0.0; blue = 0.0; }`
	`        // set the color to pure green for the middle button`
	`        else if (button == GLUT_MIDDLE_BUTTON) {`
	`            red = 0.0; green = 1.0; blue = 0.0; }`
	`        // set the color to pure blue for the right button`
	`        else {`
	`            red = 0.0; green = 0.0; blue = 1.0; }`
	`    }`
	`}`						

Answer							

Table 7. Recognized primitive, recognition rate

	Triangle	Square	Line	Polygon	Quads	Circle
Gesture record						
Recognized shape						
Recognition rate	88%	80%	91%	75%	78%	87%

4.2. System Comparison

Table 9 displays comparison results of our system with several exiting systems from H. C. Yang et al. (Yang, H. C. et al., 2007), H. B. Chang et al. (Chang, H. B. et al., 2008), M. B. Ibanez et al. (Ibanez, M. B. et al., 2011), B. D. Homer et al. (Homer B. D. et al., 2014), and L. Hall et al. (Hall, L. et al., 2012) showing the enhanced capabilities of the proposed system. The proposed system creates promising opportunities for educators to offer students easier and more intuitive ways to interact with the system.

From Table 9 we can see that our system is rich comparing to the other solutions with respect to features implemented. We have implemented all of the interactions of the QTI standard and designed more interactions based on the gesture and voice recognition as well.

Table 8. Accuracy and answer time

Assessment Item	Interaction	Success (out of 30)	Accuracy (%)	Spend Time (s)
True/False	[Gesture Based] [Simple]	22	73	3
Single response	[Gesture Based] [Text-Based]	28	93	5
Multiple response	[Gesture Based] [Miscellaneous] [Text-Based]	25	83	10
Fill in blank	[Gesture Based] [Miscellaneous] [Text-Based]	26	86	8
Pattern match	[Gesture Based] [Miscellaneous] [Text-Based]	24	80	6
Kinect Angle	[Gesture Based] [Text-Based] [Graphical]	29	96	4
Voice	[Gesture Based] [Text-Based] [Graphical]	23	76	3
Drawing	[Gesture Based] [Graphical]	28	93	5
Result			85	5.5

Table 9. Comparison of proposed system

Feature/System	Our system	H. C. Yang et al.	H. B. Chang et al.	M. B. Ibanez et al.	B. D. Homer et al.	L. Hall et al.
System feature						
Environment	3D	Web	TV	Second life	PC	PC
Course Authoring tool	☑					
Item Authoring tool	☑			☑		
Rich, Multimedia Content	☑	☑	☑	☑	☑	☑
Smart Classroom Component	☑			☑		
Assessment feature						
Implemented Item Type	8	6	6	4	4	5
Interaction	☑	☑	☑	☑	☑	☑
Simple	☑	☑			☑	☑
Text-based	☑				☑	
Graphical	☑		☑	☑	☑	☑
Miscellaneous	☑			☑	☑	☑
Gesture based	☑				☑	☑
Voice Recognition based	☑			☑		☑

4.3. User Satisfaction Evaluation

This section is focused on the evaluation of user satisfaction of the proposed system and its features. A usability questionnaire which is modified from IBM computer usability satisfaction questionnaire proposed by (Lewis, J. R., 1995) was used to evaluate the satisfaction of the users of the system after the usage. The study was conducted at the MINE Lab, Department of Computer Science and Information Engineering, National Central University, Taiwan (R. O. C.) and the data were collected from lab

Table 10. The result of user's usability satisfaction from questionnaire (n=20)

	Item	Mean	SD
General Opinion	1. It was simple to use this system.	3.90	0.85
	2. I feel comfortable using this system.	4.05	0.89
	3. It was easy to learn to use this system.	3.95	0.83
	4. The interface of this system is pleasant.	4.30	0.80
	5. Overall, I am satisfied with how easy it is to use this system.	3.90	0.79
	6. Overall, I am satisfied with this system.	3.80	0.89
The System facilitate teacher for teaching (presentation)	7. This system has all the functions and capabilities I expect it to have.	3.85	0.81
	8. This system makes your presentation easy and smooth.	3.85	0.88
	9. Voice commands help the presentation more functionality.	4.00	0.79
The system motivate student to learn by assessment	10. I like using the interface of this system.	4.05	0.83
	11. This system has all type of question that I can easily understand.	4.40	0.88
	12. I think this system make me interest in doing interactive-quiz.	4.00	0.92

members and professors who have teaching experience or familiarity with the pedagogy. 20 participants engaged in Computer Science related works or studies were took part in this experiment, including one Professor, postgraduate and undergraduate students. Out of total 20 participants 3 were females and rest were males, and whereas 10 were Ph. D. students, 6 were M. Sc. Students and the rest were undergraduate students. Most of them, that is, 14 participants were 20-29 years, 5 were 30-39 years and one was 50-60 years of age. Before performing the experiment, the participants were introduced to the system and were given 1 hour assisted training about the system. For each subject introduced above were tested with all available functions of the system and was asked to perform like a real situation in the classroom, in total participants engaged with the system 10 hours during two week as 1 hour per a week day. After subjects tested the system, we collected the usability satisfaction from the users. The result of the questionnaire indicates that the users were satisfied of the overall usability of this system (Table 10). The participants agree about functions and the ease of use of the presentation application. For assessment application, most of users satisfied about the types of question covered for the assessment and expressed that it is easy to understand.

5. CONCLUSION AND FUTURE WORK

In this paper we have presented an interactive framework using Kinect for e-learning specific in assessment. We proposed a set of gesture commands for practical usage in classroom such as interactive question answering. We created new interactive question items supporting QTI-based assessment. The proposed system is easy to understand and easy to setup. The system was evaluated by usability questionnaire collected from 20 participants who have an experience related to pedagogy and students in smart classroom. Based on the questionnaire, the results are encouraging in terms of functionality and simplicity. And the results indicate that this interactive framework facilitate the teacher for teaching and motivate students to learn by interactive assessment. The most comments and suggestions of users are about the convenience of the user navigating interface and the functions such as play or pause video.

We plan to refine the user interface to improve user experience and to provide more intuition in future works, for example, introduction of a tutorial mode for beginners, guiding step-by-step instructions. In addition, we will design more gestures for presentation and assessment, and add more question types for assessment section. Furthermore, we can apply the system to the Holodeck room to create a virtual environment of smart classroom enhancing the classroom more interactive and exciting. Further evaluating the use of the system in different environments with different aged students is planned to perform.

ACKNOWLEDGMENT

Authors would like to express their gratitude for all the members of MINE Lab, Department of Computer Science and Information Engineering, National Central University, Taiwan (R. O. C.) for the support provided in participating in the questionnaire.

REFERENCES

Anthony, L., & Wobbrock, J. O. (2012). N-Protractor: A fast and accurate multistroke recognizer. In *Proceedings of Graphics Interface* (pp. 117–120). Toronto, Ontario: Canadian Information Processing Society.

Arroyo, D. M., Rodríguez, P. S., Calle, D. P., Kloos, C. D., Espiga, M. I., & Hernández-Leo, D. (2010). *Assessment in 3D virtual worlds: QTI in Wonderland* (pp. 410–417). Congreso Iberoamericano de Informátia Educativa.

Catuhe, D. (2012). *Programming with the Kinect for Windows Software Development Kit*. Redmond, Washington: Microsoft Press.

Chang, H. B., Liu, P. L., Shih, T. K., & Chen, Y. L. (2008). Developing QTI compliant assessment platform on digital TV. In *IEEE International Symposium on IT in Medicine and Education* (pp. 786-789). doi:10.1109/ITME.2008.4743974

Deshpande, S. G., & Hwang, J. N. (2001). A real-time interactive virtual classroom multimedia distance learning system. *IEEE Transactions on Multimedia*, *3*(4), 432–444. doi:10.1109/6046.966115

Dillenbourg, P., Schneider, D., & Synteta, P. (2002). Virtual learning environments. In *Proceedings of the 3rd Hellenic Conference Information & Communication Technologies in Education* (pp. 3-18).

GAST. (2011). GAST research group. Retrieved April 23, 2012, from http://www.gast.it.uc3m.es/

GTI. (2011). Interactive technologies research group. Retrieved May 10, 2012, from http://gti.upf.edu

Hall, L., Aylett, R., Hume, C., Krumhuber, E., & Degens, N. (2012). Incorporating multi-modal evaluation into a technology enhanced learning experience. *Twelfth International Conference on Intelligent Virtual Agents*. Retrieved March 5, 2013 from http://fastnet.netsoc.ie/ma3_2012/program_files/2_Paper.pdf

Homer, B. D., Kinzer, C. K., Plass, J. L., Letourneau, S. M., Hoffman, D., Bromley, M., & Kornak, Y. (2014). Moved to learn: The effects of interactivity in a Kinect-based literacy game for beginning readers. *Computers & Education*, *74*, 37–49. doi:10.1016/j.compedu.2014.01.007

Ibanez, M. B., Kloos, C. D., Leony, D., Rueda, J. J. G., & Maroto, D. (2011). Learning a foreign language in a mixed-reality environment. *IEEE Internet Computing*, *15*(6), 44–47. doi:10.1109/MIC.2011.78

IMS Global Learning Consortium. (2013). IMS question and test interoperability specification. Retrieved February 20, 2013, from http://www.imsglobal.org/question/

Learn3. (2011). Learn3 project. Retrieved May 10, 2012, from http://www.gast.it.uc3m.es/

Lewis, J. R. (1995). IBM computer usability satisfaction questionnaires: Psychometric evaluation and instructions for use. *International Journal of Human-Computer Interaction*, *7*(1), 57–78. doi:10.1080/10447319509526110

Martınez, A., Dimitriadis, Y., Rubia, B., Gómez, E., & De La Fuente, P. (2003). Combining qualitative evaluation and social network analysis for the study of classroom social interactions. *Computers & Education*, *41*(4), 353–368. doi:10.1016/j.compedu.2003.06.001

Microsoft. (2013). Kinect for Windows SDK: Communicate with computers naturally. Retrieved March 15, 2012, from http://www.microsoft.com/en-us/kinectforwindows/

Navarrete, T., Santos, P., Leo, D. H., & Blat, J. (2011). QTIMaps: A model to enable web maps in assessment. *Journal of Educational Technology & Society*, *14*(3), 203–217.

Sommool, W., Battulga, B., Shih, T. K., & Hwang, W. Y. (2013). Using Kinect for holodeck classroom: A framework for presentation and assessment. In *Advances in Web-Based Learning* (pp. 40–49). Springer Berlin Heidelberg.

Vermun, K., Senapaty, M., Sankhla, A., Patnaik, P., & Routray, A. (2013). Gesture-based affective and cognitive states recognition using Kinect for effective feedback during e-learning. In *IEEE Fifth International Conference on Technology for Education* (pp. 107-110). doi:10.1109/T4E.2013.34

Webb, J., & Ashley, J. (2012). *Beginning Kinect programming with the Microsoft Kinect SDK*. Apress. doi:10.1007/978-1-4302-4105-8

Wobbrock, J. O., Wilson, A. D., & Li, Y. (2007). Gestures without libraries, toolkits or training: A $1 recognizer for user interface prototypes. In *Proceedings of the 20th annual ACM symposium on user interface software and technology* (pp. 159-168). New York: ACM. doi:10.1145/1294211.1294238

Yang, H. C., Chang, Y. T., & Shih, T. K. (2007). Using AJAX to build an on-line QTI based assessment system. In *Proceedings of the International Conference on Computer Engineering and Applications* (pp. 69-74). Gold Coast, Australia: World Scientific and Engineering Academy and Society.

Yang, M. T., & Liao, W. C. (2014). Computer-assisted culture learning in an online augmented reality environment based on free-hand gesture interaction. *IEEE Transactions on Learning Technologies*, PP (99), 1-11.

This research was previously published in the International Journal of Distance Education Technologies (IJDET), 13(2); edited by Maiga Chang, pages 34-53, copyright year 2015 by IGI Publishing (an imprint of IGI Global).

APPENDIX

Steps of the implemented gesture for assessment guidelines are shown in Table 11.

Table 11. Assessment gesture guidelines

Gesture	Steps and description			
True/False	1. Start position	2. Gripping both hands	3-A. False	3-B. True
Drag and drop	1. Start position	2. Focus object	3. Gripping hand	4. Move into target
Draw angle	1. Start position	2. Gripping hand	3. Rounding	4. Open hand
Swipe (to left or to right)	1. Start position (right hand)	2. Move hand to left (next)	3. Start position (left hand)	4. Move hand to right (back)
Drawing	1. Gripping single hand to start to writing	2. Drawing shape	3. Drawing shape	4. Open hand to finish record, recognize symbol
Rotate	1. Left hand gripping	2. Move out (rotate to left)	3. Right hand gripping	4. Move out (rotate to right)
Zoom	1. Start position	2. Gripping both hand	3. Move hands	4. Open hands (finish)

Chapter 20

Interactive Boards in Schools:
Middle and High School Teachers' Uses and Difficulties

Wajeeh Daher
Al-Qasemi Academic College of Education, Israel & An-Najah National University, Palestine

Essa Alfahel
Al-Qasemi Academic College of Education, Israel & Achva Academic College of Education, Israel

ABSTRACT

This chapter examines middle school and high school teachers' use of interactive boards in the classroom, as well as the goals behind this use and the difficulties encountered throughout it. Ten middle school and high school science and mathematics teachers who use the interactive board for teaching science and mathematics were interviewed to elicit their practices, goals, and difficulties when using interactive boards in the classroom. The first two stages of the constant comparison method were utilized to analyze the collected data. The research findings show that science and mathematics teachers made different uses of the interactive board, which could be related to treating scientific relations, phenomena, and experiments, as well as practicing learned materials and engaging students in building activities in games and in discussions. Utilizing the different options of the interactive board, the participating teachers had various goals: giving students the ability to investigate, motivating them to learn, attracting them to the lesson, making them enjoy their learning, encouraging their collaboration, shortening the teaching time, and loading previously taught lessons. Using the interactive board in the classrooms, the teachers encountered some difficulties, such a: technical difficulties, owning the appropriate skills for using effectively the interactive board's different options, preparing appropriate activities, fulfilling students' expectations, and keeping class order.

DOI: 10.4018/978-1-5225-2589-9.ch020

INTRODUCTION

The interactive whiteboard is a large interactive display that combines a whiteboard, a computer and front projection. As learning tools they engage students with multimodal resources, as images, video and audio. Further, they enable what is done on a computer screen to be projected onto an interactive whiteboard. According to Smart Technologies Company, the first interactive board was introduced by Smart Technologies in 1991 (Smart technologies, 2006). Since then, they are becoming an integral part of the educational scene in schools in the western countries and are not considered just an additional aid to teaching (Kent, 2004a, 2004b). This also has been the case for the last couple of years in the Arab schools in Israel; what necessitates examining different educational aspects associated with the interactive board presence in the classrooms. One aspect of this learning is the teachers' perception of the interactive boards as tools for teaching and learning. This research will attempt, using quantitative methods, to examine such perceptions regarding didactic and pedagogic issues. It will examine whether there are differences between (1) teachers in public schools vs. teachers in private schools; and (2) teachers who use computers in their teaching vs. teachers who do not. Further the research will examine teachers' reasons for not using the interactive boards in their teaching and whether there are differences in these reasons between teachers in public schools vs. teachers in private schools.

BACKGROUND

Researchers point at the interactive boards as tools which contribute to teaching and learning in the classroom. We describe below those researches differentiating between them regarding the subject of the benefit (teacher/ student) and the aspect of the benefit (adding resources, adding motivation, etc.).

Researchers point that interactive boards help change, improve or add to the teaching methods of teachers who use them in the classroom (Cuthell, 2002; Latham, 2002; Levy, 2002; Jones & Vincent, 2010). Cuthell (2002), for example, administered a questionnaire in internet sites about teachers' opinions regarding the use of interactive boards in learning in elementary and middle schools. The findings show that when the interactive boards are installed in the classrooms and when the teachers have the required skills for using those interactive boards, a technological environment will be created which will support teachers and enable the transformation of their teaching methods to diversified ones.

Interactive boards add more resources and strategies to the teaching methods of teachers, enabling them to use more efficiently learning resources (Campbell & Kent, 2010; Cuthell, 2002; Glover & Miller, 2001; Levy, 2002). Specifically, they help teachers provide the students with more challenging learning opportunities (Latham, 2002). Levy (2002), for example, found that teachers looked at the interactive boards as aiding in presenting information and learning resources (as the easiness with which it is possible to draw on a greater number and wider variety of information and learning resources), in facilitating classroom interaction and activity (as freeing up time for interaction and task-related activity), and in their educational impact (as helping teachers to give more effective explanations).

Interactive boards not only contribute to the teacher but to the student too, supporting his learning - enabling understanding, concentrating, presenting information, remembering, thinking processes, and playing, and causing motivation (Kuzminsky, 2008; Levi, 2002; Schmid, 2008; Wall, Higgins, & Smith,

2005); stimulating learning - through increasing motivation, fun, self confidence, attention, and interest (Beeland, 2002; Wall, Higgins, & Smith, 2005); providing preferred learning approaches - through supporting different learning styles: visual, audio, verbal-social, and kinesthetic (Schmid, 2008; Wall, Higgins, & Smith, 2005); making students involved more interactively in learning and more focused on the learning material (Latham, 2002; Levi, 2002); enabling connectedness in an easy way - with the software, the hardware, and the multimedia (Wall, Higgins, & Smith, 2005); enabling wide range of learning resources and materials (Cuthell, 2002; Schmid, 2008) and increasing the student's achievement (Kuzminsky, 2008; Lewin, Somekh, & Steadman, 2008).

Researchers, as described above, point at the advantages of using interactive boards in the classroom, while other researchers report that interactive boards had no significant impact on the educational scene in schools, for example, Solvie (2001) found no significant difference in student attention and motivation when using an interactive whiteboard as opposed to when one was not used. In addition, Fisher (2006), examined fourth grade student academic performance before and after exposure to IWB use, where no significant gains were identified.

Barriers to using the interactive board in the classroom: According to various researchers, the lack of teachers' competence in ICT (information and communication technology) is a major barrier to their integration of ICT in their education (Bingimlas, 2009; Keong, Horani, & Daniel, 2005; Sharma, 2003; Slay, Sieborger, & Hodgkinson-Williams, 2008; Watson, 2001). Sharma (2003) found that one of the main barriers to the use of ICT in education was the low level of teacher ICT knowledge. Watson (2001) extended this finding saying that the application of ICT skills does not follow immediately from the mere knowing of them. Slay, Sieborger and Hodgkinson-Williams (2008) added that in some cases, teachers may be ICT literate, but not competent enough to apply the skills in their teaching. So, it can be concluded that mastering ICT skills and practicing them are conditions for successful use of these skills in teaching.

Keong, Horani, & Daniel (2005) conducted survey to study the barriers to the integration of ICT in teaching a specific subject: mathematics. They identified six major barriers: lack of time in the school schedule for projects involving ICT, insufficient teacher training opportunities for ICT projects, inadequate technical support for these projects, lack of knowledge about ways to integrate ICT to enhance the curriculum, difficulty in integrating and using different ICT tools in a single lesson and unavailability of resources at home for the students to access the necessary educational materials.

Murcia and McKenzie (2008) also emphasize the importance of teachers' proficiency in ICT and having appropriate time for this use as conditions for the success of their ICT use in the classroom: "inadequate professional development and lack of time to develop skills and plan lessons have been identified as barriers to the successful integration of interactive whiteboards into the classroom".

Bingimlas (2009) conducted a meta-analysis of relevant literature about barriers to technology integration in science education. The author pointed, in addition to the lack of teachers' competence, at teachers' lack of confidence and lack of access to resources as the main barriers for the integration of ICT in education. The author concluded that these barriers indicate that ICT resources including software and hardware, effective professional development, sufficient time, and technical support need to be provided to teachers in order that they integrate successfully ICT in their teaching. Navarrete (2011) confirms these conditions, in addition to leadership involvement.

THE RESEARCH RATIONALE AND GOALS

The interactive boards are becoming an integral part of the educational system in schools, where money and time are spent to utilize these new electronic tools in the classroom. Many researches, as described above, involved the benefits of using the interactive boards in the classroom, where little research has concentrated on the various uses of these boards in the classrooms. This research attempts to shed more light on this issue, specifically it examines teachers' didactical goals for using the interactive board, as well as their actual uses of this new technological tool in the classroom. In addition, the current research examines the barriers to using the interactive boards in the classroom from the teachers' point of view. These barriers could be those hindering teachers from using ICT in general in the classrooms, as well as those that are related specifically to the interactive boards. This research tries to clarify this issue. The results of this study would benefit teachers coming to use the interactive boards in their classroom, especially those who intend to use it for the first time. These teachers would be exposed to different aspects of the interactive board's use, and thus be better prepared for this use.

The Research Questions

1. What uses do science and mathematics teachers make of the interactive boards in the classrooms?
2. What goals encourage science and mathematics teachers to use the interactive boards for teaching and learning?
3. What barriers hinder science and mathematics teachers' use of the interactive boards in the classrooms?

METHODS

This research is qualitative because we want to explore through interviews the uses that teachers make of the interactive board, why they use it and what hinders them from using it. Quantitative research will not be open enough to cover teachers' various goals and uses of the interactive board, because such quantitative research will be limited to the themes which the researcher confines himself / herself to.

Participants

The research participants were ten middle school and high school science teachers who used the interactive board for teaching science and mathematics. There were four mathematics teachers and six science teachers. The distribution of the teachers regarding the school type was: six teachers in the middle school and four teachers in the high school. The teachers were chosen according to three conditions: (1) they use the interactive board in their teaching; (2) they teach in middle or high school; and (3) they approved to be interviewed. The sample of teachers interviewed was a convenience sample, for we could not locate many teachers who use the interactive board at the time of conducting the research interviews: February 2012.

The Research Tool

Data Collection: We conducted interviews with the participants to know what encourages the teachers to use the interactive boards in the classroom, what uses they make of the interactive boards in the classrooms, and what barriers hinder this use. The interviews were semi-constructed starting from questions that probed teachers' use of the interactive board. Getting a teacher's answers, new questions were asked to deepen the understanding regarding teacher's uses of the interactive board and goals of this use. Some of these questions were: How do you use the interactive board in your teaching? What are the barriers to using the interactive board in your teaching?

The list of questions is attached to appendix 1. These questions were developed by the two researchers and were but initiatives for the following more probing questions.

Data Analysis: The first two stages of the constant comparison method (Glaser & Strauss, 1967) were used to analyze the data regarding teachers' use of the interactive boards. These stages were:

Categorizing data: In this stage we put together data expressions or sentences that implied reasons for the use of interactive boards, the goal from the use or a barrier to this use. For example, regarding teachers' goal from the use of interactive boards, we searched for words like 'because', 'for', 'to', 'due to', etc., where these words, we noticed, were used to indicate a goal behind teachers' use of the interactive board. Other indicators that we looked for were words like 'goal', 'reason', 'make', etc.

Comparing data: In this stage we compared expressions or sentences within each previously built category. This gave rise to sub-categories. Let's take for example the category 'using the interactive board to get to the internet', comparing expressions or sentences in this category may give rise to the subcategories: using the interactive board to watch a video from the internet, using the interactive board to work with an applet, using the interactive board to look up a scientific term, etc.

Theoretical Saturation

Theoretical saturation should be kept in qualitative research methods which examine themes and categories in qualitative data (such as data produced in interviews) (Strauss and Corbin, 1998). This theoretical saturation occurs in data collection when: (a) No new relevant data seem to emerge regarding a category; (b) The category is well developed in terms of its properties and dimensions, demonstrating variation; and (c) The relationships among categories are well established and validated (ibid, p. 212). In the current research we kept analyzing the interviews data till the three conditions were met.

Inter-Rater Reliability of the Coding

To ensure inter-rater reliability of the coding, two coders coded 40% of interviews. The coding decisions of the two coders were evaluated for inter-rater reliability using Holsti's (1969) coefficient of reliability and Cohen's (1960) Kappa. Holsti coefficient of reliability and Cohen's Kappa were computed for the coding done to arrive at the coding categories of teachers' uses of the interactive board, the coding done to arrive at the teachers' goals from using the different options of the interactive board, and the coding done to arrive at the difficulties encountered by the teachers when using the interactive board in the classroom. Holsti coefficients of reliability were found to be 0.81, 0.79 and 0.75, respectively, while Cohen's kappa results were found to be 0.80, 0.71 and 0.69, respectively.

FINDINGS

In this research we were interested to examine three issues regarding teachers' use of the interactive board: their different uses, goals of their uses and difficulties confronted during their uses. Below, the findings regarding each issue are described. This description is done in tables, where the left column of each table includes the categories found, while the right column includes examples from the teachers' saying on the category.

Science and Mathematics Teachers' Use of Interactive Boards in the Classroom

The participating teachers made different uses of the interactive board in their classrooms. These uses could be categorized as:

Representing Scientific Phenomena: Seven out of the ten participating teachers mentioned that they use the interactive board to represent scientific phenomena which are difficult to watch or visualize. For example, Farid, a science teacher, said: Sometimes it is difficult for the students to visualize a scientific phenomenon, for example the structure of the cell, so it is easy to use the interactive board to present this phenomenon, usually using the video.

Showing How to Perform a Scientific Experiment: Three out of the ten participating teachers stated that they use the interactive board to show the procedures of carrying out scientific experiments which could be dangerous to perform physically in the lab. For example, Salam, a science teacher, declared: I use the interactive board to show the students scientific experiments that could be difficult or dangerous to perform, for example using ammonia or working with concentrated acidic and basic substances.

Investigating a Scientific Relation: Five out of the ten participating teachers pointed at the interactive boards as enabling students to investigate mathematical and scientific relations. This use was done through two means: simulations and dynamic tools. Farid stated: I use the interactive boards to show the students scientific simulations, so they discover a specific scientific relation, for example the states of the matter: solids, liquids, and gases. Halim, a mathematics teacher stated: I use the interactive board to let the students work with a dynamic tool, so they discover collaboratively a mathematical relation. We did that to discover the relation between the quadratic function parameters and its graph.

Practicing Learned Material: Four out of the ten participating teachers stated that they use interactive boards to make students practice the learning material. Sami, a mathematics teacher, said: I let my students practice what they learned using the interactive board. I noticed that when they did that after they learned about solving mathematical equations it made them enthusiastic.

Engaging Students in Building Activities: The interactive boards have working tools that enable students to build scientific and mathematical objects. Five out of the ten participating teachers mentioned using this option in their classrooms. Ahlam, a mathematics teacher, declared: My students use the interactive board to build collaboratively geometrical solids according to some conditions.

Engaging Students in Games: The interactive board is also an environment in which students can play games. Two out of the ten participating teachers mentioned that they use the interactive board to engage their students with learning games. Amin, a mathematics teacher stated: My students use the interactive board to play games. This makes the whole class attentive to follow the different actors' steps.

Engaging Students in Discussions: Seven out of the ten participating teachers mentioned that the interactive board motivates their students to discuss issues related to the subject matter. Eman, a science teacher, said: I noticed that my students engage more enthusiastically in a classroom discussion during or after their work with the interactive board. This makes me want to engage them in scientific discussions more and more.

Teachers' Goals from Using the Different Options of the Interactive Board in the Classroom

The participating teachers had different goals for using the interactive board options in in their classrooms. These goals could be categorized as:

*Making students visualize a scientific or mathematical phenomenon or relation:*The interactive board, as six out of the ten participating teachers mentioned, has different multimedia utilities which help students visualize scientific and mathematical phenomena. Ahlam said: the visual facilities of the interactive boards make it wonderful to show the students the graph of a function and the relation between this graph and the function rule. Thus I use the interactive board for these visual facilities.

Motivating students to learn: The different multimedia utilities of the interactive boards, as five out of the ten participating teachers mentioned, also motivate students to engage actively in learning mathematics and science. Eman said: the multimedia in the interactive board enables to show the scientific phenomena as in real life, which motivates students to study these phenomena actively. This motivation is behind my goal of using the interactive board in my teaching.

*Attracting students' attention to the lesson:*The pen's colors in the interactive board, as four out of the ten participating teachers mentioned, help teachers attract students' attention to the lesson. Kholoud, a science teacher said: One reason for my using the interactive board is the pen's colors option which makes it easier for me to attract students' attention to the lesson.

*Making students concentrate on a topic:*The pen's colors, as three out of the ten participating teachers declared, not only help the teacher attract students' attention to the lesson, but they also help the students concentrate on the science or mathematics topic. Nadera, a mathematics teacher, said: the pen colors help students concentrate on the geometric figure and thus arrive faster at the relations in the figure. This is a wonderful option which makes me use the interactive board.

*Making students enjoy their learning:*The multimedia options of the interactive board, as three out of the ten participating teachers declared, also affected positively students' emotions while learning. Asil, a science teacher, declared: I prefer using the interactive board in the classroom to make my students enjoy their learning, probably because of it multimedia options.

*Encouraging students' collaboration:*Students' active learning described above encourages them to collaborate in investigating new phenomena and relations. Omar, a science teacher and one of four teachers who mentioned this goal, said: I use the interactive board for it encourages students' collaboration. The whole class collaborates wonderfully when we use the interactive board to investigate scientific phenomena. This is actually what happened when we investigated the 'work phenomenon'.

*Shortening the teaching time:*The various potentialities, options and tools in the interactive board makes the teaching time of the teacher shorter, as four out of the ten participating teachers mentioned.

Salam declared: The interactive options in the board help the teacher explain the lesson in a shorter time. This encourages me to use the interactive board to utilize all its tools during the lesson.

Loading previously taught lessons: An interactive option which was popular in the classroom is to load a previously taught lesson. Amin, one of eight teachers who mentioned this goal as behind his use of the interactive board, said: Sometimes I use the interactive board to load a lesson which was given one or two lessons before to remind my students of a rule or an example.

Making students more attentive in the lesson: The possibility to save the lesson taught with the interactive board encourages the student to be more attentive in the lesson, for they do not have to copy every word which the teacher mentions. Kholoud, one of four teachers who mentioned this goal, declared: Some of my students do not copy the material written on the interactive board, for I send them the whole lesson by email. This makes them more attentive during the lesson. This is a great option which makes me use the interactive board in my teaching.

Difficulties Confronted by the Participating Teachers in Using the Interactive Board In Their Teaching

The participating teachers reported different difficulties that they encountered using the interactive board in their teaching. These difficulties can be categorized in the following categories.

Technical difficulties: These difficulties could be divided into the difficulty to write clearly using the board's pen and the difficulty to use the board because of its sensitiveness to dirt. Amin, one of four teachers who mentioned this difficulty, complained: Students have difficulty reading my or other students' writing on the interactive board. Further, Kholoud said: Once, one of my students made the board dirty, and thus disabled it.

Owning the appropriate skills for using effectively the interactive board's different options: Feeling in control of the various options of the interactive board worried four out of the ten participating teachers. Salam confessed: Though I have the basic skills for using the interactive board, I do not feel I own the appropriate skills for using its different options effectively in my teaching.

Preparing appropriate activities: Preparing appropriate activities for the new technological tool worried seven out of the ten participating teachers. Ahlam admitted: I have to spend long time in preparing lessons that utilize the different options of the interactive board. This makes me use it sometimes as regular board only.

Fulfilling students' expectations: Fulfilling students' expectations from the activities learned with the interactive board also burdened six out of the ten participating teachers. Eman complained: Students expect every lesson to include a multimedia application, and it is hard to convince them that this not always necessary.

Keeping the class order: Three teachers pointed that the activity and interactivity of the students, which the interactive board encourages, sometimes make it hard for the teacher to maintain the class order. Asil said: Every student wants to participate in the interactive board's activities, so it is hard sometimes to keep the class order. I think we should find creative ways for overcoming this difficulty.

DISCUSSION

Teachers' uses of the interactive board: Looking at teachers' uses of the interactive board, it could be seen that the interactive board enabled teachers to perform varied teaching actions recommended by educational institutions and by researchers and expected to benefit students' learning. One of these actions is the ability of science teachers to use simulations to make students investigate scientific ideas. This teaching action is supposed to influence positively students' learning, for it enables them "to observe, explore, recreate, and receive immediate feedback about real objects, phenomena, and processes that would otherwise be too complex, time-consuming, or dangerous." (Bell & Smetana, 2007, p. 23). Another teaching action enabled by the interactive board is working with scientific phenomena, where the participants in the research were highly aware of this action and performed it in their classrooms. The importance of working with scientific and/or natural phenomena is attended to in various researchers, for example in Bell and Smetana (ibid), as well as in Kolokouri and Plakitsi (2009) who emphasize that understanding scientific concepts related to natural phenomena and developing, as a result, scientific argumentation will contribute to students' increasing responsibility and decision making.

The participating teachers were also highly aware of the contribution of the interactive board to encouraging discussion in their classroom, and thus this use was one of the most uses performed with the interactive board in their classes. This use of the interactive board by the participating teachers will probably influence positively students' learning (National Academy of Science, 1997; National Council of Teachers of Mathematics, 2000). Further, Roth and Garnier (2006) studied the "TIMSS Video Study of Science" in five countries: the Czech Republic, Japan, Australia, and the Netherlands. The authors address the issue of classroom discussion, saying that Japan classroom discussions helped students link learning activities to science ideas, while in the Netherlands, class discussions supplemented the text. In Australia, teachers initiated classroom discussions that challenged students' thinking. The previous findings of Roth and Grnier (ibid) point at the positive contribution of the interactive board if used to promote classroom discussions.

Teachers' goals for using the interactive boards in the classroom: Teachers' goals for using the interactive boards in the classroom could be related to various aspects of teaching and learning: the cognitive aspect (for example making students visualize a scientific phenomenon or relation), the emotional aspect (for example making students enjoy their learning), the social aspect (for example encouraging the collaboration of students), the behavioral aspect (for example making students more attentive in the lesson), and the management of learning aspect (for example shortening teachers' time). Thus the interactive board can support the teacher in her/his attempts to attend to the various aspects of learning, and as a result make students' learning more fruitful. This attendance to the various aspects of learning is described by various researchers as influencing positively students' learning, for example, Russo and Benson (2005) say that the cognitive outcome of learning is an important issue in most learning contexts, while Pekrun (2007), for example, concludes, based on theoretical considerations and evidence, that emotions in academic settings are critical to college students' scholastic development. In addition, Dixon, Crooks and Henry (2006) say that social presence is necessary for building and sustaining communities of learning. Students' behavior in the classroom is another aspect of learning which is connected to the previous aspects and which influences the outcomes of learning.

The most mentioned goals for using the options of the interactive board in the classroom was connecting to previously learned lessons and enabling students' visualizing of scientific phenomena. These two goals realized by the use of the interactive board are related to two main aspects of teaching, where the first goal is related to 'providing a supportive learning environment ', while the second is related to the same aspect and to another aspect: 'nurturing processes and strategies which foster learning'. These two aspects are recognized in the literature as significant in terms of students' learning (Jaworski, 1992). This means that the participating teachers were aware that utilizing the options of the interactive board can contribute positively to their students' learning.

*Difficulties of using the interactive boards in the classrooms:*The difficulties described by the participants in this research could be related to the tool (technical difficulties), to the teacher (Owning appropriate skills and the readiness to prepare appropriate activities) and to the student (students' expectations). Previous researches reported similar difficulties regarding the use of interactive boards in the classroom, but without categorizing them in the current categorization: tool-teacher-student.

The most mentioned difficulties the participating teachers reported were preparing appropriate activities and fulfilling students' expectations. These two difficulties are two sides of the same difficulty which is fitting the educational context to the interactive board potentialities. Regarding this compound difficulty, BECTA (2003) reported that expectations students have regarding the use of the interactive board in the classroom put pressure on teachers, having to continually improve the presentation and content of lessons. BECTA (ibid) points at other factors which influence the use of interactive boards in the classroom. Amongst these are appropriate training and ongoing technical support to teachers and schools. Difficulties encountered for the absence of the factors described above could be overcome by planning actions by the ministry of education (for example planning appropriate workshops) from one side and educational institutions (for example planning appropriate lessons) from the other side. Ensuring appropriate preparation of the teacher and appropriate activities for the interactive board would ensure that the teacher utilizes the interactive board in a way which attends to the different aspects of students' learning, and thus makes this learning fruitful.

CONCLUSION AND FUTURE RESEARCH DIRECTIONS

This research intended to verify the different uses of the interactive board in the classroom by science teachers. The research findings show that science teachers make different uses of the interactive board: Representing scientific phenomena, showing how to perform a scientific experiment, investigating a scientific relation, practicing learned material, engaging students in building activities, engaging students in games, and engaging students' in discussions.

These uses enabled by the interactive board (learning through phenomena, learning through investigating and through simulation, learning through discussions) are recommended by researchers as practices which help students learn independently and connect their learning to real life (Bouillion & Gomez, 2001). Garofalo, Drier, Harper, Timmerman, & Shockey, 2000).

Utilizing the different options of the interactive board, the participating teachers had the following goals: Enabling students to visualize a scientific phenomenon or relation, motivating students to learn, attracting students' attention to the lesson, making students concentrate on a topic, making students more attentive in the lesson, making students enjoy their learning, encouraging the collaboration of students, shortening the teaching time and loading previously taught lessons. The ability of the interactive board to facilitate teachers' realization of these goals points that by utilizing it properly, teachers can attend to the different aspects of students' learning: the cognitive, the affective, the social and behavioral.

Using the interactive board in the classrooms, the teachers encountered some difficulties:

Technical difficulties: (The difficulty to write clearly using the board's pen and the board sensitiveness to dirt), owning the appropriate skills for using effectively the interactive board's different options, preparing appropriate activities, fulfilling students' expectations and keeping the class order. Probably, the technical difficulties will be resolved with new versions of the interactive board, while the other difficulties can be resolved by actions from the side of the ministry of education (for example planning appropriate workshops), and from the side of educational institutions (for example planning appropriate lessons).

In this research we interviewed middle and high school teachers regarding their practices, goals and difficulties when using the interactive board in the classroom. It is our conviction that teachers' practices and difficulties should also be examined inside the classroom itself, by observing these practices and difficulties during the actual teaching in the classroom, not only for the middle and high school, but also for the primary school.

REFERENCES

Beeland, W. D. (2002). Student engagement, visual learning and technology: Can interactive whiteboards help? *Action Research Exchange, 1*(1). Retrieved February 20, 2013 from http://chiron.valdosta.edu/are/Artmanscrpt/vol1no1/beeland_am.pdf

Bell, R. L., & Smetana, L. K. (2007). Using computer simulations to enhance science teaching and learning. In R. L. Bell, J. Gess-Newsome, & J. Luft (Eds.), *Technology in the secondary science classroom* (pp. 23–32). Washington, DC: National Science Teachers Association Press.

Bingimlas, K. A. (2009). Barriers to the successful integration of ICT in teaching and learning environments: A review of the literature. *Eurasia Journal of Mathematics. Science and Technology Education, 5*(3), 235–245.

Bouillion, L. M., & Gomez, L. M. (2001). Connecting school and community with science learning: Real world problems and school-community partnerships as contextual scaffolds. *Journal of Research in Science Teaching, 38*, 878–898. doi:10.1002/tea.1037

British Educational and Communication Technology Agency (BECTA). (2003). *What the research says about interactive whiteboards*. Retrieved February 20, 2013 from http://www.mmiweb.org.uk/publications/ict/Research_ClassroomOrg.pdf

Campbell, C., & Kent, P. (2010). Using interactive whiteboards in pre-service teacher education: Examples from two Australian universities. *Australasian Journal of Educational Technology, 26*(4), 447-463. Retrieved February 20, 2013 from http://www.ascilite.org.au/ajet/ajet26/campbell.html

Cohen, J. (1960). A coefficient of agreement for nominal scales. *Educational and Psychological Measurement, 20*(1), 37–46. doi:10.1177/001316446002000104

Cuthell, J. P. (2002). *Interactive whiteboards: New tools, new pedagogies, new learning?* Retrieved February 20, 2013 from http://www.virtuallearning.org.uk/changemanage/iwb/IWB%20Survey%202004.pdf

Dixon, J. S., Crooks, H., & Henry, K. (2006). Breaking the ice: Supporting collaboration and the development of community online. *Canadian Journal of Learning and Technology, 32*(2), 99–117.

Fisher, S. (2006). *Using technology to prepare for future scientists.* (Unpublished master's thesis). Wichita State University, Wichita, KS.

Garofalo, J., Drier, H., Harper, S., Timmerman, M. A., & Shockey, T. (2000). Promoting appropriate uses of technology in mathematics teacher preparation. *Contemporary Issues in Technology & Teacher Education, 1*(1), 66–88.

Glaser, B., & Strauss, A. (1967). *The discovery of grounded theory.* Hawthorne, NY: Aldine Publishing Company.

Glover, D., & Miller, D. (2001). Running with technology: The pedagogic impact of the large scale introduction of interactive whiteboards in one secondary school. *Journal of Information Technology for Teacher Education, 10,* 257–276. doi:10.1080/14759390100200115

Holsti, O. R. (1969). *Content analysis for the social sciences and humanities.* Reading, MA: Addison-Wesley.

Jaworski, B. (1992). Mathematics teaching: What is it? *For the Learning of Mathematics, 12*(1), 8–14.

Jones, A., & Vincent, J. (2010). Collegial mentoring for effective whole school professional development in the use of IWB technologies. *Australasian Journal of Educational Technology, 26*(4), 477–493.

Kent, P. (2004a). e-Teaching: The elusive promise. In R. Ferdig et al. (Eds.), *Proceedings of Society for Information Technology & Teacher Education International Conference 2004* (pp. 520-522). Chesapeake, VA: AACE.

Kent, P. (2004b). *E-teaching and interactive whiteboards: Technology used to enhance effective pedagogy - Creating a significant impact on classroom practice and student learning.* Paper presented at the Australian Computers in Education Conference. Adelaide, Australia.

Keong, C. C., Horani, S., & Daniel, J. (2005). A study on the use of ICT in mathematics teaching. *Malaysian Online Journal of Instructional Technology, 2*(3), 43–51.

Kolokouri, E., & Plakitsi, K. (2009). Scientific literacy and nature of science in early grades using cartoons. In G. Cakmakci & M. F. Taşar (Eds.), *Contemporary science education research: Scientific literacy and social aspects of science* (pp. 113–123). Ankara, Turkey: Pegem Akademi.

Kuzminsky, T. V. (2008). *Interactive whiteboard technology within the kindergarten visual arts classroom.* (Unpublished master's thesis). Georgia Public University, Atlanta, GA. Retrieved February 20, 2013, from http://etd.gsu.edu/theses/available/etd-04122008-104815/unrestricted/kuzminsky_tracy_v_200805_maed.pdf.pdf

Latham, P. (2002). *Teaching and learning primary mathematics: The impact of interactive whiteboards.* BEAM Research Papers. Retrieved February 20, 2013 from http://www.beam.co.uk/uploads/discpdf/ RES03.pdf

Levy, P. (2002). *Interactive whiteboards in learning and teaching in two Sheffield schools: A developmental study.* Retrieved April 20, 2011 from http://dis.shef.ac.uk/eirg/projects/wboards.htm

Lewin, C., Somekh, B., & Steadman, S. (2008). Embedding interactive whiteboards in teaching and learning: The process of change in pedagogic practice. *Education and Information Technologies, 13*(4), 291–303. doi:10.1007/s10639-008-9070-z

Murcia, K., & McKenzie, S. (2009). Finding the way: Signposts in teachers' development of effective interactive whiteboard pedagogies. *Australian Educational Computing, 24*(1), 23–29.

National Academy of Science. (1997). *Science teaching reconsidered: A handbook.* Washington, DC: National Academy Press.

National Council of Teachers of Mathematics. (2000). *Principles and standards for school mathematics.* Reston, VA: Author.

Navarrete, C. (2011). Identifying affordances and barriers to student-centered, collaborative learning in the integration of interactive whiteboard technology. In M. Koehler & P. Mishra (Eds.), *Proceedings of Society for Information Technology & Teacher Education International Conference 2011* (pp. 2996-3001). Chesapeake, VA: AACE.

Pekrun, R. (2007). Emotions in students' scholastic development. In P. Perry & J. C. Smart (Eds.), *The Scholarship of Teaching and Learning in Higher Education: An Evidence-Based Perspective* (pp. 553–610). Dordrecht, The Netherlands: Springer. doi:10.1007/1-4020-5742-3_13

Roth, K., & Garnier, H. (2006). What science teaching looks like: An international perspective. *Science in the Spotlight, 64*(4), 16–23.

Russo, T., & Benson, S. (2005). Learning with invisible others: Perceptions of online presence and their relationship to cognitive and affective learning. *Journal of Educational Technology & Society, 8*(1), 54–62.

Schmid, E. C. (2008). Potential pedagogical benefits and drawbacks of multimedia use in the English language classroom equipped with interactive whiteboard technology. *Computers & Education, 51*(4), 1553–1568. doi:10.1016/j.compedu.2008.02.005

Sharma, R. C. (2003). Barriers in using technology for education in developing countries. In *Proceedings of the International Conference on Information Technology: Research and Education* (ITRE 2003) (pp. 512 - 516). ITRE.

Slay, H., Sieborger, I., & Hodgkinson-Williams, C. (2008). Interactive whiteboards: Real beauty or just lipstick? *Computers & Education, 51*(3), 13–21. doi:10.1016/j.compedu.2007.12.006

Smart Technologies. (2006). *Interactive whiteboards and learning: Improving student learning outcomes and streamlining lesson planning.* Retrieved from http://downloads01.smarttech.com/media/research/ whitepapers/int_whiteboard_research_whitepaper_update.pdf

Solvie, P. A. (2004). The digital whiteboard: A tool in early literacy instruction. *The Reading Teacher*, *57*(5), 484–487.

Strauss, A., & Corbin, J. (1998). *Basics of qualitative research: Techniques and procedures for developing grounded theory* (2nd ed.). Thousand Oaks, CA: Sage.

Wall, K., Higgins, S., & Smith, H. (2005). The visual helps me understand the complicated things: Pupil views of teaching and learning with interactive whiteboards. *British Journal of Educational Technology*, *36*(5), 851–867. doi:10.1111/j.1467-8535.2005.00508.x

Watson, D. (2001). Pedagogy before technology: Re-thinking the relationship between ICT and teaching. *Education and Information Technologies*, *6*(4), 251–266. doi:10.1023/A:1012976702296

KEY TERMS AND DEFINITIONS

Constant Comparison Method: This method was described by Glaser and Strauss (1967). It consists of actions that seek to find appropriate themes important for the research and then to group these themes in categories that reflect the topic of the research.

Holsti Coefficients of Reliability: A method that computes the inter-rater reliability of coding.

Interactive board: an interactive whiteboard is a large interactive display that combines a whiteboard, a computer and a projector.

Inter-Rater Reliability of Coding: It is the degree of agreement among raters that interpret the research data. It gives a score of how much homogeneity or consensus there is in the ratings given by judges.

Scientific Phenomena: Phenomena related to one of the sciences, for example the states of the matter in chemistry and the relation between the parameters of a function and its graph in mathematics.

Teachers' Goals: These are the goals behind teachers' decisions regarding their teaching strategies and the different aspects of their students' learning.

Technical Difficulties: Difficulties related to operating a technological tool.

This research was previously published in Transforming K-12 Classrooms with Digital Technology edited by Zongkai Yang, Harrison Hao Yang, Di Wu, and Sanya Liu, pages 306-319, copyright year 2014 by Information Science Reference (an imprint of IGI Global).

APPENDIX

The Interview Questions

1. What makes you use the interactive board in your teaching?
2. How do you use the interactive board in your teaching?
3. For what targets do you use the interactive board?
4. Which tools in the interactive board do you use?
5. For what targets do you use each tool in the interactive board?
6. What are the barriers to using the interactive board in your teaching?

Section 5
Urban Spaces and Energy Optimization

Chapter 21
Visualising Data for Smart Cities

Michael Batty
University College London, UK

Stephan Hugel
University College London, UK

Andrew Hudson-Smith
University College London, UK

Flora Roumpani
University College London, UK

ABSTRACT

This chapter introduces a range of analytics being used to understand the smart city, which depends on data that can primarily be understood using new kinds of scientific visualisation. We focus on short term routine functions that take place in cities which are being rapidly automated through various kinds of sensors, embedded into the physical fabric of the city itself or being accessed from mobile devices. We first outline a concept of the smart city, arguing that there is a major distinction between the ways in which technologies are being used to look at the short and long terms structure of cities, and we then focus on the shorter term, first examining the immediate visualisation of data through dashboards, then examining data infrastructures such as map portals, and finally introducing new ways of visualising social media which enable us to elicit the power of the crowd in providing and supplying data. We conclude with a brief focus on how new urban analytics is emerging to make sense of these developments.

DEFINING SMART CITIES

The term 'smart cities' has emerged very quickly over the last five years[1]. First, this has been a consequence of the rapid spread of computation into public and open environments, into what Hardin (1968) and others have called the 'commons', spaces that are used and exploited collectively. Second, it has been spurred on by the miniaturisation of computable devices to the point where tiny sensors can be embedded into objects of many different sizes, from buildings to our own bodies, thus generating digital information concerning the status, the condition, location and so on, of the objects in question. This feature of the smart cities movement is often referred to as the Internet of Things (Sterling, 2005). A third force is the emergence of digital data in space and time, that is, in terms of how an object's status varies in real time and across different spatial locations, and this data is invariably orders of magnitude bigger than anything we have dealt with in the human domain so far. This 'big data' is providing a very different perspective on the way we might understand our cities while also revealing how new information tech-

DOI: 10.4018/978-1-5225-2589-9.ch021

nologies are changing the very behaviour patterns that make up the contemporary city (Kitchin, 2014a). Google Trends reveals that this interest concerning smart cities and big data is still rising exponentially, as an analysis of the relevant search terms demonstrates (Batty, 2013).

A smart city also implies some degree of intelligence, some set of computable and automated functions that act intelligently with respect to the way the city actually functions through its populations. In this sense, smart cities have been embraced as the new frontier by the world's largest IT companies whose products, which have evolved from hardware to software and data, are further evolving into systems that might be embodied in the public domain where the obvious applications involve making collective actions more efficient. To an extent, the smart city movement barely touches the traditional questions of equity and distribution which have dominated city planning for over a century, although some lip service is currently being paid to the fact that new information technologies might make cities more prosperous in terms of income and wealth and, as a consequence, perhaps more evenly distributed.

'Smart cities' is a label that is now being used generically to cover a very wide range of applications of computers, sensors, and related computation and interaction that has any link whatsoever to the city. It is such a broad domain that it is essential, in any discussion, to bound the area and define its scope. The focus here is on the immediacy of new data and functions that define the smart city with an emphasis on their use and understanding using visualisation, but to set this in context it is worth providing some overall structure for different approaches to the idea of the smart city. For more than a century, the general concern for cities as regards urban planning has been on how cities can be improved over relatively long time spans. In this sense, the knowledge that is brought to bear on cities can be somewhat abstract, conceived in terms of how locations and interactions through transport can be orientated to thinking of future forms and functions for cities that might optimise some quality of life. Every planning instrument, from new towns to green belts, has been predicated with these goals in mind, where the emphasis is not particularly on the routine but on the strategic. Insofar as planning has dealt with routine functions, this has tended to be subsumed under organisational and management structures that say little or nothing about how cities might become more equitable. The focus on short-term management goals is in fact more geared to improved efficiency. To date, many of these routines have not been informed by digital technologies, in contrast with longer-term plan-making which has been so informed, albeit crudely, but not without considerable debate and controversy.

There is thus a major distinction between digital technologies being used for the short-term routine management of cities and those for longer-term strategic planning, and this difference is reflected in much of the data, information and knowledge that pertains to the functions that smart city technologies are able to inform. Furthermore, there is a distinction between public and private use. In the past, data on individuals, insofar as they provided information about their own functioning in cities, was produced for aggregates of population using traditional surveys such as censuses. Individually specified data tended to be in terms of the role of citizens in participating in the decision process. This has changed radically in that individuals are now able to record their own behaviours passively or actively using multiple personalised devices which are extensively linked through digital networks. In turn, these provide massive amounts of data that can be mined to facilitate a better understanding of how cities function, at present mainly in the short term, but in time as this kind of data accumulates, in the longer-term too.

In fact, the term smart cities pertains much more to the routine management of cities in the very short term: with respect to how cities function in the next 5 minutes, the next 5 hours, the next 5 days rather than the next 5 years or 50 years. This is largely because smart city technologies which lie at the leading edge of current computable devices are strongly orientated to sensors with big data generated, if not used, in real time. Instant messaging and related website presence also implies various kinds of social network, while telephone traffic is fast merging with other media, and consumer purchase data of all kinds is also being generated on short time cycles. Combine all this with financial information in real time and the shortening of our attention spans with respect to the emergence of the smart city is clearly evident. Of course, there are some attempts to look at longer-term data, which can be assembled from individual responses such as house and land prices, income data, retail prices, employment, migration and so on, but so far most of the focus in smart cities has not been on these traditional concerns. Smart cities tend to be all about how big data can be used to examine mobility, social networks and individual preferences data by way of crowd-sourcing, and, to an extent, online citizen participation. It may not always be the case but currently this is the dominant preoccupation in this domain and quite unashamedly we will exploit this here in our focus on how new visual technologies are able to capture this new concern.

We will begin by sketching the rudiments of a conceptual approach to smart cities, concentrating on short-term issues which involve how computation is changing the way we deal with routine travel and communications using embedded sensor technologies to mobile devices operated through a range of media, from machines to humans. The focus of the smart city in this domain is on control and management from the data that is generated in real time and this 'big data' provides a new level of complexity with respect to the way we make sense of mobility and interaction in terms of anything we have been able to do hitherto. Visualisation is the obvious medium for its simplification and abstraction and this is leading to many kinds of infographic that are being used for the control as well as the automation of these kinds of system, particularly transit. New varieties of analytics are emerging to make sense of such data and we will focus on how new ways of computing are being used to make such systems more efficient through real-time control.

In fact, so far many of these technologies have not been realised. The larger computer companies, which see these markets as their domain, have only a limited number of solutions that have been tried and the history of these applications to date has not been a happy one. In short, real-time control, interoperability of systems, and the use of big data to provide a seamless understanding of how such systems can be made more efficient is more myth than reality and the promise of these systems is yet to be realised on anything other than the very small scale. We will sketch possibilities in this chapter making the point that the simplest and most straightforward of smart city technologies are those that currently exist, such as dashboards and control centres. To conclude, we will examine the prospects for developments in this domain and point the way to how technologies for short-term control might lead to longer-term strategic management and policy-making once such systems become established and more long-lived. Reviews of smart city applications so far are highly diffuse but readers who wish to review the wider context are referred to the paper by Batty et al. (2012) where the range of tools and methods used to understand and implement smart city ideas are reviewed.

A CONCEPTUAL MODEL OF THE SMART CITY: ROUTINE FUNCTIONS, NETWORKS, AND NEW MEDIA

The first signs of computational technologies (that we define as digital rather than analogue) becoming embedded into cities came in the late 1980s with the emergence of local and wide area networks (LANS and WANs) and the development of digital mobile phones. This represented one aspect of the convergence of computers with telecommunications which in itself was unexpected when digital computers were first invented. Miniaturisation also played its part and, combined with the development of widespread interactive computing during those years, provided a new sense in which those living and working in cities could communicate. In fact, cities are all about communication and thus flows and networks are central to any model of the smart city. Equivalent new technologies have of course existed since the telegraph and telephone were invented in the 19th century, but it was only when these technologies became interactive and, indeed, all-pervasive that the notion of the city itself becoming computable heralded in the age of the smart city. In the 1980s, the idea that economic development could be spurred by the location of fibre optics was widely explored as a basis for improving the prosperity of cities, and early municipal information systems were proposed as technologies to deliver public services. But it was not until the mid-1990s with the widespread development of mobile devices and wireless networks coming into their own that the idea of the computable city became a reality (Batty, 1997). The web, of course, was the progenitor of the smart city but the idea too that these technologies were replacing or at least complementing traditional physical and analogue technologies also suggested that smart cities, the key to a post-industrial world, might be much more complex than cities of the industrial and pre-industrial past.

What is very clear from the embedding of computational devices into the very fabric of the city across many scales is that cities are not managed or controlled from the top down. The emergence of social media is enough to convince one that cities do not function from top-down control no matter how many proposals are implemented that assume this to be the case. It has long been agreed amongst urbanists that cities grow and evolve from the bottom up (Jacobs, 1961), through the action of millions of individual decisions with more aggregate decisions still being generated by individuals no matter how much these may look like top-down control. Individual actions of course range from the simplest decisions about where to move to on a daily basis to where to locate for longer term advantage, but all such decisions are grounded in real time. These are being dramatically informed and transformed by new information technologies and this has heralded a shift in our thinking about cities to the short-term, to actions and decisions that happen on a diurnal cycle or shorter time intervals, in contrast to decision making that in the past had only been possible to observe over much longer time periods.

There is an irony in all of this. We do not have a good conceptual model of how a city functions in the very short term, where all the current activity associated with the smart city is taking place, whereas we do have models, albeit not very good ones, of how cities evolve in the longer term. Essentially, our vision of how cities evolve in terms of the structuring of their land use in organised spatial clusters and how their densities react to changes in demand and supply for land and capital, are based on models that examine how decisions that take time are made. Insofar as we have models that deal with short- and long-term decision-making, we simply assume a disconnection between how we act in the short term with long-term decisions, although it is increasingly clear that there are important feedbacks taking place that we should account for between the short- and long-term.

There are almost as many theories of the city as there are individuals attempting to make sense of these phenomena, with the field being clearly multi-paradigmatic or pluralistic. No good theories of the smart city in the short- or long-term exist, but to make progress here we can define some elements that pertain to the dynamics and structure of cities in the short term involving activities and interactions that take place in cycles that cluster around mobility during the working day and the delivery of services that take place over time periods on monthly cycles. These merge, of course, into longer-term change but our focus here is on how these shorter-term cycles are being 'informated' by new technologies. We have already noted that complexity science, with its focus on understanding systems from the bottom up, is key to our approach and this is manifest by the rapid growth of ideas about how networks are formed and how new technologies are reinforcing and generating networks of flows. These range across social and economic functions that involve interactions between people, but they are increasingly measured in non–physical terms – not in terms of people, energy or commodity flows but in terms of information flows, the flow of ideas, and the flow of money, which is a virtual commodity in itself. These are extremely hard to observe and our accounting systems are quite inadequate to provide any degree of comprehension which might underpin the way individuals and groups are making decisions based on electronically transmitted information.

This is best seen in the rise of social media. Much emphasis in the smart city is on making sense of how cities function from the vast volumes of interactions that individuals now organise through web services. These range across everything from Facebook to Google searches, through tagging mobile phone calls (from Call Detail Records – CDRs) to locations that can be associated with particular attributes such as work and play, but also through the variety of short text messaging and related services, of which Twitter is the example par excellence. Much of this data is highly ambiguous and can be positively misleading and, although interesting in its own right as we reveal below, there are considerable barriers to its use in understanding its meaning for the functioning of the contemporary city.

The single biggest problem in developing strategies for developing new technologies that make cities more efficient is that their effect involves a degree of invisibility that is different from traditional urban functions that depend on traditional technologies. In terms of how labour and capital are deployed in the industrial city to generate work, physical movements of activities – people and goods – predominate and these are comparatively easy to observe. Information flows, which have dramatically expanded through the internet, now provide massive input into production and consumption and their impact on physical flows and interactions is extremely hard to disentangle. This merger of the real and the physical makes the smart city considerably more complex to engage and understand than any city in any previous era. This transfer of atoms to bits, as Negroponte (1995) so presciently called it, is the dominant signature of the contemporary city and one of its consequences is that interactions within the population have multiplied massively as new and more immediate modes of communication have proliferated. This is seen clearly in the proliferation of social media, which is being used for a very wide range of functions which are increasingly almost too cryptic and complex to disentangle.

Automation in physical interactions is also a key feature of the smart city. Technology in cars enables better driving and communication with systems that enable better navigation utilising GPS, crowd-sourcing and other data pertaining to the transportation systems, such as that provided by services such as Waze (https://www.waze.com/). There are many developments which merge the physical and virtual in terms of the way information about the state of the physical system influences the way users engage with it and this is complicating analysis in ways that are unprecedented and for which we have a paucity of new approaches. Many new forms of information system are being introduced into cities in an attempt to control public access to services and one of the goals of many of the large IT companies, such as IBM and Cisco, in their smart cities projects is to ensure good integration between diverse systems, thus adding value to the entire enterprise. But a lot of this is mere hype. It is difficult, if not impossible, to correctly merge data sets that do not have common keys, and although there are ways of approximating such linkages, the state-of-the-art in this remains primitive. In the geospatial domain, address points, zip codes or their equivalent, is the usual way but even in relatively unambiguous contexts, where such a common key exists between two or more data sets, there are often problems of quality and completeness. In short, the notion of a seamless set of information systems where different activities in the city can be controlled from some common portal or frame remains a dream of the smart city optimists and is likely to remain so. An extreme version of such integrated technologies is the notion of an operating system for the smart city such as that proposed by PlanIT (http://living-planit.com/UOS_overview.htm). But such plans must be treated in somewhat allegorical terms as their realisation is simply impossible, sometimes betraying the naïve idealisation about how cities work that tends to characterise many of those thinking, writing and trying to implement technologies that compose the smart city. A generous interpretation of much of this hyperbole would be to assume that it represents directions for debate rather than serious practical proposals for action.

There have been attempts at bringing new technologies to the city to deal with routine events before. In the 1960s, technologies developed for dealing with political strategies in the Cold War – game theory, operations research, and information systems – were applied quite widely to the problems of the emergency services particularly in large US cities where the focus on deprivation and local resourcing had become urgent due to de-industrialisation, poor infrastructure and ethnic conflict. Various models of resource allocation for quite well-defined problems had been researched and applied at places like the RAND Corporation in the 1950s and 1960s and it appeared that the judicious application of these tools to urban emergency services might provide efficient methods for resolving key urban problems. It is important to note that these represented the application of computer models to problems where the data was adequate and which were controlled by agencies entirely within the purview of local municipalities, such as police and fire services. In fact, the experience of these first applications of smart city technologies was disastrous largely due to the inability of all the stakeholders involved to appreciate the many different perceptions of the problem, the politics involved in terms of traditional and new ways of working, and the generally volatile context of these problems, which were part of the wider decay in US cities due to factors well beyond the control of the municipalities themselves. Flood (2011), amongst others, paints a picture of classic wicked problems that get worse as seemingly more sophisticated methods were put to work on solving and alleviating them. Given this history, the portents for the current generation of smart city technologies are not good, particularly as this time around the key actors in the process – the large software and networking technology companies – are in the game so that they can make money. 50 years ago this profit motif was not to the fore in quite the same way (Greenfield, 2013).

It is quite clear that we do not really have a comprehensive theory which provides us with an integrated view of how new digital technologies are affecting the form and function of the contemporary city, apart from the straws in the wind noted here. There is little sense of joined-upness in the way new network technologies are being developed and how these might integrate different human behaviours which, in turn, will change the way the city is structured. To an extent, this is because many of these technologies are potentially disruptive, providing new modes of working that do not replace but simply add to conventional ways of doing things. In a sense, those who have attempted to look at these in a wider context have been forced back to first principles in terms of thinking what cities are for, how they work and how they act as social and economic drivers to increase prosperity and quality of life. Harrison et al. (2010) have sketched a context for the approach to smart cities through infrastructure, and extended this to embrace wider issues that tend to see these developments in context (Harrison & Donnelly, 2011). But our sense of the terrain is still extremely patchy and this discussion seems to miss so much of what cities are all about while at the same time appearing to pervade every aspect of the city as any universal technology will surely do.

IMMEDIATE VISUALISATIONS

Using our narrower perspective on the smart city, which focuses on the use of computation and sensors to automate routine systems which operate at high frequencies, real-time data streams tend to dominate the development of integrated systems for control and management. This is the focus of IT companies such as IBM through their Smart Planet initiative and it is therefore not surprising that those responsible for the wider coordination of such technologies, largely municipalities and public agencies of various kinds, have jumped on the notion that such real-time data can provide a picture of the city's functioning useful to its management. The web provides an essential enabling agent in this quest and a range of visual interfaces are rapidly emerging from the 'passive' dashboard that gives an instant picture of what is happening through real-time data feeds to the city to more fully equipped control centres where operators interact more directly in the control of systems whose performance is largely assessed using visualisations from such real-time feeds.

Data is key to these immediate visualisations and, in fact, the smart cities movement in general is dominated by the collection of data in real time and its potential use for real or near real-time control and management. In the next section, we will explore how data is driving the development of infrastructures that are coordinating and integrating diverse urban data but in its most basic form, dashboards and control centres of which individual web sites through which data is organised and visualised are central.

With the emergence of instant access to networks, at the time of writing (August 2014) around 100000 tweets are sent every minute with a total of 7 trillion in 2012, Google receives 2000000 search requests every minute, while users share almost 700000 pieces of content on Facebook (Mashable, 2012). There are upwards of 3.5 billion mobile phone users, some 700 million users of Facebook each month, 120 m Twitter users, 30 m Foursquare, and 46 m Linked-In users (Kearney, 2013). The sheer volumes of data being generated in this way are mind-boggling and as much of this data is without real structure as it is generated as a by-product of the devices used to produce it, there is a massive problem of making sense of it all. The obvious first step is simply to classify it through dashboards that simply take a series of data streams and display the quantities of the data involved with respect to the time over which it is generated. Temporal comparisons are thus the essence of how these dashboards might be used. In Figure 1, we show an associated infographic which collates much of this information together and provides a wider picture of this volume. An increasing amount of this data stream is geo-located, from check-ins via social networks sites like Foursquare through to Tweets and searches via Google Now. The data that cities and individuals emit can be collected and viewed to make it visible, thus aiding our understanding not only of how urban systems operate but opening up the possibility of the continuous real-time viewing of the city at large (Hudson-Smith, 2014). Cities across the world are at various stages of both releasing and utilizing such datasets as both producers and consumers of urban information. It is part of our realization that smart cities are no longer places where city governments act as the top-down drivers of development; rather, they act as one of the players in a much wider ecosystem of data and information

A key role that a city government plays in this emerging ecosystem is as a provider of data. The London Data Store is a prime example of how such an archive can provide an impetus to the creation of services and added value from data. Developed by the Greater London Authority and part of the EU **iCity** project, which involves building a platform of linked open applications for innovation in smart cities (http://www.icityproject.eu/), the data store has stimulated over 70 mobile applications linking to more than 500 datasets from a combination of the 27 real-time live traffic and transport data feeds.

Figure 1. The Dataverse: An infographic summarising the picture in June 2012 (Source: http://mashable. com/2012/06/22/data-created-every-minute/)

Through these feeds, we have created a City Dashboard as a means of viewing a key number of live data feeds. This essentially is a dumb interface to a visualisation of these data streams updated in real time, and delivered in a web-based manner. The dashboard collates and simplifies over 20 live feeds from air pollution through to energy demand, river flow, the FTSE 100, the number of buses in service, the status of the subway networks and so on, which we illustrate below in Figure 2 (a).

The dashboard is an early example of collating and visualising data feeds to provide a view of how a city is currently performing. Not only limited to London, the dashboard has also been built for Birmingham, Brighton, Cardiff, Edinburgh, Glasgow, Leeds and Manchester with a version for Venice also under development. But in these different cities, the types of streaming data can be a little different as the dashboard highlights the variability in the availability of feeds from city to city. London, at the present time, is the location for the majority of data feeds with their number updated on a second-by-second basis. The majority of this data is either collected via an Application Programming Interface (API) which is an interface, usually through a web site, where a user can query the status of the system with the live data delivered to the user (or its client), or the data mined in accordance with a data provider's terms and conditions (O'Brien et al., 2014). The ability to tap into these API feeds allows the city dashboard to provide a view of the particular city at a glance with the use of simple colour coding to indicate the positive or negative connotations of the current state of the data. A custom-made version of the London

Figure 2. Live Data Feeds (a) Into a Dashboard (b) Disaggregated into an iPad wall (Source: http:// citydashboard.org/london/)

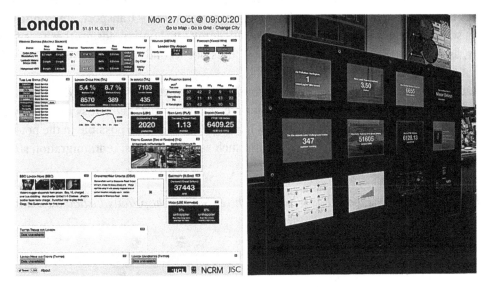

dashboard has been developed for internal use by the London Mayor's Policy Office at the Greater London Authority. Designed around 12 iPads and mounted into a single system, the board allows each iPad to display historic and live data relating the city as we show in Figure 2(b).

The historic nature of the iPad wall version of the dashboard requires an element of data graphing to examine trends in the feeds, and this has led to the next stage of the development of the **Citydashboard**, moving towards an archive system for city data. At its initial conception, the city dashboard was created as a simple viewer of city-related data feeds. The introduction of basic analytics has created a unified database with over 1 billion rows of data collected at the time of writing. With varying terms and conditions for each of the data streams, it is not however possible to redistribute the historic data. The variety of terms around data redistribution and republishing of feeds has resulted in a city dashboard system built around a custom developed '*cityapi*' that at this moment in time cannot be redistributed. The *cityapi* was produced to simplify the construction of data visualisation, collection and analytics from live feeds with each section of the API relating to specific feeds. The publishing of data streams via systems such as the London Data Store is creating a new landscape in data availability and arguably the development of a new kind of city-wide information system. The ability to refine and redistribute feeds is perhaps the next step to their wider user. While we have focused on the distribution of feeds, it should be noted that it is however possible to view these streams as a new data archive and plug them directly into systems for building various kinds of urban model ranging from simple 2-D and 3-D physical visualisations to mathematical abstractions of urban functions such as traffic, rental values, house prices and so on. Such data has the potential to enable us to develop a series of indicators which measure the performance of the city in both the short- and long-term. Indicators covering aspects of the city from urban flow, such as transport and pedestrian movement, through to a city's economic flows and onwards to more social inputs such as well-being and happiness, are on the horizon. To an extent, all these developments involve analytics that are currently at various stages of development but most are still very primitive and we will thus postpone their discussion until a little later in this chapter.

An example of a dashboard that goes beyond our own physically-orientated data streaming technology is being developed for Amsterdam. This is organised in terms of socio-economic data and is an archive rather than a live stream of outputs. Divided into five sections – transport, environment, population, culture, social-political, sport, security and the economy –it shows trends for these counts over the working day, as in Figure 3. The speed of refresh is hours not seconds and thus this dashboard is more like a state of the nation report.

In fact users can plot the data in mappable form so the dashboard has simple GIS functionality and users can thus get a picture of how these categories are changing spatially across the city, which is divided into 50 or more small zones. In a sense, this implies what might be possible in the not-too-distant future as new sources of open data come on stream, such as house prices, rent, migration statistics and

Figure 3. The Amsterdam Dashboard as a living archive (Source: http://citydashboard.waag.org/)

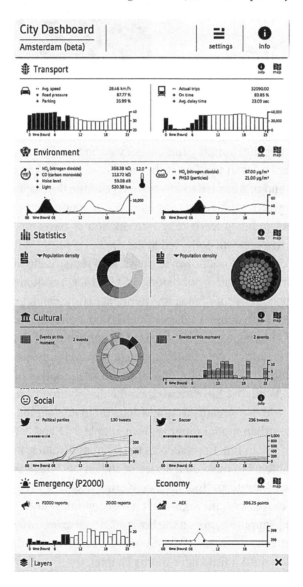

so on, which potentially might be delivered and updated on a day-by-day basis or at least a cycle which is much shorter than the typical year, approaching the second-by-second focus on dashboards based on streamed physical data. In fact, dashboards merge into more formalised control centres where there is more interactive usage and where operators are employed with a mandate to control various systems which take the real-time feeds from these various systems and employ simple functionality to make key decisions. These have been available for many years for real-time traffic control and currently there are many new systems being developed, the poster-child of which is the IBM system for Rio-de-Janeiro. To date, the analytics associated with such systems are quite rudimentary, largely indicators that are derived directly from raw data (Kitchin, 2014b), and the degree of intelligence or smartness embodied in such systems is not particularly advanced on traditional intuitive responses to crises that have been used for a long time. As we get a better sense of how all these real-time systems interact with one another then doubtless these control centres will improve, but currently the smartness which is potentially associated with such technologies is in its infancy. In fact, their smartness is largely based on the smartness of their users.

SMART DATA INFRASTRUCTURES

Kitchin (2014a) makes the point that the smart cities movement is as much about data infrastructures as it is about data. It is about how systems are designed that capture, process, and deliver data through various kinds of visualisation and then the construction of analytics – methods and models – that turn this data into information that can be used to predict and then control the system(s) of interest. So far, there is not much infrastructure that stitches together data that is captured in real time, largely due to the fact that the data sources are not coordinated and have no common keys for their integration. A good example involves transit data in London where demand for travel is logged in real time through the smart card system which 85% of travellers on public transport – bus, tube and light rail, and heavy overground suburban rail – use in payment for the service. This data is captured when travellers tap in and out on the tube and rail and tap in on the bus. There is an immediate problem of linking bus data to tube data; although it is possible to construct journeys using rail then bus using simple analytics, it is hard to predict user trips that use bus then rail because there is no tap out on bus. In short, these two closely related data sources cannot be easily collated. The system also records the position and time and status of any bus and train through APIs which deliver that data to any user with a three-minute latency but it is impossible, without some very brave assumptions, to link this supply data to demand data from the smart card. The missing data relates to the time and position when a traveller gets on and off a train and this data, which is within the complex network of underground stations, is simply not available. Moreover, assumptions need to be made about what trains travellers get on as there are many combinations of routes that fulfil the same travel objectives. Our point here is that despite there being very good data from these real-time feeds, it is impossible to construct a portal that integrates this data so that the trip system can be studied in its entirety. Of course it goes without saying that this data cannot be linked to demographic and related attributes and thus it is not possible to generate analytics that would help us understand how demand might be changing.

Building portals which introduce structure into data is a major quest in developing protocols and analytics that let both users and planners of the smart city function more intelligently. Since the web was developed during the last 20 years, geospatial data has become central and the first systems with widespread use dating back to the mid 1990s were map interfaces providing simple animation. Google maps is now 10 years old and it has become the *de facto* standard with usage figures in the order of one billion users each month, although this figure is complicated by repeat users and different ways in which these maps are interfaced in various portals. To date, the best data infrastructures developed which pertain to smart cities are those that deal with the less routine but regular and well-organised tranches of public data that inform us how cities function, in particular population census data. A good example of the kind of portal that takes state-of-the-art visualisation techniques and uses them to display, query and construct simple indicators of geospatial data is the **DataShine** 2001 Census portal developed by O'Brien and Cheshire (see http://datashine.org.uk/), which enables users to pull up and query a very wide variety of map data across many spatial scales pertaining to characteristics of the population built at the finest scale available for the UK.

In fact, although portals such as **DataShine** could be constructed with access to the raw data or semi-processed archives available as open data from various agencies such as the ONS, NOMIS and OS[2] in the UK, it is much easier and cleaner to download the data and organise it for rapid access. In **DataShine**, bulk data downloads from NOMIS are stitched together and then placed in a PostgreSQL database. The map base is taken from OS Open Data and thus the portal builds on several public data sources that have recently become more easily available through the open data movement. The typical interface is shown in Figure 4 where the population with educational level 2 skills is displayed at the scale of Greater London. Users can zoom in and out very rapidly and it is easy to get a picture of the whole nation (at least England and Wales, which is the current implementation) in this manner.

The interface is organized so that as much data as possible is displayed on the screen, while users can move the windows around and the ultimate map can be downloaded as a PDF at a higher level of resolution than the screen display. The colour spectrum can be changed on the fly and in this way users

Figure 4. The DataShine Portal for the 2011 population census

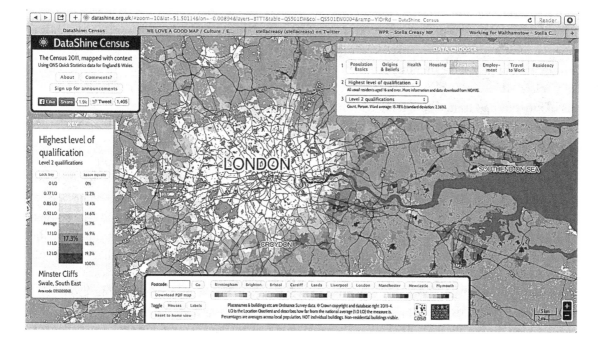

Figure 5. *Visualisations of the distribution of professional and managerial occupations in the biggest cities in England and Wales from the DataShine Portal. Going clockwise: Greater London; Birmingham; Liverpool and Manchester; England and Wales.*

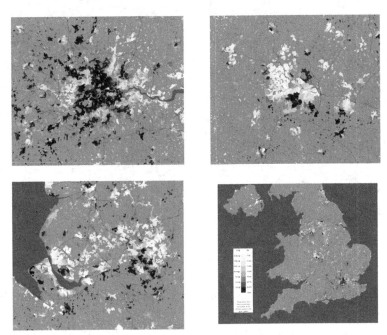

can explore the data in a remarkably flexible manner producing exactly what they require with ease. Of course, all data exploration and queries demand a degree of ingenuity but **DataShine** is an example of a portal that is immediately useful for those involved in understanding the variation in different attributes of the population and their relation to policy. The system is also able to produce excellent graphics for research purposes and in Figure 5 we show how we can generate a series of maps at different scales that reflect how the morphology of cities at these scales is reflected by a population attribute based on the percentage of professional occupations by ward.

A good deal of analysis using geospatial data is now being included in web-based GIS and there are portals emerging which enable users to create their own maps, uploading data in standard formats such as shapefiles, XML formats and so on, and then manipulating and merging data in various ways to enhance their analysis. Our own portal, called **MapTube,** which is billed as a 'Place for Maps', has been under development for several years and acts as a workhorse for simple map analysis and storage. When users are able to use web software which is entirely open in the way **MapTube** is, we need to guard against violations of copyright. To this end, **MapTube** creates maps for the users from their own data, delivers the map to their web site and then keeps a pointer to the site so that the user retains or is responsible for any copyright. In fact, **MapTube** mainly contains maps that we have created and for it to gain widespread use we need to broadcast its availability. The fact that portals such as these are queried and accessed many thousands of times does not imply widespread usage for there is still a learning curve and the number of professionals dealing with data that pertains to smart cities is still quite small. Most municipalities, for example, still do not have the professional capabilities to deal with smart city technologies of which big data and web interaction are key, and thus there is a growing gap between

Figure 6. A typical MapTube interface displaying OAC data

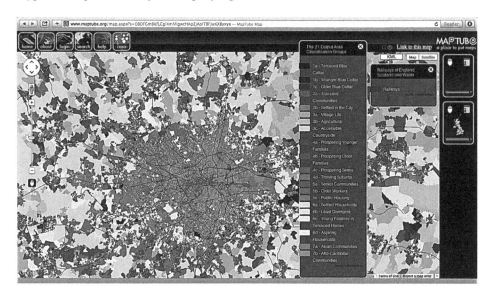

data analysis and the kind of urban analytics that portals like **DataShine** and **MapTube** offer, despite the fact that they are fairly basic.

We show the interface to the **MapTube** site (http://www.maptube.org/) in Figure 6 where the user is able to access various parts of the site that let them upload their map (with quite straightforward help facilities), display it and then merge it through overlay with any other map that is on the system. As many overlays of different maps as the users wishes can be created with transparency-fading facilities so that spatial correlations and comparisons can be made. In Figure 6 we show the geodemographic structure of the population of Greater London as the output area classification (OAC), which takes the various indices and profile of the population in each ward and then produces a summary of this according to various social and economic descriptors. We also overlay railway lines on this map so that the user can make sense of any radial or circumferential bias in the spatial distribution of population types. In this way, a user can build up a picture of a place. In both **DataShine** and **MapTube**, users can dig down and pull up the raw data thereby having full control over any understanding that can be gleaned from this kind of casual spatial analysis.

What we have shown so far are somewhat straightforward but robust portals to data that pertains to the spatial distribution of various functions in the city. The common mode of integration is spatial where the common key is the geocode. It has taken 20 years or more to reach the stage where portals such as these are now widely available to inform urban analysis, and more integrated systems have been slow in coming. The scale of hyperbole in this domain is enormous with many proposals for integrated systems that are simply not possible. With unstructured data and few common keys, integrated systems that merge many different streams of data are rare and in any case, in terms of data delivered in real time, there are often no strong reasons why such data should be integrated. In fact, it is more likely that the device itself acts as the integrator or platform on which many applications can be developed, and it is the user who will perform any integration with the device acting as its own portal to many different kinds of data.

There is another important reason why integrated data portals will also remain the exception rather than the rule. Cities are built from the bottom up, being the product of countless decisions that are made individually, even if within a social context. Their structure is one of self-organisation and there is little reason to think that millions of people making decisions about how to develop and use new information technologies will self organise in any different way. In fact, the development of computing has followed a similar path to all other human endeavours with surprising twists and turns, and the notion of top-down coordinated systems that function perfectly is fanciful. In fact, systems need to be designed so that they are able to accept and deal with error and this usually requires human intervention. Of course, some transaction processing systems dealing with highly routinised data such as automated banking, the control of automated vehicles such as trains, the control of energy in home environments and such like are capable of being highly centralised and operated accordingly. But in general most of the functions that characterise the contemporary city require a mix of automation and human decision making to enable their successful functioning and the kind of urban ecology that is resulting – that is, the urban ecology that we might call the smart city – is just that: it is an ecology which situates organisms in their environment, structured so that it maintains diversity and resilience to various changes that optimise its functioning.

DATA STREAMS FROM SOCIAL MEDIA

Here we will define social media as any kind of medium through which individuals communicate with one another in space and time. To an extent, this defines the city itself for as everyone from Plato to Jane Jacobs (1961) has argued, cities are places where people come together to improve their quality of life through communication which leads to the sharing and pooling of their talents. As cities evolve from the bottom up with their subsystems continuing to function as they grow, traditionally they are best articulated in terms of distinct communities or neighbourhoods which are arranged in hierarchical order with this hierarchy elaborating itself as a city scales in size. In the last 100 years, onto this pattern have come new ways of interacting and communicating in which the role of physical distance has been tempered and, in some way, by-passed through the telegraph, telephone, television and so on. Most of these media have been passive or at least interactive in a modest way, but with the rise of the net, the web, and our ability to connect up using portable/mobile devices there has been a veritable explosion in new ways of interactive communications. Their impact on the ways we behave in cities with respect to one another is not at all clear. As these new forms of communication work themselves out, we are increasingly able to record and archive these new forms of interaction and the quest is to now to consider the ways in which this media is improving the quality of urban life or otherwise. Moreover, such communications are having an impact on the form of the city and are certainly changing the way we travel in physical terms. We are at the beginning of a revolution in the way cities are structured with new patterns of communication layered on top and alongside traditional ones, and the impact on where we locate and how we travel is becoming ever more complex.

So far, the most serious attempts at exploring these new media have been through access to mobile phone calls, which have the prospect of revealing all kinds of communication, from social networks to travel patterns. CDTs usually contain geocoded information that logs the origin and destination of the call and judicious analysis of the time and length of calls can provide some probability of the call being of a particular type. If attribute data about the user is available from the mobile phone provider (which it usually isn't because of confidentiality and/or commercial reasons) then an even better prediction of what the mobile phone call relates to can be generated. This is about as good as it gets and in cases where this level of data is available, there is the possibility that such data might be used as a 'proxy' for travel and interaction. However, this new data would appear to be most useful as a complement to existing travel data of the conventional kind. When it comes to recreational usage, such as short text messaging, then the big problem is that only a very small proportion of such messages are tagged to location and an even smaller number can be related to an origin and a destination. The content of such messages is problematic because they are short and cryptic and although these data sets can be enormous – we noted above that there are more than 150 million tweets per day globally – the usable content is tiny. When it comes to other social media sites, such as Foursquare and Facebook, the problems multiply because the use of such media is much less obvious in terms of the physical space in which such communications take place.

The attraction of working with these new types of social media is that they contain data at the individual level which can be aggregated to search for patterns and correlations, and they are usually coded at a very fine level of space – coordinates, for example, or the finest level of zip code – and at temporal frequencies of minutes or even seconds. A picture of the city evolving in the very short term can thus be assembled if the data is judged to have any relevance whatsoever. A good example of this data is the pattern of ethnicity in a large city – London in this case – which is extracted from an analysis of geo-located tweets with respect to the language used. This has been mined and displayed by Cheshire and Manley (2012) and Figure 7 displays the pattern that they extracted for Greater London over 5 summer months from May until September of 2012 (covering the Olympic Games weeks). This is based on 3.3 million usable tweets from the 6 million or so which gave a GPS location. In fact, during this period there were more than 300 million tweets in London but only 1% of these appear to have a GPS location and thus the sample is hardly representative (Betanews, 2012). In fact, this map betrays the basic problem with social media and the possibility of generating useful and informative data from it that can say something about the smart city. The problem relates more widely to mobile phone data where very often the data available is only from one provider and in most cases the market for mobile phones is partitioned between two or more providers. Thus the data can be highly biased and, in the case of Twitter usage, it is also very clear that when we take age into account the bias is greatly exacerbated as it is widely known that the number of Twitter users declines precipitously with age, for example.

In Figure 7, the scale of the illustration blurs the colours somewhat and it is necessary to zoom in and manipulate the transparency of the map to get a good understanding of the clustering. It is also worth noting that when writing about visualisation in the smart city, we are not able to show the diverse range of visualisation tools that are possible because they depend on animating maps and related infographics; for this readers must turn directly to the web or to archived videos such as those on *YouTube*. Nonetheless, the pattern generated in the static map in Figure 7 is similar to that pertaining to the various ethnic group clusters that have been provided in the Output Area Classification (OAC) (http://ukdataexplorer. com/census/).

Many digital methods and models have been derived in parallel to the smart city movement in that the focus is on the longer-term analysis of factors affecting a city's economy, demography, transportation systems and so on. Iconic models, which are 3-D representations of the city in digital form, and more abstract mathematical models, which attempt to predict the location and interaction between different land uses and activities, are being slowly informed by new data that originates from shorter term real-time feeds such as those associated with mobile phones, smart cards, and various sensors embedded in places of continuous activity. Some of the tools used for visualisation in 2-D from GIS and 3-D from computer-aided design are now being used to visualise real-time streamed data such as Twitter feeds. One of our projects takes geolocated tweets and associates them with specific locations which can be identified as land and building parcels, as we show in Figure 8. By placing this data into a procedural

Figure 7. Geolocated tweets in central and inner London mined according to language using Google Translate and collected in the summer of 2012

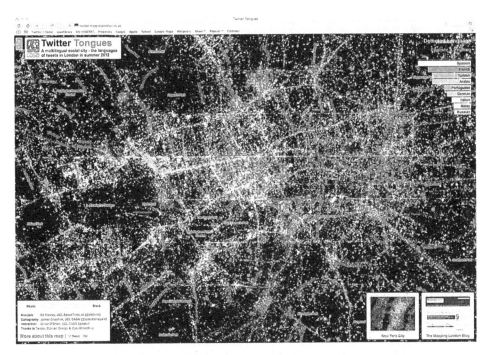

system, the 'Tweet City' project is an ongoing visualisation which utilizes the Twitter API in an attempt to create a new 3-D urban landscape. In addition, the project augments already existing GIS spatial data with real-time Twitter feeds using a custom-developed 'tagging' methodology. This allows the user not only to develop different visualizations by editing simple rules but also to develop more sophisticated types of analysis based around city data feeds.

Figure 8. Live Twitter feeds in London visualized as building heights

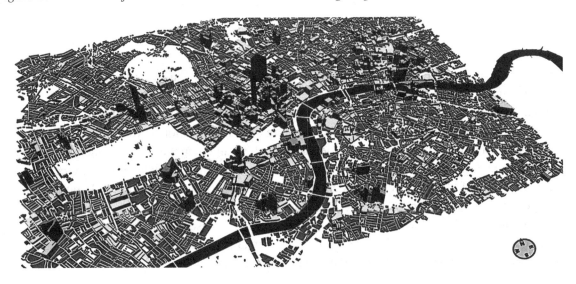

This visualisation, in fact, makes use of an augmented 3-D GIS called **City Engine** which embodies a procedural modelling system that lets the user associate given rules for the development of each object in the GIS. The key advantage of moving city data feeds into a procedural geographic information system is the ability to introduce more advanced spatial analysis functions within real-time data mining. The project aims to include multiple feeds, such as air-quality readings, by tracking down enough air-quality sensors to form accurate, pinpoint pollution estimates. The system operates online and, as it is linked to a 3-D representation of the city, has the potential to augment the **Citydashboard** concept towards one of integrating wider feeds such as those being explored in **iCity**. Emerging trends can be visualised on a city-wide or hyper-local scale via the move to a 3-D interface. Moving to a more 'urban' view of the data and placing it in a geo-located position, whilst still maintaining the real-time reporting, further develops the concept. Tweet City developed by Flora Roumpani and Stephan Hugel can be downloaded at http://urschrei.github.io/CityEngine-Twitter/ where the user can engage in various explorations of the data and its visualisation.

Our last visualisation involves generating big data in quite a different way by sampling the 'crowd' eliciting responses to various events which can be captured and imported into visual models that let users and analysts explore the movement of crowds in motion. This is not quite crowdsourcing in the traditional way but it is sampling data pertaining to live scenes and then augmenting their analysis though visual models of the kind that are available using **City Engine**. An increasing number of urban information systems which can be visualised in 2-D or 3-D form rely on variants of crowd-sourcing for their data through a form of citizen science. As Haklay (2010) states, "… using citizen science can take a form in which volunteers put their efforts to a purely scientific endeavour, such as mapping galaxies, or a different form that might be termed 'community science' in which scientific measurements and analysis are carried out by members of local communities so they can develop an evidence base and set action plans to deal with problems in their area". With almost ubiquitous mobile phone ownership in urban areas, 'the crowd' is becoming both a provider and user of data. Many crowd-sourced applications are still at the prototype stage but with the ability to ask a crowd to share their location as they move across a city, and this has core implications for urban monitoring and management.

Figure 9 details a live capture of crowd-sourced location data during the Lord Mayor's Show in the City of London in 2011. The aggregated data of all participating visitors – those who line the route of the parade – is used to create a real-time overview of the crowd density at the event locations. Organizers can subsequently use the system's output to identify potential hot spots before they turn into hazards. Situations can thus be defused by sending visitors location-based advice either via a push notification or SMS text (SIS, 2013). In fact, taking this visualisation into a real-time context is difficult as restrictions on bandwidth will remain critical for a long time to come as yet in capturing and transmitting data back to users with no appreciable lag.

Another feature of the smart city in terms of our definition as self-monitoring, analysis and reporting is volunteered location-sharing. This is similar in nature to adding location to a social network; it allows a new generation of data-miners and data scientists to collect and map location, expanding the view of how we not only use space and place but through additional information as to how we perceive space. The measurement of happiness, emotions and well-being in space is an emerging field but one that is perhaps central to the concept of a self-monitoring, analysing and reporting city. One example is the LSE 'Mappiness' project which is an iPhone application that asks users at random points during the day the extent to which they are feeling happy (http://www.mappiness.org.uk). The application associates each response with key spatial and environmental indicators using the GPS location data. As MacKer-

Figure 9. Mapping the crowd and visualising its density in city engine

ron and Mourato (2013) state, they can calculate the habitat type at each reported point location which they then classify in the nine broad habitat categories used in the UK National Ecosystem. Using data from Weather Underground, which collates data from 280 weather sensors across the UK, they link each response with weather conditions reported by the station nearest to the response location at the moment nearest the response timestamp. They also calculate whether it was daylight at the response date, time and location. Finally, the application allows the user to record a sample of sound and to take a picture of their location. The application has over 3 million users and is an example of extracting new sources of information using mobile devices. The mapping of emotions opens up our ability to explore how we actually feel about our built environment. Applications such as Mappiness are, of course, subjective, yet represent a new type of self reporting tool for the inhabitants of the city. It is these new sources of data, combined with the perhaps more traditional datasets, that hold the key to the development of a smart city. A city where the current status quo can be monitored and fed into urban models to develop a predictive view of the future of a city system.

THE FUTURE OF SMART CITIES AND THE NEW URBAN ANALYTICS

In this chapter, we have taken a relatively low key approach to smart cities in terms of the new urban analytics that are being composed to ensure that better analysis, policy-making and ultimately a better quality of life contribute to the outcomes that the smart city is able to generate. Our focus has been on new data sets that provide the context for new forms of understanding and we have not focused on the tools – the simulation models and methods – that might be used to articulate this understanding, and articulate new modes of control and management. These analytics loosely form part of what many call 'urban informatics', which is defined as the application of computers to the functioning of cities; Foth et al. (2011), for example, define urban informatics as the study, design, and practice of urban experiences across different urban contexts that are created by new opportunities of real time, ubiquitous technology and the augmentation that mediates the physical and digital layers of people networks and urban infrastructures. This is strictly the narrower focus that we have adopted here; it pertains to the ways in which computers are being embedded into cities as hardware and software so that routine functions can be made more efficient, not only through automated responses but through the data that such computation generates, which is central to policy analysis. This narrow focus is on control and the kinds of analytics that would best pertain to this area are models that deal with rapid movements and location in cities that occur in almost real time. In its wider focus, it is concerned with the use of computers and communications to enable services to be delivered across many domains and to enable populations to engage and interact in policy issues that require citizen participation. Urban informatics is thus intimately tied up with monitoring, analysis, reporting and thence control and management, which are the key elements that we have used in this perspective on the smart city.

The kinds of analytics that now form the cutting edge in realising smart city technologies are not new. Half a century ago, after the rise of operations research, which involved the applications of mathematical and statistical tools to search for patterns and to optimise the organisation of industrial and military systems, the tools involved in optimising short-term resource allocations using various kinds of queuing theory, optimisation such as linear programming, scheduling systems based on graphs and path analysis, were applied to routine functions in cities, particular police, fire and related emergency services. Urban operations research, as this came to be called (Larson & Odoni, 1981), was quite widely applied in urban contexts in the US as we indicated earlier and some of these tools have remained embedded in the routine functions of these services. In fact, as we also implied, although these kinds of tools deal with quite well-defined protocols, their application over the last few decades has not been a roaring success and their interaction with the political and bureaucratic process has been problematic. This poses a stark warning for the smart cities movement, and although this is not the place to discuss these wider issues, they are important (Batty, 2014). Here we will conclude with a short summary of the kinds of technologies that lie at the basis of new urban analytics, as these are rapidly developing at the present time and there are many opportunities as well as pitfalls.

The range of analytics that pertain to the kinds of data that we have reviewed here is wide in that it ranges from statistical methods that seek to extract patterns in such data to simulation models that are validated to such data and thence used for prediction. Prescriptive or design methods also map onto these analytics to an extent, the new class of geodesign methods emerging from GIS being a case in point. These analytics are also surrounded by various minimalist tools which relate to the extraction of indicators and performance measures from data, such as those that are implied in data streamed into dashboards and control centres and then transformed into measures useful in providing users and policy makers with some sense of how the city is performing relative to various baselines. There is now a wide class of multivariate methods that fall under the rubric of data mining tools that are sometimes referred to as machine learning. These range from basic component and factor analysis, which have been around for 50 years, to newer techniques such as neural networks and evolutionary algorithms that extract patterns in large data sets by learning through iterative exploration. These techniques tend to be non-causal in focus: they work by extracting correlations and some, such as Anderson (2007), have gone so far as to argue that the search for causal relationships is a thing of the past in the age of big data and data mining. But we, amongst others, would consider this a controversial stance, born of a lack of understating of the complexity of cities. It may be relevant in some contexts where routine patterns are dominant and unvarying but it is unlikely to be the case in searching for ways in which to understand and control systems as complex as the city.

Important elements in this range of tools are large-scale integrated models of various kinds. To an extent, these tend to be developed for longer-term, more intricate aspects of city systems which do not focus on the sorts of cybernetic control that short-term analytics for the management of energy and transit relate to. This makes it important to see the smart city in a somewhat wider context than we have emphasised here. A more complete review of analytics, data and visualisation would cover these kinds of model where the definition of the system of interest is more ambiguous and unclear than in the kinds of routine system developed here. This needs more comprehensive review but it is important to conclude this chapter by noting that the term 'smart cities' is being used to cover a very wide range of spatial and temporal scales. These cover a range of processes relating to how cities function and it is important to be aware that the tools being developed cut across these scales, being developed in ways that make their usage and relevance quite different between different types of application. In fact, our vision for urban analytics is extremely diffuse in that there is a deep hierarchy of tools that are being slowly fashioned to deal with many different aspects of urban systems. Such technologies thus need to be finely adapted to the many different perspectives on the smart city which now exist while being focussed on the many different policy (and political) contexts which dominate all discussions about future cities.

ACKNOWLEDGMENT

Thanks to Steven Gray, James Cheshire, Ed Manley, Richard Milton, and Oliver O'Brien whose examples of map technologies we have included here. This chapter was part financed by the ESRC Talisman Project ES/I025634/1.

REFERENCES

Anderson, C. (2007). The End of Theory: Will the Data Deluge Make the Scientific Method Obsolete? *Wired Magazine*. Retrieved from http://www.wired.com/science/discoveries/magazine/16-07/pb_theory

Batty, M. (1997). The Computable City. *International Planning Studies, 2*, 155-173. Retrieved from https://web.archive.org/web/19980124005925/http://www.geog.buffalo.edu/Geo666/batty/melbourne.html

Batty, M. (2013). Big Data, Smart Cities, and City Planning. *Dialogues in Human Geography, 3*(3), 274–279. doi:10.1177/2043820613513390

Batty, M. (2014). *The Smart Cities Movement, forthcoming CASA working papers series*. London: UCL.

Batty, M., Axhausen, K., Fosca, G., Pozdnoukhov, A., Bazzani, A., Wachowicz, M., & Portugali, Y. et al. (2012). Smart Cities of the Future. *The European Physical Journal. Special Topics, 214*(1), 481–518. doi:10.1140/epjst/e2012-01703-3

Betanews. (2012). *Twitter: 500 million accounts, billions of tweets, and less than one percent use their location*. Retrieved from http://betanews.com/2012/07/31/twitter-500-million-accounts-billions-of-tweets-and-less-than-one-percent-use-their-location/

Cheshire, J. A., & Manley, E. (2012). *Twitter Tongues*. Retrieved from http://twitter.mappinglondon.co.uk

Flood, J. (2011). *The Fires: How a Computer Formula, Big Ideas, and the Best of Intentions Burned Down New York City and Determined the Future of Cities*. New York, NY: Riverhead Trade.

Foth, M., Choi, J. H., & Satchell, C. (2011). Urban Informatics. *In Proceedings of the ACM Conference on Computer Supported Cooperative Work* (pp. 1-8).

Greenfield, A. (2013). *Against the Smart City. Amazon Media Kindle*. New York, NY: Do Projects.

Haklay, M. (2010). Geographical Citizen Science – Clash of Cultures and New Opportunities. In *Proceedings of Workshop on the Role of Volunteered Geographic Information in Advancing Science*. Retrieved from http://web.ornl.gov/sci/gist/workshops/2010/papers/Haklay.pdf

Hardin, G. (1968). The Tragedy of the Commons. *Science, 162*(3859), 1243–1248. doi:10.1126/science.162.3859.1243 PMID:5699198

Harrison, C., & Abbott-Donnelly, I. (2011). A Theory of Smart Cities, Annual Meeting of the ISSS. Retrieved from http://journals.isss.org/index.php/proceedings55th/article/viewFile/1703/572

Harrison, C., Eckman, B., Hamilton, R., Hartswick, P., Kalagnanam, J., Paraszczak, J., & Williams, P. (2010). Foundations for Smarter Cities. *IBM Journal of Research and Development, 54*(4), 1–16. doi:10.1147/JRD.2010.2048257

Hudson-Smith, A. (2014). Tracking, Tagging and Scanning the City. *Architectural Design, 84*(1), 40–47. doi:10.1002/ad.1700

Jacobs, J. (1961). *The Death and Life of Great American Cities*. New York: Random House.

Kearney, A. T. (2013). The Mobile Economy 2013. Retrieved from http://www.gsmamobileeconomy.com/GSMA%20Mobile%20Economy%202013.pdf

Kitchin, R. (2014a). *The Data Revolution: Big Data, Open Data, Data Infrastructures and Their Consequences*. London: Sage. doi:10.4135/9781473909472

Kitchin, R. (2014b). *Knowing and Governing Cities Through Urban Indicators, City Benchmarking and Real-Time Dashboards*. Retrieved from https://www.maynoothuniversity.ie/progcity/

Larson, R. G., & Odoni, A. R. (1981). *Urban Operations Research*. NJ: Prentice-Hall.

MacKerron, G., & Mourato, S. (2013). Happiness is Greater in Natural Environments. *Journal of Global Environmental Change, 23*(5), 992–1000. doi:10.1016/j.gloenvcha.2013.03.010

Mashable. (2012). *How Much Data is Created Every Minute?* Retrieved from http://mashable.com/2012/06/22/data-created-every-minute/

Negroponte, N. (1995). *Being Digital. New York, NY*. Alfred: Knopf.

O'Brien, O., Batty, M., Gray, S., Cheshire, J., & Hudson-Smith, A. (2014). On City Dashboards and Data Stores. In *Proceedings of Workshop on Big Data and Urban Informatics*. University of Illinois at Chicago, Chicago, IL.

SIS. (2013). *Mapping the Crowd, The Lord Mayors Show, SIS Software*. Retrieved from http://www.sis.software.co.uk/

Sterling, B. (2005). *Shaping Things*. Cambridge, MA: MIT Press.

KEY TERMS AND DEFINITIONS

Crowd-Sourcing: Sampling a population with respect to their opinions using internet-related technologies such as web questionnaires.

Data Infrastructures: Combinations of hardware, software, dataware and organisational-ware that provide the structures that deliver data and make it computable.

Map Portals: Web-sites and/or standalone software systems that enable users to display, query, locate and visualise spatial data in map form as layers.

Social Media: Digital media that pertains to social interactions between people and places such as short text messages and web-based social networking sites.

Urban Analytics: Methods of mathematical and symbolic modelling that generate insights into existing data as well as predictions of future data.

Urban Dashboards: Portals, usually web-enabled, that collate continuous feeds of data which are produced in real time.

Visualisation: Methods of turning data and analysis into images that can be near real such as 2D maps and 3D scenes as well as more abstract such as networks and graphs.

ENDNOTES

[1]   The adjective 'smart' in this context is a peculiarly American term. It was first used in an urban context with respect to urban growth. 'Smart growth' evolved as a term for managed urban sprawl in the 1980s and 1990s (http://www.smartgrowthamerica.org/) and its usage in IT applied to cities – smart cities – was an obvious extension (Batty et al., 2012). Earlier definitions, from wired cities to information cities, intelligent cities, digital cities and virtual cities, cover the same domain tending to merge into one another but all covering the wider context. The term 'smart' is much more widely used in American everyday language than British everyday language, but it is rapidly being adopted globally.

[2]   **ONS**: Office of National Statistics; **NOMIS**: National Online Manpower Information System; **OS**: Ordnance Survey.

This research was previously published in the Handbook of Research on Social, Economic, and Environmental Sustainability in the Development of Smart Cities edited by Andrea Vesco and Francesco Ferrero, pages 339-362, copyright year 2015 by Information Science Reference (an imprint of IGI Global).

Chapter 22
Wireless Access Networks for Smart Cities

Hervé Rivano
Inria, France

Khaled Boussetta
Université Paris 13, France & Inria, France

Isabelle Augé-Blum
INSA Lyon, France & Inria, France

Marco Fiore
CNR, Italy & Inria, France

Walid Bechkit
INSA Lyon, France & Inria, France

Razvan Stanica
INSA Lyon, France & Inria, France

Fabrice Valois
INSA Lyon, France & Inria, France

ABSTRACT

Smart cities are envisioned to enable a vast amount of services in urban environments, so as to improve mobility, health, resource management, and, generally speaking, citizens' quality of life. Most of these services rely on pervasive, seamless and real-time access to information by users on the move, as well as on continuous exchanges of data among millions of devices deployed throughout the urban surface. It is thus clear that communication networks will be the key to enabling smart city solutions, by providing their core support infrastructure. In particular, wireless technologies will represent the main tool leveraged by such an infrastructure, as they allow device mobility and do not have the deployment constraints of wired architectures. In this Chapter, we present different wireless access networks intended to empower future smart cities, and discuss their features, complementarity and interoperability.

INTRODUCTION

Since 2009, more than half of the world's population now lives in urban areas, a proportion that exceeds 75% in developed countries and will grow to 60% worldwide by 2030 (United Nations, 2012). The rapid rise of cities yields new societal challenges with strong scientific and technological implications. As the population density starts to exceed 5.000 inhabitants per km^2, all type of living resources face a dramatic growth in demand. This applies to natural goods, such as water or gas, as well as to infrastructures, such as transportation systems, energy grids and telecommunication networks. The problem is the availability

DOI: 10.4018/978-1-5225-2589-9.ch022

of such resources will not increase at the same rate as their demand, as testified by recent forecasts on sustainable development (United Nations, 2013), on road capacity and energy distribution (International Energy Agency, 2012), and on global mobile data traffic (Cisco, 2013).

The answer to the needs of mass urbanization lies then in the way the resources at our disposal are managed, and Information and Communication Technologies (ICT) are expected to play a key role in that process. The complete list of use cases for ICT in future smart cities is vast and varied, with a large number of applications that promise to have a significant impact on the efficient management of urban resources in just a few years from now. In fact, most such applications strongly rely on communication. The mobility and pervasiveness of the devices participating in the process commend that data transfers – at least those including end users – are mainly wireless. However, the nature of network access (by hundreds of thousands of autonomous or mobile devices) and the type of traffic generated (from small-size periodic data to high-definition video streaming) define new usages over large (i.e. metropolitan) scales, which cannot be accommodated solely via the traditional communication infrastructure. This makes the case for original networking solutions that can efficiently cope with the future communication demands of smart cities. On the one hand, there is the necessity to enhance the existing cellular infrastructure, especially in terms of radio access. Although connection speeds are expected to augment 7-fold by 2017 (due partly to the additional capacity provided by heterogeneous deployments, as well as to traffic offloading via femtocells and Wi-Fi), this will not suffice to manage the overall 13-fold increase in mobile data traffic by the same date (Cisco, 2013). On the other hand, short-range wireless technologies, such as Wi-Fi, DSRC, and Zigbee will empower ubiquitous meshed architectures, based on the M2M paradigm and specifically designed to manage the load offered by smart city services.

As a result, there is a clear need for innovative communication network models in the wireless last mile, i.e. that bridging end terminals – be they autonomous devices or mobile appliances under the control of users – to the wired network. In fact, the network paradigms envisioned to enable smart cities are not far from those studied by the research community over the last decade. One can find glimpses of the vision that accompanied studies on wireless sensor networks, mesh networks, vehicular networks, and ad hoc networks in general. However, there is more to smart city communication infrastructure than the direct implementation of state-of-the-art protocols proposed for the aforementioned wireless networks.

In this Chapter, we present wireless last-mile communication technologies for upcoming smart cities. The *"Background"* section presents the technologies that are currently employed to provide wireless access to users and devices. Such technologies, falling into the two wide categories of cellular and wireless local-area networks, have been dominating the market for over a decade: the presentation of their architecture and major features represents the natural starting point for our treatise. The *"Emerging wireless access technologies"* section presents a wide range of diverse solutions that are gaining momentum nowadays in the context of ICT for urban environments. Our discussion includes both direct evolutions of the cellular and wireless local area network paradigms as well as innovative and disruptive solutions, based on communication to, from and among sensors, vehicles and mobile terminals. The section provides a comprehensive overview of the underlying technologies that may contribute to the overall ICT architecture in upcoming smart cities. The *"Future research directions"* section outlines how the different technologies presented before – each dedicated to a specific need in terms of the smart city wireless communication infrastructure, and typically regarded in isolation – need ultimately to coexist. We thus introduce a unifying paradigm for wireless technologies in smart cities, under the term of *capillary networking*. We discuss future research challenges arising from such a holistic viewpoint on emerging wireless access. The *"Conclusion"* section closes the Chapter, summarizing the main points emerging from the discussion.

BACKGROUND

Wireless access infrastructures are currently based on two complementary network paradigms, i.e. cellular and local-area architectures. In order to better understand their evolution within the smart city context, below we provide a brief overview of the technologies they build upon.

Cellular Network Infrastructure and Technologies

Cellular networks are based on architectures operated by telecommunications companies. They are designed to provide telephony services, such as voice calls, fax and Short Messages Services (SMS), as well as data traffic services to *mobile* users, with a *pervasive* coverage. Support of mobility is enabled by the use of wireless technologies that allow users to freely travel (possibly over large distances and at high speed) while carrying and using their communication devices. Pervasive coverage means instead that a user is able to receive or initiate a cellular phone call or data session from any place. Cellular networks are intended to provide different Quality of Service (QoS) levels to users, in return for an access fee charged by the operator.

In order to allow complete user mobility, the communication occurs between a user-carried mobile terminal and a so-called fixed base station – both equipped with radio transmitter(s) and receiver(s), and capable of emitting and receiving radio-frequency signals. The communication occurs over reserved portions of the electromagnetic spectrum, and exchanges are bidirectional, as the radio signal carrying the information can be emitted by the mobile user's terminal and received by the base station (uplink direction), or be emitted by the base station and received by the terminal (downlink direction). Each communication occupies one specific portion of such a spectrum, also referred to as a *channel*.

The physical properties of radio-frequency signal propagation result in a significant attenuation of the same with the distance between the transmitter and the receiver. Theoretically, the attenuation is at least proportional to the square of the distance, but it is often much greater due to the environment in which the base station and the mobile terminal are located. Indeed, the presence of static and mobile obstacles around and between the transmitter and receiver causes reflections, refraction, diffraction, Doppler and multipath effects. In turn, these lead to a finite maximum distance between the transmitter and receiver. As a consequence, each base station can serve users within a limited geographical area, named *cell*. Pervasive coverage is then guaranteed by deploying base stations so that the superposition of the corresponding cells covers the whole target territory.

The tessellation of space into cells allows different base stations to use the same channels to serve different users. This operation must however be performed with care, since radio-frequency signal propagation cannot be precisely controlled and thus typically trespasses the cell boundaries. This implies that simultaneous transmissions occurring within nearby cells and over the same channels risk interfering with each other and disrupting both communications. The way channels are allocated within the spectrum and the mechanisms used to manage this so-called co-channel interference are the main differences between the different technologies that have characterized subsequent generations of cellular

Figure 1. Cellular network architectures in GSM (top), UMTS (middle) and LTE (bottom)

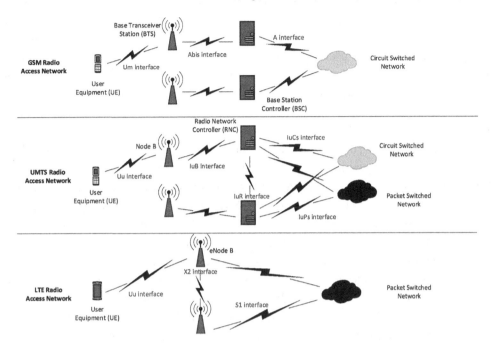

networks. Below, we introduce the features of the second- and third-generation architectures that are dominant in today's deployments.

Second Generation Cellular Networks: GSM, GPRS and EDGE

The second generation of cellular networks (often referred to as 2G) maps to GSM (Global System for Mobile Communications), whose share exceeds 90% of the total 2G market. GSM only supports mobile telephony services, and defines channels as time-frequency slots, and thus adopts mixed Time Division Multiple Access (TDMA) and Frequency Division Multiple Access (FDMA) techniques to make multiple base station-to-user communications co-exist within the available spectrum.

More precisely, the GSM standard defines several carrier frequency ranges in the ISM band. Most current deployments use the 850-900 MHz band, and some include the 1800-1900 MHz band. The GSM band is then divided into two sub-bands, dedicated to uplink and downlink communication respectively. To carry a phone call, the system has to allocate one GSM downlink channel and one GSM uplink channel, which are released once the call is terminated.

Different cells can use the same GSM channels. However, in order to avoid co-channel interference, channel reuse – which in fact translates into frequency channel reuse in GSM – is not allowed among cells that are too close to one another. Specifically, the larger the distance between cells reusing the same frequencies, the lower the interference (and the better the QoS); however, larger distances among these cells also mean that the same channels can be used fewer times throughout the network, which negatively affects the capacity to accommodate user demand. The planning of frequency allocation in GSM networks is thus quite a complex task, aiming at maximizing frequency reuse while maintaining co-channel interference below a minimum threshold.

A typical GSM infrastructure, shown in the top plot of Figure 1, relies on a set of Base Transmitter Stations (BTS) that are connected through wired Pulse-Code Modulation (PCM) lines to a set of switches called Base Station Controllers (BSC). BSC are responsible for timeslot allocation for voice traffic, managing the handover of users between adjacent cells and radio resource monitoring. BSC are connected to the core GSM network, which is composed of a set of gateways and databases that provide several functions in addition to managing radio interface e.g. interconnecting with the public switched telephone network, identifying and locating mobile subscribers, routing calls, billing and securing communications).

The GSM infrastructure was designed by telecommunication actors following the telephony circuit switched model in order to ensure interconnection with public switched telephone networks. However, the rapid development of Internet and its tremendous popularity among users in the 1990s led standardization bodies – namely ETSI – to extend the GSM standard in order to support data traffic. The first extension to meet with some success was GPRS (General Packet Radio Service). GPRS introduces several upgrades at the radio interface and in the core infrastructure. To ensure retro-compatibility with previous GSM versions, as well as interoperability with the emerging Internet, GPRS extends the core network with new components to enable packet switching. In particular, gateways (called GGSN and SGSN) are added within the core network to allow external Internet connectivity. Also, a Packet Control Unit (PCU) is added to the BSC. The PCU is responsible for allocating GSM channels to data traffic in a dynamic fashion, i.e. only when there are data bursts. Moreover, the PCU implements a scheduling mechanism that is used to share available channels among concurrent data sessions. A later GPRS upgrade consisted of introducing Coding Schemes (CS) at the radio interface in order to increase the bit rate according to the signal quality, by transmitting bursts with a certain redundancy rate.

Despite these enhancements, the maximum GPRS bit rate was, in the late 1990s, at least one order of magnitude lower than that promised by emerging wireless local area network technologies such as Wi-Fi. To reduce this gap, ETSI proposed an updated version of GPRS, named Enhanced Data Rates for GSM Evolution (EDGE). This standard introduced limited modifications to the GPRS infrastructure. The main innovation is the support of adaptive modulation schemes at the radio interface: by adapting the number of modulated carriers, a transmitter can adjust its bit rate depending on the quality of the signal. EDGE defines up to eight combinations of modulation and coding schemes, with bit rate per time-slots ranging from 8.8 to 59.2 Kbit/s, and a maximum bit rate per downlink connection up to 384 Kbit/s.

Third Generation Cellular Networks: UMTS and HSDPA

EDGE/GPRS standards were also denoted as 2.5G technologies, a prelude of the actual third generation, or 3G technologies. The latter were embodied by UMTS (Universal Mobile Telecommunications System), which was standardized by 3GPP in the early 2000s.

UMTS introduced major modifications to cellular architectures. Firstly, the radio interface was substantially modified, moving from a TDMA/FDMA scheme to a WCDMA (Wideband Code Division Multiple Access) scheme, as detailed by Holma and Toskala (2001) in a dedicated book. WCDMA is based on Direct Sequence Spread Spectrum (DSSS), a spread spectrum technique that encodes each data bit with a chip sequence – or code. This operation spreads the bits over the available spectrum, with the result that the transmitted signal occupies a much larger bandwidth than the original bandwidth of the data signal. However, it also allows multiple transmissions to simultaneously use the same frequency bandwidth by using orthogonal codes. The result is a range of advantages over FDMA/TDMA, including higher spectrum efficiency, reduced power transmission levels and greater robustness to multipath effects and inter-symbol interference. DSSS also makes it possible to relax the orthogonal code constraint (and thus to accommodate more codes within the same spectrum, increasing the system capacity) at the expense of some interference.

From a networking viewpoint, although most of the GSM entities were maintained in UMTS (possibly with a new terminology, see the middle plot in Figure 1), the associated protocols were updated so as to complete the switch from a circuit switched to a native packet switched architecture. Several interfaces and protocols, such as ATM or IP, were introduced in the UMTS core network protocol stack to replace circuit switched lines.

The increase in access capacity (with up to 2 Mbit/s transfers in the first release of UMTS) and the evolution of the core network toward a packets switched architecture deeply modified the utilization of cellular networks and enlarged the number of offered services. Since the introduction of UMTS, cellular data traffic has seen a continuous increase, especially with the success of smartphones and mobile applications. Accommodating such an increasing demand has required the 3GPP to release several enhancements of UMTS, which led to so-called 3.5G standards. Among these releases, High Speed Downlink Packet Access (HSDPA) has been widely deployed by cellular operators. Similarly to the evolution from 2G to 2.5G, the HSDPA technology did not introduce any major modifications to the network infrastructure. Most of the upgrades were instead at the radio interface and eNodeBs (i.e. the equivalent of BTS in GSM). In particular, HSDPA moved some functions, such as radio resources allocation, from the core network to the eNodeB, with the aim of improving the system's responsiveness to the fast-changing radio channel conditions. Moreover, new and denser coding schemes, including 16QAM, were added, enabling a maximum downlink bit rate of 14.4 Mbit/s.

Wireless Local Area Network Infrastructure and Technologies

With the rapid acceleration of the computer industry, and with the introduction of personal computers, the 1980s also saw an increased demand for interconnection and communication capabilities. At that point, Local Area Networks (LAN) were already a reality, implemented via wired technologies such as Ethernet. However, wireless networks, with their ease of deployment and reduced material cost, were also becoming technically feasible.

Encouraged by a decision made by the US Federal Communications Commission, which in 1985 allowed the unlicensed use of 100 MHz of spectrum in the 2.4 GHz band (one of the so-called Industrial, Scientific and Medical (ISM) radio bands), equipment manufacturers began proposing their solutions for wireless local area networks (WLAN), mostly operating in this ISM band. However, inter-connection problems soon emerged, and different standardization organizations decided to address the issue. In 1997, the Institute of Electrical and Electronics Engineers (IEEE), which had already standardized an Ethernet-like solution for wired networks, published the IEEE 802.11 standard, specifying the Medium Access Control (MAC) and Physical (PHY) layers of wireless LANs.

Easy to implement and quickly brought to the market by manufacturers supporting the standard, IEEE 802.11 soon emerged over competing technologies and became the de-facto standard for WLANs. However, early IEEE 802.11 products still had inter-operability problems, mostly because different manufacturers were giving different interpretations of some parts of the standard. As IEEE lacked the resources needed to test equipment compliance, companies supporting the IEEE 802.11 standard created an independent organization, the Wi-Fi alliance, to test and certify IEEE 802.11 products. This also led to the commercial name of Wi-Fi, generally used today to designate certified IEEE 802.11 equipment.

The specifications are being continuously adapted to the dynamic wireless market, allowing Wi-Fi to operate today on different frequency bands, from the 700 MHz band freed by the switch from analog to digital television broadcast, to the 60 GHz ultra-wide band, which allows a significant increase in transmission data rate. Most Wi-Fi WLANs operate however at 2.4 and 5 GHz (the latter band being first used by amendment IEEE 802.11a), where 3 to 12 non-overlapping 20-MHz frequency channels are available. The standard was also adapted to a number of specific environments, such as mesh networks, vehicular communications, or direct device-to-device transmissions. These functions are added to the standard through so-called *amendments*, discussed and drafted by different working groups within IEEE.

At the physical layer, the standard initially used spread spectrum techniques, such as Direct Sequence Spread Spectrum (DSSS in the original standard) or Frequency Hopping Spread Spectrum (FHSS in the IEEE 802.11b amendment). However, Orthogonal Frequency Division Multiplexing (OFDM), introduced by amendments IEEE 802.11a/g, has become the prevalent choice in the last decade, and all recent devices use this technique, sometimes with complementary mechanisms, such as transmission and reception through multiple antennae.

The IEEE 802.11 standard describes two MAC layer protocols, Distributed Coordination Function (DCF) and Point Coordination Function (PCF). The latter is a deterministic channel access method, where a central master station (STA), typically the Wi-Fi Access Point (AP), polls all the regular STAs, granting them transmission opportunities. On the other hand, DCF is a contention-based method, using Carrier Sense Multiple Access (CSMA), whose main principle is that every STA listens to the channel before attempting a transmission and refrains from doing so if another station is already using the channel. DCF uses acknowledgement (ACK) messages to detect failed transmissions, and takes a binary back-off approach to reduce the collision probability between STAs, implementing a Collision Avoidance (CA) mechanism – hence the name CSMA/CA, generally used to describe this medium access solution.

Although described in the standard, and despite the greater quality of guaranteeing finite channel access time, PCF is not typically implemented in off-the-shelf Wi-Fi devices, which only run DCF and its evolutions. One of these evolutions, Evolved Distributed Channel Access (EDCA), has been defined in the IEEE 802.11e amendment, and later included in the recent IEEE 802.11-2012 standard (IEEE Computer Society, 2012). It proposes the use of transmission queues with different priorities, making it possible to distinguish between data traffic with real-time constraints and classical *best effort* data at the MAC sub-layer.

Building on these continuous improvements and the development of wireless communications, in less than a decade Wi-Fi has become the most successful wireless technology worldwide. According to the Cisco Data Meter application (CDM, 2014), Wi-Fi is the main wireless technology used to access Internet services, transporting three to four times more data than cellular networks. While this difference is more significant in the case of tablets, as depicted in Figure 2, it is interesting to notice that even in the case of smartphones Wi-Fi largely dominates as an access technology, as shown in Figure 3.

Figure 2. Average monthly worldwide tablet data traffic transported through Wi-Fi (in blue) and cellular (in green) technologies (Courtesy of Cisco Systems, Inc. Unauthorized use not permitted. Captured from http://www.ciscovni.com/data-meter/ on July 8th, 2014.).

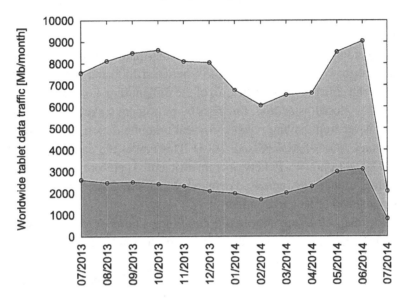

Figure 3. Average monthly worldwide smartphone data traffic transported through Wi-Fi (in blue) and cellular (in green) technologies (Courtesy of Cisco Systems, Inc. Unauthorized use not permitted. Captured from http://www.ciscovni.com/data-meter/ on July 8th, 2014.)

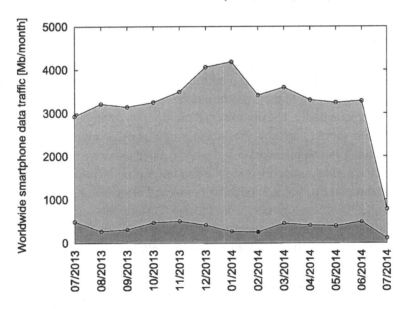

EMERGING WIRELESS ACCESS TECHNOLOGIES

Second- and third-generation cellular and Wi-Fi access networks are designed to accommodate a type of mobile traffic that is rapidly becoming outdated.

On the one hand, we are witnessing a growth in data traffic demand from mobile users which was barely predictable only a few years ago. The success of smartphones and mobile apps led to a mobile traffic compound annual growth rate (CAGR) of 146% between 2006 and 2013 – a performance surpassing even that of the overall data traffic over the turn of the millennium, i.e. when the Internet first started to pervade our lives. This notwithstanding, forecasts by prominent stakeholders tell us that the mobile communication hype is far from having reached its peak: mobile data traffic is still expected to grow 11-fold by 2018, with a CAGR of 61% (Cisco, 2013). This makes the data rates offered by the 2G/3G cellular network and 802.11a/b/g Wi-Fi networks insufficient. Therefore, both access technologies are being improved in order to meet the increased demand, which promises to be especially challenging in ever-more-densely populated urban environments.

On the other hand, smart cities are expected to introduce a number of services that rely heavily on wireless access, but introduce traffic demands of an unprecedented nature. These include direct communication among mobile devices, novel types of end users such as connected vehicles, and a massive number of data flows consisting of periodic, high-frequency, small-sized messages generated by metering or crowdsensing applications.

In this section, we discuss the most prominent emerging technologies intended to address the future evolution of mobile traffic, with a focus on smart city services.

Evolution of Cellular Access Technologies

The huge popularity of mobile smart terminals such as smartphones or tablets and the rapid development of mobile services have marked the end of the last decade. This tremendous success was supported by the evolution of 3G cellular networks toward HSDPA, which allowed the support of IP services. In addition, Android, iOS and other mobile operating platforms have greatly facilitated the development and the distribution of mobile applications. Since then, the number of available mobile applications and services has continued to grow exponentially. The ubiquity and multiplicity of mobile services have deeply modified user habits, and most services are now available for mobile users anywhere and anytime. Attracted by the increasing growth of the mobile market and its associated lucrative revenues, new operators have emerged and entered the highly competitive mobile and telecommunication sector, championing novel technologies. Within this context, several consortia composed of mobile ICT actors already anticipated the saturation of 2G and 3G access networks a decade ago. Different technologies began to be proposed at that time as candidates for the fourth generation of cellular networks.

Long Term Evolution (LTE) is the technology that was retained for 4G cellular infrastructures. The first LTE version was specified in 2008 by the 3GPP release number eight, and it was soon considered a 3.9G technology designed to provide a smooth transition to actual 4G systems. As shown in the bottom plot of Figure 1, most of the specifications introduced innovations at the radio interface, named eUTRAN. The key elements include Orthogonal Frequency Division Multiple Access (OFDMA), Adaptive Modulation and Coding (AMC) schemes, Multiple Input Multiple Output (MIMO) techniques, beamforming, turbo codes and Hybrid Automatic Repeat Request (H-ARQ).

In 2010, release 10, referred to as LTE Advanced (LTE-A), was recognized by the ITU as a true 4G technology. In addition to some enhancements to the radio interface, such as the capacity to aggregate several carriers, the main novelty of LTE-A lies in replacing the two tier 2G/3G core networks (composed of a circuit switched and packet switch sub-systems) with a unique flat all-IP core network, facilitating the support of IP-based protocols and mobile services. The IP-enabled entities that compose the core network provide operators with the capability to deploy at reduced cost and to manage a 4G infrastructure that can adapt flexibly to customer demand.

LTE/LTE-A operates in conventional 3GPP/3GPP2 bands (e.g. 800/900 MHz), but it also supports many new frequencies between 600 MHz and 3.8 GHz. The allocated bandwidth per operator is flexible and can range from 1.4Mhz to 100Mhz. The theoretical maximum downlink bit rate per user in LTE and LTE-A can attain 300 Mb/s and 1Gb/s respectively.

Overall, many smart city services will rely on cellular access. Specifically, cellular technologies offer anywhere, anytime connectivity that is secure, has QoS guarantees, and enjoys ever-growing bitrates. These features make cellular access the baseline solution for wireless communication in digital urban environments. The main downside, however, remains the economic cost for the end user: to cope with this issue, diverse generations of cellular technologies can be leveraged to satisfy the needs of different applications. For instance, resources (e.g. water, electricity, gas) can be monitored using integrated sensors and GSM chipsets; residential and office building can be managed through M2M services supported by 3G technologies; high-end mobile applications can instead resort to 4G.

Finally, it is worth mentioning the emergence of so-called Ultra Narrow Band (UNB) networks. UNB is a recent technology allowing wireless transfers over long distances (tens or even hundreds of Km) at very low bitrates (10 to 1000 bps). The UNB network architecture mimics that of a traditional cellular network, however the extended communication range makes is possible to dramatically reduce the number of base stations: as an example, the whole of France is covered using just 1000 antennas, whereas the same number of antennas is used in the same country to provide UMTS/LTE access to the city of Lyon alone. In turn, this cuts down capital and operational expenses linked to building and maintaining the network. When compared to traditional cellular systems, UNB technology is also inexpensive from other perspectives. On the one hand, it operates on an unlicensed spectrum (e.g. 868 MHz in Europe and 915 MHz in the US – frequencies often used by cordless phones), which makes it possible to reduce subscription fees to $1 per year. On the other hand, its communication chips are especially cheap to produce, being sold at $1 each today. Clearly, the low bitrate limits the applications of UNB. The technology is thus devoted to so-called Internet of Things (IoT) applications, as UNB could enable Internet connection for countless energy-constrained devices that need to transmit small amounts of information. These include toys, heart rate monitors, energy grid meters, underground pipe monitors, or parking space monitors.

Evolution of Wi-Fi Access Technologies

Nowadays Wi-Fi is the most common wireless access technology in the indoor environment, and it also accommodates a non-negligible share of outdoor-generated mobile traffic. The result is that large portions of urban areas are characterized by a pervasive presence of Wi-Fi APs. Although outdoor Wi-Fi hotspots or WLANs are deployed and managed by operators or companies, in many cases Wi-Fi equipment is installed and configured by private end users, without any coordination. The consequence is the saturation of Wi-Fi channels, especially on the unlicensed 2.4 GHz frequency band. This, jointly with the 54 Mb/s data rate cap of IEEE 802.11a/g, makes current Wi-Fi standards unable to cope with the surge in traffic demand.

IEEE 802.11n

In order to address this situation in 2009 IEEE standardized an enhancement of the IEEE 802.11 family, known as 802.11n. The upgrades make it possible to increase the maximum bit rate per channel to 600 Mbit/s. The major source of improvements lies in the introduction of Multiple Input Multiple Output (MIMO) transmissions: by leveraging the presence of multiple antennae at the sender and receiver, MIMO techniques exploit diversity to make signal reconstruction more efficient and robust to multipath. An introduction to MIMO communication is provided by Tse and Viswanath (2005). The 802.11n standard defines several multi-antenna scenarios, such as 1x2, 3X3, and 4X4.

Another improvement introduced by IEEE 802.11n is the possibility of merging two adjacent 20-MHz channels to form a single 40-MHz channel, basically doubling the maximum capacity of a single data transfer. This allows a further 4% gain, due to the use of the frequency guard band that previously separated the two joined 20-MHz adjacent channels.

Last but not least, IEEE 802.11b/g can only operate at the 2.4 GHz band, whereas IEEE 802.11a only works at the 5 GHz band. IEEE 802.11n allows the user to choose any of these two bands, the main advantage being that of balancing the load among the overcrowded 2.4 GHz band and the not-yet-saturated 5 GHz band. The latter portion of the frequency spectrum also has the advantage of not being subject to interference from the many devices operating at 2.4 GHz, such as Bluetooth, cordless phones, baby monitors, or microwave ovens. Moreover, the number of non-overlapping available channels is much larger at 5 GHz (e.g. 8 in the US) than at 2.4 GHz (e.g. 3 in the US).

IEEE 802.11ac

IEEE 802.11n products are now widely sold at affordable costs. Anticipating the increasing demand for data traffic, in 2014 IEEE announced a new upgrade, called 802.11ac. IEEE 802.11ac targets a maximum cell capacity of 1 Gbit/s and is clearly positioned as a competing technology with the Gigabit Ethernet.

Technically speaking, there is no major technological breakthrough in IEEE 802.11ac. This new evolution of Wi-Fi pushes further the capacity increase already attained in IEEE 802.11n, by allowing the merging of adjacent channels to create 80-MHz and even 160-MHz band channels. Additionally, whereas IEEE 802.11n does not allow MIMO configurations exceeding 4x4, IEEE 802.11ac supports up to 8x8 MIMO. Finally, the denser modulation technique 256QAM is supported by 802.11ac.

Wireless Sensor Communication Technologies

With the turn of the millennium, significant advances in technology for micro-scale electromechanical systems, along with the emergence of low-power wireless communication circuits, enabled the production at industrial level of small-sized, low-cost nodes with sensing, computational and wireless communication capabilities. Akyldiz et al. (2002) provide a first survey of these devices. The deployment of a significant number of sensor nodes – often referred to as *motes* – leads to the formation of a wireless sensor network (WSN), whose goal is to collect information on a physical phenomenon within the supervised geographical area. Nowadays, WSNs are becoming increasingly popular in a number of domains, including the military, medical and environmental sectors. From a different perspective, technologies related to WSNs have also found a large number of applications within the context of smart cities, where they find usage in parking availability monitoring, air pollution monitoring, urban traffic monitoring, or smart street lighting.

The reason for such a success lies in the substantial benefits offered by WSNs: (i) the lack of infrastructure and of associated capital and operational costs; (ii) the self-organization capability of network components, which eases the deployment operation; (iii) the limited cost and size of the sensors themselves, which contributes to both the advantages above. These advantages appear especially profitable for urban applications such as pollution monitoring, public lighting control, smart parking, and smart metering of water, gas, or electricity. A thorough discussion of the potential applications of sensor technologies for smart urban environments, including technical requirements, can be found in (ETSI TR 103055, 2011).

Clearly there are challenges as well, especially in terms of limited resources: the battery lifetime, the communication range, the storage and computation capabilities of sensors are severely constrained, and must be managed carefully – even more so when considering that sensor nodes are typically expected to operate autonomously for timespans from months to years. Fortunately, most WSN-based services concern low-duty-cycle monitoring and tracking, and thus do not require frequent or high-rate data transfers. Driven by the low-power and low-complexity requirements of WSN on one hand, and by the low-data rate and latency requirements of the overlying applications on the other, much attention has been devoted to developing new specifications and protocols at all layers of the protocol stack, as detailed by Wagner (2010), among others.

In the following, we present the main standardized protocols, with a focus on the lower layers of these standards, i.e. the physical (PHY), the medium access control (MAC), and the routing standards, since they are the most relevant in terms of access network technologies.

IEEE 802.15.4 and Upper Networking Stacks

The most popular protocol stack used in WSN architecture is based on definitions provided in the IEEE 802.15.4 standard, which describes the operations at the PHY and MAC layers. It is often coupled with standards that define higher-layer (i.e. network) protocols such as Zigbee or 6LowPan. In order to provide a comprehensive overview, we will first present the IEEE 802.15.4 standard, and then introduce the most popular higher-level standards.

IEEE 802.15.4 was the first open standard designed for low-rate wireless personal area networks (LR-WPAN). The targets of IEEE 802.15.4 are low-complexity and low-power PHY and MAC layer specifications for low data rate wireless communication between low cost devices. At the physical layer, the first version of IEEE 802.15.4, released in 2003, specifies the use of unlicensed bands at 868-868.6 MHz (Europe), 902-928 MHz (North America), and 2400-2483.5 MHz (worldwide) with data rates of 20, 40 and 250 Kb/s respectively (IEEE Computer Society, 2003). The IEEE 802.15.4a standard, released in 2007, introduces enhancements and corrections, along with support for higher data rates; it also reduces unnecessary complexity and considers additional portions of the frequency spectrum (IEEE Computer Society, 2006). In 2009, two new amendments, IEEE 802.15.4c and IEEE 802.15.4d, were released: they mainly introduced two new frequency bands (314-316 MHz and 430-434 MHz).

At the MAC layer, IEEE 802.15.4 defines two channel access modes: a non-beacon-enabled mode and a beacon-enabled one. In the non-beacon-enabled mode, data is transmitted using an unslotted CSMA-CA scheme. Similar to what happens in IEEE 802.11 networks, each node listens to the channel prior to transmitting in order to determine whether the latter is free. If this is not the case, the node waits for a binary exponential back-off before attempting retransmission. In the beacon-enabled mode, a slotted

CSMA-CA scheme is used, where a super-frame structure makes it possible to coordinate access to the medium. To that end, a coordinator starts the operations by sending a beacon, which synchronizes nearby nodes and advertises the structure of the super-frame. The latter is composed of: (i) an inactive period; (ii) a Contention Access Period (CAP), where nodes use a slotted CSMA/CA to access the channel; (iii) a Contention-Free Period (CFP), which contains a number of guaranteed time slots (GTS) allocated to specific stations by the coordinator node.

As pointed out above, one of the main design guidelines of IEEE 802.15.4 is the low power consumption. To reach this goal, the standard defines energy-efficient management schemes, mainly including the ability to reach very low duty cycling (i.e. the ratio of the active period to the full active-sleep period). It was shown that most energy consumption at sensor nodes is due to active radio transceivers: therefore, low-duty cycling is the most effective technique to save energy. Beside energy efficiency, IEEE 802.15.4 adapts to time-sensitive WSN applications thanks to the guaranteed time slots (GTS), which are reserved and do not require prior negotiation; these aspects are thoroughly discussed, among others, by Sohraby et al. (2007) and Buratti (2010).

The IEEE 802.15.4e amendment, approved in 2012, introduced some MAC-layer enhancements to the IEEE 802.15.4a standard. It mainly supersedes the use of a single channel mandated by IEEE 802.15.4a, as it favors interference and multi-path fading. Instead, IEEE 802.15.4e introduces a time-slotted channel-hopping mode, which is especially intended for industrial applications.

The success of IEEE 802.15.4 has encouraged the development of many standards to specify upper stacks. Below we present two popular standards, Zigbee and 6LowPan.

Zigbee is a high-level standard-based technology for low-cost, low-power radio devices. It is designed by the industry consortium Zigbee Alliance and is based on the IEEE 802.15 standard, as shown in Figure 4. Zigbee supports both operation modes of IEEE 802.15.4 presented above. It defines three types of devices: the Zigbee Coordinator (ZC), a single node per network that represents the root of the network tree; the Zigbee router (ZR), which relays packets; the Zigbee End Device (ZED), which runs applications, mainly related to sensing and actuation services. ZED nodes are usually battery-powered and do not relay packets; they are allowed to have very low-duty cycles to reduce their energy consumption and enhance their lifetime.

Figure 4. 802.15.4 and two popular upper stacks: Zigbee (left), and 6LowPan (right)

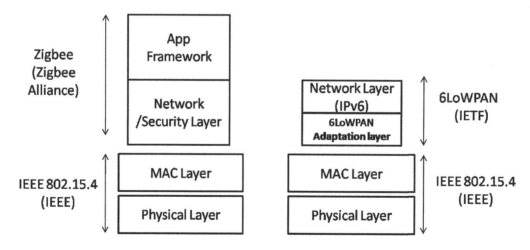

Zigbee supports three types of topology: star, tree and mesh. The multi-hop routing in tree topologies is guaranteed by a specific address assignment scheme, which makes it possible to deduce the relationships between nodes and their ancestors and descendants. In this way, Zigbee avoids having to build and maintain routing tables. In the mesh topology case, multi-hop routing is performed through an AODV-like reactive routing protocol: the source initiates a route discovery phase by broadcasting a route request, and a shortest path is built using packet loss probability on each link as the cost metric (Zigbee Alliance, 2008). Recently, Zigbee has become increasingly popular in the context of short-range, low-rate WSN applications, including home entertainment and control, building automation, smart parking, and industrial control.

6LowPan stands for low-power wireless personal area networks. It is an IETF working group that aims to adapt IPv6 to support low-cost low-power radio devices. To that end, it builds on top of the IEEE 802.15.4 standard. 6LowPan is motivated by the fact that IP can and should be supported by low-power devices such as sensor and actuator nodes, so as to guarantee their interoperability within a global Internet of Things, as also discussed by Mulligan (2007). The problem statement was introduced in the RFC 4919, as per Kushalnagar et al. (2007), and specifications were released in RFC 4944, as per Montenegro et al. (2007), and later updated in RFC 6282, as per Hui and Thubert (2011).

In order to be able to support IP while reducing energy consumption, 6LowPan offers the following main features. First, it proposes an adaptation layer that makes it possible to fragment IP packets and reassemble them into IEEE 802.15.4 frames. This adjustment is needed since IPv6 packets can be larger than the maximum IEEE 802.15.4 frame size. Second, in order to reduce the length of data packets, 6LowPan proposes to compress the IPv6 header (40 bytes). Third, 6LowPan defines two routing strategies: a mesh-under approach and a route-over one. In the mesh-under strategy, the routing of packets is implemented at the 6LowPan adaptation layer, as shown in Figure 3, based on the IPv6 fragments before the reconstruction. In the route-over strategy, the routing is implemented at the IPv6 layer, where packets are routed after the reconstruction. The mesh-under approach makes it possible to reduce the transmission delay, whereas the route-over strategy is more suitable to loss-prone environments. A detailed discussion is provided by Montenegro et al. (2007), and Hui and Thubert (2011).

Even though 6LowPan presents higher complexity and delay compared to Zigbee, it has recently grown in popularity thanks to the emergence of the Internet of Things and the growing need for interoperability between devices.

DASH7

Although IEEE 802.15.4 and the associated protocols have attracted significant attention, their usage remains limited to significantly localized applications. With these technologies, transmission ranges do not exceed 100 meters, and are more often around 30-40 meters, which may be too limited for many smart city services. This has motivated the development of new standards such as DASH7, which is currently attracting more and more attention. As explained by Norair (2009), DASH7 is based on the standard ISO 18000-7 and is promoted by the DASH7 alliance, an industry consortium formed in 2009. The first standard DASH7 Mode 2 was announced in 2009 as the next-generation version of ISO 18000-7. Dash7 Alliance Mode Draft 2 was released in 2013 (DASH7 Alliance, 2013).

DASH7 introduces specifications for all the layers of the network stack, from the physical to the application one. At the physical layer, DASH7 operates at the 433 MHz ISM band, where the spectrum is organized into 15 channels grouped into five channel types: Base, Legacy, Normal, Hi-Rate and Blink.

These channels have different bandwidths and use different modulation schemes. At the MAC layer, two modes are used according to the channel class. The normal and high-rate classes, referred to as *guarded* channels, are controlled by a CSMA/CA process, whereas access to the other channels, called *non-guarded* channels, can be achieved at any time using a pure ALOHA access mechanism without prior negotiation. For these classes, the use of CSMA/CA is in fact optional.

At the network layer, DASH7 proposes to use a background network protocol called D7A Advertising Protocol (D7AAdvP) and two foreground network protocols, D7A Network Protocol (D7ANP) and D7A DataStream Protocol (D7ADP). D7AAdvP is a broadcast transmission-only protocol used exclusively for fast ad-hoc group synchronization thanks to very short background frames (DASH7 Alliance, 2013). D7ADP is a generic data encapsulation protocol without any addressing or routing information. Communication and routing are thus entirely managed at the upper layers. Finally, D7ANP is an addressable and routable protocol that supports unicast, broadcast, anycast and multicast communication. As an alternative, DASH7 can support IPv6 addressing using a simple adaptation layer, which makes it easily interoperable with other systems. In both cases, we stress that DASH7 specifications define a simple two-hop routing approach and allow integration with other standards like IETF RPL in that sense, as discussed by Weyn et al. (2013).

At the radio level, the main advantage of DASH7 is the good trade-off between the transmission range – reaching up to 2 Km of distance – and the data rate – up to 200 Kb/s, while using low-power communications. This occurs mainly thanks to an operating frequency with good propagation characteristics, and makes it possible to penetrate water and concrete. However, it also mandates the use of larger antennas compared to those employed by technologies adopting higher frequencies.

DASH7 technology has met with significant success over the past few years. As for other technologies, success has been stimulated by military applications: the U.S. Department of Defense awarded a huge multi-million contract for DASH7 devices in January 2009, and NATO is also expected to deploy DASH7 infrastructures. However, DASH7 is also used in several civil applications, with a particular focus on urban services such as home automation and automotive systems.

IEEE 802.11 Power Saving Mode (Low-Power Wi-Fi)

Instead of developing brand new sets of specifications, a different strategy for wireless sensor connectivity lies in the adaptation of well-known standards, via the optimization of their performance in terms of energy consumption. The IEEE 802.11 standard has received a lot of attention in this sense, and a significant amount of work has been devoted to the study of the viability of low-power IEEE 802.11 for wireless sensor networks.

Specifically, modifications of IEEE 802.11 that enable power saving have been proposed both in the case of traditional AP-based DCF communication and in the presence of self-organizing STAs (the so-called *ad hoc* mode). In the presence of an AP, mobile nodes go periodically to a power saving mode where they turn off their transceivers. They then wake up periodically, on a listen interval basis, to check for incoming packets. The AP sends a beacon message at every beacon interval, such that the listen interval is a multiple of the beacon interval. The beacon contains the identifiers of nodes with buffered packets. The latter are assumed to stay awake to receive their packets, as described in Tseng et al. (2002) and Tozlu et al. (2012).

In power saving mode using the ad hoc mode, mobile nodes are supposed to be synchronized and contend at the beginning of the active period to send the beacon packets containing, among other fields, the source address and the destination address of buffered packets. Tseng et al. (2002) showed that the power saving mode initially designed for single-hop ad-hoc communications brings more challenges and complexity in multi-hop networks, mainly due to clock synchronization, neighboring discovery, packet delays, and network partitioning issues.

The use of low-power 802.11 in wireless sensor networks offers the main advantage of native IP compatibility, which facilitates the integration of sensor nodes in the Internet of Things. For this reason, the use of 802.11 may be profitable in single-hop AP-based architectures, such as home environments and building automation scenarios, where sensor nodes send data to a sink while in power-saving mode. However, WSN dedicated standards remain more suitable today for large-scale wireless sensor deployments.

Networked Vehicle Technologies

Increased safety and efficiency in both private and public road transportation is one of the major challenges to be addressed by future smart city technologies. Not only are urban areas growing in terms of population size, but their inhabitants also tend to be increasingly mobile and expect to be able to travel to, from and within cities more and more easily and rapidly. The result is a surge in road travel demand, which can barely be accommodated by traditional solutions, i.e. by augmenting the capacity (e.g. adding lanes to existing roads, or planning and deploying more effective road signalization) and extent (e.g. constructing brand new streets and beltways) of the road infrastructure. Although largely adopted in the past, such practices are now approaching their limits within metropolitan areas in developed countries, where road infrastructures are already very comprehensive, and further physical extensions are unfeasible or unpractical.

A game-changing contribution is thus expected to come from the integration of ICT into road transportation systems. This implies an important goal shift, from increasing the capacity of the road network to using the existing capacity more efficiently – and, incidentally, in a safer way. The objective is to simultaneously reduce road accidents, travel times, and pollutant emission by road vehicles, the three points being clearly correlated. To that end, a number of ICT-enabled smart transportation services are expected to significantly improve our ability to leverage the road infrastructure. These include collision or generic warning notification, reliable and real-time traffic condition information, near-future and long-term anticipation of road network utilization and travel times, traffic light state broadcasting and speed adaptation, automated and transparent tolling, approaching emergency vehicle alert, and nearby point-of-interest advertising.

All of the aforementioned services rely on the capability of vehicles to receive and/or transmit data, anywhere and anytime. They thus depend on the so-called *networked vehicle* principle, i.e. equipping vehicles with one or more wireless communication interfaces, so that they are fully integrated within the smart city telecommunication network. Multiple radio interfaces may be needed on each vehicle since different services entail diverse information sources and destinations: for example, live traffic information services rely on information generated by an Internet-based server (or, as some may refer to it, in the Cloud), which then needs to be multi-casted to subscriber vehicles; on the contrary, collision notifications concern circumscribed geographical areas and have tight delay constraints, which makes direct communication among vehicles a more fitting option.

As a result, the vehicular communication environment requires that different wireless networking approaches are taken in parallel. Here, the main distinction is between services that need pervasive access to remote resources, and those that require localized access. The former are expected to leverage the existing cellular infrastructure, whereas the latter depend on dedicated communication paradigms that are specific to vehicular environments. Below we present architectures following these two paradigms and discuss the associated access network technologies separately.

Cellular Communication-Enabled Vehicles

Vehicles can easily be equipped with cellular radio interfaces and exploit the existing 2G/3G/LTE infrastructure to send/receive data. This approach to vehicular networking is especially convenient in the case of services provided by or requiring the intervention of servers on the Internet. In fact, its implementation is trivial from a technical viewpoint, and the first networked cars embedding cellular interfaces are already on the market. Moreover, the integrated interfaces can be easily replaced by those already available on, for example, smartphones or high-end navigation systems present onboard, which dramatically increases the penetration rate of the technology at basically no cost.

As a result, cellular access is the current de-facto standard in communication-enabled vehicles, and a number of already deployed services rely on a vehicle-to-cellular infrastructure data transfer model. One example is that of *remote monitoring* of vehicle status, a service offered by many automobile manufacturers, e.g. BMW Assist, Ford SYNC, General Motor OnStar, Toyota Safety Connect and Mercedes-Benz mbrace, to cite a few. Another successful application is that of quasi-real-time traffic estimation and notification, where vehicles act as mobile sensors in a *crowdsensing* system, by periodically communicating their speed and direction (and possibly information about accidents, road works, etc.). This information is gathered and processed by a central controller, and finally broadcasted back to the vehicles, which thus have an up-to-date vision of the road traffic conditions (TomTom, 2010). A final example is provided by insurance services: by installing *black boxes* on vehicles, the behavior of drivers can be constantly monitored, and liability can be determined in case of accidents.

All the services introduced above require information from vehicles to be uploaded to the Internet. Their success raises two main questions. The first is of economic nature. Cellular communication occurs on a licensed spectrum, and has thus a financial cost. The question concerns which of the entities involved (the service provider, the car manufacturer, the telecommunication operator, or the end user – either directly or indirectly) will pay for such a cost. In other words, business models must be identified that make cellular access by vehicles economically viable. The second question is instead technical, and it is thus of more interest within the context of this Chapter. It concerns how to accommodate vehicle-generated data – typically referred to as Floating Vehicle Data, or FVD – through cellular upload. Sommer et al. (2010) and Bazzi et al. (2011) have considered exploiting the Random Access Channel (RACH) of 3G UMTS access networks. RACH is a shared direct-access channel normally employed for signalization; however, by transmitting small-sized FVD directly on RACH, rather than asking for a dedicated channel, vehicles reduce delays and increase communication efficiency. The solution appears viable, yet important issues also exist: only a few tens of small packets can be uploaded per second within each cell, RACH does not support inter-cell handover (which occurs frequently in the case of high-speed vehicles), and the solution generates RACH congestion – thus reducing the QoS of traditional mobile voice and data services. Mangel et al. (2010) and Ide et al. (2012) have instead studied the impact of FVD on LTE access networks technology. Although better performing than UMTS, LTE also has limitations when it comes to FVD upload: specifically, it suffers delays of up to 50 ms and its capacity is constrained to 100 packets per second on a dedicated 5-MHz channel.

In order to mitigate the effect of FVD on cellular access networks, Stanica et al. (2013) and Ancona et al. (2014) have suggested complementing cellular communication with dedicated vehicle-to-vehicle communication. The latter is also a more fitting technology in the case of information dissemination constrained to vehicular devices, i.e. where the data is generated by, and destined to vehicles. Here, cellular communications do not appear a convenient solution, as they force the content to unnecessarily transit (twice or more) through the radio access network. Below we describe dedicated wireless technologies enabling direct and distributed communication among vehicles.

Dedicated Communication-Enabled Vehicles

Wireless communication technologies dedicated to vehicular environments have not yet hit the market, even though they feature a very long history of research and development with its roots in early proposals during the 1970s. Prototype solutions were developed in parallel in the USA, with the Electronic Route-Guidance System (ERGS) introduced by Rosen et al. (1970), based on vehicle-to-instrumented intersection communication, as well as in Japan, where the Comprehensive Automobile Traffic Control System (CACS) national project (launched in 1973), targeted the same road efficiency goals we still pursue today. A number of activities in the USA, Japan and Europe followed during the next 30 years, and Hartenstein and Laberteaux (2008) provide quite a complete overview of the field. However, the limitation of wireless technologies available at the time, the complexity of shifting the whole automotive industry towards the networked vehicle paradigm, the excessive costs of building the dedicated roadside infrastructure needed by many proposed architectures, and the lack of ultimate proof of the effectiveness of dedicated vehicular communications led to a failure to bring these proposals to the industrial production stage.

At the turn of the century the study of vehicular communication technologies started to gain momentum. This was due to the combination of two main factors: first, the success of IEEE 802.11 as a local area network technology, which demonstrated how high-performance wireless communication could be easily and widely deployable; second, the allocation of a reserved frequency band for Dedicated Short-Range Communication (DSRC) in vehicular environments, first in the USA and subsequently in Japan

Figure 5. 5.9-GHz frequency spectrum reserved for DSRC by FCC

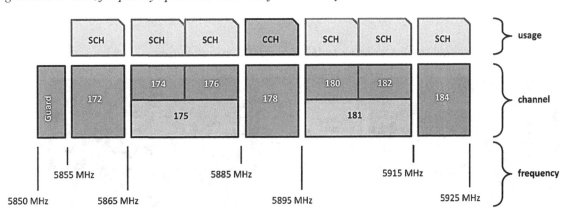

and Europe. As a result, adapting the IEEE 802.11 standard to operate in the DSRC frequency band appeared as a convenient solution to finally enable vehicular communication.

According to the specifications of the US Federal Communications Commission (FCC), the DSRC spectrum consists of 75 MHz at 5.9 GHz, divided into seven 10-MHz channels, with the lower 5 MHz reserved as a guard band. Two pairs of channels can be combined into 20 MHz channels, as per the diagram. One of such channels, namely channel 178, is designated as the Control Channel (CCH), whereas all the others are Service Channels (SCH). The former is intended for signaling purposes and for broadcasting information relevant to all vehicles. The latter are designated for specific services provided or consumed by vehicles. Transmission power can reach 28.8 dBm for an expected communication range of 1 km. We note that experimental assessments, such as those carried out by Bai et al. (2010) and Martelli et al. (2012) have found such ranges to be rather optimistic, with practical communication distances falling in the 50-300 m range. In Europe, the European Commission has standardized a slightly different spectrum allocation, with a reserved band limited to the three central channels of the FCC specifications. These are also referred to as the ETSI ITS-G5 channels.

Building on such dedicated spectrum availability, ten years of standardization efforts have led to different bodies producing several specifications. Figure 6 presents the network protocol stacks proposed by IEEE and ETSI.

The IEEE stack, on the left in Figure 6, is expected to be adopted in the US, and is based on different protocol families. The Physical (PHY) layer and Medium Access Control (MAC) sub-layer are direct evolutions of those described in the popular IEEE 802.11 standard for wireless local area networks. The draft standard for DSRC has long been known as IEEE 802.11p, however such an amendment has recently been superseded and its features included in the latest release of the IEEE 802.11 standard, known as IEEE 802.11-2012. Since the legacy IEEE 802.11 standard and its different variants have been described previously in this Chapter, here we limit ourselves to highlighting the main features inherited from IEEE 802.11p that have been included in IEEE 802.11-2012:

- Compliance with the 10-MHz PHY channel structure dictated by FCC specifications.
- An *ad-hoc* communication mode outside the context of a Basic Service Set (BSS), i.e. the elementary building block of IEEE 802.11 networks, typically managed by an Access Point (AP). This mode allows direct communication between any device, removing the association and authentication phases: these are time-consuming operations that are not compatible with the short-lived links established by high-speed vehicles.

Figure 6. DSRC protocol stack according to IEEE and ETSI specifications

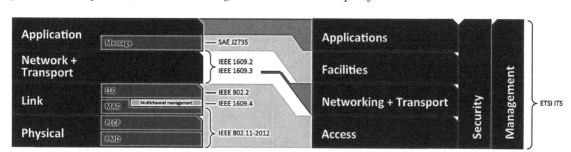

- Adoption of the Quality of Service (QoS) specifications introduced earlier by amendment IEEE 802.11e, concerning the use of four traffic priority categories that devices can use to access the channel, depending on the kind of data they have to transmit.

The management of the multiple available channels in Figure 6 is constrained by the availability of a single radio interface at each vehicle, and IEEE 1609.4 describes its operation. The standard recommends that all vehicles – synchronized via GPS, for example – alternately listen (or transmit) on the CCH and on a SCH of interest according to a time-division mechanism. More precisely, time is divided into 100-ms intervals, during which all vehicles spend the first 50 ms on the CCH and the next 50 on a SCH. This approach has long been questioned by the research community, due to the latency and temporal unbalance in the channel access load it may generate; different approaches have thus been proposed, such as those by Campolo et al. (2011) and Di Felice et al. (2012).

At the network and transport layers, the complexity of the traditional TCP/IP model is deemed useless in vehicular environments, where long-lived unicast flows are absent. Therefore, the IEEE 1609.3 standard replaces TCP (or other transport protocol) and IP headers and operations with a much more compact message structure. The resulting WAVE (Wireless Access for Vehicular Environments) Short Message Protocol, or WSMP, makes it possible to: (i) reduce the packet overhead from the 52 bytes of TCP/IPv6 to 11 bytes; (ii) control lower-layer parameters directly from the application layer, as the data transmission rate, the transmit power, and the channel number can be explicitly indicated in the WSMP packet. The IEEE 1609.2 standard integrates IEEE 1609.3, by defining the security measures to be adopted to ensure privacy, authentication and integrity of data exchanged via DSRC. Finally, the SAE J2735 standard defines a DSRC message set dictionary, i.e. a list of standard message types that can be used to exchange different kinds of information in the vehicular network.

The ETSI stack, on the right in Figure 5, is expected to be adopted in Europe, and it is based on a single standard called ETSI ITS. The ETSI ITS standard was developed after the different protocols that compose the IEEE stack, and thus makes large reuse of mechanisms defined in the IEEE stack – also to ensure compatibility between DSRC implementations in the US and Europe. Specifically, the *access* layer of ETSI ITS, built on top of the ITS-G5 channels mentioned before, covers PHY and MAC specifications, and basically relies on the specifications of IEEE 802.11-2012. The *networking and transport* layer accommodates any layer-3 and layer-4 solutions, including TCP/IP, those specifically defined by IEEE 1609.3, and so-called Geo-networking solutions introduced by ETSI itself. The *facilities* layer implements all functions that support interoperability between the vehicular network and external systems, such as those composed by in-vehicle electronic control units or roadside units. As such, this layer specifies periodic (Cooperative Awareness Messages, or CAM) and event-triggered (Decentralized Environmental Notification Messages, or DENM) messages that can be used for road safety and traffic management purposes. The ETSI architecture also includes additional *security* and *management* layers that are orthogonal to the previous layers, and define (i) cryptographic and algorithmic solutions to guarantee secure operations, and (ii) interfaces among the different layers respectively.

The IEEE and ETSI architectures have served as a basis for the development of a large body of literature on applications, algorithmic solutions, and protocols dedicated to vehicular environments. Many of these are targeted at road safety, and implement services such as collision avoidance, on-road danger warning, approaching emergency vehicle notification, real-time traffic congestion information and routing, and accident liability attribution. Others are not directly related to road safety and include the dissemination of content to users onboard cars, the unicast routing of data within the vehicular network, the deployment of DSRC-based roadside units, the gathering, fusion and exploitation of FVD concerning the vehicles themselves as well as the surrounding environment, making vehicles active participants of urban sensing processes. A thorough discussion of the many and varied works on specific aspects of communication and networking techniques for vehicular environments would require a book per se, and is out of scope in the brief overview we provide here. We refer the interested reader to complete volumes on these subjects, such as those by Olariu and Weigle (2009), Moustafa and Zhang (2009), Hartenstein and Laberteaux (2010), and Beylot and Labiod (2013).

Direct Mobile Device Communication Technologies

Direct communication between wireless devices is an important opportunity to offer new, cheaper services to mobile end users. This communication paradigm bypasses operators, which are instead at the center of traditional mobile network models, and allows two devices in proximity to directly exchange data traffic. Moreover, as the mobile traffic load grows, even cellular operators are beginning to integrate device-to-device communication capabilities in their architectures, so as to meet user demand more effectively. Below we provide a survey of currently available technologies providing direct connectivity between mobile devices.

Bluetooth 3.0 and 4.0

Legacy Bluetooth has been the main technology used for device-to-device communication for a long time. Integrated in all mobile phones for more than a decade now, Bluetooth interfaces allow file exchange, data synchronization and the connection of peripheral devices. Originally standardized by the IEEE as the 802.15.1 standard, Bluetooth specifications are now defined by the Bluetooth Special Interest Group (SIG), while the IEEE working group is no longer maintained.

Bluetooth operates on the 2.4 GHz band, and proposes a centralized medium access method, where a master node forms a so-called *piconet*, which can be joined by up to seven slave nodes. The master node is in charge of regulating access to the wireless channel, and thus polls the slaves, granting them transmission opportunities. The Bluetooth standard describes not only the channel access technology, but also an entire communication architecture. Specifically, the protocol stack is divided into two parts: the *controller stack* and the *host stack*. The controller stack includes the physical and link layers, usually implemented on the chipset, while the host stack covers upper layers, including mandatory and optional protocols. The two host mandatory protocols are the Logical Link Control and Adaptation Protocol (L2CAP) and the Service Discovery Protocol (SDP).

In the last few years, Bluetooth has been adapted to two different scenarios. First of all, wireless technology is required to interconnect devices in a home network, more and more popular for audio and video streaming. While Bluetooth interfaces were present on most devices, the throughput offered by the technology was not enough for video streaming purposes. Bluetooth 3.0, a standard published by the SIG in 2009 (Bluetooth SIG, 2009), addresses this issue by reaching a theoretical throughput of 24 Mb/s. However, these high data speeds are not actually provided through the Bluetooth interface. Instead, Bluetooth 3.0 introduces a Generic Alternate MAC/PHY (AMP) concept, in which Bluetooth is used for the negotiation and establishment of a collocated IEEE 802.11 link, used for data transmission. Initially, Bluetooth 3.0 adopted IEEE 802.11g as an alternative technology, with IEEE 802.11n being added as an alternative in 2011.

A second important Bluetooth use-case is represented by the Internet of Things, an inter-connection of small wireless nodes, which are very often energy constrained. Traditional Bluetooth proposes a connection-oriented link layer, where a link created between devices is maintained until an explicit disconnection, even if there is no data flowing between the two connected devices at a given time. Based on the observation that this mode of operation consumes a significant amount of energy, Bluetooth 4.0 describes different energy saving mechanisms (Bluetooth SIG, 2013). The new features include a totally redesigned PHY layer with larger channel bandwidth, and an asynchronous connection-less MAC protocol. Bluetooth 4.0 achieves a throughput of up to only 1Mb/s, but it is optimized for small, discrete data transfers, ideal for small, energy-constrained nodes, such as those forming a wireless sensor network.

With these two adaptations, new Bluetooth-based applications are expected to emerge. The increased throughput in Bluetooth 3.0 is particularly interesting for video and audio streaming, and also for file exchange, either in the context of a home network, or to interconnect personal devices (e.g. transferring photos or contacts between smartphones, use on a smart-watch content stored on a smartphone, watching videos from a tablet directly on a smart-TV, etc.). At the same time, Bluetooth 4.0 is expected to have a significant impact on the personal fitness and health market, by allowing devices such as smart-watches or electronic bracelets to monitor human activity and upload data to more powerful personal equipment, such as a smartphone or tablet.

LTE Direct

Despite the significant challenges that such a shift brings, device-to-device communication is on the verge of breaking into cellular network architectures. Pushed by the exploding adoption of smartphones and the dramatic growth of data traffic, cellular operators are considering utilizing direct communication in order to offload data from their network, especially in the context of ambient awareness, i.e. the continuous and passive monitoring of relevant phenomena in the user's proximity.

The LTE Direct system operates on a licensed spectrum and it is composed of two main functions: Device-to-Device Peer Discovery and Device-to-Device Data Communication. In Peer Discovery, described in more detail by Lin et al. (2014), a small part of the time-frequency resource, generally less than 1%, is dedicated to LTE Direct discovery. This is based on the concept of *expressions*, which describe the services proposed by a device and are transmitted using the discovery resources functionality. The cellular Radio Access Network (RAN) assigns these discovery resources to authorized LTE Direct devices. In practice, the devices broadcast their expressions locally using 128-bit identifiers, then wake up periodically to discover all devices within range that are interested in the services it may offer.

Once the discovery phase succeeds, two devices that detected a common expression need to communicate with each other. The cellular network is used in this case for control-plane operations, such as synchronization, configuration or authentication, while the actual communication can take place either through the cellular network, or directly between the devices. The RAN controls the communication type in order to optimize network capacity, and assigns the necessary time-frequency resources in both situations. LTE Direct has a very high discovery capacity (almost 3000 services can be discovered in only 64 ms), with a negligible impact (0.3% reduction) on LTE uplink capacity.

LTE Direct can be used to disseminate information with a local geographic scope, such as service advertisements or coupons. Restaurants and shopping centers are expected to adopt the technology widely for marketing purposes. LTE Direct can also be used to interconnect vehicles in a certain area, covering safety and road monitoring applications, as explained by Gallo and Härri (2013).

Wi-Fi Direct

The first version of the IEEE 802.11 standard proposed an ad-hoc mode. The main concept used in ad-hoc mode consisted of a normal device declaring itself to be an Access Point (AP), allowing communication with other devices in a transparent manner. However, the IEEE 802.11 ad-hoc mode had limited success, especially because of the difficulties of inter-connecting an ad-hoc network with other IEEE 802.11 networks.

Indeed, in IEEE 802.11, the access points broadcast a so-called *Basic Service Set (BSS) identifier*, generally defined as the MAC address of the AP. A Wi-Fi device attaches to a BSS and, while the device can switch from one BSS to another, it must be connected to a single BSS at a given time. In the case of an ad-hoc Wi-Fi network, the device that becomes an AP cannot leave the BSS it has created, and the other devices cannot belong to more than one BSS, so communication will remain local, without any possibility of exiting the BSS.

With the IEEE 802.11 working groups reluctant to modify this feature, the Wi-Fi alliance decided to define its own specification for device-to-device communication using Wi-Fi, under the name of Wi-Fi Direct (Wi-Fi Alliance, 2014). Just as in IEEE 802.11 ad-hoc mode, a Wi-Fi Direct device embeds a *soft AP*, which allows it to act as an access point. The main difference comes from the fact that the device can belong to two BSS at the same time, once as an AP and once as a normal station. A device in this situation needs to switch between the two networks, very likely established on different physical channels. However, while the device acts as a normal station on the second network, the first network remains practically without an access point. In order to stop any data exchange in the network during an absence period, the AP device uses a virtual carrier sense mechanism to declare the medium as busy for all possible transmitters.

Due to these enhancements, Wi-Fi Direct has already replaced IEEE 802.11 ad-hoc mode in the market, and is already integrated into most commercial mobile devices. Wi-Fi Direct is considered a solution to provide fast wireless connections to peripherals (e.g. printers, displays, speakers, scanners, cameras, etc.), while still being connected to an AP, which is impossible with traditional Wi-Fi. File sharing applications could also benefit from Wi-Fi Direct, particularly in scenarios where two-way data transfer between multiple devices is needed.

Ultra-Wide Band

With communication becoming possible at higher frequencies of the radio spectrum, previously unused large portions of spectrum can be used. Ultra-Wide Band is a radio technology that makes use of this available spectrum, and is able to achieve high-speed short-range communications. UWB was intensively researched in the early years of the millennium, with several standards being adopted (ETSI, 2004). While the expected market breakthrough did not occur, interest in UWB was revived by potential uses in wireless sensor networks, as pointed out by Zhang et al. (2009).

Unlike traditional radio technologies, which use the signal's power, frequency or phase to modulate information on a narrow band channel, UWB transmits *pulses* on a large bandwidth (over 500 MHz) channel using pulse-position or pulse-time modulation. This allows throughputs of up to 1 Gb/s over distances of a few meters, under line-of-sight conditions.

This type of pulse-based UWB has long been used for radar and imaging systems. This brings an important advantage to the technology, as the same signals can be simultaneously used for communication and localization purposes. Due to this property, UWB is a good candidate technology for surveillance and monitoring systems. When the 60GHz band is used to transmit information, the pulses do not penetrate the human body, making UWB suitable for body area networks, used for example by eHealth applications. On the other hand, when functioning at lower frequencies (between 3 and 10 GHz), the pulses can penetrate through intervening bodies, making UWB particularly appealing for connecting peripherals to a computer, for example by using the Wireless Universal Serial Bus (USB) standard (USB Implementers Forum, 2010).

Near Field Communication

Radio-Frequency Identification (RFID) is a technology allowing a reader device to send radio waves to a passive device, also known as a *tag*. The tag uses the radio waves to recover energy and modulate locally stored information, which is transmitted back to the reader, allowing identification and authentication applications. Near Field Communication (NFC) builds on RFID standards (ISO/IEC/ECMA, 2013) to achieve two-way communication, allowing for low-speed data transfer over very short distances (less than 10 cm).

NFC is especially used in contactless payment systems, but also as an access token for restricted areas. Another important use of the technology takes advantage of its low-energy consumption: NFC can be used to detect the proximity of another device and activate energy-consuming interface, such as Wi-Fi Direct, for a high-speed data exchange.

A number of wireless communication technologies have been proposed in the last few years for direct device-to-device data transfer. These technologies cover many different scenarios, from communication ranges of a few centimeters (NFC), up to several hundred meters (LTE Direct), and from transfer speeds of a few Mb/s (Bluetooth 4.0), up to more than 1 Gb/s (Wi-Fi Direct, UWB). With commercial smartphones already integrating interfaces for several of these technologies, device-to-device communication is only waiting for the *killer application* to change the urban networking paradigm.

FUTURE RESEARCH DIRECTIONS

In the previous section, we reviewed wireless access technologies for smart cities. Table 1 summarizes the main features of such technologies, as well as their expected usages in digital urban environments. In the light of our discussion, we draw the following main considerations.

- Firstly, network paradigms – including the associated communication technologies – for the wireless last mile cannot be studied in isolation from each other, but must be fully integrated, so as to achieve a coherent deployment that leverages the strengths and makes up for the deficiencies of each networking approach.
- Secondly, network architectures for the wireless last mile cannot be separated from the application use cases, nor can they be specific to one single application, but they must be designed with a clear set of requirements from the largest possible number of smart city services in mind.

Table 1. Summary of wireless technologies for smart cities, ordered by achievable bitrate

Technology	Range (m)	Bitrate (Mbps)	Applications
GSM	< 35000	0.0144	voice, sms
GPRS/EDGE	< 35000	0.144	email, machine-to-machine, telemetering
UMTS	< 100000	2	web browsing, social media
HDSPA	< 100000	40	streaming, smartphone applications
LTE/LTE-A	< 100000	300-1000	broadband mobile Internet access (streaming, cloud services, pervasive access, high-mobility device connectivity)
IEEE 802.11 a/b/g/n/ac	100-500	1-1000	broadband Internet access, local area networks, home networks
Wi-Fi Direct	100-500	1000	peripherals connection, file transfer
UWB	< 10	1000	surveillance and monitoring, peripheral connection
Low Power Wi-Fi	25	1-54	home control, building automation
Bluetooth 3.0	10-100	24	video streaming, peripheral connection, file exchange
DSRC	50-1000	3-27	road safety, traffic management, vehicular communications
Bluetooth 4.0	10-100	1	personal fitness, eHealth, sensor networks
LTE Direct	500	1-10	service discovery, vehicular communications
NFC	< 1	1	ePayment, access restriction, device discovery
IEEE 802.15.4	75	0.25	home entertainment and control, building automation, smart parking, and industrial control
DASH7	250-1000	0.02-0.2	military applications, monitoring, building automation, in-vehicle automotive services
UNB	undisclosed	0.001	very low bitrate Internet-of-Things services

- Thirdly, network solutions for the wireless last mile of smart cities cannot be abstracted from the urban tissue, but must be developed and evaluated considering the geography of metropolitan areas, as well as the spatiotemporal dynamics of human mobility, habits and interests that characterize them.

These observations lead to the introduction of a novel, unifying networking paradigm for wireless access in smart urban environments. We refer to it as *capillary networking*, a term that is reminiscent of the pervasive penetration of different technologies for wireless communication in future digital cities. Indeed, capillary networks represent the very last portion of the data distribution and collection network, bringing Internet connectivity to every endpoint of the urban tissue in the same exact way capillary blood vessels bring oxygen and collect carbon dioxide at tissues in the human body. Capillary networks inherit concepts from the self-configuring, autonomous, ad hoc networks so extensively studied in the past decade, but they do so in a holistic way, considering multiple technologies and applications simultaneously and accounting for the specificities of the urban environment.

Capillary Networks

Capillary networks employ manifold wireless communication technologies to provide a flexible link between the core network and mobile devices. The different access paradigms discussed above come together and are strongly intertwined within capillary networks, coexisting and co-operating in the context of arising digital cities. As argued by Augé-Blum et al. (2012), this has three major implications, as follows.

Firstly, capillary networks arise from the interaction of all the technologies that are part of it. As an example, state-of-the-art smartphones integrate a growing number of sensors (e.g. environment sensing, resource consumption metering, movement, health, noise or pollution monitoring) and multiple radio interfaces (e.g. 3G, LTE, Wi-Fi, Bluetooth, NFC, etc.): all these sensing and communication capabilities must be considered as a whole when designing services as well as the network solutions deemed to support them. Similar trends are also observed in privately owned vehicles (TomTom, 2010), public transports as outlined by Zu et al. (2009), commercial fleets (Cabspotting, 2014), and even city bikes (Copenhagen Wheel, 2014). In the same way, access network sites tend to implement heterogeneous (e.g. 2G, 3G, LTE, Wi-Fi, etc.) communication technologies so as to limit capital expenses. There is thus a need for holistic approaches to the study and deployment of capillary network solutions.

Secondly, the capillary network paradigm necessarily accounts for the specificities of urban environments. These include actual urban mobility flows, city land-use layouts, metropolitan deployment constraints, and routine or extraordinary activities of the population. Often, these specificities do not arise from purely networking features, but relate to the study of city topologies and road layouts, social acceptability, transportation systems, energy management, or urban economics.

Thirdly, the scope of digital and smart cities applications is not restricted to Internet of Things use cases supported by Machine-to-Machine (M2M) communications. Indeed, a city is, above all, the gathering of its citizens. Digital services and mobile Internet are primarily used to increase the quality of life, empowerment, and entertainment opportunities for citizens. Communication patterns in smart cities are thus not restricted to M2M. In some cases, data flows should be gathered to, or distributed from, a centralized information system. In other situations, data should be disseminated within a geographically or temporally constrained perimeter. Future usage may even lead to direct data exchange among neighboring end users. These user-centric services are tightly correlated with the usage of the urban environment, which induces a strong spatial and temporal heterogeneity in data traffic patterns.

As a result, a number of open issues remain to be addressed, in order to turn the large set of currently available communication interfaces and infrastructures from a mass of independent technologies into an actual capillary network, capable of answering the challenges of the smart city.

Open Issues

The urban environment is especially challenging for wireless networking technologies, yet capillary communications need to take place at the heart of urban activity. Current research activities seldom consider the unreliability of radio links or the heterogeneity of the urban environment when proposing dedicated solutions for smart city access networks. An important challenge is thus that of properly understanding and characterizing the fundamental features of urban capillary networks. These include the network infrastructure topologies, the dynamics of user mobility and activities, and the traffic patterns generated by smart city services. Models and datasets are required for the evaluation of relevant scenarios of urban networks, as proposed by Uppoor et al. (2014) for the case of vehicular mobility.

In terms of pervasive urban sensing, a major challenge lies in shifting the current common practice of designing a dedicated sensor network for each application. Such an approach would not scale, and needs to be superseded by the rise of multi-service data collection networks capable of fulfilling the QoS requirements of each application. The notion of Service Level Agreement (SLA) for traffic differentiation, QoS support (in terms of delay, reliability, etc.) is central here, both for scalability purposes and resource-sharing effectiveness. A proper definition of this notion and the related network mechanisms, in particular in the settings of low-power wireless devices and mobile Internet-of-Things devices, needs to be developed, as proposed by Gaillard et al. (2014). Furthermore, even though they are not designed to carry such low payload traffic, cellular networks could be used to collect M2M traffics. In particular, when a cell is fully loaded or, at the other extreme, when there are few access requests, there is a considerable amount of small, unused bandwidth slots on the random access RACCH channels. The challenge is then to piggyback few bits of data within the access signaling procedures, without saturating the resources needed by legacy mobile users.

More generally, QoS must be accounted for at both MAC and routing layers. Recent proposals, such as those by Barthel et al. (2012), target the improvement of QoS performance while preserving energy efficiency. Yet, for critical applications, QoS performance is not enough: in this case, fully deterministic protocols are needed so that worst-case delays can be predicted, as done, for example, by Mouradian et al. (2014).

Significant challenges also emerge with respect to network robustness and energy efficiency. As a matter of fact, the dramatic increase in mobile data traffic imposes an ever-growing densification of micro-cell coverage, as pointed out by Fehske et al. (2009), which raises energy issues. Indeed, current 3G and LTE eNodeB's or relays, whatever their state – idle, transmitting, or receiving – are known to drain a vast majority of the power consumed within the mobile network; moreover, this represents a growing trend (ITU, 2014). For a sustainable deployment of the micro-cell infrastructure which does not lead to a surge in the access network energy consumption, but yields instead a significant decrease in the same, an operator has to be able to dynamically switch on or off radio access equipment depending on mobile demand, as originally indicated by Marsan et al. (2009). To this end, self-organization mechanisms typically proposed for wireless sensor networks can be adapted to the energy models of the micro-cells and the requirements of the cellular infrastructure, as proposed by Tunaru et al. (2013). Again, the main challenge lies in designing and assessing solutions with realistic environmental conditions in mind, including infrastructure deployment, the geographical coverage of each antenna, or mobile traffic demand.

Energy efficiency is an open issue not only in the case of cellular networks, but also when it comes to sensing infrastructures. Here, an interesting approach to solving the problem is energy harvesting, which can significantly increase the network lifetime by allowing nodes to recharge over time using power sources made available by the surrounding environment.

Finally, the sheer growth in mobile traffic demand will represent a problem per-se in years to come, and the issue will be more evident in urban scenarios where user density is significantly higher. In this regard, the capillarity of heterogeneous wireless access networks needs to be leveraged so as to diversify the routes data take and balance the load among the different infrastructures. The ubiquity of Wi-Fi access in urban areas makes it an especially interesting solution to cellular offloading, and many studies, such as that by Lee et al. (2010), have focused on its potential, concluding that more than 65% of the data can be offloaded from the cellular infrastructure in high-density areas. However, most public Wi-Fi networks are optimized for connectivity and not for capacity: more research is needed in this area to correctly assess the potential of this technology. Moreover, handovers among diverse technologies are currently managed by mobile terminals alone, and more efficient results might be achieved if the client and network sides collaborated in taking decisions about such vertical handovers. Direct opportunistic communication between mobile users can also be used to offload an important amount of data, as stressed by Han et al. (2010). In this case, one has to face a number of major problems concerning the role of social information and multi-hop communication in the achievable offload capacity. Finally, the last key challenge related to accommodating mobile data traffic demand is the deployment of an architecture of hotspot access points tailored for user-centric applications, including urban sensing or connected vehicles.

CONCLUSION

In this Chapter, we overviewed current and future technologies providing communication and networking support to smart city services. The infrastructures contributing to such an effort are many and varied, and this heterogeneity can be both a richness and an impediment towards the deployment of pervasive smart city solutions. On the one hand, the availability of wireless access technologies with diverse properties makes it possible to support applications with dissimilar requirements. On the other hand, deploying a large number of independent network infrastructures based on mutually blind technologies is hardly a possibility, due to interference on the shared portions of the spectrum and the multiplication of capital and operation expenses.

The solution lies in reducing mobile access technologies to a limited set with orthogonal properties, and – most importantly – designed with interoperability in mind. Enabling interaction among different wireless architectures leads to an ideal network support for smart city services; however, it also poses a number of technical and engineering challenges. Our ability to answer such challenges may make the difference between the deployment of expensive yet barely useful communication infrastructures, and that of effective and efficient smart city solutions.

REFERENCES

Akyildiz, I. F., Su, W., Sankarasubramaniam, Y., & Cayirci, E. (2002). Wireless sensor networks: A survey. *Computer Networks*, *38*(4), 393–422. doi:10.1016/S1389-1286(01)00302-4

Ancona, S., Stanica, R., & Fiore, M. (2014). Performance Boundaries of Massive Floating Car Data Offloading. In Proceedings of IEEE/IFIP WONS. doi:10.1109/WONS.2014.6814727

Augé-Blum, I., Boussetta, K., Rivano, H., Stanica, R., & Valois, F. (2012). Capillary Networks: A Novel Networking Paradigm for Urban Environments. In Proceedings of UrbaNE. doi:10.1145/2413236.2413243

Bai, F., Stancil, D. D., & Krishnan, H. (2010). Toward understanding characteristics of dedicated short range communications (DSRC) from a perspective of vehicular network engineers. In *Proceedings of ACM MobiCom*. doi:10.1145/1859995.1860033

Barthel, D., Lampin, L., Augé-Blum, I., & Valois, F. (2012). Exploiting long-range opportunistic links to improve delivery, delay and energy consumption in Wireless Sensor Networks. In *Proceedings of IEEE MASS*.

Bazzi, A., Masini, B. M., & Andrisano, O. (2011). On the Frequent Acquisition of Small Data Through RACH in UMTS for ITS Applications. *IEEE Transactions on Vehicular Technology*, *60*(7), 2914–2926. doi:10.1109/TVT.2011.2160211

Beylot, A.-L., & Laboid, H. (2013). *Vehicular Networks: Models and Algorithms.* Wiley. doi:10.1002/9781118648759

Bluetooth SIG. (2009). *Specifications of the Bluetooth System, Covered Core Package: 3.0 + HS.*

Bluetooth SIG. (2013). *Specifications of the Bluetooth System, Covered Core Package: 4.1.*

Buratti, C. (2010). Performance analysis of IEEE 802.15.4 beacon-enabled mode. *IEEE Transactions on Vehicular Technology*, *59*(4), 2031–2045. doi:10.1109/TVT.2010.2040198

Cabspotting. (2014). Retrieved from http://cabspotting.org/api

Campolo, C., Molinaro, A., & Vinel, A. V. (2011). Understanding the performance of short-lived control broadcast packets in 802.11p/WAVE Vehicular networks. In *Proceedings of IEEE VNC.*

CDM. (2014). *Cisco Data Meter.* Retrieved from http://www.ciscovni.com/data-meter/

Cisco. (2013). *Global Mobile Data Traffic Forecast Update.*

DASH7 Alliance. (2013). *DASH7 Alliance mode draft 02 release: An advanced communication system for wide-area low-power wireless applications and active RFID.*

Di Felice, M., Ghandour, A. J., Artail, H., & Bononi, L. (2012). On the impact of multi-channel technology on safety-message delivery in IEEE 802.11p/1609.4 vehicular networks. In *Proceedings of IEEE ICCCN.*

ETSI TR 101 994-1. (2004). *Short Range Devices (SRD); Technical Characteristics for SRD Equipment using Ultra Wide Band Technology (UWB); Part 1: Communications Applications.*

ETSI TR 103 055-1.1.1. (2011). *Electromagnetic compatibility and Radio spectrum Matters (ERM) - System Reference document (SRdoc): Spectrum Requirements for Short Range Device, Metropolitan Mesh Machine Networks (M3N) and Smart Metering (SM) applications.*

Fehske, A., Richter, F., & Fettweis, G. (2009). Energy efficiency improvements through micro sites in cellular mobile radio networks. In *Proceedings of IEEE GLOBECOM Workshops.* doi:10.1109/GLO-COMW.2009.5360741

Gaillard, G., Barthel, D., Theoleyre, F., & Valois, F. (2014). Service Level Agreements for Wireless Sensor Networks: a WSN Operator's Point of View. In *Proceedings of IEEE/IFIP NOMS.* doi:10.1109/NOMS.2014.6838261

Gallo, L., & Härri, J. (2013). A LTE-Direct Broadcast Mechanism for Periodic Vehicular Safety Communications. In *Proceedings of IEEE VNC.* doi:10.1109/VNC.2013.6737604

Han, B., Hui, P., Kumar, V., Marathe, M., Pei, G., & Srinivasan, A. (2010). Cellular Traffic Offloading through Opportunistic Communications: A Case Study. In *Proceedings of ACM CHANTS.* doi:10.1145/1859934.1859943

Hartenstein, H., & Laberteaux, K. (2008). A tutorial survey on vehicular ad hoc networks. *IEEE Communications Magazine*, *46*(6), 164–171. doi:10.1109/MCOM.2008.4539481

Hartenstein, H., & Laberteaux, K. (2010). *VANET - Vehicular Applications and Inter-Networking Technologies.* Wiley.

Holma, H., & Toskala, A. (2001). *WCDMA for UMTS: Radio Access for Third Generation Mobile Communications*. Wiley.

Hui, J., & Thubert, P. (2011). Compression format for IPv6 datagrams over IEEE 802.15.4-based networks. *RFC 6282*.

Ide, C., Dusza, B., & Wietfeld, C. (2012). Performance Evaluation of V2I-Based Channel Aware Floating Car Data Transmission via LTE. In *Proceedings of IEEE ITSC*. doi:10.1109/ITSC.2012.6338753

IEEE Computer Society. (2003). *Local and Metropolitan Area Networks - Specific Requirements Part 15.4: Wireless Medium Access Control (MAC) and Physical Layer (PHY) Specifications for Low-Rate Wireless Personal Area Networks (LR-WPANs). 802.15.4-2003 - IEEE Standard for Information Technology*.

IEEE Computer Society. (2006). *Local and Metropolitan Area Networks - Specific Requirements Part 15.4: Wireless Medium Access Control (MAC) and Physical Layer (PHY) Specifications for Low Rate Wireless Personal Area Networks (WPANs). 802.15.4 802.15.4-2006 - IEEE Standard for Information technology*.

IEEE Computer Society. (2012). *802.11-2012 - IEEE Standard for Information Technology--Telecommunications and Information Exchange between Systems. Local and Metropolitan Area Networks--Specific Requirements Part 11: Wireless LAN Medium Access Control (MAC) and Physical Layer (PHY) Specifications*.

USB Implementers Forum. (2010). *Wireless USB Specification Revision 1.1*.

International Energy Agency. (2012). *Energy Technology Perspectives 2012*. Executive Summary.

ISO/IEC/ECMA. (2013). Near Field Communication Interface and Protocol - 2, 3rd Edition.

ITU. (2014). *ITU-T and Climate Change, Technology Watch Report*.

Kushalnagar, N., Montenegro, G., & Schumacher, C. (2007). IPv6 over low-power wireless personal area networks (6LowPan): Overview, assumptions, problem statement, and goals. *RFC 4919*.

Lee, K., Lee, J., Yi, Y., Rhee, I., & Chong, S. (2010). Mobile Data Offloading: How Much Can Wi-Fi Deliver? In *Proceedings of IEEE/ACM CoNEXT*.

Lin, X., Andrews, J., Ghosh, A., & Ratasuk, R. (2014). An Overview of 3GPP Device-to-Device Proximity Services. *IEEE Communications Magazine*, *52*(4), 40–48. doi:10.1109/MCOM.2014.6807945

Mangel, T., Kosch, T., & Hartenstein, H. (2010). A Comparison of UMTS and LTE for Vehicular Safety Communication at Intersections. In *Proceedings of IEEE VNC*.

Marsan, M., Chiaraviglio, L., Ciullo, D., & Meo, M. (2009). Optimal energy savings in cellular access networks. In *Proceedings of IEEE ICC Workshops*.

Martelli, F., Renda, M. E., Resta, G., & Santi, P. (2012). A measurement-based study of beaconing performance in IEEE 802.11p vehicular networks. In Proceedings of IEEE INFOCOM.

Montenegro, G., Kushalnagar, N., Hui, J., & Culler, D. (2007). Transmission of IPv6 packets over IEEE 802.15.4 networks. *RFC 4944*.

Mouradian, A., Augé-Blum, I., & Valois, F. (2014). RTXP: A Localized Real-Time MAC-Routing Protocol for Wireless Sensor Networks. *Computer Networks*, *67*, 43–59. doi:10.1016/j.comnet.2014.03.020

Moustafa, H., & Zhang, Y. (2009). *Vehicular Networks - Techniques, Standards, and Applications.* Auerbach Publications. doi:10.1201/9781420085723

Mulligan, G. (2007). *The 6lowpan architecture.* EmNets. doi:10.1145/1278972.1278992

Norair, J. P. (2009). Introduction to DASH7 technologies. Retrieved November 30, 2014, from https://dash7.memberclicks.net/assets/PDF/dash7%20wp%20ed1.pdf

Olariu, S., & Weigle, M. (2009). *Vehicular Networks from Theory to Practice.* Chapman Hall/CRC. doi:10.1201/9781420085891

Rosen, D., Mammano, F., & Favout, R. (1970). An electronic route-guidance system for highway vehicles. *IEEE Transactions on Vehicular Technology*, *19*(1), 143–152. doi:10.1109/T-VT.1970.23442

Sohraby, K., Minoli, D., & Znati, T. (2007). *Wireless Sensor Networks: Technology, Protocols, and Applications.* Wiley. doi:10.1002/047011276X

Sommer, C., Schmidt, A., Chen, Y., German, R., Koch, W., & Dressler, F. (2010). On the Feasibility of UMTS-based Traffic Information Systems. *Ad Hoc Networks*, *8*(5), 506–517. doi:10.1016/j.adhoc.2009.12.003

Stanica, R., Fiore, M., & Malandrino, F. (2013). Offloading Floating Car Data. In *Proceedings of IEEE WoWMoM*.

The Copenahagen Wheel. (2014). Retrieved November 30, 2014, from http://senseable.mit.edu/copenhagenwheel

TomTom. (2010). Travel Time Measurements using GSM and GPS Probe Data. In *Proceedings of 16th ITS World Congress and Exhibition on Intelligent Transport Systems and Services.* Stockholm, Sweden

Tozlu, S., Senel, M., Mao, W., & Keshavarzian, A. (2012). Wi-Fi enabled sensors for Internet of Things: A practical approach. *IEEE Communications Magazine*, *50*(6), 134–143. doi:10.1109/MCOM.2012.6211498

Tse, D., & Viswanath, P. (2005). *Fundamentals of wireless communication.* Cambridge University Press. doi:10.1017/CBO9780511807213

Tseng, Y.-C., Hsu, C.-S., & Hsieh, T.-Y. (2002). Power-saving protocols for IEEE 802.11-based multi-hop ad hoc networks. In Proceedings of IEEE INFOCOM.

Tunaru, I., Rivano, H., & Valois, F. (2013). WSN-inspired Sleep Protocols for Heterogeneous LTE Networks. In *Proceedings of PE-WASUN.* doi:10.1145/2507248.2507267

United Nations Development Policy and Analysis Division. (2013). *World Economic and Social Survey 2013 - Sustainable Development Challenges.*

United Nations Economic and Social Affairs. (2012). *World Urbanization Prospects. The 2011 Revision.*

Uppoor, S., Trullols-Cruces, O., Fiore, M., & Barcelo-Ordinas, J. M. (2014). Generation and Analysis of a Large-scale Urban Vehicular Mobility Dataset. *IEEE Transactions on Mobile Computing*, *13*(5), 1061–1075. doi:10.1109/TMC.2013.27

Wagner, R. S. (2010). Standards-based wireless sensor networking protocols for spaceflight applications. In *Proceedings of IEEE Aerospace Conference*. doi:10.1109/AERO.2010.5446672

Weyn, M., Ergeerts, G., Wante, L., Vercauteren, C., & Hellinckx, P. (2013). Survey of the DASH7 Alliance protocol for 433 MHz wireless sensor communication. *International Journal of Distributed Sensor Networks*, *2013*, 1–9. doi:10.1155/2013/870430

Wi-Fi Alliance. (2014). *Wi-Fi Peer-to-Peer (P2P) Technical Specifications v1.5*.

Zhang, J., Orlik, P. V., Sahinoglu, Z., Molisch, A. F., & Kinney, P. (2009). UWB Systems for Wireless Sensor Networks. *Proceedings of the IEEE*, *97*(2), 313–331. doi:10.1109/JPROC.2008.2008786

Zhu, H., Li, M., Zhu, Y., & Ni, L. M. (2009). Hero: Online real-time vehicle tracking. *IEEE Transactions on Parallel and Distributed Systems*, *20*(5), 740–752. doi:10.1109/TPDS.2008.147

Zigbee Alliance. (2008). *Zigbee specifications*. ZigBee Document 053474r17.

KEY TERMS AND DEFINITIONS

Cellular Network: Wireless communication system providing pervasive and seamless service to mobile users through a set of base stations, each covering one or more of the cells in which the geographical space is tessellated.

Mobile User: Individual carrying a communication device, which he/she possibly uses while moving.

User Terminal/Equipment: Communication device carried by a mobile user.

Vehicular Network: Wireless communication system composed of vehicles equipped with radio interfaces, and capable of exchanging data among them as well as with the cellular network or other fixed infrastructures.

Wireless Network: Communication network using radio frequency signals to convey data between sources and destinations.

Wireless Sensor Network: Wireless communication system composed of wireless sensors.

Wireless Sensor: Low-cost battery-powered device featuring limited computational and memory resources, as well some sensing and wireless communication capabilities.

This research was previously published in the Handbook of Research on Social, Economic, and Environmental Sustainability in the Development of Smart Cities edited by Andrea Vesco and Francesco Ferrero, pages 266-297, copyright year 2015 by Information Science Reference (an imprint of IGI Global).

Chapter 23
Smart CCTV and the Management of Urban Space

Jung Hoon Han
University of New South Wales, Australia

Scott Hawken
University of New South Wales, Australia

Angelique Williams
University of New South Wales, Australia

ABSTRACT

This chapter briefly describes the proliferation of CCTV over the last few decades with particular reference to Australia and discusses the limits of the technology. It then focuses on new image interpretation and signal processing technologies, and how these advanced technologies are extending the reach, power, and capabilities of CCTV technology. The advent of "Smart" CCTV has the ability to recognize different human behaviours. This chapter proposes a typology to assist the application and study of Smart CCTV in urban spaces. The following four typologies describe different human behaviours in urban space: 1) Human-Space Interaction, 2) Human-Social Interactions, 3) Human-Object Interactions, and 4) Crowd Dynamics and Flows. The chapter concludes with a call for future research on the legal implications of such technology and the need for an evidence base of risk behaviours for different urban situations and cultures.

I. INTRODUCTION

Smart Cities aim to make urban areas more livable, efficient and safe through the integration of information and communication technology (ICT). Smart technologies within Smart Cities can either act as new innovative infrastructure in their own right, or more frequently, are implemented to transform the way traditional infrastructure and services are accessed and used. ICT facilitates networking and engagement with the urban system, and can improve the quality of life for people in urban areas (Han & Lee, 2013; Lee, at al. 2014; Neirotti, et al. 2014). A range of these smart technologies have been adapted to transform

DOI: 10.4018/978-1-5225-2589-9.ch023

urban infrastructure into "smart" infrastructure. Examples include the city-wide collection of digital data on parking spaces and urban services; security cameras that identify pedestrian risk behaviours; and GPS systems that identify traffic congestion, taxi locations and traffic lights. Such advances give urban residents access to real-time information so they can make better decisions whether it be: selecting the fastest driving route and avoiding congestion, or identifying and visiting nearby services, or avoiding crime or disaster scenes (Yigitcanlar & Han, 2010). Smart technology is changing the way urban residents use traditional cities and urban infrastructure. The range of smart technology is proliferating rapidly with new software and algorithms transforming technology that has been around for many decades.

One such technology, in the process of being transformed, is Closed Circuit Television (CCTV). This chapter briefly discusses the use CCTV technology during the last few decades and outlines the limits of its effectiveness. It then focuses on the transformation of this technology by new innovations. Finally a four category typology to help with the application of this technology in urban space is proposed. The categories that make up the typology are:

1.   Human-Space Interaction;
2.   Human-Social Interactions;
3.   Human-Object Interactions; and
4.   Crowd-Dynamics and Flows.

Traditional CCTV technology consists of two parts:

1.   The camera or sensor, and
2.   The interpretation or signal processing of the image sequence that the video camera takes.

There have been recent advances in both these areas. Image interpretation and signal processing technologies are now employing advanced algorithms to capture changes in the images recorded by the sensors, and the sensors themselves are also becoming more sensitive and so extending the reach, power and capabilities of CCTV technology. These two aspects of CCTV technology are significant for the continued rollout of new CCTV technology and the transformation of existing technology already deployed in cities around the world.

II. THE PROLIFERATION OF CCTV IN GLOBAL CITIES

The emergence of Closed Circuit Television (CCTV) systems occurred in the 1960s, Its subsequent proliferation in the 1980s and 1990s, has been documented by various authors (Fyfe and Bannister, 1996; Norris, Moran and Armstrong, 1998; Webster, 2004a). Especially since 9/11, CCTV technology has been adopted by urban governments. This reflects growing pressures to guarantee community and public safety in urban spaces, and changing socio-political government agendas. In Australia uses of CCTV technology have been most prevalent in the law and order context (Australian Institute of Criminology, 2004). The attractiveness of CCTV as a tool for the management of urban spaces can be explained by reference to three categories of justification: first, as having a predictive, preventative or deterrent function; second, in assisting on-the-spot responses to emergency situations as they occur; and third, in forensically identifying what has occurred in the past (Waters, 1996). Further attention is devoted to these applications of CCTV technology later in the chapter.

Sociologists have recognized that the increasing ubiquity of CCTV has been propelled by broader socio-economic and political forces which characterise the changing urban spaces of post-industrial cities (McCahill, 2013). Specifically, technological advances in mass surveillance coincided with economic restructuring and associated private outsourcing of government functions, which occurred in neo-liberal states from the 1970s (Webster, 2004b; McCahill, 2013). The phenomenon of modern "surveillance societies" has been accounted for by drawing together three theoretical strands: first, the 'electronic panopticon' (Giddens, 1987; 1990); second, 'post-Fordism' (Harvey, 1989); and third, the 'risk society' (Beck, 1992).

In terms of the 'electronic panopticon', new surveillance technologies such as CCTV have altered the Benthamite architectural norm for social discipline by removing traditional spatial and temporal barriers, and dispensing with the need for the physical co-presence of the observer. This technological innovation suited changed socio-economic and political conditions in urban spaces from the 1970s. Following from this, post-Fordist literature suggests that such changes encouraged local business and local elites to utilise surveillance technology to protect and facilitate commercial exchange in new urban areas of consumption (McCahill, 2013).

And lastly, changing attitudes towards risk have occurred in law and order politics within Western neo-liberal states from the early 1990s. Government-industry cooperation in providing 'proactive intelligence-led policing' present a new paradigm of urban space management through a focus on crime (Webster, 2004a; Griffin, Trevorrow & Ialpin, 2007). A particular characteristic of this new approach is the promotion of social exclusionary practises. Analysing the installation of CCTV systems in the city centre of Liverpool, England, Coleman and Sim (2000) note the centrality of the private sector in 'constructing definitions of risk and danger in the city and who should be targeted to avoid these risks and dangers' (2000: 627).

In accordance with this political-economic philosophy of urban space management through 'intelligence-led policing', it can be observed how the embrace of mass surveillance technologies in global cities has additionally been influenced by Beck's theory of the 'risk society' (Beck, 1992). According to Beck's theory, actuarial reasoning and technology are linked and operationalized in the management of urban criminogenic spaces. The database that results from such methods in turn produces informational intelligence to support the development of strategies for situational crime prevention.

Extensive British-based public perception surveys, undertaken for technology companies (Crockard & Jenkins, 1996; Ross & Hood, 1998), as well as by the Home Office (Honess & Charman, 1992; Brown, 1995) and independent academics (Bennet & Gelsthorpe, 1996; and Ditton, 2000) have indicated the community's support for the presence of CCTV, which is perceived to be necessary for crime reduction. Despite general public support for CCTV in overseas contexts, Australian social scientists have acknowledged the privacy implications for civil liberties that are associated with the 'real-time' surveillance capacity of CCTV in public areas (Brown, 1995). Indeed, in the absence of public perception studies to quantify the assumed populist support for CCTV in Australian urban spaces, it is relevant to note the considerable criticisms of civil libertarians in this field.

Concerns raised by civil libertarians concerning the unacceptable invasions of privacy perpetrated by privately owned and operated CTTV cameras in urban spaces were clearly voiced in the case of *SF v Shellharbour City Council* [2013] NSWADT 94, Australia. This case involved an application in the New South Wales Administrative Decisions Tribunal by a Nowra resident who had objected to police use of live footage in the Nowra city area. In particular, it was argued that the respondent council had breached various Information Protection Principles under the *Privacy and Personal Information Act 1998* (NSW) ("PPIA Act"). The court held in favour of the applicant, finding that the respondent council had failed to provide sufficient information in signage concerning the information collection process and the purposes for the information collected, in contravention of relevant privacy principles under the PPIA Act. This case demonstrates the important legal parameters within which CCTV footage can be lawfully applied. Further, it demonstrates legal recognition of the importance of striking a balance between the communal good and privacy concerns when considering uses of CCTV in urban space management.

III. CCTV AS A TOOL FOR THE MANAGEMENT OF URBAN SPACE

As the previous section indicates, despite its drawbacks, CCTV has been enthusiastically taken up in various cities, London being the best known example. In London CCTV technology is used to detect and deter both criminal and anti-social behaviour (ASB). It is important to note that anti-social behaviour is a contested concept and largely depends on a society's "behavioural expectations for a particular space and time" (Millie 2008, p.379). Anti-social behaviour is therefore culturally specific. ASB can be defined as behaviour that causes alarm or distress to others not in the same household as the perpetrator but nevertheless that such behaviour is a) not prohibited by the criminal law and b) in isolation such behaviour constitute relatively minor offences (Millie 2008). As a tool to facilitate urban crime detection, prevention and prosecution, as well as a technology to manage urban anti-social behaviour, the adoption of CCTV technology is based on the premise that formal surveillance modifies the urban environment in such a manner as to deter crime and anti-social behaviour due to an increased risk of detection (Clarke, 2004; Baum et al., 2014).

In addition to this crime and anti-social behaviour prevention role, CCTV cameras in urban spaces have the pro-active function of encouraging potential victims to take security precautions (Armitage, Smyth & Pease, 1999). Two prominent theories, the routine activities theory (Cohen & Felson, 1979) and the rational choice theory (Clarke & Cornish, 1985), underpin these justifications for the role of CCTV in reducing crime. First, the occurrence of a crime depends on the convergence of three factors: a motivated offender, a suitable victim and the absence of a capable guardian (Cohen & Felson 1979). Second, the characteristics of a motivated offender typically include some degree of rational decision-making in the immediate situational context of crime (Clarke & Cornish 1985). In summary CCTV increases opportunity for detection of the crime, thus de-motivating the offender, making potential victims more security conscious and allowing for the quicker response rate of emergency services.

The sense of social control inspired by the installation of CCTV cameras, can beneficially generate community cohesion and pride, thus decreasing crime through more positive methods (Welsh & Farrington, 2002). In the Australian context, this explanation has been extended to include theories which link CCTV guaranteed safety to urban rejuvenation and to stimulation in local trade and investment (Coleman & Sim, 1998, 2000; Mackay, 2003; Martin, 2000; Reeve, 1998). This position was made clear in the City of Perth's 2001 CCTV Information Kit, which explained the context for the installation of CCTV systems in terms of economically-desirable safety goals: "The Central Business District was suffering a retail decline in the mid-1980s and the best efforts of the Council to rejuvenate the area were often offset by emotional stories in the media which generated an undesirable image of the city" (City of Perth, 2000).

IV. THE LIMITS OF TRADITIONAL CCTV TECHNOLOGY AND THE NEED FOR SMART TECHNOLOGY

The relevance of smarter uses of CCTV systems in Australian cities is highlighted by the concession made in the literature as to the questionable effectiveness of traditional CCTV as a singular tool for crime prevention (Kruegle, 2011). For example whilst the deterrence effect of CCTV can be strong in the initial installation period, it is acknowledged that this factor is difficult to sustain in the longer term. The effectiveness of CCTV systems can be improved by progressively modifying it for particular situations and types of anti-social behavior according to changing requirements. There are ways of fine tuning CCTV's impact. For example "smart" algorithms may be applied to CCTV systems for purposes of detecting entry into prohibited areas, loitering, vandalism, aggressive human exchanges, "man-down" situations, and pedestrian-vehicular accidents. CCTV technology has the potential to become a key component of digital policing strategies designed to more efficiently coordinate early emergency responses for serious incidents.

In the US, research has found that the deployment of CCTV on city streets has the potential to reduce crime. For instance Baltimore city government gains $1.06 in cost avoidance for every $1 spent on CCTV (Urban Institute, 2011). However this reduction is dependent on how the surveillance system is set up and monitored. Although the presence of CCTV has been found to reduce crime, if there is a perception that cameras are not monitored, such technology has little impact. This has led to a call for a more intelligent deployment, integration and monitoring of such systems. The study area included Baltimore, Chicago and Washington, D.C. and compared the monthly average crime reports in areas with CCTV. The cameras were deployed to areas of similar crime volume, land use and demographics. The report generally showed that urban crime decreased following introduction of CCTV, even controlling for an overall reduction in crime. However, CCTV had no effect in West Garfield Park, Chicago as the residents have a perception that "police do not watch the cameras" in their neighborhood. The mismatch between the widespread deployment of CCTV technology and human capacity to monitor the images captured by the cameras has been documented in behavioural studies. Generally a human's maximum attention span, when faced with the visual challenge of monitoring such screens, is 10 minutes before there is a sharp decrease in ability to identify visual anomalies within image sequences (Medina, 2014; Dukette & Cornish, 2009).

The study that investigated the effectiveness of CCTV also found that the impact of such technology may be limited by the methods of deployment. Cameras had no effect on crime in Washington D.C. due the deployment of the technology. CCTV in the area was not able to capture significant crime scenes due to inappropriate pre-programmed panning functions and inadequate resolution that did not allow for enlargement of crime scenes captured on the cameras (Urban Institute, 2011). Although CCTV technology enables the deployment of hundreds of "eyes" focused upon the city, if there is no mechanism for interpreting such data the net result is visual "noise". A common sight in security and urban management departments around the world are enormous banks of monitors being fed images from different locations. Such monitor arrays produce meaningless data unless these images are able to be processed, interpreted and monitored effectively.

Smart CCTV (SCCTV) systems are based on integrating emerging signal processing technologies with more traditional CCTV technology to empower the interpretative power of urban authorities and limit the production of "noise streams". SCCTV technology reduces the likelihood of human error and oversight through the use of sophisticated algorithms designed to identify anomalies within image sequences and trigger a range of alarms. For example a SCCTV might identify a traffic incident with a pedestrian, call an ambulance, determine the best route for the ambulance and redirect traffic away from the incident area.

SCCTV systems integrate a series of cameras that are networked through a sophisticated wireless infrastructure to a control room, where images captured are recorded, monitored and stored. In addition traditional CCTV technology has evolved from static, low-resolution sensors, to high quality sensors capable of panning, tilting and zooming in accordance with complex behavioural-based algorithms set by remote operators. The broad adoption of SCCTV technology has occurred against an institutional backdrop that increasingly favours problem-oriented monitoring of space (Clarke, 2004; Goldstein, 2003). In this context, SCCTV has functioned as an integrated way to manage urban space issues such as crime detection, disaster response, and traffic incidents prevention (Ratcliffe, 2008).

Figure 1. One police officer monitors 412 CCVTs in South Korea
Source: Donga Newspaper (20/02/2009).

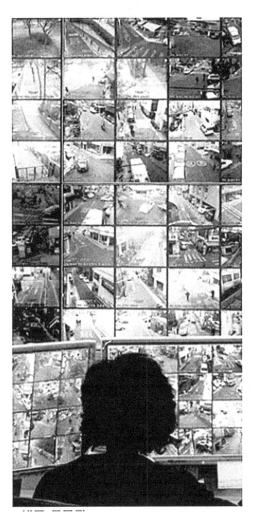

V. THE INTEGRATION OF CCTV WITH SMART IMAGE RECOGNITION AND SIGNAL PROCESSING TECHNOLOGY

SCCTV can be applied to the process of human behaviour recognition. Typologies of such behaviour may be devised to distinguish between different urban situations and human actions. This chapter proposes a typology to assist the application and study of Smart CCTV in urban spaces. The following four typologies describe different human behaviours in urban space:

1. Human-Space Interaction;
2. Human-Social Interactions;
3. Human-Object Interactions; and
4. Crowd-Dynamics and Flows.

In the last decade numerous advances have been made in image or "signal processing" that promise new, more powerful ways to use CCTV to monitor and manage urban space. The application of smart technologies for the management of human behaviour in urban space varies according to the type of human behaviour under investigation. Thus, technologies facilitating motion detection are suited to Human Space Interaction. Alternatively, technologies that provide action recognition may be utilised to monitor Human-Social Interaction and Human-Object Interaction. Finally, technologies that seek to track objects are relevant to Crowd-Dynamics and Flows. The application of such technologies to the various situations of human behaviour in urban spaces is discussed below.

Figure 2. Typologies of the different situations of human behaviour in urban spaces

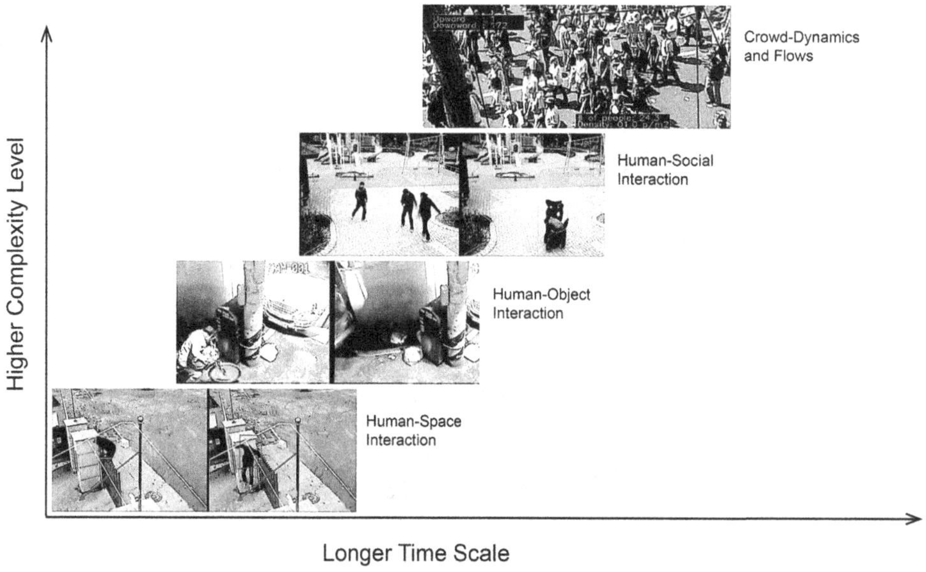

Situations of Human Behaviour in Urban Spaces

1. Human-Space Interaction

Signal processing technologies, which target motion detection and generate digital intelligence, can be used to inform policy-makers of relevant human interactions in urban spaces. Human motion information collected from CCTV cameras is of interest for the purposes of urban space management due to the potential provision of baseline measurements of a human presence in public as opposed to private areas.Motion detection can indicate the movement of humans from a private area (i.e. city office) to a public space (i.e. train station).

Motion detection in video images aims to segment regions corresponding with a person from the rest of an image. Motion segmentation is a notoriously difficult task. Several conventional approaches to motion detection include background subtraction (Haritaoglu, Harwood & Davis, 2000); statistical methods (Kim, Sakamoto, Kitahara, Toriyama, & Kogure, 2007); temporal distancing (Bayona, SanMiguel, & Martínez, 2010); and optical flow (Shibata, Yasuda & Ito, 2008).

Background subtraction requires a raw subtraction to be performed in relation to a target in stationary scenes (Sheikh, Javed & Kanade, 2009). Due to the constant changes that occur in dynamic scenes, a morphological operation must further be applied in order to obtain accurate detection (Camplani & Salgado, 2011). The statistical method represents a developed form of background subtraction, with such strategies as dual foreground involving the application of statistics to individual pixels or a group of pixels (Porikli, Ivanov & Haga, 2008). This method is sufficiently robust to tolerate illumination changes and occlusion, as well as deal with environmental conditions including noise and shadow (Ibid).

In order to identify human moving targets from other possible non-human moving targets across successive frames, temporal distancing is utilised. Under this approach, the current image frame is subtracted from either the preceding or the following frame of the image sequence (Bayona et al., 2010). Through the application of thresholds to remove pixel changes across successive image sequences, this method successfully adapts to a dynamic scene (Ibid). Figure 3 shows that different algorithms apply to the areas divided by a gate. The human activity moving from the 'outside' (left image) to the 'inside' of the gate (right image) is programmed to signal an alert with the presence of an intruder.

Figure 3. Intruder Alert! human space interaction
Source: National Information Society in Korea (2013).

Finally, the optical flow method operates as a strategy to measure the spatial arrangement of objects based on their individual velocities, and is used for both motion detection and object detection (Denman, Chandran & Sridharan, 2007). The method is based on optical flow vectors, which are analysed to determine the apparent velocities of movement derived from patterns of brightness in an image (Ibid). Specialised hardware such as FPGA and GPU cards are required for the operation of the optical flow method in order to satisfy the demands of the processes computationally data-intensive nature (Ishii, Taniguchi, Yamamoto & Takaki, 2010).

As indicated in the above discussion, strategies for motion detection face various challenges in the analysis of dynamic scenes. Further innovation is required in order to minimise issues associated with illumination changes, occlusion and environmental changes caused by noise and shadow. Furthermore, additional limitations are represented by the computational data-intensive nature of strategies such as optical flow.

2. Human-Social Interaction and 3. Human-Object Interaction

Significant insights into the social and object-based interactions of humans in urban spaces may be obtained through technologies that provide human activity recognition. Uses of technology to facilitate signal processing of CCTV footage may, for instance, reveal both positive and negative patterns of human social interaction within a particular urban space. Positive interactions that may be captured through SCCTV include hand-shaking and sitting in grouped clusters, so as to infer the conduciveness of a particular urban space to cordial greetings and informal human social gatherings. Alternatively, SCCTV may be programmed to identify aggressive encounters, including fighting and burglary, in turn indicating events of inter-personal aggression and conflict in urban spaces.

Behavioural analysis obtainable through smart technological manipulation of CCTV data for urban space management extends not only to social patterns, but also to patterns of human interactions with inanimate objects. Particularly relevant to the context of Human-Object Interactions in urban spaces are architectural discourses, which enable post-occupancy assessment of urban design features. In addition, more ad hoc situations of human object-based interactions may be monitored, such as dumping of rubbish and suspicious objects in urban spaces. The algorithm applied in SCCTV detects when an unidentified object appears in the monitoring site. It is programmed to alarm (left photo image) if the possessor leaves the site and does not return within a set time (refer to Figure 4).

Figure 4. Motion detection of garbage dumping
Source: National Information Society in Korea (2013).

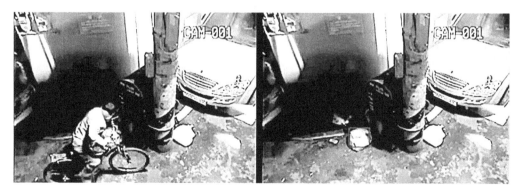

When using image processing technology in the application of human interaction identification in urban spaces, it is necessary to note that approaches to human activity recognition can be divided into two broad categories: non-hierarchical and hierarchical (Aggarwal & Ryoo, 2011). The non-hierarchical approach is divided into two classes: a space-time approach (Bobick & Davis, 2001) and a sequential approach (Darrell & Pentland, 1993). Three classes apply to the hierarchical approach: statistical (Zhang et al., 2006; Nguyen et al, 2005), syntactic (Ivanov & Bobick, 2000), and description-based (Intille & Bobick, 1999) approaches.

In analysing the overall advantages of respective hierarchical and non-hierarchical approaches to individual human and crowd activity recognition, strengths lie in the capacity of the strategies to model either periodic or non-periodic and more complex activities. Thus, spatial-temporal approaches have been shown to be effective in recognising periodic actions, whereas description-based approaches are better adapted to identifying more complex, multiple and concurrent human activities.

Digital modelling of CCTV systems in order to generate an understanding of human behaviours seeks to isolate and analyse the normality or abnormality of individual human behaviours. This modelling requires a combination of the signal processing techniques outlined above, as well as artificial intelligence techniques (Leordeanu and Collins, 2005). Suspicious or endangering behaviour is "detected" through appropriate algorithms and rules, which are modelled according to different categories of human activities (Lalos and Anagnostopoulos, 2009). Various taxonomies have been developed for the purpose of classifying a hierarchy of human actions. For example, Moeslund et al (2006) propose the following abstract levels of an observable suspicious behaviour: action-primitive; action; and activity. An action-primitive may involve "raising the left hand", an action may involve "waving the hand", and an activity may involve "punching someone". Thus, in this example, the raising, waving and punching actions converge in the one course of conduct (Ibid). Action recognition algorithms developed for SCCTV accordingly alert human operators to such crimes as burglary and group fighting in public places (affray). Figure 5 shows an example of a conflict event. Algorithms are developed to distinguish between playing and serious violent activities. The left image shows that SCCTV alerts when a person falls down after the other person punches him.

Figure 5. Person falls down as a result of fight
Source: National Information Society in Korea (2013).

4. Crowd-Dynamics and Flows

Initial uses of computer technology as part of the advancement of smarter CCTV involved the estimation of global properties of urban crowds, including density and flow (Davies, Yin and Velastin, 1995). Development of individual human tracking technology provided a platform for the study of the movement of individuals within a dynamic crowd scene. Such SCCTV applications are beneficial for policymakers in the field of urban space management due to the generation of useful information relating to group and individual human behaviours in "rush-hour" type situations (Davies & Velastin, 2005). In particular, benefits include the provision of data crucial in informing policy related to threat assessment, emergency response procedures, and amenity/resource allocation in various public urban spaces, such as train stations. Figure 5 illustrates SCCTV crowd monitoring.

Crowd density can be estimated by a ratio that measures the 'background area' against the 'crowd area' in a single area covered by the footage. Where densities are low, the individual 'edges' of all pedestrians may be extracted from the image (Velastin et al., 2006). For purposes of crowd density, basic motion data can be obtained by use of a gradient method to monitor changes in colour brightness from one image to the next, expressed as a vector field. Block matching the pixels in alternate images further produces similar results for monitoring crowd flows. Digital models for assessing both crowd density and flow are to be distinguished on the basis that they establish general models of crowd behaviour and do not seek to isolate individual behaviours (Davies, Yin and Velastin, 1995).

Technologies focusing on the tracking of individual human targets within a dynamic crowd scene aim to maintain the identity of the moving human target (Aggarwal and Cai, 1999; Haritaoglu et al., 2000). The tracking process typically establishes a correspondence between the image structure of two consecutive frames in what is referred to as a 'sliding window' approach (Benfold & Reid, 2011). This involves taking measurements from the scene of interest at a discrete time, and making a distinction between a target and all unwanted movements (referred to as clutter), so as to deduce information about the object being tracked (Cavallaro, Steiger & Ebrahimi, 2005).

Figure 6. Crowd monitoring
Source: www.evitech.com.

Algorithms to track objects can be classified into six categories (Vishwakarma & Agrawal, 2013). First, algorithms can track objects by identifying variations in the image regions that correspond to the moving object (Meyer & Bouthemy, 1994; Schmaltz et al., 2012) Second, algorithms can provide for contour-based non-rigid object tracking (Yokoyama & Poggio, 2005; Yilmaz et al., 2006). Third, maths tools can be used to support both static (Comaniciu et al., 2003) and dynamic (Lin et al. 2009) feature-based object tracking. Fourth, model recognition can be used to track human motion (Gavrila & Davis, 1996). Fifth, hybrid tracking can be utilised, and has involved the combination of feature and model-based approaches (Lalos & Anagnostopoulos, 2009). Sixth, optical flow-based tracking may be achieved through intensive computation (Denman et al., 2005; Ince & Konrad 2008).

Hybrid tracking has been suggested as a particularly robust approach to dealing with occlusions of tracked entities (Vishwakarma and Agrawal, 2013). In order to minimise problems associated with changes in the velocity of the object, referred to as 'occlusion', use of a Kalman filter can be applied to provide estimates of future trajectories in an occluded zone (Corvee, Velastin & Jones, 2003). Alternatives to the avoidance of occlusion issues include Bayesian random-sampling techniques (Narayana & Haverkamp, 2007), the adaptive background subtraction method (Luo, Li & Gu, 2007) and a perspective multi-scale approach (Nieto, Ortega, Cortes & Gaines, 2014). In addition to overcoming problems of occlusion, hybrid tracking may furthermore remove problems associated with background clutter and loss of an object due to rapid movements. Figure 7 demonstrates tracking technology in the context of school zones. It first identifies the school children (blue squares in the photo image) and then traces their pathways with a zoom-in (left image).

VI. DISCUSSION AND CONCLUSION

As this chapter notes, the shortcomings of traditional CCTV systems are well documented in scholarly literature. The increasing presence of CCTV in public places globally and the large amounts of money spent on its deployment warrant a comprehensive analysis of both the effectiveness of such technology and the legal implications of such technology. It is no longer so much a question of applying an unblink-

Figure 7. Tracking children in outer school zones
Source: National Information Society in Korea (2013).

ing surveillance gaze in search of a simple security fix, but more a question of what should be watched, and why, and by whom. SCCTV technology provides the technological means to address these questions through its increased precision and capabilities.

Considering current investment trends in urban security it is likely that Smart CCTV systems will develop as an integral component of Smart Cities in order to address the limitations of traditional CCTV. SCCTV systems have the potential to play a substantial role in the management of urban space through intelligence led policing. In applying this smart technology attention must be devoted to associated risks, such as the potential for false alarms and privacy breaches. Nevertheless when compared to conventional CCTV, intelligence-led policing via SCCTV offers a more flexible and focused approach through targeting specific risk behaviours. Rather than the unfiltered monitoring of urban space offered by traditional CCTV, SCCTV provides the technology to select specific risk behaviours and generate appropriate alarms.

Figure 8. Evaluation of CCTV image interpretation technologies

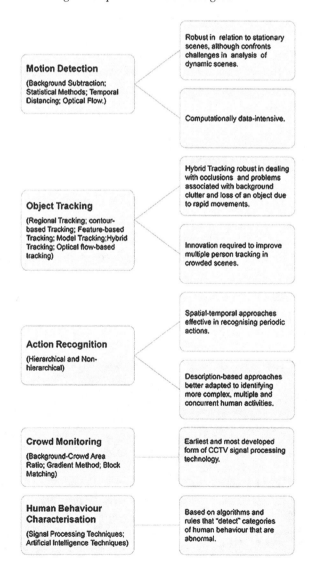

To achieve this, an evidence base of risk behaviours needs to be compiled in the form of a database. The four categories proposed in this chapter offer an initial framework for such a database. However beyond these four categories the culturally specific nature of urban space and behaviour, pose limitations for the application of this technology in urban areas globally. Any database must be adjusted to account for the different human behaviours, evident in different geographic contexts and different cultures. SCCTV itself has the potential to assist in generating this evidence base of urban human behaviour through a systematic program of research preceding the rollout of the technology.

The advent of SCCTV indicates a substantial increase in the power and sensitivity of traditional CCTV technology and the potential to transform both the management and design of urban space. This power needs to be guided by a technological vision of city-wide data management within a sophisticated legal framework cognisant of the culturally specific nature of urban space.

REFERENCES

Aggarwal, J. K., & Cai, Q. (1999). Human motion analysis: A review. *Computer Vision and Image Understanding, 73*(3), 428–440. doi:10.1006/cviu.1998.0744

Aggarwal, J. K., & Ryoo, M. S. (2011). Human activity analysis: A review. *ACM Computing Surveys, 43*(3), 1–43. doi:10.1145/1922649.1922653

Armitage, R., Smyth, G., & Pease, K. (1999). Burnley CCTV evaluation. In K. Painter & N. Tilley (Eds.), *Surveillance of public space: CCTV, street lighting and crime prevention* (pp. 225–250). Monsey, NY: Criminal Justice Press.

Australian Institute of Criminology. (2004). Closed Circuit Television (CCTV) as a crime prevention measure. *AICrime Reduction Matters, 18*, 1.

Baum, S., Arthurson, K., & Han, J. H. (2014, July). Tenure social mix and perceptions of antisocial behaviour: An Australian example. *Urban Studies (Edinburgh, Scotland), 22*. doi:10.1177/0042098014541160

Bayona, A., SanMiguel, J. C., & Martínez, J. M. (2010). Stationary foreground detection using background subtraction and temporal difference in video surveillance. In *Proceedings of IEEE 17th Int. Conf. on Image Processing*. IEEE. doi:10.1109/ICIP.2010.5650699

Beck, U. (1992). *Risk society: Towards a new modernity*. London: Sage.

Benfold, B., & Reid, I. D. (2011). Stable multi-target tracking in real-time surveillance video. In *Computer vision and pattern recognition* (pp. 1–8). Colorado Springs, CO: CVPR.

Bennett, T., & Gelsthorpe, L. (1996). Public attitudes towards CCTV in public places. *Studies on Crime and Crime Prevention, 5*(1), 72-90.

Bobick, A. F., & Davis, J. W. (2001). The recognition of human movement using temporal templates. *IEEE Transactions on Pattern Analysis and Machine Intelligence, 23*(3), 257–267. doi:10.1109/34.910878

Brown, B. (1995). *CCTV in town centres: Three case studies*. London: HMSO.

Camplani, M., & Salgado, L. (2011). Adaptive background modelling in multicamera system for real-time object detection. *Optical Engineering (Redondo Beach, Calif.), 50*(12), 1–17. doi:10.1117/1.3662422

Cavallaro, A., Steiger, O., & Ebrahimi, T. (2005). Tracking video objects in cluttered background. *IEEE Transactions on Circuits and Systems for Video Technology, 15*(4), 575–584. doi:10.1109/TC-SVT.2005.844447

City of Perth. (2000). *Closed circuit TV information kit*. Perth, Australia: Perth City.

Clarke, R. V. (2004). Technology, criminology and crime science. *European Journal on Criminal Policy and Research, 10*(1), 55–63. doi:10.1023/B:CRIM.0000037557.42894.f7

Clarke, R. V., & Cornish, D. B. (1985). 'Modelling offenders' decisions: A framework for research and policy. In M. Tonry & N. Morris (Eds.), *Crime and justice* (pp. 147–185). Chicago: University of Chicago Press.

Cohen, L. E., & Felson, M. (1979). Social change and crime rate trends: A routine activity approach. *American Sociological Review, 44*(4), 588–608. doi:10.2307/2094589

Coleman, R., & Sim, J. (2000). You'll never walk alone: CCTV surveillance, order and neo-liberal rule in Liverpool city centre. *The British Journal of Sociology, 51*(4), 623–639. doi:10.1080/00071310020015299 PMID:11140887

Colman, R., & Sim, J. (1998). From the dockyards to the Disney stores: Surveillance, risk and security in Liverpool city centre. *International Review of Law Computers & Technology, 12*(1), 27–45. doi:10.1080/13600869855559

Comaniciu, D., Ramesh, V., & Meer, P. (2003). Kernel-based object tracking. *IEEE Transactions on Pattern Analysis and Machine Intelligence, 25*(5), 564–577. doi:10.1109/TPAMI.2003.1195991

Corvee, E., Velastin, S. A., & Jones, G. A. (2003). Occlusion tolerant tracking using hybrid prediction schemes. *Acta Automatica Sinica, 29*(3).

Crockard, S., & Jenkins, D. (1998). *An independent evaluation of Chelmsford town centre CCTV scheme*. Chelmsford: Anglia Polytechnic University.

Darrell, T., & Pentland, A. (1993). Space-time gestures. In *Proceedings of IEEE Computer Society Conf. on Computer Vision and Pattern Recognition* (pp. 335–340). IEEE.

Davies, A. C., & Velastin, S. A. (2005). A progress review of intelligent CCTV surveillance systems. In *Proceedings of IDAACS 2005 Workshop*. IDAACS. doi:10.1109/IDAACS.2005.283015

Davies, A. C., Yin, J. H., & Velastin, S. (2005). Crowd monitoring using image processing. *Electronics and Communication Engineering Journal, 7*(1), 37–47. doi:10.1049/ecej:19950106

Denman, S., Chandran, V., & Sridharan, S. (2007). Adaptive optical flow for person tracking. *Pattern Recognition Letters, 28*(10), 1232–1239. doi:10.1016/j.patrec.2007.02.008

Ditton, J. (2000). Crime and the city: Public attitudes to CCTV in Glasgow. *The British Journal of Criminology, 40*(4), 692–709. doi:10.1093/bjc/40.4.692

Dukette, D., & Cornish, D. (2009). *The essential 20: Twenty components of an excellent health care team*. RoseDog Books.

Fyfe, N. R., & Bannister, J. (1996). City watching: Closed circuit television in public spaces. *Area*, *28*(1), 37–46.

Gavrilla, D., & Davis, L. (1996). 3D model-based tracking of humans in action: A multi-view approach. In *Proc. of the Computer Vision and Pattern Recognition* (pp. 73–80). Academic Press.

Giddens, A. (1987). *Social theory and modern sociology*. Palo Alto, CA: Stanford University Press.

Giddens, A. (1990). *The consequences of modernity*. Cambridge, MA: Polity Press.

Goldstein, H. (2003). On further developing problem-oriented policing: The most critical need, the major impediments, and a proposal. In J. Knutsson (Ed.), *Problem-oriented policing: From innovation to mainstream* (pp. 13–47). Monsey, NY: Criminal Justice Press.

Griffin, D. (2007). *Trevorrow, P. and Halpin, E.* Amsterdam, Netherlands: Developments in E-Government.

Han, J. H., & Lee, S. (2013). Planning ubiquitous cities for social inclusion. *Int. J. of Knowledge-Based Development*, *4*(2), 157–172. doi:10.1504/IJKBD.2013.054092

Haritaoglu, I., Harwood, D., & Davis, L. S. (2000). W4: Real-time surveillance of people and their activities. *IEEE Transactions on Pattern Analysis and Machine Intelligence*, *22*(8), 309–330. doi:10.1109/34.868683

Harvey, D. (1989). From managerialism to enerpreneurialism: The transformation in urban governance in late capital-ism. *Geografisk annaler. Series B. Human Geography*, *71*(1), 2–17.

Honess, T., & Charman, E. (1992). *Closed circuit television in public places: Its acceptability and perceived effectiveness*. London: Home Office.

Ince, S., & Konrad, J. (2008). Occlusion-aware optical flow estimation. *IEEE Transactions on Image Processing*, *17*(8), 1443–1451. doi:10.1109/TIP.2008.925381 PMID:18632352

Intille, S. S., & Bobick, A. F. (1999). A framework for recognizing multiagent action from visual evidence. In Proceedings of AAAI-99. AAAI Press.

Ishii, I., Taniguchi, T., Yamamoto, K., & Takaki, T. (2010). 1000 fps real-time optical flow detection system. In *Proc. SPIE*. SPIE.

Ivanov, Y. A., & Bobick, A. F. (2000). Recognition of visual activities and interactions by stochastic parsing. *IEEE Transactions on Pattern Analysis and Machine Intelligence*, *22*(8), 852–872. doi:10.1109/34.868686

Javed, O., & Shah, M. (2002). Tracking and object classification for automated surveillance. In *Proceedings of 7th European Conference on Computer Vision*. Springer. doi:10.1007/3-540-47979-1_23

Kim, H., Sakamoto, R., Kitahara, I., Toriyama, T., & Kogure, K. (2007). Robust silhouette extraction technique using background subtraction. *MIRU*.

Kruegle, H. (2011). *CCTV surveillance: Video practices and technology*. Boston: Butterworth-Heinemann.

Lalos, C., & Anagnostopoulos, V. (2009). Hybrid tracking approach for assistive environments. *Int. Conf. Proc. Series, 39*(64), 5.

Lee, S. H., Leem, Y. T., & Han, J. H. (2014). Impact of ubiquitous computing technologies on changing travel and land use patterns. *International Journal of Environmental Science and Technology.*

Leordeanu, M., & Collins, R. (2005). Unsupervised learning of object features from video sequences. In Proceedings of IEEE Computer Society Conf. on Computer Vision and Pattern Recognition. IEEE. doi:10.1109/CVPR.2005.359

Lin, F., Chen, B. M., & Lee, T. H. (2009). Robust vision-based target tracking control system for an unmanned helicopter using feature fusion. In *Proceedings of 9th IAPR Int. Conf. on Machine Vision Applications* (vol. 13, pp. 398–401). IAPR.

Luo, R., Li, L., & Gu, I. Y. (2007). Efficient adaptive background subtraction based on multi-resolution background modelling and updating. Springer.

Mackay, D. (2003). Multiple-targets: The reasons to support town-centre CCTV systems. In M. Gill (Ed.), *CCTV* (pp. 23–25). Leicester, UK: Perpetuity Press. doi:10.1057/palgrave.cpcs.8140154

Martin, C. (2000). Crime control in Australian urban space. *Current Issues in Criminal Justice, 12*(1), 79–92.

McCahill, M. (2013). *The surveillance web*. Devon, UK: Taylor and Francis.

Medina, J. (2014). *Brain rules: 12 principles for surviving and thriving at work, home, and school*. Pear Press.

Meyer, F., & Bouthemy, P. (1994). Region-based tracking using affine motion models in long image sequences. *CVGIP. Image Understanding, 60*(2), 119–140. doi:10.1006/ciun.1994.1042

Millie, A. (2008). Anti-social behaviour, behavioural expectations and an urban aesthetic. *The British Journal of Criminology, 48*(3), 379–394. doi:10.1093/bjc/azm076

Moeslund, T. B., Hilton, A., & Kruger, V. (2006). A survey of advances in vision-based human motion capture and analysis. *Computer Vision and Image Understanding, 104*(2-3), 90–126. doi:10.1016/j.cviu.2006.08.002

Narayana, M., & Haverkamp, D. (2007). A Bayesian algorithm for tracking multiple moving objects in outdoor surveillance video. In *Proceedings of CVPR* (pp. 1–8). New York: IEEE Press.

National Information Society Agency. (2013). *2012 yearbook of information society statistics*. Retrieved from http://eng.nia.or.kr/english/eng_nia.asp/

Neirotti, P., Marco, A., Cagliano, A., Mangano, G., & Scorrano, F. (2014). Current trends in Smart City initiatives: Some stylised facts. *Cities (London, England), 38*, 25–36. doi:10.1016/j.cities.2013.12.010

Nguyen, N.T., Phung, D.Q., Venkatesh, S., Bui, H. (2005). Learning and detecting activities from movement trajectories using the hierarchical hidden Markov model. In *Proceedings of IEEE Computer Society Conf. on Computer Vision and Pattern Recognition* (vol. 2, pp. 955–960). IEEE.

Nieto, M., Ortega, J. D., Cortes, A., & Gaines, S. (2014). Perspective multiscale detection and tracking of persons. *LNCS, 8326,* 92–103.

Norris, C., Moran, J., & Armstrong, G. (Eds.). (1998). *Surveillance, closed circuit television and social control.* Aldershot, UK: Ashgate.

Porikli, F., Ivanov, Y., & Haga, T. (2008). Robust abandoned object detection using dual foregrounds. *EURASIP Journal on Advances in Signal Processing,* (8): 197875.

Ratcliffe, J. H. (2008). *Intelligence-led policing.* Cullompton, UK: Witlan.

Reeve, A. (1998). The panopticisation of shopping: CCTV and leisure competition. In Surveillance, closed circuit television and social control. Aldershot, UK: Ashgate.

Ross, D., & Hood, J. (1998). Closed circuit television (CCTV) - The Easterhouse case study. In L. Montanheiro, B. Haigh, D. Morris, & N. Hrovatin (Eds.), *Public and private sector partnerships: Fostering enterprise* (pp. 497–516). Sheffield Hallam University Press.

Sheikh, T., Javed, O., & Kanade, D. (2009). Background subtraction for freely moving cameras. In *Proceedings of IEEE 12th Int. Conference on Computer Vision.* IEEE.

Shibata, M., Yasuda, Y., & Ito, M. (2008). Moving object detection for active camera based on optical flow distortion. In *Proc. of the 17th World Congress the International Federation of Automatic Control* (pp. 720–725). Academic Press.

Urban Institute. (2011). *Evaluating the use of pulic surveillance cameras for crime control and prevention* (Final Technical Report). Author.

Velastin, S., Boghossian, B., & Vicencio-Silva, M. (2006). A motion-based image processing system for detecting potentially dangerous situations in underground railway stations. *Trans. Research Part C, 14*(2), 96–113. doi:10.1016/j.trc.2006.05.006

Vishwakarma, S., & Agrawal, A. (2013). A survey on activity recognition and behaviour understanding in video surveillance. *The Visual Computer, 29*(10), 983–1009. doi:10.1007/s00371-012-0752-6

Waters, N. (1996). Street surveillance and privacy. *PLPR, 3,* 48.

Webster, W. R. (2004). *The policy process and governance in the information age: The case of closed circuit television.* (Unpublished PhD Thesis). Glasgow Caledonian University, Glasgow, UK.

Webster, W. R. (2004). The diffusion, regulation and governance of closed-circuit television in the UK. *Surveillance and Society, 2*(2/3), 230-250.

Yigitcanlar, T., & Han, J. H. (2010). Ubiquitous eco cities: Telecommunication infrastructure, technology convergence and urban management. *International Journal of Advanced Pervasive and Ubiquitous Computing, 2*(1), 1–17. doi:10.4018/japuc.2010010101

Yilmaz, A., Javed, O., & Shah, M. (2006). Object tracking: A survey. *ACM Computing Surveys, 38*(4), 1–45. doi:10.1145/1177352.1177355

Yokoyama, M., & Poggio, T. (2005). A contour-based moving object detection and tracking. In *Proceedings of 2nd Joint IEEE Int. Workshop on Visual Surveillance and Performance Evaluation of Tracking and Surveillance* (pp. 271–276). IEEE. doi:10.1109/VSPETS.2005.1570925

Zhang, D., Gatica-Perez, D., Bengio, S., & McCowan, I. (2006). Modeling individual and group actions in meetings with layered hmms. *IEEE Transactions on Multimedia*, *8*(3), 509–520. doi:10.1109/TMM.2006.870735

KEY TERMS AND DEFINITIONS

Closed Circuit Television (CCTV): CCTV refers to a surveillance camera which transmits an image to a specific place where it is displayed on a limited set of monitors. The digital signal is not openly transmitted but may employ point to point (P2P), point to multipoint, or mesh wireless links.

Human–Computer Interaction: Human-computer interaction refers to the intersection of computer science and behavioural sciences, involving planning and design of the interaction between people (users) and computers.

Image Processing: Image processing is any form of digital signal processing for which the input is an image, such as a photograph or video frame.

Motion Detection: The process of detecting a change in position of an object relative to its surroundings or moving objects, particularly people.

Smart CCTV: Smart CCTV builds knowledge in the form of testable explanations and predictions about human movement and actions by a set of algorithms that computers use to perform specific operations or to prevent urban crime and antisocial behaviours.

Smart City: Smart Cities uses digital technologies and technological convergence to reduce costs and resource consumption and enhance urban areas to achieve more livable, efficient and safe cities.

This research was previously published in the Handbook of Research on Digital Media and Creative Technologies edited by Dew Harrison, pages 430-447, copyright year 2015 by Information Science Reference (an imprint of IGI Global).

Chapter 24
Urbanizing the Ambient:
Why People Matter So Much in Smart Cities

H. Patricia McKenna
AmbientEase, Canada

ABSTRACT

The purpose of this chapter is to develop and explore the ambient urbanizing concept as a way to shed light on what happens at the urban level when people become more aware and attuned to smartness and ambience in everyday city spaces. The research design for this work includes a case study approach and multiple methods of quantitative and qualitative data collection and analysis. In parallel with this study, anecdotal evidence gathered from individuals across the city through informal individual and group discussions enabled further analysis, comparison, and triangulation of data. This chapter makes a contribution to the research literature across multiple domains; sheds light on the emerging relationships of awareness in the people – technologies – cities dynamic, highlighting the critical role of people, in their everyday urban activities, interactions, and experiences; and offers a proposed ambient urbanizing framework for enriching spaces, things, and designs in smart cities.

1. INTRODUCTION

This chapter explores aware technologies and aware people in the formulation of emerging understandings of urbanizing the ambient in 21st century cities. Building upon Sassen's work on urbanizing technology in the context of smart cities and Weiser & Seely Brown's (1995) work on calm technology design, this chapter explores the ambient urbanizing concept through the constructs of awareness, attention, and attunement. Calm technology, as in, invisible or ubiquitous computing, is variously known as pervasive computing, ambient computing, to name a few, depending upon the research lab (Dourish & Bell, 2011). Using a minimally viable city-focused platform as a space with real-time, real-world, social media components, the ambient and ambient urbanizing concepts are explored. The mechanisms of noticing, idea-generation, and the sharing of content about the city contribute insight into the ambient-related constructs under study – awareness, attention, and attunement.

DOI: 10.4018/978-1-5225-2589-9.ch024

The significance of this chapter is that it provides a conceptualization of ambient urbanizing in the context of 21st century smart cities with an emphasis on the combination of aware people and aware technologies. As such, the objectives of this chapter are to: a) explore emerging understandings of aware-enabled smart cities; b) shed light on what happens at the urban level when people become more aware and attuned to smartness and ambience in everyday city spaces; and c) explore urban level activities contributing to urbanizing the ambient, giving rise to the ambient urbanizing concept as emerging perspectives on the importance of people in smart cities.

The research design for this work incorporates a case study approach and multiple methods of quantitative and qualitative data collection and analysis. Use of a minimally viable city-focused platform as a space for thinking and sharing about the city is followed up with an interview about use experience of the tool and semi-structured questions about the city as smart. In parallel with this study, anecdotal evidence gathered from individuals across the city through informal individual and group discussions enabled further analysis, comparison, and triangulation of data. A more detailed discussion of the methodology for this work is described in section 4. A selective review of the ambient, urbanizing, and smart cities research literature in section 3 provides a theoretical perspective for the chapter in support of the deductive portion of qualitative data analysis, to complement emergent aspects of the inductive analysis portion.

Section 2 provides additional background and context for this chapter in terms of motivation; the ambient, urbanizing, and smart city concepts, incorporating emerging and developing perspectives and challenges from the research literature; along with definitions for key terms used in this chapter.

2. BACKGROUND AND CONTEXT

This chapter is motivated by the need for engaging people in more meaningful discussions about smart city phenomena. In response to the unprecedented challenges associated with rapid urban growth in the 21st century (Charoubi et al., 2012), Nam and Pardo (2011) articulate the smart cities concept as a way for cities to innovate themselves using information and communications technologies (ICTs). Gil-Garcia, Pardo, and Nam (2016) advance smarter as the new urban agenda while Ojo, Dzhusupova, and Curry (2016) identify current gaps in the smart cities research literature. Relevant to this chapter are the research gaps (Ojo et al, 2016) pertaining to the *dimensions* of education and of people and the *research approach* of living lab, as in real world everyday life. The smart city topic is present on the agenda of policy-makers, technology companies, and academics, yet city inhabitants do not seem to be involved in meaningful discussion about the concept and its implications for surveillance, privacy, inclusion and many other issues (Craglia & Granell, 2014). Further, the smart cities concept is said to be unfamiliar to more than 61% of the 1000 surveyed by Frost & Sullivan (Gamble, 2014). The concept has emerged as contested and controversial in the smart cities research literature (Greenfield, 2013) with utopian and dystopian visions (Townsend, 2014; Marvin, Luque-Ayala, and McFarlane, 2016, Hollands, 2016) and is articulated in terms of tensions and implications by futures researchers (IFTF, 2011). Smart cities have been evolving over the last decade (Scholl, 2016) yet Brandt (2015) notes a kind of obliviousness in the United Kingdom where "nearly 100 percent do not notice smart cities growing around them."

Smart cities are enabled by a confluence of at least four developments: the emergence of information and communication technologies (ICTs) (Charoubi et al., 2012) including smart/ambient technologies

(Weiser & Seely Brown, 1995); the openness movement, encompassing open source, open data, open access; the emergence of citizen science and crowdsourcing (Craglia & Granell, 2014; Sasso, Konomi, Arikawa, & Fujita); and the concept of inverse infrastructure (Egyedi & Mehos, 2012), with ad hoc, user-driven, adaptive development from the bottom up, broadening the potential scope of agency and involvement (Angus, Lane, & Roussos, 2014). It is worth noting that many of the key elements and indicators of smart cities such as livability, walkability, sustainability, resilience to name a few (UN, 2015; Cohen, 2014) can be found in the city planning literature and new urbanism works pre-dating the smart cities movement (Jacobs, 1961; Gehl, 1968, 1980; Whyte, 1988; De Certeau, 1984).

William, Robles, and Dourish (2009) argue for an emphasis on urban experience and users embedded as actors in the global networks of interactions and flows. To this end, Williams et al. (2009) explore 'urbane-ing' in terms of the concept of city in the context of urban informatics. Seely Brown (2014) refers to a forthcoming work co-authored with Pendleton-Julian (Design unbound) that will bring forward the complex challenges, as in 'wicked problems', facing education (Johnson et al., 2016) and characterizing 21st century cities (Charoubi et al., 2012) and the need for "skillfully reading the currents and disruptions of the context around us." Where Sassen (2013) articulates the need for an urbanizing of technology, this chapter focuses more specifically on the urbanizing of ambient technologies with an emphasis on the importance of people in a people-technologies-cities dynamic.

Further context for this chapter is provided in the key terms and definitions section, with definitions for key terms used. A selective review of the smart cities and ambient research literature provides a theoretical perspective for the chapter, focusing on the constructs of awareness, attention, and attunement. The research design for the study upon which this chapter is based is described in the methodology section, followed by an overview of findings and a discussion of the analysis and results. The implications for practice and research that this chapter makes are identified followed by study challenges and mitigations and the conclusion.

3. THEORETICAL PERSPECTIVE

This section presents a selective review of the research literature for smart cities in terms of issues, controversies, and problems as they relate to the theme of urbanizing technologies and more particularly, ambient technologies, in 21st century cities. The literature on ambience and the ambient will be presented along with the related constructs of attunement, awareness, and attention to shed light on the relationships between aware people and aware technologies. The city literature is reviewed at the intersection of urbanism and smart cities, touching on theories around people; urban environment interactions; perceptions and experiences of everyday life; urban planning; and placemaking. A discussion of the urbanizing of technology (Sassen, 2012) follows and more specifically, urbanizing the ambient.

3.1 Ambience and the Ambient

Rickert (2013) claims that "we are entering an age of ambience" where "boundaries between subject and object, human and nonhuman, and information and matter dissolve" pushed further, in part, by ubiquitous technology, affecting our interactions and what we know "about self and the world." More than two decades ago, Weiser (1994) described ubiquitous computing as working toward the highest ideal of making computing invisible where it becomes "so imbedded, so fitting, so natural, that we use it without even thinking about it." Weiser referred to work on the "building of versions of the infrastructure-to-come" at Xerox PARC "in the form of inch-, foot-, and yard-sized computers we call Tabs, Pads, and Boards." Much of this infrastructure in the form of smartphones, sensors, outdoor jumbotron displays we now take for granted.

Rickert (2013) suggests that, "ambience allows us new perspectives" and is "an ensemble of variables, forces, and elements that shape things in ways difficult to quantify or specify" since, the elements are "simultaneously present and withdrawn, active and reactive, and complexly interactive among themselves as much as with human beings." Rickert (2013) describes ambience as "less driven by connection and more resonant with immersion and permeation" and like a network "connotes distribution, coadaptation, and emergence." In the context of urban form, Lynch (1989), in defining settlement form, refers to ambiences, and later describes this as "the set of encompassing conditions" in the city, as in, "light, noise, microclimate, smell" (Lynch, 1996). It is worth noting that Smith (2015) identified "four emerging sources of authority" in relation to health and well-being as, "computation, narratives, networks, and ambience" adding that these sources "will fundamentally transform who we trust and what interventions will be available."

Rickert (2013) argues that "ambience is itself ambient" and McCullough (2013) suggests that, "when you feel renewed sensibility to your surroundings you might try calling this ambient." In articulating how to arrive at an understanding of ambient, McCullough itemized 12 possible ways, three of which are highlighted here for their relevance to this chapter. First, McCullough describes ambient as, "that which surrounds but does not distract"; second, "a continuum of awareness and an awareness of continuum"; and third, "rampant availability of opportunities to shift attention." The first description brings to mind Weiser's (1994) notion of computing as imbedded, fitting, and natural, suggestive of attunement. The second description of ambient makes a connection and association with awareness and persistence. The third description is noteworthy because it makes a connection with attention. The ambient will now be discussed in terms of the three associated constructs of attunement, awareness, and attention.

3.1.1 Attunement

Rickert (2013) claims that "ambience involves more than just the whole person" and "is inseparable from the person in the environment that gives rise to ambience" and as such, involves the notion of attunement. Rickert (2013) describes attunement as "not additive" but "a fundamental entanglement," arguing that, "what is public is as ambient as it is salient." For Rickert, "ambience guides, calls, or suggests according to our ability to attune to our emergence in the situation." Weiser and Seely Brown (1995) suggested that it is how technologies "engage our attention" that gives rise to whether they will be encalming, as in, ambient. And as such, calm or ambient technology "engages both the center and the periphery of our attention," moving "back and forth between the two" where periphery refers to, "what we are attuned to without attending to explicitly." Weiser and Seely Brown (1995) argue that "by placing things in the periphery we are able to attune to many more things" and "by recentering something formerly in the periphery we take control of it" enabling awareness and control from the periphery.

3.1.2 Awareness

Discussing awareness in human-computer interaction and computer-supported collaborative work (CSCW) environments, Dourish and Bellotti (1992) claim that, "awareness information is always required to coordinate group activities, whatever the task domain." Dourish and Bellotti point to "an awareness of the activity of others" as providing "a context for your own activity" and through information sharing in a mode encompassing synchronous, asynchronous, and semi-synchronous, the "workspace becomes a persistent space in which collaborators can interact" in support of active or passive awareness. Dourish and Bellotti (1992) argue that, "awareness information provided and exploited passively through the shared workspace, allows users to move smoothly between close and loose collaboration and to assign and coordinate work collaboratively."

Weiser and Seely Brown's (1995) notion of calm technology, as in ambient, is described in terms of the three characteristics of "motion between center and periphery, peripheral reach, and locatedness." Windows within an office space are used as a design example "that enhances peripheral reach and locatedness." The inner office window is for Weiser and Seely Brown (1995) "a metaphor for what is most exciting about the Internet" and by extension, social media spaces, in terms of "the ability to locate and be located by people passing by on the information highway." Internet multicast video is used by Weiser and Seely Brown (1995) as an example of a "window of awareness" with continuous, two-way interaction enhancing presence and responsiveness with added attunement opportunities.

Erickson and Kellogg (2000) focus on visibility, awareness, and accountability in the development of socially translucent systems to support graceful "communication and collaboration among large groups of people over computer networks." Jacobs (1961) noted the importance of visibility on a city and community level. Where Jacobs speaks in terms of just enough control to decide what and to whom to reveal details about self, Erickson and Kellogg point to the importance of constraints enabling adjustments, where socially translucent is proposed rather than socially transparent in response to the "tension between privacy and visibility," thus the need for awareness and accountability. As such, Erickson and Kellogg point to the importance of technologies with windows rather than walls that, "mesh with human behavior" at "individual and collective levels." This type of translucence allows "users to 'see' one another, to make inferences about the activities of others, to imitate one another" in order for "new social forms" to be "invented, adopted, adapted, and propagated."

Dourish (2004) noted that in CSCW "visibility is generally addressed as the support for awareness in collaborative systems" and that "awareness is the informal, often tacit, understanding that collaborators have of each other's activities." Dourish (2004) adds that awareness technologies "provided group members with views or representations of each other and their work, to help them coordinate their actions smoothly." Bellotti & Sellen (1993) provide a design framework to address privacy issues in ubiquitous systems from a technical rather than a social or policy solution perspective, serving also to "elucidate the delicate balance that exists between awareness and privacy."

Through studies with audio-video communication Dourish, Adler, Bellotti, & Henderson (1996) argue that "the media-space world *is* the real world" and as such, "it is a place where real people, in real working relationships, engage in real interactions." Baude (2015) lends further support to the real world nature of online environments by claiming that the Internet is an innovation of space.

McCullough's (2013) description of ambient as "a continuum of awareness and an awareness of continuum" possibly gives ways to Seely Brown's (2014) description of designing a technology "that lets us look through the screen instead of at the screen" leveraging the "synergistic relationship between the center and the periphery" in order to "look through the information and on to the world" and the larger context.

3.1.3 Attention

Contributing to the notion of the attention economy, Simon (1971) articulated the scarcity of attention in relation to information, stating that "in an information-rich world, the wealth of information means a dearth of something else: a scarcity of whatever it is that information consumes." For Simon, information "consumes the attention of its recipients" and as such, "a wealth of information creates a poverty of attention." However, Weiser and Seely Brown (1995) point to the paradox of how what appears to be information overload can be overcome in that "the way to become attuned to more information is to attend to it less." As such, peripheral awareness supports "an increased sense of locatedness" making way for social interactions and human empowerment (Weiser & Brown, 1995).

Bellotti, Back, Edwards, Grinter, Henderson, & Lopes (2002) address interaction issues in 'sensing' systems from a human-human design perspective by focusing on communication. Posing five questions, Belloti et al. (2002) present design challenges related to smart/sensing systems, one of which focuses on attention. McCullough (2013) notes that Seely Brown (2014) "emphasized the attentional principle of 'periphery'" and for both Weiser and Seely Brown (1995) "periphery was everything you were aware of that didn't consume your attention, and that could be brought to the center of focus if necessary." McCullough (2013) notes the importance of "attention to surrounding" and that it is a "fundamental theme in urbanism." Lynch (1960), describing the moving elements of the city, referring in particular to people and their activities, points to the importance of *legibility,* as in, the clarity, safety, and ease with which the city can be navigated. Lynch describes the physical form of cities in terms of five elements – paths, edges, districts, nodes, and landmarks, noting that this contributes to heightening attention and enriching experience.

3.2 Urbanizing Technology and the Transitioning From Cities to Smart Cities

The works of many can be seen to form the essence of the people dimension of smart cities assisting in the transitioning from cities to smart cities.

3.2.1 Cities and Everyday Life

Jacobs (1961), concerned with "how cities work in real life" addressed the ordinary and everyday "to promote social and economic vitality." Also concerned with everyday life, De Certeau (1984), discussing spatial practices in "walking in the city", describes the city as "a place of transformations and appropriations" that is "the object of various kinds of interference but also a subject that is constantly enriched by new attributes." It is instructive to note that discussion of urban form by Lynch (1989) in terms of *settlement form* or the physical environment is described as "the spatial arrangement of persons doing things." Lynch adds to this, "the resulting spatial flows of persons, goods, and information and the physical features which modify space in some way significant to those actions, including enclosures, surfaces, channels, ambiences, and objects." Whyte (1988) spent hours walking around New York City during the 1970s and 80s rediscovering public spaces and the city at the street level and observing their use by people. Whyte credits the proselytizing work of architect Gehl (1968) with contributing dramatically to the pedestrianizing of the city center in many cities around the world.

3.2.2 Smart Cities and Urbanizing Technology

In 2008, Hollands explored the 'real smart city' in terms of, "intelligent, progressive or entrepreneurial" and more recently (2016) points to the diversity of ideas, debates, and understandings pertaining to the smart cities concept. Hollands (2016) questions what he sees as the trend of cities increasingly "becoming a backdrop to corporate advertising and the privatisation of public spaces." Hollands points to Harvey's (1989) notion of a shift in city governance from managerial welfare to urban entrepreneurialism where cities capitalize on the smart city movement. In terms of alternatives, Hollands, drawing on the work of Hill (Ampatzidou, 2013) and de Waal (2013), points to the importance of "people and citizens" and to "social learning and social cooperation." Hollands (2016) provides alternative examples of community projects involving people and social media, highlighting the "right to use the technology" and the "right to shape the city using human initiative and technology for social purposes," As such, the notion of 'urbanizing' comes into play as well as the concern with the people and learning dimensions of smart cities (Nam & Pardo, 2011).

Sassen (2012) articulates the urbanizing concept in relation to technology and the need for smart city technologies to be able to "work within a particular urban context." An example of urbanizing a new addition to the city, albeit extreme, was enacted and later documented by Petit (2002) through a high-wire walk between the Twin Towers in New York City. Controversial from conception, when the Twin Tower structures were finally completed, owners had difficulty attracting people to the new space. However, Philippe Petit was fascinated with the structures from the early stages of their development. After considerable planning and preparation, Petit emerged early one morning to perform aerial artistry in a high-wire walk between the two structures, at the 1,350-foot level for 45 minutes. Thousands of people on their way to work took notice of the spectacle, with the Mayor of the city among the viewers. Arrested for this illegal and arresting act of creativity, Petit was later released and instead, was assigned community duty to perform for the children in Central Park. Among the outcomes from this event that captured the attention and imagination of people in the city was the effect of humanizing the structures, as in, urbanizing and warming people to this new space encompassing many types of technology including that of verticality.

Issues associated with smart cities and the urbanizing of cities, include, but are not limited to, privacy, surveillance, visibility, and translucence.

3.2.2.1 Privacy and Surveillance

Greenfield (2013) is critical of smart city initiatives and solutions that place an emphasis on technology over people, contributing a space of controversy to the smart cities movement. Townsend (2014) presents utopian and dystopian perspectives on smart cities, identifying three key issues of concern – the buggyness of software driven systems; the brittleness of systems that may not be highly adaptive, responsive, or resilient; and being bugged by a surveillance society. As if in anticipation of Townsend's third concern, Mann (2013) proposes the perspective of sousveillance enacted by people in cities with the increasing presence of mobile/wearable cameras/recording devices such as smartphones. Jacobs (1961) noted that, "people's love of watching activity and other people is constantly evident in cities everywhere." Jacobs goes on to point out the critical role of 'watching' in the city and the importance of densification and diversity to support social and economic vitality in the city. Jacobs makes the connection between city surveillance and city safety where city design supports people to keep an eye on spaces in their neighborhoods as part of intense daily activities and use. Jacobs notes that "privacy is precious in cities" and that sharing much of nothing does not work but being in control of what is shared and of how much, matters.

Addressing issues of brittleness, Sassen (2012) argues for the urbanizing of technology if smart cities are to be successful and overcome the challenge of closed systems obsolescence. As a solution, Sassen proposes that open source be extended and applied not just to technologies but also to cities, as in, open source urbanism. Townsend (2014) details a range of open source efforts in terms of the open-source metropolis. For Sassen, open source urbanism accommodates the software of people's practices. Sassen questions whether the very complexity of urban spaces when combined with the software of people's practices may leverage what is needed to overcome the buggyness and brittleness of smart cities. The incompleteness of cities is emphasized by Sassen (2012) and it may be that as the urban is continually in-the-making, this buggyness can be understood as a space and opportunity for creativity, intervention, and collaboration in making cities smarter.

Combining the terms urban and capability, Sassen (2013) seeks to "capture an elusive mix of space, people, and particular activities" as constituting urban capability. For Sassen, this social and material physics of the city gives way to a kind of speech, enabling the city to talk back. Supporting the argument for urbanizing technologies is the concern identified by Sassen with three forces contributing to deurbanization – inequality, privatizing urban spaces, and surveillance systems. It may be that Mann's notion of sousveillance as undersight (2013) is a way of urbanizing technologies of watching in the city. Mann & Ferenbok (2013) point to the use of wearable and mobile technologies as enabling "unprecedented 'on the ground' watching of everyday life" to provide undersight and the potential for balancing the oversight of surveillance systems in the city.

3.2.2.2 Visibility and Translucence

Gehl (2010) notes the importance of translucence, as in, "being able to see through windows" as an enhancer for people in the city, both from the inside and outside of buildings. This is reminiscent of Weiser & Seely Brown's window metaphor for technologies that enable visibility and a seeing through to the information and the world, and of the translucence work of Erickson and Kellogg (2000).

Gehl is concerned with the livability of cities and with "human quality in the public realm" from a humanistic planning perspective, calling for "lively, safe, sustainable, and healthy" cities (2010) and highlighting concern for the human dimension. For Gehl, designing cities for people must take into consideration two fundamentals – human mobility and human senses as the "basis for activities, behavior and communication in city spaces." Whyte (1988) placed an emphasis on people, in designing urban environments, informing contemporary urban initiatives around placemaking in the context of Project for Public Spaces.

Gehl claims "there is much more to walking than walking" noting that "it is also – and most particularly about – the city as meeting place," As such, enabling "direct contact between people and the surrounding community" and "experiences and information," walking is fundamentally "a special form of communion between people who share public space as a platform and framework." Gehl makes reference to activities associated with walking in the city in terms of their versatility and complexity, "with much overlapping and frequent shifts" in the type of walking along with unpredictability and unplanned, spontaneous actions." Oldenburg (1999) makes the case for the importance of informal public life and meeting places. Oldenburg's (2001) third place or space as "a setting beyond home and work in which people relax in good company" is needed "to construct the infrastructures of human relationships." Memarovic, Fels, Ancieto, Calderon, Gobbo, & Carroll (2014) provide a rethinking and extending of third places in the context of ICTs with implications for visibility and presence awareness.

Sassen (2012) challenges the development of smart cities such as Masdar City in Abu Dhabi, United Arab Emirates as costly and difficult to replicate examples, functioning as a kind of lived-in laboratory. The concept of arcology advanced by Solari (Solari et al., 2012) is a combining of architecture and ecology and Masdar City is said to be inspired by arcology principles (Dellesky, 2014). Mone (2015) claims that new smart cities are beginning to emerge, drawing on the combined efforts of "academics, civic leaders, businesses, and individual citizens working together to create urban information systems." With sensor embedded technology, Mone (2015) refers to gadgets "talking to the city itself" yet, emphasizes the importance of people in this ecosystem and the endless possibilities of open data. Cohen (2015) identifies multiple generations of smart cities as: 1.0 where technology is driven by providers; 2.0 as city-driven, technology enabled; and 3.0 as involving citizen co-creation with the city.

3.3 Ambient Urbanizing

Ambient urbanizing is advanced in this chapter as an approach to theorizing the urban on the one hand and as a type of methodology on the other, contributing to a larger area of emerging cities methodologies (UCL, 2015). The combining of resources, skills, and disciplines opens the way for theorizing around ambient urbanizing in this chapter. As technologies become more aware and are being pervasively and ambiently used by people and cities, the potential exists for enhanced awareness.

3.3.1 Ambient Public Displays

Cuff, Hansen, & Kang (2008) pointed to the possibilities for pervasive computing enabled by cell phones as "passive sensors that can silently collect, exchange, and process information all day long." Gehl noted the importance of active facades that encourage people to slow down or stop, noting that people were seen to interact more with their cell phones. Memarovic, Langheinrich, & Alt (2012) offer an interacting places framework (IPF) for promoting community interaction and place awareness (CIPA) using public displays that incorporate ubiquitous wireless communication and sensing. Memarovic et al. (2012) explore the challenges and opportunities of this type of open networked pervasive display, highlighting the four elements of: content providers, content viewers, interacting places communication channels, and an awareness diffusion layer. Memarovic et al. (2012) make reference to implicit awareness diffusion "through the effect of Legitimate Peripheral Participation (Lave & Wenger, 1991) where people learn about a place and its community by observing interests of others." Synthesis of research in this area (Memarovic, 2015) contributes to an understanding of challenges going forward.

3.3.2 Ambient Sensing and Spectacle

Ambient urban visualization has been discussed in different contexts, from participatory sensing of environmental data in the city (Kuznetsov, Davis, Paulos, Gross, & Cheung, 2011) to the legal, and the privacy implications of sensing going public and "making the invisible visible" (Cuff et al., 2008). Kuznetsov et al. (2011) provide an example of urbanizing the ambient in the form of colored balloons containing sensors reflecting environmental quality by color as the balloons are moved around the city performing as sensors in the sky. Kuznetsov et al. (2011) identify this type of visualization as spectacle computing, enabling participatory sensing, focused on air quality in the city, activating attention and awareness.

Focusing on everyday practices, Stengers (2010) points to their dynamic and performative nature where people "adapt, improvise, and experiment." Weiser (1994) highlighted Jeremijenko's 'dangling string' display as a new direction in invisible or ubiquitous computing, providing an early example visualizing ethernet packets physically and in an ambient way.

Lynch (1996) noted that artificial light "now offers largely unexploited resources of color, form, and sequential change" adding that "prevailing microclimates, by small areas, and the intensity, character, and rhythm of city sound affect all observers." Artificial light is also an important consideration in relation to urban display screens from large jumbrotron to small handheld devices. Microclimates will also be important in terms of spaces enabled by ambient screen displays.

As theorized in this chapter, ambient urbanizing calls for increased thinking and discussion about awareness and aware technologies in the creation of smarter cities. Utilizing a people-technologies-cities interactive dynamic, this work contends that increasing awareness and understanding about aware-enabled technologies is critical since such technologies are intricately interwoven into and throughout everyday life (IFTF, 2015). As such, aware people when combined with aware-enabled technologies, is theorized to contribute to the enhancing of human potential and the enriching of urban experiences and spaces.

In this chapter, the ambient urbanizing concept is operationalized using the activities of noticing in the city and the sharing of ideas for the city as proxies for the constructs of awareness, ambience, and smartness. What people do with an early-stage urban-focused social media space like AboutTheCity-i2 is designed to contribute to discussions, understandings, and potentials for ambient urbanizing. This exploration of ambient urbanizing gives rise to three research questions identified in section 3.4.

3.4 Research Questions

Q1: Why is urbanizing the ambient important in 21st century cities?
Q2: How does urbanizing the ambient occur in contemporary cities?
Q3: What approaches to urbanizing the ambient serve to enrich urban experiences and spaces?

4. METHODOLOGY

The research design for this work includes an exploratory case study approach and multiple methods of quantitative and qualitative data collection and analysis. Webspace use, interview, and open-ended survey form the basis for qualitative data collection, analyzed using content analysis. Survey (closed-ended) and use experience activity data constitute the quantitative collection portion.

This study spans a 7-month timeframe from mid 2015 into 2016, across multiple cities (Langford, Ottawa, Toronto, Victoria, and Jyväskylä) of small to medium to large sized populations, mostly in Canada but also extending to Finland in northern Europe. Interest and involvement was sought from individuals 18 years of age or older. In parallel with this study and beginning 5 months earlier, anecdotal evidence was gathered over a 1-year period through informal individual and group discussions with people across the city. The study methodology is described in terms of the process, sources of evidence, and the data analysis.

4.1 Process

People across six sectors of the city were invited to participate in the study (e.g., city officials, local business, educators, community members, students, and visitors to the city) and given a link to the city-focused web platform for AboutTheCity-i2. People who registered to participate in the study were then given access to three spaces: a Noticing page for contributing content; an Ideas page for contributing content; and TheCity page where contributed content is dynamically displayed. Participants were then invited to talk about smartness in their city in an interview. In this study, i-2 refers to iteration 2, featuring a mobile platform with direct accessibility, by-passing the need to download or install an application. Figure 1 presents the user interface for the AboutTheCity-i2 platform in two screenshots.

The screenshot on the left in Figure 1 provides a space for participants to contribute information about noticing in the city in the form of text, links that may connect to other sites and multi-media, and tags. Similarly, a space is available for generating and contributing ideas about the city. Contributed content is immediately viewable, with one click, by other participants as shown in the screenshot on the right in Figure 1. At a glance, participant responses pertaining to noticing and ideas are viewable and browsable, along with the date of the contribution; the city name; the anonymized ID of the contributor (e.g., AtC00); why what is noticed matters; what the idea is about; and a description of the idea.

Figure 1. AboutTheCity-i2: User interface screenshots

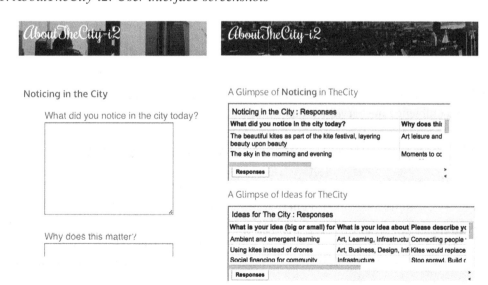

In concept, this platform, when used with a mobile smartphone for example, is intended to foster noticing, thinking, and discussion about the city. In design, this platform is minimalist, intentionally under-designed, and is intended to foster and enable attention to, awareness of, and attunement with the city through sharing moments of noticing and idea generation about the city. As a user interface this platform is limited in capability, enabling the capture and display of data through the use of embedded Google forms. Regarding use, this space offers a combining of content and context as a quick, easy-to-use, in-the-moment tool to possibly engage, give pause for thought, and inspire.

Respondents were also given the option to complete an online survey about their use experience with AboutTheCity-i2 and about smartness in their city.

4.2 Sources of Evidence

Sources of evidence for this chapter consist of data collected through activity tracking of the About-TheCity-i2 webspace including artifacts generated in the form of content, links, and tags contributed by respondents. Data were collected through in-depth interviews with participants using a semi-structured interview protocol. An online survey instrument with open and closed-ended questions provided an additional source of quantitative and qualitative data.

Data were collected from informal discussions with individuals and groups across the city constituting anecdotal evidence. Sharp (2014) argues for the necessity of accessing "the diversity and ambiguity of human experience" in order to "learn what matters."

4.3 Data Analysis

Data analysis consisted of content analysis for qualitative data relying on a combination of techniques for the development of terms that on the one hand, emerge from the data (inductive) and on the other hand are advanced by the research literature (deductive). Coding terms contribute to the generation of a coding glossary in support of the coding process. Overall, data were analyzed for an n=16 spanning all age ranges from 20s to 70s including 45% female and 55% male.

5. FINDINGS

Key findings presented in this section are organized around the three research questions, enabling insight into what is occurring at the urban level when people become more aware, attentive, and attuned to smartness and ambience in everyday urban spaces.

5.1 Importance of Urbanizing the Ambient in 21st Century Cities

In exploring the importance of urbanizing the ambient in 21st century cities, a highly active community member in Toronto, admitted to being caught off guard by the "smart cities thing," commenting that the "predictive aspect of technology has got me on edge a little bit." While smart technologies were described as "extraordinarily convenient", concern with trust was expressed and the "ethical implications of letting technology make decisions for us." The individual added, "that conversation I don't think has been had thoroughly yet and I can't wait until it is", while also expressing shock at "how quickly this concept of self driving cars has come about and this issue of drones."

Individuals from business, the local community, and postsecondary institutions in Greater Victoria tended to associate the smart cities concept with technology, while smartness and aware technologies were associated with the notion of the automaton, as in, robotics. A community member observed that aware technologies provide affordances, "helping us to understand our communities differently, not better, but differently."

The smartness term contributes to concerns with the need for balance associated with technologies and how important it is to "rely upon our senses" as in, "our innate sense of the way in which we engage with aspects of the city." For example, it was suggested that awareness pertains to "everyday signs and signals" such as obvious signs of the usage of paths and not just "the current day smart signs." As such, awareness was seen as important for keeping in touch with "a part of ourselves" and "a part of that connection that makes the dynamic city come alive."

Assessment of AboutTheCity-i2 and its potential for urbanizing aware spaces emerged as neutral. However, AboutTheCity-i2 was assessed as having possibilities for attuning to urban spaces and for heightening urban sensibilities.

5.2 Occurrences of Ambient Urbanizing in 21ˢᵗ Century Cities

Ambient urbanizing emerged as occurring in contemporary cities in a range of ways through a variety of mechanisms. Referring to city data displays tracking bike path usage, one educator commented that, relying solely on the quantification of activities in the city with numbers tends to scare people. Instead, it was suggested that new awarenesses associated with "seeing differently" be leveraged so as to educate and "to begin to enrich or enhance or permit our communities to evolve in ways they need to." A business person commented on the additional potential of the urban data display in terms of "how can we improve" and "where are you from?" commenting that, "I think it would be interesting to have that interactivity." A community leader described the use of infrared cameras by the city business association, capturing street data that "records the blobs" as people move around specific parts of the city.

A community member highlighted the placing of large jumbotron screens outside of sports events in Toronto, as a city experiment, extending the event inside that drew 20,000 people to include an additional 10,000 people outside.

Looking for "an opportunity maybe for making the city a little smarter" an engineering student described how "I hope to change people's minds so they follow a more green way." In developing a course project, the student commented that, "it would be nice if the city itself could be more interactive" and "not only the profit making companies."

Mobility was discussed in terms of multi-modal and multi-directional uses of transport and infrastructure in a large city like Toronto by a community member who commented that "you're not moving one way, you are walking, I'll ride my bike somewhere, I'll jump on a streetcar, the subway." The PATH series of passages and tunnels underneath the city of Toronto was described as an almost game-like design so that "the city is allowing you to play in it." A Placemaker described a library box for the free exchange of books and how the idea served to engage in diverse and unexpected ways, involving people, urban spaces, technologies (e.g., GPS, Google maps, timelapse video, social media), things in the form of books, and unexpected connection and sharing.

Using online technologies for a City Hall meeting was beneficial in the view of a Victoria City Councilor in being able to "definitely create discussion and connections" and "extend conversations on issues and ideas." Described as a back channel by an educator, the idea of including a Twitter feed behind a conference speaker where you may have 500 people in attendance is being enriched by up to any number of additional people online.

In the context of placemaking and pop up events, a community leader commented that, "we like to do those to demonstrate how a space can change" using the example of a temporary Sunday afternoon street closure to traffic to create a pedestrian space.

A postsecondary educator pointed to "urban spaces embedded within suburban communities" as "gathering and sharing places" accommodating "unhurried and quiet" interactions. Using the example of an elaborate fountain that the city could "orchestrate with color and sound" the educator described the experience of noticing "the sounds of the fountain as I walk to catch the bus" and provided a webpage link with an image. The fountain was highlighted because this "provides a touchstone for people in the area" as a point of interaction.

Table 1 provides an overview of public spaces amenable to the making of smarter cities through ambient urbanizing initiatives across multiple cities and urban voices.

Another factor enabling ambient urbanizing, in the words of a postsecondary educator, is "recognizing that we can turn anything into anything, so what do you want?"

5.3 Approaches to Ambient Urbanizing: Enriching Urban Experiences and Spaces

Approaches to fostering discussion and thinking about ambient urbanizing are identified in Table 2, along with emergent observations about each. People were encouraged to focus on five elements that potentially serve to enrich urban experiences and spaces, as in: what they notice about the city and why this matters; ideas they have for the city; how they feel the pulse of the city, what contributes to the vibrancy of the city, and how they sense the city.

Regarding noticing, for one community member it is the architecture, for another it is the people and their faces and whether they are friendly or happy or welcoming, and for others it is the state of the city itself in terms of "how clean it is." For one educator it is the urban events (e.g., markets) and for another

Table 1. Summary of public spaces for making cities smarter through ambient urbanizing

	Business	**Community**	**Educators**	**Gov'mt**	**Students**	**Visitors**
Data displays	✓	✓	✓	✓	✓	✓
Entertainment screens	✓	✓	✓	✓	✓	✓
Green urban apps	✓	✓	✓	✓	✓	✓
Mobility/Things/Tech	✓	✓	✓	✓	✓	✓
Online/Conf/Twitter	✓	✓	✓	✓	✓	✓
Pedestrian events	✓	✓	✓	✓	✓	✓
Third places (fountain)	✓	✓	✓	✓	✓	✓

Table 2. Summary of approaches to ambient urbanizing in smart cities

	Emergent Observations
Noticing	Architecture, Events (markets), Objects/spaces (fountain, screens), People, State of things
Ideas	Infrastructure, Social financing for community centres, Mobile cloud app
Pulse	Buildings, Mobility/movement, Night life, People, Students, Businesses
Sensing	Connectivity, Lost, Relaxed, Safe, Scared, Senses
Vibrancy	Connections, Dynamic, Mixed use, Multi-purpose, People

it is the example of a fountain with sound and color that becomes an enriching space, a focal point where people take notice, stop, look at each other, talk, interact, and slow down.

In terms of ideas, infrastructure was a key focus with one community leader pointing to social financing for community centers in new communities. One educator opts not to share ideas because of ownership concerns and another advances a "mobile cloud app to capture and share insights for instant awareness" adaptable for "business, design, health, infrastructure, learning, safety, sport, tourism."

The pulse of the city "is the face of the buildings" and "the actual street that you are walking on" stated one community member who added that "you can see the life." For an educator, the pulse of the city is found in "the way people walk and talk and engage each other" and in – "the coffee shops, the businesses – the people and daily goings on." A city councilor added that "people interacting with each other and with their surroundings, I think that's when you get the pulse" and "when people actually say hi to each other because its creating activity."

Sensing in the city is described by one educator in terms of enabling a getting in touch with a range of senses through, "a second of connectivity" as in, "it causes people to go, did you hear that." A Victoria community Placemaker referred to the example of the Bastion Square Parkade Stairwell sensors project (Chamberlain, 2015) by a local technology company, in partnership with the city, other technology companies, local business, artists, and community events. Designed by Monkey C Interactive, this public artwork is described as being "about people interacting with each other" to "compose and create." A local city councilor (Chamberlain, 2015), commented that such artworks are "designed to ensure civic parkades are safe and welcoming."

An for vibrancy, an educator commented that, "I've always found an urban setting is dynamic, the energy is just electric." A city councilor observed that, "vibrancy is created by people and connections between people and the way that comes to life – whether through arts and culture, sitting and having a coffee discussing the city and things you are passionate about." Noting the traditional separation between work and play in the city, one participant suggested that "successful cities are everything" as in, multi-purpose spaces. As such, cities are enriched by the creation of mixed-use spaces and "it's the people" that contribute to the vibrancy and enrichment of the city.

6. DISCUSSION

Discussion about smartness, aware technologies, and smart cities revealed a willingness to engage with the topic and to share ideas and information. However, a desire to learn and be more involved and part of the conversation, debate, and movement emerged. While awareness of smart city initiatives emerged, the extent and depth was found to be limited, along with mechanisms for becoming more actively involved.

Public spaces identified and summarized in Table 1 for making cities smarter through ambient urbanizing reveal a meshing and interweaving of people, technologies, and urban spaces. The value of noticing in the city was recognized as assisting people to become more aware and to see how things change, evolve, and grow. Contributing insight into why people matter so much in smart cities, emergent observations in Table 2 reveal that people figure into all approaches used in this study for exploring ambient urbanizing. For example, through discussions on noticing in the city, sharing ideas for the city, feeling the pulse of the city, sensing the city, and the vibrancy of the city, a circling around and interweaving of the awareness, attention, and attunement constructs emerged.

Responses are city specific and focused on the individual or group's local city. However, it is worth noting that without exception, urban discussions and thinking about smart cities and aware technologies extended to experiences in other larger cities (e.g., Barcelona, Detroit, Helsinki, London (UK), Los Angeles, Montreal, Moscow, New York, Oulu, Paris, Portland (OR), San Francisco, Seattle, Sydney, Thailand, Vancouver, and Vietnam). This finding contributes further to contemporary urban theorizing regarding where the urban begins and ends (Brenner & Schmid, 2015).

6.1 Role and Potential of Ambient Urbanizing

Urbanizing the ambient emerges in this chapter as important in 21st century cities for at least three reasons, in that: greater awareness is generated about aware technologies; greater awareness is developed about the smart city concept; and an urban discourse including spaces for action are generated and generative. Findings in this study enable the formulation of a proposed conceptual ambient urbanizing framework for enriching spaces, things, and designs in smart cities, as illustrated in Figure 2.

Through the interactive dynamic of people – technologies – cities, a city-focused social media space is used to explore awareness – ambiance – smartness. The ambient urbanizing framework is intended to activate awareness through noticing and sharing in the city as enrichment mechanisms for fostering smarter designs, spaces, and things. As such, this proposed framework is intended to mitigate, provide alternative perspectives, and possibly obviate concerns raised by Greenfield (2013) and others (Townsend, 2014) regarding utopian and dystopian perspectives on smart cities.

Figure 2. Ambient urbanizing framework for enriching spaces, things, and designs in smart cities

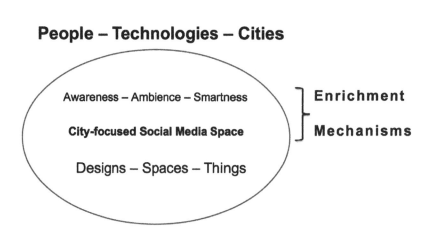

6.2 Summary

As theorized and then explored in this chapter, the combining of aware people with aware-enabled technologies opens spaces and possibilities for ambient urbanizing and the potential for contributing to the enhancing of human potential and the enriching of urban experiences and spaces. Through learning about and coming to understand ambient urbanizing, the words of Weiser & Seely Brown (1995) on learning to design calm technologies, as in ambient, echo forth, "we will enrich our opportunities for being with other people" making way for ambient technologies "to play a central role in a more humanly empowered twenty-first century."

7. IMPLICATIONS FOR PRACTICE AND RESEARCH

Based on study findings, this chapter makes recommendations for ambient urbanizing going forward, in terms of both practice and research.

7.1 Practical Recommendations

- **Ambient Urbanizing Hackathons:** Building on local initiatives (Chamberlain, 2015), creatively explore the potential and enriching nature of ambient urbanizing.
- **Exploration, Testing, Learning, and Demonstrations:** Leverage social media and other aware technologies as city-focused noticing and awareness spaces (e.g., AboutTheCity-i2, CitizenLab, Jaxber, PlaceSpeak) in real world urban environments to engage in ambient urbanizing, generating opportunities for all while identifying emerging trends.

7.2 Research Recommendations

- **Ambient Urbanizing Framework:** The proposed ambient urbanizing framework is intended for smart city developers, planners, community members, and researchers alike. The framework will benefit from further use, testing and development, with the potential to open future research and practice opportunities in a number of domains including smart cities, urban design, ambient computing, awareness research, and the Internet of Things (IoT).
- **Ambient Urbanizing Research:** This work suggests that while the use of aware-enabled, as in, ambient technologies is well advanced, the extent and sufficiency of ambient urbanizing may be lagging, opening an area for further research.
- **Theory Development:** Insights emerging in this chapter about ambient urbanizing provide opportunities for further research and theory development.

8. CHALLENGES AND MITIGATIONS

Discussing abstract concepts such as ambient, smartness, aware technologies, and urbanizing provided challenges for many which were mitigated by interactive discussion about their cities and the presence and enriching potential of interacting with technology in public spaces. Challenges of this exploratory study pertaining to small sample size and the number, size, and geographic locations of cities are mitigated by the in-depth interviews yielding rich data along with the potential to extend this research to other locations, cities of greater scale (e.g., megacities), and urban contexts.

9. CONCLUSION

This chapter assists in coming to understand the ambient and ambient urbanizing concepts; the potential of ambient urbanizing as an enrichment mechanism for designs, spaces, and things in the context of smart cities; and why people matter in the people – cities – technologies dynamic. An ambient urbanizing framework is advanced as a way of engaging people in meaningful discussions about the smart cities phenomena. Increased awareness of the city is generated through involvement in city-focused social media spaces and other aware technologies for noticing and sharing about the city while contributing insight into enrichment mechanisms for designs, spaces, and things in urban environments.

This chapter makes several contributions, including: a) conceptualization of ambient urbanizing for the 21st century; b) further development of the research and practice literature for smart cities, awareness, and the ambient; and c) creation of a discourse space for fostering enrichment mechanisms for ambient urbanizing of designs, spaces, and things in smart cities. The key take away from this chapter pertains to how development and use of ambient urbanizing provides a way of articulating why people matter so much to the enrichment of urban designs, spaces, and things in technology-rich, 21st century smart cities. It is expected that his chapter will be of interest to a wide range of city-focused practitioners and researchers and anyone concerned with liveable, resilient, sustainable, and humanly empowered cities.

REFERENCES

Ampatzidou, C. (2013). *Smart cities vs smart citizens: PBL expert meeting on smart cities with Dan Hill. The Mobile City*. Rotterdam: The New Institute. Retrieved 20 March 2016 from http://themobilecity. nl/2013/11/01/smart-cities-vs-smart-citizens/

Angus, A., Lane, G., & Roussos, G. (2014). Public goods: Using pervasive computing to inspire grassroots activism. *IEEE Pervasive Computing / IEEE Computer Society [and] IEEE Communications Society, 13*(2), 44–51. doi:10.1109/MPRV.2014.33

Beaude, B. (2015). Internet: A unique space of coexistence. In EPFLx: SpaceX Exploring Humans' Space: An Introduction to Geographicity. Massive Open Online Course (MOOC), edX, Fall.

Bellotti, V., Back, M., Edwards, W. K., Grinter, R. E., Henderson, A., & Lopes, C. (2002). Making sense of sensing systems: Five questions for designers and researchers. CHI '02. *Proceedings of the SIGCHI Conference on Human Factors in Computing Systems*. New York, NY: ACM. doi:10.1145/503376.503450

Bellotti, V., & Sellen, A. (1993). Design for privacy in ubiquitous computing environments. In G. de Michelis, C. Simone, & K. Schmidt (Eds.), *Proceedings of the Third European Conference on Computer-Supported Cooperative Work*. doi:10.1007/978-94-011-2094-4_6

Brandt, J. (2015). Oblivious in the UK? Nearly 100 percent do not notice smart cities growing around them. *SmartGridNews*. Retrieved 8 September 2015 from http://bit.ly/1O066La

Brenner, N., & Schmid, C. (2015). Towards a new epistemology of the urban? *City*, *19*(2-3), 151–182. doi:10.1080/13604813.2015.1014712

Chamberlain, A. (2015). Bastion Square parkade stairwell sensors will trigger songs, lights. *Times Colonist*. Retrieved 18 March 2016 from http://www.timescolonist.com/news/local/bastion-square-parkade-stairwell-sensors-will-trigger-songs-lights-1.2048706

Charoubi, H., Nam, T., Walker, S., Gil-Garcia, J. R., Mellouli, S., Nahon, K., & Scholl, H. J. et al. (2012). Understanding smart cities: An integrative framework. In *Proceedings of the 45th Hawaii International Conference on System Sciences* (pp. 2289-2297). Washington, DC: IEEE Computer Society Press.

Cohen, B. (2014). *The smartest cities in the world 2015: Methodology*. FastCo-Exist.com. Retrieved 14 March 2016 from http://www.fastcoexist.com/3038818/the-smartest-cities-in-the-world-2015-methodology

Cohen, B. (2015). The three generations of smart cities: Inside the development of the technology-driven city. *FastCompany CoExist*. Retrieved 25 August 2015 from http://www.fastcoexist.com/3047795/the-3-generations-of-smart-cities

Craglia, M., & Granell, C. (Eds.). (2014). *Citizen science and smart cities*. European Commission, Joint Research Center, Institute for Environment and Sustainability, JRB Technical Reports, Report of Summit, Ispra. Retrieved 15 March 2016 from http://digitalearthlab.jrc.ec.europa.eu/Citizen_Science_and_Smart_Cities_Full_Report.pdf

Cuff, D., Hansen, M., & Kang, J. (2008). Urban sensing: Out of the woods. *Communications of the ACM*, *51*(3), 24–33. doi:10.1145/1325555.1325562

De Certeau, M. (1984). *The practice of everyday life*. Berkeley, CA: University of California Press.

De Waal, M. (2013). *The city as interface: How new media are changing the city*. Rotterdam: NAI Uitgevers/Publishers Stichting.

Dellesky, C. (2014). *The futuristic, sustainable cities inspired by arcology*. Washington, DC: TheCityFix, World Resources Institute. Retrieved 14 July 2015 from http://thecityfix.com/blog/friday-fun-futuristic-sustainable-cities-arcology-arconsanti-paolo-soleri-masdar-endless-harvest-boston-carrie-dellesky/

Dourish, P. (2004). *Where the action is: The foundations of embodied interaction*. Cambridge, MA: MIT Press.

Dourish, P., Adler, A., Bellotti, V., & Henderson, A. (1996). Your place or mine? Learning from long-term use of audio-video communication. *Computer Supported Cooperative Work*, *5*(1), 33–62. doi:10.1007/BF00141935

Dourish, P., & Bell, G. (2011). *Divining our digital future: Mess and mythology in ubiquitous computing*. Cambridge, MA: MIT Press. doi:10.7551/mitpress/9780262015554.001.0001

Dourish, P., & Bellotti, V. (1992). Awareness and coordination in a shared workspaces. In *Proceedings of the ACM Conference on Computer-Supported Cooperative Work*. ACM Press. doi:10.1145/143457.143468

Egyedi, T. M., & Mehos, D. C. (Eds.). (2012). *Inverse infrastructures: Disrupting networks from below*. Edward Elgar Pub. doi:10.4337/9781781952290

Erickson, T., & Kellogg, W. A. (2000). Social translucence: An approach to designing systems that support social processes. *ACM Transactions on Computer-Human Interaction*, *7*(1), 59–83. doi:10.1145/344949.345004

Gamble, R. (2014). *Survey says: General population lacks awareness on smart cities*. Meeting of the Minds, Urban Age Institute. Retrieved August 21, 2015 from http://cityminded.org/survey-says-general-population-lacks-awareness-smart-cities-11670

Gehl, J. (1968). *Pedestrians*. Copenhagen: Arkitekten.

Gehl, J. (1980). *Life between buildings: Using public spaces*. Washington, DC: Island Press.

Gehl, J. (2010). *Cities for people*. Washington, DC: Island Press.

Gil-Garcia, J. R., Pardo, T. A., & Nam, T. (Eds.). (2016). *Smarter as the new urban agenda: A comprehensive view of the 21st century city*. Springer. doi:10.1007/978-3-319-17620-8

Greenfield, A. (2013). *Against the smart city: The city is here for you to use*. Seattle, WA: Amazon Digital Services.

Harvey, D. (1989). From managerialism to entrepreneurialism: The transformation in urban governance in late capitalism. *Geografiska Annaler. Series B, Human Geography*, *71*(1), 3–17. doi:10.2307/490503

Hollands, R. G. (2008). Will the Real Smart City Please Stand Up?: Intelligent, progressive or entrepreneurial? *City: Analysis of Urban Trends, Culture, Theory, Policy Action*, *12*(3), 303–320.

Hollands, R. G. (2016). Beyond the corporate smart city?: Glimpses of other possibilities of smartness. In S. Marvin, A. Luque-Ayala, & C. McFarlane (Eds.), *Smart Urbanism: Utopian vision or false dawn?* (pp. 169–185). London, UK: Routledge.

IFTF. (2011). *A planet of civic laboratories: The future of cities, information, and inclusion*. Palo Alto, CA: Institute for the Future. Retrieved 20 June 2015 from http://www.iftf.org/our-work/global-landscape/human-settlement/the-future-of-cities-information-and-inclusion/

IFTF. (2015). *Automated world. Technology Horizons 2015*. Palo Alto, CA: Institute for the Future. Retrieved 21 August 2015 from http://www.iftf.org/iftf-you/programs-initiatives/technology-horizons/

Jacobs, J. (1961). *The death and life of great American cities*. New York, NY: Random House.

Johnson, L., Adams Becker, S., Cummins, S., Estrada, V., Freeman, A., & Hall, C. (2016). *NMC horizon report: 2016 higher education edition*. Austin, TX: The New Media Consortium.

Kuznetsov, S., Davis, G. N., Paulos, E., Gross, M. D., & Cheung, J. C. (2011). *Red balloon, green balloon, sensors in the sky. UbiComp '11*. Beijing, China: ACM.

Lave, J., & Wenger, E. (1991). *Situated learning – Legitimate peripheral participation*. New York, NY: Cambridge University Press. doi:10.1017/CBO9780511815355

Lynch, K. (1960). *The image of the city*. Cambridge, MA: MIT Press.

Lynch, K. (1989). *Good city form*. Cambridge, MA: MIT Press.

Lynch, K. (1996). *City sense and city design: Writings and projects of Kevin Lynch* (T. Banerjee & M. Southworth, Eds.). Cambridge, MA: MIT Press.

Mann, S. (2013). Veillance and reciprocal transparency: Surveillance versus sousveillance, AR glass, lifelogging, and wearable computing. *Proceedings of the IEEE International Symposium on Technology and Society (ISTAS2013)* (pp. 1-12).

Mann, S., & Ferenbok, J. (2013). New media and the power politics of sousveillance in a surveillance-dominated world. *Surveillance & Society*, *11*(1/2), 18–34.

Marvin, S., Luque-Ayala, A., & McFarlane, C. (Eds.), *Smart Urbanism: Utopian vision or false dawn?* (pp. 169–185). London, UK: Routledge.

McCullough, M. (2013). *Ambient commons: Attention in the age of embodied information*. Cambridge, MA: The MIT Press.

Memarovic, N. (2015). *Understanding future challenges for networked public display systems in community settings*. C&T'15, Limerick, Ireland. Retrieved 12 March 2016 from http://www.ifi.uzh.ch/zpac/people/memarovic/ct2015.pdf

Memarovic, N., Fels, S., Ancieto, J., Calderon, R., Gobbo, F., & Carroll, J. M. (2014). Rethinking third places: Contemporary design with technology. *The Journal of Community Informatics*, *10*(3). Retrieved from http://ci-journal.net/index.php/ciej/article/view/1048/1116

Memarovic, N., Langheinrich, M., & Alt, F. (2012). Interacting places – a framework for promoting community interaction and place awareness through public displays. *Pervasive Computing and Communications Workshops (PERCOM Workshops), 2012 IEEE International Conference*.

Mone, G. (2015). The new smart cities. *Communications of the ACM*, *58*(7), 20–21. doi:10.1145/2771297

Nam, T., & Pardo, T. A. (2011). Smart city as urban innovation: Focusing on management, policy, and context. In *Proceedings of the 5th International Conference on Theory and Practice of Electronic Governance (ICEGOV2011)* (pp. 185-194). New York, NY: Association for Computing Machinery (ACM).

Ojo, A., Dzhusupova, Z., & Curry, E. (2016). Exploring the nature of the smart cities research landscape. In J. R. Gil-Garcia, T. A. Pardo & T. Nam, T. (Eds.), Smarter as the new urban agenda: A comprehensive view of the 21st century city. Springer. doi:10.1007/978-3-319-17620-8_2

Oldenburg, R. (1999). *The great good place: Cafes, coffee shops, bars, bookstores, hair salons, and other hangouts at the heart of a community*. New York, NY: Marlowe and Company.

Oldenburg, R. (2001). *Celebrating the third place: Inspiring stories about the 'great good places' at the heart of our communities*. New York, NY: Marlowe and Company.

Petit, P. (2002). *To reach the clouds: My high wire walk between the Twin Towers*. New York, NY: Macmillan, North Point Press.

Rickert, T. (2013). *Ambient rhetoric: The attunements of rhetorical being*. Pittsburgh, PA: University of Pittsburgh Press.

Sasao, T., Konomi, S., Arikawa, M., & Fujita, H. (2015). *Context weaver: Awareness and feedback in networked mobile crowdsourcing tools. The International Journal of Computer and Telecommunications Networking*. doi:10.1016/j.comnet.2015.05.022

Sassen, S. (2012). *Urbanizing technology*. LSE Cities. Retrieved May 26, 2015, from https://lsecities.net/media/objects/articles/urbanising-technology/en-gb/

Sassen, S. (2013). Does the city have speech? *Public Culture, 25*(2), 209–221. doi:10.1215/08992363-2020557

Scholl, H. J. (2016). Foreword. In J. R. Gil-Garcia, T. A. Pardo, T. Nam, T. (Eds.), Smarter as the New Urban Agenda: A Comprehensive View of the 21st Century City. Springer.

Seely Brown, J. (2014). Calm tech, then and now: Re:form interviews John Seely Brown on the paradox of information overload and designing for the periphery. *Re:form*. Retrieved 10 March 2016 from http://www.johnseelybrown.com/calmtech.pdf

Sharp, C. (2014). *Calling time on 'anecdotal' evidence*. Alliance for Useful Evidence. Retrieved 18 January 2016 from http://www.alliance4usefulevidence.org/calling-time-on-anecdotal-evidence/

Simon, H. (1971). Designing organizations for an information-rich world. In M. Greenberger (Ed.), *Computers, communications, and the public interest* (pp. 37–72). Baltimore, MD: The Johns Hopkins Press.

Smith, S. (2015). The future of health + well-being: A presentation by Institute for the Future for the Department of Health and Care, Aarhus Municipality, Denmark. Palo Alto, CA: IFTF. Retrieved 1 March 2016 from https://www.aarhus.dk/~/media/eDoc/1/8/9/1891077-2850164-1-pdf.pdf

Soleri, P., Kim, Y., Anderson, C., Nordfors, A., Riley, S., & Tamura, T. (2012). *Lean linear city: Arterial arcology*. Mayer, AZ: Cosanti Press.

Strengers, Y. (2010). *Conceptualizing everyday practices: Composition, reproduction and change*. (Working Paper No. 6). Melbourne, Australia: Carbon Neutral Communities, Centre for Design, RMIT University and University of South Australia. Retrieved 17 August 2015 from http://mams.rmit.edu.au/6p1hikrdei2rz.pdf

Townsend, A. (2014). *Smart cities: Big data, civic hackers, and the quest for a new utopia*. New York, NY: W.W. Norton.

UCL. (2015). *Cities methodologies. London: UCL Urban Laboratory*. Retrieved 26 August 2015 from http://www.ucl.ac.uk/urbanlab/latest/events/cities-methodologies

UN. (2015). *Habitat III Issue Papers, 21 – Smart cities. United Nations Conference on Housing and Sustainable Urban Development*. New York, NY: UN-Habitat, UNDP, and ITU.

Weiser, M. (1994). *Creating the invisible interface: (invited talk)*. New York, NY: UIST '94 Proceedings of the 7th Annual ACM Symposium on User Interface Software and Technology.

Weiser, M., & Seely Brown, J. (1995). *Designing calm technology*. Palo Alto, CA: Xerox PARC. Retrieved 9 March 2016 from http://www.ubiq.com/weiser/calmtech/calmtech.htm

Whyte, W. H. (1988). *City: Rediscovering the center*. New York, NY: Doubleday.

Williams, A., Robles, E., & Dourish, P. (2009). Urbane-ing the city: Examining and refining the assumptions behind urban informatics. In M. Foth (Ed.), *Handbook of research on urban informatics: The practice and promise of the real-time city* (pp. 1–20). Hershey, PA: Information Science Reference; doi:10.4018/978-1-60566-152-0.ch001

KEY TERMS AND DEFINITIONS

Ambient: The increasing presence of aware-technologies in and around human activity affecting the nature and experience of information, attention, attunement, and awareness.

Ambient Urbanizing: Ambient urbanizing refers to how people adapt and leverage aware technologies to enhance and enrich interactions, awareness, experiences, and communications in the city.

Attention: Attention in an ambient context refers to a more fluid, porous, dynamic space involving peripheries where focus can shift awareness of something in the periphery to the foreground as needed.

Awareness: The concept or quality of being aware as it applies to people on the one hand and to technologies on the other. Noticing, for example, can be used by people as a way of becoming more aware of their environments, of others, and themselves. Social media technologies such as Facebook display presence-awareness by showing which of your friends are currently active in the space.

Engagement: Engagement refers to informed involvement in an activity, enabling meaningful and thoughtful contribution(s).

Practice: Practice refers to the methods and approaches used to accomplish a particular activity. In an ambient urbanizing context, the potential exists for ad hoc, emergent, and adaptive solutions, possibly contributing to ambient practices.

Smart Cities: Smart cities are urban areas characterized by aware people who are engaged, in combination with and aided by the use of, awareness enhancing technologies. For example, using a smartphone with location-awareness to quickly and effectively navigate in the city while using the device to share with others your noticing, discovery, or reimagining of urban spaces.

Smartness: Smartness pertains to the awareness of people, of technologies, and of people interacting with technologies in urban spaces as noted in the smart cities definition.

This research was previously published in Enriching Urban Spaces with Ambient Computing, the Internet of Things, and Smart City Design edited by Shin'ichi Konomi and George Roussos, pages 209-231, copyright year 2017 by Engineering Science Reference (an imprint of IGI Global).

Chapter 25
Optimized Energy Consumption and Demand Side Management in Smart Grid

Sadiq Ahmad
COMSATS Institute of Information Technology, Pakistan

Ayaz Ahmad
COMSATS Institute of Information Technology, Pakistan

Raziq Yaqub
NIKSUN Inc., USA

ABSTRACT

This chapter reviews prevailing methodologies and future techniques to optimize energy consumption. It discerns that smart grid provides better tools and equipment to control and monitor the consumer load, and optimize the energy consumption. Smart grid is essentially composed of smart energy equipment, advance metering infrastructure and Phasor Measurement Units (Synchrophaors) that helps to achieve optimized energy consumption. The chapter also places focus on demand side management and optimized energy consumption scheduling; and establishes that both, the utilities, as well as the users can play a vital role in intelligent energy consumption and optimization. The literature review also reveals smart protection, self-healing systems and off-peak operation result in minimizing transmission and distribution losses, as well as optimizing the energy consumption.

Abbreviation:

- **DSM:** Demand Side Management
- **IT:** Information Technology
- **AMI:** Advance Metering Infrastructure
- **DERs:** Distributed Energy Generations
- **DRM:** Demand Response Management

DOI: 10.4018/978-1-5225-2589-9.ch025

- **ECS:** Energy Consumption Scheduling
- **ECA:** Energy Consumption Algorithm
- **PMU:** Phase Measuring Unit
- **PAPR:** Peak to Average Power Ratio
- **HEC:** Home Energy Controller
- **HEM:** Home Energy Management
- **HAN:** Home Area Network
- **ZNEBs:** Zero Net Energy Buildings
- **DLM:** Direct Load Management
- **DLC:** Direct Load Control

INTRODUCTION

Smart grid is an emerging topic in today's research community. It provides range of solutions to optimize the energy consumption. It is the collection of conventional generation, transmission and distribution network, communication network, energy storage devices, distributed generation, advance network control, decision support applications and home energy management systems. In simple words, it is the integration of Information Technology (IT) with electrical power system to improve the power production and utilization (Fang, Misra, Xue, & Yang, 2012, Ghafurian, 2011). In order to improve the production, optimize the energy consumption, and to reduce the transmission and distribution losses, the existing system should be made efficiently (Fadlullah et al., 2011). To provide reliable and efficient as well as optimal energy supply to the end user, we need to change our traditional grid into smart grid. The concept of smart grid technology getting importance due to the fact that it can efficiently manage the consumers load according to the restriction imposed by the supplier. The reduction in energy consumption and the increase in the efficiency mainly depend upon the electric appliances in the residential, commercial and industrial area. Therefore, to achieve both of these goals, the existing appliances should be replaced by smarter ones (Stragier, Hauttekeete & De Marez, 2010). Smart grid technology is based on advance and smart control system that can utilize the potential of two way communication. In this new technology, a continuous and effective communication module needed between two control center i.e., one at the consumers end the other at grid end. It is the smart grid which can gathers information about all the ongoing actives of power supplier and can shape, monitor the consumers load by employing different controlling and monitoring scheme. The components of the smart grid i.e., advance metering infrastructure (AMI), demand response management (DRM), smart protection system, and self-fault detection and correction. Self-fault detection and correction can help in optimizing the energy consumption and can improve the system efficiency (Deng et al., 2011). Energy consumption and optimal energy management refers either to reducing energy consumption directly or shifting the high power appliances from peak hours to off-peak hours. In case of residential area the direct load reduction in energy consumption can be achieved by training the end users and by installing smarter appliances in that area. To shift peak load to off-peak hours, the utilities communicate with the consumers to inform them about high price per kWh in peak hours and incentivize them to shift the high load appliances to off-peak hours (Mohsenian-Rad, Wong, Jatskevich & Schober, 2010). To efficiently utilize the available power and to reduce the line losses the energy consumption or peak hours demand should be minimized because in peak hours when the demanded current increase, the line losses also increase, as the line losses are directly proportional to the square of the demanded current. That is, at lower peaks, line losses will be less and the grid will be stable and more efficient and vice versa. Similarly, if the user uses smart appliances, the peak demand will be low and as a result the grid efficiency will be increased. The peak energy demand can be optimized both by using smart equipments and by using optimal demand side management. As in (Law et al., 2012), the authors propose that user demand can be managed by providing them with incentives to lower the electricity demand in peak hours and shift their high load appliances to off-peak hours. In this chapter, we also reviewed different incentive based energy consumption scheduling (ECS) algorithm to reduce the peak demand. In demand side management, we review different paper for optimal electricity (energy) consumption planes at the consumer end.

The rest of the chapter is divided into three sections. In Section II, we present a survey on the smart equipment, smart technology and demand side management to optimize the energy consumption on user and demand side. In Section III, we review the existing energy consumption scheduling algorithms (ECA). Section IV concludes the chapter.

COMPONENTS OF SMART GRID AT DISTRIBUTION LEVEL

In this section we discuss the general components that is use to optimize the energy consumption of consumers. The advance metering infrastructure is one of the important components of smart grid technology.

Advance Metering Infrastructure

Advance metering infrastructure (AMI) is an active area of research that is used to monitor the consumers load. AMI is the most important parameter among smart grid technology. It is the name of complete infrastructure which can integrate various components both at consumers as well as at supplier side. The smart meters and smart appliances are the consumers side components while the communication networks among all these appliances, i.e., meters and between consumers and supplier, and a data management system are the supplier end components (Mohassel, Fung, Mohammadi & Raahemifar, 2014, Mohassel, Fung, Mohammadi, & Raahemifar, 2014). It is the AMI which provide a complete infrastructure to implement the smart grid technology. AMI is a unit which can be used to monitor consumers load and operation in real time. With the help of AMI load switching and operation can be achieved remotely (Roy, Bedanta & Dawnee, 2015). The authors in (Yu, Zhang, Mohammad, Nguyen & Sato, 2014, Popovic & Cackovic, 2014, Bian, Kuzlu, Pipattanasomporn & Rahman, 2014, Jiang, et al., Li, et al.,) presented AMI with different perspectives and according to them AMI consists of smart meters that is used to observe the power usage, it can efficiently control and optimize the energy usage, it can store data and process metering by operating different data management systems. Another description of AMI is given by the authors in (ETSI TR, 2012). According this report, the AMI consists of smart meters, data concentrators, central data collection point, local area network and wide area network. Smart meter may be a local electronic meter, data concentrators may process the data from various meters, while the local area network and wide area network provides bi-directional communication between the smart meter and the data concentrators and communication between data concentrators and central data collection point. AMI can be used to achieve distribution automation using supervisory control and data acquisition system (Nunoo & Ofei, 2010). It can also be used to manage consumers' energy consumption, phase identification and distributed state estimation (Sui, Sun & Lee, 2011, Nthontho, Chowdhury & Winberg, 2011, Short, 2013, Chen & Lin, 2013).

SMART EQUIPMENTS AND DEMAND SIDE MANAGEMENT

To reduce the energy consumption, first and mandatory step is to replace the conventional equipment of the traditional grid by smarter ones. In this section, we review smart equipments, different energy consumption algorithms and demand side management as explain below.

Smart Equipment and Smart Technologies

Smart Meter, AMI

Smart meter or advance meter is the key component of the smart grid technology. Smart metering is the momentous part for the realization of the concept of smart grid. Smart metering is basically the deployment of meters that can enable the bi-directional communication between consumers and supplier (Finster & Baumgart, 2014).

To reduce energy consumption and to optimize energy consumption, the conventional meter should to be replaced by smart meter. Smart or advance meter is similar to conventional energy meter with additional features of communicating with the utility as well as with the consumer to better handle the energy consumption. Smart meters are categories on the basis of three different perspectives: electrical, thermal and fluid. In each category there are numerous sensors which can be used to measure different factors which include humidity, temperature and light. Smart meters can perform two functions: communication and measurements. Therefore, each of the smart meters has two sub part calibration and communication part. The calibration part is depending upon disparate factors including precision and accuracy, measured phenomenon, data security level, technical requirement, application, etc., while the communication encryption and security is depending on the second sub-part i.e., communication (Smart, "no date"). The authors in (De Capua, Lipari, Lugara & Morello, 2014) explored that the smart energy meter is a conventional energy meter having ability to measure the quality energy, conveying information to the energy supplier in real time and having the capability to prevent malfunctions. Smart meter can facilitate both the consumers as well as the supplier through real time energy consumptions control and real time monitoring. Moreover, smart meter also provide the consumers with real time pricing and analyzed the consumers energy usage information and share it with utility (Subhash & Rajagopal, 2014).

Smart metering is also useful to avoid the energy theft (Efthymiou, & Kalogridis, 2010). Various techniques can be utilized to avoid energy theft. The authors in (Hashmi & Priolkar, 2015) suggested a novel method to minimize energy theft by locating the energy theft location. The authors used power line communications and AMI to find out the approximate energy theft's location. Smart meter can also enable the local utility to connect and disconnect electrical services of the consumers. Anti-theft smart meter is the most important and the elementary component of the smart and intelligent transmission and distribution system (Krishnan, 2008). Other privacy techniques regarding energy theft's is given by the authors in (Stallman, 2010, McLaughlin, Holbert, Fawaz, Berthier & Zonouz, 2013, McLaughlin, Podkuiko & McDaniel, 2010). Advance meter is the primary components of advanced metering infrastructure (AMI). Advance meter along with AMI can also be utilized for consumers load management and load monitoring. The authors in (Hart, 1992) proposed different algorithms to control and monitor the load demand. For optimize energy consumption system, AMI plays an important role. AMI should have the following key features (Hart, 2008).

- Automatic registration of the meter's point.
- Ability to detect fault and rectify it.
- Interconnection of outage management and utility billing

When the consumer service is lost due to some reason, the AMI will notify the supplier trouble call center in order to rectify it, and similarly, when it comes to its normal status, the AMI will register that point automatically and will notify the utility. In conventional power system, the outage and faults are detected by the consumer and are rectified by calling to the supplier trouble call center which affects the energy consumption. In addition, AMI localizes fault automatically and notifies the utilities. Similarly, by using AMI, the outage management and utility will communicate each other and will rectify the fault as soon as possible to optimize the system. Through AMI, utilities can get basic information about the demand side management and revenue projection, etc. AMI in the smart grid is also responsible to provide all the consumer information to local utility, and to provide updated information about the updated agreement, controlling algorithm, load shedding schedule and real time pricing at different times to consumers to optimize the energy consumption (Farhangi, 2010). AMI interacts with the utility and management section to provide the distribution grid all the information about the voltage, current, power and losses (Hart, 2008). By using the smart appliance, energy demand can be reduced. In summary, by using smart equipments, advance appliances and use of AMI, the energy consumption can be reduces up to a great extent.

Smart Fault Detection and Correction

Fault detection and correction affect the energy consumption. In the smart grid, fault detection and correction is very important and the most challenging task. Because a small fault generally delocalizes the whole system and becomes a base for a bigger fault which can disturb the whole power system. So for smart grid to have stable and to optimize the energy consumption, early fault detection is very important (He & Zhang, 2011). Fault detection in transmission line is also a difficult task. The authors in (León, Vittal, & Manimaran, 2007; León et al.; Gungor, Lu, & Hancke, 2010) explored that installation of the sensor networks in power grid is one of the source for detecting the faults on time. Along with energy theft, line outage is another source of the degradation of the optimality of energy consumption and also increases the line losses. In order to enhance the optimal energy consumption the authors in (Tate & Overbye, 2008; Borghetti, Nucci, Paolone, Ciappi & Solari, 2011), proposed the phasor measurement unit (PMU) to measure the line outage and how to minimize it. Moreover, the authors investigate that outage can be measured by computing the phasor angle across the busses and can be compared with the fault events to determine the outage of the transmission line.

Smart Protection

Power system protection is the most important and paramount parameter in smart grid technology. In the literature various protection schemes are available to protect smart grid. The authors in (Fadul, Hopkinson, Andel & Sheffield, 2014) discussed a toolkit based on communication protection system. The proposed toolkit composed of three modules, i.e., assignment module, detection module and decision module. The assignment module determines the effected node by collecting its complete information. The detection module detects the faulty system by using traditional relays and frequency disturbance monitoring device, while the decision module takes proper decision to rectify the faulty system. Similarly, protection of smart grid based on distributed energy is discussed in (Ates, Uzunoglu & Karakas, 2014). The proposed framework is based on IEEE 13 bus system, where different protection scheme is recommended for different fault scenarios. The authors in (Shipman, Hopkinson & Lopez, 2015) suggested con-resistant trust mechanism. The proposed mechanism contributes in transients' instabilities mitigation. Another protection scheme is presented by the authors in (Garlapati, Lin, Sambamoorthy, Shukla & Thorp, 2010). The proposed framework is based on to improve the performance of zone 3 relay protection.

In smart grid, it is very important to have smart and advance controlling and protection algorithms to get optimal energy consumption schedule. These algorithms collect the data from the distribution grid and after analyzing the grid components data, it provides the probable solution. Beside this optimal energy consumption can be achieved through optimal demand side management.

Optimal Demand Side Mangement

Demand side management (DSM) refers to reducing the energy consumption and peak electricity demand by designing algorithm on consumer's side (Masters, 2013). DSM is a set of flexible and coordinated program/algorithms that can provide an opportunity to the customer to efficiently shift their electricity demand during peak hours into off-peak hours. By employing such programs and algorithms consumers' can reduce his/her electricity consumption, which can in turn reduce his/her electricity bills and can improve his/ her living standard (Davito, Tai & Uhlaner, 2010). These algorithms are further divided into subclasses such as fuel substitution algorithm, direct load algorithm and demand response algorithm (Ramanathan, & Vittal, 2008; Pedrasa, Spooner & MacGill, 2009). These entire algorithms are used to reap the optimal energy consumption i.e., to reduce the commercial, industrial and residential energy consumption. These algorithm benefits both the consumer as well as the suppliers. From consumer perspective, these algorithms reduce the electricity bills and as a result reduce the individual expenditures (Obaidat, Anpalagan, & Woungang, 2012). For example (as in (Savings, "no date")), if a 100W light bulb in USA is turned on all the month would cost $7.92 if the cheapest price is 11 cent/kWh, and would cost $25.20 if the highest price is 35 cent /kWh as per unit price increases with increasing units consumption. So, if the consumer reduces its energy consumption, it would save $17.28 in a month. On the other hand, from supplier perspective, these algorithms can reduce the generation, transmission and distribution costs and also can improve the system efficiency and stability, ensuring reliable energy supply. Table 1, shows the benefits of DSM algorithm.

To manage residential load, demand response algorithms can either directly reduces the energy consumption or shifts the high load appliance to the off-peak hours. The first one can be achieved by constructing energy efficient building and by using energy efficient appliances as discuss earlier in this section. Optimality of DSM depends on the peak-to-average load ratio (PAR). PAR ratio can be reduced by shifting the high load appliances to the off-peak hours (Mohsenian-Rad, Wong, Jatskevich, Schober & Leon-Garcia, 2010).

Table 1. Benefits of DSM

Consumer Benefits	Supplier Benefits
Required demand will be fulfilled.	Generation, transmission and distribution cost will be reduced.
Reliable service.	Less capital will be required for generation etc.
Reduction in electricity bills.	System will be more efficient and flexible.
Improved life style.	Better services for consumer.

To optimize the energy consumption by reducing the PAR, Cisco has designed hardware in 2010 known as home energy controller (HEC) that is shown in Figure 1. The HEC has 1.1GHz of Intel Atom processor with Ubantu or LINUX operating system. For supplier, the HEC provide home energy management (HEM) solutions that include the effective handling and implementation of the demand management, scheduling of the outage and real time pricing algorithms (Costanzo, 2012).

The authors further exploited that, HEM manages the energy consumption by shaving the peak hour's demand, i.e., by shifting the peak load to off-peak hours. HEM system consists of three sub system: 1) Sensor and other controlling devices, 2) Monitoring and controlling system, and 3) Energy management algorithm. The sensors in the HEM detect the fault and other events of different appliances connected through home area network (HAN) which may be either wired or wireless, and send these information to the control units which takes an appropriate action (León, Vittal, & Manimaran, 2007; Gungor, Lu, & Hancke, 2010). Monitoring and controlling section monitors the real time load and corresponding real time pricing and informs the consumer about the high load and its high pricing. The energy management algorithm in HEM also based on by reducing the load directly, or by shifting the peak hour's loads to the off-peak hours. The idea of the authors in (Costanzo, 2012) can better understand from the Figure 2, which shows the block diagram of HEM.

In order to better handle and optimize the energy consumption, the demand response algorithm is divided into two categories. These two categories are elaborated as follows.

Figure 1. Cisco HEC device

Figure 2. Block diagram of HEM

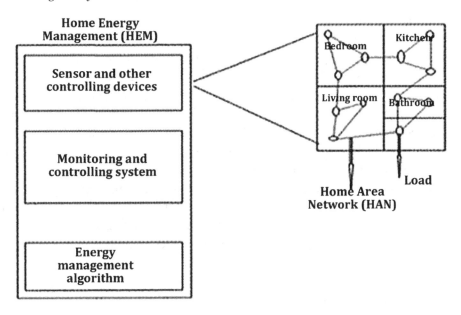

DSM in Smart Building

Smart home or smart building is another hot topic in current research community. A smart home contains major home appliances that are interconnected through different communication networks. All these home appliances can be accessed, monitored and controlled remotely. In smart homes various home automation and controlling techniques can be used to manage various household appliances. DSM in smart building is a sub category of DSM, which can be used as one of the monitoring and controlling scheme.

In this sub category of DSM, the energy consumption is managed by a prominent concept circulating in recent research area called Zero Net Energy Buildings (ZNEB's). The objective of ZNEB's is to reduce the energy consumption by balancing the energy consumption and the cost. In order to balance and reduce the energy demand, the distributed energy resources (DERs) are required to be installed in the ZNEB's (Stadler, Siddiqui, Marnay, Aki, & Lai 2011). In (Stadler et al.,), the authors further investigated that the DERs in ZNEB's mostly recover its initial capital cost and also reduce the operation cost. For optimal DSM, the HEM provides the coordination between different buildings devices and DERs (Costanzo et al.,). The function of the DSM is to optimize and ensure the availibity of energy at minimum cost in peak hours.

Direct Load Management (DLM)

Direct load management (DLM) is a subclass of DSM demand response algorithms. To optimize the energy consumption by DLM algorithms, the utility company imposes constraints on some of the consumer's high energy household appliances to be controlled and managed remotely by the supplier to minimize the energy consumption. In this subsection, we review direct load control (DLC) algorithms. The purpose of these algorithms is to control consumer devices and to get minimum energy consumption (Ruiz, Cobelo & Oyarzabal, 2009). All the available algorithms are based on linear or dynamic programming, having the objective to minimize peak load which is equal to the maximization of the load reduction at minimum cost (Lee, & Wilkins, 1983, Cohen & Wang, 1988). To develop DLC algorithms, it is mandatory step to study the load in order to determine the type and nature of the load and extract user's normal consumption patterns and plot the curves. The idea of the authors in (Ruiz et al.,) is shown in Fig.3 and Fig.4. These curves are depending upon the type of building and the environmental condition such as temperature, humidity and appliances used inside the building, etc. In the following, we review an optimal DLC algorithm that can be used to reduce the demanded load. In this algorithm, let we have *h* type of consumers having both base load as well as peak load type of appliances. Moreover, we have to control the total load which is the sum of base load plus peak hour's load. The main objective of this algorithm is to control the peak hours load appliances to minimize the total load. We start calculating the load by applying the control strategy *s* between initial and final time steps c_i & c_f. Figure 3 shows load versus time graph of a single consumer. To understand the idea of (Ruiz et al.,) let in Figure 3, from 0 to 13 o'clock we have only base load and from 13-17 o'clock the demand becomes higher and the curve goes higher. Therefore, to optimize the whole energy consumption of that consumer the peak load should be controlled. The total load for Figure 3 will be equal to

$$L_1 = (hours_B \times kW_B) + (hours_P \times kW_P) \tag{1}$$

where for Figure 3 the $hours_B=20h$ and $kw_B=2kW$ and similarly, for peak hour the $hours_P=4h$ and $kw_P=4kW$. By putting values in equation (1) the energy consumption of a single consumer in 24 hours can be calculated as follows.

Figure 3. Single consumer demand load curve

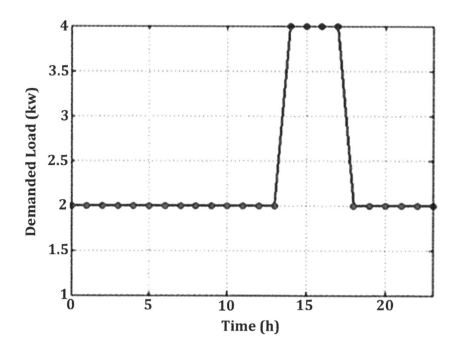

$$L_1 = ((13+7) \times 2) + (4 \times 4)$$

$$L_1 = 56kWh$$

So, the consumer 1 is consuming 56 units in 24 hours. Similarly, if we use the cheapest price scheme as in (Saving, "no date"), would cost $6.16 in 24 hours. Similarly, if we have *n* users, we have to calculate and plot the demand load versus time curve for each individual user.

To optimize the energy consumption and reduce the demanded load the peak hours' interval is shifted from 13 to 15 o'clock and ended at 17 o'clock and as a result the peak hour demand load is reduced from 4 kW to 3 kW. In addition, the peak hour's duration decreases from 4 hours to 2 hours, which is shown in Figure 4. And from Figure 4 the total energy consumed by consumer 1 can be calculated by putting the corresponding values in equation 1 as given below.

$$L_1 = ((15+7) \times 2) + (2 \times 3)$$

$$L_1 = 50kWh$$

From this calculation it is clear that by applying strategy *s* only a single consumer can save 6 kWh in 24 hours and if compare in cost would save $0.66 by a single consumer. In the following, the author in (Ruiz et al.,) suggests formulation of this energy consumption algorithm in general form.

Figure 4. Single consumer load curve after applying strategy s

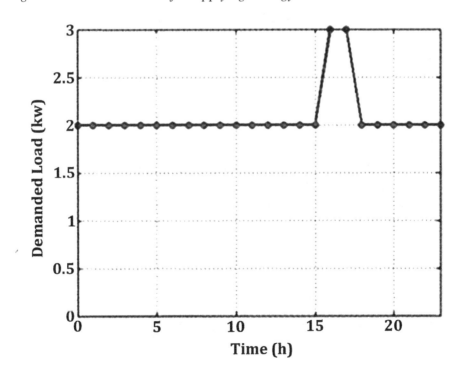

The mathematical formulation of the aforementioned scheme is provided as follows. Following are the variables used in the formulation.

c_i initial time step of the control period.

c_f final time step of the control period.

Δc time step duration.

Bl_c base load at time step c.

h customer type.

$jDev_h$ number of device to be controlled in group of customer.

$E_{hst}(c) = A_{hst}(c) - A_{h0}(c)$ Where $E_{hst}(c)$ is load consumption variation.

$A_{hst}(c)$ expected device consumption at time step c of h type customer when strategy s is applied at time step t.

$A_{h0}(c)$ expected device consumption at time step c of h type at no control action.

s control action, which turns off the device or shift the load.

O_{hsc} number of controlled/peak load devices with optimal strategy s starting at time step c of h customer.

O_{hst} number of controlled/peak load devices with optimal strategy s starting at time step t of h customer.

O_{h0} number of uncontrolled/base load devices with optimal strategy s starting at time step c of h customer.

v_c total number of O_{hst} variables in which the control action starts at time step c.

v_t total number of O_{hst} variables in which the control action starts at time step t.

The mathematical formulation for the DLC of the (Ruiz et al.,) is shown below and the objective of this formulation is to maximize the load reduction or to minimize the demand load over a specified controlled period.

$$min \sum_{c=c_i}^{c_f} l_c \qquad (2)$$

where l_c is the final demand load at time step c after applying the control action s.

Final demand load l_c is the sum of base load and change in peak load at each time step c when the control action is applied

$$l_c = Bl_c + \Delta l_c$$

where

$$\Delta l_c = \sum_{k=1}^{h} \sum_{v=1}^{v_c} O_{hsc} E_{hsc}(c) + \sum_{k=1}^{h} \sum_{t=c_i}^{c-\Delta c} \sum_{v=1}^{v_t} O_{hst} E_{hst}(c) \tag{3}$$

By putting the above two value in (2) we get

$$min \sum_{c=c_i}^{c_f} \left[Bl_c + \sum_{k=1}^{h} \sum_{v=1}^{v_c} O_{hsc} E_{hsc}(c) + \sum_{k=1}^{h} \sum_{t=c_i}^{c-\Delta c} \sum_{v=1}^{v_t} O_{hst} E_{hst}(c) \right] \tag{4}$$

Subject to

1. $O_{hst} \geq 0$ for all h, s, t
2. $jDev_h = O_{h0} + \sum_{j=1}^{jVar} O_{hst}$ for all h
3. O_{hst} and O_{h0} should have only integer values
4. $l_c \leq l$ limit for all c

where *jVar* is the total number of control variables in the problem i.e., $jVar = \sum_{t=c_i}^{c_i} h_c$

REDUCTION IN ENERGY CONSUMPTION BY USING ENERGY CONSUMPTION SCHEDULING

Consumer loads can be divided into three sub parts (1) Base line load e.g., lighting and cooking. (2) Burst load e.g., dryer, washing machine etc. (3) Regular load e.g., heating, ventilation and air conditioning (HVAC) etc, (Costanzo, 2012, Heshmati, 2014). In this section, we review different ECS algorithms, which are normally used for smart pricing. ECS is a unit which is installed inside the smart meter connected to both power line and communication line for data communication. These devices run on distributed algorithms to provide the consumer with optimal energy consumption by optimal scheduling, to ensure the minimum PAR in the system (Eksin, Deliç & Ribeiro, 2014). Game theoretic analysis provides incentive based pricing schemes for end user to improve the performance of the system and minimize the PAR. The block diagram of ECS is shown in Figure 5 (Mohsenian-Rad et al.,). By the use of ECS, the following actions can be performed.

- Cost minimization.
- Consumer load controlling.
- Peak to average power ratio reduction.
- Optimal scheduling.

Figure 5. Block diagram of ECS device and its usage

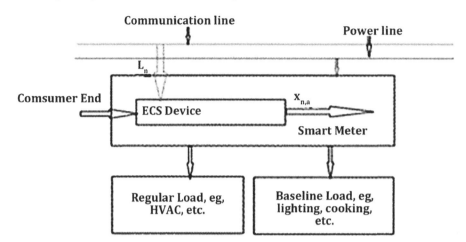

Cost Minimization

Consumer energy demand increases in peak hours and to meet that peak hour's demand, the generation companies run peaker power plants which charge higher prices per kilowatt hour and as a result energy cost increases (Photovoltaics, 2011). From consumer perspective, it is necessary to get the energy at minimum cost. For minimum cost, the consumers have to minimize their peak hour's demand. Cost minimization is very important outcome of ECS. The basic objective of the ECS is to control and schedule the consumer peak loads and also to provide the consumer with power at minimum cost. In the literature various scheduling algorithms like in (Jalali & Kazemi, 2015, Eksin, Deliç, & Ribeiro, 2014, Chavali, Yang & Nehorai, 2014, Mohsenian-Rad et al.,) are available which can be utilized to minimize the consumer energy cost by scheduling the load properly. For example we have a scheduling algorithm presented by (Mohsenian-Rad et al.,) as follows. Here first the load is scheduled according to the proposed framework.

Figure 6. Distributed power and communication line with ECS

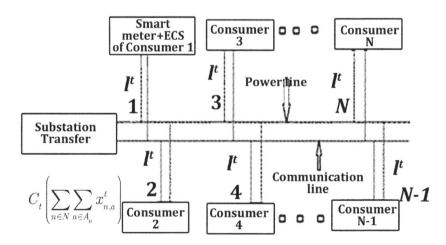

Once the load is scheduled properly, then by solving the following optimization problem, the peak load and cost can be minimized.

$$Min \sum_{t=1}^{T} C_t \left(\sum_{n \in N} \sum_{a \in A_n} x_{n,a}^t \right) \qquad (5)$$

where $C_t \left(\sum_{n \in N} \sum_{a \in A_n} x_{n,a}^t \right)$ is cost function and $x_{n,a}^t$ is energy consumed by appliance a of consumer n in time t hour. The above problem is an integer programming problem and by solving this problem the PAR ratio can be reduce up to a great extent. A.H Mohsenian-Rad in (Mohsenian-Rad et al.,), considers a substation transformer, which is connected to different consumers via ECS device as shown in Figure 6. In this figure, $l_{1....}^t$ up to l_N^t are load of N consumers at time t hours, where $t = \{1,2,3....24\}$. The total load of any consumer n is $l_n = \{l_n^1 + l_n^2 +,,,,,,,,,l_n^{24}\}$. The total load of all consumers at time t is given as follows.

$$L_t = \sum_{n \in N} l_n^t \qquad (6)$$

The daily average and peak load can be calculated as follows.

$$L_{peak} = \max_{t \in T} L_t \qquad (7)$$

$$L_{avg} = \frac{1}{T} \sum_{t \in T} L_t \qquad (8)$$

Similarly, the PAR can be calculated by the following formula.

$$PAR = \frac{\max_{t \in T} L_t}{\frac{1}{T} \sum_{t \in T} L_t} \qquad (9)$$

PAR minimization problem can be written as,

$$\min \frac{\max_{t \in T} L_t}{\frac{1}{T} \sum_{t \in T} L_t}$$

Which is min max problem, and as the average load is constant so the corresponding problem becomes as

$$\min_{t \in T} \max L_t \tag{10}$$

At the end by solving this min max problem the cost can be reduce.

Consumer Load Control

To reduce the energy consumption and to optimize the power system, it is very important to control the load on consumer end. Specially, controlling the peak load is very important because peak load can change the PAR and also affect the cost of energy on consumer end. To control consumer load, let we have A_n appliances. Now the energy consumed by appliance a such that $a \in A_n$ in t hour of consumer n is $x_{n,a}^t$.

At any time t the total load of any consumer n will be equal to the summation of the energy consumed by all appliances of that consumer which can be represented as

$$l_n^t = \sum_{a \in A_n} x_{n,a}^t \text{, where } t \in T \tag{11}$$

In order to optimize the energy consumption, the authors in (Mohsenian-Rad et al.,, Mohsenian-Rad et al., 2010, Ipakchi & Albuyeh, 2009), proposed different schemes, where the utility companies puts some restriction on consumers side, i.e., the power level used by consumers will be within certain limits. For optimal energy consumption, the consumers have to keep their load within these limits. The upper bound of these limits, is supposed to be $\gamma_{n,a}^{\max}$ which means that all the appliances of a consumer are on during 24 hours, and lower bound $\gamma_{n,a}^{\min}$ which means that only necessary appliances of the consumer are on during 24 hours. Moreover, there will be the starting and ending scheduling time of each appliance to better schedule the consumer load. Let $\alpha_{n,a}$ and $\beta_{n,a}$ be the starting and ending times of appliance a of user n that should be scheduled. From times $\alpha_{n,a}$ to $\beta_{n,a}$ the $\sum_{a \in A_n} x_{n,a}^t$ will be equal to the daily energy consumption i.e., $E_{n,a}$, elsewhere $\sum_{a \in A_n} x_{n,a}^t = 0$.

$$\gamma_{n,a}^{\min} \leq \sum_{a \in A_n} x_{n,a}^t \leq \gamma_{n,a}^{\max} \text{ } for \forall t \in \{\alpha_{n,a}, \ldots \ldots \beta_{n,a}\} \tag{12}$$

Keeping in view the above constraint, the authors define a feasible space for energy consumption of user n, as given by

$$\chi_n = \left\{ X_n \left| \begin{array}{l} \sum_{t=\alpha_{n,a}}^{\beta_{n,a}} x_{n,a}^t = E_{n,a} \text{, } \sum_{a \in A_n} x_{n,a}^t = 0 \forall t \in T \setminus T_{n,a} \\ \gamma_{n,a}^{\min} \leq x_{n,a}^t \leq \gamma_{n,a}^{\max}, \forall t \in T_{n,a} \end{array} \right. \right\} \tag{13}$$

where X_n is energy consumption scheduling vector.

Peak to Average Power Ratio Minimization

Energy efficiency refers to using minimum energy by consumer at specific time, even in peak hours. To achieve reliable and efficient electric grid, it is very important to reduce the peak hour demand. Moreover, PAPR also depends on peak hour's power demand. For optimal and low energy consumption Peak to average power ratio must be kept low. PAPR reduction is a hot topic in current research community. Various articles can be found on PAPR reduction e.g., in (Bakker, Bosman, Molderink, Hurink & Smit, 2010, Caron & Kesidis, 2010, Chen, Li, Low & Doyle, 2010). The authors in (Soliman & Leon-Garcia, 2014, Chai, Chen, Yang & Zhang, 2014) introduced game theoretic based algorithms to minimize the generation cost and PAPR. To reduce energy consumption, demand load and to get energy at minimum price, the PAPR should be minimized. The daily peak and average power consumed can be calculated by the following formula.

$$P_{peak} = max \left(\sum_{n \in N} \sum_{a \in A_n} x_{n,a}^t \right)$$

$$P_{avg} = \frac{1}{T} \sum_{n \in N} \sum_{a \in A_n} x_{n,a}^t$$

Peak to average power ratio can be written as

$$PAPR = \frac{max \left(\sum_{n \in N} \sum_{a \in A_n} x_{n,a}^t \right)}{\frac{1}{T} \sum_{n \in N} \sum_{a \in A_n} x_{n,a}^t} \tag{14}$$

to minimize PAPR, equation (14) can be written as

$$\min_{X_n \in \chi_n} \frac{max \left(\sum_{n \in N} \sum_{a \in A_n} x_{n,a}^t \right)}{\frac{1}{T} \sum_{n \in N} \sum_{a \in A_n} x_{n,a}^t} \tag{15}$$

Equation (15) is min max problem, and as the denominator is constant, so the above problem becomes as

$$\min_{X_n \in \chi_n} max \left(\sum_{n \in N} \sum_{a \in A_n} x_{n,a}^t \right) \tag{16}$$

Optimal Scheduling

Optimal schedule can be achieved by joint cost minimization and consumer load controlling. From equation (5) and (13), ECS units can efficiently schedule the energy consumption by solving the following optimization problem.

$$\min_{X_1 \dots X_N} \sum_{t=1}^{T} C_t \left(\sum_{n \in N} \sum_{a \in A_n} x_{n,a}^t \right)$$

Subject to

$$X_n \in \chi_n \text{ for } \forall n \in N$$

as the constraint in the above problem are linear (convex), it can be solved optimally if the cost function is strictly convex (Mohsenian-Rad et al.,)

CONCLUSION

This chapter summarized different scenarios and methodologies used to optimize energy consumption by using smart techniques. From the literature review, we concluded that the energy consumption can be optimized by the replacement of the conventional grid components by advance ones. We also discerned that the energy consumption can be further optimized by using smart protection and fault detection systems. We also identified that the use of advance control algorithms can reduce the demand. Furthermore, we also established that to ensure efficient and better electricity availability, the peak load should be shifted to the off-peak hours. We further noticed that different techniques are employed on the DSM for minimizing the peak demand that consequently results in minimizing transmission and distribution losses, as well as optimizing the energy consumption. Also we reviewed DER in ZNEB's to balance the peak load. By deployment of ECA, the cost can be minimized, the load can be controlled and the PAPR can be reduced.

REFERENCES

Ates, Y., Uzunoglu, M., & Karakas, A. (2014, March). The case study based protection analysis for smart distribution grids including distributed generation units. In *Developments in Power System Protection (DPSP 2014), 12th IET International Conference on* (pp. 1-5). IET. doi:10.1049/cp.2014.0144

Bakker, V., Bosman, M. G. C., Molderink, A., Hurink, J. L., & Smit, G. J. M. (2010, October). Demand side load management using a three step optimization methodology. In *Smart Grid Communications (SmartGridComm), 2010 First IEEE International Conference on* (pp. 431-436). IEEE doi:10.1109/SMARTGRID.2010.5622082

Bian, D., Kuzlu, M., Pipattanasomporn, M., & Rahman, S. (2014, July). Analysis of communication schemes for Advanced Metering Infrastructure (AMI). In *PES General Meeting| Conference & Exposition, 2014 IEEE* (pp. 1-5). IEEE.

Borghetti, A., Nucci, C. A., Paolone, M., Ciappi, G., & Solari, A. (2011). Synchronized phasors monitoring during the islanding maneuver of an active distribution network. *Smart Grid. IEEE Transactions on*, 2(1), 82–91.

Caron, S., & Kesidis, G. (2010, October). Incentive-based energy consumption scheduling algorithms for the smart grid. In *Smart grid communications (SmartGridComm), 2010 First IEEE international conference on* (pp. 391-396). IEEE. doi:10.1109/SMARTGRID.2010.5622073

Chai, B., Chen, J., Yang, Z., & Zhang, Y. (2014). Demand response management with multiple utility companies: A two-level game approach. *Smart Grid. IEEE Transactions on*, 5(2), 722–731.

Chavali, P., Yang, P., & Nehorai, A. (2014). A distributed algorithm of appliance scheduling for home energy management system. *Smart Grid. IEEE Transactions on*, 5(1), 282–290.

Chen, L., Li, N., Low, S. H., & Doyle, J. C. (2010). Two market models for demand response in power networks. *IEEE SmartGridComm*, 10, 397–402.

Chen, S. J., & Lin, C. H. (2013, July). Integrating SVM Classifier and Distribution State Estimation for Detection and Identification of AMI Customer's Meter Data. In *Computer Software and Applications Conference (COMPSAC), 2013 IEEE 37th Annual* (pp. 278-279). IEEE. doi:10.1109/COMPSAC.2013.47

Cohen, A. I., & Wang, C. C. (1988). An optimization method for load management scheduling. *IEEE Trans. Power Syst., 3*(2), 612-618.

Costanzo, G. T. (2012, April). Demand side optimization in smart and green buildings. In *2012 in International Conference Towards Net Zero Energy buildings*.

Davito, B., Tai, H., & Uhlaner, R. (2010). The smart grid and the promise of demand-side management. *McKinsey on Smart Grid*, 38-44.

De Capua, C., Lipari, G., Lugara, M., & Morello, R. (2014, May). A smart energy meter for power grids. In *Instrumentation and Measurement Technology Conference (I2MTC) Proceedings, 2014 IEEE International* (pp. 878-883). IEEE. doi:10.1109/I2MTC.2014.6860868

Deng, R., Maharjan, S., Cao, X., Chen, J., Zhang, Y., & Gjessing, S. (2011, October). Sensing-delay tradeoff for communication in cognitive radio enabled smart grid. In *Smart Grid Communications (SmartGridComm), 2011 IEEE International Conference on* (pp. 155-160). IEEE.

Efthymiou, C., & Kalogridis, G. (2010, October). Smart grid privacy via anonymization of smart metering data. In *Smart Grid Communications (SmartGridComm), 2010 First IEEE International Conference on* (pp. 238-243). IEEE. doi:10.1109/SMARTGRID.2010.5622050

Eksin, C., Deliç, H., & Ribeiro, A. (2014, May). Distributed demand side management of heterogeneous rational consumers in smart grids with renewable sources. In *Acoustics, Speech and Signal Processing (ICASSP), 2014 IEEE International Conference on* (pp. 1100-1104). IEEE. doi:10.1109/ICASSP.2014.6853767

ETSI TR 102 935 V2.1.1. (2012). *Machine-to-Machine communications (M2M); Applicability of M2M architecture to Smart Grid Networks; Impact of Smart Grids on M2M platform, 2012.* doi:10.1109/ENERGYCON.2014.6850622

Fadlullah, Z. M., Fouda, M. M., Kato, N., Takeuchi, A., Iwasaki, N., & Nozaki, Y. (2011). Toward intelligent machine-to-machine communications in smart grid. *Communications Magazine, IEEE, 49*(4), 60–65. doi:10.1109/MCOM.2011.5741147

Fadul, J. E., Hopkinson, K. M., Andel, T. R., & Sheffield, C. (2014). A Trust-Management Toolkit for Smart-Grid Protection Systems. *Power Delivery. IEEE Transactions on, 29*(4), 1768–1779.

Fang, X., Misra, S., Xue, G., & Yang, D. (2012). Smart grid—The new and improved power grid: A survey. *IEEE Communications Surveys and Tutorials, 14*(4), 944–980. doi:10.1109/SURV.2011.101911.00087

Farhangi, H. (2010). The path of the smart grid. *Power and Energy Magazine, IEEE, 8*(1), 18–28. doi:10.1109/MPE.2009.934876

Finster, S., & Baumgart, I. (2014). Privacy-Aware Smart Metering: A Survey. *IEEE Communications Surveys and Tutorials, 17*(2), 1088–1101. doi:10.1109/COMST.2015.2425958

Garlapati, S., Lin, H., Sambamoorthy, S., Shukla, S. K., & Thorp, J. (2010, October). Agent based supervision of zone 3 relays to prevent hidden failure based tripping. In *Smart Grid Communications (SmartGridComm), 2010 First IEEE International Conference on* (pp. 256-261). IEEE. doi:10.1109/SMARTGRID.2010.5622051

Ghafurian, R. (2011). Smart grid: The electric energy system of the future. *Proceedings of the IEEE, 99*(6), 917–921. doi:10.1109/JPROC.2011.2124210

Gungor, V. C., Lu, B., & Hancke, G. P. (2010). Opportunities and challenges of wireless sensor networks in smart grid. *Industrial Electronics. IEEE Transactions on, 57*(10), 3557–3564.

Hart, D. G. (2008, July). Using AMI to realize the Smart Grid. In *2008 IEEE Power and Energy Society General Meeting-Conversion and Delivery of Electrical Energy in the 21st Century.* doi:10.1109/PES.2008.4596961

Hart, G. W. (1992). Nonintrusive appliance load monitoring. *Proceedings of the IEEE, 80*(12), 1870–1891. doi:10.1109/5.192069

Hashmi, M., & Priolkar, J. G. (2015, May). Anti-theft energy metering for smart electrical distribution system. In *Industrial Instrumentation and Control (ICIC), 2015 International Conference on* (pp. 1424-1428). IEEE. doi:10.1109/IIC.2015.7150972

He, M., & Zhang, J. (2011). A dependency graph approach for fault detection and localization towards secure smart grid. *Smart Grid. IEEE Transactions on, 2*(2), 342–351.

Heshmati, A. (2014). Demand, Customer Base-Line and Demand Response in the Electricity Market: A Survey. *Journal of Economic Surveys, 28*(5), 862–888. doi:10.1111/joes.12033

Ipakchi, A., & Albuyeh, F. (2009). Grid of the future. *Power and Energy Magazine, IEEE, 7*(2), 52–62. doi:10.1109/MPE.2008.931384

Jalali, M. M., & Kazemi, A. (2015). Demand side management in a smart grid with multiple electricity suppliers. *Energy, 81*, 766–776. doi:10.1016/j.energy.2015.01.027

Jiang, R., Lu, R., Wang, Y., Luo, J., Shen, C., & Shen, X. S. (2014). Energy-theft detection issues for advanced metering infrastructure in smart grid. *Tsinghua Science and Technology, 19*(2), 105–120. doi:10.1109/TST.2014.6787363

Krishnan, R. (2008). Meters of tomorrow [in my view]. *IEEE Power and Energy Magazine, 2*(6), 96-94.

Law, Y. W., Alpcan, T., Lee, V., Lo, A., Marusic, S., & Palaniswami, M. (2012, November). Demand response architectures and load management algorithms for energy-efficient power grids: a survey. In *Knowledge, Information and Creativity Support Systems (KICSS), 2012 Seventh International Conference on* (pp. 134-141). IEEE. doi:10.1109/KICSS.2012.45

Lee, S. H., & Wilkins, C. L. (1983). A practical approach to appliance load control analysis: a water heater case study. *IEEE Trans. Power Appar. Syst., 5*(3), 64-64.

León, R. A., Vittal, V., & Manimaran, G. (2007). Application of sensor network for secure electric energy infrastructure. *Power Delivery. IEEE Transactions on, 22*(2), 1021–1028.

Li, H., Lin, X., Yang, H., Liang, X., Lu, R., & Shen, X. (2014). EPPDR: An efficient privacy-preserving demand response scheme with adaptive key evolution in smart grid. *Parallel and Distributed Systems. IEEE Transactions on, 25*(8), 2053–2064.

Masters, G. M. (2013). *Renewable and efficient electric power systems.* John Wiley & Sons.

McLaughlin, S., Holbert, B., Fawaz, A. Q., Berthier, R., & Zonouz, S. (2013). A multi-sensor energy theft detection framework for advanced metering infrastructures. *Selected Areas in Communications. IEEE Journal on, 31*(7), 1319–1330.

McLaughlin, S., Podkuiko, D., & McDaniel, P. (2010). Energy theft in the advanced metering infrastructure. In *Critical Information Infrastructures Security* (pp. 176–187). Springer Berlin Heidelberg. doi:10.1007/978-3-642-14379-3_15

Mohassel, R. R., Fung, A., Mohammadi, F., & Raahemifar, K. (2014, June). Application of Advanced Metering Infrastructure in Smart Grids. In *Control and Automation (MED), 2014 22nd Mediterranean Conference of* (pp. 822-828). IEEE. doi:10.1109/MED.2014.6961475

Mohassel, R. R., Fung, A. S., Mohammadi, F., & Raahemifar, K. (2014, May). A survey on advanced metering infrastructure and its application in Smart Grids. In *Electrical and Computer Engineering (CCECE), 2014 IEEE 27th Canadian Conference on* (pp. 1-8). IEEE.

Mohsenian-Rad, A. H., Wong, V. W., Jatskevich, J., & Schober, R. (2010, January). Optimal and autonomous incentive-based energy consumption scheduling algorithm for smart grid. In Innovative Smart Grid Technologies (ISGT), 2010 (pp. 1-6). IEEE. In Innovative Smart Grid Technologies (ISGT), 2010 (pp. 1-6). IEEE. doi:10.1109/ISGT.2010.5434752

Mohsenian-Rad, A. H., Wong, V. W., Jatskevich, J., Schober, R., & Leon-Garcia, A. (2010). Autonomous demand-side management based on game-theoretic energy consumption scheduling for the future smart grid. *Smart Grid. IEEE Transactions on, 1*(3), 320–331.

Nthontho, M., Chowdhury, S. P., & Winberg, S. (2011, October). Smart communication networks standards for smart energy management. In *Telecommunications Energy Conference (INTELEC), 2011 IEEE 33rd International* (pp. 1-9). IEEE. doi:10.1109/INTLEC.2011.6099798

Nunoo, S., & Ofei, A. K. (2010, September). Distribution automation (DA) using supervisory control and data acquisition (SCADA) with advanced metering infrastructure (AMI). In *Innovative Technologies for an Efficient and Reliable Electricity Supply (CITRES), 2010 IEEE Conference on* (pp. 454-458). IEEE.

Obaidat, M. S., Anpalagan, A., & Woungang, I. (Eds.). (2012). *Handbook of green information and communication systems*. Academic Press.

Pedrasa, M. A. A., Spooner, T. D., & MacGill, I. F. (2009). Scheduling of demand side resources using binary particle swarm optimization. *Power Systems. IEEE Transactions on, 24*(3), 1173–1181.

Photovoltaics, D. G. (2011). *IEEE Guide for Smart Grid Interoperability of Energy Technology and Information Technology Operation with the Electric Power System (EPS), End-Use Applications, and Loads*. IEEE.

Popovic, Z., & Cackovic, V. (2014, May). Advanced metering infrastructure in the context of smart grids. In Energy Conference (ENERGYCON), 2014 IEEE International (pp. 1509-1514). IEEE.

Roy, S., Bedanta, B., & Dawnee, S. (2015, August). Advanced Metering Infrastructure for real time load management in a smart grid. In *Power and Advanced Control Engineering (ICPACE), 2015 International Conference on* (pp. 104-108). IEEE. doi:10.1109/ICPACE.2015.7274926

Ruiz, N., Cobelo, I., & Oyarzabal, J. (2009). A direct load control model for virtual power plant management. *Power Systems. IEEE Transactions on, 24*(2), 959–966.

Shipman, C. M., Hopkinson, K. M., & Lopez, J. (2015). Con-Resistant Trust for Improved Reliability in a Smart-Grid Special Protection System. *Power Delivery. IEEE Transactions on, 30*(1), 455–462.

Short, T. A. (2013). Advanced metering for phase identification, transformer identification, and secondary modeling. *Smart Grid. IEEE Transactions on, 4*(2), 651–658.

Silicon Laboratories, Inc. (n.d.). *Smart Metering Brings Intelligence and Connectivity to Utilities, Green Energy and Natural Resource Management, Rev.1.0*. Available at: http://www.silabs.com/Support%20 Documents/TechnicalDocs/Designing-Low-Power-Metering-Applications.pdf

Soliman, H. M., & Leon-Garcia, A. (2014). Game-theoretic demand-side management with storage devices for the future smart grid. *Smart Grid. IEEE Transactions on, 5*(3), 1475–1485.

Stadler, M., Siddiqui, A., Marnay, C., Aki, H., & Lai, J. (2011). Control of greenhouse gas emissions by optimal DER technology investment and energy management in zero-net-energy buildings. *European Transactions on Electrical Power, 21*(2), 1291–1309. doi:10.1002/etep.418

Stallman, R. (2010). Is digital inclusion a good thing? How can we make sure it is? *Communications Magazine, IEEE, 48*(2), 112–118. doi:10.1109/MCOM.2010.5402673

Stragier, J., Hauttekeete, L., & De Marez, L. (2010, September). Introducing Smart grids in residential contexts: Consumers' perception of Smart household appliances. In *Innovative Technologies for an Efficient and Reliable Electricity Supply (CITRES), 2010 IEEE Conference on* (pp. 135-142). IEEE.

Subhash, B., & Rajagopal, V. (2014, March). Overview of smart metering system in Smart Grid scenario. In *Power and Energy Systems Conference: Towards Sustainable Energy* (pp. 1-6). IEEE. doi:10.1109/PESTSE.2014.6805319

Sui, H., Sun, Y., & Lee, W. J. (2011, July). A demand side management model based on advanced metering infrastructure. In *Electric Utility Deregulation and Restructuring and Power Technologies (DRPT), 2011 4th International Conference on* (pp. 1586-1589). IEEE. doi:10.1109/DRPT.2011.5994150

Tate, J. E., & Overbye, T. J. (2008). Line outage detection using phasor angle measurements. *Power Systems. IEEE Transactions on, 23*(4), 1644–1652.

Yu, K., Zhang, D., Mohammad, A., Nguyen, N. H., & Sato, T. (2014, October). A key management scheme for secure communications of information centric advanced metering infrastructure in Smart Grid. In *Power System Technology (POWERCON), 2014 International Conference on* (pp. 2019-2024). IEEE.

ADDITIONAL READING

Ali. A, Shabbir, A., Hassan, N.U., Yuen, C., Ahmad, A., & Tushar, W., (2015, in Press). Understanding Customer Behavior in Multi-tier Demand Response Management Program. *IEEE Access (in press)*.

Bae, H., Yoon, J., Lee, Y., Lee, J., Kim, T., Yu, J., & Cho, S. (2014, February). User-friendly demand side management for smart grid networks. In *Information Networking (ICOIN), 2014 International Conference on* (pp. 481-485). IEEE.

Baldauf, A. (2015, May). A smart home demand-side management system considering solar photovoltaic generation. In *Energy (IYCE), 2015 5th International Youth Conference on* (pp. 1-5), IEEE. doi:10.1109/IYCE.2015.7180731

Barbato, A., Capone, A., Chen, L., Martignon, F., & Paris, S. Distributed Demand-Side Management in Smart Grid: how Imitation improves Power Scheduling (pp. 6163-6168). In IEEE ICC 2015.

Barooah, P., Buic, A., & Meyn, S. (2015, January). Spectral decomposition of demand-side flexibility for reliable ancillary services in a smart grid. In *System Sciences (HICSS), 2015 48th Hawaii International Conference on* (pp. 2700-2709). IEEE. doi:10.1109/HICSS.2015.325

Belhaiza, S., & Baroudi, U. (2015). A Game Theoretic Model for Smart Grids Demand Management. *Smart Grid. IEEE Transactions on, 6*(3), 1386–1393.

Chai, B., Chen, J., Yang, Z., & Zhang, Y. (2014). Demand response management with multiple utility companies: A two-level game approach. *Smart Grid. IEEE Transactions on, 5*(2), 722–731.

Chavali, P., Yang, P., & Nehorai, A. (2014). A distributed algorithm of appliance scheduling for home energy management system. *Smart Grid. IEEE Transactions on, 5*(1), 282–290.

Cicek, N., & Delic, H. (2015). Demand Response Management for Smart Grids With Wind Power. *Sustainable Energy. IEEE Transactions on, 6*(2), 625–634.

Eksin, C., Deliç, H., & Ribeiro, A. (2014, May). Distributed demand side management of heterogeneous rational consumers in smart grids with renewable sources. In *Acoustics, Speech and Signal Processing (ICASSP), 2014 IEEE International Conference on* (pp. 1100-1104). IEEE. doi:10.1109/ICASSP.2014.6853767

Erol-Kantarci, M., & Mouftah, H. T. (2015). Energy-Efficient Information and Communication Infrastructures in the Smart Grid: A Survey on Interactions and Open Issues. *IEEE Communications Surveys and Tutorials, 17*(1), 179–197. doi:10.1109/COMST.2014.2341600

Graditi, G., Di Silvestre, M. L., Gallea, R., & Riva Sanseverino, E. (2015). Heuristic-based shiftable loads optimal management in smart micro-grids. *Industrial Informatics. IEEE Transactions on, 11*(1), 271–280.

Jalali, M. M., & Kazemi, A. (2015). Demand side management in a smart grid with multiple electricity suppliers. *Energy, 81*, 766–776. doi:10.1016/j.energy.2015.01.027

Javaid, N., Khan, I., Ullah, M. N., Mahmood, A., & Farooq, M. U. (2013, October). A survey of home energy management systems in future smart grid communications. In *Broadband and Wireless Computing, Communication and Applications (BWCCA), 2013 Eighth International Conference on* (pp. 459-464). IEEE. doi:10.1109/BWCCA.2013.80

Kinhekar, N., Padhy, N. P., Li, F., & Gupta, H. O. (2015). Utility Oriented Demand Side Management Using Smart AC and Micro DC Grid Cooperative. *Power Systems. IEEE Transactions on, 99*(1), 1–10.

Ma, J., Deng, J., Song, L., & Han, Z. (2014). Incentive mechanism for demand side management in smart grid using auction. *Smart Grid. IEEE Transactions on, 5*(3), 1379–1388.

Mou, Y., Xing, H., Lin, Z., & Fu, M. (2015). Decentralized Optimal Demand-Side Management for PHEV Charging in a Smart Grid. *Smart Grid. IEEE Transactions on, 6*(2), 726–736.

Nguyen, H. K., Song, J. B., & Han, Z. (2015). Distributed Demand Side Management with Energy Storage in Smart Grid, in Parallel and Distributed Systems, IEEE Transactions on, 26(12), 3346-3357. doi:10.1109/TPDS.2014.2372781

Pan, J., Jain, R., & Paul, S. (2014). A Survey of Energy Efficiency in Buildings and Microgrids using Networking Technologies. *IEEE Communications Surveys and Tutorials, 16*(3), 1709–1731. doi:10.1109/SURV.2014.060914.00089

Puradbhat, S., & Banerjee, R. (2014, May). Estimating demand side management impacts on buildings in smart grid. In Innovative Smart Grid Technologies-Asia (ISGT Asia), 2014 IEEE (pp. 635-640). IEEE. doi:10.1109/ISGT-Asia.2014.6873866

Qela, B., & Mouftah, H. T. (2014). Peak Load Curtailment in a Smart Grid Via Fuzzy System Approach. *Smart Grid. IEEE Transactions on, 5*(2), 761–768.

Ramachandran, B., & Ramanathan, A. (2015, March). Decentralized demand side management and control of PEVs connected to a smart grid. In *Power Systems Conference (PSC), 2015 Clemson University* (pp. 1-7), IEEE. doi:10.1109/PSC.2015.7101679

Rasoul, M., Abdi, H., Rezaei, S., & Rahimzadeh, H. (2015, June). Demand side management and charging and discharging for multiple PHEVs to reduce cost and reduce fossil fuel using game theory in smart grid. In *Environment and Electrical Engineering (EEEIC), 2015 IEEE 15th International Conference on* (pp. 128-132), IEEE. doi:10.1109/EEEIC.2015.7165499

Refaat, S. S., & Abu-Rub, H. (2015, September). Implementation of smart residential energy management system for smart grid. In Energy Conversion Congress and Exposition (ECCE), 2015 IEEE (pp. 3436-3441), IEEE. doi:10.1109/ECCE.2015.7310145

Roy, S., Bedanta, B., & Dawnee, S. (2015, August). Advanced Metering Infrastructure for real time load management in a smart grid. In *Power and Advanced Control Engineering (ICPACE), 2015 International Conference on* (pp. 104-108), IEEE. doi:10.1109/ICPACE.2015.7274926

Shabbir, A., Hassan, N. U., Yuen, C., Ahmad, A., & Tushar, W. (2015, November). Multi-tier Incentive Scheme for Residential Customer Participation in Demand Response Management Programs. 2015 Proceedings of the IEEE ISGT ASIA, Bangkok (pp. 1-5), IEEE.

Sheikhi, A., Rayati, M., Bahrami, S., & Mohammad Ranjbar, A. (2015). Integrated Demand Side Management Game in Smart Energy Hubs. *Smart Grid. IEEE Transactions on*, 6(2), 675–683.

Sheikhi, A., Rayati, M., Bahrami, S., & Ranjbar, A. M. (2015, February). Demand side management in a group of Smart Energy Hubs as price anticipators; the game theoretical approach. In *Innovative Smart Grid Technologies Conference (ISGT)*, 2015 IEEE Power & Energy Society (pp. 1-5). IEEE. doi:10.1109/ISGT.2015.7131836

Soliman, H. M., & Leon-Garcia, A. (2014). Game-theoretic demand-side management with storage devices for the future smart grid. *Smart Grid. IEEE Transactions on*, 5(3), 1475–1485.

Tsiamitros, D., Stimoniaris, D., Poulakis, N., Zehir, M. A., Batman, A., Bagriyanik, M.,... Dialynas, E. (2014, October). Advanced energy storage and demand-side management in smart grids using buildings energy efficiency technologies. In Innovative Smart Grid Technologies Conference Europe (ISGT-Europe), 2014 IEEE PES (pp. 1-6). IEEE. doi:10.1109/ISGTEurope.2014.7028841

Vidal, A. R., Jacobs, L., & Batista, L. S. (2014, December). An evolutionary approach for the demand side management optimization in smart grid. In*Computational Intelligence Applications in Smart Grid (CIASG), 2014 IEEE Symposium on* (pp. 1-7). IEEE. doi:10.1109/CIASG.2014.7011561

Wang, Z., Zhang, W., Zhang, L., Chen, G., Dong, Z., & Huang, T. (2015, March). Impact of different penetrations of renewable sources and demand side management on Australian future grid. In *Smart Grid and Renewable Energy (SGRE), 2015 First Workshop on* (pp. 1-6), IEEE. doi:10.1109/SGRE.2015.7208723

Yaqub, R., Ahmad, S., Ahmad, A., & Amin, M. (2015, in press). Smart Energy-consumption Management System Considering Consumers' Spending Goals (SEMS-CCSG). In WILEY International Transactions on Electrical Energy Systems (in press).

Ye, F., Qian, Y., & Hu, R. A Real-Time Information Based Demand-Side Management System in Smart Grid.

KEY TERMS AND DEFINITIONS

Advance Metering Infrastructure: It is the basic component of smart grid technology, in which the utilities companies as well as the consumers can communicate in bi-direction.

Demand Response Management: It is a management scheme used for energy management normally controlled and devised at supplier or at utility side. Or it is the response of consumers to the energy management schemes design by the utility companies.

Demand Side Management: In the smart grid, managing the consumers demand at consumers' end is called demand side management.

Direct Load Control: Direct load control is a subsection of direct load management. Here in this scheme the utility company imposes constraints on some of the consumer's high energy household appliances to be controlled and managed remotely by the supplier to minimize the energy consumption.

Direct Load Management: It is also an energy management scheme, in which the ON/OFF control of the consumer appliances' is under the management who provided the scheme.

Distributed Energy Resources: Beside the central power generation, the smart grid support the distributed electricity (energy) generation normally install near to the consumers end. These resources may be renewable or not, e.g., solar, wind, diesel generator, etc.

Energy Consumption Algorithms: Different methods and algorithms are used to manage the consumers demand. These methods can be define as energy consumption algorithms.

Home Area Network: In smart grid technology, for efficient energy management it is mandatory that all the appliances at the consumers end are interconnected through different communication networks. These communication networks are known as home area network. These networks may be either wired or wireless.

Home Energy Controller: It is device designed by Cisco, install at consumers premises to manage the energy consumption.

Home Energy Management: Home energy management is a scheme that is devised for consumers to manage residential load.

Peak to Average Power Ratio: It is the ratio normally used for reliability and low cost energy production. Lower the peak to average power ratio, the more will the power system stable and the lower will be the production cost of energy.

Phasor Measurement Unit: It is a unit used to measure the outage between two line.

Zero Net Energy Building: It is the new concept circulating in current research community. The objective of ZNEB's is to reduce the energy consumption by balancing the energy consumption and the cost. In ZNEBs, the buildings are designed energy efficient in such manner to minimize the energy consumption by utilizing energy efficient appliances.

This research was previously published in Smart Grid as a Solution for Renewable and Efficient Energy edited by Ayaz Ahmad and Naveed Ul Hassan, pages 1-25, copyright year 2016 by Information Science Reference (an imprint of IGI Global).

Chapter 26
Implementation of Flooding Free Routing in Smart Grid:
VCP Routing in Smart Gird

Saad Afzal
COMSATS Institute of Information Technology, Pakistan

ABSTRACT

Smart Grid is a communication and automatic control capabilities in electric power grid system for improving efficiency, reliability, management, capabilities and security of electric power grid. Routing is important in Smart Grid to send data from one point to another point. Routing in Smart Grid is necessary to search /identify destination point/node for communication and to computer the best available route in the network topology among which the data to be sent during communication. Smart Grid can be a combination of fixed nodes (home appliances, smart meter, control centre, etc.) but the nature of communication between fixed nodes is dynamic due to the switch on/off or the fluctuation in electricity flow. Therefore the fixed nodes can also be disappeared from the network topology in Smart Grid. Existing routing protocols for Smart Grid are based on flooding mechanism. We would like to examine the feasibility of flooding free routing in Smart Grid. Then we will propose a flooding-free routing for Smart.

INTRODUCTION

Introduction of Smart Grid

Energy is a main source of modern economic development world. More energy is required with the increasing of world's population needs. The global demand for energy grows with the growth of developing countries as they enter industrial and services stages of development. The Smart Grid is a complete system that includes the operational and energy measures such as Smart Meters, Smart Home Appliances, different renewable energy sources such as solar & wind energy system and energy efficiency resources. The generation of electricity as per customer requirement and distribution of electricity are the most important aspects of smart grid technology. Smart Grid is a solution of drawbacks in current electric

DOI: 10.4018/978-1-5225-2589-9.ch026

grid and is a full suite that can solve the problems form production to distribution in current electric grid. Smart Grid is an addition of Information Technology (IT) in current electric grid. The important part of the motivation of the use of IT in Electric grid for Smart Grid is to be able to provide two way flow of information for communications in Smart Grid among different components. Through Smart Grid solutions the energy requirements can be fulfilled however for this purpose the complete implementation of Smart Grid from the production to consumption point and the necessary communication between all the parts of Smart Grid is necessary.

Smart Grid Requirements and Challenges

In current Electricity System the control centers for monitoring the power grid components are used. This system is called Supervisory Control and Data Acquisition (SCADA). This system provides communication between these control centers and substations of Smart Grid. Smart Grid is the introduction of communications and automatic control capabilities in electric power grid for improving efficiency, reliability, environmental, economics, management, security and safety of electric power grid. Smart Grid can be used for better management of electricity generation, transformation, distribution and load balancing. The reliable, scalable, robust, and secure communication network is important component for the successful operations of Smart Grid. The results of improvement in Electric Grid the resultant Smart Grid have following features/benefits:

- The decrement of rate and deduction in length of outages due to customer awareness of electricity use and prices though smart meters.
- Improvement in Power quality issues that result the reduction in number of disruptions.
- Reduction in Electricity prices due to awareness of lower prices in electricity use information.
- Smart Grid is automatic system therefore the maintenance cost is reduced.
- Smart Grid can use available assets bitterly.
- Security of Smart Grid is improved cyber and physically than Electricity Grid.
- Smart Gird provides safety of electricity Hazards.

In Figure 1 the electricity Power Control is displayed the communication & control management converts traditional electricity system into modern Smart Grid power control system. The Smart Grid is fully accommodating traditional (hydraulic, oil, nuclear etc) and renewable (wind, solar and water etc) energy sources then the electricity is transmitted from generation points to distribution points by Transmission Control Center. The Distribution Control Center communicates with Transmission Control Center and distributes electricity power between industrial, commercial and residential areas. All levels of electricity power are connected through communication network and managed/supervised through control systems.

Applications of Smart Grid

The Smart Grid is an enhancement of traditional electric power grid. The overview of some applications of Smart Grid is as per following for understating the system.

Figure 1. Smart grid power control system

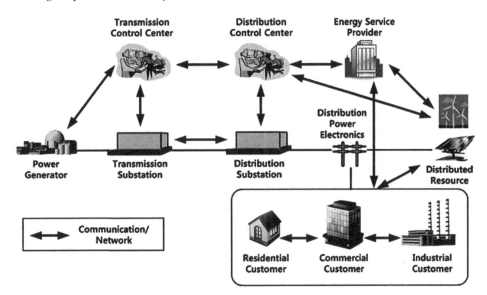

Advanced Control

Samad T., and Annaswamy A. (2011) found Smart Grid can have a complete control system over the electric power grid and its communication. This control system can be used to analyze the performance of whole smart grid by using distributed, independent reinforcement learning controllers that have learned successful strategies to manage the behavior of the Smart Grid. This can be able to face the situation of changing environment such as equipment failure.

Fault Detection and Isolation

TECHNOLOGIJA, S. ELECTRONICS AND ELECTRICAL ENGINEERING (2011) has showed that the management of the Smart Grid system will be required digitally controlled, programmed analysis of problems, and automatic switching capabilities to avoid or mitigate power outages, blackout, power quality problems, and system collision. To predict, detect and respond to the system problems automatically, the system managers/controllers can use the real time information which comes from embedded sensors and automated controls deployed in the smart grid.

Outage Management

Outage management is a main feature of the Smart Grid. Amin S. M., and Wollenberg B. F. (2005) described that the outage management can works on several levels such as to aware the utility for an outage, to automatically report the location of an outage and to minimizing the effect of an outage by using techniques and technologies to route the power in whole area.

Substation Automation and Diagnosis

The Operation Center Supervisory Control and Data Acquisition (SCADA) receive data from several substations and process data to take suitable action. According to Wang W., Xu Y., & Khanna M. (2011), the Smart Grid can be distributed and centralized architecture and Smart Grid can also be more than one main station to control the Smart Grid actions. The different network topologies can be used for communication between these stations. Each master station (manned) has a support of backup/emergency master station to update and synchronized a data.

Demand Response Management

Balijepalli V. S. K. M., Pradhan V., Khaparde S. A., and Shereef R. M. (2011) has described that the Demand Response (DR) application can collect information from various sources in system such as forecast, MDM and Supervisory Control and Data Acquisition (SCADA). Based on inputs that collected by DR, the power demand supply is determined for real time and also for the next time. Based on the surplus/deficit demand response signals are sent out to the consumers. The Demand Response Management system helps to make the Smart Grid much more efficient and balanced because the generation of more electricity power can be generated if the system controllers already know the high demand of the electric power in peak hours.

Distribution Automation

Brown R. E. (2008) has showed that the Distribution Automation (DA) is a technology of Smart Grid that can be implemented for the distribution of electric power grid for both local power lines and neighborhood substations. Through implementation of DA in Smart Grid the grid reliability with real-time monitoring and intelligent control can be assured. DA can be allowed to individual devices to sense the operation conditions of electricity grid and to adjust power flow for improving & optimized performance of Smart Grid.

Advanced Meter Reading (AMR) and Infrastructure (AMI) Overview

Advance Meter Reading (AMR) is a feature of Smart Grid described by Yan Y., Qian Y., Sharif H. and Tipper D. (2013). In Smart Grid the meter reading can be obtained through automatic system and no need to send a person that reads meters and collect data manually. Automated Meter Reading also some time called the interval meters. The idea of an interval meter comes from the fact that the meter (AMR and AMI) can be captured electricity usage information on a timely basis and is able to transmit same data to the utility company from the consumer point. The main difference between AMI and AMR is that an AMR device only provides a one-way communication path. Demand response, price, and other operational signals cannot be transmitted from the utility company to an AMR meter as it can with an AMI meter.

Introduction of Mobile Ad Hoc Network (MANET):

Mobile ad hoc network (MANET) is a type of ad hoc network, the nodes exists in MANETS change their locations and configures themselves on the fly basis. There is no predefined infrastructure for MANETs. The devices communicating in MANETS are mobile in nature and the nodes used wireless connections for their connectivity to various networks. This can be a standard as a Wi-Fi connection, or another medium, such as a cellular, Microwave or satellite transmission etc.

Some MANETs are restricted to a local area of wireless devices (such as a group of computers and laptop in any building) However, the others networks may be connected directly with the internet. For example, Vehicular Ad Hoc Network (VANET) is a MANET network that allows vehicles to communicate with roadside equipments while the vehicles may not have internet connection directly in themselves, the wireless roadside equipments can be connected to the Internet and able to allow vehicles to send their data on Internet. The vehicle data may be used to measure traffic conditions or to keep track of trucking fleets. Due to dynamic nature of MANETs, the MANETs are typically not secure therefore, it is important to be careful what data is being send over a MANET. Patel V. and Lathigara A. presented the working of AODV for multipath extensions.

Applications of MANET

The battlefield and disaster-recovery networks are the mostly discussed applications scenario for MANET. The following are main applications for MANET:-

Mesh Networks

Mesh Network is the combination of mobile and fixed nodes that are interconnected via wireless links in a form of multi-hop ad hoc network. Wireless network contains a architecture of hierarchy network by adding special nodes such as mesh routers. Wireless Mesh Network can be used for intelligent transportation system, Public safety through law enforcement public safety agencies and Nortel Wireless Mesh Networks etc,

Opportunistic Networks

The Opportunistic Networks can utilize any possible in-range device near to destination to forward messages. The wildfire networks are interesting example of Opportunistic routing wherein it uses for tracking wild species to deeply investigate the behaviour, interactions and influences on each other. Opportunistic Networks can also be used in developing areas through providing broken internet connectivity to rural developing areas.

Wireless Sensor Networks

Wireless Sensor Networks contain the small, wireless, battery powered smart sensor nodes. These nodes have communication capabilities and also can filter, share, combine and operate on the data they sense.

Civilian and Environmental applications are the main topics for WSN, that includes habit monitoring networks, Envisense GlacsWeb Project, Health Monitoring, Tracking Applications, Intelligent Home Environment and Localization Applications.

Vehicular Ad Hoc Networks

Vehicular Ad Hoc Network (VANETs) is advancement or variation of Mobile Ad Hoc Networks (MANETs). In VANETs the nodes moved on a proper pattern with compare to movement of nodes in MANETs. Therefore through a movement on specific patterns the safety and better management for Vehicles can possible. The vehicles can be captured from GPS, accelerometers, magnetometers, or the available sensors in vehicles and the data can be transmit to other vehicles or to road side equipments through the cellular, Bluetooth, WiMAX, Wi-Fi, or DSRC networks. In VANET, every participating node/Vehicle participate as a wireless router or node, that can allow connectivity of vehicles with approximately range of 100 to 300 meters and through this connectivity vehicles create a wide range network. The self-safety, Traffic Management, Driver Assistance Management and Travel Information Guidance etc are the main applications of VANETs.

Introduction of Routing

Routing is a procedure of computing best suitable path in the network from source to destination for the delivery of data packets. The term routing is also referred to forwarding a data packet from one node to another node through a best path in the network till the data reaches at the destination node. Routing have been using in several types of networks like the electronic data networks (such as the Internet), telephonic network (circuit switching) and the transportation networks smart grid device-to-device communication etc. All this about wireless sensor networks has been defined by Akyildiz I. F., Su W., Sankarasubramaniam Y., and Cayirci E. (2002).

Routers are used for forwarding data from one router to another on the path from source to destination. The routing protocols decide the routes to be taken for delivery of data packets. It is important that the routes must have knowledge of the network topology in order to select the best available route for communication between sender and receiver. The route depends on the cost criteria and may also depend on the current network conditions. Router used routing tables to store the address/location of other nodes and routers for communication. Extra time for searching node can be avoided through the record maintained in routing tables. Mostly the routing table maintains the one entry for each destination network. Routers update routing tables, when found any change in nodes on the basis of change in location, failure of node, joining of node etc. Each entry in routing table is a step next node towards the destination. The record for complete route in one routing table is unnecessary. Each routing table in a router has the records of the neighbors of that router. The network topology can be contained of fixed nodes and can be maintained by the moveable/dynamic nodes.

The Figure 2 is an example of simple routing between routers/nodes. The routers are used best available shortest path for the communication from sender to receiver. Every node will communicate to its neighbor node then will communicate with destination by crossing nodes hope by hope. When the multiple paths are available then the node/router will be select the shortest/best path through any algorithm for communication. The processing, Storage, connectivity option and the routing/forwarding mechanisms are requirements of the network for routing.

Figure 2. Routing between routers in a network

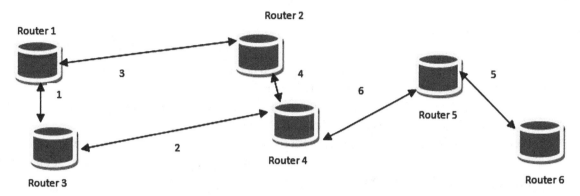

The Table 1 is maintained by every router and update table accordingly in case of any change (joining of new node, node failure, new shortest available path etc). In a network every table has the next hope address for performing communication between nodes. The table is maintained for the address of next hope for every node of a network.

Classification of Routing Protocols

Routing can be classified into four common basis, these are Routing Updates, Temporal Information, topology Organization and Resource organization. Every network topology/protocol deal with these four basics of routing however every protocol have their own merits and boundaries. The some details of these classifications are given below:

Table 1. Routing Tables of Routers in a Network 1

Router 1 Table			Router 2 Table			Router 3 Table	
1	0		1	1		1	1
2	2		2	0		2	1
3	3		3	1		3	0
4	3		4	4		4	4
5	3		5	4		5	4
6	3		6	4		6	4
Router 4 Table			Router 5 Table			Router 6 Table	
1	3		1	4		1	5
2	2		2	4		2	5
3	3		3	4		3	5
4	0		4	4		4	5
5	5		5	0		5	5
6	5		6	6		6	0

Routing Updates

Routing Updates have following further three types:

- **Pro-Active Routing:** This routing gets information about all possible/acceptable routes from one node to another node before the need of that route.
- **Re-Active Routing:** This routing gets the information of nodes connected in a network topology when the route is needed from one to other node. This is called On-demand routing.
- **Hybrid Routing:** This is the combination routing of Pro-active and Re-active routing protocols. In this protocol every node knows its neighbors before demand and gets information about other nodes as per demand requirements.

Temporal Information

This information contains the past history of connectivity or can be based on prediction of future connectivity through the lifetime of nodes and their location for movements.

Topology Organization

Any network topology can be organized into two ways Flat or Hierarchical. The Flat network topology based on global addresses such as 802.11 etc. The Hierarchical network topology based on the Geographical positions of node or the Hop distance between nodes.

DHT Based Routing and its Advantages

The functionality and advantages of DHT based Ad Hoc routing is following:

Fully Distributed

DHT based Ad Hoc routing is fully distributed routing. Ad Hoc routing does not have any central or leader node therefore the any single node or leader is not responsible for all the communication in network topology. Every node is responsible for his communication therefore in DHT based routing there is no communication load on any single node or line.

Local Maintenance

Maintenance performs at local nodes mostly in DHT based protocols. The joining of new node or leaving of a node not affects the working of whole network. The joining and leaving of nodes maintains locally so it is not expensive.

Loop Free Routing

DHT based routing is decentralized network therefore the routing between nodes is loop free routing. There is no head or leader in network that pass all the communication. This functionality removed loops from DHT routing.

Minimize Route Acquisition Delay: Proactive

DHT based routing also provide the functionally of proactive routing. The route between nodes can be defined before the route requirement. This functionality reduced the path finding overhead when the route is required.

Quick Route Reconfiguration

The Ad Hoc based DHT routing is adaptive to frequent changes. Any change in network does not affect the whole network. The change in unrelated parts of network should not impact a node.

Energy Conservation

In network, if the nodes are not busy in communication then they are in sleeping mode and again become active when there communication in network is necessary. This functionality enhanced the energy conservation of nodes in network topology.

Unidirectional Link Support

Ad Hoc based DHT routing in wireless network presented by Abid S. A., Othman M., and Shah N. (2014). In Ad Hoc based DHT routing the Nodes are connected wirelessly and are able to communicate for Uni-directional communication in network.

Importance of Routing in Smart Grid

To send data from one component to another component in smart grid would be necessary to search/ identify destination and to computer a best route in the network along witch the data is to be sent. The communication in Smart Grid can be divided into three layers: Home Area Network (HAN), Neighbor Area Network (NAN) and Wide Area Network (WAN) presented by Saputro N., Akkaya K. and Uludag S. (2012). Home Area Network: Home Area Network (HAN) can enable automatic network for monitoring and controlling the home appliances, Han also can generate Power Supply Demand (DR). HAN is basically a domain of the customer and provides access facility to applications under the home. The home devices can send their electricity use and power reading to the smart meter or to the point of AMI application. Home area network is a combination of sensors and home appliance. Home appliances can be categorized into four categories due to their communication requirements.

- First group contains small load appliances such as lights, mobile chargers, laptops etc. These small devices do not have a load or significant data for network.
- Second group contains the uncontrollable large load appliances such as a stove. These types of appliances are used as per their requirements and it is difficult to manage the use of these devices.
- Third group contains controllable large appliances such as dryers, air conditioners etc. The control center requires the complete information about this group.
- The fourth group contains the Electric Vehicles (EVs). EVs requires large load and the management of charging is big challenge for Smart Grid.

Neighbor Area Network: Neighbor Area Network (NAN) provides connectivity of smart meters to local access points for the use of AMI applications. The network topology can have a mesh network of smart meters with local access points. NAN is connecting Building Area Network with Mobile Workforce and also communicates the HAN with Wide Area Network.

Wide Area Network: Wide Area Network (WAN) is a communication link provider between utility systems and to productions departments directly. Blackhaul and Core are two types of WAN. Table 2 can describe basic difference between HAN, NAN and WAN.

Routing is required in all these types of networks. In HAN the routing is required between Smart meters and Home Devices (appliances) for communication, between smart meter and a local access point and between local access points and meter data management system. However these all devices are almost static but their behavior is dynamic. i.e. they may fail due to the heavy load of traffic or due to power failure etc.

Our focus is Home Area Network, and we will present flooding free routing communication network for Home Area Networks.

Communication Technologies for Smart Grid

Several communication technologies such as cellular, WiMAX, power line communications (PLC) etc, can be used in Smart Grid as shown by Usman A. and Shami S. H. (2013). However, there is no clear consensus by the research community on a single technology so far because each of these technologies has its own pros and cons. For example, cellular networks are primarily optimized for conventional human-to-human (H2H) communication. To use cellular network technology for communication in

Table 2. Difference b/w HAN, NAN and WAN 1

Networks	Data Rate	Communication Range	Protocols	Applications
HAN	1-10 Kbps	Thousands of square feet	IEEE 802.15.4 and 802.11 PLC etc.	Advanced Metering Infrastructure Demand Resource etc
NAN	10-1000 kbps	1-10 square miles	801.11s RF Mesh WiMax 3G, 4G and LTE etc	Advanced Metering Infrastructure Demand Resource Load Management
WAN	10-100 Mbps	Thousands of square miles	WiMax 3GPP RF Mesh	Demand Resource Load Management

Smart Grid, it would have following challenges (i) Radio resource management between H2H users and smart meters would become a challenging as both (users and smart meters) have different quality of services (QoS) requirements. (ii) secondly, a large number of smart meters in a community can create traffic overload on the uplink random access channel. (iii) Thirdly, packet of smart meter type traffic can be much smaller due to small data packets due to this the signaling traffic resulting in low efficiency. Last, but not the least, cellular coverage penetration is an important issue that needs to be considered due to the variability in smart meter locations (e.g., some meters may be installed at places such as garages, under the stairs, or may be present inside metal cages). Similarly some challenges exist for WiMAX based solutions. Apart from this, the security issues of WiMAX are still under investigation for researches. Moreover, utility providers are still not comfortable with the fact that their data travels through a third party networks, it could be a high risk for consumers and also for utilities. This issue is common to both cellular and WiMAX based networks. PLC appears to be an attractive solution due to the use of already existing power grid infrastructure. However, the underlying communication medium will not be available in case of power outage which is a serious issue. Moreover, in some parts of the world regulatory authorities have banned the use of PLC due to the possible detrimental effect on military High Frequency Radio Communications.

Power Line Communication presented by Yousuf M. S., Rizvi S. Z. and El-Shafei M. (2008), Fiber Optics Communication has described by Sörries B. (2013) and Wireless Communication Technologies can be used in Smart Grid.

The Table 3 (Source: GTM Research) will describe the advantages and constraints of various Network Architectures for Smart Grid communications:-

Related Work, Research Motivation

Virtual Cord Protocol (VCP) is proposed by Awad A., Sommer C., German R. and Dressler F. (2008). This is a DHT based protocol which offers a routing mechanism for efficient routing in addition to standard DHT functions (e.g., insert, get, and delete). The VCP scheme requires the first node of the network should be pre-programmed with smallest value of the address space of predefined range [S-E] say S and the next joining node will get the largest value of predefined range say E. All other nodes that will join VCP required at-least one hello message from the nodes that are already part of the network topology. The following points describe different joining cases:-

- If a newly added node can communicate with any end node that is existing at lower or higher virtual position(S or E), then the new node gets this end value i.e (S or E) and becomes the successor/predecessor of the old node (S or E). The old node (S or E) gets a new position between the new end value and its successor or predecessor depends on its old position. The new node becomes predecessor of the old node if it received position S.
- If the newly added node can communicate with two adjacent nodes in the VCP network then the new node gets the virtual position between the values of that two adjacent nodes and becomes the successor of one node and the predecessor of the second node.
- If the newly added node can only communicate with any one node in the network then the new node ask the node to create a virtual node. Now the new node gets the position between real node and the position of virtual node.

Table 3. Pros. and Cons. of various networks 1

Manner	Advantages	Constraints	Effect of Failure
Mesh	Few message losses when network paths disrupted	Topologically complex network	Often automated network reconfiguration
	Less training required to manage	Substantial additional equipment needed	Data overloads
	Inherently reliable via path redundancy		Loss of data if in rural areas
Point-to-Point	Simple architecture	Excessive stress or malfunctions can result in loss of coverage to wide area	Temporary re-mapping of endpoints to different collectors
	Fewer collection points	May require additional relays when towers not available	Can lose communications to significant portions of the network
	Less additional equipment		Manual reconfiguration from control center requires more network management employees
PLC	Low maintenance	No communications in the event of an outage	Loss of all downstream communications
	Very little additional equipment	Device communications paths must be re-mapped when reconfiguration of the distribution grid occurs	Loss of communications to critical protection devices
	Simple configuration		Manual reconfiguration from control center requires more network management employees
Cellular	Low maintenance	High per-endpoint operational costing	Complete loss of communications
	Strong existing network	Poor coverage in rural areas	Overloaded during natural disasters
	Management staff requirements are minimal	Cannot unilaterally improve service to poor coverage area	No ability to independently fi x the network
	Low capital cost	May not be first priority in the event of a down network	

The joining algorithm of VCP can understand better by an example. The first node of the VCP network gets the lowest position and the second node gets the highest position in the predefined range of address space. The new node is near to node having position (virtual coordinate) 1, now the new node gets the maximum position and the old node becomes the predecessor of the new node and gets the ID 0.5. Now, examine the fifth new node joining the network, this node can communicate with two adjacent nodes (having consecutive virtual coordinates) 0.5 and 0.75. This newly node gets the position 0.6 which is between 0.5 which acts as its predecessor and 0.75 which acts as its successor. The newly joining sixth node can only communicate with node having position 0.5. Now the node (0.5) creates a virtual node (0.55) having position between its successor node (0.6). Now the new node gets the position (0.52) between the virtual node (0.55) and the real node (0.5).

In case of routing packets from source to destination, each node must know its predecessor and successor as well as its local physical neighbors. Routing is performed by utilizing the virtual cord. Each node sends the packet to its neighbor which has relative position closest to the virtual position of the destination node. For Example: If a node (0.25) has a data item then it hashes the data item and gets 0.781. Now node (0.25) checks adjacent neighbors as well as physical neighbors having position close to 0.781. Node (0.25) sends it to node (0.5) which is its local physical neighbor which further sends it to node (0.75) which is a local physical neighbor of node (0.5). Finally, the node (0.75) sends it to its adjacent neighbors having position 0.78 which stores the data item which makes 0.78 responsible for the data item 0.781.

In case of node failure there are two cases:

- The failing node could be the final destination
- The failing node could be the next hop towards the final destination but not the final destination itself.

The first case is handled by either by dropping or replicating the data items at the neighbors of the final destination. In second case the scheme utilizes an alternative path approach. Neighbors of the failed node locally creates a no path interval (NP-I: consisting of IDs that the dead node was responsible for) and sends a no path packet (NP) (consisting of NP-I) to another active node in its neighbor which is close to NP-I. Now each node having NP-I either sends it to the destination using greedy approach or continue sending no path packets (NP). If a node, that already has NP-I, receive no path packet then it sends no path back (NPB) packet for avoiding loops. An interval is maintained at each node which describes the range of data packets that can be stored at each node and is evaluated by calculating the distance between the current node and its adjacent neighbors in the cord.

The main idea of Virtual Ring Routing (VRR) has found Caesar M., Castro M., Nightingale E. B., O'Shea G. and Rowstron A. (2006). VRR based on location independent hierarchy, without flooding in network. Virtual Ring Routing provides both traditional point to point network routing and DHT routing to the node. VRR never floods the network and uses only location independent identifiers to route. The nodes in VRR organized into a virtual ring arranged order as per network topology by their identities allocated to those nodes. VRR uses random unsigned integers to identify its nodes and organizes these nodes into a virtual ring in ascending order. Each node maintains a small number of routing paths to its neighbors in the ring. VRR uses these routing tables to route packets for packet forwarding between source nodes to destination nodes in network topology. VRR forwards data packets along the ring and also take shortcuts if available in that route. In VRR logical location assigns independently from the physical location for each node. Nodes maintain address records of next hop to 2 predecessor and 2 successor (clockwise & counter clockwise) virtual neighbors. The every node in VRR also keeps a routing table record for physical neighbors, virtual neighbors, next hop and intermediate paths of desired node (from sender to destination node). The routing table is tuple with End A, End B, Next A, Next B, Path id). A node in VRR forwards packets on Next A (Next B) of entry with closest End A (End B) to destination. If both available paths tie, then VRR uses smallest (End A, Path id), Path id assigned by End A during (Setup, pair globally unique).

Virtual Set Paths

In Virtual Routing Ring the virtual set paths are multi hop in most of cases and is bidirectional because members in the Vset are symmetrical. Vset-paths can be used to route packets between any pair of nodes. VRR routes and send messages to numerical keys of each node whose identifier is numerically closest to the key from among all the endpoints in their routing table.

Joining of Nodes

When a new node joins the Virtual Routing Ring network, the node initializes its Physical Neighbors (Pset) and Virtual Neighbors (Vset) and sets up Vset paths to its virtual neighbors. The new node sends periodic local "Hello" messages to find its physical neighbors. For easy understanding suppose, we have nodes from 1, 2, 3, 4, 5, 6, 7 and node 18 join the ring, it send "Setup Request" to random physical neighbor suppose to node 2. The node 2 Forwards "Setup Request" around ring with destination node 18. Then the "Setup Request" eventually arrives at node 7 (closest to node 18), node 7 sends "Setup" message to node 20 (via node 2) with node 7's virtual neighbor set. After receiving "Setup" reply, the node 18 sends "Setup" message to node 7's neighbors: node 6, node 1 and node 2. Now the node 18 has joined the ring and setup with its neighbors. The Table 4 describes the routing for node 8F6.

Packet Forwarding

In Virtual Routing Ring every node maintains a routing table with information about the Vset paths to its virtual neighbors and other Vset Paths that are routed through the node. Each entry contains the identifiers of the two endpoints of the path, the identifier of the physical neighbors to be used as the next hop towards each end point and a Vset path identifier. The first end point identifier in an entry is always the identifier of the node that initiated the Vset path setup. The first four entries are for the Vset paths from the node to its four virtual ring neighbors. Since node 8F6is an endpoint in these paths, the identifier of the next hop towards the node is null. The 5th and 6th entries in the above table are for two

Table 4. Routing Table in VRR maintained by node 1

Endpoint$_A$	Endpoint$_B$	next$_A$	next$_B$	Path id
8F0	8F6	20E	null	03
8E2	8F6	F01	null	2F
8F6	90E	null	7E2	1E
910	8F6	F01	null	2F
35F	37A	20E	7E2	12
A01	A10	F01	FC1	F0
8F6	20E	null	20E	FF
8F6	F01	null	F01	FF
8F6	7E2	null	7E2	FF
8F6	FC1	null	FC1	FF

Vset paths that are routed through node 8F6. VRR maintains the invariant that the next A and next B files in a node's routing table entries are in the Pset of the node. The last four entries are one-hop paths to physical neighbors. The communication between nodes of Virtual Ring Routing is given in Figure 3.

Failure Detection

The Hello message broadcasted in T seconds is an indication of whether a node is active or not. Whenever a 'Linked # Active' node is found a physical neighbor path is inserted in the routing table. The failures detected by each node using only direct communication between physical neighbors. Every node maintains state for each neighbor [Linked, Pending, Failed, Unknown] by considering Pset as the set of nodes in the Linked state. A node is marked 'Failed' if no Hello message is received for T seconds. Two hop paths determined from these rules are also recorded and uses per hop acknowledgement.

Dynamic Access Routing Protocol (DART) defined by Eriksson J., Faloutsos M., & Krishnamurthy S. (2004) and again by Eriksson J., Faloutsos M., & Krishnamurthy, S. V. (2007). DART is proactive routing protocol. DART is similar to Tribe at a high level. DART and Tribe work in the basis of addresses of the node by separating the address into two parts, one part is Dynamic for routing and second part is Static for node identification. There are three major Functions of DART:

First is address allocation that maintains one routing address per network interface to locate network location. Second is routing that delivers packets from a node to a given routing address and the third is Node Lookup that is a distributed lookup table that mapping every node identifier to its current network address.

DART Maintain a unique address for every node and ensures that all prefix sub graphs are connected (Address Invariant). Therefore DART has minimized communication overhead. DART is a decentralize protocol that require no centralized sources infrastructure. By traversing node (step by step) the requirement of address size (in bits) keep prefixes small.

The joining node picks an address with a prefix common with one of its neighbors. When a node joins the network, it listens to the periodic routing updates of its neighboring nodes. By using this listening new node identify an unoccupied address.

Figure 3. Virtual Ring Routing network

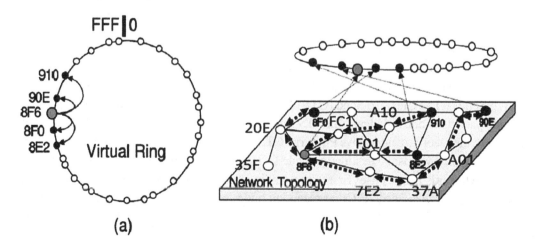

The new node registers its unique identifier and the newly obtained address in the distributed node lookup table. The node lookup table has following features:-

1. Each node registers and updates its entry.
2. Due to mobility, the address may subsequently be changed and then the lookup table needs to be updated.
3. When Node moves, change the address. Nodes Change routing tables periodically.
4. ID to address mapping. Given ad ID, Find the address.
5. Maps identifier to current routing address.

The routing in DART is Proactive and Scalable therefore don't have overhead to detect a path for establishing a connection between source and destination nodes. Due to its scalability DART provides more connectivity for a large ad-hoc network. Routing is simply, Address tells where we are now and where to go (left or right). The nodes with similar addresses are near to each other.

Delivery of packets is simple in DART. When a node wants to send packets to a node known only by its identifier, it will use the lookup table to find its current address. When the address are known then the routing function care of the communication. The Address Tree visualizes the network from the address space point of view. Addresses are L bit binary numbers, the address space can be thought of as a binary address tree of L+1 levels. The leaves of the address tree represent actual node address. Nodes are stored in increasing address order from left to right. The actual physical links are represented by dotted lines connecting leaves.

Location Assisted Routing (LAR) by M Biagi M. & Lampe L. (2010) is used for PLC in low- and medium-voltage distribution grids to connect network nodes (e.g., meters, actuators, sensors) via multihop communication. Routing in LAR is based on geographic coordinates of nodes. In LAR, it is assumed that the nodes are static and their geographic location is known a priori. By using the geographic information of nodes, it can assist in routing in a way that nodes know in which direction a message is intended to flow in network. The following techniques have been discussed.

Beacon-Less Routing (BLR) presented by Heissenbüttel M., Braun T., Bernoulli T. & WäLchli M. (2004). In BLR, nodes have knowledge about topology map but not have the knowledge of geo location of current neighbor nodes. To deliver a data packet to the destination, the sender node broadcasts the data packet to its neighbors by including the geographic location of destination in the packet, an intermediate node again rebroadcasts the packet after a delay that is chosen inversely proportional to the distance gain towards the destination node. If another intermediate node says Q overhears the retransmission made of same data packet made by P, then Q will not retransmit.

Implicit Geographic Forwarding with GPSR presented by Son S., Blum B., He T. & Stankovic J. (2003) to avoid possible redundant packet transmission experienced in BLR, the IGF approach proposes a Request to Send (RTS)/Clear To Send (CTS) procedure before data packet transmission at a node. To send the data packet, a node broadcasts an RTS frame which contains location of destination node. After receiving RTS, the receiving node says P returns CTS with a delay that is set according to the receiving node's distance gain towards the destination node D. Hence, the receiving node says P that provides the largest advance towards D responses first to the sending node. Thus sending node will select P as a next hope and forwards the message to P. Other receiving nodes overhearing CTS frames from P would avoid responding to the RTS. Though IGF avoids redundant transmission, there is a chance of collision of CTS frames, which may require a collision resolution stage. Similar to BLR, also in IGF a chosen route may not connect to D because of inactive nodes (A ⊂ N) or adverse channel conditions.

Galli S., Scaglione A. & Wang Z. (2010) described the better role of PLC in Smart Grid system. The Narrow Band (NB) and Broad Band (BB) PLC can provide bi-directional communication for fast communication system. The PLC have a big role in distribution side of grid because the transformation in Micro Grids, Distributed Generation (DG) and consumer participation contributes here. PLC can provide the point to point connectivity for Medium Voltage (MV) configuration for transformer substations At the other side PLC provides the point to multipoint connectivity between transformer and smart meters by using Low Voltage (LV).

The role of PLC for MV and LV has been presented by Benato R., Caldon R. & Cesena, F. (2003). In traditional system, substations at the MV level have not capability for proper communication. In the case of any fault on any location in the electric power system, it is must that the substations communicate for the solution. With the help of PLC capabilities, it can possible to communicate at MV network for substations in smart grid. The electricity generation, Fault Detection and monitoring and safety etc for smart grid can possible in MV network through PLC. The PLC can transform a signal in the MV network with less cost compared to other methods.

The use of Advanced Metering Infrastructure (AMI) in NB-PLC is in focus for PLC based LV networks.. The NB-PLC is a good choice for smart meter applications in Smart Grid system. The PLC based AMI network is able to avoid network jamming e.g the real time Energy Management via power lines and the project internet has experimentally demonstrated the possibility of using HDR NB-PLC in transforming channel contention into channel cooperation by using a single frequency network with flooding based routing described by Bumiller G., Lampe L. & Hrasnica H. (2010). PLC-LV can implement in Vehicle-to Grid communications. The instantly recognizable physical association between the vehicle and a specific EVSE can be established via PLC for vehicle-to-grid communication

BB-PLC can be a primary application on the LV side for Demand Response (DR) in smart gird. The link between the utility and appliances under the home required to establish a proper link (wired / unwired) for the implementation of DR application. The interest is growing for the use of LV networks in DR application.

The best suited technology for PLC in smart grid application can be NB and BB-PLC. The BB-PLC based technology can be the more efficient choice in application scenarios that are used in smart grid application under the home. The usage of NB-PLC for low complexity, low power, low data rate in applications of AMI and DR has several advantages. The considerable advantages of NB-PLC over BB-PLC can be described in Table 5.

Biagi M., Greco S., & Lampe L. (2012) presented the multihop routing using location information of the PLC devices i.e., geographic routing (geo-routing) for PLC is described. The benefits of using knowledge about immediate connectivity in a local neighborhood of a device is investigated as well as power adaptation for economical energy consumption for fast and multi-hop geo-routing is described.

The nature of nodes in Smart Grid is static therefore the network topology is also static. The connectivity of nodes described links for possible communication between network nodes are variant according to time. The network topology does not change so that a pro-active routing scheme is required. This pro-active scheme can reliable to update network topology with a certain frequency for guaranteed delivery of packet from source to destination.

Table 5. Comparison of NB-PLC and BB-PLC 1

Fields	NB-PLC	BB-PLC
Ease of Upgrade to Future	The solutions can be easily implemented as "soft" modems by using DSP.	Not possible with scaled down versions of BB devices
Worldwide Harmonization	Available band for PLC in the whole world is the CENELEC band.	The use of frequencies above than 2 MHz is prohibited in outdoor environments in some countries
Coexistence	Devices Operating in the CENELEC/FCC/ARIB bands would naturally coexist via FDM with BB HAN technologies.	In High Frequencies (HF) band, segregating two different bands the technologies supporting two very different sets of applications
Optimized Design	BB-PLC solutions like IEEE 1901 or ITU-T G. hn were not originally designed for SG applications but for home networking or Internet access applications only	HDR NB-PLCs solutions being developed in G.hnem and IEEE 1901.2 are explicitly targeting SG applications and requirements

The delivery of packet from source node say P to destination node say Q depends on the neighborhood knowledge of source node P. The node P evaluates the next possible relays. After selecting of next relay, the node P will send the packet, the packet contains the address of the selected relay. The next relay proceeds in the same manner until the packet reaches to the destination node Q.

The level of neighborhood knowledge determines how far the next node can look form source node. This lookup can make choice for the next possible relay. The larger lookup can deliver packet fast, since the relay must contain information about more neighborhoods.

The role of PLC for large scale networks has discussed by Bumiller G., Lampe L. & Hrasnica H. (2010). PLC can be enabler for sensing, control and automation in large systems comprising tens or even hundreds of components spread over relatively wide network area such as a smart grid network. The use of Power lines for communication is not new concept. The power lines can be used by electricity utilities for the transmitting of control signals at low rates for several home automatic appliances. PLC can enable utilities to retrofit their power line networks for communication purpose at only little additional cost. The PLC is required for the connectivity of large numbers of devices such as switches, intelligent sensors, intelligent meters and home appliances. The design and performance requirement for PLC in large-scale control and automation system is different form PLC indoor system. Geographical coverage or the number of network nodes and different required applications for the communication are the different work parameters.

Energy Management System (EMS) is an intelligent system to use energy efficiently in Smart Grid presented by Garrity T. (2008). EMS works on the basis of situation-aware network of the interconnected sensors and actuators. The real time prices of energy consumption to balance electricity can be managed through intelligent energy meters. The central control communication center can manage this network. If every home in a specific area has an equipped with intelligent energy meters then the PLC based network can communicate between meters and the common transformer station. Automation and Grid management system mainly have a master-slave concept structure due to organized structure of network. In Smart Grid the many applications and devices are communicated with central control center that are time variant. Hence, resource efficient transport of data to and from the central node is mandatory to achieve sufficient network coverage in Smart Grid.

Problem Statement

The different ways to communicate in Smart Grid has been discussed. The Smart Grid needs a way to communicate in which the nodes communicate without extra flooding cost and the communication is also guaranteed. For this the following is a statement of problem.

The addressed Problem statements of this chapter can be described as per following:

- Flooding is a costly that wasted bandwidth of network. To reach a message till destination it has to pass from approximately all nodes that is wasting of time and bandwidth. The message can also be broadcast by every receiver that increases the duplication of same data in network and cause to a drawback for network. Moreover the Duplicate packet may circulate forever, unless certain precautions are taken.
- Let us consider Figure 4 the nodes in geographic network communicates through Becon-Less Routing (BLR) Now If the Sender Node 5 communicates to Destination node 9. In BLR nodes have knowledge about topology map but not have the knowledge of geo location of current neighbor nodes. To deliver a data packet to the destination node 9, the sender node 5 broadcasts the data packet to its neighbor nodes 4 and 6 by including the geographic location of destination in the packet, an intermediate node have to again rebroadcasts the packet after a delay that is chosen inversely proportional to the distance gain towards the destination node 9. However the sender node 5 is closest to Destination node 9 in network but node 5 cannot communicate with node 9 directly and no other node in network is closest to node 9. Therefore the node 5 will never communicate with node 9 by using BLR in given situation.
- The Ad-hoc on Demand Vector (AODV) routing protocol based on four Control messages types to operate AODV communication. Each message contains routing information for a specific role: Route Request (RREQ), Route Reply (RREP) and Route Reply Acknowledgement (RREP ACK). The time consumes for all these types of messages during communication.

Figure 4. Problem statement figure

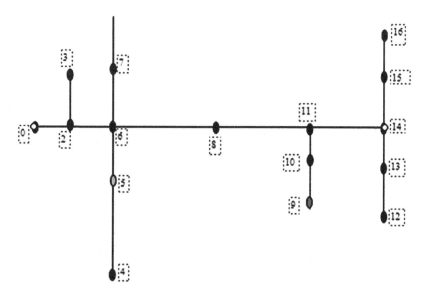

Research Objectives and Proposed System and Proposed Solution

The author research objective is to address all above mentioned problems and to provide a better solution. Author will implement our scenario in Smart Grid communication system and will show flooding free routing in Smart Grid. For the purpose the author will use the MANET's protocol for flooding free communication in Smart Grid. To support this chapter, the author will consider the paper by Yoon S. G., Jang S., Kim Y. H. & Bahk S. (2014).

PROPOSED SOLUTION

Author has implemented Virtual Cord Protocol (VCP) to solve above mentioned problems. The joining of all nodes in a VCP network topology is shown in two parts Figure 5 and Figure 6.

As described above the functionality of VCP routing protocol that the nodes will join network same as mentioned above about joining of nodes in VCP in section 'Related Work, Research Motivation'.

The all given nodes of problem statement have joined the network through VCP protocol. Now all the nodes are in sequence and arranged in ascending orders that's why every node is knows that the desired destination node is at which side. The nodes are also connected in a row therefore it is easy to know that the node is missing/failed or not.

Figure 5. Joining in VCP part 1

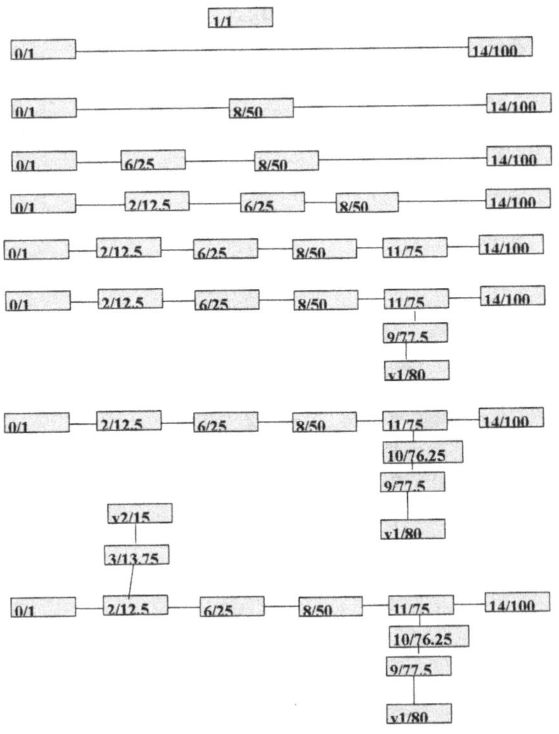

Figure 6. Joining in VCP part 2

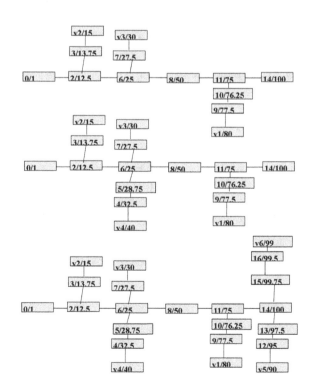

CONCLUSION

- Flooding free joining of nodes in Smart Grid through VCP has been implemented and now we are able to see that every node will communicate with other nodes without flooding because there is no need to find nodes location. Every node knows that the destination's node address is higher or lower than his own address, therefore the sender node will send message towards destination directly without flooding. The receiver also send message towards destination without flooding. We have save cost of flooding and bandwidth of the network. The duplication packets also been reduced. Now the communication between nodes is a straight and duplication of packets has been reduced.

- The communication problem of diagram mentioned in Problem Statement section at point ii has also been solved. Now through VCP every node is able to communicate with any other node in network topology. All nodes have joined VCP and they are in proper sequence therefore the communication problem is removed.

- The time consumption that has been seen in Ad-hoc on Demand Vector (AODV) routing protocol (based on four Control messages types) has also been solved. Now in VCP protocol there is no need to routing information, Route Request (RREQ), Route Request Reply (RREP) and Route Reply Acknowledgement (RREP ACK). Now the communication in Smart Gird is simple and every node knows his location in network. The node wills simple compare the value of destination address with his own address and if he is receiver then he will keep that data packet. Otherwise the packet will be forwarded to up direction or down direction according to the destination address.

REFERENCES

Abid, S. A., Othman, M., & Shah, N. (2014). A Survey on DHT-Based Routing for Large-Scale Mobile Ad Hoc Networks. *ACM Computing Surveys*, *47*(2), 20. doi:10.1145/2632296

Akyildiz, I. F., Su, W., Sankarasubramaniam, Y., & Cayirci, E. (2002). Wireless sensor networks: A survey. *Computer Networks*, *38*(4), 393–422. doi:10.1016/S1389-1286(01)00302-4

Amin, S. M., & Wollenberg, B. F. (2005). Toward a smart grid: Power delivery for the 21st century. *Power and Energy Magazine, IEEE*, *3*(5), 34–41. doi:10.1109/MPAE.2005.1507024

Awad, A., Sommer, C., German, R., & Dressler, F. (2008, September). Virtual cord protocol (VCP): A flexible DHT-like routing service for sensor networks. In *Mobile Ad Hoc and Sensor Systems, 2008. MASS 2008. 5th IEEE International Conference on* (pp. 133-142). IEEE.

Balijepalli, V. S. K. M., Pradhan, V., Khaparde, S. A., & Shereef, R. M. (2011, December). Review of demand response under smart grid paradigm. In Innovative Smart Grid Technologies-India (ISGT India), 2011 IEEE PES (pp. 236-243). IEEE. doi:10.1109/ISET-India.2011.6145388

Benato, R., Caldon, R., & Cesena, F. (2003, June). Application of Distribution Line Carrier-based protection to prevent DG islanding: an investigating procedure. In *Power Tech Conference Proceedings, 2003 IEEE Bologna* (Vol. 3, pp. 7-pp). IEEE. doi:10.1109/PTC.2003.1304393

Biagi, M. M., & Lampe, L. (2010, October). Location assisted routing techniques for power line communication in smart grids. In *Smart Grid Communications (SmartGridComm), 2010 First IEEE International Conference on* (pp. 274-278). IEEE.

Biagi, M., Greco, S., & Lampe, L. (2012, March). Neighborhood-knowledge based geo-routing in PLC. In *Power Line Communications and Its Applications (ISPLC), 2012 16th IEEE International Symposium on* (pp. 7-12). IEEE. doi:10.1109/ISPLC.2012.6201303

Brown, R. E. (2008, July). Impact of smart grid on distribution system design. In Power and Energy Society General Meeting-Conversion and Delivery of Electrical Energy in the 21st Century, 2008 IEEE (pp. 1-4). IEEE. doi:10.1109/PES.2008.4596843

Bumiller, G., Lampe, L., & Hrasnica, H. (2010). Power line communication networks for large-scale control and automation systems. *Communications Magazine, IEEE, 48*(4), 106–113. doi:10.1109/MCOM.2010.5439083

Caesar, M., Castro, M., Nightingale, E. B., O'Shea, G., & Rowstron, A. (2006). Virtual ring routing: Network routing inspired by DHTs. *Computer Communication Review, 36*(4), 351–362. doi:10.1145/1151659.1159954

Eriksson, J., Faloutsos, M., & Krishnamurthy, S. (2004, March). Scalable ad hoc routing: The case for dynamic addressing. In *INFOCOM 2004. Twenty-third AnnualJoint Conference of the IEEE Computer and Communications Societies* (Vol. 2, pp. 1108-1119). IEEE.

Eriksson, J., Faloutsos, M., & Krishnamurthy, S. V. (2007). DART: Dynamic address routing for scalable ad hoc and mesh networks. *IEEE/ACM Transactions on Networking (TON), 15*(1), 119-132.

Galli, S., Scaglione, A., & Wang, Z. (2010, October). Power line communications and the smart grid. In *Smart Grid Communications (SmartGridComm), 2010 First IEEE International Conference on* (pp. 303-308). IEEE. doi:10.1109/SMARTGRID.2010.5622060

Garrity, T. (2008). Getting smart. *IEEE Power and Energy Magazine, 2*(6), 38–45. doi:10.1109/MPE.2007.915181

Heissenbüttel, M., Braun, T., Bernoulli, T., & Wälchli, M. (2004). BLR: Beacon-less routing algorithm for mobile ad hoc networks. *Computer Communications, 27*(11), 1076–1086. doi:10.1016/j.comcom.2004.01.012

Samad, T., & Annaswamy, A. (2011). *The Impact of Control Technology: Overview, Success Stories, and Research Challenges*. IEEE Control Systems Society.

Saputro, N., Akkaya, K., & Uludag, S. (2012). A survey of routing protocols for smart grid communications. *Computer Networks, 56*(11), 2742–2771. doi:10.1016/j.comnet.2012.03.027

Son, S., Blum, B., He, T., & Stankovic, J. (2003). IGF: A state-free robust communication protocol for wireless sensor networks. Tec. Report Depart. Comput. Sci. Univ. Virginia.

Sörries, B. (2013). *Communication technologies and networks for Smart Grid and Smart Metering*. CDG 450 Connectivity Special Interest Group (450 SIG).

Usman, A., & Shami, S. H. (2013). Evolution of communication technologies for smart grid applications. *Renewable & Sustainable Energy Reviews*, *19*, 191–199. doi:10.1016/j.rser.2012.11.002

Wang, W., Xu, Y., & Khanna, M. (2011). A survey on the communication architectures in smart grid. *Computer Networks*, *55*(15), 3604–3629. doi:10.1016/j.comnet.2011.07.010

Yan, Y., Qian, Y., Sharif, H., & Tipper, D. (2013). A survey on smart grid communication infrastructures: Motivations, requirements and challenges. *IEEE Communications Surveys and Tutorials*, *15*(1), 5–20. doi:10.1109/SURV.2012.021312.00034

Yoon, S. G., Jang, S., Kim, Y. H., & Bahk, S. (2014). Opportunistic routing for smart grid with power line communication access networks. Smart Grid. *IEEE Transactions on*, *5*(1), 303–311.

Yousuf, M. S., Rizvi, S. Z., & El-Shafei, M. (2008, April). Power line communications: an overview-Part II. In *Information and Communication Technologies: From Theory to Applications, 2008. ICTTA 2008. 3rd International Conference on* (pp. 1-6). IEEE. doi:10.1109/ICTTA.2008.4530268

ADDITIONAL READING

Bouhafs, F., Mackay, M., & Merabti, M. (2012). Links to the future: Communication requirements and challenges in the smart grid. *Power and Energy Magazine, IEEE*, *10*(1), 24–32. doi:10.1109/MPE.2011.943134

Chen, X., Jones, H. M., & Jayalath, D. (2011). Channel-aware routing in MANETs with route handoff. Mobile Computing. *IEEE Transactions on*, *10*(1), 108–121.

Fan, Z., Kalogridis, G., Efthymiou, C., Sooriyabandara, M., Serizawa, M., & McGeehan, J. (2010, April). The new frontier of communications research: smart grid and smart metering. In *Proceedings of the 1st International Conference on Energy-Efficient Computing and Networking* (pp. 115-118). ACM. doi:10.1145/1791314.1791331

Fan, Z., Kulkarni, P., Gormus, S., Efthymiou, C., Kalogridis, G., Sooriyabandara, M., & Chin, W. H. et al. (2013). Smart grid communications: Overview of research challenges, solutions, and standardization activities. *IEEE Communications Surveys and Tutorials*, *15*(1), 21–38. doi:10.1109/SURV.2011.122211.00021

Gharavi, H., & Hu, B. (2011). Multigate communication network for smart grid. *Proceedings of the IEEE*, *99*(6), 1028–1045. doi:10.1109/JPROC.2011.2123851

Gharavi, H., & Hu, B. (2011, March). Multigate mesh routing for smart grid last mile communications. In *Wireless Communications and Networking Conference (WCNC), 2011 IEEE* (pp. 275-280). IEEE. doi:10.1109/WCNC.2011.5779140

Güngör, V. C., Sahin, D., Kocak, T., Ergüt, S., Buccella, C., Cecati, C., & Hancke, G. P. (2011). Smart grid technologies: communication technologies and standards. Industrial informatics, IEEE transactions on, 7(4), 529-539.

Jaisankar, N., & Saravanan, R. (2010). An extended AODV protocol for multipath routing in MANETs. *IACSIT International Journal of Engineering and Technology*, *2*(4), 394–400. doi:10.7763/IJET.2010.V2.154

Laverty, D. M., Morrow, D. J., Best, R., & Crossley, P. (2010, July). Telecommunications for smart grid: Backhaul solutions for the distribution network. In Power and Energy Society General Meeting, 2010 IEEE (pp. 1-6). IEEE. Frikha, M. Routing in MANETs. Ad Hoc Networks: Routing, QoS and Optimization, 23-47.

Qin, L., & Kunz, T. (2003). On-demand routing in MANETs: The impact of a realistic physical layer model. In Ad-Hoc, Mobile, and Wireless Networks (pp. 37-48). Springer Berlin Heidelberg.

Saputro, N., Akkaya, K., & Uludag, S. (2012). A survey of routing protocols for smart grid communications. *Computer Networks*, *56*(11), 2742–2771. doi:10.1016/j.comnet.2012.03.027

Wang, W., Xu, Y., & Khanna, M. (2011). A survey on the communication architectures in smart grid. *Computer Networks*, *55*(15), 3604–3629. doi:10.1016/j.comnet.2011.07.010

Wang, Y., & Singhal, M. (2007). On improving the efficiency of truthful routing in MANETs with selfish nodes. *Pervasive and Mobile Computing*, *3*(5), 537–559. doi:10.1016/j.pmcj.2007.02.001

KEY TERMS AND DEFINITION

Geo Routing: This routing is used in network when the no direct connection or path is available for the communication of nodes.

Home Area Network (HAN): HAN is home level network with the purpose to facilitate the communication among digital devices inside the home.

Hybrid Routing: This is a combination of pro-active and re-active routing. Hybrid Routing have advantages of both routing techniques.

MANET: Mobile Ad-hoc network is useable in the environment where the proper infrastructure for communication is not available.

Neighbor Area Network: NAN is an offshoot of Wi-Fi hotspots and wireless local area networks, used for connectivity at whole building level instead of home level.

Power Line Communication: PLC is a communication type in Smart Grid that use already available infrastructure of electricity to communicate Smart Grid devices.

Pro-Active Routing: This routing gets information about all possible/acceptable routes from one node to another node before the need of that route for communication between nodes.

Re-Active Routing: This routing gets the information of nodes connected in a network topology when the route is needed from one to other node. This is called On-demand routing.

Routing: Routing is necessary to find the destination node for communication when the location of destination node is unknown for sender node.

Wide Area Network: The big network that make able to connectivity of devices from any desired location at distance level with HAN/NAN.

This research was previously published in Smart Grid as a Solution for Renewable and Efficient Energy edited by Ayaz Ahmad and Naveed Ul Hassan, pages 298-322, copyright year 2016 by Information Science Reference (an imprint of IGI Global).

Index

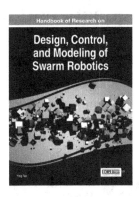

Stay Current on the Latest Emerging Research Developments

Become an IGI Global Reviewer for Authored Book Projects

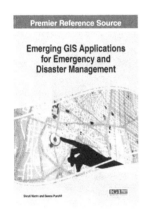

The overall success of an authored book project is dependent on quality and timely reviews.

In this competitive age of scholarly publishing, constructive and timely feedback significantly decreases the turnaround time of manuscripts from submission to acceptance, allowing the publication and discovery of progressive research at a much more expeditious rate. Several IGI Global authored book projects are currently seeking highly qualified experts in the field to fill vacancies on their respective editorial review boards:

Applications may be sent to:
development@igi-global.com

Applicants must have a doctorate (or an equivalent degree) as well as publishing and reviewing experience. Reviewers are asked to write reviews in a timely, collegial, and constructive manner. All reviewers will begin their role on an ad-hoc basis for a period of one year, and upon successful completion of this term can be considered for full editorial review board status, with the potential for a subsequent promotion to Associate Editor.

If you have a colleague that may be interested in this opportunity,
we encourage you to share this information with them.

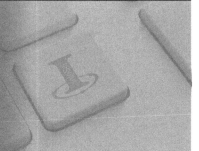

Printed in the United States
By Bookmasters